The Cornwallis Papers

The Campaigns of 1780 and 1781

in

The Southern Theatre of the American Revolutionary War

Volume III

Arranged and edited by

Ian Saberton

The Naval & Military Press Ltd

Published by
The Naval & Military Press Ltd

Unit 10 Ridgewood Industrial Park,
Uckfield, East Sussex,
TN22 5QE England

Tel: +44 (0) 1825 749494
Fax: +44 (0) 1825 765701

www.naval-military-press.com
www.military-genealogy.com
www.militarymaproom.com

ISBN Volume I 9781845747923
ISBN Volume II 9781845747916
ISBN Volume III 9781845747909
ISBN Volume IV 9781845747893
ISBN Volume V 9781845747886
ISBN Volume VI 9781845747879

CONTENTS

Editorial method

Subject to the following modifications, the editorial method remains the same as described in volume I.

Omitted papers

Though belonging to the period covered by this volume, the following papers in the series PRO 30/11/- are omitted on the ground that they do not relate to the southern campaigns or are too inconsequential: 4(21), (45), (47), (88), (244), (305), (380), and (392); 5(5), (7), (10), (17), (40), and (42); 62(10); 66(27); 71(11) and (13); 72(68); 83(23); 84(55); 93(10); 99(17); 104(7) and (9); 105(3); 106(3), (5), (11), (17) and (22); 107(1); 270(122); and 275(20).

Footnotes

As a general rule biographical footnotes on persons who are not the subject of such notes in this volume will be found in volume I or II.

Titles of works cited in abbreviated form in footnotes

Appletons'
Appletons' Cyclopædia of American Biography (New York, 1888-)

Army Lists
A list of the general and field officers... (London, 1754-77), together with *A list of all the officers of the army...* (London, 1778-)

Bass, *The Green Dragoon*
Robert D Bass, *The Green Dragoon: The Lives of Banastre Tarleton and Mary Robinson* (Sandlapper Press Inc, 1973)

Bass, *Swamp Fox*
Robert D Bass, *Swamp Fox: The Life and Campaigns of General Francis Marion* (The Sandlapper Store Inc, 1976)

Boatner, *Encyclopedia*
Mark Mayo Boatner III, *Encyclopedia of the American Revolution* (D McKay Co, 1966)

Cashin, *The King's Ranger*
Edward J Cashin, *The King's Ranger: Thomas Brown and the American Revolution on the Southern Frontier* (Fordham University Press, 1999)

Cashin Jr and Robertson, *Augusta*
Edward J Cashin Jr and Heard Robertson, *Augusta and the American Revolution: Events in the Georgia Back Country 1773-1783* (Richmond County Historical Society, 1975)

Clark, *Loyalists in the Southern Campaign*
Murtie June Clark, *Loyalists in the Southern Campaign of the Revolutionary War,* volume I (Genealogical Publishing Co, 2003)

The Clinton Papers
The Papers of Sir Henry Clinton (William L Clements Library, University of Michigan)

Coldham, *Loyalist Claims*
Peter Wilson Coldham, *American Loyalist Claims* (National Genealogical Society, 1980)

DAB
Dictionary of American Biography (New York, 1928-1958)

Davie, *Revolutionary War Sketches*
William R Davie, *The Revolutionary War Sketches of William R Davie,* edited by Blackwell P Robinson (NC Department of Cultural Resources, Division of Archives and History, 1976)

Davies ed, *Docs of the Am Rev*
K G Davies ed, *Documents of the American Revolution 1770-1783,* volume XVIII (Irish Academic Press, 1978)

DeMond, *Loyalists in NC*
Robert O DeMond, *The Loyalists in North Carolina during the Revolution* (Duke University Press, 1940)

DGB
Dictionary of Georgia Biography, edited by Kenneth Coleman and Charles Stephen Gurr (University of Georgia Press, 1983)

DNB
Dictionary of National Biography (London, 1885-1901)

Draper, *King's Mountain*
Lyman C Draper, *King's Mountain and its Heroes* (Cincinnati, 1881)

Fortescue, *British Army*
Sir John Fortescue, *A History of the British Army,* volume III (Macmillan & Co Ltd, 1902)

Garden, *Anecdotes* (1st Series)
Alexander Garden, *Anecdotes of the Revolutionary War* (Charleston, 1822)

Garden, *Anecdotes* (2nd series)
Alexander Garden, *Anecdotes of the American Revolution, Second Series* (Charleston, 1828)

Gibbes, *Documentary History*
Robert W Gibbes, *Documentary History of the American Revolution* (The Reprint Company, 1972)

'Joseph Graham's Narrative', *The Murphey Papers*
Joseph Graham, 'Narrative', in William Henry Hoyt ed, *The Papers of Archibald D Murphey* (Publications of the NC Historical Commission, 1914)

The Greene Papers
The Papers of General Nathanael Greene, volumes VI-IX, edited by Richard K Showman, Dennis M Conrad, Roger N Parks, et al (University of North Carolina Press, 1991-7)

Gregg, *The Old Cheraws*
Alexander Gregg, *History of the Old Cheraws* (The Reprint Company, 1975)

Hanger, *An Address to the Army*
George Hanger, *An Address to the Army in reply to Strictures of Roderick M'Kenzie (late Lieutenant in the 71st Regiment) on Tarleton's History of the Campaigns of 1780 and 1781* (London, 1789)

Hay ed, *Soldiers from NC*
Gertrude Sloan Hay ed, *Roster of Soldiers from North Carolina in the American Revolution* (Reprint, Genealogical Publishing Co Inc, 1988)

Heitman, *Historical Register*
Francis B Heitman, *Historical Register of the Officers of the Continental Army during the War of the Revolution* (Reprint, Clearfield Publishing Co Inc, 2000)

Hunter, *Sketches of Western NC*
C L Hunter, *Sketches of Western North Carolina, Historical and Biographical* (Raleigh, 1877)

James, *Marion*
William Dobein James, *A Sketch of the Life of Brig Gen Francis Marion* (Reprint, Continental Book Co, Marietta GA, 1948)

Johnson, *Greene*
William Johnson, *Sketches of the Life and Correspondence of Nathanael Greene* (Charleston, 1822)

Johnson, *Traditions*
Joseph Johnson, *Traditions and Reminiscences chiefly of the American Revolution in the South* (Charleston, 1851)

Johnston, *Commissioned Officers in the Medical Service*
William Johnston, *Roll of Commissioned Officers in the Medical Service of the British Army: 20 June 1727 to 23 June 1898* (Reprint, The Wellcome Historical Medical Library, 1968)

Lambert, *SC Loyalists*
Robert Stansbury Lambert, *South Carolina Loyalists in the American Revolution* (University of South Carolina Press, 1987)

Landrum, *History of Upper SC*
J B O Landrum, *Colonial and Revolutionary History of Upper South Carolina* (Greenville SC, 1897)

Lee, *Memoirs*
Henry Lee, *Memoirs of the War in the Southern Department of the United States* (Revised edition, New York, 1869)

Lossing, *Pictorial Field-Book*
Benson J Lossing, *The Pictorial Field-Book of the Revolution* (New York, 1855)

Marshall, *Royal Naval Biography*
John Marshall, *Royal Naval Biography* (London, 1823-35)

McCowen Jr, *Charleston, 1780-82*
George Smith McCowen Jr, *The British Occupation of Charleston, 1780-82* (University of South Carolina Press, 1972)

McCrady, *SC in the Rev 1775-1780*
Edward McCrady, *The History of South Carolina in the Revolution 1775-1780* (The Macmillan Co, New York, 1901)

McCrady, *SC in the Rev 1780-1783*
Edward McCrady, *The History of South Carolina in the Revolution 1780-1783* (The Macmillan Co, New York, 1902)

Moss, *SC Patriots*
Bobby Gilmer Moss, *Roster of South Carolina Patriots in the American Revolution* (Genealogical Publishing Co Inc, 1983)

Moultrie, *Memoirs*
William Moultrie, *Memoirs of the American Revolution* (New York, 1802)

ODNB
Oxford Dictionary of National Biography (Oxford University Press, 2004)

Rankin, *Marion*
Hugh F Rankin, *Francis Marion: The Swamp Fox* (Thomas Y Crowell Company, 1973)

Raymond, 'British American Corps'
W O Raymond, 'Roll of Officers of the British American or Loyalist Corps', *Collections of the New Brunswick Historical Society*, ii, 1899

Robinson, *Davie*
Blackwell P Robinson, *William R Davie* (University of North Carolina Press, 1957)

Rogers Jr, *Georgetown County*
George C Rogers Jr, *The History of Georgetown County, South Carolina* (University of South Carolina Press, 1970)

Ross ed, *Cornwallis Correspondence*
Charles Ross ed, *Correspondence of Charles, First Marquis Cornwallis*, volume I (London, 1859)

Sabine, *Biographical Sketches*
Lorenzo Sabine, *Biographical Sketches of Loyalists of the American Revolution* (Boston, 1864)

Salley Jr, *Orangeburg County*
A S Salley Jr, *The History of Orangeburg County, South Carolina, from its first Settlement to the close of the Revolutionary War* (Orangeburg, 1898)

Stevens, *Clinton-Cornwallis Controversy*
Benjamin Franklin Stevens, *The Campaign in Virginia 1781: the Clinton Cornwallis Controversy* (London, 1887-8)

Syrett and DiNardo ed, *The Commissioned Sea Officers*
David Syrett and R L DiNardo ed, *The Commissioned Sea Officers of the Royal Navy 1660-1815* (Navy Records Society, 1994)

Tarleton, *Campaigns*
Banastre Tarleton, *A History of the Campaigns of 1780 and 1781 in the Southern Provinces of North America* (London, 1787)

Valentine, *The British Establishment*
Alan Valentine, *The British Establishment, 1760-1784: An Eighteenth-Century Biographical Dictionary* (University of Oklahoma Press, 1970)

Wheeler, *Historical Sketches*
John Hill Wheeler, *Historical Sketches of North Carolina from 1584 to 1851* (Reprint, Clearfield Company Inc, 2000)

Wheeler, *Reminiscences*
John Hill Wheeler, *Reminiscences and Memoirs of North Carolina and Eminent North Carolinians* (Reprint, Genealogical Publishing Co, 1966)

Willcox, *Portrait of a General*
William B Willcox, *Portrait of a General: Sir Henry Clinton in the War of Independence* (Alfred A Knopf, 1964)

Samuel Cole Williams, *Tennessee during the Revolutionary War* (University of Tennessee Press, 1974)

PART SIX

Refitment at Winnsborough

Commencement of the Winter Campaign

1st November 1780 to 31st January 1781

CHAPTER 29

Introduction to the rest of Part Six

As this Part unfolds, we see Cornwallis continuing to wait at Winnsborough in the hope of being joined by Leslie, a junction on which the winter campaign depended.

Bound for the Chesapeake and placed under the orders of Cornwallis, Leslie had sailed from New York on 16th October with a medley of some 1,900 troops and entered Hampton Road six days later. The principal objects of his expedition were to cooperate with Cornwallis, make a diversion in his favour, and establish a post on Elizabeth River. Complying with Cornwallis's tentative summons to come south, he did not quit the Chesapeake before 22nd November and it was not till 13th December that he arrived off Charlestown bar. His reinforcement, which was inadequately composed, required some remodelling on landing.

A younger son of the Earl of Leven and Melville, the Hon Alexander Leslie (1731-1794) had entered the army in 1753 as an ensign in the 3rd Regiment of Foot Guards (the Scots Guards). By 1768 he had risen to the lt colonelcy of the 64th Regiment stationed at Boston. In 1776 he played a prominent part as a brigadier general in the New York campaign and recently had accompanied Clinton to the south, having been promoted to the local rank of major general. On conclusion of the Charlestown campaign he had gone back with Clinton to New York.

Leslie's return now to South Carolina, his junction with Cornwallis, and his involvement in subsequent operations are more or less dealt with in these Papers. In late July 1781, while at Portsmouth, Virginia, he was appointed by Cornwallis to command at Charlestown and at the same time was notified of his promotion to the local rank of lt general. He did not sail for Charlestown directly but called first at New York, where he took part in the councils of war convened in response to the developing crisis in Virginia. He did not reach Charlestown until November. With the fate of the war now decided, he proceeded to evacuate the town and Savannah in 1782, a year in which he was promoted to the regular rank of major general.

Leslie's end came at Beechwood House about three miles west of Edinburgh. As second in command in Scotland, he had been involved in suppressing a mutiny among fencible troops at Glasgow, where he was knocked down by a missile thrown by a riotous mob. On his way back to headquarters he became dangerously ill and died on 27th December 1794. A portrait of him by Gainsborough is in a private collection surveyed by the Scottish National Portrait Gallery in 1964.

Now arriving in Charlestown, shortly before Leslie, was Charles O'Hara (*c.* 1737-1802), who was to command the Brigade of Guards forming part of Leslie's reinforcement. Comprising some 750 men, it consisted of three detachments from the Grenadier, Coldstream, and Scots Guards.

An illegitimate son of Lord Tyrawley, O'Hara was educated at Westminster School and was appointed a cornet in the 3rd King's Own Regiment of Dragoons in December 1752. Some three years later he was promoted to a lieutenancy in the 2nd Regiment of Foot Guards (the Coldstream Guards) and saw service in Portugal and Germany during the Seven Years' War. He went on to become Lt Colonel of the Africa Corps of Foot and Governor at Senegal, where he remained until he was dismissed from the Governorship in 1776. In the meantime he had been promoted to captain in the Coldstream Regiment, a rank which carried with it a lt colonelcy. Coming out to North America at the beginning of 1777, he was eventually promoted by Clinton to the local rank of brigadier general but played a relatively inconsequential part in the war. Returning home on leave in February 1779, he had arrived back at New York in October 1780. He would now go on to distinguish himself for courage and leadership in the winter campaign, being severely wounded at the Battle of Guilford.

O'Hara was a friendly, larger-than-life character with immense personal charm, described by his contemporaries as handsome, with a dark and ruddy complexion, a facile tongue, and a ready grin. It would fall to his lot to deliver up the troops at Yorktown after Cornwallis had feigned a temporary indisposition. Wounded and captured in 1793 by the French at Toulon, he would die a full general while Governor of Gibraltar, beset in his final months by illness and constant pain from old war wounds. 'Few men,' according to *The Gentleman's Magazine*, 'possessed so happy a combination of rare talents. He was a brave and enterprising soldier, a strict disciplinarian, and a polite accomplished gentleman.'

While Leslie was awaited at Charlestown, all possible means were employed to put South Carolina into a better state of defence, but it was an uphill, largely unrewarding struggle. Yes, the navigation of the Santee was secured, enabling the safe conveyance of supplies to Camden and Winnsborough, yet despite the quiescent effect of Tarleton's brief incursion in early November, the vast territory east of the Wateree and Santee remained almost totally outside British control. Admittedly, a small garrison occupied Georgetown, the 64th and other troops operated between Nelson's Ferry and Camden, and Cassells' militia regiment was advanced to Black River, but neither they nor Tarleton, outside their immediate areas of operation, had a material effect on this virulently disaffected region, the hunting ground of Marion.

Of Huguenot descent, Francis Marion (*c.* 1732-1795) was born at Goatfield Plantation, St John's Parish, Berkeley County, and was no more than six years old when his family moved to a plantation on Winyah Bay. Having received a rudimentary education, he went to sea

when aged about fifteen but on a return passage from the West Indies his ship foundered and he lost his appetite for the nautical life. He remained on the family plantation until 1761, when he took a courageous part in the Cherokee War as a lieutenant of militia. He went on to farm leased lands along the west bank of the Santee before purchasing in 1773 a plantation, 'Pond Bluff', four miles below Eutaw Springs. Less than two years later he was elected to the Provincial Congress and in June 1775 was commissioned a captain in its second regiment. In February 1776 he was promoted to major and four months later commanded part of the heavy guns at Fort Sullivan during the failed British attempt on Charlestown. At the same time his regiment was transferred to the Continental establishment and in November 1776 he became its lt colonel, a rank he would hold till almost the end of the war. A strict disciplinarian, he would bravely lead his men during the failed assault on Savannah in October 1779. Five months later, as the British menaced Charlestown, he broke his ankle and, being unfit for duty, was ordered to quit the town. By mid August he had recovered and it was then that he was appointed by Gates to command the revolutionary irregulars east of the Wateree and Santee. His subsequent operations in 1780 are more or less adverted to in these Papers, and though they involved him in only relatively minor actions, his presence contributed effectively to keeping alive the spirit of revolt in that quarter. At the close of 1780 he was appointed a brigadier general of militia, and in 1781 he *inter alia* collaborated with Lee in reducing Forts Watson and Motte, occupied Georgetown, and led his brigade at the Battle of Eutaw Springs. He proceeded to attend the revolutionary assembly at Jacksonborough and served for many years in the legislature after the war.

A principled man of short, unprepossessing appearance, Marion, unlike Sumter, was opposed to plunder and wanton cruelty, impressing on his men to forgo such activities. Yet as volunteers they could come and go as they pleased. Once away from camp they 'found it difficult to stifle the strong urge for vengeance and often satisfied their blood lust on those loyalists who were so unfortunate as to meet up with them.' These poor creatures were 'chased from their homes, hunted thro' the woods, and shot with as much indifference as you would a buck'. Their possessions were rifled.

By the beginning of November 1780 the situation in the Low Country to the west of the Santee had also begun to deteriorate. So many small parties of revolutionary irregulars were entering the territory from the east, crossing the river above and below Nelson's Ferry, that Balfour was obliged to detach fifty men to Monck's Corner with orders to move on to Nelson's if necessary, despite there being already very strong posts at both locations. The ferry at Manigault's he directed to be secured by Fisher's Orangeburg militia, and those on the lower parts of the Santee by the militia of Ball and Wigfall, but no assistance was forthcoming from Lechmere's and Ballingall's militia, who were totally disaffected and refused to turn out to a man. Together with the move of the 64th and other troops to the eastern side of the river and the posting of an additional 120 Hessians and convalescents at Monck's Corner, these measures appear to have stabilised the situation, though the threat of incursions remained.

In the Back Country the post at Camden was initially in much need of improvement. When Rawdon arrived on 13th November to supersede Turnbull, he found matters in so backward a state that he anticipated some difficulty in making the post tolerably convenient and pretty secure before the bad weather set in. As the village was by no means capable of holding the number of men who required quarters in it, he promptly sent for a quantity of planks and boards so that barns, stables etc might be speedily converted into some kind of barracks for the troops and huts erected contiguously for the officers. By the close of November the redoubts, though defensible, were by no means completed, while arrangements were in train for constructing a strong log house to defend the mill and for putting up a stockade around the body of the village, which would secure the stores. By the close of December he had laid up a sufficient stock of provisions to support the garrison for many days in case he was reduced to keeping close within the works, and was continually adding to the hoard by collecting more than was necessary for the garrison's immediate consumption.

In this Part Rawdon goes some way towards amplifying what he would later assert were 'the extraordinary disadvantages which attended it [*Camden*] as an individual position'[1]. He now explains why, in short, the post 'was always an infamous one'.

Garrisoning the village on Rawdon's arrival were the 7th Regiment (Royal Fusiliers), the New York Volunteers, the Royal North Carolina Regiment, the South Carolina Royalist Regiment, and the Volunteers of Ireland. If we allow for the sickness prevalent among them, the rank and file present fit for duty amounted in all to approximately 1,050 men, to whom should be added Harrison's irregulars and 150 convalescents fit for the defence of the redoubts. On 25th November the 7th Regiment was dispatched to reinforce Cornwallis, and one day later Rawdon assured him, 'Should the enemy attempt this post, I hope they will find neither want of vigilance nor of firmness in the garrison.' On 5th December the 63rd arrived to replace the 7th.

In January the troops under Rawdon's command were set out in two returns which appear later in this Part.

As the enemy nearly always kept at a distance in his front, Rawdon was able to push frequent detachments through the districts around him, which greatly checked any growing combinations. At the close of December he was confident that, by fitting out a part of the New York Volunteers as cavalry, he would enable his force to acquire a more active quality.

Some 30 miles west-north-west of Camden lay Winnsborough, the post occupied by Cornwallis. With him at first were 600 men composed of the 23rd, 33rd and 2nd Battalion, 71st, to whom, as we have seen, were soon added the remnants of the 7th, which had been much depleted by sickness. McArthur with the 1st Battalion, 71st, had been earlier detached to the eastern bank of Brierley's Ferry, where he arrived on 12th November. It was situated low down on Broad River some 16 miles west-south-west of Winnsborough. With orders to watch the motions of the enemy and secure the communication with the mills he remained in its vicinity till early January, apart from a brief excursion to join Tarleton after the action at Blackstocks. From the beginning of December the British Legion lay close by.

Together, the posts at Brierley's, Camden and Winnsborough effectually secured the lower part of the territory between the Broad and Catawba or Wateree Rivers, but no control was exercised over the mid to northern part, where the enemy was free to operate.

---

1 See vol I, page 32.

West of the Broad River the situation remained precarious. By the beginning of November the whole country to the north of the Enoree was in the enemy's possession, and despite the actions at Fishdam and Blackstocks it remained preponderantly so. Between the river and the Saluda was only one post, Williams's stockaded house, which was occupied, first by Kirkland with 100 of his militia, and then by Cunningham with 200 or so of his. On 30th December Cunningham evacuated the house after the enemy routed a party of militia seven miles above. Next day the enemy burnt it. As a result control of the remaining country between the Enoree and the Saluda was lost.

From the Enoree to Long Cane few of the royal militia had been willing to turn out, and of those that did, many were ill equipped and short of arms and ammunition. Almost all were dispirited and could not be depended on. Yet, exceptionally, a party of some 210 had performed well when they participated with Allen and 150 rank and file of the Ninety Six garrison in routing Clark and McCall near White Hall on 12th December.

Continuing to occupy the village of Ninety Six were the 1st Battalion, De Lancey's Brigade, and the 3rd Battalion, New Jersey Volunteers, under the overall command of Lt Colonel John Harris Cruger. Near 300 men were fit for duty. By 9th December the extensive fortifications were well nigh complete, at which time Lt Haldane, an engineer, reported to Cornwallis, 'I arrived at this place on Wednesday morning and found the works in a much better state than I expected. Tho' they are not so entirely conformable to rule, yet they may answer the present purpose as well as the best executed work.' He recommended that an abatis be constructed, which was promptly begun. The artillery to be kept by the garrison was for a time uncertain, but on 4th January Haldane confirmed that its two field pieces were to remain and that an iron six-pounder had been ordered up. The problem, if the post was besieged, would be the want of water.

Although Allen – Cruger's second – took part in two brief excursions, the post was fit for little more than a bare defensive. To detach troops in force that could keep the field a reinforcement was necessary, a fact recognised by Cornwallis when he assigned the 7th to Cruger's command at the beginning of January. It comprised 167 rank and file. In addition Dunlap was busy at Ninety Six in forming two or three troops of 40 loyalist dragoons each. Unfortunately, while the 7th were on their march to join the garrison, they were temporarily placed under Tarleton and captured at the Battle of Cowpens. They were not replaced.

Having obtained leave of absence from Cornwallis, Cruger departed on 17th or 18th December for Charlestown, where he arrived late on the 21st. It was not until 9th January that he set out on his way back.

Immediately south of the Congaree was the post which became known as Fort Granby. It appeared to Balfour to be of great importance. Writing to Cornwallis on 26th December, he remarked, '... if I receive no orders to the contrary [*and he received none*], shall immediately send up Mr Maxwell there and give him sixty men of Brown's corps[2] and one hundred of the Orangeburgh militia, which are forming upon the new plan and in which I have confidence. A redoubt round Hampton's house with this garrison will not be forced

---

2 *Brown's corps*: the Prince of Wales's American Regiment.

except by cannon and can act offensively against small partys. The ferrys over the Congarres and Saluda will be covred by this post, as also the communication betwixt Camden and Ninety Six and the District of Orangeburgh, which induces me to wish it as strong as possible.'

On 17th December Balfour set out for Winnsborough, where he arrived late on the 20th. While there, he settled with Cornwallis a mass of business too extensive to be dealt with in correspondence. He arrived back in Charlestown late on the 28th.

Busy in the Back Country on the enemy side were a number of actors. Sumter, who on 6th October had been formally commissioned a brigadier general of militia, now returned to the fray. At the beginning of November he advanced to the east side of Broad River with several hundred men, and while posted at Fishdam Ford, he was surprised in the early hours of the 9th by Wemyss and a party of the 63rd and British Legion. It was an inconclusive engagement, but due to the inexperience of a junior officer Wemyss, who was wounded, was captured and paroled, together with a number of his wounded men. Crossing to the west side of the river, Sumter claimed a victory, was widely believed, and many flocked to his standard, increasing his command to reputedly 1,000 men. Among others also in the field were Brandon, McCall, Candler, Clark, John Thomas Jr, and Twiggs, who united under Sumter in repulsing Tarleton on 20th November in the action at Blackstocks. Of Tarleton's men some 50 were killed or wounded, while the enemy's casualties came to only seven. If it had not been that Sumter was severely wounded, the affair would have been rightly classed as an enemy victory.

Besides the actions at Fishdam and Blackstocks, the behaviour of the revolutionaries toward the loyalists and uncommitted was equally important in their retaining control of most of the territory beyond Broad River. Not to put too fine a point on it, a reign of terror was instigated. On 23rd November Cornwallis, who had no reason for lying to a subordinate, advised Cruger that Sumter's men 'have been guilty of the most horrid outrages'. Not only was Sumter responsible but also Brandon, Clark and others, who, as Cornwallis explained on 3rd December to Clinton, 'had different corps plundering the houses and putting to death the well affected inhabitants between Tyger River and Pacolet.' Next day he observed to Clinton, 'I will not hurt your Excellency's feelings by attempting to describe the shocking tortures and inhuman murders which are every day committed by the enemy, not only on those who have taken part with us, but on many who refuse to join them... I am very sure that unless some steps are taken [*by the enemy*] to check it, the war in this quarter will become truly savage.' The upshot was of course inevitable, as Cornwallis stated on 17th November to Balfour: 'our friends terrified beyond expression, either flying down the country or submitting tamely to the insults and cruelties of the enemy, all the disaffected and many who had been neutral and some pretended friends flocking to the enemy's standard.'

The developing barbarity was graphically described in a letter of 6th January from O'Hara to the Duke of Grafton: 'The violence and the passions of these people are beyond every curb of religion and humanity. They are unbounded, and every hour exhibits dreadful wanton mischiefs, murders, and violences of every kind, unheard of before. We find the country in great measure abandoned, and the few who venture to remain at home in hourly expectation of being murdered or stripped of all their property.' Perhaps needless to say, it was the revolutionary irregulars who were preponderantly the guilty party. Until King's Mountain

Ferguson had used his best endeavours to suppress the irregularities of the Back Country loyalists, quite a few of whom had begun to plunder the opposing party after the capture of Charlestown. From King's Mountain onwards the situation radically changed. Now, over much of the Back Country, there was an open door for the revolutionaries to do with the loyalists as they willed – and many did.

Towards the end of December the enemy in the Back Country received a welcome accession of strength when Pickens broke his parole and went off with some 100 men from the Long Cane settlement. Assiduously courted until then by the British, he was a man of influence whose militia regiment, according to Allen, 'was always esteemed the best in the rebel service.' He would soon take part in the Battle of Cowpens.

In the Ceded Lands above Augusta matters had taken a turn for the better by November. Of the inhabitants there, 255 loyalists had been formed into a militia under Thomas Waters, whereas there remained in the settlement 57 persons whose characters were unknown and 159 for whom 21 hostages had been carried to Savannah. Of the rest, 42 prisoners had been sent to Charlestown, 49 notorious and active revolutionaries were lying out, and 140 had gone off with Clark in September.

Between Augusta and Savannah the developing situation was not so rosy. Nominally a revolutionary, but more bent on plunder, a freebooter named James McKay[3] began to haunt the swamps along the Savannah River, capturing supplies bound for Augusta and eventually cutting the communication. In mid January Brown detached Lt John Camp and ten rangers to see that the militia provided proper escorts, but they were captured by McKay and all but one given a Georgia parole, that is to say, stripped, tortured, and put to death. Brown responded by detaching Captain Alexander Wylly with 40 rangers to Matthews' Bluff on the Savannah, but learning there that the whole of Beaufort District had revolted under William Harden to the tune of 500 men, Wylly prudently retreated. Fearing a general insurrection, Brown joined Wylly by forced marches with a further 40 rangers, about the same number of native Americans, and a body of royal militia. Encamped at Wiggan's plantation some 30 miles from Black Swamp, he was attacked by Harden and McKay, who were routed, notwithstanding that all but ten of the royal militia fled or defected.

Brown hanged twelve men who had been involved in the torture and murder of Camp and his detachment, handed over to the native Americans another who had been traitorously complicit, and destroyed any settlement where he found plundered goods concealed. Harden would soon return to the fray, while McKay would continue to infest the Savannah.

In November Sir James Wright, the Governor of Georgia, had pressed Cornwallis to equip and bear the expense of a troop of 50 horse which would otherwise be raised on the Georgia establishment. Its purpose would have been to patrol the vast territory between Savannah and Augusta, which – Brown's excursion apart – was bereft of troops. Despite the risks, the request seems in retrospect to have been eminently reasonable, but in January Cornwallis turned it down on the grounds that cavalry was very expensive and useless if not well commanded. So, as Cornwallis began his winter campaign, Georgia was left with only 211

---

3 Pronounced 'McKoy'.

troops fit for duty at Savannah, together with the remains of 250 King's Rangers at Augusta.

Across the northern border of South Carolina Gates and his men had been keeping well out of harm's way. By late November the Continentals, who had been reinforced with recruits from the north, numbered 1,450, of whom 400 had been formed into a light corps under Brigadier General Daniel Morgan. Gates had also been joined by William Washington and 70 dragoons, besides having at his disposal 1,150 militia. He had advanced to Charlotte, to the south of which were posted Morgan, Washington and the militia, their front guarded by Davie and other irregular corps, who, according to Cornwallis, 'have committed the most shocking cruelties and the most horrid murders on those suspected of being our friends that I ever heard of.'

The situation south of Virginia began markedly to change in favour of the revolutionaries after Nathanael Greene superseded Gates on 4th December. A native of Rhode Island, Greene (1742-1786) had been brought up as a Quaker but was expelled from the Society of Friends in 1773 for attending a military parade. Commissioned a brigadier general in the Continental Army on 22nd June 1775, he served through the siege of Boston and on 9th August 1776 was promoted to major general. He went on to play a prominent part in northern operations, notably in the action at Trenton and the Battles of Brandywine, Germantown, and Monmouth. Having displayed at Boston a talent for not only gathering and conserving military supplies but also working tactfully amid intercolonial jealousies, he reluctantly became Quartermaster General on 25th February 1778 and served until 3rd August 1780. During this period his arrangements for supplying the army were a great improvement and much increased its mobility. Yet it is on his campaigns in the Carolinas that his reputation firmly stands. In them he would, as we shall see, display patience, resolution, profound common sense, and a keen insight into Cornwallis's mistakes, 'qualities which go far towards making a great commander'. Admittedly, he would never be victorious in battle, but in each case the strategic effect turned out decidedly to his advantage. Fortescue, who was singularly qualified to assess the merit of an officer, concluded, '... Greene, who was a very noble character, seems to me to stand little if at all lower than Washington as a general in the field.' He would not live long after the war, dying on 19th June 1786 of sunstroke at his plantation in Georgia.

The troops found by Greene at Charlotte were in a wretched, disorderly state, almost bereft of provisions in an area that had been stripped clean. An immediate change of location was necessary. He therefore moved with the bulk of his troops to Hick's Creek, nearly opposite to Cheraw Hill, on the Pee Dee. Arriving there on 26th December, he established a "camp of repose" to refit and discipline the men, expecting to be provided with an abundance of provisions by the zealous revolutionaries in the neighbourhood. As to the rest of his troops, he had come to a risky decision that was to have a profound effect on the war.

Conscious that his move to the south might dishearten the Back Country revolutionaries in South Carolina, Greene had detached Morgan to the area beyond Broad River under their control, the object being 'to give protection to that part of the country and spirit up the people, to annoy the enemy in that quarter'. Morgan's command comprised 320 Continental light infantry, 200 Virginia militia, and about 80 dragoons under William Washington. Quitting Charlotte on 21st December, Morgan encamped four days later on the north bank of the Pacolet at Grindal's Shoals, where he remained for much of the time until pressed by

Tarleton. According to Graham, by 17th January Morgan had been joined by about 380 Georgia, North Carolina, and South Carolina militia, but if allowance is made for sickness and detachments, the total force he brought to the field on that momentous day did not exceed 850 men.

As evinced by Ferguson, the war had shown that distant detachments beyond the reach of support were fraught with danger. In Morgan's case, the risk would pay off.

Two or three days after Morgan had taken post on Pacolet a spy reported that Thomas Waters and some 250 Georgia loyalist militia had penetrated and were laying waste the habitations of revolutionaries on Fair Forest Creek. What occurred next is perhaps best summarised in Morgan's own words: 'On the 29th I dispatched Lt Colonel Washington with his own regiment and two hundred militia horse, who had just joined me, to attack them. Before the colonel could overtake them, they had retreated upwards of twenty miles. He came up with them next day about 12 o'clock am at Hammond's Store House about 40 miles from our camp. They were alarmed and flew to their horses. Washington extended his mounted riflemen on the wings and charged them in front with his own regiment. They fled with the greatest precipitation without making any resistance. 150 were killed and wounded and about 40 taken prisoners. What makes this success more valuable, it was attained without the loss of a man.' Morgan omits to say that many of the unresisting loyalists were given no quarter, being quite simply butchered. This affair, the burning of Williams's stockaded house, and the threat in general posed by Morgan set in motion the train of events that culminated in the disaster at the Cowpens. Besides what is set out later in this volume, so much has been written about the battle and the events leading up to it that it is unnecessary to elaborate here, save to state the basic facts.

Reacting promptly to Morgan's presence, Cornwallis ordered Tarleton on 2nd January 'to push him to the utmost'. Crossing to the west side of Broad River at Brierley's Ferry, Tarleton proceeded to do so, advancing with the British Legion (451 rank and file), the 1st Battalion, 71st (249), the light company, 71st (69), the 7th (Royal Fusiliers) (167), and the 3rd company, 16th (attached to the guns) (41). In all, the rank and file numbered 977.[4] When allowance is made for officers, serjeants and drummers, the total force came to some 1,150 men.

On the 17th Tarleton came up with Morgan at the Cowpens and was comprehensively defeated in the ensuing battle. All his men were killed or captured apart from some 200 officers and men of the British Legion cavalry who fled. The day was lost due partly to the impetuosity of Tarleton but pre-eminently to the superlative generalship of Morgan, who, despite fewer numbers, inferior troops and unpromising terrain, disposed and led his men in a masterly way.

Daniel Morgan (1736-1802) was probably born in New Jersey, but some say in Pennsylvania, and in his youth moved to the Shenandoah Valley in Virginia, where he became an independent waggoner, accompanying Braddock's ill-fated expedition. Impulsive and hot-

---

[4] These and later figures are taken from those present fit for duty as stated in the first return, vol IV, ch 42, p 61. The totals for all ranks are extrapolated from the totals for rank and file by using a factor of 17.5%.

tempered, he received 500 lashes for striking a British subaltern. He went on to serve as a lieutenant in Pontiac's War and in 1774 accompanied Lord Dunmore's expedition to western Pennsylvania. At the outbreak of the revolutionary war he was commissioned captain of a Continental company of Virginia riflemen and within three weeks arrived at Boston. He then took part in the expedition to Quebec, where he was captured during the assault in the face of overwhelming odds, having temporarily succeeded to the overall command. Exchanged, he was commissioned on 12th November 1776 as colonel of a Virginia regiment to be raised on the Continental establishment. Five months later he organised a corps of 500 sharpshooters and in August was ordered north to join Gates in the Saratoga campaign. His troops played a decisive role in the battles of 19th September and 7th October. Dissatisfaction at not being promoted to command an infantry brigade led him to resign on 18th July 1779, but on learning of the disaster at Camden, he put aside personal grievances and joined Gates at the beginning of October. The rest is history. After the war he prospered and by 1796 owned more than 250,000 acres on the Monongahela and Ohio Rivers. In 1794, as commander of the Virginia militia, he helped to suppress the Whiskey Insurrection and three years later began to serve for one term in Congress.

Morgan was stout and active, six feet in height, and 'exactly fitted for the toils and pomp of war'. Wild in his youth, he became in later years a devout member of the Presbyterian Church.

Cornwallis had by now commenced the winter campaign, having left Rawdon to command in the field from Georgetown to Augusta. Marching from Winnsborough on 8th January, he received news of Cowpens on the 18th, the day on which he was joined by Leslie at Turkey Creek. 'The late affair,' he confessed to Rawdon, 'has almost broke my heart.' His situation was indeed critical, yet practice in the school of adversity had strengthened him. Despite seeing infinite danger in proceeding, he saw certain ruin in retreating and was therefore determined to press on in pursuit of Morgan. Finding it impossible to take on waggons, he would soon burn all except those laden with rum, salt, spare ammunition, and hospital stores. In the meantime Morgan crossed the Catawba at Sherrald's Ford.

With the loss of so many of Tarleton's detachment Cornwallis's remaining troops present fit for duty were the Brigade of Guards (690 rank and file), the 23rd (Royal Welch Fusiliers) (286), the 33rd (328), the 2nd Battalion, 71st (237), the Regiment of Bose (347), the Jägers (103), the Royal North Carolina Regiment (256), and the remains of the British Legion (174), making in all 2,421 rank and file. If we allow for officers, serjeants and drummers, his total remaining force for the winter campaign came to some 2,850 men.

Cowpens was a turning point in the war. As may soon be seen, it would lead, by an unbroken chain of consequences, not only to defeat in the Carolinas and Georgia but also to the catastrophe at Yorktown. Those consequences we shall address in later volumes.

§ - §

Principal papers and works consulted in the writing of this chapter

Margaret Baskin, 'Charles O'Hara (1740?-1802)' and 'Alexander Leslie (1731-1794)' (www.banastretarleton.org, 30th June 2005)

Mark Mayo Boatner III, *Encyclopedia of the American Revolution* (D McKay Co, 1966)

Edward J Cashin, *The King's Ranger: Thomas Brown and the American Revolution on the Southern Frontier* (Fordham University Press, 1999)

The Cornwallis Papers (UK National Archives, Kew)

Dictionary of American Biography (New York, 1928-1958)

Sir John Fortescue, *A History of the British Army*, volume III (Macmillan and Co Ltd, 1902)

The Gentleman's Magazine, lxxii (1802), 278

James Graham, *The Life of Daniel Morgan* (New York, 1856)

Anne King Gregorie, *Thomas Sumter* (The R L Bryan Co, 1931)

Don Higginbotham, *Daniel Morgan: Revolutionary Rifleman* (The University of North Carolina Press, 1961)

John Kay, *A Series of Portraits and Caricature Etchings... With Biographical Sketches and Illustrative Anecdotes* (Edinburgh, 1838)

Paul David Nelson, *General Horatio Gates* (Louisiana State University Press, 1976)

Hugh F Rankin, *Francis Marion: The Swamp Fox* (Thomas Y Crowell Co, 1973)

Banastre Tarleton, *A History of the Campaigns of 1780 and 1781 in the Southern Provinces of North America* (London, 1787)

Theodore Thayer, *Nathanael Greene: Strategist of the American Revolution* (Twayne Publishers, NY, 1960)

Christopher Ward, *The War of the Revolution* (The Macmillan Co, NY, 1952)

Franklin and Mary Wickwire, *Cornwallis: The American Adventure* (Houghton Mifflin Co, 1970)

O H Williams, 'A Narrative of the Campaign of 1780', Appendix B to volume I of William Johnson, *Sketches of the Life and Correspondence of Nathanael Greene* (Charleston, 1822)

§ - §

CHAPTER 30

Letters to or from England, New York or Virginia

---

1 - To or from Clinton

Clinton to Cornwallis, 5th November 1780 *4(55): LS*

New York
5th November 1780

Lt General Earl Cornwallis

My Lord

I had the honor of receiving your Lordship's dispatches of the 29th August[1] by the *Keppel* brig soon after I had closed mine of the 20th September[2]. I am now to acquaint your Lordship that the expedition under Major General Leslie sailed on the 16th ultimo and I understand was seen entering the Chesapeake on the 19th with a fair wind. Having already apprized you of his destination, your Lordship will be able to form a tolerable just idea as to the time of his arrival.

I inclose to your Lordship the copies of several original letters which were lately intercepted in a rebel mail going to the eastward.[3] And I have also the honor to transmit the

---

1 *your Lordship's dispatches..*: see vol II, p 41.

2 *mine of the 20th September*: see vol II, pp 48-54.

3 The copies are not extant.

copy of a letter said to be written by Lord Rawdon to Major Rugely and of an extract of one from your Lordship to Lt Colonel Balfour, which the rebels pretend to say were intercepted; but as I have some doubts of their authenticity, I beg your Lordship will be so good to inform me if any such letters were actually written.

I inclose to your Lordship a copy of my letter to General Washington in answer to his which accompanied the copy and extract of the letters alluded to. And I likewise send you a pamphlet that has been lately published, together with copies of my correspondence with Mr Washington in continuation.[4]

Sir George Rodney is still here but proposes leaving us in a few days. The French squadron commanded by Monsieur Ternay remains blocked up at Rhode Island by Admiral Arbuthnot, at which place the French troops also continue fortifying.

Brigadier General O'Hara arrived in the last fleet from England and will immediately join the Guards, who formed a part of the force that went on the expedition. Your Lordship will find by my last dispatch, a duplicate whereof is herewith transmitted, that General Leslie is wholly under your orders; and if the present instructions (a copy of which is inclosed[5]) are not such as you approve, your Lordship will of course alter them as you please.

A convoy will sail immediately for Charles Town with the recruits belonging to the several regiments under your Lordship's command.

I have the honor to be
Your Lordship's most obedient and most humble servant

H CLINTON

Enclosure (1)
Washington to Clinton, 6th October 1780 — *3(195): C* *98(1): C*

Head Quarters
6th October 1780

His Excellency Sir Henry Clinton

Sir

Congress, having received information that there were good grounds to believe that a number of respectable citizens of South Carolina, prisoners of war by the capitulation of Charlestown, had been seized upon and confined on board a ship of war, have directed me

---

4 Copies of the pamphlet and further correspondence are not extant

5 The copy bears the date 12th October but is otherwise identical to enclosure (1), vol II, p 50.

to enquire of your Excellency whether such arrests and confinements have been made and for what reasons. You will oblige me by making the communication as soon as convenient.

I have the honor to be with respect
Your Excellency's most obedient and humble servant

G° WASHINGTON

Enclosure (2)
Clinton to Washington, 9th October 1780 — *3(201: C* *98(3): C*

New York
October 9th 1780

General Washington

Sir

Persuaded it is for the interest of mankind that a correspondence should exist between generals commanding adverse armies, I do, without waiting your return to applications of an earlier date made on my part on a subject very interesting to me[6], answer without delay your letter of the 6th instant.

I have heard the report you mention that a number of persons under the capitulation of Charlestown had entered into a plot for the destruction of the place where they were protected and that the officer commanding there had found it necessary to interfere. I have this only from common fame; no formal report has been made to me on the subject.

But as I am well acquainted with Lord Cornwallis's humanity, I cannot entertain the least apprehension that he will stain the lustre of the King's arms by acts of cruelty. The friends of those persons under the description you give of them need be under no fears for their safety. Lord Cornwallis is incapable of straining the laws to take away the lives or liberties of the innocent. If any forced construction be put upon the laws by his Lordship, it will be in favor of the accused, and every plea their friends can offer for them will be humanely heard and respected.

I am, sir,
Your most humble servant

H CLINTON

---

[6] This and following enclosures allude to Washington's decision to execute Major John André, Clinton's aide-de-camp, on the ground of espionage.

Enclosure (3)
Washington to Clinton, 16th October 1780

3(235): C
98(7): C

Head Quarters
October 16th 1780

His Excellency Sir Henry Clinton

Sir

I have received your two letters of the 9th and 13th.[7]

On the same principle upon which that of the 9th is founded, it has been my endeavour to conduct the correspondence between us on the terms which politeness and the nature of the intercourse demanded. In the affair to which you allude I persuade myself all the attentions were observed which the peculiarity of the circumstances would justify.

In my letter of the 6th ultimo I barely made an enquiry about the persons who are the subject of it. I stated no particular report, much less the one you mention of a supposed plot for the destruction of Charles Town, which, I cannot but believe, will on investigation appear as ill founded as it does to me, in the present situation of things, improbable. I wish I could agree in opinion with you on the spirit which actuates your officers in southern command, but I must conceive the enclosed intercepted letters of Lord Cornwallis and Lord Rawdon breathe a very different temper. They not only profess a flagrant breach of the capitulation of Charles Town and a violation of the laws of nations, but under whatever forced description the unhappy objects of the severity are placed, it is in a form and carried to an extreme at which humanity revolts. I flatter myself you will interfere your authority and influence to prevent a prosecution of measures which cannot fail to aggravate the rigors of war and involve the most disagreeable consequences.

Major General Phillips in his letter in consequence of your orders proposes an interview between himself and General Lincoln or some other officer for the settlement of the intended exchanges, but as the business is, I apprehend, too simple and too desireable on both sides to admit of difficulty, I think the meeting of the commissaries will answer every purpose. I shall extend the instructions given to mine to your last proposition in favor of Major Generals Phillips and Riedesel[8] with their families.

---

7 The letter of the 13th (3(218) and 98(5)) imparts Clinton's intention immediately to exchange Major Generals Phillips and Riedesel with their suites. It also advises that Phillips has Clinton's full authority to agree to exchanges generally.

8 Major General Friedrich Adolphus the Baron Riedesel (1738-1800) had commanded the Brunswick troops forming part of Burgoyne's offensive. Taken prisoner with Phillips at Saratoga in October 1777, he was now to be exchanged with him.

I am, sir,
Your most obedient humble servant

G[O] WASHINGTON

Enclosure (4)
Purported extract from Cornwallis to Balfour, Commandant of Ninety Six, undated[9] *98(10): C*

I have given orders that all the inhabitants of this province who have subscribed and have taken part in this revolt should be punished with the greatest rigour, and also those who will not turn out, that they may be imprisoned and their whole property taken from them or destroyed. I have likewise ordered that compensation should be made out of their effects to the persons who have been injured and oppressed by them. I have ordered in the most positive manner that every militia man who has borne arms with us and afterwards joined the enemy shall be immediately hanged. I desire you will take the most rigorous measures to punish the rebels in the district in which you command and that you will obey in the strictest manner the directions I have given in this letter relative to the inhabitants of this country.

Enclosure (5)
Rawdon to Rugeley, 1st July 1780 *98(9): C*

Head Quarters
Camden
July 1st 1780

H Rugely Esq
Major of Militia

Sir

So many deserters from this army have passed with impunity thro' the districts which are under your direction that I must necessarily suspect the inhabitants to have connived at, if not facilitated, their escape. If attachment to their Sovereign will not move the country people to check a crime so detrimental to His Service, it must be my care to urge them to their duty as good subjects by using invariable severity towards every one who shall shew so criminal a neglect of the public interest. I am therefore, sir, to request of you that you will signify to all within the limits of your command my firm determination in this case. If any person shall meet a soldier straggling without a written pass beyond the piquets and shall not do his utmost to secure him or shall not spread an alarm for that purpose, or if any person shall give shelter to soldiers straggling as above mentioned or shall serve them as a guide or shall furnish them with horses or any other assistance, the persons so offending may assure themselves of

9 A fabrication. See Cornwallis to Clinton, 4th December, p 27. For Cornwallis's actual letter, see vol II, p 19.

rigorous punishment either by whipping, imprisonment or by being sent to serve His Majesty in the West Indies according as I shall think the degree of criminality may require. I have ordered that every soldier who passes the piquets shall submit himself to be examined by any of the militia who have any suspicion of him. If a soldier therefore attempts to escape when ordered by a militia man to stop, he is immediately to be fired upon as a deserter. Single men of the light horse need not be examined as they may often be sent upon expresses, nor is any party of infantry with a non commissioned officer at the head of it to be stopped.

I will give the inhabitants ten guineas for the head of any deserter belonging to the Volunteers of Ireland, and five only if they bring him in alive. They shall likewise be rewarded (tho' not to the same amount) for such deserters as they may secure belonging to any other regiment.

I am confident that you will encourage the country people to be more active in this respect, and am, sir, with much esteem

Your very humble servant

RAWDON

Enclosure (6)
Clinton to Washington, 23rd October 1780[10] ***3(265): C***
98(11): C

New York
23rd October 1780

General Washington

Sir

I have received your letter of the 16th instant inclosing copies of an extract of a letter from the Earl Cornwallis to Lt Colonel Nisbett Balfour and of a letter from Lord Rawdon to Major Rugely.

I must always consider an extract from a letter as partial and not always a candid description of a correspondence, but admitting the authenticity of these papers, I am to suppose that Lt General the Earl Cornwallis had determined to punish with a just severity certain persons who, after subscribing to and taking a test oath of allegiance and service to His Majesty, had committed crimes in violation of such test oath so taken and subscribed to by them. And it seems to me both natural and proper that loyal subjects who have been injured and oppressed on account of their zeal for the King's Service should receive compensation in such cases by a discrimination between them and the avowed enemies to the British Government.

10 Published in Ross ed, *Cornwallis Correspondence*, i, 60-1.

I perceive no reason why a militia man who has joined the King's army and is afterwards taken in that of the enemy should be discriminated from other deserters. I need not point out to you, sir, the right the laws of arms give over such offenders. And this will serve as the only necessary remark I have occasion to make on what is called a letter from Lord Rawdon, which concerns only deserters. For the style or terms in which it may be written he is in the first instance answerable only to the King's Lt General commanding in the Southern District, finally to me.

It has been my invariable line of conduct always to soften so far as possible, never to aggravate, the rigors of war. Such has been also the desire of every general officer in His Majesty's Service acting in this unhappy war; but proper punishment upon guilty persons may become sometimes necessary. By guilty persons I profess to mean those who shall have been convicted upon the clearest grounds and justest principles of *real*, not *supposed*, crimes. A conduct so founded leaves me in no apprehension of becoming involved in any disagreeable consequences.

I desire to conclude this subject by informing you, sir, that I esteem myself accountable for my public conduct to His Majesty the King, to my country, and my own conscience. The latter, being a principal mover of all my actions, will, I flatter myself, approve me to His Majesty and the Government I serve, consequently to the world. The King's general officers serving on expeditions, or in different districts under me, act from my orders, and I will observe respecting them generally, as I did in a late letter concerning Lord Cornwallis's conduct, such as his Lordship would assuredly govern himself by towards the conspirators at Charles Town, that I am well acquainted with the humanity of the general and other officers of the King's army and cannot entertain the least apprehension that they will *stain* the lustre of the King's arms by acts of cruelty. They are incapable of *straining* the laws to take away the lives or liberties of the *innocent*. If any *forced* construction be put upon the laws, it will be in *favor* of accused persons, and every plea their friends can offer for them will be *humanely* heard and respected.

I will imagine this letter may be considered as a full answer to the subjects your letter of the 16th treats of, both as it relates to them in the present instance or in any future one.

I have the honor to be etc

H CLINTON

Clinton to Cornwallis, 6th November 1780[11] *4(35): LS*

New York
November 6th 1780

Lt General the Earl Cornwallis

My Lord

Immediately after my arrival at New York I received certain information that the French armament consisting of seven ships of the line and 5,800 land forces would assemble at Rhode Island, which I communicated to Admiral Arbuthnot; and notwithstanding its being on the coast was confirmed to him by his cruizers on the 7th of July, one of which had fired upon the French admiral's ship, we got no certain account of its arrival at Rhode Island till the 18th, eight days after the French troops had landed. I received the first account and transmitted it to the Admiral, who sailed in consequence the day following. I will not trouble your Lordship with all the particulars. Suffice it to say (with which your Lordship will, I am sure, be well pleased) that if any thing was left unattempted, not the least blame can fall to the share of the army.

Monsieur Ternay still remains at Rhode Island and the troops are of course fortifying. The arrival of this French armament has certainly hurt our affairs much. It has enabled Washington to compleat his army with six and three months men. That immediately under his orders consists of 11,400 men, which, with the French and militia of five very populous provinces, makes him very formidable. Your Lordship can guess at the strength of this part of the army by that under your own orders and will agree with me that it is scarcely possible for me to detach a greater force from it or of our being able to make such efforts in Chesapeak Bay as are now almost become necessary. However, when I know your Lordship's success in North Carolina and your determination respecting a post on Elizabeth River, I will then consider what additional force I can spare. If your Lordship determines to quit that post, I shall in that case think your present force, including General Leslie's, quite sufficient. The diversion I have thought proper to make in your favor will, I hope, answer the purpose. By all accounts I have received, Petersburg is their principal depot, and Gates's public letter[12] since confirms it. If General Leslie succeeds, I think Gates must quit the Yadkin, which, by his letter, it seems he means to dispute with you. I inclose your Lordship that same letter of Gates's.[13] I think 'tis possible Ferguson may have met with a small cheque, but I will not suppose it possible that any thing can have happened to him as therein mentioned.

---

11 Extracts from the second and third paragraphs, containing no material differences, are published in Stevens, *Clinton-Cornwallis Controversy*, i, 287-9.

12 *Gates's public letter*: of 12th October to Governor Jefferson of Virginia, it reported Ferguson's defeat and Gates' intended move to the Yadkin. It is published in Draper, *King's Mountain*, 521.

13 Of the enclosures referred to in this letter, only the copy of Clinton's later instructions to Leslie is extant.

By the copy of instructions last sent[14] and those now forwarded to General Leslie, your Lordship will perceive I mean that you should take the command of the whole. If my wishes are fulfilled, they are that you may establish a post at Hillsborough, feed it from Cross Creek, and be able to keep that of Portsmouth (a few troops will do it) and carry on desultory expeditions in Chesapeak till more solid operations can take place, of which I fear there is no prospect without we are considerably reinforced. The moment I know your Lordship's determination to keep a post at Portsmouth, I will, as I said before, consider what additional force I can spare. Once assured of our remaining superior at sea, I might possibly send 2,000 more for this winter's operation, but if those people get the command of Long Island Sound, they will immediately pass over to that island, the disloyalty of which you are no stranger to, and then our situation will be critical. In short, as I was of opinion that not less than 15,000 would defend this post even against the force that Washington alone could collect, I cannot suppose that less will do when he is joined by 6,000 French. Respecting operations in Chesapeak, they are but of two sorts: solid operation with a fighting army to call forth our friends and support them; or a post, such as at Portsmouth, carrying on desultory expeditions - stopping up in a great measure the Chesapeak, and, by commanding James River, prevent the enemy from forming any considerable depots upon it or moving in any force to the southward of it. Such, my Lord, are the advantages I expect from a station at Portsmouth, and I wish it may appear to you in the same light. You may in that case probably take up (for this winter at least) your head quarters there. As I have often said, except as a visitor, I shall not move to Chesapeak, without Washington goes there in great force, which he does not seem inclined to do, nor indeed to send a single man there except Green to command.

There is no material news from Europe except private talk of a peace with Spain. By the inclosed intercepted letters I do not think that impossible.

Haldimand[15], thinking us hard pressed, did all he could to ease us by two attacks on our frontiers. Had our important attempt upon the Highlands succeeded, this diversion would have been wonderfully well timed, but of that unfortunate affair I say nothing. General Phillips has at my request mentioned it and other matters to you at large.

Haldimand is I think safe for this year, except the French should move against him in the winter, which I am far from thinking impossible.

I refer your Lordship to the inclosed intercepted letters. By Hamilton's[16] you will see Washington's aim, which must occasion jealousy in Congress. God grant us peace with Spain and a reinforcement of 10,000 men, and then your Lordship and I may see a speedy end to

---

14 *instructions last sent*: see p 15, note 5.

15 Frederick Haldimand (1718-1791) was Governor and Commander-in-Chief in Canada.

16 Born on the isle of Nevis in the Leeward Islands, Lt Colonel Alexander Hamilton (1757-1804) was Washington's aide-de-camp and trusted adviser. He would resign in February 1781, take command of an infantry regiment in Lafayette's corps, and at the siege of Yorktown lead a brilliant attack on one of the two principal British redoubts. After the war he would pursue a glittering political career, the high points of which were his influential involvement in promoting the federal convention of 1787 and his most effective tenure of the secretaryship of the Treasury from 1789 to 1795. His end came when he was mortally wounded in a duel with Aaron Burr. (*DAB*)

this unhappy war.

I have the honor to be
Your Lordship's most obedient and most humble servant

H CLINTON

Enclosure
Clinton to Leslie, 2nd November 1780[17] *4(1): C*

New York
November 2nd 1780

The Hon Major General Leslie

Sir

Having already put you under the orders of Lord Cornwallis, who must of course be the best judge of operations to the southward, it may be needless to say any thing more; but least you should not receive any orders from his Lordship, or obtain *certain* intelligence relative to him, or have reason to suppose you can better assist his operations by a diversion made nearer to him, I think it necessary to give you some hints respecting Cape Fear River and how far the acting upon that river will operate. Should Lord Cornwallis have passed the Yadkin and be advanced towards Hillsborough, I think you cannot act any where so well as in James River, approaching sometimes towards the Roanoke, but not passing that river without orders from Lord Cornwallis. If you have every reason to believe that his Lordship meets with opposition at his passage of the Yadkin, I think a move on Cape Fear River will operate effectually. I have had much conversation with General O'Hara on this subject. I have given him every information respecting that move, and I trust, after consulting him, you will act in the best manner possible to fulfill the object of all *your* instructions, a diversion in favor of Lord Cornwallis. That you may [be] the better judge of his plan, I send you copies of such of his letters which give any hints towards it.

Should you determine to quit Chesapeak totally, you will apply to the officer commanding in the naval line, to whom Sir George Rodney intends giving corresponding instructions. As you will meet of course in Cape Fear River a considerable number of gallies, armed vessels etc, I wish, in case you quit Chesapeak, that all those now with you may be sent back to us. You will of course cautiously avoid inrolling any of the militia of Princess Ann or elsewhere without you determine to establish a post. Those, however, who voluntarily join you must be taken care of.

I have the honor to be etc

H CLINTON

---

[17] Published in Stevens, op cit, i, 285. There are no material differences.

Cornwallis to Clinton, 3rd December 1780[18] *72(57): ADf*

Camp at Wynnesborough
December 3rd 1780

Sir

I am just honoured with your letters of the 5th and 6th of last month. Lord Rawdon during my illness informed your Excellency in his letters of the 28th and 31st of October[19] of the various causes which prevented my penetrating into North Carolina. I shall not trouble you with a recapitulation, except a few words about poor Major Ferguson. I had the honour to inform your Excellency that Major Ferguson had taken infinite pains with some of the militia of Ninety Six. He obtained my permission to make an incursion into Tryon County whilst the sickness of my army prevented my moving. As he had only militia and the small remains of his own corps without baggage or artillery, and as he promised to come back if he heard of any superior force, I thought he could do no harm and might help to keep alive the spirits of our friends in North Carolina, which might be damped by the slowness of our motions. The event proved unfortunate without any fault of Major Ferguson. A numerous and unexpected enemy came from the mountains. As they had good horses, their movements were rapid. Major Ferguson was tempted to stay near the mountains longer than he intended in hopes of cutting off Colonel Clarke on his return from Georgia. He was not aware that the enemy was so near him, and in endeavouring to execute my orders of passing the Catawbaw and joining me at Charlottetown, he was attacked by a very superior force and totally defeated on King's Mountain.

Wynnesborough, my present position, is an healthy spot, well situated to protect the greatest part of the northern frontier and to assist Camden and Ninety Six. The militia of the latter, on which alone we could place the smallest dependence, was so totally disheartened by the defeat of Ferguson that of that whole district we could with difficulty assemble one hundred, and even those, I am convinced, would not have made the smallest resistance if they had been attacked. I determined to remain at this place untill an answer arrived from General Leslie, on which my plan for the winter was to depend, and to use every possible means of putting the province into a state of defence, which I found to be absolutely necessary whether my campaign was offensive or defensive. Bad as the state of our affairs was on the northern frontier, the eastern part was much worse. Colonel Tynes, who commanded the militia of the High Hills of Santee and who was posted on Black River, was surprised and taken and his men lost all their arms. Colonel Marion had so wrought on the minds of the people, partly by the terror of his threats and cruelty of his punishments and partly by the promise of plunder, that there was scarce an inhabitant between the Santee and Pedee that was not in arms against us. Some parties even crossed the Santee and carried terror to the gates of Charlestown. My first object was to reinstate matters in that quarter, without which Camden could receive no supplies. I therefore sent Tarleton, who pursued Marion for several days,

---

18 Published in Stevens, op cit, i, 302. The only material difference is a reference there to Tarleton's force at Black Stocks consisting of 190 cavalry and 80 infantry.

19 *his letters..*: see vol II, pp 57 and 60.

obliged his corps to take to the swamps, and, by convincing the inhabitants that there was a power superior to Marion who could likewise reward and punish, so far checked the insurrection that the greatest part of them have not dared openly to appear in arms against us since his expedition.

The 63rd Regiment under Major Wemys had been mounted on indifferent horses of the country for the purpose of reducing and disarming the Cheraws. It had afterwards been sent by Lord Rawdon for the security of Ninety Six. When I sent Lt Colonel Tarleton to the Low Country, I ordered Major Wemys to come down to Broad River to keep constantly moving on either side of the river he might think proper for the protection of the mills from which the army subsisted and for the preservation of the country. Sumpter then lay with about 300 men, partly of militia and partly of the banditti who have followed him ever since the reduction of this province, near Hill's Iron Works between the Catawba and Broad River, about forty miles in our front. Branan, Clarke and others had different corps plundering the houses and putting to death the well affected inhabitants between Tyger River and Pacolet. Major Wemys, who had just past Broad River at Bryerley's Ferry, came to me on the seventh of last month and told me that he had information that Sumpter had moved to Moore's Mill within five miles of Fishdam Ford and about twenty five miles from the place where the 63rd then lay, that he had accurate accounts of his position and good guides, and that he made no doubt of being able to surprise and rout him. As the defeating so daring and troublesome a man as Sumpter and dispersing such a banditti was a great object, I consented to his making the trial on the 9th at day break and gave him forty of the dragoons which Tarleton had left with me, desiring him, however, neither to put them in the front nor to make any use of them during the night. Major Wemys marched so early and so fast on the night of the 8th that he arrived at Moore's Mill soon after midnight. He then had information that Sumpter had marched that evening to Fishdam Ford, where he lay with his rear close to Broad River on a low piece of ground. The major immediately proceeded to attack him in his new position and succeeded so well as to get into his camp whilst the men were all sleeping round the fires, but as Major Wemys rode into the camp at the head of the draggoons and the 63rd followed them on horseback, the enemy's arms were not secured and some of them, recovering from the first alarm, got their rifles and with the first fire wounded Major Wemys in several places and put the cavalry into disorder. The 63rd then dismounted and kill'd and wounded about seventy of the rebels, drove several over the river, and dispersed the rest. The command, however, devolving on a very young officer who neither knew the ground nor Major Wemys's plan nor the strength of the enemy, some few of which kept firing from the wood on our people who remained in the enemy's camp and who were probably discovered by their fires, our troops came away before day break, leaving Major Wemys and 22 serjeants and rank and file at a house close to the field of action. In the morning those who were left with a flag of truce with the wounded found that the enemy were all gone, but on some of their scouting parties discovering that our people had likewise retired, Sumpter returned and took Major Wemys's parole for himself and the wounded soldiers. Major Wemys is gone to Charlestown and is in a fair way of recovery.

The enemy on this event cried victory and the whole country came in fast to Sumpter, who passed the Broad River and joined Branan, Clarke etc. I detached Major McArthur with the 1st Battalion of the 71st and the 63rd Regiment, after having sent my aid de camp, Lieutenant Money, to take the command of it, to Brierley's Ferry on Broad River in order to cover our mills and to give some check to the enemy's march to Ninety Six. At the same time I recalled Lt Colonel Tarleton from the Low Country. Tarleton was so fortunate as to pass not only the Wateree but the Broad River without General Sumpter's being apprized of it, who, having increased his corps to one thousand, had passed the Ennoree and was on the point of attacking our hundred militia at Williams's House, fifteen miles from Ninety Six, and where I believe he would not have met with much resistance. Lt Colonel Tarleton would have surprised him on the south of Ennoree had not a deserter of the 63rd given notice of his march. He, however, cut to pieces his rear guard in passing that river and pursued his main body with such rapidity that he could not safely pass the Tyger and was obliged to halt on a very strong position at a place called Black Stocks close to it. Tarleton had with him only his cavalry and the 63rd mounted, his infantry and 3 pounder being several miles behind. The enemy, not being able to retreat with safety and being informed of Tarleton's approach and want of infantry by a woman who passed him on the march and contrived by a nearer road to get to them, were encouraged by their great superiority of numbers and began to fire on the 63rd who were dismounted. Tarleton, to save them from considerable loss, was obliged to attack, altho' at some hazard, and drove the enemy with loss over the river. Sumpter was dangerously wounded, three of their colonels killed, and about 120 killed, wounded or taken. On our side about 50 were killed and wounded. Lieutenants Gibson and Cope of the 63rd were amongst the former, and my aid de camp, Lieutenant Money, who was a most promising officer, died of his wounds a few days after. Lt Colonel Tarleton, as soon as he had taken care of his wounded, pursued and dispersed the remaining part of Sumpter's corps, and then, having assembled some militia under Mr Cunningham, whom I appointed brigadier general of the militia of that district and who has by far the greatest influence in that country, he returned to the Broad River, where he at present remains, as well as Major McArthur in the neighbourhood of Brierley's Ferry.

It is not easy for Lt Colonel Tarleton to add to the reputation he has acquired in this province, but the defeating 1,000 men, posted on very strong ground and occupying log houses, with 90 cavalry and 80 infantry is a proof of that spirit and those talents which must render the most essential services to his country. Lt Colonel Tarleton commends much the good behaviour of the officers and men under his command and he particularly mentions Lieutenant Skinner[20] of the 16th Regiment of Infantry, who does duty with the Legion, as having distinguished himself.

Lt Colonel Balfour, by putting the prisoners on board of ships, was enabled to spare the 64th Regiment from Charlestown and sent them to secure the navigation of the Wateree from Nelson's Ferry and to communicate with Camden. This is the present state of our affairs. Smallwood had been encamped from the beginning of last month, with about 13 hundred militia, a corps of 250 Continentals under Morgan and 70 dragoons commanded by Washington, about 12 miles on this side of Charlottetown, his front guarded by Davie and other irregular corps, who have committed the most shocking cruelties and the most horrid murders on those suspected of being our friends that I ever heard of. Gates joined the week before last with about 12 hundred Continentals and six and eighteen months men, and 300 cavalry under White and Armand. Morgan's infantry and Washington with 100 cavalry came down on the 1st in the evening to attack a block house built by Colonel Rugeley in which he

---

20 Commissioned an ensign in the 16th Regiment on 4th September 1772, John Skinner had been promoted to a lieutenancy there on 23rd November 1775. (*Army Lists*)

had placed himself with 100 militia. Lord Rawdon, who commands at Camden and had notice of their approach, sent to Rugeley to order him to retire to Camden, but he answered that, as the enemy had no canon, he was determined to defend himself to the last extremity and had no fear of being taken. The enemy's infantry did not advance within six miles of his block house, but the cavalry surrounded it and summoned him and he instantly surrender'd without firing a shot. I am informed that Green is expected in a few days to relieve Gates.

As it will be necessary to drive back the enemy's army and at the same time to maintain a superiority on both our flanks, and as I thought that the cooperation of General Leslie even at the distance of the Cape Fear River would be attended with many difficultys, I have sent cruisers off the Frying Pan to bring him into Charlestown and I hourly expect his arrival. After every thing that has happened, I will not presume to make your Excellency any sanguine promises. The force you have sent me is greater than I expected and full as much as I think you could possibly spare unless the enemy detached in force to the southward. The utmost exertion of my abilities shall be used to employ them to the best advantage.[21]

Whenever our operations commence, your Excellency may depend on hearing from me as frequently as possible, and it is from events alone that any future plan can be proposed.

I have the honour to be etc

[CORNWALLIS]

Cornwallis to Clinton, 4th December 1780[22] *72(65): ADfS*

South Carolina
December 4th 1780

His Excellency Sir Henry Clinton KB etc etc etc

Sir

I received from your Excellency the copies of two letters which were sent to you from General Washington of the 6th and 16th of October, complaining of the cruelty and injustice of the measures pursued by the officers serving under your command in the southern colonies.

In regard to the complaint contained in the letter of the 6th of the removal of some of the citizens from Charlestown to St Augustine, I have only to say that the insolence of their behaviour, the threats with which they in the most daring manner endeavoured to intimidate our friends, the infamous falsehoods which they propagated through the town and country, and the correspondence which they constantly kept up with the enemy rendered it

21 The following passage is deleted: 'Whatever progress the King's troops may make, the war here must ultimately terminate in the defensive. I sincerely hope that the zeal and fidelity of our North Carolina friends may give us a safe and easy defensive.'

22 Published in Ross ed, *Cornwallis Correspondence*, i, 72-3.

indispensably necessary that they should either be closely confined or be sent out of the province. The milder measure was adopted and they were sent, with every convenience which their situation admitted of, to a better climate than South Carolina.

In answer to that of the 16th I have the honour to inclose to your Excellency my genuine letter to Lt Colonel Cruger at Ninety Six[23], for it was to him and not to Lt Colonel Balfour that it was addressed, dated on the 18th of August. Your Excellency will see that either General Washington or his correspondent in the Southern District has been pleased to make several very material alterations in my letter, which in its original state only directed the commanding officer to punish in the most rigorous manner and to take or destroy the property of those who, having submitted to the British Government and taken the oaths and protection in the months of June and July, went into rebellion in the month of August; to hang those who had voluntarily enrolled themselves in the royal militia and received arms and amunition from the King's Stores and had taken the first opportunity of deserting with them to the enemy; and lastly to use the most vigorous measures to extinguish the rebellion in his district. In what manner this letter professes a flagrant breach of the capitulation of Charlestown and a violation of the laws of nations, I am at a loss to find out. However provoked by the horrid outrages and cruelties of the enemy in this district, I have always endeavoured to soften the horrors of war and received the acknowledgements of General Gates and the principal officers of the enemy's army for the tenderness and attention shewn to their wounded and prisoners taken on the 16th and 18th August. Far different was the treatment of the unhappy men who were taken with Major Ferguson. I will not hurt your Excellency's feelings by attempting to describe the shocking tortures and inhuman murders which are every day committed by the enemy, not only on those who have taken part with us, but on many who refuse to join them. I cannot flatter myself that your representations will have any effect, but I am very sure that unless some steps are taken to check it, the war in this quarter will become truly savage.

I have the honour to be etc etc etc

CORNWALLIS

Cornwallis to Clinton, 22nd December 1780[24] — *72(69): ADfS*

Wynnesborough
December 22nd 1780

His Excellency Sir Henry Clinton KB etc etc etc

Sir

I have the pleasure to inform your Excellency that Major General Leslie arrived with his whole fleet at Charlestown on the 14th of this month with no other loss than the dragoon horses and a great part of those for the Quarter Master General. The species of troops which

---

23 *my genuine letter..*: see vol II, p 19.

24 Published in Stevens, op cit, i, 313. There are no differences.

compose the reinforcement are, exclusive of the Guards and Regiment of Bose, exceedingly bad. I do not mean by representing this to your Excellency to insinuate that you have not sent every assistance to me which you could with prudence and safety spare from New York. From the account which your Excellency does me the honour to send me of the situation and strength of General Washington's army and the French force at Rhode Island, I am convinced that you have done so; but I think it but justice to the troops serving in this district to state the fact lest the services performed by the southern army should appear inadequate to what might be expected from the numbers of which it may appear to consist. The fleet from New York with the recruits arrived a few days before General Leslie.

It was entirely owing to accident that so many oat ships were left at Charlestown. They were very near being lost in a gale of wind off the bar and were obliged to come in to refit. I have ordered some of them to be ready to sail with the first convoy, which will go as soon as the officers of the navy think they can proceed with safety.

As soon as the victuallers are unloaded I shall apply to the commanding officer of the navy for a convoy to return with them to England, taking also such transports as are unfit to continue longer in the service, on board of which the invalids will be embarked.[25]

The want of specie in this province puts us under the greatest difficulties. Every method has been pursued to keep the money in the hands of the contractors for Government and to prevent the imposition of the merchants, but the sum actually in the province is so inadequate to the necessary demands that we have scarcely been able to pay the subsistance of the troops.

I do not quite understand the state of the cartel, but the number of prisoners at Charlestown is a great inconvenience.

Lt Colonel Balfour informs me that Major Delancey requested in your Excellency's name that he would endeavour to procure some horses to be sent to General Vaughan; but the great demand for the service of this province for horses for cavalry, mounted infantry and the Quarter Master General's Department has put it out of his power to do it. Cavalry accoutrements at Charlestown are very dear and bad. Should your Excellency have received from England more than are wanted for the service of New York, they will be very usefull here.

I am afraid the expence of quartering the troops at Charlestown will be very great, but I do not know how it can be avoided without breaking the capitulation in regard to the property in town.

I have the honour to be with great respect
Your most obedient humble servant

CORNWALLIS

---

25 Although Cornwallis does not say so, he is complying with a direction to him of 29th July 1780 from HM Treasury (2(391) enclosing 2(204)). It required the speedy return to England of victualling transports in view of an acute shortage.

Cornwallis to Clinton, 29th December 1780[26] *72(71): C*

Head Quarters
Wynnesborough
29th December 1780

His Excellency Sir Henry Clinton KB etc etc etc

Sir

When the numerous and formidable body of the Back Mountain men came down to attack Major Ferguson and shewed themselves to be our most inveterate enemies, I directed Lt Colonel Brown to encourage the Indians to attack the settlements of Watoga, Holstein, Caentuck and Nolachuckie, all which are new encroachments on the Indian territories. The good effects of this measure have already appeared. A large body of the mountaineers marched lately to join the rebels near King's Mountain but were soon obliged to return to oppose the incursions of the Indians. I have the honour of inclosing to your Excellency copies of letters from Lt Colonel Brown, Major General Campbell and Major De Peister with the intercepted ones from the Governor of Virginia to Don Galvez and his answer[27].

If the account given of the behaviour of the Indians by Lt Colonel Brown is true, their humanity is a striking contrast to the shocking barbarities committed by the mountaineers.

I have the honour to be with great esteem
Your most obedient and most humble servant

[CORNWALLIS]

Cornwallis to Clinton, 3rd January 1781 *72(73): ADfS*

Wynnesborough
January 3rd 1781

His Excellency Sir Henry Clinton KB etc etc etc

Sir

Captain Cotton of the 33rd Regiment being dead of his wounds, I beg leave to recommend Captain Lieutenant *Ingram* to succeed to the company, Lieutenant *George Anson Nutt* to the captain lieutenantcy and Ensign *William Fenwick* to the lieutenantcy. In case Lieutenant *St Leger* should have been promoted to a company in England, I take the liberty of recommending Ensign *Ralph Gore* to succeed him.

---

26 An extract from this letter is published in Ross ed, *Cornwallis Correspondence*, i, 76.

27 For the enclosures, see pp 295-305.

If Lieutenant *Nutt* should succeed to the captain lieutenantcy, I should be very glad to have him exchanged. He commanded a detachment of recruits in General Burgoine's army and consequently is in the Convention. I can with truth assure your Excellency that Lieutenant *Nutt* is an officer of merit and from his character and services very deserving of promotion.

As Ensign *Swayne* of the 33rd Regiment was drowned on his passage from England, there will be three ensigncys vacant in the regiment even if Lieutenant *St Leger's* preferment should not have taken place. Whenever your Excellency shall have fulfilled your obliging intentions in regard to Lt Colonel Webster, I should wish to recommend Volunteer *James Talbot*, who served with the regiment on the 16th of August, and Adjutant *John Fox* for ensigncys in the 33rd Regiment.

I have the honour to be
Your most obedient and most humble servant

CORNWALLIS

Clinton to Cornwallis, 13th December 1780[28] ***4(316): LS***

New York
December 13th 1780

Lt General the Earl Cornwallis

My Lord

I was honoured with your Lordship's dispatches of the 3rd and 22nd September[29] by the *Thames*, which arrived here on the 12th ultimo, and on the 5th instant I received by the *Beaumont* those from Lord Rawdon and Colonel Balfour to General Leslie[30]. As that general received your Lordship's first invitation on the 7th ultimo, I naturally supposed that he would have sailed soon after to join you at Cape Fear, but am sorry to find he did not move from the Chesapeak before the 22nd. Inclosed I send your Lordship a return[31] of the force that embarked with him. It was all I could spare, but I thought it fully adequate to the service required. My first instructions to General Leslie put that corps entirely subject to your Lordship's orders. I did not, I confess however, suppose it would move to Cape Fear, but having afterwards too good reason to dread by rebel accounts poor Ferguson's fate, I in a second instruction recommended that measure as the only salutary one under the circumstances I apprehended Ferguson's defeat would place your Lordship. By a letter of

28 Published without the postscript in Stevens, op cit, i, 310. There are no other material differences.

29 *your Lordship's dispatches..*: see vol II, pp 43-7.

30 For Rawdon's letters, see vol II, pp 55 and 59. For Balfour's, see Stevens, op cit, i, 301.

31 *a return*: not extant.

Colonel Balfour's to General Leslie (without date) are these expressions: 'I have only to repeat that the *safety* of this province *now* is concerned in your getting as fast as possible near us.' I should be sorry to understand from this that the province is really in danger. Wishing, however, to give your Lordship's operations in North Carolina every assistance in my power, tho' I can ill spare it, I have sent another expedition into the Chesapeak under the orders of Brigadier General Arnold, Lt Colonels Dundas and Simcoe. The force by land is not equal to that which sailed with General Leslie, but I am not without hopes it will operate essentially in favor of your Lordship either by striking at Gates's depot at Petersburg, which I have still reason to think is considerable, or finally by taking post at Portsmouth, which I have ever considered as very important for reasons most obvious. If we take post there, fortify, and assemble the inhabitants, it ought not afterwards to be quitted, and therefore I cannot suppose your Lordship will wish to alter the destination of this corps without absolute necessity. On the contrary, I flatter myself that, should your success be such as your Lordship will I hope *now* have reason to expect, that you will reinforce that corps and enable it to act offensively. When that is your intention, I am to request that the following corps may, in their turn, be considered for that service, viz, the troop of 17th Dragoons, the Yagers, the detachment of the 17th Foot, and the Provincial light infantry etc. I need not tell your Lordship that those detachments have left me very bare indeed of troops; nor that Washington still continues very strong, at least 12,000 men; that he has not detached a single man as yet to the southward except Lee's cavalry, about 250. I need not tell you also that there are 6,000 French already at Rhode Island, but I must acquaint your Lordship that six compleat regiments more are expected under convoy of a number of capital ships. Whatever may have been the intention of the French in sending a reinforcement to this country, I think, however, the season is now too far advanced to expect the last, and was I not clearly of that opinion I should scarcely dare detach as I do. As I have always said, I think your Lordship's movements to the southward most important; and as I have ever done, so I will now give them all the assistance I can. It remains to be proved whether we have friends in North Carolina – I am sure we had three years ago. That experiment now will, however, be fairly tried. If it succeeds and we hold the entrance of the Chesapeak, I think the rebels will never attempt either of those provinces.

I am very happy to find by your letter to General Leslie[32] that your Lordship is so well recovered from your late indisposition, which gave me the greatest pain and concern.

As your Lordship's dispatch of the 12th November and Lord Rawdon's and Colonel Balfour's letters to General Leslie, brought here by the *Beaumont*, were addressed *On His Majesty's Service*, I took the liberty to break the seals, supposing they might contain intelligence necessary for my information.

Should your Lordship at any time judge it expedient to reinforce the corps under Brigadier General Arnold, you will of course either continue it under his orders or send any other general officer you think proper to take the command whenever you may think such alteration necessary.

---

[32] *your letter..*: of 12th November, p 39.

I have the honor to be
Your Lordship's most obedient and most humble servant

H CLINTON

PS

I am happy in this opportunity of introducing to your Lordship Major Craig[33] of the 82nd Regiment, an officer whose services in the light infantry at Boston and with northern army were very meritorious. I beg leave to refer your Lordship to him for any other particulars respecting the present situation of affairs here that you may wish to be informed of.

Cornwallis to Clinton, 6th January 1781[34] — *72(75): ADfS*

Wynnesborough
January 6th 1781

His Excellency Sir Henry Clinton KB etc etc etc

Sir

I am just honoured with your letter of the 13th ultimo. I have written several letters in the course of last month to give your Excellency an account of the state of the provinces of South Carolina and Georgia and of the military transactions; I fear they are all still at Charlestown, as no opportunity has offered of transmitting them to New York. The present addition to the naval force in this quarter will I hope enable me or, if I am too distant, Lt Colonel Balfour to transmit reports more frequently.

The difficulties I have had to struggle with have not been occasioned by the opposite army. They always keep at a considerable distance and retire on our approach, but the constant incursions of refugees, North Carolinians and Back Mountain men, and the perpetual

---

33 Of an eminent Scottish family, James Henry Craig (1748-1812) was born in Gibraltar, where his father was serving as a judge. Having entered the army as an ensign in 1763, he became a captain in the 47th Foot in 1771 and accompanied his regiment to North America three years later. He went on to participate gallantly at Bunker Hill and Trois-Rivières before taking such a distinguished part in Burgoyne's offensive that he was sent home with Burgoyne's dispatches after Saratoga. Shortly afterwards he was rewarded by promotion (without purchase) to the majority in the newly raised 82nd Regiment. After being involved with it in the Penobscot expedition in the summer of 1779, he was now commanding the remnants of its two flank companies and two other companies which had now been sent from New York to Charlestown. Soon he would be placed in command at Wilmington, where he remained until its evacuation in November 1781. His service there, for which he is justly famous, is partly set out in *The Cornwallis Papers*. After the war he saw service as a major general in Cape Colony and Bengal before becoming a lt general and Governor General of Canada. He attained the rank of full general eleven days before his death. According to Sir Henry Bunbury, he was 'very short, broad, and muscular, a pocket Hercules, but with sharp, neat features, as if chiselled in ivory. Not popular, for he was hot, peremptory, and pompous... [He was] clever, generous to a fault, and a warm and unflinching friend to those he liked.' (*ODNB*; Boatner, *Encyclopedia*, 301-2; *DNB*)

34 Published without the enclosure in Stevens, op cit, i, 315. There are no other material differences.

risings in different parts of this province, the invariable successes of all these parties against our militia, keep the whole country in continual alarm and render the assistance of regular troops every where necessary. Your Excellency will judge of this by the disposition of the troops which I have the honour to inclose to you.

I shall begin my march tomorrow (having been delayed a few days by a diversion made by the enemy towards Ninety Six) and propose keeping on the west of Catawba for a considerable distance. I shall then proceed to pass that river and the Yadkin. Events alone can decide the future steps. I shall take every opportunity of communicating with Brigadier General Arnold.

I have directed Lt Colonel Balfour to apply to the commanding officer of the navy to send a force immediately into Cape Fear, and to embark about 200 men and establish some post for the protection of the victuallers and vessels in the river.

The expression made use of in the letter from Lt Colonel Balfour to Major General Leslie was only meant to convey his private opinion of the necessity of his complying with my request and of the danger to which the province would be exposed if it was again left as destitute of troops as in October last. He certainly had no apprehensions whilst the army remained on the frontiers. I can with truth assure your Excellency that Lt Colonel Balfour does not hold the language of despondency and that his spirited exertions and constant attention to the good of the service have rendered me the most effectual assistance. In the hurry of business your Excellency omitted answering the following paragraph in my letter of the 30th of June[35]: 'Mr Graham, Lt Governor of Georgia, has presented an account of money advanced for refugees, to which is added a charge of twenty shillings per diem to the 24th of June as Inspector of Refugees in Georgia, but as he informs me that his commission for that office is not signed, I beg to know your pleasure whether this account is to be allowed.'

I have the pleasure to inform your Excellency that the army here is perfectly healthy and in good order.

I have the honour to be with great esteem
Your most obedient and most humble servant

CORNWALLIS

Enclosure — *72(75): Df*

Disposition of the Troops in the Southern District

Lord Rawdon to command on the frontier of South Carolina, having under his command the following corps and stations:

---

[35] *my letter..*: see vol I, p 160.

–	at Augusta	Lt Colonel Brown's corps – Florida Rangers
–	at Ninety Six	7th Regiment, Cruger's and Allen's battalions
–	at Camden, to move occasionaly and protect the frontier	63rd, 64th, Volunteers of Ireland, New York Volunteers, Watson's corps, Innes's corps
–	at George Town	Fanning's corps
–	at Congarees and Nelson's Ferry	The remains of the Prince of Wales's and ninety five rank and file from the garrison of Charlestown
–	at Pocotaligo	Light company of the 84th
–	garrison of Charlestown	Ditfurth, Huyne, Angeleli, 82nd, 84th
–	To march with the army into North Carolina	Guards, 23rd, 33rd, 71st, Bose, Yaghers, Hamilton's, and Legion.

Cornwallis to Clinton, 18th January 1781[36] *5(47): ADfS*

Camp on Turkey Creek
Broad River
January 18th 1781

His Excellency Sir Henry Clinton KB etc etc etc

Sir

In my letter of the sixth of this month I had the honour to inform your Excellency that I was ready to begin my march for North Carolina, having been delayed some days by a diversion made by the enemy towards Ninety Six. General Morgan still remained on the Pacolet. His corps, by the best accounts I could get, consisted of about five hundred men - Continental and Virginia State troops – and one hundred cavalry under Colonel Washington, and six or seven hundred militia, but that body is so fluctuating that it is impossible to ascertain its number within some hundreds for three days following. Lt Colonel Tarleton, with the Legion and corps annexed to it, consisting of about 300 cavalry and as many infantry, and the 1st Battalion of the 71st Regiment and one three pounder, had already passed the Broad River for the relief of Ninety Six. I therefore directed Lt Colonel Tarleton to march on the west of Broad River, to endeavour to strike a blow at General Morgan, and at all events to oblige him to repass the Broad River. I likewise ordered that he should take with him the 7th Regiment and one three pounder, which were marching to reinforce the garrison of Ninety Six, as long as he should think their services could be usefull to him. The remainder of the army marched between the Broad River and Catawba. As General Greene

[36] Published in Stevens, op cit, i, 319. There are no differences.

had quitted Mecklenburgh County and crossed the Pedee, I made not the least doubt that General Morgan would retire on our advancing. The progress of the army was greatly impeded by heavy rains which swelled the rivers and creeks, yet Lt Colonel Tarleton conducted his march so well, and got so near to General Morgan, who was retreating before him, as to make it dangerous for him to pass Broad River, and came up with him at 8 o'clock am on the 17th instant. Every thing now bore the most promising aspect. The enemy were drawn up in an open wood and, having been lately joined by some militia, were more numerous[37], but the different quality of the corps under Lt Colonel Tarleton's command and his great superiority in cavalry left him no room to doubt of the most brilliant success. The attack was begun by the first line of infantry consisting of the 7th Regiment, the infantry of the Legion and corps of light infantry annexed to it; a troop of cavalry was placed on each flank; the 1st Battalion of the 71st and the remainder of the cavalry formed the reserve. The enemy's line soon gave way and their militia quitted the field, but our troops having been thrown into some disorder by the pursuit, General Morgan's corps faced about and gave them an heavy fire. This unexpected event occasioned the utmost confusion in the first line, the 1st Battalion of the Seventy First and the cavalry were successively ordered up, but neither the exertions, intreaties or example of Lt Colonel Tarleton could prevent the panic from becoming general. The two three pounders were taken and I fear the colours of the Seventh Regiment shared the same fate. In justice to the detachment of the Royal Artillery I must here observe that no terrors could induce them to abandon their guns and they were all either killed or wounded in the defence of them. Lt Colonel Tarleton with difficulty assembled fifty of his cavalry, who, having had time to recollect themselves and being animated by the bravery of the officer who had so often led them to victory, charged and repulsed Colonel Washington's horse, retook the baggage of the corps, and cut to pieces the detachment of the enemy who had taken possession of it, and, after destroying what they could not conveniently bring off, retired with the remainder unmolested to Hamilton's Ford near the mouth of Bullocks Creek. The loss of our cavalry is inconsiderable but I fear about 400 of the infantry are either killed, wounded or taken. I will transmit the particular account of the loss as soon as it can be ascertained.[38]

It is impossible to foresee all the consequences that this unexpected and extraordinary event may produce, but your Excellency may be assured that nothing but the most absolute necessity shall induce me to give up the important object of the winter's campaign. I shall direct Lt Colonel Balfour to transmit a copy of this letter by the first opportunity to the Secretary of State.

I have the honour to be
Your most obedient and most humble servant

CORNWALLIS

§ - §

---

37 The following words are deleted: 'than the corps under Lt Colonel Tarleton'.

38 The following sentence is deleted: 'Major McArthur of the 71st and Captain Newmarsh of the 7th are taken, the latter wounded, Captain Helger of the 7th killed.'

2 - To or from Leslie before his arrival at Charlestown

Leslie to Cornwallis, 24th October 1780[39] — *3(275): ALS*

Hampton Road, Virginia
On board the *Romulus*
24th October 1780

Earl Cornwallis etc

My Lord

Commodore Gayton[40] in the *Romulus, Blonde, Delight, Otter, Hallifax,* and sloop *Beaumond* sailed from the Hook the 17th instant and arrived here two days ago with transports with the following corps: Guards, Bose, Fanning's, a corps of Provintial light infantry commanded by Colonel Watson (who is left sick behind), part of the 82nd, and 84th, and 100 Yagers – in all, about 1,900 men.

Colonel Bischhausen[41] of the Regiment of Bose and Lt Colonel Howard[42] act as brigadiers.

I am order'd to correspond with your Lordship and put myself under your command. From every intelligence I can get I don't hear of your being nearer than Camden. Sir Henry flatter'd himself you had been far in North Carolina. I have two different parties on shore,

---

39 Cornwallis received this letter on 12th November. See his letter of that date to Balfour, p 71.

40 George Gayton (?-1797) was a long-standing naval officer who had been commissioned a lieutenant in 1744, rising to commander in 1759 and to post-captain nine years later. Recently, as captain of the 44-gun *Romulus*, a new frigate which had been launched in December 1777, he had formed part of the naval force involved in the siege and capture of Charlestown. Now, as commodore, he was commanding the squadron which had escorted Leslie's corps to Virginia. He would accompany the corps to Charlestown, from where, while proceeding to the Chesapeake on 19th February, he would be captured with his ship. He was honourably acquitted by a court martial on 26th September. He died an admiral of the red. (Syrett and DiNardo ed, *The Commissioned Sea Officers*, 172; Michael Phillips, 'Ships of the Old Navy' (Internet, 10th January 2006); *The Cornwallis Papers*)

41 Carl von Bischhausen was colonel of the Hessian grenadier regiment which bore his name. Now placed in command of the Regiment von Bose with the rank of brigadier, he would soon arrive with it at Charlestown as part of Leslie's reinforcement. The regiment would accompany Cornwallis on the winter campaign, but Bischhausen would not. Seized with gout, he would remain in town, leaving the regiment to be ably commanded by Major Johann Christian du Buy, an officer acknowledged by Cornwallis to be 'of superior merit'. (*The Cornwallis Papers*)

42 Now temporarily acting as a brigadier general in command of the Brigade of Guards (soon to be superseded by Charles O'Hara), John Howard had been commissioned an ensign in the 1st Regiment of Foot Guards (the Grenadier Guards) on 13th June 1756. He was promoted in the regiment to lieutenant on 23rd July 1760 and to captain on 22nd February 1773, a rank which carried with it a lt colonelcy. After the Battle of Guilford he would be commended in dispatches by Cornwallis 'for his spirited example on all occasions'. About the same time he would receive news that with effect from 17th November 1780 he had been promoted to a colonelcy by brevet. (*Army Lists*; *The Cornwallis Papers*)

one at Hampton and another in Elisabeth River to get intelligence and *pilots*, for not a white person has come off.

By the Williamsbourg papers sorry to hear of Major Ferguson's fate. It may, I am affraid, stop your Lordship's progress towards us, and you are at such a distance it is not adviseable for me to penetrate towards you, not knowing your situation, and the nature of troops under my command.

I intend to try at Richmond or Petersburgh, but I am much in the dark for want of certain intelligence.

I was in hopes of finding something here from Charles Town, as Sir Henry six weeks ago informed your Lordship of this move.

The English fleet arriv'd the day we left New York with 4,000 recruits etc. General O'Hara came in it. Nothing new. The combined and our fleet were both at sea, and every thing quiet in London. They had hanged a number of the rioters. Lord George Gordon's tryal not come on. The Cork fleet much want'd and hourly expected. Sir Henry was anxious to hear from your Lordship and I am informed some of our ships, the day we sail'd, spoke with a vessell from you for York. It was unlucky we did not stay a couple of days longer, for I was promis'd some more troops if the fleet arriv'd.

I am sent away in a starved manner – little or no small craft, the men of war short, if the first intention, of a 64 and 2 frigates. You will observe they culled the army for me excepting the Guards and the Hessian. In short, the Commander in Chief has another scheme of more importance in view, otherwise I should have fared better. He told me I should be soon support'd.

I inclose your Lordship a copy of my instructions[43]. By them you are sure of finding me near our present situation. I intend to send some one off by land to inform you where I am and what I am about.

Mr Townsend is wrote to for rice, which I hope they will send as soon as possible. I write Balfour on that head. McKenzie[44] appointed Major to the 23rd, but poor André's

---

43 *my instructions*: see p 15, note 5.

44 The son of a Dublin merchant and his Huguenot wife, Frederick MacKenzie (*c.* 1730-1824) was commissioned an ensign in the 23rd Regiment (Royal Welch Fusiliers) in 1745. In April 1775 he had been serving as a 1st lieutenant in the regiment for more than seventeen years and took part in the actions at Lexington and Concord, of which he has left a valuable and fair account, as indeed he has of his entire involvement in the revolutionary war. Promoted to captain in the 23rd eight months later, he went on briefly to act as Deputy Adjutant General under Howe before serving three years at Newport, Rhode Island. Now acting as an aide to Clinton, he had been promoted to the majority in his regiment, backdated to 9th August, in consequence of the death of Thomas Mecan. After the war he would successively command the 37th Regiment and the Exeter Volunteers before becoming Secretary of the Royal Military College. (Richard M Ketchum, 'Men of the Revolution XV - Frederick MacKenzie', *American Heritage* magazine, xxvi, 6 (October 1975); Frederick MacKenzie, *Diary of Frederick MacKenzie*, 2 vols (Harvard Press, 1930); *Army Lists*; *The Cornwallis Papers*)

unfortunate fate will keep him some time yet in office. De Lancy[45] Deputy Adjutant General.

This goes by the *Beaumond*[46] sloop, and it may bring the rice for the army and Negroes.

I have the honor to assure your Lordship of being
Your most obedient and most humble servant

A LESLIE

NB

2 officers and 40 dismounted of the 17th Light Dragoons are with us. Commodore Gayton desires his best respects to your Lordship.

Cornwallis to Leslie, 12th November 1780[47] *82(32): CS*

Camp at Wynnesborough between Broad River and Wateree
November 12th 1780

Hon Major General Leslie

Dear Sir

You will, I hope, have receiv'd some letters written by Lord Rawdon during my illness. I am now perfectly recover'd and almost as strong as ever. Had I attempted to penetrate into

---

45 Born in the city of New York, Oliver De Lancey Jr (1752-1822) was educated in England and entered the 14th Dragoons as a cornet on 1st October 1766. He was promoted to lieutenant in the 17th Light Dragoons on 12th December 1770 and to captain in the regiment on 15th May 1773. The following year he sailed for North America to pave the way for his regiment, joining up with them on their arrival at Boston on 24th May 1775. At the Battle of Long Island on 27th August 1776 he led a detachment of the 17th which captured an enemy patrol and seized Jamaica Pass, facilitating the British victory. He went on to serve in Pennsylvania and New Jersey and was promoted to major in the 17th on 3rd June 1778. Now, with the execution of John André, he had been assigned to the office of Deputy Adjutant General, having recently served on secondment as a deputy quartermaster general during the Charlestown campaign. He would be promoted to lt colonel and Adjutant General in 1781. After the war he eventually became Colonel of the 17th and a full general besides serving for many years in the Commons as the Member for Maidstone. He died in Edinburgh at the home of his sister Charlotte, who was married to Sir David Dundas, the Commander-in-Chief of the British Army after the Duke of York. (*Army Lists*; *Appletons'*; Boatner, *Encyclopedia*, 326-7)

46 Since 11th May 1780 the *Beaumont* sloop of war had been commanded by Thomas Macnamara Russell (*c.* 1738-1824), who on that date had been promoted to commander, a rank which carried with it the courtesy title of captain. (*ODNB*)

47 A version of this letter containing self-evident inaccuracies is published in Stevens, op cit, i, 295. The letter, and copies of earlier ones to Leslie, were dispatched from Charlestown in the *Beaumont* sloop of war at daybreak on 17th November (see Balfour's letter of that date, p 83), but miscarried. They were conveyed to New York and opened by Clinton (see his letter of 13th December, p 31). Copies carried by the *Galatea, Roebuck* and *Loyalist*, which were also sent out to meet Leslie, may have miscarried too (see Balfour's letter of 15th December, p 113).

the farther part of North Carolina, my small army wou'd have been exposed to the utmost hazard and it wou'd have been as impossible to have cooperated with you in the Chesapeak as with Sir Henry Clinton at New York.

If you come to Cape Fear (of which at present I have little doubt), by the help of galleys and small craft which will be sent from Charlestown you will easily secure a water conveyance for your stores up to Cross Creek. I will, on hearing of your arrival in Cape Fear River, instantly march with every thing that can be safely spared from this province, which, I am sorry to say, is most exceedingly disaffected, to join you at Cross Creek. We will then give our friends in North Carolina a fair trial. If they behave like men, it may be of the greatest advantage to the affairs of Britain. If they are as dastardly and pusillanimous as our friends to the southward, we must leave them to their fate and secure what we have got. If you find it difficult from contrary winds to get into Cape Fear, the entrance of which is not easy to vessels coming from the northward by the projection of the Frying Pan Shoal, it will be very little out of your way to look into Charlestown; and *perhaps*, though not probably, Balfour may give you the 64th[48] instead of some of the *corps d'élite* which you have brought with you. At any rate we may settle our operations more fully, and you will enter Cape Fear River with every assistance that can be procured from thence. All the men of war with you except the *Romulus* can go into Cape Fear if wanted, but I believe that will not be the case, and the *Sandwich* will be of more use than any of them. I can only say that most impatiently I long for the day of meeting with you.

I cannot help now mentioning a thing which has given me the greatest concern. Some of my letters from the northward have made me suspect that you thought that your removal from Carolina was owing to an application from me. I most solemnly declare upon my honor that nothing can be more false. When I came to town after the surrender, Sir Henry mention'd my going with him to the northward. I said that I was ready to serve wherever he thought fit to employ me, and had no objection to remain in Carolina if he thought my services cou'd be usefull in that province. He said something civil about the climate. On my assuring him that it was no objection, he then wished me to take this command. However painfull and distressing my situation has been, and however dark the prospect then was, it cannot be supposed that as a military man I shou'd not rather chuse to command to the southward than be third at New York, but so far from expressing a desire to have any other officer remain with me in preference to you, I shou'd have wished for you in preference to all others; but I did not interfere in any degree with Sir Henry's arrangement, nor did I say more or express myself stronger on the subject of my own staying than I have described in this letter. I therefore hope that we shall meet with the same cordiality, and continue on the same footing of friendship, which has hitherto subsisted between us, and that you will believe me to be

Most truly and faithfully yours

CORNWALLIS

---

[48] *the 64th*: immediately before the war Leslie had been lt colonel of this regiment.

Leslie to Rawdon, 9th November 1780 *4(78): ALS*

Portsmouth, Virginia
9th November 1780
9 in the morning

Rt Hon Lord Rawdon

My Lord

Yesterday I had the honor of your Lordship's letter by Lieutenant Gratton[49]. Very sorry at Lord Cornwallis' indisposition. Hope soon to take him by the hand in better health.

I wrote his Lordship the 25th ultimo by the *Beaumond* armed sloop, informing him I intended going up James River after securing pilots and gaining intelligence (for Sir Henry flatter'd us by assuring me Lord Cornwallis would send the *Sandwich* here to wait for us).

The Williambourg paper of the 22nd October mentioned Ferguson's unhappy fate. This made us determine to establish a post here, for we forsaw your army under those circumstances could not penetrate so near to Petersbourgh as I expected. I've sent off two messengers by land to you. The works here are now almost compleated, and I intended to have made little excurtions untill I heared or made myself master of the situation of your army.

The country all round seem happy at our arrival, and some wished to take arms, which I never encouraged, for I always inwardly suspected his Lordship might call on me to go to Cape Fear or Charles Town. It hurts me *once* more to come here, and then to forsake them, but I see the necessity of it, and in 4 days the troops shall be all on board and loose no time in getting to Cape Fear River, but I have neither pilots nor guides for that country and no small craft but a few old horse sloops. I have wrote Colonel Balfour to send round all the above requisitions, and provisions, for we sailed only with 60 days' allowance.

I shall wait in Cape Fear River untill I have his Lordship's orders or hear for certain where he is so that I can make a junction. I hope some intelligent person may be sent of that country from Colonel Balfour. I leave this open for his perusal.

A General Mulenberg[50] is at McKie's Mills near Smithfield with 1,500 men. Colonel

---

[49] *your Lordship's letter..*: that of 24th October. See vol II, p 55.

[50] Of German descent, John Peter Gabriel Mühlenberg (1746-1807) was an influential Lutheran minister who had forsaken the cloth in 1776 in order to raise and command the 8th Virginia Continental Regiment composed largely of Germans from the Shenandoah Valley. In February 1777 he was promoted to brigadier general in the Continental line and went on to see distinguished service in the northern theatre of operations, notably in the Battles of Brandywine and Germantown. Sent by Washington to Virginia in December 1779, he had been overseeing the recruitment of Continental troops when Leslie's expedition arrived at Portsmouth in late October. He immediately took command of troops opposing the invasion. Shortly after Leslie's imminent removal to South Carolina Mühlenberg was placed by Greene under Steuben and he was again involved in opposing the British incursions into Virginia in the coming months. He remained in the field until Cornwallis's capitulation at Yorktown. Towards

Stuart[51] of the Guards forced a post the other day at the North West Landing 12 miles beyond Great Bridge. He took 4, 4 iron pounders, and killed 8 or 10 men. He had 2 killed and 2 wounded of his party. I make every one imagine I am going up the river. Pilots are getting for all ports of the Chesapeak so they will be pusled as to our intentions.

I here inclose a state of the troops[52]. Your Lordship will observe it is a medley.

I beg my best respects to Lord Cornwallis and all friends, and

I have the honor to assure you that I am, my Lord,
Your Lordship's most obedient and most humble servant

A LESLIE

PS

I forwarded a copy of your Lordship's letter and one of my own[53] by an express vessell just going off when Gratton arrived.

Cornwallis to Leslie, 21st November 1780[54] *82(75): C*

Camp at Wynnesborough
November 21st 1780

Hon Major General Leslie

Dear Sir

I have just had the satisfaction of receiving your letter to Lord Rawdon of the 9th of this month. I wrote to you on the 12th by the *Beaumont* sloop but think it very doubtful whether you will receive my letter.

---

the end of the war he settled in Philadelphia and pursued a successful political career at state and federal level. Dying on his birthday, he was buried at the Augustus Church, Trappe. (*DAB*; *The Greene Papers*, vi-viii, *passim*)

51 The Hon James Stuart was a captain in the 1st Regiment of Foot Guards (the Grenadier Guards), a rank which carried with it a lt colonelcy. He would be killed at the Battle of Guilford, where, according to Henry Lee, he fell by the sword of a Captain Smith of Gunby's Maryland Regiment. (*Army Lists*; Return of casualties in the Battle of Guilford, ch 42, vol IV; Lee, *Memoirs*, 280)

52 *state of the troops*: not extant.

53 *one of my own*: of 7th November to Clinton. An extract is published in Stevens, op cit, i, 289.

54 This letter was dispatched from Charlestown in the *Loyalist* but miscarried. Leslie may have received copies of it and of earlier letters by the *Roebuck*, which was also sent out to meet him.

As you must on account of the Frying Pan Shoal come very near to Charlestown Bar, and as your corps composed of such various materials may want some modelling, and that[55] it will give me the greatest satisfaction to talk over with you our future plan of operations, I could wish, unless you have entered Cape Fear Harbour, that you would come on to Charlestown. It will lose but little time, and in my opinion it will be time very well lost. I can assure you that the thoughts of meeting with you so soon gives me the greatest satisfaction, and that

I am with very sincere regard
Your most obedient and faithful servant

CORNWALLIS

§ - §

3 - To or from Germain

Cornwallis to Germain, 18th December 1780 ***76(24): ADfS***

Wynnesborough
December 18th 1780

Rt Hon Lord George Germain etc etc etc

My Lord

As your Lordship will doubtless be glad to hear by every safe opportunity the state of affairs in the Southern District, I have the honour of transmitting to you by the *Blonde* frigate copies of the letters written by Lord Rawdon during my illness to the Commander in Chief and to Major General Leslie and of one written by myself to the Commander in Chief on the 3rd of this month[56]. As these letters explain fully our past operations and present situation, I have only to add that Major General Leslie is safely arrived with his whole fleet at Charlestown.

I have the honour to be
Your Lordship's most obedient and most humble servant

CORNWALLIS

---

55 *that*: the meaning is 'as'. As in modern French, a subordinate conjunction, if repeated in 18th-century English, was often replaced by 'that'.

56 *copies of the letters*..: see p 24 and vol II, pp 55-61.

Germain to Cornwallis, 3rd November 1780 *65(5): LS*

Whitehall
3rd November 1780

Earl Cornwallis

My Lord

This letter will be delivered into your hands by Lt Governor Bull[57], whose respectable character, long and faithful services in South Carolina, and great property in that province must be well known to your Lordship. He now returns to take possession of his estate, of which he was deprived by the rebels during their usurped government, and to be ready to resume his former station whenever the King's Service may require it. I beg leave to recommend him to your Lordship as a person very deserving of the favor and protection of Government, as your Lordship may safely rely upon his zeal and loyalty.

I am, my Lord,
Your Lordship's most obedient humble servant

GEO GERMAIN

Germain to Cornwallis, 9th November 1780[58] *65(7): LS*

(N° 1)

Whitehall
9th November 1780

Earl Cornwallis

My Lord

I had the very great pleasure to receive from Captain Ross, who arrived in London on the 9th of last month, your Lordship's dispatches N°s 1 and 2[59], which I immediately laid before the King, who read with the highest satisfaction the account contained in the latter of the very

---

57 William Bull (1710-1791) had served as Lt Governor of South Carolina from 1759 till the revolution, acting for eight years during this period as head of the administration. Born and reared in South Carolina, he had a true understanding of colonial prejudices but had remained loyal to the Crown, vainly attempting to stem the growing revolutionary sentiment. Having now returned to Charlestown, he would be appointed Intendant General of Police. Notwithstanding his politics, he was held in great affection in South Carolina and was so great a favourite that parents frequently named their children after him. One such person was a tailor named Frog, who was persuaded to christen his son John Bull, much to his later dismay. Although not subjected to banishment and confiscation by the revolutionary assembly at Jacksonborough, Bull would leave Charlestown in 1782 and spend the last nine years of his life in London. (*DAB*; McCowen Jr, *Charleston, 1780-82*, 19; Johnson, *Traditions*, 62)

58 Published without the enclosure in Stevens, op cit, i, 290. There are no other differences.

59 *your Lordship's dispatches..*: see vol II, pp 7 and 11.

glorious and complete victory obtained by your Lordship over the rebels near Camden on the 16th of August.

The great superiority of the enemy in numbers over the forces under your command, His Majesty observed, distinguished this victory from all that have been atchieved since the commencement of the rebellion, and though it might have been expected that the long continuance of the war would have increased the military skill and discipline of the enemy, your Lordship's complete success is a brilliant testimony that the spirit and intrepidity of the King's troops will always triumph over them and that, however they may exceed in numbers, the vigor and perseverance of the British soldiers will overcome all resistance when led on by an able and determined commander seconded by gallant and judicious officers. It is therefore particularly pleasing to me to obey His Majesty's commands by signifying to your Lordship His royal pleasure that you do acquaint the officers and soldiers of the brave army under your command that their behaviour upon that glorious day is highly approved by their Sovereign, and you will particularly express to Lord Rawdon, Lt Colonels Webster and Tarleton His Majesty's approbation of their judicious and spirited conduct. The latter indeed has a double claim to praise for his great alertness in overtaking General Sumpter's detachment before they were apprised of Gates's defeat and by their destruction rendering the victory at Camden still more decisive. Captain Ross's services have been rewarded in consequence of your Lordship's recommendation with a brevet of major, but you will perceive by the inclosed copy of Lord Amherst's letter to me that it is not judged fit at present to give Lt Colonel Tarleton the same rank in the army which he holds in the Provincials.

The steps your Lordship immediately took for improving your victory were highly judicious and must be attended with the most important consequences, nor was your determination to inflict exemplary punishment on those traitors who had repeated the violation of their oaths of allegiance or broken their parole and taken arms against the King less wise or promotive of the great object of the war, the restoration of the Constitution, for the most disaffected will now be convinced that we are not afraid to punish and will no longer venture to repeat their crimes in the hope of impunity should they be detected; and those who are more moderate will be led to withdraw from a cause which is evidently declining before it becomes desperate and they expose themselves to the consequences they may reasonably apprehend will fall upon such as persist in rebellion to the last.

The civil regulations you have made for South Carolina, as far as I am informed of them by your Lordship and Mr Simpson, appear extremely prudent and proper, and I am glad to find they are satisfactory to the merchants here who are deeply connected with that province. Such of the civil officers as are in England have received orders to return and the greatest part will sail with the first convoy. As the province is not yet restored to peace, it is not judged proper to appoint a Governor, but as the Lt Governor is going out, he can exercise all the functions of a Governor in Chief in consequence of His Majesty's commission to Lord William Campbell, which devolves to him, and as it is the King's wish to convince the people of America that no abridgement of their former liberties is intended, but that they will be restored to all the privileges of their former Constitution, the exercise of such powers as it may be fitting to allow the civil authority to possess, in the present situation of affairs, being in the hands of the constitutional officers of the province must have a good effect. Your Lordship will therefore endeavour to throw the conduct of civil matters into their former channels as far as you shall judge expedient to permit the civil officer to act. I impatiently expect to hear of your further progress and that Sir Henry Clinton and Vice Admiral Arbuthnot have found means of sending a force into the Chesapeak to co-operate with you, for, if that be done, I have not the least doubt, from your Lordship's vigorous and alert movements, the whole country south of the Delaware will be restored to the King's obedience in the course of the campaign.

I understand the Congress evade an exchange of the Convention troops with the garrison of Charles Town under the pretence that the time of service of the greatest part of it will expire in a little time and the men will then be no longer soldiers and not entitled to be considered as prisoners of war; and as the expence of maintaining these people is enormous, some means must be found of relieving the public from it and counteracting the chicane of that faithless body. What appears to me the most practicable measures for these purposes are the inducing the prisoners to enter on board the ships of war or privateers or to go as recruits to the regiments in the West Indies or as volunteers to serve upon the expedition against the Spanish settlements from Jamaica; and your Lordship will therefore take the proper steps for disposing of as many of them as possible in these several ways or in such others as may occur to you as more practicable and effectual.

I am, my Lord,
Your Lordship's most obedient humble servant

GEO GERMAIN

Enclosure
Amherst to Germain, 6th November 1780 ***71(5): C***

Whitehall
6th November 1780

Rt Hon Lord George Germain etc etc etc

My Lord

I have had the honor to receive your Lordship's letter of the 4th instant with the extract from Lord Cornwallis's letter of the 21st of August last therein inclosed. When I laid before the King the names of Major Tarleton and Captain Ross, His Majesty was pleased to direct that the latter should be promoted to the rank of major, of which I have had the honor to acquaint your Lordship, and His Majesty was pleased to express His sense of Major Tarleton's services in very flattering terms but did not think proper to give him any additional rank, he having very lately only been appointed to the rank of major.

I have the honor to be, my Lord,
Your Lordship's most obedient and most humble servant

AMHERST

Cornwallis to Germain, 18th January 1781 — *76(26): ADfS*

Camp on Turkey Creek
Broad River
January 18th 1781

Rt Hon Lord George Germain etc etc etc

My Lord

I think it necessary to transmit to your Lordship a copy of my letter to Sir Henry Clinton lest the exaggerated accounts from the rebels should reach Europe before your Lordship could hear from New York. I shall only say in addition to what I have said to Sir Henry Clinton that this event was extremely unexpected, for the greatest part of the troops that were engaged had upon all former occasions behaved with the most distinguished gallantry.

I have the honour to be with great respect
Your Lordship's most obedient and most humble servant

CORNWALLIS

§ - §

4 - From Amherst

Amherst to Cornwallis, 7th November 1780 — *71(7): ALS*

Whitehall
7th November 1780

My Lord

I had the honour of receiving your Lordship's letter[60] by Captain (now Major) Ross, whose arrival here with the accounts from your Lordship gave a more general joy and satisfaction than I have seen on any other event. I beg leave to offer my most sincere congratulations on the very eminent and signal success on the 16th August with my best acknowledgements for the letter your Lordship honoured me with, which, as it mentioned and recommended the services of particular officers, I took the earliest occasion of laying before the King, and His Majesty was pleased to receive it in the most gracious manner. Major Ross is now returning to your Lordship agreeably to your desires, and as you will receive from the

---

60 *your Lordship's letter*: see vol II, p 21.

Secretary of State every particular regarding the intended reinforcements to North America, I will not take up your Lordship's time with a repetition of the intentions or trouble your Lordship with what is passing in this capital, as Major Ross will give a much better account than I can in writing. I shall only add that if there is any thing in this country by which I can obey your Lordship's commands, I shall be exceedingly glad in executing them and proving to your Lordship that

I am with great regard and respect, my Lord,
Your Lordship's most humble and most obedient servant

AMHERST

§ - §

5 - From Arbuthnot

Arbuthnot to Cornwallis, 2nd December 1780 — *66(17): LS*

Charon off Staten Island
the 2nd December 1780

Earl Cornwallis etc etc etc

My Lord

I cannot express the very high sense I entertain of your Lordship's attention in honouring me with your correspondence particularly at times so critical and interesting that the object immediately before you might justly be presumed to engage all your attention.

I should have been supremely happy to have had it in my power at this moment to communicate any decisive event in the naval way, but the French have as usual kept out of our reach and the King's squadron of the line have been solely occupied in attending their movements.

Admiral Sir George Rodney has been here for some time in the autumn. It is a month since he sailed for the Leeward Islands.

I do myself the honor to inclose to your Lordship a copy of the orders the different commanding naval officers engaged in co-operation with you serve under.

The Chevalier de Ternay and his squadron yet continue at Rhode Island and are like to winter there.

I am with every sentiment of affection, respect and esteem, my Lord,
Your Lordship's most faithful and devoted servant

M^{T} ARBUTHNOT

Enclosure (1)
Arbuthnot's instructions to Barkley, 4th December 1780 *66(19): C*

By Mariot Arbuthnot Esq,
Vice Admiral of the Blue,
Commander in Chief etc etc etc

To Captain Barkley[61] of His Majesty's Ship the *Blonde*

Blonde
Hyæna
Galatea
Sandwich
Loyalist
and
Gallies

You are hereby required and directed to take the ships and vessels named in the margin under your command and to employ them in such manner as to give every possible effect to the operations of his Excellency Lt General Earl Cornwallis in the Carolinas as that officer may suggest. Particular attention is to be paid to the port of Charlestown, and one coppered ship always left there for the purposes of carrying on the King's Service and giving weight to the secondary and collateral measures which the commanding officer of the King's troops in that district may have to carry on in concert with his Lordship.

Given on board the *Charon* off Staten Island
4th December 1780

M^{T} ARBUTHNOT

By command of the Admiral

WILL GREEN[62]

---

61 Andrew Barkley (?-1790) had been commissioned a lieutenant in the Royal Navy in 1758, rising to commander in 1766 and to post-captain four years later. Presently captain of the *Blonde*, he would command on the Charlestown station after the departure of George Gayton for the Chesapeake. He had arrived in port as part of the squadron recently escorting Leslie's corps. In late January, with the *Blonde* and the *Delight* and *Otter* sloops of war, he would take charge of the convoy carrying Craig's detachment of some 300 men to Wilmington. There he would co-operate in the capture of shipping and leave 60 marines to form part of Craig's command. Nevertheless, he and Craig did not see eye to eye, and Craig would be glad to see the back of him when Barkley sailed for Charlestown on 18th February. (Syrett and DiNardo ed, *The Commissioned Sea Officers*, 21; *The Cornwallis Papers*)

62 William Green was Arbuthnot's secretary. If Clinton is believed, he was thoroughly dishonest and, starting as a nobody, had risen to a position of such power that he presumed to act in the Admiral's name. 'That blockhead of a secretary,' remarked Clinton, 'does all he can to keep us at variance, that his misconduct may not be discovered.' Many years later Green would write his memoirs, of which a part has survived. According to Willcox, it is factually unreliable but does imply that Arbuthnot was strongly under Green's influence, with other

Enclosure (2)
Arbuthnot's instructions to Symonds, 4th December 1780 — *66(21): C*

Secret

By Mariot Arbuthnot Esq,
Vice Admiral of the White,
Commander in Chief etc etc etc

To Captain Symonds, Commander of His Majesty's Ship the *Charon*

Charon
Amphitrite
Charlestown
Thames
Medea
Fowey
Bonetta
Swift
Hope
Vulcan fireship
Independance armed brig

WHEREAS a secret expedition is on foot for the annoyance of the rebels in Virginia which is to be conducted by Brigadier General Arnold at the head of a detachment of His Majesty's forces, and whereas I have thought fit that His Majesty's Ship the *Charon* and the ships and vessels named in the margin should be employed in cooperation on that service,

You are therefore hereby required and directed to take the said ships and vessels under your command and to proceed with them and the transports etc named in the annexed list to the Chesapeak Bay, and having seen the whole armament thither in safety and the troops landed, you will leave the conduct of the expedition to Captain Gayton of the *Romulus*, which ship is cruizing with the *Delight* off the Capes of Virginia, to whom you are to deliver the inclosed packet and with the ships and vessels named in the margin to take such a position off the Capes of Virginia, at a distance of from fifty to one hundred leagues, as may best enable you to fall in with the escort, and intercept the convoy, under the command of Paul Jones[63].

Charon
Medea
Charlestown
Amphitrite
Roebuck
Raleigh

Should you not fall in with the *Romulus*, you are to continue with the expedition and to direct Captain Duncan[64] of the *Medea* to cruize as before mentioned.

On your arrival off the Capes of Virginia you are to detach the *Bonetta* to Cape Fear, and afterwards to Charlestown with the inclosed dispatches, with directions to Captain Gambier[65] of His Majesty's

---

evidence suggesting that the influence was misused. (Willcox, *Portrait of a General*, 312; Henry S Fraser ed, *The Memoranda of William Green...* (Providence, 1924), 36 etc)

63 A heroic figure in the revolutionary navy, John Paul Jones (1747-1792) had set sail from France in December after most distinguished service in European waters. Commanding the *Ariel*, he would arrive at Philadelphia on 18th February. He saw no further active service in the war. (*DAB*)

64 Commissioned a lieutenant in the Royal Navy in 1759, Henry Duncan (?-1814) was promoted to commander in 1768 and to post-captain eight years later. He was now commanding the 28-gun *Medea*, a new vessel launched at Bristol in 1778. Having served as a controller of the navy between 1801 and 1806, he retired as a superannuated captain in 1811. (Syrett and DiNardo ed, *The Commissioned Sea Officers*, 135; Michael Phillips, 'Ships of the Old Navy' (Internet, 10th January 2006))

Ship the *Raleigh* and to Captain Douglas[66] of His Majesty's Ship the *Roebuck* to join you according to the rendezvous you shall transmit them therewith.

You are to take these ships on their junction under your command and to cruize with them on that station for six weeks, when you are to return to this port.

But should you not fall in with the *Romulus*, you are to leave the execution of your cruizing orders to Captain Duncan of the *Medea* and, opening the orders addressed to Captain Gayton, to take and abide by them for your future guidance until you shall be releaved by that ship, when you are to join the cruizing squadron, and ordering Captain Duncan, in case of his falling in with her, to deliver a copy of my orders for him, which you will furnish him with for that purpose.

Romulus
Thames
Fowey
Swift
Hope
Delight
Vulcan
Independance armed brig

The ships to remain in the Chesapeak are those named in the margin.

The cooperation of the army is to be hearty, animated, extensive and effectual both with the King's ships and men in every possible instance of service.

You will direct the *Bonetta* to return to this port after the delivery of her orders at Charlestown.

Given on board His Majesty's Ship the *Charon* off Staten Island
the 4th December 1780

M^T ARBUTHNOT

By command of the Admiral

WILL GREEN

---

65 James Gambier (1756-1833) was born at New Providence in the Bahamas, where his father was serving as Lt Governor. Brought up in England by an aunt, he went to sea at an early age, became a lieutenant in 1777, and one year later was promoted successively to commander and post-captain. Now commanding the *Raleigh*, a 32-gun frigate captured from the French on 17th June 1778, he had recently been involved with it in the reduction of Charlestown. In later life he would play a distinguished part in the naval war against Napoleon and in 1808 was rewarded with a peerage for his capture of the entire Danish navy. Subsequently, as a peace commissioner, he helped to end the Anglo-American War of 1812. A committed Christian who did much to evangelise the lower decks of the navy, he died an admiral of the fleet. (*ODNB*; Syrett and DiNardo, *The Commissioned Sea Officers*, 169; Michael Phillips, 'Ships of the Old Navy2' (Internet, 10th January 2006))

66 John Leigh Douglas (?-1810) had been commissioned a lieutenant in the Royal Navy in 1760 and had risen to commander in 1777 and to post-captain in April 1779. Lately, as captain of the *Roebuck*, a 44-gun frigate, he had formed part of the naval force involved in the siege and capture of Charlestown. He died an admiral of the red. (Syrett and DiNardo ed, *The Commissioned Sea Officers*, 129; McCrady, *SC in the Rev 1775-1780*, 459)

[*Subscribed*:]

As Brigadier General Arnold is under the orders of Earl Cornwallis, the co-operation with one is considered a co-operation with the other.

Enclosure (3)
Arbuthnot's instructions to Gayton, 8th December 1780 *66(23): C*

By Mariot Arbuthnot Esq,
Vice Admiral of the White,
Commander in Chief etc etc etc

To Captain Gayton, Commander of His Majesty's Ship *Romulus*

Romulus
Thames
Fowey
Swift
Hope
Delight
Vulcan
Independance armed brig

You are hereby required and directed to take the ships and vessels named in the margin under your command and to employ them in full and extensive co-operation with Brigadier General Arnold commanding a detachment of His Majesty's forces upon a secret expedition to annoy the rebels in the Chesapeak.

You are to give every possible aid, protection and effect to the measures of the army both with the King's ships and seamen upon every occurrence of your service.

When the Brigadier General or officer commanding the detachment shall signify his desire of extending his operations to any other of the colonies, you will reembark the troops and escort him accordingly with your whole force.

You are by no means to permit the ships or vessels under your command to be frozen up.

Given on board His Majesty's Ship *Charon*
the 8th December 1780

M^{T} ARBUTHNOT

By command of the Admiral

WILL GREEN

Enclosure (4)
Arbuthnot's instructions to Dawson, 8th December 1780 *66(24): C*

By Mariot Arbuthnot Esq,
Vice Admiral of the White,
Commander in Chief etc etc etc

To Captain Dawson, Commander of His Majesty's Ship the *Iris*

Iris *Halifax* *Otter* *Cornwallis* *Dependance*	You are hereby required and directed immediately to proceed to Cape Fear and, taking the ships and vessels named in the margin under your command, to remain with them in Cape Fear River and cooperate as far as lies in your power to promote the objects of the army under Lt General Earl Cornwallis as he shall suggest, for which this shall be your order.

Given on board His Majesty's Ship the *Charon* off Staten Island
the 8th December 1780

M[T] ARBUTHNOT

By command of the Admiral

WILL GREEN

Arbuthnot to Cornwallis, 13th December 1780 *66(35): ALS*

Caron
New York
December the 13th 1780
Fleet in Gardner's Bay

My dear Lord

I have suffered a thousand different passions upon your account since we parted. Some times reports have been received that your Lordship's life have been in danger from ill health, which that horrid climate of South Carolina rendered too probable for the ease of your Lordship's numerous friends. Imediately after, we were intoxicated with joy on that memorable victory over our enemies near Camden obtained by the very great officership your Lordship produced against such superiority of numbers. We are, however, (I know that I am) again relapsing by seeing in the rebel papers the capture of Major Wemyss and 25 prisoners, which accident had obliged your Lordship to retire into South Carolina to cover that province.

No man can possibly be more interested in every thing that concerns your Lordship's success than your humble servant. Accordingly my spirits are soon elevated at your success and as easily depressed when even doubtfull intelligence leaves me any thing to dread.

Your reinforcement under General Arnold is on the way and employs all my ships, and I hope by the time of their arrival your Lordship will be at perfect ease with respect to the enemy.

Sir George Rodney has been in these seas since the 14th of September and remained till the begining of November, in the course of which I understand a correspondence was carrying on between the Commander in Chief and General Arnold thorough Major André which ended in a personal interview at the General's post, West Point, that was to be given up, but on Mr André's return, which was fataly by land, he was arrested (plans of the fortresses and other papers found upon him), tryed, condemned and hanged. Thus unhapily finished the life of a very good youth, as fame says.

I have been employed a float, ever since I left you, in watching and blocking up Monsieur Tierney at Rhode Island, during which the Commander in Chief and Sir George was transacting business without taking notice of me, particularly the Admiral, who created himself Comander in Chief without authority otherwise than the bare seniority of his flag, which I deny. Your Lordship will perceive by my wandering from subject to subject that I am much hurried. The captain waites who is to carry this letter. I must therefore pray that your Lordship will apologise for me to Lord Rawdon, to whom I have not time to write, or I would assure his Lordship the liberty that I have lately taken in writing to Lord Huntington[67] respecting his Lordship's health proceeded from no motive but the aprehension I laboured under at the time for him, whose life I think of too much consequence to his country and friends to omit any means for his preservation. I hope you will both long live as a pattern of virtue to this giddy age and reap those laurels you are so justly intitled to. I most ardently wish I could be near you, who I long to serve with. Give me a hint and I will come with the fleet to the Chessapeake. Adieu.

I am in the sincerest manner, my dear Lord,
Your faithfull and most obedient most humble servant

M^T ARBUTHNOT

[*Subscribed*:]

Tiernie still at Rhode Island. Destang in the West Indies. Lately arrived in a frigate.[68]

§ - §

---

67 Educated at Westminster and Oxford, Francis Hastings (*c.* 1729-1789), 10th Earl of Huntington, had played a fairly inconsequential role in public life. An avowed whig, he was an opponent of the North ministry. (Valentine, *The British Establishment*, i, 426)

68 D'Estaing had sailed for France in early 1780 after the siege of Savannah had been broken. He never again appeared in North American or Caribbean waters.

6 - To Arnold

Clinton to Arnold, 14th December 1780[69] *4(331): C*

Head Quarters
New York
December 14th 1780

Brigadier General Arnold[70]

Sir

You will be pleased to proceed with the troops which are embarked under your command, a return whereof you will receive herewith, to Chesapeak Bay, and if a favorable opportunity of striking at any of the enemy's magazines should offer itself, you are at liberty to attempt it provided it may be done without much risque, but if there should be no prospect of effecting that or any other essential service, you are as soon as possible to establish a post at Portsmouth on Elizabeth River in Virginia, make known your intention of remaining there, distribute the proclamations you take with you, which are to be addressed to the inhabitants of Princess Ann and Norfolk Counties, and assemble and arm such of those people as you have reason to believe are well affected to His Majesty's Government and are inclined to join you. It is, however, by no means my intention that you should invite the inhabitants of other districts to join you till such time as you establish yourself and afford them the like protection as is held out to those of Princess Ann and Norfolk Counties.

After having established yourself at Portsmouth, I would not have you make any excursions from thence unless they can be effected without the smallest danger to the safety of that post, which is always to be considered as the primary object of this expedition.

Having sent Lt Colonels Dundas[71] and Simcoe, officers of great experience and much in

---

69 This letter was presumably enclosed with Clinton's of the 13th to Cornwallis, p 31. An extract, omitting the last three paragraphs, is published in Davies ed, *Docs of the Am Rev*, xviii, 256. It also omits the word 'all' which appears here in the fourth paragraph. There are no other material differences.

70 Until recently Benedict Arnold (1741-1801) had been a major general in the Continental line with an outstanding record of military service. Angry at repeated slights from Congress, resentful at actions of the Pennsylvania authorities leading to his court martial, short of ready money, and indignant at the French alliance, he began in May 1779 to enter into that betrayal of the revolutionary cause which is indelibly associated with his name. Discovered in September 1780 while conspiring to deliver up his command at West Point to the British, he fled to New York and was promptly commissioned a brigadier general on the Provincial establishment. He was now about to command the expedition to Virginia. (*DAB*)

71 Thomas Dundas (1750-1794) was born into a family of minor Scottish gentry whose seat was at Fingask and Carron Hall, Stirlingshire. Educated at Edinburgh High School, he entered the 1st Dragoon Guards as a cornet on 25th April 1766. Three years later he purchased a captaincy in the 63rd Regiment and in April 1775 sailed with it from Cork to reinforce Boston. In January 1776 he went on to purchase the majority in the 65th Regiment, then

my confidence, with you, I am to desire that you will always consult those gentlemen previous to your undertaking any operation of consequence.

You will be able to judge from appearances on your arrival in Chesapeak whether it may be expedient to immediately establish the intended post. Should Lord Cornwallis, who will have been informed of your move, require any co-operation on your part before that is done, you are directed to obey his Lordship's commands, but after you have established the post as before mentioned, it is (as I have already said) my request that you do not undertake any operation with the least risque to that important station unless, after consulting the above mentioned gentlemen, your reasons should be such as you shall all think sufficient for so doing or Earl Cornwallis should positively direct.

Some blank warrants for holding general courts martial will be delivered to you, and I do hereby authorize and impower you to approve of the several sentences of said courts, unless in such cases as are capital or may extend to the cashiering of commissioned officers.

You will receive one thousand pounds sterling on account to defray the contingent expences that may occur on this command, and care will be taken to send a supply in due time for the subsistence of the troops etc on this service, who are already paid up to the 23rd of February next.

In order that I may be furnished with every information necessary to be communicated to the Secretary of State for His Majesty's information, I am to request you will from time to time communicate to me such intelligence as you may think interesting to the King's Service.

Most heartily wishing you success, I am, sir, etc etc

H CLINTON

---

at Halifax, Nova Scotia, before being promoted to the lt colonelcy of the 80th Regiment, which in early 1778 was being raised by the Corporation of Edinburgh. With it he arrived at New York some eighteen months later. Now accompanying Arnold to Virginia, he would remain there with the 80th and be appointed one of two British commissioners who settled the articles of capitulation at Yorktown. After the war he was placed on half pay, serving as MP for Orkney and Shetland from 1784 to 1790, but returned to active service in 1793, being appointed a major general and taking a leading part in Sir Charles Grey's successful expedition to reduce the French Windward Islands. Appointed Governor of Guadeloupe, he died at Basse Terre shortly afterwards of yellow fever and was buried in the principal bastion of Fort Matilda. When the French recovered Basse Terre in December 1794, they disinterred his remains, which were, according to Victor Hugues, the notorious republican commissioner, 'given as prey to the birds of the air'. The following year a monument to Dundas was voted by Parliament and placed in St Paul's Cathedral. (*ODNB*)

Cornwallis to Arnold, 6th January 1781 *84(16): C*

Wynnesborough
South Carolina
January 6th 1781

Brigadier General Arnold etc etc etc

Sir

I was this day informed by a letter from the Commander in Chief that you was appointed to command a force in Chesapeak Bay. By the junction of the corps under General Leslie I am enabled to leave the provinces of South Carolina and Georgia in perfect security and to march into North Carolina with 3,000 good troops. My future operations must depend on events and the exertions of our friends in that province. I shall take every opportunity of communicating with you and shall be glad to hear frequently from you. I enclose a cypher which is very easy and at the same time very safe.

I propose sending immediately some armed vessels and a small land force to possess the harbour of Cape Fear. I have desired Lt Colonel Balfour to send such of the Virginia refugees as he thinks may be usefull to you, amongst whom I beg leave to mention Captains Parker and Blair[72], who have been represented to me as men of merit. I have likewise ordered Captain Saunders[73] of the Queen's Rangers to join you.

---

72 George Blair had migrated from Britain to Virginia in 1762 and gone into a mercantile partnership six years later at Smithfield in Isle of Wight County. Of the loyalist persuasion, he was commissioned a captain on 15th November 1775 in the Queen's Own Loyal Virginia Regiment raised by Lord Dunmore, the royal Governor. In mid April 1776 he came to be aboard a six-gun privateer which crossed Ocracoke Bar, North Carolina, and captured two prizes. While at anchor, the privateer was very soon boarded and taken, and the prizes recaptured. Blair was sent a prisoner to Suffolk, and then to Williamsburg, Virginia, and after spending nine months in captivity, he was dispatched under guard to Philadelphia. On reaching Alexandria, he escaped and made his way 300 miles to HMS *Roebuck*, which took him to New York. Besides being employed in gaining intelligence in the interior, he was placed in command of a company of guides and pioneers and in May 1779 accompanied Mathew and Collier's successful expedition to Virginia. Now in South Carolina, he would, like James Parker (see vol II, p 347, note 53), embark to join Arnold in Virginia but be captured at sea on 19th February. After six months' imprisonment on the American coast, he was confined at Santo Domingo until January 1782 and then sent on to France, where he remained captive until the peace treaty. Placed on the Provincial half-pay list, he proceeded to seek compensation from the royal commission for his property confiscated in Virginia. (Coldham, *LoyalistClaims*, 39,40; *The Pennsylvania Gazette*, 8th and 15th May 1776; WO 65/165(16) (National Archives, Kew))

73 At the outset of the revolution John Saunders (1754-1834) had been a planter owning an estate of 1,200 acres in Princess Anne County, Virginia. A steadfast loyalist, he refused to subscribe to the Continental Association subversive of the Crown and went on to raise a company in the Queen's Own Loyal Virginia Regiment, with which he accompanied the deposed royal Governor, Lord Dunmore, to New York. Commissioned a captain by Dunmore, he would serve in the same capacity when his regiment came to be incorporated into the Queen's Rangers. At the Battle of Brandywine he was wounded. A cavalry officer, he had in late 1780 accompanied Leslie with a detachment of some twelve men, first to Virginia, and then to South Carolina, with orders to complete a troop to serve to the southward. He did not go on to join Arnold in Virginia and until mid 1781 was stationed at Georgetown. The following year he sailed for England, where he sought compensation for his confiscated property from the royal commission, entered the Middle Temple, and was admitted to the bar in 1789. Soon afterwards he was appointed a Judge of the Supreme Court in New Brunswick, where he also became a member of the legislative assembly, a lt colonel in the militia, and a Member of HM Council. From 1822 till his death he occupied the

I am, sir,
Your most obedient and most humble servant

CORNWALLIS

§ - §

office of Chief Justice of the province. (The John Saunders Papers (microfilm), The Loyalist Collection, Harriet Irving Library, University of New Brunswick; *The Cornwallis Papers*)

CHAPTER 31

Correspondence between Cornwallis and Balfour

Cornwallis to Balfour, 1st November 1780 ***82(1): C***

Camp at Wynsborough
November 1st 1780

Lt Colonel Balfour
Commandant of Charlestown

Dear Balfour

This is the first time I have taken up a pen and of course shall be short. I find Cunningham declines attempting his corps, so that we must make the most of the militia. They must have pay when employ'd: a captain £50 a year, a lieutenant £30 and an ensign £20; the privates three dollars a month; and those that have been employed under Ferguson to be paid three months back. Some allowance of medicines to be made to the doctor at Ninety Six who attends on the sick. The troops of horse of 40 men each to be rais'd; Dunlap to have the rank of major and to have the temporary command of them. I mention all this that you may talk it over with Cunningham. That part of the country must be kept at all events and I think no reasonable expence should be spared. Besides, Georgia depends entirely upon it. The letters you have received fully explain our situation. Our subsistance is attended with a thousand difficulties, which do not help me to sleep sound. The army, thank God, is well and despises all hardships.

Yours most affectionately

[CORNWALLIS]

PS

Lord Cornwallis desires me to acquaint you that any arrangements you may have made with Colonel Cunningham respecting the militia he will gladly approve of.

JM

Cornwallis to Balfour, 4th November 1780 *82(6): C*

Wynnesborough
November 4th 1780

Lt Colonel Balfour
Commandant of Charlestown

Dear Balfour

We still continue to subsist here but I fear it cannot last long. In the mean time my thoughts are turned to putting Camden and Ninety Six into the best state possible. I am convinced that cavalry is necessary for 96 and could wish to have two or three troops raised as soon as possible. Dunlap, who is an active, gallant officer, will have the rank of major and command the whole.

I understand that appointments are arrived at Savannah for 300 cavalry. I should fear that they may be damaged. In all probability the vessel by this time is got to Charlestown. Tarleton is to have the best of the appointments and give up the worst of his own. However, as it would be of great importance to have something on horseback as soon as possible at 96, I would give forty sets immediately to Captain Dunlap. He must likewise have about £150 advanced to him to begin upon the bounty money. He will come to you in town, when all these things may be settled by you. The 96 militia must have considerable encouragement; I mean to give three months' back pay to those who have been in constant service with Ferguson according to the rates I mentioned to you in my last. I foresee that it will draw us into great expence but I cannot help it, for should the militia of this country absolutely refuse to serve, the consequences would indeed be fatal. I think if Cunningham, who by all accounts is the most popular man amongst them, was appointed brigadier general of militia, it would be attended with the best of consequences. His pay might be 15 shillings a day. The sooner he is sent down the better.

I have sent Haldane to Camden and hope soon that the works there will be in a good state. I have ordered a good redoubt on each side of the river to command the ferry. I mean to give the command of that post to Wemyss and mount the York Volunteers and send them to 96. Poor Turnbull is quite worn out and anxious to get away.

In answer to Governor Dalling's request[1], it is not in my power to give him leave to enlist prisoners and I do not know of any others whom he can get, nor can I think it can ever answer for them to have recruiting parties in this province. I would, however, wish to shew all possible civility and attention to Governor Dalling's request, and if it can be managed, I would exchange the officers as they may be much wanted.

Yours sincerely

CORNWALLIS

PS

The militia officers ought to have commissions. If you could get a number printed and sent to me, I would sign them and give them to Cunningham to fill up. Sir Henry left a number as far as captains. I believe they are at my quarters at Charlestown.

Balfour to Rawdon, 1st November 1780 — *4(9): ALS*

Charles Town
1st November 1780

My Lord

I did myself the honor to write you a few days ago[2] and to send some letters for Lord Cornwallis from England, his seal, and some lemon juice.

Since my letter left this, I have received many acounts of the numbers of the different rebell partys having increased considerably, and that they had crossed the Santee both above and below Nielson's Ferry in small but many partys. In consequence of this intelligence I have been obliged to detach fifty men to Monk's Corner, and to move on to Nielson's if necessary, at both of which places there is very strong posts. The ferry at Manigault's I have directed to be secured by the Orangeburgh militia, and those on the lower parts of Santee by Ball's and Wigfall's regiments.

But the numbers and spirits of the rebell partys so far outballances that of our militia that a post at the High Hills of Santee or King's Tree Bridge is now absolutely necessary, otherwise the communication is at an end betwixt the army and this town. Indeed, the successes of smaller partys seems to have induced the enemy to make these plundering partys a serious object, to increase them by every means they can, and lateraly[3] to put them under a form and Continental officers to command. Their numbers betwixt the Pedee and Santee

---

1 *Governor Dalling's request*: see his letter of 14th July, vol II, p 122 et seq.

2 See vol II, pp 131-9.

3 *lateraly*: latterly.

are much exagerated, but from the best acounts they exceed a thousand divided into three partys, which are so often shifted that it is impossible to give any acurate acount of their situation. However, I fear much that they are become so formidable that nothing less than a very strong detachment from the army with cavalry can shew themselves in that country, which must not remain if possible in its present situation, otherwise our posession of the province will be of little consequence.

The officers for the necessarys are here and were ordered to leave town tomorow, but as I am informed there is no soldiers' shirts in town, and some being in a ship just coming up the harbour, I have kept them for the arrival of the vessel. But from Monk's Corner nothing can stirr untill we hear of the communication being safe. I shall take care to have every thing there ready and to press every waggon in the country when it is in our power to move. I fear some rum must have fallen into their hands.

Detaching more men from this garrison in our present sickly state I apprehend would be by no means *proper*. Lieutenant Bluck's detachment and that today has distressed me a little. However, if two or three hundred men are wanted for a short time, I think I could keep things here quiet, although I would not wish it unless absolutely necessary.

I have apprised Turnbull of the situation as far as I know. His detachment, I fear, he thinks too small at present to venture a movement towards Nielson's.

The news lately is, by a letter from Governor Maxwell from Providence: Monsieur Guichen[4] sailed from the Cape[5] to join Monsieur Ternay at Rhode Island.

A ship acount of many ships bound to the West Indies and three East India men of ours being captured by a squadron of the enemy's fleet. I long to hear of Lord Cornwallis. I fear some dispatches have fallen into the enemy's hands.

I have the honor to be
Your Lordship's most obedient servant

N BALFOUR

---

4 Luc Urbain de Bouëxic (1712-1790), Comte de Guichen, was a French admiral who had arrived with a squadron in the West Indies in March 1780. The following month he was involved in an indecisive engagement with Rodney off Martinique. Contrary to Balfour's information, de Guichen had sailed, not for Rhode Island, but for France, where he arrived at Brest in September. (Boatner, *Encyclopedia*, 459-460; Fortescue, *British Army*, 336)

5 Cape François on the north coast of Haiti.

Cornwallis to Balfour, 6th November 1780 *82(9): ACS*

Winsborough
November 6th 1780

Dear Balfour

I am rather sorry that opportunity offered immediately of sending the first letter, the second being more material.[6] We find difficulty subsisting here but hope to stay until the Legion returns. Could you send some pilots for Cape Fear to Leslie.

Duncan Macrae in the service of Mr Cruden knows the river.

Yours etc

CORNWALLIS

Balfour to Cornwallis, 5th November 1780 *4(27): ALS*

Charles Town
5th November 1780

With most unfeigned sincerity I congratulate your Lordship on your recovery. We never knew how very ill you was untill you was greatly better. The rebells has buried you regularly every day for some time past. May all their wishes respecting you turn out as vain and fruitless.

Before I mention any circumstances of the situation of affairs here, I acknowledge the receipt of Lord Rawdon's letters of the 30th and 31st[7] with the letters for the Commander in Chief and General Lessly[8] with the duplicates.

Unluckily the ships were under way and the *Thames* just at the barr when my request got to Captain Howe for his deferring his departure, and therefore they could not, as he said in his *answer*, be detained. However, I have only to assure you that an express boat went to him the moment I had time to read Lord Rawdon's letter and write to him.

The forwarding General Lessly's letter[9] has been very difficult and I am at last obliged to hire a fast sailing sloop at forty shillings per diem with a lieutenant of one of the galleys

6 The letters referred to are Rawdon's of 24th and 31st October to Leslie, vol II, pp 55 and 59.

7 See vol II, pp 128 and 130.

8 See vol II, pp 59-61.

9 Rawdon's to Leslie of 31st October, vol II, p 59.

(who knows that coast) and eight volunteers from the transports to navigate her. They will sail tomorow morning certainly[10], and I shall send one of the letters to the Commander in Chief by them to put into any ship of war they may meet or to be forwarded by General Lessly. Getting dispatches from hence at present by sea is allmost impossible without hiring vessells at an enormous price, and we have nothing in the small armed way or from the navy to asist us. However, if you wish me to hire one for York, be so good as let me know.

When I received the letter from Lord Rawdon first for General Lessly[11], I own I thought it so undecisive that, knowing *his* disposition, was sure that it would distress him much and perplex him exceedingly. I therefore, being throughly convinced I was doing a benefit to the service, took the liberty to send Gratton of the 64th, in whom he has great confidence, and wrote him a strong letter[12] pressing his coming to the place you wished and in such terms that I thought would *decide* him unless his instructions *interfered*. Gratton was also instructed fully upon the head, and I have no doubt, unless that he is absolutely ty'd down, that we shall hear of him very soon by the *Iris*, who has had very fine winds and sailed instantly upon the requisition. At present I am certain *this* letter[13] will bring him and have therefore preferred sending it to sending *that*[14] to New York for the Commander in Chief.

The garrison at St Augustine being in want of provisions, I am obliged again to request the *Galatœa* (just come in from Savannah) to go there with a convoy, with which request Captain Read writes me he will comply.

Nothing after her will remain but the *Sandwich* and *Loyalist*, the last being just come in from a cruise and in want of repair.

When Captain Symonds was here in the *Carron* convoying the fleet, I fully told him what a situation we were in, for want of asistance, in the navy affairs, harbour, cruisers etc etc. He promised me faithfuly to explain things to the Admiral and I doubt not he will. Indeed, a commanding officer is wanted exceedingly, and it would but tire you to say how very much I have been plagued about their affairs.

Permit me to assure you that I have felt the greatest satisfaction in observing the line you have followed. The leaving this province in the situation things proved to be in, with the general dissafection of allmost all ranks, would have been attended, I am convinced, with fatal consequences, and in attempting to gain two provinces, one if not both might have been lost. The most earnest desire for a forward movement and an offensive war prevented my mentioning any sort of obstructions, being more earnestly anxious that your operations should

---

10 The sloop was to be delayed. See Balfour to Cornwallis, 10th November, p 69.

11 Rawdon to Leslie, 24th October, vol II, p 55.

12 *a strong letter*: see p 31, note 30.

13 *this letter*: Rawdon to Leslie, 31st October, vol II, p 59.

14 *that*: Rawdon to Clinton, 31st October, vol II, p 60.

not be retarded by any objections of mine unless I saw and felt difficultys too obvious to be overlooked for the general safety and your success.

The general appearance of things at present is exactly *that* of every one part I have ever seen in America: a general distrust, and a kind of calm, to observe what side is to preponderate, the *friends* of Government anxious to palliate the faults of rebells and willing to make as much of their own equivocal merit as possible.

Cunyngham is here. I had sent for him, finding that he was not going on with his corps. He says that his raising men is now impossible. Whether he is disgusted with the stoppage that was put to his former warrant or desirous of being at the head of the militia of that country as principal, I am at a loss to know. Part of both weighs, I believe. However, he is certainly by every title best meriting protection and asistance. I have pressed him as much as possible upon the subject of his corps, but he insists upon its being out of his power etc. Kirkland seems to be taken up by Crugar, which surprises me, as undoubetly he is by no means a man of influence or reputation in the country. However, he says that he has been more active than any other man in that district.

The idea of militia being of consequence or use as a military force I own I have now totaly given up. That they are of use so far in appearance as being in arms for us, persecuting plunderers, and having the appearance of a force in support of Government must undoubetly serve an essential purpose. When I mentioned Crugar's plan of a draft of young men to be pay'd and clothed under the command of a good officer with some regulars to asist in forming them, I conceived they might have answer'd a good purpose for a time, when you was advancing, but certainly they would have been still militia and of course of little real service. Upon the whole I am at present from experience convinced that no militia of this province will be of any use to us as a military force and can only be of service in keeping the peace of the country against plunderers etc. To raise and form corps is then only the service to be procured from them; and to allow them to remain under the *old Provincial laws*, which are as well adapted as any others for the purposes I have mentioned, giving them upon particular occasions rum, blankets and salt, will in all probability encourage and keep them up.

Major McLaurin, late of Innis's corps, is a man of sense and some influence in the Back Country; also he is connected with many principal people of it. He has proposed upon good terms to attempt raising a regiment thereabouts and comes with his plan to your Lordship in a few days.

In regard to it I have only to observe that he must not call it a battalion of Innis's, otherwise he will not succeed; that as to himself he has but one fault as I am assured, which is that he drinks sometimes rather hard. In other respects he is unexceptionable, and if your Lordship gives him a commission, I rather think he will succeed. Cunnyngham also comes to you to lay before you his reasons of declining the corps. If you have no objections and think to leave the militia to their former laws, Cunyngham, I think, surely is the best man in the country to command the whole, and if he was allowed pay of some kind, it would retrieve his fortunes, at present very low. Crugar has begged to come a few days to town upon business, and Williamson, Pickens etc come with him.

If Wemyss could be prevailed upon to stay under the command of Crugar, it would be of much service, for I find a diffidence, allarm and despondancy that would but ill suit us in case of your being at a distance. Brown is also very ill adapted for that post, and I look upon the whole unfortunate insurrection of the mountaineers, Ferguson's defeat and all the other bad consequences to have originated in his stubborn and unpardonable indolence at the beginning when he came to Augusta. However, if Wemyss or any other regular corps remains at Ninety Six with Allen's and Crugar's, it must be secure unless attacked by an army. Some horse will be necessary, which will be got (as Crugar writes me) easily and will be well commanded by a militia major, one Clarey. McLaurin's or any other corps can be forming there and the militia ready for any purpose they *can* serve under Cunyngham. This appears to me the best and only plan left for that country. The advanced posts can easily be fixt upon by the officer commanding.

I wrote fully to Lord Rawdon my ideas concerning the defence necessary for the eastern district betwixt George Town and Camden[15], and am now of opinion that either Cheraw Hill or King Tree Bridge should be formed immediately into a post. Colonel Gray seems to me by much the best militia man I have seen, and if a detachment could be spared for him, it would be of service, as I realy think he would yet make something of that militia from his zeal and spirit. How far the Cheraws are too much exposed and too far advanced I am not able to judge. As to George Town District, Cassells, I hope, will under the protection of Bluck's detachment and Balingall's regiment (if I can get them there) be able to keep posession with his militia of the ferrys upon Pedee pretty high up and adjoining to Cheraws, or otherwise upon Port's Ferry and others which cover that country. As I look upon this as the only time for fixing and taking posession of all the leading and principal posts of the province, I hope you will excuse the tiresomness of my dwelling so long upon that subject.

An object of consequence appears to me *now* in the communication being kept and the army well supply'd from this at present.

It is with great reluctance that I assure you of my feeling every distress you can suppose from the want of active and trusty officers in allmost every situation and department. Pressing opportunitys are every day appearing and demanding good people to act in, but where or how to get them God knows, for, Moncrief excepted, there is not a man I can trust with the dutys of his department.

I hope your Lordship will believe me sincere when I assure you I only mean this as an appology for any want of exertion you may have found from this, and not a wish to make demands or difficultys. My most earnest and anxious desire while I stay here is to plague you as little as possible with either.

Upon the most accurate acount I can get of our strength in waggons I find it will be quite impracticable to go near supplying you with rum, salt, and carrying up the necessarys sent for, which indeed are so very immense in bulk and quantity that it will be hard to say when they can be got up. A weekly small supply of rum and the most useful necessarys I have ordred first up, and the cloathing etc in turn, but some small petihaugres with boats, and a large

---

15 *I wrote..*: on 26th October, vol II, p 131.

quantity of rum and salt, I am about to send off round by the mouth of Santee, which I am well informed will not be more than twenty four days in getting to Congarees. Whether that place or McCord's Ferry will best suit you to send waggons to must be determined with you and orders sent immediately to McCord's to inform there, as henceforth every thing will proceed to Congrees unless stopped by you at McCord's. The sending all the way to the army from Monk's Corner by land is now absolutely impracticable, and indeed any farther than Nielson's. As to safety, the movement of Tarleton and the detachment from hence will fully answer that purpose, but a corps must remain somewhere towards Black River or King's Tree to keep the river, otherwise nothing will remain safe, however it may be for a time, and it is now realy an object for these plundering partys, who are swelled to a great degree and perfectly masters of that country.

Dunlapp is an officer I think might be of very great use at present by permitting him to raise cavalry, which can be got both here and in the country, and by placing him betwixt George Town and Camden. Indeed I know of no *other* fitt for that service but himself. I mentioned in a letter to Lord Rawdon my having demanded in your name all the cavalry acoutrements that are arrived in Georgia from England; and this day Colonel Clarke writes me that he will send all that there is, as it seems many has been plunder'd from the ship, which was taken by the privateer and retaken. Tarleton's demands here, I am told by Innis, are amazingly great. However, I have desired them to be comply'd with, as I have ever understood it your desire to supply the cavalry with what they may want.

The want of cash is become very hard upon us. Gordon is gone to New York to replace Crouder[16], who goes home, and he has promised me faithfully a supply. I have sent to Georgia but expect little from the Governor and Council, who are the most absurd of all people.

Cruden's business is begun, as you wish, but finding the very great danger of Negroes and property being carried off (which practice was already begun), he has extended his seizures very much. A list of them shall be sent next opportunity.

I have now mentioned every thing I can think of worth troubling your Lordship about. Many, many others I have decided on according to the commands you laid upon me of doing for the best from myself. I have only now to add that the communicating with General Lessly and giving him your ideas and instructions will be an object soon to be thought of. The *Sandwich* is ready for sea and might lay in Cape Fear with any letters or person you thought proper to send – as soon as, I mean, as it is known when he may be expected. If you think you cannot send him any confidential person from the army, and if you think such a person is necessary, you know I am allways willing to be employ'd where you think me of most service. The Congarees is but two days and a half journey from hence if your Lordship wishes to see me on that or any other business. I can safely and easily meet you there on any day you will appoint.

---

[16] Crowder would have been an assistant or deputy paymaster general at New York.

Inclosed is a letter from Jamaica[17], and I hope from Captain Cornwallis.

Lemmon juice was sent some time ago. I hope it is arrived safe, as well as the Madiera, claret, spruce and molasses I sent from thinking your illness had prevented your servants thinking of them.

Crabtree is arrived, and shall equip him as quickly as possible. I hope the watch and seal arrived safe and are as you wanted. We are now very strong in salt pork and flour in case General Lessly may want. I forgot to say that a gun boat will convoy the large boats up the Santee. No news from New York or any thing late from England.

Lord Rawdon will, I hope, excuse my not answering his Lordship's letter, as I understood from Colonel Tarleton you had reassumed the command of the army, which gives me most sincere satisfaction, and that I can now say to yourself that

I am with unfeigned attachment
Your most faithful servant

N BALFOUR

[*Subscribed*:]

Eleven oat ships are come in here, being most of them drove from their anchors and unable to reach their convoy. How many shall we keep here? Mr Townshend has sent some people to drive cattle to Camden and desires me to say that he can contract for any quantity of salted pork of the country to be deliver'd at Camden.

Cornwallis to Balfour, 10th November 1780 — *82(18): C*

Winsborough
November 10th 1780

Lt Colonel Balfour
Commandant of Charlestown

Dear Balfour

I this day received your letter of the 5th and am infinitely obliged to you for the steps you have taken in regard to Leslie. You have, as you always do, prevented my wishes. You will have heard of the unfortunate accident of poor Wemys. Had he not fallen at the first five shots, it would have been a very compleat stroke. His arm is broke and he is shot in the knee, notwithstanding which Sumpter had the inhumanity to put him into a waggon and carry him off[18]. Sumpter has passed Broad River and I believe joined Clarke and Brannon, making in all about 6 or 700. I have sent Money to command the 63rd and detached that

---

[17] *letter from Jamaica*: not extant.

[18] Cornwallis retracted this charge. See his letter to Balfour of 16th November, p 73.

regiment and the 1st Battalion of the 71st to Shirar's Ferry to watch the motions of the enemy and secure our communication with our mills. I do not think, whilst we keep our present situation, that they will attempt 96. The security of the country east of Santee puts me under the greatest difficulties. I do not know how to fix a post that will be both usefull and safe at Kingstree Bridge. Unless it is a post of some strength, it will only protect the ground it stands on. When Tarleton returns, I shall send Lord Rawdon and his corps to Camden and mount the New York Volunteers and as many more as he chooses and can conveniently equip. I think he must have a detachment of the Legion, but really without Tarleton they are of little value. I cannot think that the large cargo of rum and salt can come safe by the mouth of Santee. The navigation is very long and cannot be protected by any floating force. I wish I could think of a corps proper to be stationed on Black River, but we are not only weak in troops but in absolute want of officers to command them, of which the transaction of the night before last was a cruel instance, when Sumpter's corps might have been annihilated. I have written fully to you about Cunningham and the cavalry requisite for 96. I could likewise wish to have at least two troops for the eastern part of the province. If Dunlap would be more usefull there than at 96, it will be easy to change him. He will be with you in town very soon. It will be unlucky if Cruger should be absent just now from his command. Smallwood is said to be about Twelve Mile Creek, and Gates expected at Charlottetown. My present position is calculated to secure Camden and 96 and is the most convenient in every respect if Mr Sumpter does not starve us. Whilst we keep it, the land communication to Camden from McChord's is perfectly safe. A large proportion of oats must go to New York. It is impossible that we ever can send any farther from town than Monck's Corner. England has great merit and, considering all our difficulties and hardships, his waggons and horses are in wonderfull good order. His thoughts are taken up with supplying the army, and not making money, which is the only object of all the departments. I am much hurried and will write again very soon.

Yours very sincerely

CORNWALLIS

[*Subscribed*:]

Perhaps it will be better that the *Sandwich* should not go into Cape Fear River 'til you hear from Leslie.

Balfour to Cornwallis, 10th November 1780 — *4(90): ALS*

10th November
11 o'clock at night

This evening the *Beaumont* arrived from General Lessly and I have not lost a moment in sending his letter[19], which Benson carrys to Monk's Corner to be forwarded by an officer with the greatest expedition and safety.

---

[19] *his letter*: Leslie to Cornwallis, 24th October, p 37.

I have not the least doubt of his coming to the place you want, especialy since *things turn out as they do*.

The fast sailing sloop is not yet gone with the second letter[20], being blocked up by two privateers, which the *Gallatœa*, having now got out, will clear, and she will sail tomorow.

I shall have pilots etc etc ready in a man of war (the *Loyalist*), with a provision ship, to lye in the mouth of the river, but wish to hear something by the *Iris* first. The duplicate of the second letter I shall send by the *Beaumont*, to cruize, and, if she does not meet the fleet, to proceed with it to the army for fear the sloop does not get safely to them. I hope every day to hear more certain acounts of them and, if I can be sure of their destination, shall send rice, provisions etc without waiting for the *Iris*. I trust much to Gratton and my letter. The *Beaumont* will be ready for sea in three days, and by her I shall send the letter to the Commander in Chief, and not by the sloop as mentioned in my last. When she joins the fleet, an opportunity will certainly soon offer to New York; but as I conceive it is more material to get the letter to General Lessly than to the Commander in Chief, my principal object shall be pointed to that end. As the coming of the army is yet uncertain to a *certain* quarter, I think sending vessells to lye there before they come may be improper, at least till we are clear of their intentions, but a pilot or two can be put on board the *Beaumont* when she sails for fear of the slow return of the *Iris*. Being affraid to detain the dispatch one moment, I shall only add that two hundred and fifty good cattle left Goose Creek this morning for the army. They are supernumerary here and can be at McCord's Ferry in eight days. Their arrival there will be notify'd to Knight[21], the commissary, in time, who must give directions for their further movement.

I hope a post will be established at King Tree before Tarleton's return, otherwise the enemy will just come back upon that unfortunate district and the Santee be unsafe for the rum and salt now loaded for the bringing up that river in quantity. Haste prevents my writing better or saying more than that I shall put every thing in train for Lessly. I think he certainly will come where you wish him, and hope to receive instructions for him as soon as possible.

Ever yours most gratefully

NB

PS

Many of my letters are yet unanswer'd.

---

20 *the second letter*: Rawdon to Leslie, 31st October, vol II, p 59.

21 *Knight*: Knecht.

Cornwallis to Balfour, 12th November 1780[22] *82(30): C*

Winsborough
November 12th 1780

Lt Colonel Balfour

Dear Balfour

I have just received your letter of the 10th and Leslie's. It convinces me that I was right not to go on. I have no doubt of Leslie's immediate compliance. Cape Fear is a port rather difficult to make on account of the *Frying Pan Shoal*. If winds should not be favorable to Leslie, he had better come to Charlestown, where we may arrange his *corps d'élite* and he may take a fresh departure. I send him a short and kind letter[23] and take my chance of your getting it to him. I wrote you a long letter on the night of the 10th answering, as I thought, every thing material as far as I could, but perhaps imperfectly. I enclose to you Tarleton's report of his expedition[24]. The state of affairs at 96 absolutely require immediate offensive measures in that quarter or every thing will be lost and not easily recovered. Our victory the other night was compleat, but by Wemys's unlucky wound and the youth and inexperience of the casual commander we have allowed the enemy to call it a triumph. Wemys is within ten miles of us and I hope in no great danger as no bone is broke. The greatest difficulty I now feel is the fixing a post at Kingstree Bridge, the utility of which I am most thoroughly sensible of. Lord Rawdon goes to morrow to take the command of Camden and will fix on some plan. I have thoughts of sending the weak light company of Brown's to join Maxwell, and the New York Volunteers mounted and Major Fraser with 100 men of Innes's, to see the post fixed. I should then hope that Maxwell with the two companies and perhaps fifty men of Innes's might be able to keep the post with the help of militia and Harrison's two companies if we can make any thing of them, which is very uncertain, being visited frequently by the mounted New York Volunteers and reinforced by a troop or two of new raised dragoons to be raised and commanded as you please. If you think it best to remove Dunlap from 96 to that part of the country, you are at liberty to do it. I had given him the rank of major, which I doubt much whether I had the power of doing, in order to make him of more consequence amongst the militia. I have given you the general outlines of our plan, which has cost us much pains and perhaps is not very sufficient. I beg you will make any addition or improvement to it that you may think will make it more efficacious or secure. I will answer for Lord Rawdon, as well as myself, that there will be no jealousy, as we all most heartily mean the same thing, the good of our distressed country.

Allow me again to repeat my sincere acknowledgements to you for the important services you have rendered me. You have in every thing done just what I could have wished and, what few officers in our service are capable of doing, have voluntarily taken responsibility upon yourself to serve your country and your friend.

---

22 Extracts from this letter are published in Ross ed, *Cornwallis Correspondence*, i, 68.

23 *a short and kind letter*: see p 39.

24 *Tarleton's report..*: of 11th November, p 336.

I am with the greatest regard
Most sincerely yours

CORNWALLIS

[*Subscribed*:]

Many thanks for your waggon, which came very opportunely. The horses made a striking contrast with ours, one of which would draw more than four of yours. We have not lost one since we came to this ground and have brought our flour, meal and forage from above twenty miles distance; but we have thought more of carrying on the King's Service than of making a fortune for General Dalrymple[25].

Balfour to Cornwallis, 7th November 1780 — *4(57): ALS*

7th November

It was with unfeigned pleasure I this moment read yours of the 1st November and that I had ocular demonstration you was again at the head of the army. The season is now so healthy that I believe there is no kind of danger, but if fortune puts you another summer in this climate, more care will be absolutely necessary for your health.

Cunyngham has been here. I gave him a hundred dollars, finding him in distress. We talkt over the militia business fully and he is exactly wishing the plan you mention. However, as General Williamson is to be here in a day or two, and Crugar I believe (who is anxious to come for a day), I did not absolutely fix any plan for your approbation untill I saw them and had their ideas upon the subject. Dunlapp is an excellent man for the horse business, but I conceived that you would place him nearer the frontiers upon Pedee betwixt Camden and George Town as being the most active situation, for undoubetly some very spirited officer must be if possible placed there. Bluck goes on well at George Town and reports his situation as exceeding strong, having repaired his redoubt and got two howitzers from the galley upon it, a good abbattis etc. Whether Lechmere or Ballingall will be able to make any thing of their regiments I begin to suspect much. For three weeks past they have been attempting to get them together in vain. I meant them to asist Cassells at George Town.

Major McLaurin, who I mentioned in my last very tedious letter, is the bearer with his plan for raising his corps. I have talkt the matter over with him, and from what I have seen of him and his knowledge of the people when at Ninety Six, I should realy think it would be worth while to give him a fair tryal. He is also very intelligent respecting the part of the country where the army now is, and may be [of] use respecting a future supply.

I have made every enquiry respecting the possibility of a large convoy of boats with pork from this being sent regularly by the Santee and have no doubt of its being very practicable

---

25 *Dalrymple*: the Quartermaster General.

in case it is wanted. We shall see how the rum and salt get up. I will not longer trouble you with this but to assure you how

Very sincerely I am yours

N BALFOUR

PS

If you wish to give me a ride, it will do me much good coming to the Congrees if you have any business to communicate.

Cornwallis to Balfour, 16th November 1780 *82(46): C*

Winsborough
November 16th 1780

Lt Colonel Balfour

Dear Balfour

Major McLaurin arrived yesterday with yours of the 7th. I am not sanguine about his success but I will give him a warrant and let him try his fortune, but not as a second battalion to Innes. Tarleton is going to relieve the 96 District. A Negroe who came in on Tuesday assured me that Smallwood was on the west side of Broad River with three pieces of cannon, but I have every reason to believe that Smallwood is on the Salisbury Road; nor do I give credit to the cannon, although the Negroe persists in saying that he is content to be hanged if it is not true. It is absolutely necessary to settle matters in that quarter in case we should be obliged to march in a hurry towards Cross Creek. I have talked much to Tarleton relative to the post at Kingstree Bridge. He does not think that fewer than 3 or 400 horse and foot would be safe from being either carried off or starved or would be adequate to the protection of the river. It is at such a distance from the Santee, and the country so disaffected, that a small body of infantry in redoubts, which by the by take some time in making, could have no communication with the river. I should think it adviseable that no attempt should be made to send up rum and salt from the mouth of the Santee; and if McKinnon can send the usual supplies to McChord's, or even to Manigault's Ferry, the patroles which Lord Rawdon will send in force from Camden will pretty well secure them. The terrible outcries from 96 made it impossible to leave Tarleton longer in the Low Country. Had any misfortune happened there, not only South Carolina but Georgia must have fallen. Indeed, the carrying any of our posts must be attended with fatal consequences, which is a strong argument against Kingstree if it was possible to establish a post there, which at present I am convinced is not the case. I tremble for the necessaries embarked at Nelson's. If McKinnon's train is totally unfit for any service and that[26] he cannot recruit it, he may receive some assistance from Camden, but unless he will buy good horses and pay a good price for them, it is better to give the matter

---

[26] *that*: the meaning is 'if'. See p 43, note 55.

up altogether. We get plenty of good, strong draft horses for ten or twelve pounds a piece, but mostly under ten. Now as Government is charged fifteen, I cannot help thinking there is still a fair profit left; besides that, I cannot think Britain engaged in this war merely for the emolument of the Quarter Master General. I fear much cannot be expected from Lechmere's and Ballinghall's militia. Those who have been out and done their duty on the Santee must have encouragement in money, blankets etc. I most anxiously expect the hearing from Leslie as on him depends our having a chance of being tolerably quiet. They may salt pork at Camden and I understand that such a scheme is in agitation. Indeed, when the army moves forward, and at all times, it would be proper that Camden, 96, and even Augusta, where there must be some work, should have always at least a fortnight's salt provisions.

I am, dear Balfour,
Yours most sincerely

CORNWALLIS

[*Subscribed*:]

I totally misrepresented in my letter the treatment Wemys met with from Sumpter etc as neither he nor the other prisoners were at all illtreated.

Cornwallis to Balfour, 16th November 1780 — *82(48): C*

Winsborough
November 16th 1780

Lt Colonel Balfour

Dear Balfour

I mentioned in one of my letters that you might, if you pleased, change the appointment of Dunlap from the 96 cavalry to that of the Low Country, but considering that matter, I am convinced that the 96 cavalry will be good for nothing if it is not commanded by him, as the best men of the country would go out with their troops only to plunder and get themselves demolished. If we move to Cross Creek, 96 will be the only part of the province much exposed, and of much greater importance than the Low Country, which we shall clear as we pass and which will be greatly covered by our position at Cross Creek.

Yours most sincerely

CORNWALLIS

Cornwallis to Balfour, 17th November 1780 — *82(55): C*

Wynsborough
November 17th 1780

Lt Colonel Balfour

Dear Balfour

No sooner do I find myself under difficulties to accomplish any very important object than I am relieved by finding that you have already done it for me. You will spoil me for acting with any other person. This was never more strongly verified than in the instance of your sending the 64th Regiment to Kingstree Bridge, where it was impossible for me to place any thing that I could think perfectly safe. I am now quite easy and satisfied, and indeed I flatter myself that so respectable a force on Black River, with the constant communication that Lord Rawdon will be very attentive to keep up and the post at George Town, will render the whole navigation of the Santee secure, and that your large convoy will arrive at Camden without any material risk. The situation of things in the 96 District was very unpleasant and distressing, our friends terrified beyond expression, either flying down the country or submitting tamely to the insults and cruelties of the enemy, all the disaffected and many who had been neutral and some pretended friends flocking to the enemy's standard. Only one hundred militia embodied for us in that extensive and *friendly* district, and those commanded by Kirkland. Tarleton, who is to day at Shirar's Ferry, will soon alter the situation of affairs. He will have the 63rd with him and I have desired him not to hurry himself but to follow up his blow. I will then lose no time in endeavouring to put that quarter into some state of defence that I may be ready for Leslie. Our troops get healthier every day, are in high spirits, and, as soon as they get their warm cloathing, will be fit for any thing. I should be very glad to have some conversation with you, but I have no cavalry and am a little afraid of being alone in the part of the country you mention. As soon as Tarleton's expedition is over and we see what turn things are likely to take, I will endeavour to settle a rendezvous with you. There is one Hampton[27], who has a store at the Congarees, who has a brother, aid de camp to Sumpter.

---

[27] Wade Hampton (1751/2-1835), the owner of the Congaree store, was born in Halifax County, Virginia, and brought before the revolution to the Back Country of South Carolina. In July 1776 his parents, who had settled on the middle fork of Tyger River, were killed, together with his brother Preston, by Cherokees. Having seen service as a junior officer in the 1st South Carolina Continental Regiment, Wade was now on the face of things content to act as a loyal subject of the Crown, pursuing his trading interests. He was, however, behaving in a duplicitous manner. Having, on the one hand, taken protection and sworn allegiance to the Crown, he was, on the other, secretly supplying the enemy and providing them with intelligence. At first suspected, he would be caught out at the time of Sumter's raid in February 1781. He was arrested but escaped, going on to serve as a colonel in Sumter's Brigade. Whatever his behaviour may lead us to think of him, he would prove to be one of Sumter's most daring, effective officers and perform especially well in the Battle of Eutaw Springs. After the war he played a prominent part in public affairs, both politically and militarily, but his many responsibilities did not keep him from advancing his private interests. He had the qualities which made for success in the Back Country of the 18th century: energy, foresight, and the frontiersman's attitude towards land, that is to say, the will to possess without an overscrupulous regard for the means of doing so. In later life he added to his South Carolina lands by taking up sugar plantations on the lower Mississippi, and when he died, he was reputed to be the wealthiest planter in America, owning 3,000 slaves. Of his four brothers, John, Henry and Richard all joined Sumter as a major and colonels respectively, while Edward, who was to be killed by 'Bloody Bill' Cunningham in October 1781, also served as a captain in the revolutionary militia. (*DAB*; Heitman, *HistoricalRegister*, 271; *The Cornwallis Papers*; McCrady, *SC in the Rev 1775-1780* and *1780-1783, passim*; Draper, *King's Mountain*, 82, 83n; *Appletons'*)

He himself is said to be a great rebel, and his store supposed to be entirely for their use. You may perhaps find out what articles he chiefly brings from town. You will have been out of humour with my last letters representing the impossibility of securing the Santee, but remember that I did not expect any assistance from you. I still think, however, that the vessel destined for the mouth of Santee will have a long voyage. You will see Dunlap and hear what he says. I fancy you will agree with me in thinking him most usefull on this frontier, where, either with Sumpter, with Mecklenburg County, or with the Back Mountain men, we are sure of having perpetual war as long as the independance of America is in dispute.

I am, my dear Balfour, with the utmost gratitude and sense of your attention to me and zeal for the service
Your truly affectionate and faithfull friend

CORNWALLIS

Balfour to Cornwallis, 15th November 1780 — *4(126): ALS*

Charles Town
15th November 1780

Major Manson would inform your Lordship of the movements of the 64th Regiment, which I hope will meet with your approbation. The risks we run here are by no means of any consequence sufficient to prevent an exertion when it is so requisite as it appeared to me to be when Tarleton was ordred back from that country. I hope *that* force, amounting to 275 rank and file with two three pounders, is sufficient to give the check that was necessary to Marrion and Herrington, who would very soon have become very formidable and the communication by Neilson's would inevitably have fallen. While no foreign fleet appears, I will be answerable for this town, even as we are, although a British regiment would be nearly absolutely necessary. I have, however, been obliged to take up some more of the violent and principal men that were upon parole and to shipp them on board the *Sandwich* just going as a convoy to St Augustine.[28] The necessity of this measure was evident to every person whom I consulted upon it and much pressed by Moncrieff and Simson. The unweried assiduity with which they keep down every movement towards the success of our affairs, the pains which they take to prevent every person over whom they have any influence to come in and become British subjects, is astonishing. A dissafection is reported to me in Balingall's and Lechmere's regiments to be principally brought about by their[29] means. Also the backwardness in the whole country to take our side, which is so very evident, can only in great measure be attributed to the hidden and powerful influence their leading men still have over them, nor do I believe the government will ever get into any strength or form while they remain. I hope I shall not ever be tempted to committ any harsh action without good reason, but situated as things are, a decisive and strict line is absolutely necessary to be kept.

---

[28] Twenty-two men were transported, among whom was Arthur Middleton. They were accompanied by Brigadier General Rutherford and Lt Colonel Isaacks of North Carolina. A full list of the transportees appears in McCrady, *SC in the Rev 1775-1780*, 857.

[29] *their*: the principal disaffected persons'.

I have therefore given our newly become subjects to know that I expect a very different conduct from them than merely a passive and negative junction with us. They must take a part and by their activity shew their wish to asist a government they have become members of. All meetings and caballs are suppressed and I think soon we will be able to hope that the town will be our own.

Many violent gentry who were sent from the country are *gone* to warn the others of what they may expect. I am sorry to tell you that Ballingall's and Lechmere's regiments were so totaly dissafected that very few assembled and *those* very soon deserted, and Ballingall is clearly of opinion it is principaly owing to the influence of the prisoners upon parole. Inclosed is a much pleasanter acount[30] of Cassells's regiment, whom you need not doubt I shall court and encourage by all means possible and hope to raise a good number of cavalry amongst them. At present I have directed them only to move up Black River and take post at an intermediate ferry, betwixt Major McLeroth[31] at King's Tree Bridge and them, called Horth's Ferry. Cassells wants much to get to the Pedee, but that at present, I conceive, would be running too great a risk, and while they are cover'd betwixt two posts, they may advance and scour the country as far as they will, having allways a support and retreat to King's Tree or George Town.

As to the 64th Regiment, as Wemiss is wounded and prisoner, if you prefer it either to the 63rd or 7th, I can only say in my opinion this garrison will be equaly well off with either of the others, although perhaps weaker a little. And should it be necessary to keep the 64th out some longer or to move them more towards you, I think there is no danger *now* here. We will be all alert and look out if you want us to be so. Tarleton's friend[32] is gone, as you ordred, with directions to return (the moment he finds Gates in motion) to you if that is the case; if not, to get all the intelligence he can and come more leisurely to the army.

---

30 *acount*: not extant.

31 A native of Argyll, Robert McLeroth had entered the 64th Regiment as a captain on 1st January 1766 and sailed with it for North America in September 1768. Promoted to major on 28th August 1776, he had commanded the regiment in the New York campaign and went on to play a distinguished part in the Battle of Brandywine, where he was wounded. Continuing to command the regiment, he took part in the Charlestown expedition and had until very recently been with it in forming part of the garrison of the town. Now sent forward with 300 of his men to Kingstree, he would operate between Nelson's Ferry and the High Hills to secure the navigation of the Santee and the communication with Camden by land, but in mid December he would repair to Charlestown on regimental business and be briefly superseded in command by Major John Campbell of Rawdon's corps. As revealed later in *The Cornwallis Papers*, Balfour would be severely critical of McLeroth's ability 'to act for himself', perhaps influencing Cornwallis to a marked degree. Rawdon for his part, while admitting to McLeroth's having 'not quite enterprize enough', would not go so far, commenting, 'B[alfour] and M[cLeroth] never liked one another, so I hope it is not quite so bad.' Whatever McLeroth's merits as an officer, there is no doubt about his benevolence and humanity towards his opponents, as evinced by the testimony of those on both sides of the political divide. He would continue to command the 64th in South Carolina till April or May 1781, when news reached Charlestown of his promotion to the lt colonelcy of the 57th, effective from 18th November 1780. He sold out his commission one year later. (*Army Lists*; Major H G Purdon, 'An Historical Sketch of the 64th Regiment' (Internet, 13th February 2006); *The Cornwallis Papers*; James, *Marion*, 97-8; Garden, *Anecdotes* (1st series), 264; Garden, *Anecdotes* (2nd series), 103)

32 *Tarleton's friend*: de Treville.

The express boat is gone and the *Beaumont* with a duplicate and *pilot* sails tonight. Rice, flour and some provisions are all ready with two galleys and the *Loyalist.* I have allways forgot to say that by the last opportunity to England I wrote to General Amherst, with whom I am in confidence, to say nearly how things were and told him of Ferguson's affair. This, I think, will cool those sanguine expectations so ready to rise every moment in Pall Mall, where I dare say it will get to. This letter went about a month ago and I hope was wrote in a manner you would have approved of. I can only say it was intended most sincerly to be in that style.

The rum and salt shall be sent as usual by Nielson's, and I think it can be got up in sufficient quantity as we are now stronger than we were on the communication. The cloathing and necessarys are all gone from Monk's Corner.

I hope the cattle I sent are near you. I have wrote fully to Crugar about the militia. My scrawl is so long and bad I can only add that I shall write soon, I hope in God, with the return of the *Iris*.

I ever am etc

N BALFOUR

PS

I wish many queries in my other letters answer'd.

Cornwallis to Balfour, 18th November 1780 — *82(59): C*

Winsborough
November 18th 1780

Lt Colonel Balfour

Dear Balfour

I this day received your letter of the 15th. In mine of yesterday's date I expressed my very sincere acknowledgements to you for establishing the post at Kingstree, the utility of which I clearly saw but which I was afraid to undertake with a motley corps of Provincials and militia.

I am perfectly convinced you will do every thing that is right and just and necessary for the King's Service in regard to the rebellious citizens, who do ten times more harm than those in arms against us. I therefore beg that my name may be used in that business and that it may be all done by my order. I was not sanguine about Balingall's and Lechmere's regiments, so that I am not much disappointed. The supineness and luke warm behaviour of those of 96 vexes me much more.

Your language to the newly become subjects is very proper, and the abolishing all meetings and cabals.

I saw Wemys to day. He will soon set out for Charlestown. I desired him to dictate an account of the business, which I will transmit to you for publication. I fear Wemys forgot he was an infantry soldier, as he owns that he did not order his men to dismount even when he was in the middle of the enemy's camp and saw them asleep at their fires; but you will soon see the best he can make of it. After all, the victory was ours if we had staid 'till daylight.

You are certainly right to keep the defence to Black River and not to let Cassels encourage you yet to think of Pedee. It makes the frontier too extensive 'till we move. If I should propose any change for the 64th, it would be the 7th, but we will settle that hereafter. I should hope to get Wemys exchanged, for altho' he was in the late instance a mad trooper, he is certainly in the main a sensible and usefull officer. I am glad the express boat is gone; my thoughts are turned constantly that way.

What you have done in writing to General Amherst is like yourself and exactly the thing in the world I would have wished you to have done. I will not tire you with a repetition of compliments.

You cannot conceive what comfort I feel in the safety of our cloathing and necessaries, without which we should really be distressed. I saw this evening the parade of the Royal Welch Fuzileers and I assure you they are in great order and the most willing and good humoured people in all hardships. I propose sending the cattle for some days to the Congarees, as neither Camden or the army are in immediate want, and they will get more food there than here. We are at present most plentifully supplied with every article but forage, which is rather scarce.

I have read over your letters for some days back and do not see any queries unanswered. If any should have escaped me that are pressing, your decision will be sure of meeting my hearty approbation.

I am sorry to hear that money is scarce at Charlestown. I shall certainly want some soon as I lend to all departments. I should therefore wish you to send some by the first good opportunity. McKinnon has directed England to give receipts for horses to be paid in Charlestown, but that is very bad economy, for a man that would take 9 guineas here ready money would not take an order on Charlestown for fourteen. Pray tell him that I say so.

I am, dear Balfour,
Most truly yours

CORNWALLIS

Cornwallis to Balfour, 19th November 1780 *82(63): C*

Wynnesborough
November 19th 1780

Lt Colonel Balfour

Dear Balfour

I have been reading your letters to day farther back than I went yesterday. I find a query relative to the pay of the police. Mr Simpson is certainly entitled to as good a salary as Mr Elliot. I think therefore, if you approve, that he should have 40 shillings a day and the other Commissioners 20. Westerhagen has likewise a good plea for some allowance. I am afraid of the Hessians in money matters, but as he commands 3 regiments, I think him entitled to brigadier's pay. I will mention it to the Commander in Chief and in the mean time wish you to give him a civil but general answer that I am fully sensible of his pretensions and will represent his case and have no doubt that some allowance will be procured for him. You likewise mention in your letter of the 29th the calls of the militia for pay, woollens etc. I think I have given you *carte blanche* on that head. However, I again repeat that where they have shewn any real merit I would give them pay according to the rates I formerly mentioned, presents and warm cloathing. I believe some of the Orangeburg who have been at Nelson's Ferry deserve encouragement. I am very sorry you are distressed for cash. I would not wish to distress Government at present, yet some is absolutely necessary, especially the payment of receipts given for forage, cattle etc to friends or people living under our protection. Unless those things are paid, our reputation and credit are totally lost. I desired those who had good receipts to apply to you if they could not obtain payment and particularly addressed one Levi Smith[33] to you, of whom we bought some rum and who has some receipts of his neighbours as well as his own for forage etc.

Tarleton crossed the Broad River yesterday without opposition. I hope he will at least scatter those gentry and drive them out of the province, but as they are all mounted, I dare not flatter myself with any thing very decisive.

I send you Wemys's narrative, which is rather too long considering the event. I leave it to your judgement to extract and print something from it. He mentions a consultation of the officers, but as I am informed that some of them absolutely deny it, I should advise leaving it out as it may produce altercation and disagreable inquiries.

You may depend on hearing from me whenever any thing happens. As soon as the Ninety Six business is tolerably settled I shall be very impatient to hear from Leslie as I feel all the inconveniences of a defensive war very strongly.

---

[33] Levi Smith was a loyalist who kept a 'back store' north of the Congaree. He would be among the garrison of Fort Motte who surrendered to Lee and Marion on 12th May 1781. Two of his compatriots were promptly strung up, another was then killed, and he himself was about to be hanged when Marion intervened and turned him over to Greene as a prisoner. He soon escaped, returned to the Low Country with Rawdon, and as late as mid November 1782 was living in Charlestown. (Lambert, *SC Loyalists*, 201, 213n; Clark, *Loyalists in the Southern Campaign*, i, 489)

I am, my dear Balfour,
Most truly yours

CORNWALLIS

[*Subscribed*:]

Cavalry swords are in universal request. I could wish that all those lately arrived, except the 46 for Dunlap, might be sent with all possible expedition to Camden that Tarleton might take what he wants and give in exchange some which he has that are too short for the Legion. I shall, however, be tempted to take some good ones for the light company of the New York Volunteers, who will in Lord Rawdon's opinion make excellent cavalry.

Balfour to Cornwallis, 18th November 1780 *4(157): ALS*

Charles Town
18th November
10 o'clock evening

An hour ago the *Blonde*, Captain Barclay, with Gratton arrived. Inclosed is Lessly's letter[34] to Lord Rawdon, which, with the return, speaks pretty plainly for his situation, but mine from him and Gratton's private acount of matters is distressing. Never was there a corps so composed or so commanded – a medley and numerous mixture of all the bad corps, without any form or officer of experience either to asist him in the field or by his advice. In short, in his own opinion he is nearly unfitt at present for any offensive service, and were he to land at Cape Fear, it would be only to take post. He mentions in his letter to me his coming here and I see he wishes it, which Gratton also assures me of, as he feels the necessity of putting some arrangement to this strange medley under your direction.

I have consulted Moncrieff and we have both cooly and deliberately determined, from considering your Lordship's last letter to Lessly[35], from examining the return of his corps, and from hearing Lessly's own opinion of it, that his coming here is clearly the most judicious step to take to consult with your Lordship upon future plans of operations, to arrange and form his army (and if necessary to leave any improper part of it here, taking in its room some troops from this garrison), to divide his force, reinforce your Lordship, or in short to fix any plan you may think best — all which, and supplying him with proper provisions, can very well be done without allmost any loss of time, as to take the barr of Cape Fear he must come very near this place. And at all events your answer to this will be in time if wrote immediately to get to him before he comes here.

---

34 *Lessly's letter*: of 9th November, p 41.

35 *your Lordship's last letter..*: of 12th November, p 39.

I shall in consequence of this opinion send the *Loyalist* or *Blonde*, by making a requisition, to cruize off Cape Fear, and write to General Lessly for fear your letter by the *Beaumont*[36] misses him, telling him the state of the case and desiring him to come here immediately. If the *Beaumont* meets him, he will come here without any further requisition, as by my letter and Gratton's acount he is very desirous for it, feeling, as I know, his own situation with such a corps, unsupported, unadvised. Should you have changed your opinion, the galleys, provision ships etc etc shall all be ready to sett off and I dare say will be in full time, as he cannot be here in all probability in less than a week.

I am sorry to tell you that the *Sandwich* is gone to St Augustine, as the state of that garrison could no longer be risked without provisions and Captain Reed[37] chose to *refuse* my three official requisitions to take the convoy and leave the *Sandwich* here for particular service. This most extraordinary and most unusual behaviour is more distressing when I find that to cruize for prizes was the only service for which he refused to comply with my request.

Should Lessly come, of course every thing but his sick will remain on board and every thing we can do shall be done for him; but I should apprehend that you would wish to see and communicate with him, which I can easily manage by bringing him to any place you will fix upon near the army.

Although accustomed to act from my opinion, yet believe me the magnitude of this present stepp would shake me exceedingly but that I have the sanction of your own opinion in your last letter to Lessly to support me, added to Moncrieff's, and Gratton's acount of every thing, which is so clear that indeed there ought not to remain any hesitation about it.

Gratton's usefulness upon this occasion, his prudence and good management would be fully rewarded by a line from your Lordship to say you are sensible of this piece of service.

Captain Barclay bids me with his respectful compliments assure your Lordship of his being happy to cooperate and to forward your Lordship's wishes in the service by every means in his power.

I ever am etc

NB

---

36 *your letter by the Beaumont*: see note 35 above.

37 *Captain Reed*: of the *Galatea*.

Cornwallis to Balfour, 21st November 1780 **82(73): C**

Wynnesborough
November 21st 1780

Lt Colonel Balfour
Commandant of Charlestown

Dear Balfour

I have just received yours of the 18th with Leslie's, which gives me the greatest satisfaction. I attribute so much of the success of this business to your good management that I can't help again repeating my most sincere acknowledgments. I inclose a letter to him[38] with a duplicate of my last, which will answer every purpose.

Indeed I am most clearly of opinion in the present state of affairs and of his detachment that his coming to Charlestown is the wisest plan. As soon as he arrives, I wish you would set out with him for the army. If I can meet you on the road, I will. If not, you will not lose much time by coming on. You will of course give me the earliest and speediest notice of your setting out, and I will take all possible precautions for your safety and send horses to meet you. I have as yet heard no news from Broad River, but I always trust that where Tarleton is things will go on well.

I am
Most faithfully yours

CORNWALLIS

PS

I will not fail to represent to the Admiral the behaviour of Captain Reed.

Say every thing civil from me to Barclay. I dare say we shall do well together.

Balfour to Cornwallis, 17th November 1780 **4(149): ALS**

Charles Town
17th November 1780

I just received your Lordship's letter of the 12th. Time enough to save the *Beaumont*, who had been detained by contrary winds. She has sailed at day break this morning.[39] I have no doubt of Lessly coming here upon your letter. As they will want much, I shall be ready

38 *a letter to him*: of the 21st, p 42.

39 See p 39, note 47.

for them with all we have; but one want, viz cash, is now absolutely so much called for that, after running as long as I could, I am very near a fair stand fast and a complete bankruptcy. The fact is that there is not now near currency enough for the country exclusive of the army, and that the merchants to procure indigo and rice give cash, which is never again heared of, and keep up the remainder to distress the publick in order that the bills of exchange may rise. In the money contract with Harley & Drummond I know *they* act only upon commission at so much per cent for money procured to be sent to this country, so that in fact it is distressing the publick, their raising the exchange, but in that, or in any other feeling where immediate gain is concerned, they are the most unfeeling and rapacious of mankind. However, at present the distress is realy very allarming for want of cash. I have ransacked Savannah, but unless some specie comes from New York, I fear for the subsistances of the regiments not being forthcoming. Every regulation to counteract the merchants' avarice and get money shall be made use of.[40]

As to the post at King's Tree, the 64th Regiment can stay to see it fixed and a respectable work erected. However, I rather conceive that all Innes's corps, with Frazer to command, joined by the York Volunteers, and the two troops to be raised, them occasionaly posted at George Town or King's Tree, would answer fully as well as Maxwell, who, although a sensible and prudent man, is certainly not so active or good an officer as Frazer. Brown's light company, I should think, might march to King Tree and so on to George Town, which is rather too weak at present, and hereafter most of that corps might be fixed there and commanded by Maxwell, but I must seriously beg your attention to Ninety Six. If possibly some regular troops with a steady officer to support and asist Crugar could be spared, I assure you it is much wanted by every thing I can learn, for all officers, especialy Provincials, who have not [*sic*] been left to act for themselves are much at a loss and so diffident that they require a support to their oppinion, instead of which Crugar has the direct reverse in Allen, who is timid to the greatest degree. One very great and serious advantage in Lessly coming here will be our being able to get some officers to take commands or asist in them, for well I know you neither can give or tell me where to get a proper man or troops for Ninety Six nor can I fix upon any one fitt to command the two troops to be raised. I wait till I see

---

40 After the fall of Quebec the supply and payment of troops in North America was at first effected by the Commander-in-Chief drawing bills of exchange directly upon the Paymaster General in London. This arrangement proved both cumbersome and unviable as it resulted in the depression of the exchange rate. To obviate such losses a contract was entered into in 1767 by the Commissioners of the Treasury with John Drummond (1723-1774), banker, and Sir Samuel Fludyer (1705-1768), Deputy Governor of the Bank of England, acting jointly as Messrs Fludyer & Drummond. Under the contract the partners would deliver all monies issued from the Treasury for remittance to America. These monies were converted into Spanish and Portuguese coin and paid over, as called for, to the deputy paymasters in the colonies. The Crown received all interest and profits and it paid all charges. Messrs Fludyer & Drummond received a commission of one per cent of all monies delivered to them. It was hoped by this arrangement that the exchange would be stabilised and the necessity for remittance of specie avoided by the contractors' agents raising funds from the sale of bills of exchange drawn on the contractors. In 1768, when Samuel Fludyer died, his share of the contract was taken by Thomas Harley (1730-1804), banker and at that time Lord Mayor of London, and in 1772 Henry Drummond (*c.* 1730-1795), banker, became involved to assist his cousin, John Drummond, due to the latter's poor health. The contractors posted agents in the principal garrisons of North America and in the West Indies. An agent also had to accompany the army on campaigns and major expeditions besides being present during the occupation of places such as Philadelphia and Charlestown. It was an agent's duty to maintain constant communication with the contractors, to whom he was entirely accountable, and to keep account books and letterbooks. From 1767 to 1783 the contractors themselves held their joint account with the London bankers, Messrs Drummond, which had been established about 1712. ('Online archive guide', Royal Bank of Scotland (Internet, 28th December 2005))

Dunlapp about all these cavalry matters. I am told that a captain of the infantry of the Legion, one Stuart[41], is extremly well calculated for the kind of business wanted for the two troops. If Tarleton could spare him, it would be a great matter to sett them on foot directly, as every hour lost is of consequence. I have wrote to Lord Rawdon respecting the post at King Tree and mentioned the same idea I have to your Lordship, and if he thinks it too much to spare all the York Volunteers, Coffin's company might be sent with Frazer and Harrison's. However, at all events the 64th, I think, may remain there untill your Lordship thinks them safely fixed. I have no fears about ourselves, with the prisoners on board and the hidden enemys disposed of. I have no objections to bargain with Lessly if you choose it, only I must have some regulars and good officers in their room, which, from what I know of him and his present opinion of the 64th, I think he will scarcely choose. I have not yet heard of the cavalry accoutrements from Georgia, where Clarke does every thing he possibly can for us in the best humoured and most agreeable manner I can describe.

Many applications have been made to me about getting some militia exchanged that have been taken in different skirmishes in this neighborhood, some of men of property and loyalty. I wish to know if you will allow any of those taken on the 16th of August – militia men - to be exchanged for them. If there is no reason particular against it, I should think it would be very useful at present. The expence of my friend Tarleton's demands at present are astonishing, but I have not stopt them to ask your sanction for fear of impeding the service of that very useful corps; but after his *dissipating* and *dispersing* account of Marion I am sorry to say that in a few days afterwards he appeared with 500 men befor George Town, where I am sorry to say he now is within a few miles. However, Bluck is not allarmed and writes in perfect security. He has orders to apply to McLeroth at King Tree if necessary, and I have apprised the major of Bluck's situation. Indeed cavalry now is so essentialy necessary that nothing will be quiett in this province without them. Marion's movement I beg Tarleton may be remembred of – it is no joke to us.

Westerhaugen's hint and Simson's I mentioned some time ago. I beg an answer.

I am sorry to make two complaints, one of a Colonel Mills and another of Colonel Cary, who I suspect have been taking good care of *themselves*. The first I have ordred down here to show how he came posessed of three hundred Negroes he is carrying across the country, pillaging and robbing every plantation he comes to. The acount the other gentleman renders of the seized effects is as enormous as it is inexplicable. I have put it into the hands of the

---

41 Patrick Stewart was, as Balfour says, a captain in the infantry of the British Legion. In the action at Hanging Rock on 6th August he had played an effective and timely part in the repulse of Sumter and Davie, and in the Battle of Camden ten days later he had commanded the Legion infantry. Many of his company would be captured in January at the Battle of Cowpens but he would not. He was taken prisoner in the capitulation of Yorktown and shortly after allowed to depart in the *Andrew* transport for New York. He died there on 18th October 1782 and was interred in St Paul's churchyard. (Donald J Gara, 'Biographical Sketches on Infantry Officers of the British Legion 1778-1782' (*The On-Line Institute for Advanced Loyalist Studies*, 5th December 2005); Tarleton, *Campaigns*, 95, 99; Muster Roll of Patrick Stewart's company of the British Legion, 25th October to 14th December 1781 (National Archives of Canada, RG8, series C, 1884(22)); *Royal Gazette* (New York), 23rd October 1782)

police for I can't unravell it. A Mr Ogilvie[42] complains loudly but it is a long story. I enclose his petition[43], which clearly demonstrates that if Ogilvie was *entitled* to the rent of his lands, Cary had no business to dispute the matter, whether it was a lease or sublett, which it seems was realy the case, Ogilvie's attorney having sublett the lands in his absence. When the police report upon Cary's accounts, shall send them to you. The *Sandwich*, I am sorry to say, is gone as convoy to St Augustine with provision vessells. A Captain Reed of the *Gallatœa*, in spite of three official requisitions, would not take them under his convoy but referred me to the *Loyalist*, who was unfitt for sea but will be now ready, and he went a-cruizing for prizes. Indeed you cannot suppose how much the service suffers for want of a naval officer to remain here in the command. Every one now does just as he thinks most convenient for himself; you know their liberal jokes concerning the service.

I have only now to assure your Lordship that, acting upon your own principles, I am not affraid of responsibility, and that to serve my country and gain your esteem are the two objects I most earnestly and sincerly shall attempt and try by every means in my power, and that I am with faithful attachment

Yours

N BALFOUR

PS

I gave two pipes of port to the Hessian Hospital in the time of their dreadful sickness, when not a guinea was to be laid out by their own hospitalls for them. Have I done right and shall I pay it?

Cornwallis to Balfour, 22nd November 1780 — *82(81): A(in part) CS*

Wynnesborough
November 22nd 1780

Lt Colonel Balfour

Dear Balfour

Tarleton came up with and defeated Sumpter on the evening of the 20th. I send you his letter[44], from which you may form a paragraph for Messrs Robertson etc.

---

42 From Cornwallis's reply it is clear that Balfour is referring, not to Charles Ogilvie (see vol II, p 333, note 22), but to George or William, both of whom, like Charles, would be banished and have their property confiscated by act of the revolutionary assembly at Jacksonborough. Whether William was related to Charles is uncertain, but George was, and while residing in England after the war, he would pursue Charles' claim for compensation after the latter's death. (SC Banishment and Confiscation Act 1782; Coldham, *LoyalistClaims*, 371; Sabine, *BiographicalSketches*, ii, 562)

43 *his petition*: not extant.

44 *his letter*: of 21st November, p 340.

Your letter of the 17th arrived this day, not having travelled so fast as that of the 18th.

The money business I can only lament. I do not understand these matters, but they tell me that 3 months ago a man might have got as much money as he pleased at par for bills on England. If that is true, which I am not sure of, the agents for the contractors might have laid in a stock. One thing I know, that it is impossible to carry on war without some money. As I trust that you and I and Leslie shall shortly meet, we shall do more good in a few hours' conversation than in many long letters. I think we must keep the 64th for some time at Kingstree unless you should want them at Charlestown, which will take place of every other consideration. I should fear Innes's corps alone there, and a detachment of 100 of the New York Volunteers is in fact the whole regiment. That corps I am endeavouring to mount, and trust to them for keeping the country quiet. I have no objection to exchanging some of our militia prisoners, but it must always be for people taken in action and not those found in their beds. I proposed some time ago to Smallwood to exchange some of them for the militia taken at Ferguson's action[45] but have received no answer. Cunningham was here to day full of zeal. I made him a brigadier general of militia[46] with colonel's full pay from the 24th of last June. I hope now we shall make something of the militia of that district, which never could have been the case under Kirkland. I do not know what Tarleton's demands at present are. Some of his infantry lost their packs on some waggons coming from Charlotte Town whose horses could not draw them any farther. As the men were then absent on an expedition, I promised to make them good. Tarleton says that every thing that he receives from the Provincial Store is totally unserviceable. I can vouch for the boots he received at Camden, very few of which could be got on by any of the men, and those were perfectly rotten. It is my opinion that for the ground they march over in a month they are not expensive cavalry. As to Marion, I do not think that Tarleton flattered himself that he had done more than stopping his immediate progress and preventing the militia from joining him, and if the accounts I hear from that country are true, his visit has not been ineffectual. The Legion are so ill off for officers that I do not believe Tarleton can spare any one that is worth having. I mentioned to you Westerhagen and Simpson.

In regard to Mills and Carey, the former I know little of and have many reasons to think ill of. He obtained to my great concern 150 stand of arms on pretence of their being for his militia, after he had assured me through Wemys that he had no hopes of raising any, and employed them only in arming a banditti to carry off his plunder. The arms of course were all lost or fell into the enemy's hands. In regard to Carey, you know I am more partial, altho' I will not be godfather to any man's honesty in this province. Mr Ogilvie's lands were let by him to Kershaw and by Kershaw to Whitaker[47], one of the most violent and criminal

---

45 See Cornwallis to Smallwood, 10th November, p 401.

46 For Cunningham's commission, see p 391.

47 The Whitakers in Camden District were members of an extended family who had come from Warwick County, Virginia, and settled mainly in Halifax County, North Carolina. The brothers James (1728-1782) and William Henry (1736-1789) had moved on to South Carolina, where William Henry obtained large land grants to the north of Camden. It is probably to him that Cornwallis is referring. With the brothers came their extensive families, including, on the one hand, James' sons William Alexander (*c.* 1744-*c.* 1817), Willis (1750-1832), John Wiggins (*c.* 1752-*c.* 1812), and James Jr (*c.* 1754-1824) and, on the other, William Henry's sons Lemuel Lawrence (*c.* 1751-

rebels in this province. I cannot take it upon me to determine a case of law whether Kershaw or Whitaker are answerable to Ogilvie for the rent. This I know, that Mr Ogilvie has not shewn any great zeal for the cause and was so unconscionable as to ask four shillings a bushel for his indian corn to supply the troops at Camden when it was sold all over this part of the country for two shillings and two and four pence[48]. I leave the decision of the cause to the police, sincerely believing Carey a most zealous loyalist and being uncertain as to the consciences of the appellant and defendant.

I most undoubtedly approve of your supplying the Hessian Hospital with the two pipes of port wine.

Macleod will deliver this to you. He goes to town to arrange artillery business. He is an excellent officer and a pleasant man to serve with in every respect. I could wish very much that he might continue to command my field train, which will always be very small, never exceeding four or six guns. They have sent the only lieutenant older than him with Leslie. I would not do any thing in this business without Leslie's full concurrence nor propose any thing to him at first that would be disagreeable to him. It is difficult to say at present exactly what arrangement will be made of artillery men. You will be kind enough to talk it all over with Macleod, whom you will find very intelligent in every particular.

Smallwood is by all accounts still at his old position about 12 miles on this side of Charlottetown.

I am, dear Balfour, with the most sincere regard
Truly yours

CORNWALLIS

1802), William (*c.* 1752-1787) and Thomas (1762-*post*-1793). No doubt all were of the revolutionary persuasion. (Whitaker Papers (Camden Archives and Museum, Camden SC))

48 *two and four pence*: two shillings and four pence.

Cornwallis to Balfour, 25th November 1780[49] *82(97): ADfS*

Wynnesborough
November 25th 1780

Lt Colonel Balfour
Commandant of Charlestown

Dear Balfour

The last night's gale kept me awake. I thought of our friends[50]. Gates is certainly come up towards Charlottetown with all the Continentals he could muster. They say from 700 to 1,000 infantry – in these are included Buford's 18 months men – and, as they report, 300 cavalry. I cannot, however, conceive that there are above half that number. I inclose a note I received this afternoon from Tarleton[51]. I saw two North Carolina men who met some of Sumpter's fugitives and who learned from them that he was speechless and certainly past all hopes.

If Leslie should come to Charlestown, which I most sincerely hope he will do, I think it will be well to land 800 or 1,000 of his men and bring them to me.[52] You may likewise keep something in present for your garrison. Consult Leslie before you come to me. He will probably chuse to go by land. The arrangement of the whole I leave to him. Lord Rawdon informs me that he placed Captain Coffin in a good position to cover the boats at a place where the enemy had formed a plan to intercept them and where a Captain Snipes[53] had taken post for that purpose. We have lost two great plagues in Sumpter and Clarke. I wish your friend Marion was as quiet.

Yours ever most sincerely

CORNWALLIS

---

49 The first paragraph and the last sentence of the second paragraph are published in Ross ed, *Cornwallis Correspondence*, i, 70.

50 *our friends*: Leslie and his corps. Among like references in other letters, see Cornwallis to Balfour, 30th November, p 95.

51 *a note..*: of 24th November, p 343.

52 The following sentence is deleted: 'It will enable us to clear the country here without the difficulty and risk that we are always forced to run of small detachments.'

53 A captain in Marion's Brigade, William Clay Snipes (?-1806) was an officer who was more active in plundering than in promoting the revolutionary cause. Insubordinate, arrogant, with an inveterate hatred of loyalists, he would lose his command in January 1781 when Marion reorganised the brigade. He 'will,' remarked Marion, 'do no other service than plunder the inhabitants, which will make more enemys...' Presenting his grievances in person to Rutledge, Snipes was promoted by Marion to a majority despite the latter's misgivings but went on to bear allegiance to William Harden, even frustrating Marion's operations. In May 1781 he was surprised near Dorchester while leading a party of twenty men. He and two of his men escaped, but the rest were put to the sword. (Moss, *SC Patriots*, 883; Rankin, *Marion, passim*; Bass, *Swamp Fox, passim*; *The Greene Papers*, vii, 208n, 230n)

[*Superscribed*:]

The original of this letter was in cypher.

Cornwallis to Balfour, 27th November 1780 *82(111): C*

Wynnesborough
November 27th 1780
One o'clock pm

Lt Colonel Balfour

Dear Balfour

I send this by Colonel Phillips's son, who promises to be in town on the 30th.

By accounts on which I think I can depend Gates joined Smallwood on the 23rd at 6 Mile Run between 12 Mile Creek and Charlottetown. Gates had, as my informant says, 2 pieces of cannon, but he did not see them, being afraid to go into the camp of the regulars. Davie's men are gone home, their time being out, but he says that Washington, White and Armand together make above 300 cavalry. He tells me that Sumpter is not dead nor likely to die but that the shoulder bone is hurt. He says that the rebels talk of 3,000 Virginia militia being on their way from Hillsborough to join them who had been stopped there on the appearance of our people in the Chesapeak. The numbers are certainly very erroneous, but if it is true that any are coming, it is a proof that Leslie is come away. Much of this intelligence is hearsay, but that Gates, Smallwood etc were encamped on Six Mile Run on Saturday night is most certain, as this person was in Smallwood's camp then, where he had many acquaintances, who shewed him Gates's camp that was within a quarter of a mile of it. I have not heard from Tarleton since I wrote last. His intelligence about Davie and Washington was certainly not true, but the Back Mountain men were expected to join Sumpter. You will, I hope, be set out with Leslie before this reaches you. If you should meet the express and not have received my letter of the 25th, you will be kind enough to send immediately orders for disembarking 800 or 1,000 men and you will place any corps you please to strengthen your garrison. The remainder I should wish to have up with me as soon as possible. In the present situation of things I cannot meet you, so that you must come all the way. This easterly wind gives me great hopes[54]. The gale the other night did not last long. Tell Macleod that he had better come down soon and that I wish he would bring me some bath rug to make a great coat. I am still in hot water about the cloathing, and indeed shall be until it arrives. The safety of it is of so great importance. The 71st are really quite naked.

I promised Colonel Phillips, who is, I believe, one of the honestest and most zealous men in this province, to let a nephew of his who is at Hetherell's Point come into the country on parole. If he makes a bad use of it, Phillips will be the first man to detect him. The

---

[54] *great hopes*: of Leslie's arrival in Charlestown.

nephew's name is Buchannan[55]. He was in the Continental regiment commanded by Sumpter.

I am, dear Balfour,
Yours most sincerely

CORNWALLIS

[*Subscribed*:]

I do not understand whether Leslie's cavalry have their horses with them. If not, I wish you could mount them by any exertion and extraordinary expence at Charlestown, as they would be a most material reinforcement to us.

Balfour to Cornwallis, 24th and 25th November 1780 — *4(193): ALS*

Charles Town
24th November 1780

Yours of the 17th, 18th and 19th are all *just* received together, and your sense of the very triffling services in my power to render you that you are so good as to mention in so friendly and warm a manner will, while I live, be felt with the most sincere and heartfelt gratitude.

In the movements of McLeroth I hoped for much satisfaction and real service to your Lordship's operations, but how I am dissapointed in my man! I will not now explain, nor how he has managed his matters. However, he now stands in a situation where he can scarcely go wrong.

By letters from Colonel Cassells I am pressed in the strongest manner to give only an opening for his people and our friends upon Little Pedee, those on the banks of Great Pedee, on the frontiers of North Carolina, as well as those on Lynches Creek, to come in to him, all which can be effected by taking posession of Port's and Britton's Ferrys upon Lynches Creek and the lower part of Pedee, which posts he means to defend with his militia, if once given to him. He assures me of many offers made him from that country, of their desire of quitting Marion (whom they all look upon only as a plunderer) and joining us.

---

55 When John Phillips came to South Carolina about 1770 from Country Antrim, Ireland, he brought with him his nephews, John and Robert Buchanan, the sons of his sister Rachel. Whereas John Phillips was a staunch loyalist and now a colonel in the royal militia, his nephews were of the revolutionary persuasion and became officers in the South Carolina Continental line. Both served in the 6th Regiment (of which Sumter had resigned the colonelcy in September 1777), John as a captain and Robert as a lieutenant, and both were made prisoners in the capitulation of Charlestown. John, apparently the subject of Phillips' representations, was released on parole and exchanged under the cartel in June 1781, but Robert was disinclined to accept any favour and died in captivity. (Judith Sandage Murphy and H Shannon Phillips Sr, 'Phillips Family' (http://www.rootsquest.com/~jmurphy/gibson/phillips.htm, 25th November 2005); Moss, *SC Patriots*, 118)

Although by no means sanguine or even giving belief to such relations in general, yet Cassells's character and his whole behaviour are much more manly and worthy of credit than any other colonel of militia I have yet seen, and as far as I have had connection with him, realy seems by no means a man of chimera or capable of undertaking any plan without a rational and well founded reason.

These two ferrys being his great object, I think McLeroth, now joined by 200 Orangeburgh and Pedee mounted militia with 100 of Major Barefield's[56] of Tynes' regiment, who has offred his services, is surely equal to take posession, there being no enemy, and put Cassells at the head of his people, which he earnestly demands.

I have therefore ventured to tell McLeroth, who is *now* joined by Grattan and Maxwell, that, a march to Port's Ferry from King Tree being so short, I wish him to take it, and that he will be joined by Cassells from George Town, who he will reinstate in safety and return to Black River.

Marrion has crossed the Pedee and has been rapid in his movements since the appearance of the 64th. The submission made to Lord Rawdon by the inhabitants of Black River and Pedee, the exertion of Cassells's men, and the spirit reviving that has been long dead against Marrion, and *his retreat*, makes this realy an opportunity of turning the scale, and I think it is a pity to lose it as we can run no great risk in so short a distance, and so many rivers in front with George Town in their rear if necessary. Also there is no kind of danger while that corps is in motion offensively, especialy as I have informed Lord Rawdon of it, *who*, if possibly he could detach to Harrison's or Ratcliffe's Bridge upon Lynches Creek, the whole country betwixt that and Santee must be secured, which is just preparatory to a forward movement and secures the communication etc etc.

McLeroth will fall back upon Black River when he has done the business, and here I must in *justice* say that he is by no means to be trusted to act for himself, but the present occasion so presents itself that it is impossible to put it off and not to take advantage of giving the turn so much wanted. Gratton and Maxwell will keep him right — I have sent them for that purpose. With any other good man I should be easy in undertaking such a movement. *With him* I am uneasy, I own, till it is over and he returns, although he has three hundred British troops, two pieces of cannon and three hundred mounted militia, a command Moncrieff envys much.

An engineer (Wilson[57]) with another galley and two pieces of cannon (iron) are on their way to George Town, where a week's work will make the redoubt absolutely impregnable to those gentry.

---

56 Balfour means Bromfield. Jesse Barefield was a captain in the revolutionary service during the first siege of Charlestown in 1779. He suffered there some indignity from a superior officer which led him to change sides and become the leader of the loyalists between the Great and Little Pee Dee, where his home lay. He died of small pox later in the war. (Gregg, *The Old Cheraws*, 338)

57 Probably John Wilson, a lieutenant in the 71st (Highland) Regiment, who is known to have acted as an assistant engineer. (WO 65/164(15) (National Archives, Kew))

The most allarming fears have haunted me about our vessell with cavalry accoutrements, who for safety is coming the inland passage from Savannah, which has been lately the prey of whale boats and rebell galleys. However, thank God, this night I hear she is safe and will be here in a few days, convoy'd by two galleys sent for her. When she comes, every thing shall be done which you wish about them immediately. Dunlapp is here, and Ninety Six I certainly think the place for him.

This moment two old Hessian general officers have left me. They are arrived in a transport who sailed in company with Sir George Rodney on the 17th instant from the Hook. A violent gale of wind seperated them the night of their sailing. The fleet consisted of seven sail of the line, four being left with Admiral Arbuthnot. The *Roebuck* and *Hyenna* were as convoy to the fleet of twelve sail bound here with recruits etc, amounting to nearly 500 men, belonging to southern regiments. O'Hara with recruits for the Guards bound for General Lessly, the men of war for the West Indies, were to leave them early.

This is nearly the amount of the Hessian intelligence, so we daily look for the remainder of the fleet, although I fear for the storm they had seperating them.

What will be done with the recruits and *Hessian generals* who are all bound for this town? It is realy too bad to send these old gentlemen here merely to get rid of them. More particulars I shall write in my next of all those affairs.

The *Gallatœa* with pilotts is cruizing off the Frying Pan for Lessly. The *Loyalist*, victualers, galleys etc etc are all waiting your express returning, and the *Sandwich* is hourly expected.

Every possible attention shall be paid to receipts from the country, and believe me no man shall impose upon the publick if possibly it can be found out. I well know many, many sad examples of lenity to those in office. Be assured I am as conscious of the dreadful and fatal consequences of the expences incurred from a want of enquiry into those publick departments as any man can be and think myself, while I command here, accountable for them. Green is come to succeed Gates, and Paul Jones arrived from France in the *Ariel*.

25th, eight o'clock in the morning

This moment your letters are arrived in answer to Lessly's[58]. It gives me much pleasure to find that you approve of Lessly coming here. However, at all events you would have had time enough to have stopped him as we hear nothing of him, and indeed I fear much he has had rough weather and some strong southerly winds.

Not an hour shall be lost in getting the meeting required, and we shall come by Camden. I shall leave Moncrieff to fill my place in carrying on matters here, and having a relay of horses, I hope little time will be lost.

---

58 *your letters..*: that of the 21st, p 42, enclosing a copy of that of the 12th, p 39.

A fast sailing ship being now about to sail for England, the *Hero*, who is also well armed, I shall venture another letter to General Amherst with very strict injunctions to a trusty passenger to throw it overboard if taken. Indeed, it will be very cautiously written at all events. Some cash shall be immediately sent up. It has often struck me that the two flank companys of the 60th Regiment might come here and be replaced by Brown's corps[59], who ought never to have his corps with him where he is.

Could one of the Hessian generals do any mischief in St Augustine? I hope soon to tell you of Lessly's arrival, which I own I fear from the weather will yet be some time longer deferred, but you shall hear the moment any accounts arrive of him or of the recruits. Those belonging to your army I wish to know what to do with.

I ever am
Most faithfuly yours

N BALFOUR

PS

I forgot to say that a skirmish has happned some time ago near George Town in which little loss happned to either side, both being militia. Marrion's nephew, a major, was killed.[60]

Cornwallis to Balfour, 29th November 1780 — *82(121): C*

Wynnesborough
November 29th 1780

Lt Colonel Balfour

Dear Balfour

I this day received yours of the 24th and 25th. You may very probably meet this letter on the road, so it shall be short. I think it will be best to give the two Hessian generals good quarters at Charlestown, to bow low to them and let them *smoke their pipes*. The recruits that appear to be at all trained to arms and fit for service had better join their regiments immediately. The others, with convalescents and men recovering from wounds, might make a good garrison for Fort Arbuthnot.

---

59 Balfour means Thomas Brown's King's Rangers, not Montfort Browne's Prince of Wales's American Regiment.

60 The skirmish occurred near White's Bridge, two miles from Georgetown, between a party of Marion's men under Captain John Melton and a body of loyalist militia from the Little Pee Dee under Major Jesse Barefield. 'In this short affair Gabriel Marion, nephew of the general, had his horse killed under him and was taken prisoner; but as soon as his name was announced, he was inhumanely shot... He had been a lieutenant in the Second Regiment, was a young gentleman of good education, of whom high expectations were formed, and who was much beloved in the brigade.' (James, *Marion*, 65-6; Gregg, *The Old Cheraws*, 343)

I heard to day that Gates had marched, and the country people said for Camden. I doubt the first part and have no faith at all in the latter. By the enclosed[61] you see we should be in a condition to make him repent it. Our troops are in the highest health and spirits. I sincerely believe for the numbers there never was so fine an army. I approve of your plan of exchanging the flank companies of the 60th for Brown's corps.

Tarleton is just come here. His corps will be at Shirar's Ferry to morrow. As I think you will have left Charlestown before this letter can reach it, I shall only add that

I am with great truth
Most sincerely yours

CORNWALLIS

Cornwallis to Balfour, 30th November 1780 *82(128): C*

Wynnesborough
November 30th 1780

Lt Colonel Balfour

Dear Balfour

By the last accounts I can get, Gates is still at Smallwood's old camp at 6 Mile Run. They talk of his making a move to his left for the sake of forage.

This fine weather and the late fair wind have, I hope, brought all our friends, and this letter will, I hope, meet you on the road.

If you can give me notice in time, I will come to Camden as it will save time in our arrangements. I enclose to you a rough sketch of my idea of the disposition of the reinforcement, submitted, however, entirely to the decision of Leslie, to be shewn to him or not as you may think most expedient. At the same time I would wish you to make any alterations you may think proper. We must begin our operations by driving Gates from the frontier, which the first forward movement will instantly effect.

I am, dear Balfour,
Most faithfully yours

CORNWALLIS

---

61 *the enclosed*: no extant copy.

Enclosure
Proposed disposition of the reinforcement — *82(123): C*

To be sent immediately to the army

The recruits for the regiments fit for service

The Guards

Regiment of Bose

Provincial light infantry and 17th infantry

Yagers

Dragoons

Convalescents from George Town

To be sent to George Town

Fanning's corps, Fanning himself to remain on leave at Charlestown or to attend head quarters

Garrison of Charlestown

82nd Regiment

To replace Hamilton's corps at Camden

84th Regiment

[*Subscribed*:]

You must not mind the Hessian guns. They must learn to move without them unless you can easily procure horses.

Balfour to Cornwallis, 29th November 1780 — *4(240): ALS*

Charles Town
29th November

My last letter gave you joy of two generals. This is only for one: *O'Hara*. The history[62] is shortly this.

---

62 *The history*: inaccurate. See Balfour to Cornwallis, 30th November, p 99.

The *Raleigh* with General O'Hara, Colonel Watson, Major J Small[63], a Colonel Campbell of Fanning's[64], Captain Barry[65] of the 52nd and some others belonging to General Lessly's army sailed on the 17th from New York for the Chesapeak, but near that port they fell in with the *Hyena*, who was convoy to the fleet of recruits. *She* made the signal for the *Raleigh* to chase, which she did and came up with the *Mifflin* privateer of 20 guns, took her, while the *Hyena* retook two briggs belonging to the fleet loaded with Provincial stores and camp equipage.

These captures and their chase brought the *Raleigh* so far down as the Cape, where she fell in with the *Gallatœa* cruizing for Leslie, when to my astonishment they oppned the dispatch for General Lessly, which immediately brought them here. This malapropos business will give suspicions, but it cannot now be helped. It is but very unacurately that I have heard

---

63 Born at Strathardle, Athol, Perthshire, John Small (1726-1796) was the son of a clergyman. After serving in the Dutch Scots Brigade, he was commissioned an ensign in the 42nd Highlanders (the Black Watch) on 29th August 1747, and having been promoted nine years later to lieutenant, he embarked with the regiment for North America and saw service in the Seven Years' War. In 1762 he became a captain in the regiment. As the revolutionary war opened, it fell to him to take part in the Battle of Bunker Hill, where his life was spared by his old friend Israel Putnam, a brigadier general in the Connecticut militia. Shortly afterwards he received the news that with effect from 13th June 1775 he had been promoted to major in command of the 2nd Battalion, 84th Regiment. With it he was now forming part of Leslie's reinforcement but would soon advise Cornwallis that the battalion was very inadequately composed. It therefore did not take part in the winter campaign but remained in South Carolina, where Small, having been promoted to lt colonel with effect from 17th November 1780, gained a lasting reputation for benevolence toward his opponents. Writing many years later, one of them remarked, 'It would be superfluous to detail particular instances of the exemplary good conduct of this gallant officer, whose constant aim was to soothe the sorrows of the afflicted and to give exercise to the beneficence of a generous heart.' Towards the end of hostilities in the south the regard in which he was held by his opponents led Greene to invite him within his camp so that he might meet Arthur St Clair, the friend and companion of his early years, who was now a major general in the Continental line. In 1793 he was appointed Lt Governor of Guernsey and one year later became a major general. (*ODNB*; *Army Lists*; *The Cornwallis Papers*; Garden, *Anecdotes* (1st series), 282-4)

64 Formerly of the Foot Guards, George Campbell had been commissioned Lt Colonel of the King's American Regiment (otherwise known as Fanning's corps) when it was raised on the Provincial establishment in December 1776. Now part of Leslie's reinforcement, he and the regiment would be posted in December to Georgetown, where in January they were attacked by Lee and Marion. Being quartered outside the garrison, Campbell was captured and paroled, but in other respects the loss was inconsiderable. On 24th February the regiment left Georgetown and by mid April had joined Rawdon at Camden, where Campbell, who had been exchanged, commanded it in the Battle of Hobkirk's Hill. He led the attack with his and the 63rd regiments, which, according to Rawdon, 'he performed with great spirit'. His character as an old Guards officer did not lend itself to easy relations with his subordinates, and by May 1783 he was court-martialled for conduct prejudicial to good order and military discipline. Found guilty, he was sentenced to be suspended without pay for six months, whereupon he petitioned Sir Guy Carleton for permission to return to Europe. (Nan Cole and Todd Braisted, 'A History of the King's American Regiment' (*The On-Line Institute for Advanced Loyalist Studies*, 7th December 2005); Colin Campbell, 'Lieutenant Colonel George Campbell, King's American Regiment', *New England Historical and Genealogical Register*, 137 (October 1983), 306-316; *The Cornwallis Papers*)

65 Henry ('Harry') Barry had entered the 52nd Regiment as an ensign on 11th March 1768 and was promoted there to lieutenant on 23rd September 1772 and to captain on 4th January 1777. On arriving at Charlestown he would be appointed Secretary to the Commandant and also serve as Deputy Adjutant General. According to Garden, he was wont to deprecate the passive courage and lack of activity displayed by revolutionary troops, but was himself taken prisoner in unflattering circumstances by Lieutenant Lawrence Manning of Lee's Legion at the Battle of Eutaw Springs. (*Army Lists*; Garden, *Anecdotes* (1st series), 145, 270-1, 311; Garden, *Anecdotes* (2nd series), 143-6; James, *Marion*, 150-1)

of it, but as they bring your dispatches[66], which, as you will see by my letter from the Commander in Chief[67], were left open, I have not delay'd a moment in sending them by an officer all the way. Tomorow another express with letters for the army, returns of what is come etc etc shall be sent and many other particulars.

As to McLeroth, it is impossible to get him to Port's Ferry as I mentioned. I wish we may be able to keep him on the other side Santee, and I must beg Lord Rawdon to communicate with him and give him the intelligences of the enemy's movements and direct *his* accordingly, as I am at such a distance, and can only say that I can spare him very well at present as long as you want him. He is now at Nielson's Ferry on the opposite side nearly, but I am obliged to say that I think the sooner he can be put into a situation where he has not to act from himself the better – otherwise I fear some accident to him. I leave this letter open for Lord Rawdon's information and that he may move the detachment as he wishes and as may appear best from his intelligence. If he is not wanted on the other side Santee, he might take post at Nielson's or Murray's on this side, which, although it must have a very bad effect in shewing the enemy our fears, yet I think it is better than run the risks I fear for, but at all events his detachment or one nearly equal to it must cover at or near Nielson's untill your movements are more forward. I send inclosed his last letter to me[68], received this day, by which Lord Rawdon may judge of his situation; and should his Lordship not want him nearer Camden or higher up the country, I realy think it will be safest to move him across the river and bring him to Murray's or Nielson's.

I ever am with sincere attachment
Your Lordship's most obedient servant

N BALFOUR

[*Subscribed*:]

The cavalry accoutrements not yet arrived, but Kinloch with armed boats sent to unload the brigg. Fifty swords, I hear, are arrived in the Provincial stores, but of all this tomorow.

---

66 *your dispatches*: Clinton to Cornwallis, 5th and 6th November, pp 14 to 23.

67 *my letter..*: not extant.

68 *his last letter to me*: not extant.

Cornwallis to Balfour, 5th December 1780 — *83(15): C*

Wynnesborough
December 5th 1780

To Lt Colonel Balfour
Commandant of Charlestown

Dear Balfour

I this morning saw your letter to Lord Rawdon. There is no occasion for the 64th joining either me or him at present; I would therefore leave it to the direction of Lord Rawdon. The recruits I should wish to join their regiments as soon as possible – I mean the stout, healthy ones — but they must come up well supplyed with necessaries and good cloathing. I think of taking McLeroth with me when I move and putting Watson's corps to act under Lord Rawdon's orders between the Santee and Pedee.

Some salt and pork came up to Friday's Ferry, said to be for Ninety Six. I have, however, taken great part of the salt and ordered the remainder with the pork to Camden. The best way of sending those articles, which will be much wanted at Ninety Six, will be by the Savannah River. Haldane is gone thither. I hear that Green is expected hourly to supersede Gates, but I do not think either will think of any offensive operations of consequence. You will have heard of that rascal Rugely. I think from the circumstance of his not retiring, when directed to do so by Lord Rawdon, and promising to defend himself to the last extremity and afterwards surrendering to a detachment of cavalry only without firing a shot is a plain proof that he must be a traitor. I long much to hear of Leslie's arrival. The wind is now again fair.

I am
Most sincerely yours

CORNWALLIS

Balfour to Cornwallis, 30th November 1780 — *4(252): ALS*

Charles Town
30th November 1780

I send now the dispatches by a private ship[69] and other letters for the army, with returns of what is sent in this fleet from New York for the Quarter Master General and Provincial Stores, the only part of which I shall meddle with will be the swords, which I shall instantly forward to Camden. The recruits are not all arrived, but the greatest part is, and I am told there are shipps in the offing.

What is become of Lessly I cannot conceive. I fear for the gal of wind, but as the *Loyalist, Beaumont, Galatœa* and *Raleigh* will be employed in searching for him and

---

69 *dispatches by a private ship*: duplicates of Clinton to Cornwallis, 5th and 6th November, pp 14 to 23.

protecting his fleet[70], I think we must get him safe soon, and indeed every hour we eagerly look for the signal.

I have put the recruits belonging to the regiments here on shore. Those for Savannah are kept on board. When the whole is come, shall send you the return, but I expect your directions concerning them as soon as possible.

You will perceive by O'Hara's letter[71] that my acount concerning the manner of his coming here was not accurate.

By my informations from North Carolina I rather think that there is some danger of an attempt upon George Town in force by Harrington and Marrion and a large emigration from North Carolina. I have therefore sent twenty men of the 64th that have recovred here since the march of the regiment to reinforce that post, which, with the two galleys (our best and pretty well manned), about 140 militia and 120 soldiers in a very strong redoubt, I hope will be in no great danger. They have provisions also laid in.

I wrote you fully of my ideas respecting the 64th, since which Gratton is come from them and confirms me in the danger of that corps's being left to act alone against *any* enemy. If Lord Rawdon could detach some mounted men towards the High Hills of Santee, they would give him confidence.

Gratton says there is nothing to oppose them, but upon the same principles as I have mentioned I own I cannot be easy untill some line is marked for him and he comes on this side the Santee, but it will be essentialy and absolutely necessary that if he comes over he must remain in the neighborhood of Nielson's, otherwise you may be assured the communication is gone – and I hope to have the cavalry accoutrements on their way to you in a day or two.

I find the allowing of stores being kept in the country produces the most dangerous effects and is only a supply to the enemy as well as a bait for the country that are dissafected to bring the enemy towards the places where they are. A proclamation prohibiting it will be published tomorow in such terms as I hope you will approve of. As I hope to see you soon, I leave a thousand querys untill I have that pleasure.

I ever am
Most faithfuly yours

N BALFOUR

---

70 See pp 39 and 42, notes 47 and 54. The *Raleigh* was delayed in port and had still not left Charlestown by 9th December. Meanwhile the *Roebuck* was employed with the *Galatea* and *Loyalist*.

71 *O'Hara's letter*: not extant.

Enclosure (1)
Invoice of camp equipage etc ***103(8): DS***

Invoice of camp equipage etc shipped on board the brigg Experiment transport, Richard Stevens master, mark'd as per margin, from the Quarter Master General's Stores, New York, November 1780		
Consignee	*Consignment Nos*	*Consignment*
23rd Regiment	6 to 10	Five hogsheads containing 134 kettles and 610 canteens
	12, 13	Two bales ditto 610 haversacks
	14	One cask ditto 134 hand hatchets
	16 to 20	Five bales ditto 134 tents
	22 to 26	Five casks ditto mallets and pins
	27	One cask ditto 10 bell tents, 16 drum cases and 8 powder bags
	28	One matted bundle ditto 10 setts bell tent poles
	29	One case ditto 10 camp colours
		Twenty one bundles ditto 134 ridge and 268 stand poles
33rd Regiment	9 to 13	Five hogsheads containing 134 kettles and 610 canteens
	15 to 16	2 bales ditto 610 haversacks
	17	One cask ditto 134 hand hatchets
	19 to 23	Five bales ditto 134 tents
	25 to 29	Five casks ditto mallets and pins
	30	One cask ditto 10 bell tents, 16 drum cases and 8 powder bags
	31	One matted bundle ditto 10 sets ditto poles

		Twenty one bundles containing 134 ridge poles and 268 stand poles
	32	One case ditto 10 camp colours
	33	1 ditto ditto officers' swords
Earl Cornwallis		Seven cases
	1 to 16	Seven casks, 2 hogsheads and seven boxes
1st Battalion, 71st Regiment	1 to 8	Eight hogsheads containing 225 kettles and 1,082 canteens
	9 to 16	Eight bales ditto 225 tents
	17 to 18	Two casks ditto 22 bell tents, 20 drum cases and 10 powder bags
	19 to 20	Two casks ditto 225 hand hatchets
	21 to 28	Eight casks ditto mallets and pins
	29 to 30	Two matted bundles ditto bell tent poles
	31	One case of camp colours
	32 to 34	Three bales containing 1,082 haversacks
		Thirty four bundles ditto 225 ridge and 450 stand poles
2nd Battalion, 71st Regiment	1 to 2	Two casks containing 225 hand hatchets
	3 to 10	Eight bales ditto 225 tents
	11 to 18	Eight casks ditto mallets and pins
	19 to 20	Two casks ditto 22 tents, 20 drum cases and 10 powder bags
	21 to 22	Two matted bundles bell tent poles
	23	1 case camp colours
	25 to 32 & 35	Nine hogsheads containing 225 camp kettles and 1,082 canteens
	24, 33 to 34	Three bales ditto haversacks 1,082
71st Regiment	70 to 77	Eight bales of bonnets, plaids and hose

NB

The camp equipage for the 23rd and 33rd Regiments is for the 8 battalion companies only, as two tenths of it was stopped for the flank companies by order of the Commander in Chief. The seven cases of wine etc for Earl Cornwallis arrived from London in the ship *Mary*, Captain Stewart, the other 16 packages in the *William and Elizabeth* with the camp equipage.

THO[S] BRANDWOOD
Store Keeper

Enclosure (2)
Abstract of clothing ***103(11): DS***

Abstract of cloathing received from New York by the Three Brothers store ship, Captain Lock, for the use of His Majesty's Provincial forces in Carolina etc, Charlestown, November 30th 1780

Serjeants	
Coats	135
Waistcoats	135
Breeches	135
Drummers' coats	50
Privates	
Coats	2,981
Waistcoats	3,031
Breeches	3,031
Stocks	4,212
Pairs of shoes	3,912
Stock buckles	4,212
Hats	3,300
Pairs of stockings	3,984
Shirts	3,400
Haversacks	3,500
Knapsacks	3,400
Caps	612

Blankets	3,500
Broad swords	70
Serjeants' sashes	135
Epaulets	105
Drummers' belts and slings	70

ALEX INNES
Inspector General, Provincial Forces

Balfour to Cornwallis, 4th December 1780 — *4(279): ALS*

Charles Town
4th December 1780

No certain acounts as yet of our friends, but such precautions are taken that I think it impossible any mistake can happen. The weather has been very bad but in general the winds have been favourable for them. With the most anxious expectation I look for them, and every thing you wish shall be done. Only one point I wish to be explained: is Lessly himself to come up with the detachment? I mean, is he to remain and not return here etc?

I fear[72] an answer to this will come before we sett out, and have time to catch us at least very near this place.

A magazine is forming at Monk's Corner, and some provisions will also be forwarded to Nielson's for the detachment, who cannot now get fresh meat in the country. A galley at Wattboo Bridge will defend the store there, and a detachment of 120 rank and file composed of Hessians and convalescents are this day at Monk's Corner in order to cover the boats and communication by Nielson's in case that circumstances might make it necessary for moving up McLeroth to Camden, which by Lord Rawdon's letter I have some reasons to think would be probable.

Marrion is too formidable to trust so near the boats and stores without something better than militia, and it is with great concern I assure you the recruits are so bad that not above a third can possibly move with a regiment or march any distance – old, lame, and decrepid without a rag to cover them.

I have directed the most that is possible to be made of them and have sent some of them to Fort Arbuthnot, which enables me to spare this detachment.

---

72 *fear*: used in the sense of 'suspect'.

I own I wished to support your corps for these *eight* or *ten* days to come particularly, although I should run risks, which indeed are so triffling that I feel not the least uneasiness.

Twelve sail is off the barr, which have been there these four days. Thick weather has prevented their getting in. They are the remainder of the convoy from New York. The *Gallatœa, Roebuck, Loyalist* and *Beaumont* are all upon one duty, as you wish.

A *flag of truce* is this day sailed for Cape Fear with naval prisoners. The *Sandwich* is not yet come back but is arrived at St Augustine.

The cavalry appointments are come. Dunlopp setts off in a day or two with his quotta, and Kinloch with his. I have sett a man a-going with advancing a little money that will make twenty five swords per week. A merchant ship is arrived from England with the latest newspapers, two of the latest of which I now send.

Lord Rawdon will of course move McLeroth as he wishes, and I have explained every thing relative to that corps to his Lordship, as also of the detachment now sent, which I was obliged to change from recruits to the troops of the garrison for the reasons I have already mentioned.

The 64th Regiment marched at a few hours' notice, therefore are not provided for a long expedition, although, if wanted for the service, a few weeks longer can be of no great moment. I hope every hour to write you when we sett out etc.

I am with most faithful attachment
Yours

N BALFOUR

Cornwallis to Balfour, 9th December 1780 — *83(31): C*

Wynnesborough
December 9th 1780

Lt Colonel Balfour

Dear Balfour

I this morning received yours of the 4th and grow very uneasy about our friends, especially as I fear their stock of provisions was very short. The weather has been lately fine. I hope all will come right.

I mean that Leslie should remain and march with the army. You have done every thing in the best manner possible as to the naval matters, the flag of truce to Cape Fear, and the magazines at Monk's Corner and Nelson's. We must trust to winds and weather.

You will soon see Cruger, Williamson and Pickens. Cruger proposed that, if the latter would accept the command of his regiment, all the doubtfull characters should be called on to declare themselves, and indeed, considering the conduct the enemy have held, I should think it necessary. Should you see them in town before I see you, which I hope will not be the case, you will settle any mode of proclamation which you may think proper for this purpose.

I find Tynes's militia has again squandered upon a vague report of Harrington, and he himself has resigned. Isham Moore has proposed raising a kind of fencible corps. I doubt much his success but shall consent to it as I am determined to let slip no occasion of trying to arm the inhabitants of this country.

I am, dear Balfour,
Most sincerely yours

CORNWALLIS

[*Subscribed*:]

The troops here are all healthy and in excellent order and spirits. Our cloathing is all come up or very near, and plenty of rum, all owing to the attention and exertions of Colonel Balfour.

Money goes very fast, and ready money, when it can be got, is very good œconomy, so that, if you can, I wish you could send or bring some to the army.

Cornwallis to Balfour, 11th December 1780 — *83(36): C*

Wynnesborough
December 11th 1780

Lt Colonel Balfour

Dear Balfour

An express going to Charlestown with some letters from the army, I take the opportunity of saying that every thing remains in the same state. Haldane, whom I sent to 96, makes a better report of the works than I expected, but rather wishes to have two iron six pounders than 3 pounders. The reason for my ordering the threes in preference was on account of the difficulty of removing ammunition. On speaking to McLeod about it, he thought it would be the easiest and best way to send up one iron six pounder with proper ammunition in addition to the two threes. If you see no objection, it shall be settled in that manner.

I received this day a letter dated the 9th from Cruger[73]. He mentions that Clarke and Twiggs had entered Long Cane settlement on Monday last and had sent for General Williamson and detained him. I hope there is no duplicity *there.* He adds that he hopes in a day or two to be able to assemble militia enough to drive off the enemy and that he proposes setting out for Charlestown.

Colonel Mills sent me a note from Major Wemys giving him one hundred Negroes, which is really a princely donation. Whatever Colonel Mills's merits may have been, we cannot yet afford those kind of presents. I therefore consider the gift as null and void and leave it to you to let him have any small proportion you may think proper. The distress of himself and family and his sufferings may be great, but when his behaviour is compared with that of many others, he does not deserve from us any distinguished favour.

I wait with the utmost anxiety to hear important news from you. I watch the wind all day and listen to it with fear and trembling at night. Most sincerely hoping that you will not receive this letter at Charlestown,

I am
Faithfully yours

CORNWALLIS

Cornwallis to Balfour, 12th December 1780 — *83(39): C*

Wynnesborough
December 12th 1780

Lt Colonel Balfour
Commandant of Charlestown

Dear Balfour

I enclose to you papers relative to Brigadier General Du Portail's exchange[74] and General

---

[73] *a letter..*: see p 280.

[74] Louis Le Bègue de Presle Duportail (1743-1802) was an officer in the French engineers who had taken leave of absence in 1777 to come to America and join the Continental Corps of Engineers. He was soon appointed Commandant of the corps with the rank of brigadier general. Having taken part in the Philadelphia and Monmouth campaigns, he was involved in the fortification of Philadephia and saw service in the Hudson Highlands. In 1780 he was sent south but arrived at Charlestown too late to play any significant role in its defence. Now exchanged, he would break the conditions of his release, being directed to make his way to Philadelphia by way of Wilmington, but instead proceeding to Greene's camp on the Pee Dee, apparently to convey intelligence. There he reviewed Greene's troops before leaving in mid January to convey letters and information from Greene to Washington about the situation in the south. He went on to command engineering operations at the siege of Yorktown, playing a vital part in its reduction. On his return to France he rose to become Minister for War and a lt general, but forewarned of political charges against him, he went into hiding for two years before fleeing in 1794 to America. Five years after his name ceased to be proscribed, he attempted to return, but died at sea and was buried there. (Boatner, *Encyclopedia*, 602-3; *The Greene Papers*, vii, *passim*; *Appletons'*)

Phillips's request for Colonel Ball[75] to go on parole. As I hope you will not be in Charlestown when this letter arrives, I have sent passports for them.[76]

This north east wind after the southerly gale must, I think, bring every thing in. If not, I shall despair. I have not heard from you since the 4th. Every thing here remains in the same state.

I am
Very sincerely yours

CORNWALLIS

Balfour to Cornwallis, 9th December 1780 — *4(302): ALS*

Charles Town
9th December

Nothing but knowing the anxiety you must feel for the arrival of our friends could induce me to write in this state of uncertainty, but they are not arrived, to my astonishment. However, a schooner came yesterday belonging to them at least, who sailed with them from the Chesapeak on the 22nd November and left them in a fog off Cape Hatteras on the 1st of this month. The captain says they were bound to Cape Fear but the rendezvous in case of seperation was here. The fleet was not on the 1st at all seperated, and except one very triffling gale of wind since, they can have mett with nothing to hurt them. Every hour I have been looking for them with the uttmost anxiety, nor can I persuade myself that any accident can happen them from the *Gallatœa's, Beaumont's, Loyalist's* and *Roebuck's* orders to cruize for them being so strict and no latitude left for these gentlemen to deviate from them. The *Raleigh* is not yet got out from contrary winds etc.

Much *must* be said on the subject of naval affairs when we meet. The service is now apparently no object to men of that profession, and the good of the publick seems to be totaly absorbed in other pursuits of their own.

I propose, when the distribution is arranged, which will be as nearly as I *can* according to what you seem to wish, that the transports should go up the Cooper and land in our flatt boats as high up as a tide will carry them, by which a delay and a town inspection will be saved and the Guards prevented paying their respects to this place.

---

75 Burgess Ball (1750-1800) had entered the Virginia Continental line in 1776 and, when taken prisoner in the capitulation of Charlestown, was Lt Colonel of the 1st Virginia Continental Regiment. He would now return on parole to Travellers' Rest, his estate to the north of Fredericksburg, Virginia, but not before calling at Greene's camp on the way, no doubt to provide intelligence in breach of his parole. He took no further part in the war. In later years he fell on hard times, had to sell his estate, and removed to Springwood, his farm in Loudoun County, where he died. His second wife, Frances, was a daughter of George Washington's brother, Charles. (Heitman, *Historical Register*, 83-4; Donna Chasen, 'Grand mansion is lost to time', *The Free Lance-Star* (Fredericksburg VA, 2004); *The Greene Papers*, vii, 228)

76 See Rawdon's and Cornwallis's letters of 10th and 12th December, pp 205-7.

The recruits under the description you mention will march on Sunday to Nielson's and, if not wanted on the communication, proceed by McCord's to the army, but I rather suppose it will be better to keep them on the communication till the army comes up. Joined to Maxwell's detachment, they will be respectable and fill the place of McLeroth's if they are moved to Camden, of which Lord Rawdon will be the judge. Should he not be wanted, I think that, untill the event we wish takes place, it would be better to keep both upon that country, and afterwards Maxwell with Brown's corps – however, of that hereafter. McLeroth complains of his regiment being kept out so long, as they are so very bare of necessarys. However, I have told him the necessity of the service he is upon, which I doubt not he must see.

It is with much concern that I find no acounts arrive of the recruits of the 33rd, which are the only part of the convoy *not arrived*. However, I hope they will cast up in a day or two, when they can be sent up to join the others at Nielson's. All the convalescents here are ordred up with the recruits on Sunday. This detachment will amount to about one hundred. I shall inspect them before they march. The convalescents at George Town cannot be sent till *relieved*.

The provisions are gone up to Monk's Corner and every thing is in readiness to receive our friends. God grant they were come!

Two orders have been given out here for officers belonging to the army to join. The necessity of such orders, I am sorry to say, was too obvious.

I have kept Captain Saumarez[77] of the 23rd here to meet Captain Peters[78], who is arrived, as he[79] is to be paymaster, and the accounts of the regiment being in his[80] hands since the death of Mecan, it was necessary to settle all our matters finaly with the old and new. Peters I know to be an attentive officer. He goes to command the regiment and I have no doubt he will acquitt himself to your approbation.

I ever am
Yours

N BALFOUR

---

77 Born at St Peter Port, Guernsey, Thomas Saumarez (?-1845) entered the 23rd Regiment (Royal Welch Fusiliers) as a 1st lieutenant on 22nd November 1777 and was promoted to captain on 13th September 1779. Of his service in the revolutionary war he las left an interesting journal. In later life he was involved with the Guernsey militia before attaining in 1811 the rank of major general. As such he commanded at New Brunswick and Halifax, Nova Scotia, during the Anglo-American War of 1812. For his services he was knighted, while his brother James became an admiral and a peer. (*Army Lists*)

78 Commissioned an ensign in the 22nd Regiment on 16th March 1775, Thomas Peters was promoted to lieutenant in the 64th on 6th June 1776 and to captain in the 23rd on 21st March 1778. (*Army Lists*)

79 *he*: Saumarez.

80 *his*: Peters'.

[*Appended*:]

12 o'clock, 9th

Since writing the enclosed, a report is just made of the arrival of the recruits of the 33rd and that the transport fell in with our friends this day week off Cape Hatteras – forty five sail – but it being in the night, nothing passed but questions of no consequence. We shall certainly hear of them tomorow.

Cornwallis to Balfour, 14th December 1780 *83(44): C*

Wynnesborough
December 14th 1780
9 o'clock pm

Lt Colonel Balfour

Dear Balfour

I yesterday morning received yours of the 9th, which gave me some satisfaction, but still our main object is wanting. It is some comfort to know they were not in the gale that dispersed the New York fleet, and as the wind has now been fair four days, and the three last the weather remarkably fine and clear, I must conclude they are arrived.

I heard from Lord Rawdon this day that McLeroth was attacked yesterday at noon by Marion at Singleton's Mills.[81] Coffin with 140 mounted men marched to his support. I hope before morning to give you a further account of that business.

As it will be most convenient for you and Leslie to come directly to the army, I will send horses to meet you half way between this and McChord's, which will help your journey very much. Give my best compliments to the General if he is with you.

Lord Rawdon wishes to bring an officer of his corps to a court martial. You will please to bring down two or three warrants for courts martial. Should this meet you on the road, you may forward that request to Benson if he can get at them. I submit to you the enclosed petition of the Chevalier de Cambray[82]. Perhaps you may not determine upon it until I see you. As I mean to take with me the 2 six pounder[s] from Camden, we shall want two there to replace them.

Yours ever most sincerely

CORNWALLIS

---

[81] See Rawdon's letter of 13th December, 8 at night, p 210.

[82] *the enclosed petition..*: no extant copy, but see de Cambray's letter of 6th January 1781, pp 409-10. He was a lt colonel in the Continental Corps of Engineers and was exchanged later that year. (Heitman, *Register*, 140)

Balfour to Cornwallis, 11th December 1780 *4(310): ALS*

Charles Town
11th December

Inclosed is a return[83] of the recruits that march tomorow morning for the army, and of those men belonging to Captain Maxwell's detachment which they will take up at Nielson's Ferry. Captain Kerr[84] of the 33rd commands the detachment.

The movement of a corps in force from Nielson's to Camden appears to me rather useful at present, and it being a country not much used by us, the corps must be better supply'd than by the other road, which is stript of every thing. I have therefore proposed that the recruits shall cross at Nielson's, be joined by Major McLeroth at Sumpter's house, and by his corps be conducted as far as the High Hills of Santee, where a mounted party from Camden might be sent to meet them. Major McLeroth will of course return, and in his absence Captain Maxwell's detachment may take care of the communication, which I know he is quite equal to.

The swamp beyond Nielson's is the only objection to this movement. I have directed Captain Maxwell to examine it, and if passable, the recruits will proceed to cross it and join the 64th, but if not, they must go the common road by McCord's etc.

This detachment will be at Nielson's on Friday, and if this march appears to Lord Rawdon in any way exceptionable, it can easily be stopt by his Lordship's sending to Nielson's for that purpose, which he will have time sufficiently to do.

I have wrote to Major McLeroth and Captain Maxwell to arrange the matter with them, and leave this letter open for Lord Rawdon's information in order that he may direct the movements of both as it may appear best, but should they receive no directions to the contrary from his Lordship, the corps will move as I have mentioned and will expect to meet a mounted detachment upon the High Hills to escort them to Camden.

Two ships from England in six weeks came off the barr yesterday and one of them unfortunately has got ashore and will be lost, a very rich cargo, thrown away by the folly of the master.

From one passenger only come on shore, I hear for certain of the arrival of the *Providence* in thirty three days from hence. This agreeable piece of news is the only one worth mentioning which I could get from this gentleman, who assures me of there being letters for your Lordship on board. If so, they shall immediately be forwarded, or if not, any news

---

83 *a return*: not extant.

84 John Kerr had spent his entire service in the 33rd Regiment. Commissioned an ensign on 2nd August 1760, he was promoted to lieutenant on 22nd February 1768 and to captain on 28th August 1775. According to Cornwallis, he 'served in Germany and is a carefull and attentive officer'. He would be killed during the siege of Yorktown. (*Army Lists*; *The Cornwallis Papers*)

worth mentioning shall be sent you.

Not a word of our friends, to my astonishment. I begin to think and fear they have got into Cape Fear, as the winds here have been all fair for turning the Frying Pan, yet I cannot suppose so many men of war can have missed them. At all events a day or two must decide it, but this unlucky wind prevents any thing getting from the northward to us. The not finding any vessells *there* from us, should they have got in, will surely bring them if nothing else will, and we have not left any possible means untry'd to get to them, as I shall explain hereafter.

Our anxiety, you may suppose, makes a thousand improbable circumstances appear likely. In my own serious opinion, and taking all circumstances together, I think they must be near us and cannot fetch the barr. God grant us a speedy sight of them!

I ever am
Yours

NB

PS

An answer to this still may be received before I move.

Balfour to Cornwallis, 13th or 14th December 1780 — *4(329): ALS*

Charles Town
Wednesday, 14th[85]

This moment forty five sail have appeared off the barr. No kind of doubt it must be them, as several small vessells spoke them that are come in.

Tomorow *he* will be here. I keep an express ready, whenever any thing is fixed, and send one *now* just to say that they are at hand. By all acounts they cannot get over the barr before tomorow, and Saturday will be the soonest, I suppose, we can sett out. However, of the exact day and our movements I shall take care to acquaint your Lordship and Lord Rawdon by express.

The recruits marched yesterday. I sent all the papers I could lay hands upon by last express and now send you one just received by a ship from England.

I am in haste.

Yours most faithfuly

NB

---

85 Either the day or the date is wrong. Wednesday was the 13th.

PS

This is left open for Lord Rawdon.

Balfour to Cornwallis, 15th December 1780 — *4(333): ALS*

Charles Town
15th December 1780

They are all arrived safe, thank God, not a vessell missing after perrills of various kinds, amongst which the want of provisions was not the least.

We have proceeded to business and this morning every thing is fixed. It will be Sunday, I think, before they can be sett a-going, as you know what arrangements are necessary in such a corps, where every thing is indeed more starved than I can possibly describe.

The Guards, Regiment of Boze, Wattson's corps, 17th infantry, Yagers etc etc compose the corps. Fanning's go to George Town, 82nd and 84th for this garrison in the room of the 64th, who join the army. Two six pounders and two Hessian three pounders attend the detachment.

Every circumstance put together, I do not think there was any alternative since the 64th was to join you. The 82nd and 84th – both *bad*, very bad – come nearly to the numbers of the 64th and take their place, and the convalescents from George Town are succeeded by Fanning's corps, who has about 230 fitt for duty, which, when reinforced by the dragoons to be raised at George Town and the remnants of Brown's corps, will, I doubt not, be quite equal to the posession of all the lower part of the Pedee.

Our only difficulty lyes with the Hessian brigadier and Colonel Fanning[86]. The first, I fear, must go, and the second, unless at Ninety Six, must be akwardly situated. However, I mean to sett out from hence alone on Saturday and get to the army by Tuesday or Wednesday when every thing shall be fully explained and can be easily altred that concerns the present arrangement. In my way up I shall get waggons, provisions etc etc, and everything I can shall

---

[86] Born on Long Island, New York, Edmund Fanning (1737-1818) had graduated at Yale College before moving on to Hillsborough, North Carolina. There he was admitted to the bar and became a person of some consequence, being elected to the legislature, commissioned a colonel in the royal militia, and appointed a Public Registrar and a Judge of the Superior Court. Eventually he was made a scapegoat by the upcountry Regulators for the high fees and excessive taxes settled on them and was treated so roughly by them that he had to resign the office of Public Registrar. He soon obtained his revenge by commanding a corps of militia in Governor Tryon's defeat of the Regulators at the Battle of the Alamance in May 1771. Dependent as he was on Tryon for support, he chose to leave North Carolina the same year and go as Tryon's private secretary to New York. In 1774 he was appointed Surveyor General of the province. A staunch loyalist, he went on to raise the King's American Regiment (otherwise known as Fanning's corps) two years later and was commissioned its Colonel. Now, as these Papers later reveal, no opportunity would arise of giving him a command in the south appropriate to his rank, leading him to think of taking a trip to England for the sake of his health. After the war he received compensation of £4,447 for the loss of his confiscated property in North Carolina and became Lt Governor, first of Nova Scotia, and then of Prince Edward Island. Having also risen to be a general in the British Army, he died at Upper Seymour Street, London. (*ODNB*; *The Cornwallis Papers*)

be got ready for the march.

General Lessly desires me to make his apology for not writing today as I was to mention the principal parts of the business. He will write by me, and as I am so soon to see you, shall not make this a bore.

A frigate was ordred from Admiral Arbuthnot to call at the Chesapeak upon General Lessly for his dispatches to England, where she was bound from Gardner's Bay. General Lessly thought it best for your Lordship's convenience to bring her here (and I shall write an official request to Captain Gayton that she may remain here untill your Lordship's dispatches by me are sent). That you will find the most sincere and hearty concurrence in the commander of this detachment I am most certain of, but that such a detachment should not be over rated, or pass upon the world for what they are *not*, I own I wish to be very clearly explained *every where*. Justice to every one demands it; and hereafter, when it is alledged (which no doubt it will be) of what stuff it was composed, it will come but with very little force in comparison with a declaration *now*, before they come to the service, of what can be expected from such a detachment and such a reinforcement.

Pardon me, I beg, for this, but acquainted as I now am with all this business, I should think my fidelity to your Lordship of little moment did I omitt telling you freely what I apprehend to be absolutely and clearly an intention to shew your force, and of course your operations, in a very unfair point of view.

I ever am with sincere regard and attachment
Yours

N BALFOUR

[*Subscribed*:]

General Lessly did not receive your letters by the *Beaumont* or *Loyalist*.[87]

Balfour to Cornwallis, 16th December 1780 — *4(341): ALS*

Charles Town
16th December

I find it will not be possible to get away before Sunday night, nor the troops to march before Munday morning.

The *gout* has seized General Bichhausen and his guns are arrested here, so that two sixes and two threes come with the army as you wished.

---

87 See pp 39 and 42, notes 47 and 54.

Colonel Fanning means to pay you a visit. When I have the pleasure of seeing you, shall explain the particular situation that he feels himself in.

On Tuesday the relief goes to George Town, and Bluck will march up the detachment to Camden on this side the Santee.

The 17th Dragoons have lost their horses – thank God, our only loss, but what to do with them we cannot settle. My idea is to send their accoutrements by water to Monk's Corner and so on to Nielson's, where fifty horses from Camden might meet them, for carrying up their accoutrements by land is impossible and the uttmost exertions in our power will, I fear, be incompetent to the moving the army. However, I will give timely notice to Lord Rawdon, who reads this, if the horses will be wanted. From all accounts his Lordship will be able to spare his mounted for a few days, and they may return, if *wanted*, immediately to Camden. The want of horses here is so great that their being mounted is out of the question, and their use with the army I know too well to keep them here a moment.

I hope to wait on you on Thursday and beg Lord Rawdon will pardon my keeping three or four mounted infantry at McCord's past my fixed time. General Lessly begs his respects to your Lordship and Lord Rawdon.

I am
Most faithfuly yours

N BALFOUR

Balfour to Cornwallis, 26th December 1780 — *4(400): ALS*

Nielson's Ferry
26th December 1780

The difficultys brought on by the movement of the 64th to the High Hills has retarded the army from crossing till this day, during the course of which we hope to get the light company of the Guards and Lt Colonel Watson's corps to the opposite side in order to relieve Major Campbell[88] at Sumpter's house. The necessity of having some indian meal to supply the army at Singleton's Mills made it necessary to march a detachment of Major Campbell's corps this evening to that place to collect corn etc. This detachment will be relieved by the light company of the Guards, who will cover the mills, while Major Campbell marches on to Camden, and untill the army comes up.

---

88 Formerly a lieutenant in the 44th Regiment, John Campbell had transferred to the Provincial establishment in 1778 and become a captain in Rawdon's newly raised Volunteers of Ireland. Now promoted to major, he and forty of its light company had been sent by Rawdon on 17th December to the High Hills of Santee, where he assumed overall command of a corps comprising his detachment, the 64th Regiment, and fifty of Harrison's irregulars. A zealous and steady officer, he had ceased to serve in the Volunteers of Irleand when it was taken on to the British establishment in August 1782. (*Army Lists*; Raymond, 'British American Corps'; *The Cornwallis Papers*)

The swamp will be passable and I have no doubt will be crossed tomorow by the troops, but I doubt much that *one* day will do all the business, and Friday morning, I fear, you must look to for their moving from Sumpter's, and Wednesday for their arrival at Camden.

Every waggon shall be taken from hence to forward them up as far as Camden, where I doubt[89] they will get to with difficulty, the horses being allmost wore out. The return of these waggons, and especialy *those* pressed from the country, I hope may appear absolutely necessary, and that the Quarter Master General may have very *strict* orders to that effect. The waggons sent from the Orangeburgh District three months ago have not yet been returned or paid, of which they do not fail to complain loudly. The only mode of silencing them I shall take whenever it is possible to get a little cash.

The recruits are this day at Thompson's house. Those belonging to Camden will proceed from thence, and the rest by the Congrees, where they will be certainly on Friday as their route and proper people are marked for them. Mr Ancrum is also wrote to there, who will take care of them and forward them to the army, which I should hope they may join on Sunday or Munday.

Inclosed is a letter from Benson shewing an intention of something against Marrion from that quarter, but as Bluck's detachment is wanted immediately for the army, I have sent to hasten him up. Should Colonel Campbell want to get him betwixt Colonel Watson's corps and his, he will find him ready and apprised of his plan, of which Lord Rawdon will also be acquainted from this. I shall not fail to press horses at Charles Town and send to Camden every sword I can get or buy for the cavalry and mounted infantry there.

The post at Congrees appears to me of great importance, and if I receive no orders to the contrary, shall immediately send up Mr Maxwell there and give him sixty men of Brown's corps and one hundred of the Orangeburgh militia, which are forming upon the new plan and in which I have confidence. A redoubt round Hampton's house with this garrison will not be forced except by cannon and can act offensively against small partys. The ferrys over the Congarres and Saluda will be covred by this post, as also the communication betwixt Camden and Ninety Six and the District of Orangeburgh, which induces me to wish it as strong as possible.

The three pounders with General Lessly are congreves with two wheels.

I shall continue the supply of rum etc as fast as my *remains* of waggons and horses will admit. There will allways be a despot here ready for Lord Rawdon's orders, and I shall not fail to give every information to his Lordship, and use every means in my power, to forward and asist the operations of his corps. I have only to add that the delay of the repair of the swamp was owing to the enemy's being left in posession of it, and the scarcity of the biscuit to[90] Major Campbell's corps being unexpectedly supply'd from this store. However, I do not doubt that there will be provisions enough for the army.

---

89 *doubt*: used in the archaic sense of 'fear'.

90 *to*: i.e. was owing to.

I have just heard of a report being spread at Charles Town that one thousand French troops have got into Cape Fear from Rhode Island. No credit is given to it, nor is it known from whence it has originated.

When every thing is perfectly clear here, I shall go to Charles Town and immediately inform you of this business and every other matter there worth mentioning.

I have the honor to be with the most sincere attachment
Your Lordship's most faithful servant

N BALFOUR

NB

The 64th etc will be at Camden, I suppose, about Sunday morning.

Enclosure
Benson to Balfour, 22nd December 1780 — *4(376): ALS*

Charles Town
December 22nd 1780

Dear Sir

In consequence of information received of Marion's situation and strength, which gives reason to suppose something decisive may be done against him, I have with the approbation of Colonel Innes sent Captain Blucke a discretionary power relative to his movements in case Colonel Cassells, Colonel Campbell and he should be of opinion that his postponing his march eight or ten days would facilitate the measure. As the informant was sent down by Colonel Cassels, whose only objection was a want of sufficient force, I return'd him with the letter to overtake Colonel Campbell on his march, recommending it to him not to attempt any thing unless there was the utmost probability of success. Colonel Cruger arriv'd in town last night. No convoy to Savannah yet. A brig from York in eleven days and no letters. An embarkation taking place there. The *Delight* sloop of war is arriv'd and the gallies. No account of the *Sandwich*. General Leslie is just setting off.

I have the honor to be with the utmost sincerity, sir,
Your faithful and oblig'd humble servant

G BENSON
Major of Brigade

[*Subscribed*:]

Mr Wright has this instant brought £500 from Savannah. I have sent it to Biddulph[91].

Cornwallis to Balfour, 29th December 1780[92] *83(95): C*

Wynnesborough
December 29th 1780

Lt Colonel Balfour

Dear Balfour

I received your letter of the 26th from Nelson's Ferry. The slow progress of Leslie is vexatious but it cannot be helped. Green marched on the 20th from Charlottetown to Haly's Ferry on Pedee. This movement – added to the account sent by Admiral Arbuthnot of five sail, supposed to be one frigate, the rest transports, getting out of Rhode Island about the 9th or 10th of November – makes me apprehend that there may be some truth in the account of the thousand French at Cape Fear. If that should be the case, it will be difficult to say what we must do, as the communication by Cape Fear, and consequently all certainty of supply, will be at an end.

Morgan with his riflemen and about 120 dragoons, commanded, I believe, by Washington, have joined Sumpter's late corps. If this French account does not interfere, I shall pursue the plan I originally intended. Tarleton will march up Broad River on Wednesday, and I shall move up the middle road on Thursday, Leslie going at the same time up the road by the Wateree. I think I must have certain accounts by that time whether the French are at Cape Fear.

I send you a packet I received from Lt Colonel Brown[93]. I am much satisfied with what he has done; it has rendered us most essential service. I beg you will signify to him from me that you have directions to give him all reasonable assistance as to money and that I wish him to encourage as much as possible the war against the Back Mountain men. I allow him to keep his brass (one pounders) in consequence of his good defence when he was attacked and to recruit in South Carolina provided he does not enlist prisoners. I do not care to speak fully to him about the Indians as the communication is not very safe to Ninety Six. I have desired Colonel Allen to send him the Ninety Six cypher, in which you may write the part of your letter which relates to them.

---

91 A reference to the Charlestown office of Francis Biddulph, a banker of Charing Cross, London, who was acting as a money contractor in association with Harley & Drummond (see p 84, note 40).

92 Extracts from this letter are published in Ross ed, *Cornwallis Correspondence*, i, 75-6.

93 *a packet..*: see pp 295-305.

I think it right to inform Sir Henry of my having employed the Indians, as there will be a considerable expence attending it. You will therefore send by the first opportunity the enclosed[94] to him with the letters from Brown, Don Galvez, Governor Henry and De Peyster.

If I march at the time I propose, I shall halt for 3 or 4 days somewhere near the Cross Roads, where letters will overtake me. This easterly wind makes me very sanguine in my hopes of seeing Ross before I part with the communication. I think I must likewise hear from New York if it is true that an embarkation is going on under Phillips for the Chesapeak.

I am, dear Balfour.
Most sincerely yours

CORNWALLIS

Cornwallis to Balfour, 1st January 1781 — *84(1): C*

Wynnesborough
January 1st 1781

Lt Colonel Balfour

Dear Balfour

I take the opportunity of a safe conveyance to Camden to say that I do not intend to move Leslie from Camden or to march far into North Carolina until I am satisfied about the Cape Fear business. Should the French keep that harbour and of course prevent any supplies to Cross Creek, it will be a serious business to go into the heart of North Carolina.

If the report should prove true, I wish you to consult the naval commander on the practicability of proceeding against them. If false, I should be very anxious to lose no time in possessing that harbour with ships of war and a detachment of troops. To make the business of 96 easy and to compensate for the mischief which Pickens, who is gone over to the rebels, may do, I have determined to leave the 7th Regiment at 96. They will have about 240 men fit for duty and consequently give Cruger more than he asks. I think you may very well make out a detachment of 200 men, including convalescents for this army, for the Cape Fear business. You must send the most intelligent commander you can find and an engineer. I will write more fully to you on this business but wish you much to lose no time in making your preparations.

Morgan, Washington etc are at Grimes's Mill 3 miles south of Pacolet, threatening and exceedingly alarming 96. You shall hear from me again soon.

Yours most sincerely

CORNWALLIS

---

94 *the enclosed*: Cornwallis to Clinton, 29th December, p 30.

Balfour to Cornwallis, 29th December 1780 — *4(424): ALS*

Charles Town
29th December 1780

After seeing every thing away from Nielson's Ferry, I got here last night with my heart so strongly impressed with all your goodness to me that, believe me, no time can ever eraze. Your confidence, be assured, shall never intentionaly be abused, and where I err, the head must only answer.

All your enclosures of the 24th, 25th and 26th[95] and all your directions shall be taken care of. The *Blonde* sails on Sunday or Munday[96].

Musket cartridges, to my astonishment, are not sent with General Lessly. A tumbrill with twenty thousand for Camden setts out tomorow morning and I shall write to Lord Rawdon for an escort to McCord's for it.

The party at George Town I fear I must bring here or keep at Nielson's Ferry, for, by the unlucky order of Innes and Benson I wrote you of, they must be too late for the army, not being yet marched from George Town from what I find here.

Captain Saunders, to my surprise, has gone to the army just at the time he ought to have gone to George Town. I shall write Lord Rawdon of it, for every hour we lose now is precious.

To shew you the attachment of the District of Ninety Six, the cannon ordred up to that post were stopped within thirty miles of the place, the trunnions knocked of, the carriadges burnt etc etc, by a party of eight or ten men. That the guns went without an escort is owing to my not knowing when or how they went.

I send an almanack and some English papers and write tomorow and every day that I think will bring my letter safe to you. Crugar is here.

My best wishes to Haldane and Governor Martin, and believe me with faithful attachment
Yours

N BALFOUR

PS

One hundred swords are gone to Lord Rawdon.

---

95 *All your enclosures..*: among them may have been Cornwallis's dispatches of 18th and 22nd December to Germain and Clinton, pp 43 and 28.

96 *The Blonde sails..*: her sailing to England was countermanded. See Balfour's and Cornwallis's letters of 2nd and 6th January 1781, pp 124 and 127.

Wynnesborough
January 3rd 1781

Lt Colonel Balfour

Dear Balfour

I received this morning yours of the 29th. We have had a great alarm in the 96 District. Washington surprised and routed some militia near Williams's and it was reported that Morgan was gone with 2 pieces of cannon to attack 96. I detached immediately Tarleton and McArthur over Broad River. All was quiet at 96 on Monday morning at 9 o'clock and I believe the enemy are retired. Cunningham abandoned Williams's house. As you mention nothing of the Cape Fear business and Lord Rawdon saw a man who spoke to one McCrae, a true friend to Government, who was at Wilmington on Christmas Eve and said he heard nothing of them in Cape Fear River, I conclude it a false story. The 7th Regiment added to 96 will make all safe there, so that I think some how or other you will make out 200 men for the Cape Fear expedition. Lord Rawdon may help you a little. They need not be good marchers. I have ordered Sutherland[97], the engineer, to go thither. You must hurry the naval department in this business. It will not only secure that important communication but pass in the country for a third large army.

I have not time now to send you my opinion on some queries presented to me by McKinnon. You will send the enclosed letter[98] to Sir Henry Clinton by the first opportunity. It contains only recommendations for the succession in the 33rd Regiment.

The following will be an improvement to our cypher[99] instead of making any particular marks which tend to discover to the enemy and are less explicit to ourselves. There is no figure in the cypher above 29. Suppose then that one, two or three or more figures as it happens from 30 to 49, both inclusive, set the cypher at *A* to the figure following them. For example, 34, 36, 43, 15 sets the cypher 15 to *A*. 33, 37, 11 sets 11 to *A*, and so on. You may change it as often as you please. Nobody who does not know the key can suspect those figures for changing the cypher, which might be the case with /, ⱡ, X and so forth. I would then insert frequently, especially in words of two or three letters, the figures from 50 to 99, both inclusive, which are to mean nothing. For example, – 11 (t), 54, 14 (h), 66, 7 (e) – 17 (o), 75, 8 (f) — 10 (o), 88, 18 (n), 76 —, which must contribute greatly to prevent decyphering. This with the help of our dictionary[100] must make our correspondence quite safe. I have explained this to Lord Rawdon.

---

97 Alexander Sutherland had been commissioned an ensign in the Corps of Engineers on 4th December 1770. He was promoted to lieutenant on 30th October 1775. (*Army Lists*)

98 *the enclosed letter*: see p 30.

99 *our cypher*: see vol II, p 82, note 42.

100 *our dictionary*: see vol II, p 65, note 11.

As the iron guns are destroyed, and the 7th going to 96, I will leave for the present the two brass ones there and perhaps may also send the old Legion 3 pounder thither if I should not have a convenient opportunity of conveying it to Camden. You shall here constantly from me while I remain in communication. I wish very much to have the letters sent off to New York as soon as possible[101]. Signify as much to Gayton. If they do not go in a safe ship, you will take care that there is some carefull person to cut away. I must not see them in a Philadelphia paper.

I am with great truth
Very sincerely yours

CORNWALLIS

NB

When I use the dictionary cypher I shall put *B*, and when I change from that again, *H*.

The same instruction with regard to the cypher was sent to Lord Rawdon.

Balfour to Cornwallis, 30th December 1780 — *4(427): ALS*

Charles Town
30th December 1780

The report of Cape Fear is certainly false and my authority is from a person who left the river a few days ago.

Inclosed is a letter which was (I suppose) forgot by some officer from New York and made its appearance here only yesterday[102].

The *Camilla*, I find, is the ship fixed on for the convoy to the victualers and decayed transports.[103]

As yet no acounts of the *Sandwich*. All the sea folks give her over. I realy think (if it proves she is lost) that some enquiry should be made about the matter, and at least that the Admiral might know by whose order she was sent upon the service to St Augustine.

I ever am
Your faithful servant

N BALFOUR

---

[101] *the letters..*: those from Cornwallis to Clinton. See ch 30.

[102] *a letter..*: not extant.

[103] See Cornwallis to Clinton, 22nd December, p 28.

Balfour to Cornwallis, 31st December 1780 *4(433): ALS*

Charles Town
31st December 1780
Eight o'clock evening

This moment a schooner is come to anchor, the master of which says that he sailed eleven days ago from New York with a fleet of forty two sail in which was embarked two thousand men commanded by General Arnold, that five days ago he parted with them off the Capes of Virginia standing into the Chesapeak, and from what he learnt they were bound up the James River.

The *Charron*, Captain Symonds, is Commodore and he knows of the names of Colonels Dundass and Simcoe being officers in the fleet on board of the transports.

The *Charron, Thames, Amphitrite* and *Bonetta* were the ships of war with the fleet, and the *Medœa* with dispatches left them the day he did and is now in sight of the bar.

Thus far the master of the schooner, whose acount I shall not comment upon nor the desultory expedition of which he brings news. The arrival of the *Medœa*, Captain Duncan, I would hope might find you still near enough for a safe communication to your letters, which shall not be stopped one moment here, nor will I keep the express but to add that

I am
Most sincerly and faithfuly yours

N BALFOUR

PS

Should the *Medœa* bring acounts or letters which I apprehend necessary for your answering or in any way communicating to England, I shall stop the sailing of the *Blonde*.

Cornwallis to Balfour, 5th January 1781 *84(14): C*

Wynnesborough
January 5th 1781

Lt Colonel Balfour

Dear Balfour

I heard from Tarleton last night. Morgan had retired and was got too far to give any hopes of overtaking him, so that I shall march as soon as possible, I believe on Sunday, and Leslie will follow on Tuesday. You see that if the account of the schooner is true I must get my dispatches in time, and indeed there can be no doubt but those dispatches will encourage me to move on. I wish I could flatter myself with seeing Ross. I think 'till the beginning of the week after next I shall be within reach of being overtaken without much risk. The addition of the 7th Regiment will make 96 perfectly secure.

I recommend to you in the strongest manner to lose no time in fitting out and sending off the expedition to Cape Fear. I think it of the utmost consequence for our own security and for the effect it will have on the minds of the people in North Carolina.

Yours most sincerely

CORNWALLIS

Balfour to Cornwallis, 2nd January 1781 *70(26): ALS*

Charles Town
2nd December 1780[104]

The dispatches now sent[105] are just brought by Captain Duncan of the *Medœa* and Major Craig of the 82nd Regiment, who is come to join his regiment here rather than remain with the unactive part at Halifax.

You will see that the letters by the *Beaumont* have been open'd at Head Quarters. This part of the business I own I should have excused[106] in respect to my letter to General Lessly *without a date*, as it was wrote with warmth at the time the army left Charlotte and without any kind of reserve.

Wishing anxiously that the General might immediately *decide* respecting his coming to Cape Fear, and conceiving it impossible that my letter should pass the *review* it has done, will acount to your Lordship for the expressions quoted in my letter by Sir Henry Clinton. I do not doubt that there are also others which are equaly warm and more imprudent, especialy as I by no means concealed my opinion of the detachment sent. *However*, as I have no objection of avowing that opinion any where, I only regret that a confidential, private letter should fall into the hands of the person it was not addressed to.

Major Craig informs me that the troops with General Arnold are principaly Dundass' and Simcoe's corps with some Yagers and Provincials, in all about fifteen hundred men. The feelings[107] of the two lt colonels, I conceive, must be somewhat strange.

---

104 Misdated, as frequently happens at the turn of a year, The letter was written on 2nd January 1781.

105 *The dispatches now sent*: Clinton to Cornwallis, 13th December 1780, p 31, and Arbuthnot to Cornwallis, 2nd and 13th December 1780, pp 48 to 54.

106 *excused*: sought to preclude.

107 *The feelings*: with respect to Arnold, who had recently defected from the revolutionary cause.

The cooperation of this detachment will not, I apprehend, effect[108] your movements. If it should, be so good as to let me know, as also whether you wish any ship of force to be sent into Cape Fear *at present* to lye there. You will see that the arrangements proposed by the Admiral were on the supposition of General Lessly's being in the Cape Fear River. The difficultys attending a new plan have been very considerable, especialy as the *Blonde* is not now to proceed to England unless you require her for your dispatches.

Captain Gayton writes you an acount of the business[109], which indeed could not be settled otherwise, as the sending away such a frigate as the *Blonde* at present might materialy effect your *future* operations, there being no acount of the *Sandwich*. I have in a great degree answred for you and as usual made free use of your name, especialy in assuring Captain Gayton that your dispatches to England are not so pressing but the convoy sailing in three weeks's time would answer nearly as well in carrying them.

Inclosed is a letter I received concerning Lieutenant Ford's court martial, which is also sent by this opportunity.[110]

Colonel Innes and Simson have both received pressing letters to come to New York and they mean to go by Gayton and take their chance of getting an opportunity from Virginia. I shall send your dispatches to Sir Henry Clinton and other letters by them. You will have time also to answer the letters now sent you before Gayton sails. I see no notice taken of the sequestration business.

By a letter from Weir I find that he means to send Major Morrison[111] here as Commissary General for the Southern District and wants to have Townshend sent back to New York.

I must here beg your interference with Weir and that you'l prevent our changing a very good commissary for a very dissagreeable, pompous fellow who is troublesome to the greatest degree and by no means equal to the business, and as this is a matter of consequence to the whole command, I beg the nabob may not erect his court here.

Colonel Crugar is here and we have had much conversation respecting his post, which is by much our most vulnerable part. Not less than five hundred men ought certainly to be placed at such a distance from support, unless you mean them not to stirr from the redoubt and leave the posession of the country to the banditti, who in their last excursion came within three miles of the place, whereas being able to detach two hundred men on an emergency

---

108 *effect*: affect.

109 *Captain Gayton writes..*: on 2nd January, p 464.

110 The letter is not extant. James Ford had been commissioned a lieutenant in the 7th Regiment (Royal Fusiliers) on 24th July 1775. (*Army Lists*)

111 A deputy commissary general, Major John Morrison would replace Captain Gregory Townsend in April 1781. As evinced by his following remarks, Balfour did not have a high opinion of him. (WO 65/164(3) (National Archives, Kew); *The Cornwallis Papers*)

effectualy gains the asistance of the militia, who, without the aid of troops, you know are of no sort of use. The inroad of two hundred men into the heart of the country betwixt this and Savanah obliged me to detach the light company of the 84th Regiment to take post at Pocotaligo, where I fear they must remain to cover that country from the mountaign men, who come down the River Savannah and return with their plunder by the Saltketchers and, being well mounted, pass easily betwixt Ninety Six and Augusta.

This detachment, with that sent today to the Congrees of sixty five rank and file, and thirty to Neilson's Ferry to cover the stores there, will put it out of my power to send any thing to Ninety Six, especialy when the corps to the *northward*[112] will move, which cannot be under one hundred men at least.

Colonel Innes's corps appears to me the best to be spared from Camden and Crugar thinks they are not by any means unpopular *now* there.

By every account from England the prosecution of this war seems determined upon and the strength gained from the new Parliament is to be shewn by the reinforcement sent here etc etc. By a letter from Weir another French squadron and army have sailed from France, bound as is supposed to America.

Six thousand pounds are come in the *Medœa*, which is not a breakfast to us. Gordon tells me that your letter[113] will bring some, as cash is to be got at New York.

By Duncan I have particulars respecting Sir William and Lord Howe[114]. The General did not stand for Nottingham and seems determined upon retirement. His brother is yet in view and more popular than ever in the navy, the state of which with respect to admirals is truly deplorable. Barrington[115] resigned and Ross[116] about to follow.

Duncan only heared of Ross's arrival, but by late acounts I find we may look for him hourly in a frigate with £50,000 for this place. Paul Jones may perhaps use a little freedom

---

112 *to the northward*: to Wilmington.

113 *your letter*: of 22nd December to Clinton, p 28.

114 Richard, Viscount Howe (1726-1799) in the Irish peerage had been Commander-in-Chief of the navy on the North American station between 1776 and 1778. Having had no active command since then, he had been frequently attending the House of Commons, where he was the Member for Dartmouth. In February 1779, on not being appointed First Lord of the Admiralty, he had become alienated from the North ministry and begun to vote with the opposition. (*ODNB*)

115 A vice admiral of the blue, Samuel Barrington (1729-1800) was an active and distinguished officer who had recently been second in command to Admiral Geary when he took over the Channnel Fleet. In August Geary fell ill through exhaustion and Barrington was ordered to take the fleet to sea. He declined to do so and was dismissed. He was a younger brother of Viscount Barrington (see vol II, p 52, note 30). (*ODNB*)

116 A rear admiral of the blue, Sir John Lockhart Ross Bt (1721-1790) had returned to the active list in 1777 after distinguished service during the Seven Years' War. In 1779 he was fourth in command in the Channel before sailing in the *Royal George* to the relief of Gibraltar under Rodney. He did not resign. (*ODNB*)

with him and the cash. Pray tell my Lord Rawdon to mention to me allways in his letters as long as[117] he thinks the communication safe betwixt him and you in case that he[118] arrives and can be got up to you before you leave us.

Tarleton's friend[119] has very near been hanged. I send you his intelligence, brought only this moment, and if possible shall get him replaced by a much surer and better man. Otherwise, it will be rendring you no great service.

Since writing the above, I am informed of a ship, the *Admiral Barrington* of sixteen guns and forty men, going on the 10th instant for England. Should you choose to send your dispatches by her, I will send some invalids as an additional force. She is a fast sailer, a letter of marque, and I apprehend by no means a bad opportunity.

I ever am, my dear Lord,
Your most faithful and sincere humble servant

N BALFOUR

Cornwallis to Balfour, 6th January 1781 — *84(17): C*

Wynnesborough
January 6th 1781

Lt Colonel Balfour

Dear Balfour

I received this day yours of the 2nd containing dispatches etc. I send you my letter to the Chief[120] open. You will seal it. My letter to England will keep very well for the convoy. I would not accustom them to expect to hear by trading ships unless there was some event of great consequence. I am clearly of opinion that the expedition to Cape Fear should take place immediately and think Craig would be a very proper man to command it. I have written to Wier on the subject you mention and enclosed a letter to Phillips. I wish you would either enclose to Wier my other letters to Phillips or give them in charge to Innes.[121] You see I have taken the business of Ninety Six entirely off your hands. Pray send Cruger down as soon as possible. We will take care to drive Morgan and Washington before us.

---

[117] *as long as*: how long that.

[118] *he*: Major Ross.

[119] *Tarleton's friend*: de Treville. His intelligence is not extant.

[120] *my letter to the Chief*: Cornwallis to Clinton, 6th January, p 33.

[121] There are no copies of the letters to Weir and Phillips. They may in part have been private.

Phillips desires[122] that on account of the great civility shewn by a Colonel Wood[123] to the Convention army his lt colonel, Jonathan Clarke[124], should be allowed to go on parole. Let it be so if you see no material objection. I should wish the letters for New York to go as soon as possible. I *hear* that I am much complained of for not writing oftener, and you are not out of that scrape. I shall not march 'til Monday as I find that Tarleton will not be quite ready.

You had better write a few lines to General Amherst by the letter of marque, mentioning the troops I have taken with me and those left in the province.

I will continue writing and will send a commission for Maxwell, altho' I am at a loss what sort of one to make out as I do not think myself empowered to grant brevets. I will manage it somehow. When money is to be had, you will secure the forage money, brigadiers' pay etc. It may be wise not to let that run in arrear.

Yours very sincerely

CORNWALLIS

PS

It will be right to send Parker and Blair and as many of the usefull refugees as you can to Arnold, and Captain Saunders and his men must go at all events.

---

122 *Phillips desires..*: his letter is not extant.

123 James Wood (1750-1813) was Colonel of the 8th Virginia Continental Regiment and in 1778 had been appointed commanding officer of the post at Charlottesville, Virginia, responsible for the captured Convention troops quartered there. After the war he would play a prominent part in the public affairs of Virginia, becoming a Member of the Governor's Council and then Governor himself. A member of the Society for promoting the abolition of slavery in Virginia, he was elected its President in 1801. Wood County, West Virginia, is named after him. (*Appletons'*)

124 Born in Albemarle County, Virginia, Jonathan Clark (1750-1811) received a fair English education before becoming a lawyer and successful businessman. A delegate to the Richmond convention which met in December 1775, he was one month later commissioned a captain in what became the 8th Virginia Continental Regiment. With it he repaired to Charlestown, South Carolina, but the regiment was not involved in the repulse of the British in June 1776. Contracting a dangerous illness shortly afterwards while at Savannah, he returned home to convalesce, but when almost recovered in spring 1777, he had the misfortune to be taken down with the small pox, which again disabled him for a considerable period. By September he had rejoined his regiment and took part in the Battles of Brandywine, Germantown, and Monmouth. A major by August 1779, he served as Henry Lee's second during the daring and mostly successful raid on the isolated British post of Paulus Hook, New Jersey. Then, having been promoted in November to Lt Colonel of the 8th Virginia (backdated to May), he was sent south with the regiment, arriving at Charlestown on 31st March, but only in time to capitulate in May. He would be granted parole under the cartel in June 1781 but would not be exchanged until after the capitulation of Yorktown. In later life he became a major general in the Virginia militia before moving to Kentucky, settling at Trough Spring near Louisville. At his death he had accumulated a large fortune in real estate and personal property, including 56 slaves. He was buried in Cave Hill Cemetery. (William Hayden English, *Conquest of the Country Northwest of the River Ohio 1778-1783 and Life of Gen. George Rogers Clark* (Indianapolis, 1896), 991-1019)

Cornwallis to Balfour, 7th January 1781 *84(25): C*

Wynnesborough
January 7th 1781

Lt Colonel Balfour

Dear Balfour

I shall march to morrow and Leslie will move on Tuesday. We shall assemble at Bullocks Creek. Tarleton will not pass Broad River until he is sure that Washington and Morgan have passed. Lee's Legion was at Guilford Court House on Wednesday sevennight. Whether it was to march to Charlottetown or Haley's Ferry is uncertain.

You will omit no opportunity of writing a line to the Commander in Chief just to state matters of fact.

I grow very anxious about Ross and am much afraid he cannot join me. If he cannot get to Bullocks Creek by the 15th or 16th, I fear there will be no chance. Lord Rawdon will give every assistance of escort, and if a speedy express is dispatched to Camden the instant Ross arrives, the escort may meet him on the Wynnesborough Road and save his going round by Camden.

I shall write you a long formal letter about the publick departments. I fear at last I shall be foiled, at least as far as the South Carolina waggons, for unless I had a person I could depend on to purchase the Quarter Master General's waggons and horses and to take care of them afterwards, I fear he would take very effectual methods to prevent my œconomy being admired.

There have been some men under sentence of death for desertion ever since the taking of Charlestown. I wish you would either put them on board a man of war or send them to the Spanish Main.

I am, dear Balfour.
Most sincerely yours

CORNWALLIS

Cornwallis to Balfour, 9th January 1781 *84(40): C*

Camp at McAlister's
January 9th 1781

Lt Colonel Balfour

Dear Balfour

I send you by this opportunity the papers relative to the Quarter Master General's Department with a letter on the subject,[125] in which I think I have been very gentle considering Mr MacKinnon's queries, which I think both foolish and impertinent.

You will receive an account from Colonel Allen at 96 of some of his men who are prisoners on parole. I should wish you to release an equal number of Continental prisoners for them.

I was desired by a friend in England to be civil to a Mr Walter Mansell[126] who had formerly been a merchant at Charlestown and lately returned thither. I beg leave to transfer the recommendation to you.

This easterly wind must produce Ross. If he sets out in the course of this week for[127] Charlestown, he will reach us. Lord Rawdon is prepared to give him every possible assistance.

I have written a very civil letter to Fanning[128], which I hope will be satisfactory.

Yours very sincerely

CORNWALLIS

[*Subscribed*:]

I have made out Maxwell's commission to command the troops to be raised by Orangeburg instead of militia. If the troops should not be raised, he is still major.

---

125 There are no extant copies of the papers and letter.

126 Walter Mansell was the proprietor of Walter Mansell & Company, a London mercantile firm with interests in South Carolina. Before the approach of the revolution it had been involved in the tea trade. Walter's support for the Crown would lead to his banishment by the revolutionary assembly at Jacksonborough and the confiscation of his property. (Dan Byrnes, 'The Blackheath Connection' (Internet, 29th December 2005); The SC Banishment and Confiscation Act 1782)

127 *for*: a miscopying of 'from'.

128 *letter to Fanning*: of 8th January, p 467.

I have not answered Sir James Wright's letter[129] relative to the raising cavalry and sending his prisoners from Augusta into Carolina. For the latter I refer him to you and wish you would be kind enough to apologise to him for my not answering the former part. You will please to tell him that I have received no proposals relative to it from Lt Colonel Clarke, that cavalry is very expensive, and useless if not well commanded, and that I cannot think it proper to allow the pay and appointments of cavalry to troops stationed in the interior part of the province. You will likewise represent to him the great force stationed at 96 and the intention of raising cavalry there. All this you will please to state in the civillest manner.

Balfour to Cornwallis, 7th January 1781 — *5(33): ALS*

Charles Town
7th January 1781

I this moment received yours of the 1st and hope you have got my letter assuring your Lordship of the falsity of the report that the French were landed in Cape Fear. Your dispatches[130] by the *Medœa* I was anxious to forward by an officer, as at that time the reports of Greene's army approaching made me wish the bearer to be extremly careful of them, which I doubt not Captain Miller has been.

Your letter of the 29th[131] with the inclosures received and shall be forwarded.

The dispatches now sent[132] came here this morning from Savannah, which place I see Clarke will leave immediately, but I own it does not appear to me of much consequence who is[133] successor is at present, and I would also hope the movement of the Spaniards is not so exactly certain as the dispatches seem to indicate.

The detaching of the 7th Regiment must put 96 out of all real hazard. Colonel Crugar setts out for that post on Tuesday and seems extremly sensible of your care of him, nor has any further wish as to military force when Dunlopp raises his cavalry, which he has been wonderfuly long in beginning. His appointments for one troop are all got up safe and the rest will be sent as quickly as the swords can be got ready.

The express today brought me also a letter from Lord Rawdon so candid and explicit respecting any future arrangements betwixt his Lordship and me that to hold back my uttmost

---

129 *Sir James Wright's letter*: of 20th November 1780, p 421.

130 *Your dispatches*: see p 124, note 105.

131 *Your letter of the 29th*: Cornwallis's of that date to Clinton, p 30.

132 *The dispatches now sent*: Clarke to Balfour, 29th December 1780 and 2nd January, and Clarke to Cornwallis, 2nd January, pp 423-431.

133 *is*: his.

and most confidential aid and exertions would be as ungenerous to him as ungrateful to you, two ideas that I hope your Lordship thinks very far from my heart.

The Cape Fear business will be all ready by Monday or Tuesday senight. At present it is fixed in the following manner: the *Blonde*, Captain Inglis, *Delight*, and *Otter*[134] with the 72nd and convalescents amounting to about 270 rank and file, four galleys, and the victualers mentioned in the enclosed return[135], besides one oat ship, an artillery vessel and some small craft.

Major Craig to command, on whose abilities and steadiness you may rely as being fully equal to the command.

Willmington, I suppose, you wish to be immediately posessed, and it is proposed to leave the *Blonde* at the Bald Head, to proceed with the sloops to Brunswick, and (there being too little water any further for them) to make the landing below Willmington with the galleys etc. The flatt boats must go and some batteaux. From all my enquirys, in which I have been aided principaly by the zeal and abilitys of Mr Cruden, I find the principal difficulty will be in getting sufficient small craft and boats up the river from Willmington to Cross Creek, which in general is a ten days' business.

Your securing Cross Creek as soon as possible will be necessary – I mean as soon as you draw near that country – as the boats usualy kept there will be of much consequence to be preserved.

The instructions I propose giving to Major Craig are that he will, after taking post at Willmington, do every thing in his power to secure small vessells and boats and hold himself in readiness to move up with the convalescents, and as much provisions as he can convey, as soon as he hears for *certain* of your approach. I shall give Ferguson's cypher to him in case you can get a communication with him.

These are the outlines of a plan only formed since I received yours this morning, but which of course will undergo some alterations and will not be put in execution untill I have your answer to this or some other explicit directions already on their way here. We prepare every thing under colour of an escort and reinforcement to General Arnold in the Chesapeak.

---

134 The name 'Creek', which is superscribed between 'and' and *'Otter'*, refers to Richard Creyk (as he signed his surname), the commander of this 14-gun sloop of war. Having circumnavigated the globe with John Byron between 1764 and 1766, he was commissioned a lieutenant in 1770 and promoted eight years later to commander, a rank which carried the courtesy title of captain. He had been actively engaged on the North American station for most of the war, being involved in the destruction of Norfolk in January 1776, the occupation of Stony and Verplanck's Points in June 1779, the Connecticut coastal raid in July of that year, and Collier's capture of much revolutionary shipping at Penobscot one month later. Promoted to post-captain in 1782, he would be appointed in 1795 Governor of the Royal Naval Hospital, and Resident Commissioner of the Victualling, at Plymouth. He became a superannuated captain in 1803 and died in 1826. (Marshall, *Royal Naval Biography*; Syrett and DiNardo ed, *The Commissioned Sea Officers*, 104)

135 *enclosed return*: not extant.

As soon as the expedition has entred the river, I should think the force in George Town might move up to Kingstown, if the enemy are not in force near it, and at once open the door to the North Carolinians, from whom I expect at least the posession of the banks of the river from Willmington to Cross Creek.

I have only now to add that from many circumstances I presume to say that the sooner we can get posession of the river the better. The approach of Paul Jones to the coast and the exertions of the French may be expected daily.

I beg your Lordship will be so good as to inform Governor Martin, with my best compliments, that I have not been able to find any letters for him in any of the opportunitys from New York.

I will not delay this express a moment longer for fear you should be getting too far for it to reach you; and that every success and happiness may attend you, be assured, is the ardent and sincere wish of

Your faithful and affectionate

N BALFOUR

Cornwallis to Balfour, 12th January 1781 — *84(51): C*

McAlister's
January 12th 1781

Lt Colonel Balfour
Commandant of Charlestown

Dear Balfour

The rains have put a total stop to Tarleton and Leslie and I do not think it right to advance too far with a large train of provision waggons and so small a corps. I hope, however, Leslie will get through all his difficulties tomorrow. I intend moving about five miles forward. You will see by my letters that you have again prevented my wishes about Craig. Lord Rawdon sent me extracts of the most material part of your letter in cypher. The original is coming with Leslie. You mention Craig's having Ferguson's cypher. I conclude, however, that you mean the *Haviland*, or more properly the *Haldane*, and shall act accordingly unless I hear from you to the contrary. I wish much to raise two troops of dragoons for the Camden District and to give the command to Captain Coffin with the same sort of majority as Dunlap and Maxwell. I would agree almost to any terms of limitation of service either as to time or place. I am convinced that the arming the country is of such infinite consequence to us that every attempt should be made. I am most sincerely rejoiced at hearing that Moncrief is lt colonel. Make my compliments to him on the occasion.

The variable winds and fine weather make me very sanguine about Ross. It would be fortunate indeed if he could catch us.

I have no faith in the Spaniards attacking St Augustine. I will write constantly 'til we lose the communication and as often as possible in cypher afterwards. I must beg of you to lose no opportunity of giving intelligence of us to *New York* and to the Chesapeake whenever it can possibly affect them, but at all times to the former.

I am, dear Balfour, etc

CORNWALLIS

[*Subscribed*:]

I send you the conclusion of one of my late letters which was left out by mistake. The only material part is the mark of the cypher.

CHAPTER 32

Correspondence with Camden

---

1 - Between Cornwallis and Turnbull

Turnbull to Cornwallis, 3rd November 1780 ***4(14): ALS***

Camden
November 3rd 1780

Earl Cornwallis

My Lord

Permitt me to congratulate you on the recovery of your health, which we all heartily rejoice at.

Tarleton crossed the river yesterday morning and proposes to set out tomorrow in search of the rebells. Two men have arrived this moment from Black Creek who assure us that Marion and Snipes have their quarters at Singleton's Mills. We have sent a spy who we expect will be back by morning, and Tarleton will regulate his route accordingly. We never can fix the numbers with those country fellows.

Colonel Davie's parties has show'd themselves within twenty miles of us, but we cannot learn that the body of Twelve Mile Creek has advanced.

Your Lordship will be surprised that our works are not in greater forwardness. The Negroes took the small pox, deserted, many died, [so] that the troops have been obliged to work there three weeks. We will do it as fast as we can.

Major Despard and Captain Haldane are arrived. We are planning which way to get in a quantity of cattle and corn from Santee, provided Colonel Tarleton takes that route.

Captain Coffin, having been taken ill at Colonel Thomson's on his way here, writes me that parties of rebells lay lurking in that country, that twenty has been seen together.

I beg pardon for not sending the inclosed letter[1] sooner. It came here by General Woodford's aid de camp last week from Hilsborough. He had obtained leave at Charlestown to go to Virginia to bring money and cloaths for the prisoners. I had him conducted by an officer of militia to the next post.

Strother, the man whom you wished to have released, died some weeks ago.

Thank God I have got all the prisoners except twenty three of[2] my hand, and I soon hope to forward them.

I am with the greatest respect
Your Lordship's most faithfull humble servant

GEO TURNBULL

Turnbull to Cornwallis, 5th November 1780 — *4(25): ALS*

Camden
November 5th 1780

Earl Cornwallis

My Lord

I had the honor of writing your Lordship two days ago, acquainting you that I had sent of twenty prisoners, four of which it seems not being able to march remained. A Lieutenant Foust[3] of Colonel Carey's set of with a guard of eleven, including himself, charged with fifteen prisoners. They put up at a house near Hunter's, the Twelve Mile House, when by some treachery the prisoners not only dissarmed the guard but paroled them.

Major Prevost, being at Hunter's and hearing there was some confusion amongst them, went up and found Mr Foust very drunk and the prisoners gone except a young boy who would not go. They were so generous to Mr Foust as to make him a present of his arms back again, which is very strong presumption that it had been a concerted scheme.

---

1 *the inclosed letter*: not extant.

2 *of*: off. Turnbull routinely spells 'off' in this way.

3 Perhaps Jacob or John Foust, who had settled in Orangeburg District by the early 1750s, or a relation of them. (Salley Jr, *Orangeburg County*, 186, 215)

Tarleton marched this morning early. I let him have our light company, and the officers of the garrison mustered up about twenty five horses to assisst him. I imagine he will be in the rear of Singleton's before day break tomorrow. Nothing new from the Waxhaws. Rudgely is arrived from town very sick. I am afraid I blamed him too rashly.

I am with the utmost respect
Your Lordship's most faithfull humble servant

GEO TURNBULL

Turnbull to Cornwallis, 8th November 1780 — *4(61): ALS*

Camden
November 8th 1780

Earl Cornwallis

My Lord

I have the honor to inclose Colonel Tarleton's letter[4] which I have this moment received.

I have sent for the person who is to go with the flag of truce and proposes sending him off this day. A sergeant from Smallwood's came here yesterday with letters for the prisoners. I sent them back instantly.

I shall execute the instructions sent me in Major England's letter relative to the rebell officers etc[5].

We are order'd to collect forage, corn and fuel and at the same time the Quarter Master General takes away our waggons.

Unless more carriadges can be got we shall be much distressed.

I beg leave to inform your Lordship that there has been grievous complaints made of Mr Kneght[6], the commissary, not paying his drivers. Such conduct hurts the service, and am credibly informed he has a large sum of money in his hands now.

I am with much respect
Your Lordship's most faithfull humble servant

GEO TURNBULL

---

4 *letter*: Tarleton to Turnbull, 5th November 1780, p 333.

5 *Major England's letter..*: no extant copy.

6 *Kneght*: Knecht.

Turnbull to Cornwallis, 8th November 1780 *4(59): ALS*

Camden
November 8th 1780

Earl Cornwallis

My Lord

I have nothing new since my writing to you this morning by Major Prevost, except that Captain Coffin arrived soon after, who informed me that all the rum etc which was at McCord's Ferry was reembarked in a boat which we might expect here in four days.

Your Lordship need not doubt but that I shall forward the rum etc for the army as soon as it arrives.

The nine waggons I had sent to McCord's Ferry cou'd not have got above twelve miles when I received this news. Of course I have order'd them back.

Captain Coffin, I understand, means solliciting your Lordship to be appointed Deputy Muster Master for the two southern provinces.

Provided you was not preengaged, I will venture to say that you will find Captain Coffin deserving of any favours that your Lordship will please to bestow.

I am with the greatest respect
Your Lordship's most faithfull humble servant

GEO TURNBULL

Cornwallis to Turnbull, 8th November 1780 *82(14): C*

Wynnesborough
November 8th 1780

Lt Colonel Turnbull commanding at Camden

Dear Sir

I have received both your letters of this date and that inclosed from Lt Colonel Tarleton. I beg you will immediately forward mine[7] to him.

Mr Knecht, the commissary, assures me he has not ninety pounds in his hands at present. He is very ill and I believe will die. I can assure you we are not without our difficulties.

---

7 *mine*: Cornwallis to Tarleton, 8th November, p 334.

I am sorry they embarked the rum. It would have been more certain to have got up the first cargo by land.

I told Captain Coffin that I intended to mount the New York Volunteers and that, as they would be constantly employed on the most active service and that[8] I looked to him to command them, I hoped that he would not think of an employment which would interfere very much with the service for which I intended him. It gives me great concern to hear of your bad state of health. I propose to release you very soon by sending Lord Rawdon to command at Camden, when I shall give you leave to go by the first opportunity for your health to New York.

I am, dear sir,
Your most obedient and faithfull servant

CORNWALLIS

Cornwallis to Turnbull, 9th November 1780 — *82(16): C*

Wynnesborough
November 9th 1780

Lt Colonel Turnbull

Dear Sir

Major Wemyss marched last night with the 63rd and 40 of the Legion to attack Sumter, who was posted at Moore's house and reported by the best intelligence we could get not to be above 2 or 300 militia. Sumpter had moved to Fish Dam Ford on Broad River, where Major Wemyss, contrary to his plan of waiting till day break, attacked him about one in the morning. He at first drove great part of them into the river, but not knowing the ground, and the enemy firing from the heights and swamps where our people could not get at them, Wemyss was wounded in the knee and about 20 men of the 63rd killed or wounded, the latter with the major obliged to be left. The loss of the Legion not ascertained. Mr Hovenden[9] wounded. Pray forward the inclosed[10] immediately by an officer to Tarleton, whose presence in these parts is absolutely necessary. If I move to my left, I will reinforce Camden.

---

8 *that*: the meaning is 'as'. See p 43, note 55.

9 Moore Hovenden (*post*-1750-1800) was a younger brother of Richard Hovenden (see vol II, p 247, note 24) and had been serving since June as a lieutenant in his brother's troop of horse, having entered it as a cornet in October 1779. Wounded in the action at Fish Dam Ford, he would recover in time to do duty with the 82nd at Wilmington under James Craig. When Cornwallis marched from there to Virginia, Hovenden accompanied him and consequently formed part of the British Legion who capitulated at Yorktown. After the war he was placed on the British half-pay list and was eventually appointed Postmaster General of San Domingo. He died at Jamaica. (Margaret Baskin, 'Richard, Moore and John Hovenden' (www.banastretarleton.org, 30th June 2005); Donald J Gara, 'Biographical Sketches on Cavalry Officers of the British Legion 1778-1782' (*The On-Line Institute for Advanced Loyalist Studies*, 24th June 2005); WO 65/164(38) (National Archives, Kew); *The Cornwallis Papers*)

10 *the inclosed*: Cornwallis to Tarleton, 9th November, p 335.

Yours etc

CORNWALLIS

[*Subscribed*:]

Send this or a copy to Colonel Balfour.

Cornwallis to Turnbull, 10th November 1780 — *82(22): C*

Winsborough
November 10th 1780

Lt Colonel Turnbull commanding at Camden

Dear Sir

I have nothing to add to the account I sent you last night except that the victory was ours but owing to Major Wemys's unfortunate fall we did not know how to make use of it. Wemys has one arm broke and a shot in his knee, yet Sumpter had the cruelty to put him into a waggon and carry him over the river[11]. The enemy, I believe, suffered very considerably. As soon as I know that Tarleton is ready to pass the river, I will send Lord Rawdon and his corps to Camden.

I am, sir,
Your most obedient and faithfull servant

CORNWALLIS

Turnbull to Cornwallis, undated[12] — *4(93): ALS*

Earl Cornwallis

My Lord

I am to acknowledge the receipt of your letters of the 6th[13], 8th and 9th instant. Colonel Tarleton's letters have been forwarded. I have not heard from him since the letter I inclosed to your Lordship, but by some of Tynes' militia, who brought in two prisoners this morning, they say that they heard that he was very near as low down as King Tree.

A deserter from Colonel Washington's dragoons, who came in two nights ago, says that General Morgan was then with 300 men, that Washington had 100 dragoons when they left

---

11 See p 68, note 18.

12 *Endorsed*: 'Received by Lancaster, November 12th.'

13 *6th*: no extant copy.

Charlotte and that only seventy remain'd, that they had retreated ten miles back on the Salisbury Road; but we find that the same party was back there yesterday and that there is likewise a detachment of rebells towards Lynches Creek. Their numbers have not yet been ascertain'd.

Captain McDonald has been very ill, which prevented the flagg going off till yesterday, and I only wait Tarleton's return to expedite those gentlemans who are to go upon parole.

I have lodged Mr Foust in the Provoost, the officer who let the prisoners escape.

Lieutenant Oldfield set out with one and twenty waggons to forage in Colonel Tarleton's rear. I expect likewise to get in some cattle from that quarter.

I am sorry for poor Wemyss. These fellows will become more impudent.

Permitt me to return your Lordship my most unfeigned thanks for your goodness in giving me hopes of going soon to New York. My health is indeed in such a state that I do believe nothing but a northern climate will reestablish it, nor do I believe that ever my constitution will bear much service in this southern climate.

If the Commander in Chief will induldge me to remain there untill my corps comes northward, I shall surely esteem it as a most interesting favor; otherwise I am afraid I must quit the service on such terms as he pleases.

I am
Your Lordship's most faithfull humble servant

GEO TURNBULL

Turnbull to Cornwallis, 11th November 1780 — *4(102): ALS*

Camden
November 12th 1780[14]

Earl Cornwallis

My Lord

I have received your letter of the 10th instant and have no certain acounts of Tarleton since that letter which I enclosed to your Lordship.

Mr Oldfield has been a-foraging about seventeen miles towards the High Hills, and the report was that Tarleton was close upon Marion's rear and was expected to come up with him before he could cross Black River.

---

14 Endorsed: 'Dated November 12th instead of 11th. Received by Lancaster, November 12th, at 8 o'clock in the morning.'

There is a man just arrived from Anson Court House, North Carolina, who says that a rebell captain of the name of Wade told him that a British army was landed in James's River in Virginia and that Harrington was with about three or four hundred men near Cheraw Hill destroying the houses and taking the property of every one who did not join.

Colonel Rudgely has collected about eighty three men and is fortifying his house at the Mills. He sent to me for ammunition. I confess I was stagger'd at the demand but Despard and Haldane advised me to try them for once.

Two men came in to Rudgely last night who informed him that Colonel Washington and Morgan with about 300 men lay at Flat Creek near Lynches Creek and that their main encampment was 14 miles below Charlotte.

Mr Oldfield sets out again this night to make another hawl of forage.

I am with the greatest respect
Your Lordship's most faithfull humble servant

GEO TURNBULL

Turnbull to Cornwallis, 11th November 1780 — *4(104): ALS*

Camden
November 12th 1780[15]

Earl Cornwallis

My Lord

Major Prevost promised me he would mention the case of Adjutant Tounsend[16] of our regiment, [who] has been in arrest about a month by Colonel Balfour's orders for trifling on the road when charged with your Lordship's dispatches.

I never mean to plead the cause of any man who is guilty of such capital offences, but I had wrote to Colonel Innes on this subject, acquainting him that Mr Tounsend had already resigned the adjutancy and wished to resign the ensigncy provided we wou'd allow him three or four months' pay to carry his family to New York, that if Colonel Balfour wished to try him I shou'd send him down to Charlestown.

---

15 Endorsed: 'Dated November 12th instead of 11th.'

16 Benjamin Townsend had been commissioned an ensign in the New York Volunteers on 5th January 1779 and until recently had been serving as its adjutant. As forecast by Turnbull, he would resign his ensigncy and therefore not be placed on the Provincial half-pay list at the close of the war. (Treasury 64/23(1) and WO 65/164(31) (National Archives, Kew))

Prevost told me that he was order'd to lay the whole matter before your Lordship.

There is a Captain Burns[17] who was put in upon us *à la suite* about three years ago. He has never attempted to raise a company, alledging that he had raised thirty men with a Colonel Stark[18], which men were all draughted into the Queen's Rangers in the beginning of the year seventy seven. He has been in disgrace in Georgia, which matter has never been cleared up. He stay'd behind in Georgia without my leave and I returned him so accordingly. He does not wish to join us because he suspects that he wou'd not be received. If your Lordship thinks him an object of charity, and not to reduce him to beggary, to second him[19] and give him five shillings a day wou'd keep him from starving; otherwise he shou'd stand tryal.

If I am happy enough to arrive at New York, I will endeavour to find out some young gentlemen for ensigns.

Our major never raised a company. He went to New York under that pretence and I am informed he has never attempted it. At the time he join'd us he promised to raise a company, and we had fewer officers for the proportion of men than any regiment. By which means they did not scruple at giving him full pay, which as long as he can receive it he never will give himself any trouble.

I am, my Lord,
Your most faithfull humble servant

GEO TURNBULL

§ - §

17 Apart from Turnbull's present remarks, little else is known of Burns. He had ceased to be an officer in the New York Volunteers by 1783 and therefore was not placed on the Provincial half-pay list at the close of the war.

18 Of Scotch-Irish descent, William Stark of New Hampshire (1724-*c.* 1777) had served in Rogers' Rangers during the Seven Years' War and fought at Ticonderoga, Louisburg, and Quebec. Disappointed at not obtaining command of a revolutionary regiment at the start of the present war, he threw in his lot with the Crown and, commissioned a major, began raising in 1777 the New Hampshire Volunteers on the Provincial establishment, a corps which, despite its name, was recruited in New York City and Philadelphia. Soon afterwards it was disbanded, with its companies being mostly drafted into the Queen's Rangers, the 2nd Battalion of the New Jersey Volunteers, and the King's Orange Rangers. Stark died after falling from a horse. In referring to him as a colonel, Turnbull appears to be confusing his rank with that of Stark's younger, more distinguished brother John, who in 1777 had been a colonel in the Continental line. (Boatner, *Encyclopedia*, 1052-3; Nan Cole and Todd Braisted, 'Loyalist Muster Rolls: New Hampshire Volunteers' (*The On-Line Institute for Advanced Loyalist Studies*, 10th December 2005))

19 *to second him*: to put him into temporary retirement with a view to a staff or other extra-regimental appointment.

2 - Between Cornwallis and Rawdon

Cornwallis to Rawdon, 13th November 1780 *82(38): C*

Winsborough
November 13th 1780

Rt Hon Lord Rawdon

My dear Lord

Since you left me I have had letters from Money and McArthur[20]. They say Sumpter is at Hawkins's Mills on Tyger River 17 miles from Shirar's Ferry, that the whole country is under the utmost terror, and all the loyal subjects instead of thinking of self defence are running as fast as possible to Congarees. The affair of Fishdam is represented by Sumpter as a compleat victory, and it is universally believed, and that the 63rd is totally cut to pieces - so much for agreable news. I enclose a line to Tarleton[21]. I should wish to see him, but his corps must keep its distance, and I believe it will be best for them to march up the Wateree as that may leave it uncertain whether his object is Davy, Smallwood or Sumpter. I flatter myself you have not got very wet. Be assured at all times, my dear Lord, of my sincere good wishes.

I am
Most faithfully yours

CORNWALLIS

[*Subscribed*:]

All here join in best wishes to our *worthy* Quarter Master General[22].

---

20 *letters..*: Money's is not extant. For McArthur's, see p 310.

21 *a line..*: Cornwallis to Tarleton, 13th November, p 339.

22 Major Richard England, Deputy Quartermaster General at Camden.

Cornwallis to Rawdon, 14th November 1780 *82(44): C*

Winsborough
November 14th 1780
11 o'clock pm

Rt Hon Lord Rawdon

My dear Lord

Having waited 'till this time in hopes of an express from Camden, I now only say that I conclude no news is good news and that I shall soon see the Legion. That Negroe was so very circumstantial that I can hardly doubt his intelligence. I have sent out on all sides, and if it proves true, I must immediately cross Broad River, as the enemy certainly means either 96 or Augusta. To be prepared for a move I send off 31 sick in waggons and about 30, if I can, on horseback. I have neither surgeon or mate that I can possibly spare. I must therefore beg that you will send a carefull mate well mounted to meet them. They will go about 12 miles to morrow. Captain King and Mr Hovenden will be of the party. I am a little uneasy for fear the enemy should attempt a blow at McArthur. I trust to your sending us a little rum, if it is arrived, with the utmost expedition. If I move, I will send you the earliest intelligence and stop every thing on the road. Tell England that Despard has bought some good waggon horses and very cheap.

Yours ever, my dearest Lord, most sincerely

CORNWALLIS

Rawdon to Cornwallis, 13th November 1780 *4(110): ALS*

Camden
November 13th 1780
8 o'clock night

Earl Cornwallis etc etc etc

I arrived here, my Lord, about an hour ago. Tarleton has not yet reached this place. He lies this night about eight miles off, but I have sent to request that I may see him very early in the morning and his corps will cross the ferry at that time.

They do not seem to have good information here respecting the enemy and they depend upon a channel of which I should be rather doubtful. A Negro who came in this afternoon says that he was carried prisoner to Morgan and Washington at Hanging Rock and escaped from them last night. He reports that in concert with Marion they were to have attacked this post and he mentions the point at which the assault was to have been directed, which is indeed the weakest in the line. The dispersion of Marion's force overturned the plan. This, however, is only conversation which he heard in the rebel camp, and he cannot say from whom. I hear much of the prowess of Harrison's rangers upon the expedition with Tarleton. A valiant friend of Government is a prodigy of which all the world talks. I will praise them very highly (if I can find room to do so) in hopes that it may stimulate them to future atchievements.

I have the honor to be, my Lord, with equal respect and affection
Your very faithful servant

RAWDON

Rawdon to Cornwallis, 14th November 1780 — *4(118): ALS*

Camden
November 14th 1780

Earl Cornwallis etc etc etc

My Lord

I have had much conversation with Lt Colonel Tarleton respecting the possibility of rendering a post at Kingstree Bridge secure. His opinion, from what he has seen of the country, is strongly against the undertaking. It will be some days before I could dispatch the detachment for that purpose, so that I may learn your Lordship's sentiments after you have heard Lt Colonel Tarleton's ideas upon the subject. In the mean time I shall send out a party in that direction, not to proceed far or to undertake any enterprize, but merely to keep alive the report of a force being still in that district. This measure is the more necessary as Lt Colonel Balfour has directed the stores for which the officers were sent to Charles Town to be embarked at Neilson's Ferry. An officer of my regiment arrived this day who saw the necessaries for the 33rd, 71st and Voluntiers of Ireland quit the ferry three days ago under care of a serjeant of the 71st and eight men of the Voluntiers of Ireland.

I find that this post was certainly to have been attacked. When we get our men mounted, we shall make the approach to it more difficult, and with the addition of my own regiment I shall have a respectable army. England and I have been hard at work this morning and have made many salutary arrangements. We shall be rather slower in mounting the New York Voluntiers than I expected. In the mean time I shall employ Harrison's as dragoons, and from what Lt Colonel Tarleton says of them I don't know whether it will not be eligible to keep them mounted. As Lt Colonel Tarleton appeared unwilling to part with the Prince of Wales's light company, I would not press it and will rather (if the post at Kingstree takes place) complete Maxwell with troops from hence than give even a shadow for discontent. I have requested Lt Colonel Tarleton to leave twelve dragoons here, whom I mean to send to Wynnesborough as soon as I can mount men to make such patroles as I think necessary.

I have had Carey with me. He thinks that he can get at some field officer of the militia under Smallwood who will give us notice of all that is intended. I have given him credit as far as an hundred guineas, according to the service. The sum may most probably be thrown away but it is well risqued for such a purpose.

General Harrington commands at Cheraws. I cannot learn his force but they do not rate him at above two hundred.

On my arrival last night I found that we were strong in cattle here and therefore ordered forty four head of remarkable fine oxen to be driven to your camp.

I have the honor to be, my Lord, with great respect
Your very faithful and affectionate servant

RAWDON

[*Subscribed*:]

I have just had the honor to receive your letter of yesterday evening.

Rawdon to Cornwallis, 14th November 1780 — *4(120): ALS*

Camden
November 14th
10 at night

Earl Cornwallis etc etc etc

My Lord

Lt Colonel Tarleton has just transmitted to me your Lordship's letter of this date[23]. He will be with you before this letter can reach you, but as I perceive by what he says to me that he gives trust to the account, I think it necessary to mention that I imagine the Negro's story to be totally false. A deserter from Washington's dragoons came in this evening. I examined him myself. He asserts that he left Smallwood's camp the day before yesterday eight miles above Twelve Mile Creek on the Salisbury Road, Washington having fallen back to Smallwood upon the news of Tarleton's being here. I believe that very deserter is now with Tarleton. As the opposite assertions of the deserter and the Negro seem both to be given so positively, I should suspect that either one or the other have been sent to give false intelligence. I think ill of the Negro because it is probable that Sumpter, acting upon the original design and not knowing the state of affairs here, is still endeavouring to draw you away from this post. I think, if the Negro was hard pressed, he would discover the business. The deserter was Irish and enlisted with Tarleton.

I have the honor to be, my Lord, very faithfully
Your affectionate humble servant

RAWDON

---

23 *your Lordship's letter*..: of 14th November to Tarleton, p 339.

Rawdon to Cornwallis, 15th November 1780 *4(132): ALS*

Camden
November 15th 1780

Earl Cornwallis

My Lord

I have been honored with your letter of the 14th dated eleven at night and was exceedingly concerned to find that you had not received a letter which I wrote immediately upon my arrival here on the evening of the 13th. Upon enquiry I find that Mr St John[24] (who was charged with it and was to have left this place very early on the 14th) was taken ill and very negligently omitted either to give me notice of the circumstance or to forward the letter. I have dispatched a mate to meet the sick and will prepare places for their reception. Matters are in so backward a state here that we shall have difficulty to get the post into a proper state before the bad weather sets in, but we will not fail in activity at least and I think we shall make it tolerably convenient and pretty secure.

Long before this reaches you I hope your Lordship will have received a letter which I dispatched last night in consequence of your letter to Tarleton respecting Smallwood's movement. From every information I believe Smallwood certainly to have been on the Salisbury Road upon Sunday last, and I am told that 200 militia whose time was out quitted him either that day or the day before. I have had no intelligence this day but I expect some.

I have detached fifty infantry and twenty mounted upon the road to Singleton's. The infantry are to halt about twelve miles from this; the cavalry are to proceed about four miles farther to inform the country people that they are a patrole from Lt Colonel Tarleton's camp and to return at night to the infantry. The whole detachment will shift its ground tomorrow and will return hither the day after. By that time I hope I shall be able to send forth a stouter corps should it appear necessary and expedient. The first embarkation of rum is within five miles of this. I will forward some with all expedition.

I have the honor to be, my Lord, very truly
Your most faithful servant

RAWDON

---

24 The Hon George Richard St John (1761-1824) was the son of Frederick, 3rd Viscount St John and 2nd Viscount Bolingbroke. He had been commissioned an ensign in the 33rd Regiment on 17th August, the day after the Battle of Camden, possibly for courageous conduct during the battle while serving as a volunteer. He would succeed to the peerage in 1787. (Valentine, *The British Establishment*, ii, 764-5; WO 65/164(8) (National Archives, Kew))

Cornwallis to Rawdon, 16th November 1780 *82(53): C*

Winsborough
November 16th 1780

Rt Hon Lord Rawdon

My dear Lord

I have received four letters from you: one of the 13th, two of the 14th, and one of the 15th. That of the 13th by Mr St John came the last. I had great doubts about the post at Kingstree Bridge before I received your letters or saw Tarleton, but delayed writing to you about it until I heard from you, as I knew it could not be established immediately. I am now convinced that a small post there would be inadequate to the protection of the river and would be in danger of being either starved or carried off, and that at present it is not in our power to establish a large one. To answer the purpose at all there ought to be at least 200 good infantry and 100 cavalry. I tremble for the necessaries embarked at Nelson's Ferry and wish at least that McKinnon could have contrived to have sent them to McChord's without the total ruin of poor General Dalrymple. I hope Balfour's large cargo of rum and salt is not set out as I think it must inevitably fall into the enemy's hands. The Negroe still persists in his story and says that he is very well contented to abide by the terms to be rewarded if the enemy have 3 six pounders on the other side of Broad River and to be hanged if they have not. However, I cannot believe him. I enclose an extract of a letter from Cruger[25]. All my accounts about Smallwood agree with yours, but mine are: 'I went as far as Fishing Creek, and there Billy McDaniel's wife told me that she saw Dicky Thomson, who said he saw young Jemmy Ridgom that just came from camps', etc etc. No offers can prevail upon any man I can find to go and see, as Hayes[26] does, with his own eyes. I will send Turnbull's leave and a letter to the Commander in Chief to morrow, being much hurried to day. Many thanks to you for all your cares and attentions, amongst others for not pressing a point that was not very essential and would have made a grievance when you knew I wished not to have any, for thinking of every thing that could be essential to us as well as your own post. In short, my dear Lord, I will not tire you with repeating the obligations which I have so often expressed. I think indeed that Camden has had a narrow escape; it cost me several sleepless nights. Tarleton is to be at Shirar's Ferry to morrow. He will pass with the Legion and 63rd and will open the country sufficiently to ascertain the material fact whether there is an army with cannon or not. If there is, it may occasion my moving. If not, he will be able, with some cooperation from 96, to clear the country very effectually. I have desired him to take time to do it, to press the enemy as much as possible that our friends may again take heart. My best wishes to England.

---

25 *a letter..*: of 14th November, p 269.

26 Hayes possessed a surname which was very common in South Carolina. He is likely to have been a person from the Back Country who, unbeknown to the enemy, had been turned by the British and was still accepted as being of the revolutionary persuasion. A candidate meeting this description is James Hayes, a captive batman in William Thomson's regiment, who deserted to the British at this time. (Moss, *SC Patriots*, 428)

I am, my dearest Lord,
Very sincerely yours

CORNWALLIS

[*Subscribed*:]

I told Balfour that I had desired you to open his letters to me but that if there were any that did not relate to publick business he might write *Private* upon them.

Rawdon to Cornwallis, 16th November 1780 — *4(139): ALS*

Camden
November 16th 1780

Earl Cornwallis etc etc etc

My Lord

I have the honor to forward the newspapers and some letters which arrived late last night from Charlestown. There were no dispatches for your Lordship.

Captain Manson of the Royal North Carolina Regiment accompanies the express, and as he was sent by the Commandant to discourse with your Lordship, I need not enter upon any business respecting the coast.

I shall communicate as early as possible with Major McLeroth and fix upon measures with him for counteracting any attempt that may be undertaken against his post. I am told that McLeroth has some mounted militia with him. If he thinks them not sufficient in number or quality, I will as soon as possible reinforce him with some of the New York Voluntiers.

Thirteen puncheons of rum arrived at the ferry this morning. I have ordered eight of them to be dispatched instantly to your camp, and as the waggons are in excellent order, they will not be long on the road. I have sent a subaltern's party to escort them.

I have not heard any thing of the enemy either yesterday or this morning, altho' I have had persons out who ought to have returned before this time. I have sent out patroles to get intelligence in the country.

Lt Colonel Turnbull sets out this morning for Charlestown. Captain Coffin has arrived here, much recovered.

I have the honor to be, my Lord, with great respect
Your very affectionate servant

RAWDON

Rawdon to Cornwallis, 16th November 1780 — *4(143): ALS*

Camden
November 16th 1780
8 at night

Earl Cornwallis

My Lord

The patroles have returned without having heard any thing of the enemy, but none of my spies have come back. I imagine by these circumstances that none of the enemy are nearer than Twelve Mile Creek. I am uneasy, however, at not having been able to procure certain intelligence about them for your Lordship's satisfaction.

Manson talks of the Commander in Chief's intention to hang some of the parole breakers in revenge for poor André. This may go farther. Might it not be well to secure the officers at Hedrall's Point. The general absolution which Gates published would be a good plea against any remonstrance respecting the capitulation[27]. As the idea struck me, I think it right to mention it, and your Lordship will weigh its expediency.

Lancaster[28] was unaccountably detained today, waiting for Captain Manson. It vexed me because he would arrive late at Wynnesborough.

I have the honor to be, my Lord,
Very faithfully and respectfully yours

RAWDON

---

27 *The general absolution..*: a reference to Gates' proclamation of 4th August. See vol II, p 38, note 3.

28 Lancaster has not been positively identified. Serving now as a courier, he may, for example, have been a non-commissioned officer or the printer to whom Rawdon refers in the postscript to his letter of 19th November. On the other hand, perhaps he was John or Thomas Lancaster, loyalists whose essential services would lead to special provision being made for them later in this volume.

Cornwallis to Rawdon, 17th November 1780 *82(57): C*

Winsborough
November 17th 1780

Rt Hon Lord Rawdon

My dear Lord

I received your letter this morning by Lancaster and the two this afternoon by Manson.[29] As Balfour can spare the 64th Regiment from Charlestown, and that[30] I understand he is, in addition to the 280 men fit for service of that regiment, to give McLeroth some Hessians and militia and 2 pieces of cannon, I am clearly of opinion that the post at Kingstree will be of the utmost utility to us and in conjunction with your patroles perfectly secure the navigation, which is of such importance to us. In short, it has relieved me from much pain and anxiety. Every account I receive certainly fixes Smallwood between Charlotte Town and Twelve Mile Creek. Tarleton will be at Shirar's Ferry this day with his corps. I have desired him to take time to follow up his blow and promised to take care of ourselves. We enjoy an affluence I hardly expected here – eight or ten days' provision before hand. I have ordered 2 of the puncheons of rum to Shirar's Ferry. I questioned Manson merely as a matter of curiosity whether he had heard that the Commander in Chief had any such intentions as you mention in cypher. He said he had never heard that he had, and seemed totally ignorant about it.

I should be happy to see so good an officer as Campbell at the head of the New York Volunteers and beg you will do what you please in that business, assuring you of my best wishes for the success of any plan which you patronize. I should recommend the putting some carefull and responsible man to superintend Camden Ferry with any allowance you may think proper to give him. If you could fix a rope across, it would facilitate the passage very much. I remember it was done at the Schuylkill opposite to Philadelphia, where the river was much wider.

I ordered Stedman to go to Camden to explain to you the state of things at the Congarees and to settle the means of conveying to Camden what you think will be particularly usefull for that post. There is some rice which it will be worth while to bring by land immediately as I understand it is much wanted for the hospital. Carey has ordered the militia from the Congarees towards Camden. If the militia are good for any thing, some of them could be usefull at the Congarees, where the whole country almost openly professes rebellion.

I am, my dear Lord,
Most sincerely and affectionately yours

CORNWALLIS

---

29 Of these three letters, only two are extant.

30 *that*: the meaning is 'as'. See p 43, note 55.

[*Subscribed*:]

It will be well to employ some persons to watch Hampton's store at the Congarees. Stedman will give you an account of it.

Rawdon to Cornwallis, 17th November 1780 — *4(145): ALS*

Camden
November 17th 1780

Earl Cornwallis etc etc etc

My Lord

I have been delaying my dispatch this morning in hopes of being able to transmit to you some certain intelligence with regard to Smallwood. To my great disappointment I have not received any information whatever. I have had patroles out for several miles upon every road this morning but they cannot hear any report of the enemy. Rugeley knows nothing and none of my emissaries have returned. A letter having arrived from Lt Colonel Balfour[31], I will forward it without waiting longer, and should intelligence arrive afterwards, I will dispatch a second express.

I have just received your Lordship's letter of yesterday. Manson will have acquainted you with Balfour's plan for the post at Kingstree. McLeroth had not arrived there yesterday, but I am easy about the stores now upon the river, having had a report (dispatched this morning) from my detachment that all was quiet. The infantry had rather exceeded my instructions, having advanced twenty miles from hence. The mounted (26 in number) had patroled several miles forwarder. The detachment returns hither today. It was composed hastily and meant only to shew itself.

I have good accounts that Marion re-crossed Black River the day after Tarleton fell back. He advanced to Gaillard's, and the next day again retired across Black River. Yesterday he lay twelve miles behind Kingstree Bridge. His numbers were accurately counted and amounted to 406. I have sent a trusty man with a letter to meet McLeroth. I hope soon to send a strong detachment of mounted to visit him, as I made Oldfield accompany our party[32] to purchase horses. I have empowered McLeroth to detain as many of those mounted as he may find requisite.

This village is by no means capable of holding the number of persons who require quarters in it. I have therefore sent for a quantity of plank and boards, with which I hope we shall speedily fit up some kind of barracks and some huts for officers. I must spare some officer, I fancy, to manage this work that it may not be made a job of.

---

31 Balfour to Cornwallis, 15th November, p 76

32 *our party*: the detachment to which the preceding paragraph refers.

By degrees we shall get into order and cleanliness, in both which points this garrison was much wanting. When one comes newly to a post, those defects strike one, and they are easily remedied if one sets about them before one becomes habituated to the sight of them.

I have the honor to be, my Lord, very faithfully and respectfully
Your affectionate servant

RAWDON

Cornwallis to Rawdon, 18th November 1780 — *82(61): C*

Wynnesborough
November 18th 1780
9 o'clock pm

Rt Hon Lord Rawdon

My dear Lord

I received this afternoon your letter of yesterday with Colonel Balfour's. His post at Kingstree, which I think must be safe, has put me quite at ease about the navigation of the river, the uncertainty of which gave me much anxiety. I have received no intelligence whatever from the other side of Catawba. A flag of truce whom I sent to Sumpter saw him and Clarke on their march between Tyger and Ennoree the day before yesterday. He said he counted about 700, all mounted with rifles, and some rusty swords. He was informed that 300 more were higher up the country. The country people told us of firing to day at Shirar's Ferry or Lisle's Ford, but as the dragoon[33], [who] was intelligent and was Tarleton's orderly man, came close by the latter and within eight miles of the former just at the time that the firing was said to have been heard and reports all quiet, and that[34] nobody in the country said any thing of it until he got within a few miles of our camp, I give no credit to it. Mr Wier[35] has had a letter from Mr Townsend relative to the cattle. We are at present pretty well off and expect another drove from the Reverend Mr Dubber[36]. If you are in no want, we had better order them to the Congarees until they are wanted and direct Stedman to procure them good pasture. Will you be kind enough to send directions to that purpose to Captain Maxwell, as Balfour said they were to wait for orders at McChord's Ferry.

---

[33] *the dragoon*: presumably the flag of truce.

[34] *that*: possibly used in the sense of 'as'. See p 43, note 55.

[35] Not Daniel Weir, the Commissary General at New York in charge of the department, but a commissary with the same surname serving at Winnsborough. (*The Cornwallis Papers*)

[36] John Frederick Dubber (?-1781) was Minister at the Appii Forum Presbyterian Church on Cedar Creek. Whether he was involved in the Weberite heresy between 1759 and 1761 is uncertain. His name was also spelt Dauber, Dowber, Dubbert and DuBard. (Harriet Imrey, 'Cedar Creek Methodist Church, SC' (Internet, 21st April 2002))

I have no doubt of your making a great alteration in the appearance as well as scent of Camden. If you find yourself pressed for time about your barracks, the log houses filled up with mud like that which I inhabit will be as warm and answer the purpose full as well. As this is only an idea suggested to me by my partiality for the house I live in, you on the spot will be best able to judge which will be most convenient and soonest made. I should think at this season of the year the last recommendation a very powerfull one. You may depend on hearing as soon as I get any accounts of Tarleton's operations.

I am, my dear Lord,
Yours most sincerely

CORNWALLIS

Rawdon to Cornwallis, 18th November 1780 — *4(155): ALS*

Camden
November 18th 1780

Earl Cornwallis etc etc etc

My Lord

I was just preparing to write to you when I received your letter of yesterday.

I have fortunately in many points prevented your Lordship's wishes. The arrangement of the ferry has already been particularly established and a rope will be fixed immediately. Oldfield visits Congarees tomorrow with an escort of twelve of the New York Voluntiers. His business is to procure horses, but I will instruct him to seize and bring hither any person who by seditious language may have lately endeavored to excite commotion in that quarter.

Forty of the New York Voluntiers are mounted and upon good horses. I cannot speak too highly of England's assiduity upon this and every other point committed to his care. If we can get swords for the light company of that regiment, they will answer better than any cavalry that we could raise, as they are dashing fellows and inured to service.

As long as the enemy keeps at a distance in my front, I shall be able to push frequent detachments thro' every district around me, which will greatly check any growing combinations. The detachment arrived last night from the Santee Road. I hope that the day after tomorrow I shall be able to send forth a more formidable corps to attempt communicating with McLeroth.

One of my spies came in last night and reports Smallwood to be still in his old position; but he never saw the enemy's camp and gives his intelligence merely from the accounts of women etc.

I have the honor to be, my Lord, with great respect
Your faithful and affectionate servant

RAWDON

Cornwallis to Rawdon, 19th November 1780 *82(67): A(in part) C*

Wynnesborough
November 19th 1780
9 o'clock pm

Rt Hon Lord Rawdon etc etc

My dear Lord

Your letter of yesterday came to me this morning. I have sent to Camden 150 stand of French arms with the ammunition belonging to them. The arms are out of repair and at any rate troublesome to convey by land carriage, and from their number are no great object. I should wish your Lordship to send them, and any of the sort that may be at Camden, by the return of the boats to Charlestown that they may be repaired as soon as possible and sent into Cape Fear River in case our forward move should take place. McLeod seems to wish to have the ammunition waggons sent all to Charlestown. I don't know the number of swords that are arrived in the sloop from Bermudas but should hope there will be enough for the light infantry of the New York Volunteers after Tarleton is supplied. At any rate they will have some tolerable ones that Tarleton has now, untill better can be made. The enemy came down yesterday to all the fords upon Broad River and to Shirar's Ferry, where they fired across at our people who were washing in the flats. We took no notice of them and they only wounded one man of the 63rd very slightly. When Tarleton's infantry arrived, he fired two or three shot with the three pounder to clear the way for their passing, which answer'd the purpose of driving away the rebels. The cavalry of the Legion passed without opposition at the Mill Ford. I shall hope in a day or two to hear some good news from that quarter, altho I must fear, as the enemy are all mounted, that nothing very decisive can happen.

I am, my dear Lord,
Yours most sincerely

CORNWALLIS

PS

I shall want to send Haldane soon to 96, so that the sooner he gives instructions to Mr Barret[37] relative to any thing you would wish to be done the better. I am told there was an idea of some little defence at the mill.

I would not take him from you as long as you think him materially usefull at Camden.

---

[37] Thomas Barrett had entered the 23rd Regiment (Royal Welch Fusiliers) as a 1st lieutenant on 23rd August 1779. He was now acting as an assistant engineer. (*Army Lists*; *The Cornwallis Papers*)

Rawdon to Cornwallis, 19th November 1780 — *4(161): ALS*

Camden
November 19th 1780

Earl Cornwallis etc etc etc

My Lord

I have had the honor of receiving your Lordship's letter for Turnbull[38] by Captain Manson as likewise the letter dated at nine last night. I find that I was mistaken in quoting Manson as my authority for what I wrote in cypher. It was Lt Colonel Hamilton who mentioned the circumstance from some letter which he had received. Every body was full of the event and I confounded the informations, otherwise I should not have attended to the matter.

I have sent to McChord's to order the cattle immediately to Congarees. We have 200 head here. All your instructions by Stedman (whom I have just seen) shall be punctually fulfilled. I have ordered the three companies of militia back to Congarees.

I have appointed Ensign Wilson[39] of my regiment to superintend the barrack business here. I had no hopes of being able to complete regular barracks, but I shall convert barns, stables etc into tolerable quarters and shall make huts contiguous to them for the officers.

I have the honor to enclose to your Lordship a letter and a memorial from Lt Colonel Doyle[40]. I think his plea very just. He has been longer in the service than either Simcoe or Tarleton and received no compensation for his commission in the line, tho' neither of those gentlemen have been subjected to the same loss.

With the most earnest desire of making myself serviceable to your Lordship,

I have the honor to remain very affectionately and respectfully
Your Lordship's most obedient servant

RAWDON

[*Subscribed*:]

Lancaster, the printer, wants to go to Charlestown. His press etc is here.

---

38 *letter for Turnbull*: no extant copy.

39 John Wilson had been commissioned an ensign in the Volunteers of Ireland in December 1778. He survived the war and had risen to be captain on the regiment's transfer to the British establishment in August 1782. (Raymond, 'British American Corps'; *Army List*)

40 *a memorial..*: no extant copy.

Enclosure
Doyle to Cornwallis, 19th November 1780 — *4(159): ALS*

Camden
19th November 1780

Lt General Earl Cornwallis etc etc

My Lord

I take the liberty of enclosing to your Lordship a memorial addressed to his Excellency the Commander in Chief which I thought it might be improper to transmit thro' any channel but the officer commanding the district.

I do not presume to sollicit your Lordship's recommendation or patronage any further than to hope that, by enclosing the memorial with your Lordship's next dispatches, it may appear that my conduct under your command has given your Lordship no reason to object against the application.

I hope that your Lordship will excuse the liberty which I have taken in making this request, and

I have the honor to remain with the highest respect
Your Lordship's most obedient and most humble servant

WELLBORE ELLIS DOYLE

Cornwallis to Rawdon, 20th November 1780 — *82(71): C*

Wynnesborough
November 20th 1780

Rt Hon Lord Rawdon

My dear Lord

On reading over Colonel Doyle's memorial, I found it impossible for me, after the conversations that have passed between the Commander in Chief and me and my declarations to the army, to enclose it without declaring at the same time that I did not adopt the substance of it.

As therefore I never have enclosed any memorials for promotion to the Commander in Chief, and that[41] he does not expect that I should do it, I rather think that I should do more

---

[41] *that*: the meaning is 'as'. See p 43, note 55.

harm than good. I have explained myself, I hope, to Colonel Doyle's satisfaction. I send to you a man who lives near Kingstree Bridge and who knows the country about it very well. The account he gives of the shallowness of the river and the facility of passing it is not much in McLeroth's favour. He will shew you some instructions that I gave him relative to a friend of his who he says was forced to go with Marion. You will make any addition you please. Not a word from Tarleton or any news of any sort. I have employed people to observe the Lands Ford and Rocky Mount. Those who undertook to go to the enemy's camp are not returned and perhaps do not mean it. If Tarleton only drives Sumpter back in a hurry, I hope it will give our friends more spirit.

Some of the puncheons of rum were very deficient. I must beg you will be kind enough to order a strict enquiry about it and proper punishment wherever the guilt may lie. They must in future be certified to be full by the person who receives them at Monck's Corner, at Nelson's Ferry, and at Camden, and then it will be easy to find out the delinquents.

I am, my dear Lord,
Most sincerely yours

CORNWALLIS

Enclosure
Cornwallis to Doyle, 20th November 1780 *82(69): C*

Wynnesborough
November 20th 1780

Lt Colonel Doyle

Sir

I shall be always happy to bear testimony to the zeal and attention which you have shewn to the good of the service and care of your regiment since you have been under my command.

I would willingly enclose your memorial to the Commander in Chief if I had not uniformly declined all applications of that sort since Sir Henry left Carolina except the succession of my own regiment. If therefore I altered my conduct in any one instance it would be difficult for me to make the army believe what is most strictly true, that I do not interfere in the recommendations or promotions of the American Army either directly or indirectly. My enclosing the memorial to the Commander in Chief, saying at the same time that I did it merely for form sake and that I was by no means interested in its success, could answer no purpose whatever. My enclosing that memorial only after rejecting all others without any such comment would be an indirect breach of my declarations.

I am, sir,
Your most obedient and most humble servant

CORNWALLIS

Rawdon to Cornwallis, 20th November 1780 — *4(164): ALS*

Camden
November 20th 1780

Earl Cornwallis etc etc etc

My Lord

I send up by Captain St Leger[42] of the 63rd Regiment 30 guineas and 20 half joes[43] for Mr Booth. It is part of a sum of two hundred pounds, which was all that I could raise for the Commissary of Captures. Mr Booth will account with Mr Stedman for the expenditure.

A Captain Reynolds[44] with eight others has come to me this morning from Great Lynches Creek. He reports that he left that place in consequence of a muster appointed there by General Harrington for the day after tomorrow. I have not horses enough, otherwise I would send visitants to join the party. Harrington has not above two hundred men.

Reynolds says that six hundred men were to join Smallwood at New Providence on the 18th to replace some who had quitted him on account of having completed their time of service – this merely the report of the country.

I have the honor to be, my Lord,
Your most faithful and affectionate servant

RAWDON

---

42 Hayes St Leger had spent his entire service in the 63rd Regiment. Commissioned an ensign on 12th December 1770, he was promoted to lieutenant on 5th March 1775 and to captain on 12th June 1777. His part in the Battle of Hobkirk's Hill would lead to a mention in dispatches. He may have been the 'Captain John Hayes St Leger' whose portrait was painted by Sir Joshua Reynolds in 1778. (*Army Lists*; *The Cornwallis Papers*; Ellis Waterhouse, *Reynolds* (Phaidon Press, 1973), plates 85-6)

43 *half joes*: Portuguese coins circulating in America. They had been minted since 1722.

44 On 30th November 1775 Richard Reynolds had been commissioned a lieutenant in George Gabriel Powell's regiment of the South Carolina revolutionary militia. He was soon after promoted to captain. The regiment's catchment area, which comprised St David's Parish, was bounded on the west by Lynches Creek. (Gregg, *The Old Cheraws*, 163, 246; Heitman, *Historical Register*, 464)

Rawdon to Cornwallis, 20th November 1780 — *4(168): ALS*

Camden
November 20th 1780
8 at night

Earl Cornwallis etc etc etc

My Lord

Isham Moore from the High Hills has just been with me. My letter to McLeroth was taken and carried to Marion. It was no consequence further than that it told my intention of raising Bromfield's militia to accompany some troops from hence to Kingstree. To prevent this Marion sent Captain William Richbourg[45] *to carry off the militia officers and stop the muster. Richbourg has an hundred men and offers thro' Moore that if I will ensure to him and his party the terms held forth by Tarleton's proclamation*[46]*, they will not only lay down their arms but Richbourg will give me the best information of Marion's strength, views and correspondence. I have given* the fullest assurances of pardon and protection, *and if it succeeds, I think the example may produce further defection from the enemy*. I fancy *Moore, by being active* in this business, *strives to retrieve* his character.

I enclose a letter from General Harrington to Lt Colonel Turnbull respecting Lowry. By the flag of truce I proposed for Tynes's exchange. I know your Lordship does not approve those partial exchanges, but I thought in the present instance the step would not be contrary to your wishes, as I conceive it might be of great advantage to get back Tynes into his district at this present juncture.

I have the honor to be, my Lord, with great respect and affection
Your most faithful servant

RAWDON

---

45 William Richbourg (*c*. 1750-*c*. 1812) and his more influential brother Henry were the grandsons of the Reverend Claude Phillippe de Richbourg, a French Huguenot who migrated to Virginia in 1700 and moved on to South Carolina. Living on or towards the High Hills of Santee, both William and Henry would be minded to support the Crown, as these Papers now and later reveal, and in March 1781 Henry as a lt colonel would serve under Watson and command royal militia in the action at Wiboo Swamp. Both would be forgiven by the revolutionaries for their sins and continue to reside in South Carolina after the war, dying at Sumter. Their other brothers James, John and Nathaniel saw service in the revolutionary forces. (Lucian F Fosdick, *The French Blood in America* (Genealogicial Publishing Company Inc, 1973), 345-357; *The Cornwallis Papers*; Rankin, *Marion*, 165; Bass, *Swamp Fox*, 235)

46 *Tarleton's proclamation*: see p 338.

Enclosure
Harrington to Turnbull, 12th November 1780 *4(108): ALS*

Cheraws
12th November 1780

Lt Colonel George Turnbull commanding New York Volunteers
Camden

Sir

I received yours of the 10th instant[47] by Captain Alexander McDonald[48]. In answer thereto I have now to acquaint you that Captain Lewis Lowry[49] was sent to Newbern on the 31st ultimo. He had full rations of good and wholesome food while in my camp and was under no other confinement than what was absolutely necessary. He had the satisfaction of seeing his wife before he was sent from here and she can best attest as to the manner he was treated. So far were we from threatening to put him to death that the mild treatment he experienced has induced his brother, Robert Lowry[50], to join our militia.

Had you been informed of the wanton cruelties committed on Peedee by Major Wemys and his party, you would have forborne to mention 'unprovoked cruelties' and 'severe retaliation'. Major Wemys here played the petty tyrant, and at the instigation of Colonel William Henry Mills, amongst a number of other inhuman acts, caused an honest man of the name of Cusack to be hanged, as I am informed on the evidence of a Negroe, spurned his

---

47 *yours..*: no copy.

48 Alexander MacDonald of Cuildreach was married to Flora MacDonald's half-sister Annabella and had settled before the revolution at Mount Pleasant more than one hundred miles up from the mouth of the Cape Fear River. In 1776 he had been commissioned a captain by Governor Martin on the Provincial establishment and had been captured at the Battle of Moore's Creek Bridge. How he came to be freed is not known, but he made his way to New York, where he had since been receiving half pay. That he had now come to Camden, South Carolina, is supported by his recent appointment as a captain in the North Carolina Highland Regiment, whose embodiment was now intended to take place during the winter campaign but would never in fact occur. His selection for his present mission towards North Carolina was no doubt due to his familiarity with the terrain over which he might have had to travel. After the war he was placed on the Provincial half-pay list and received £340.16*s*.0*d* compensation for his losses in North Carolina. (Marjorie Taylor, 'Flora MacDonald in America', *The Kintyre Antiquarian and Natural History Society Magazine* (Web Edition, 14th February 1998); Robert Archibald Logan, 'Flora and Allen MacDonald in America', *Clan Donald Magazine*, iv (1968); Clark, *Loyalists in the Southern Campaign*, i, 346, 409, 426, 469; Treasury 64/23(32) (National Archives, Kew); DeMond, *Loyalists in NC*, 253)

49 Before the revolution Lewis Lowry had settled at Jones Creek in Anson County, North Carolina, not far from the Pee Dee River. Now a captain in the loyalist irregular militia there, he would gain his freedom, perhaps in mid 1781 under the cartel with Greene. Making his way to Charlestown, he would be paid as a refugee militia captain from North Carolina until the evacuation. (Clark, *Loyalists in the Southern Campaign*, i, 354, 357, 502)

50 Robert Lowry had settled in the upper part of what is now Chesterfield County, South Carolina, and in 1777 was elected a vestryman for St David's Parish. In late 1780, as Harrington now relates, he entered the North Carolina revolutionary militia as a private in Samuel Jarvis's regiment, but he did not stay long, as he went on to serve as a private in Marion's Brigade for sixty-six days in 1781 and 1782. (Gregg, *The Old Cheraws*, 179 and note, 410; Hay ed, *Soldiers from NC*, 621; Moss, *SC Patriots*, 585)

suppliant wife and children from his feet, and, not contented with the life of the father, burnt and destroyed the houses and effects of the distressed widow and helpless innocents. Britons have not long been accustomed to countenance such savage acts as these. To them it as of right belonged to protect the oppressed and set the nations free. I am willing to believe the major and his worthy colleague Mills exceeded their orders, yet should the actual perpetrators of these horrid crimes fall into the hands of an enraged people, I cannot promise that it will be in my power to ensure to them the same treatment that Captain Lowry received from me.

I am, sir,
Your most humble and most obedient servant

H W HARRINGTON
Brigadier General commanding on Peedee

Rawdon to Cornwallis, 21st November 1780 — *4(171): ALS*

Camden
November 21st 1780

Earl Cornwallis etc etc etc

My Lord

I have just taken a step of some consequence, but as I thought no harm could arise from the failure of the attempt, I imagined it was better not to lose time in applying for your sanction. Colonel Robert Goodwin's brother[51] *is now with Smallwood and is sick. Upon pretence of visiting his brother, the colonel goes to the enemy's camp directly. He has promised to sound several persons of influence there and thinks he shall be able to make converts. He is certain at least that his brother will come over. I have authorised him to offer good terms where he can speak plain, and instructed him to drop vague hints where he is not sure of his ground. I bid him ask his brother how far it might be safe to tamper with Smallwood. At worst he will bring information*.

My intelligence says that Smallwood has fallen back to Charlotteburg and that he has collected a good deal of corn at that place.

I have been honored with your Lordship's letter of yesterday. There has been some mistake about the man who was dispatched with it. I thought he was affecting secrecy and argued for half an hour with him. He still persisted that he knew no more of Black River, Marion and Kingstree than the child unborn.

---

51 Robert Goodwin had two brothers, James (1741-?) and William (1745 ?). It is William to whom Rawdon is referring, as he was serving under Brandon or Sumter. (Information from Charles Ferdinand Carson Jr, 9th October 2005; Moss, *SC Patriots*, 370)

The deficiency in the rum casks happened before they arrived here. I suspect Bagnall on that head, but it shall be very particularly enquired into. It is I that am to make excuses for your Lordship's having been troubled with Lt Colonel Doyle's memorial, as I really did not know whether it would be proper to make an application of that nature to the Commander in Chief without its bearing evidence of being done with your Lordship's knowledge, tho' there was not the least meaning that your Lordship should interest yourself further in the fate of it. Upon this ground I advised Doyle to send it to your Lordship. He feels exceedingly obliged by the honor which your sentiments do him.

In the defence of the mill I have requested Haldane to construct a strong log house to contain a serjeant and 12. It will prevent any petty attempt.

I have been interrupted in this letter by a curious incident. *Harrison's people have long been impatient for cloathing. It arrived yesterday. Last night some of them started a notion that if they took cloathing they were liable to be drafted into regular regiments. In consequence three fourths of the corps have gone off. I have been talking to those who remain, but they don't seem satisfied. They want to plunder and not to do regular duty. I hope I shall settle it without difficulty*.

I have the honor to be, my Lord, with great respect and affection
Your very faithful servant

RAWDON

[*Subscribed*:]

I have the honor to enclose a letter which I have received from Balfour[52].

Cornwallis to Rawdon, 22nd November 1780 — *82(87): C*

Wynnesborough
November 22nd 1780

Rt Hon Lord Rawdon

My dear Lord

I received your two letters of the 20th – one by Captain St Leger, the other by express - and one of yesterday by express. I must begin by telling you that Tarleton has come up with and defeated Sumpter. Money wounded and Gibson and Cope of the 63rd killed.

I approve very much of all you have done about R[53]. The person who came to you shall not only retrieve his character but be received into favour. I shall also be very glad to get

52 *a letter..*: addressed to Rawdon, it is not extant.

53 *R*: Richbourg.

Tynes exchanged. I received a letter from Balfour by the Congarees much to the same effect as that you enclosed to me[54]. However, as Balfour says he is safe in town without the 64th, we must leave them for the present at Kingstree. It is no wonder that my poor express denied all knowledge of Black River etc. I expressed myself awkwardly, but the man I meant did not leave this place 'til yesterday and, being sickly, is very probably not yet arrived at Camden. The negotiation you mention in the first part of the cypher of your letter of yesterday must meet with my most hearty approbation. Every thing of that sort should be tried. We have every thing to gain by the trial and nothing to lose. I cannot, however, imagine there can be any hopes of the last person you mentioned. You may be assured I shall not grudge any expence incurred in a business of this sort.

The incident you mention in the last part of your cypher is curious indeed. I should hope, on a promise under your hand of not drafting them, all will be settled. If not, they must go their own way, but we must try to get as many of their horses as we can.

I am, my dear Lord,
Most sincerely yours

CORNWALLIS

[*Subscribed*:]

Macleod goes to Charlestown to morrow morning. I wish you would be kind enough to write him thither to say what iron guns you wish to have at Camden. It may be well to give you a brass 3 pounder in addition to your two six pounders, which will be very usefull for your detachments. I shall write to Balfour by Macleod and tell him that it is impossible for you to spare Innes's corps and one hundred of the New York Volunteers, which would make a deep cut in that corps. I should not like to station two brass guns with the former corps only. Macleod will not stay above three or four days at Charlestown.

Rawdon to Cornwallis, 22nd November 1780 — *4(175): ALS*

Camden
November 22nd 1780
3 afternoon

Earl Cornwallis etc etc etc

My Lord

I have just received your Lordship's dispatch of yesterday containing the letters for General Lesslie etc[55]. I have sent for an officer, by whom it shall be forwarded in less than half and hour, that there may be the more assurance of its going safe.

---

[54] *a letter from Balfour..*: of 17th November, p 83.

[55] *your Lordship's dispatch..*: Cornwallis to Balfour, 21st November, p 83.

If your Lordship gives me notice of the time and place of meeting, I will send thither a strong escort of the New York Voluntiers.

A trusty emissary has just returned from the country to me. He could not get into Smallwood's camp, but he sent others and says their report is to be trusted. Smallwood lay yesterday morning at the old place above Twelve Mile Creek, Morgan and Washington at Crawford's, Davie at Waxhaw Meeting House, with a post at Blair's Mill. They are all much distressed for corn and forage; they have stripped the whole country near them; and Smallwood now draws his corn from Great Lynches Creek, fifteen miles from his camp. It is asserted in the country that Gates's corps lies just on this side of Salisbury under the command of a General Green.

All is quiet about this post. It will, however, require unremitting activity to get matters here into the state which your Lordship wishes; but that it shall be exerted is faithfully promised by

Your Lordship's affectionate and very humble servant

RAWDON

[*Subscribed*:]

I have opened this letter to mention that another of my spies confirms the account of the enemy's positions, only he says that Smallwood's corps are detached in parties at the distance of five or six miles from each other for the convenience of subsistence.

Your dispatch is gone by Lieutenant Burrowes[56] of the Fuziliers.

Cornwallis to Rawdon, 23rd November 1780 *82(91): C*

Wynnesborough
November 23rd 1780
9 o'clock pm

Rt Hon Lord Rawdon

My dear Lord

I received yours dated yesterday 3 o'clock pm. I am sorry to find my express was so long getting to you but am much obliged to you for the precautions you have taken to prevent any further delay.

---

[56] James Burroughs had been promoted to a captaincy in the 7th (Royal Fusiliers) with effect from 18th September, but news had not yet reached Charlestown. (*Army Lists*)

I enclose a letter I have just received from Tarleton[57]. The express who brought it tells me that an account was brought in just before he came away that Sumpter was at a house four miles from our camp and that a party was going out for him.

My intelligence – as far as it goes, but I am ashamed to say how bad it is – agrees with yours as to Smallwood, but says there was no guard of the enemy at Lands Ford on Monday night, and that, the time of Davy's people being out, they were to be relieved by some other at Waxhaw Meeting House. I expect a man to morrow morning who was to be at Lands Ford last night.

I beg you will desire Colonel Carey to order a small quantity of forage to some house on the road for the use of the expresses whose horses are incapable of performing the journey for want of it. I should think Perry's would be most convenient. We live well here and succeed in getting forage beyond my most sanguine expectations. I have desired Cruger to send the Indian horses to Camden directly under an escort of militia[58].

I am, my dear Lord,
Most sincerely yours

CORNWALLIS

Rawdon to Cornwallis, 23rd November 1780 — *4(185): ALS*

Camden
November 23rd 1780

Earl Cornwallis etc etc etc

My Lord

Tho' I have nothing of consequence to communicate, I will not let slip an opportunity of informing your Lordship that every thing is quiet at this post.

By a person whom I sent to Cheraws I am informed that three days ago General Harrington received an express from Wilmington acquainting him with the appearance of a fleet off Cape Fear. Harrington wanted to persuade the people that it was a French fleet but they were not inclined to give credit to him. My informant understood that the beginning of last week was the time when the fleet was supposed to be seen. He was told at Cheraws that Gates was under arrest.

---

57 *a letter..*: of 22nd November, p 341.

58 *I have desired Cruger..*: on 23rd November, p 272.

I have the honor to be, my Lord, with great respect
Your affectionate and faithful servant

RAWDON

[*Subscribed:*]

I have just received your Lordship's letter with the account of Tarleton's brilliant success, upon which I congratulate your Lordship most heartily.

Cornwallis to Rawdon, 24th November 1780 — *82(95): C*

Wynnesborough
November 24th 1780
9 o'clock pm

My dear Lord

I have just received yours of yesterday. I think the intelligence from the Cheraws cannot be true from dates. If you look at the almanack and at that letter I sent you[59], I think you will be of that opinion.

I saw a person to day who said he parted with Gates about Tuesday seenight about fifteen miles beyond the Yadkin, he was coming with the cavalry, and that his infantry was about two or three days' march before him. He positively says he spoke to Gates. I have sent every body I could find to learn the truth of this. My accounts place Smallwood yesterday at his old position.

They assure me that Colonels Clarke and Chandler[60] were killed in the late action and that Sumpter is certainly mortally wounded, some say dead.

Tarleton has sent to McArthur to come to him. I have sent Manley to get him back as soon as he can be spared, but as this is uncertain and I feel myself very weak, I wish you could lend me the 7th Regiment for a few days. If you can do this, I beg you would lose no time. *You may depend on their being returned and the march will do the men good*.

---

59 *that letter..*: no extant copy.

60 Born in Ireland, William Candler (1738-1789) was brought as a child to Virginia. In 1762 he moved on to Georgia and nine years later was a deputy surveyor. Now, he had been named in the Georgia Disqualifying Act 1780 passed by the royal assembly and, whether as a major or colonel, had served under Elijah Clark in the September assault on Augusta and in the action at Blackstocks in mid November. He had also led a small band of thirty Georgians at the Battle of King's Mountain. In December he would accompany Clark to the Long Cane settlement and may have been among those with Clark who were later routed by Isaac Allen. After the war he represented Richmond County for two years in the Georgia legislature and served as a judge. (Draper, *King's Mountain*, 214, 469; *The Cornwallis Papers*; The Georgia Disqualifying Act 1780)

I am, my dear Lord,
Most sincerely yours

CORNWALLIS

Rawdon to Cornwallis, 24th November 1780 *4(187): ALS*

Camden
November 24th 1780

Earl Cornwallis etc etc etc

My Lord

The letter from Captain Coffin to me, which I have the honor to enclose, will give your Lordship the best information respecting the High Hills and that neighborhood. Upon information that Captain Snipes with his troop had passed Black River and advanced towards the Wateree, I detached Captain Coffin with sixty of the New York Voluntiers to endeavor to cut him off. Snipes has escaped, but it appears that my intelligence was very exact. I have this morning sent twenty more of the New York Voluntiers to Coffin, directing him to put Upton Hill in a proper state of defence and to fix Tynes firmly in his seat of government before he returns hither.

I think the navigation of the Santee seems at present tolerably secured, but I think you will have difficulties on account of the very bulky articles which are now embarked upon it. I wish to know whether the cloathing of the 71st Regiment should stop at McChord's or should come up in the boats to this place. From either there will be much labor in conveying it by land to Wynnesborough.

I think five light iron guns will be full enough for this place in addition to two small ones which we have now mounted upon a kind of swivel. I have written to McLeod about it.

Colonel Porterfield is very ill, and imagining that he shall not recover, he is very anxious to see his brother[61], a captain in the 7th Virginia Regiment and prisoner at Hedrall's Point. Supposing that your Lordship could have no objection, I have written to Lt Colonel Balfour to allow Captain Porterfield to come hither.

---

[61] Born, like his wounded brother, in Frederick County, Virginia, Robert Porterfield (1752-1843) was, as Rawdon says, a captain in the 7th Virginia Continental Regiment and had been a Continental officer since December 1776. Having served under Daniel Morgan from 1777 to 1779, he became aide-de-camp to Brigadier General William Woodford and accompanied him to Charlestown, where both fell prisoner under the articles of capitulation. He would be exchanged in December, transfer to the 2nd Virginia, and serve till the close of the war. In the War of 1812 he was appointed a brigadier general in the Virginia militia and commanded at Camp Holly. He died in Augusta County, Virginia, having served for more than fifty years as a county magistrate and for two terms as a high sheriff. (*Appletons'*; Heitman, *Historical Register*, 448)

Harrison's people are all in good humor and most of the absentees have rejoined him. The man *really* acquainted with Kingstree etc has been here and is gone forward.

I have the honor to be very faithfully
Your Lordship's affectionate and very humble servant

RAWDON

[*Subscribed*:]

I send a specimen of Harrison's corps.

Enclosure
Coffin to Rawdon, 23rd November 1780 *4(183): ALS*

Upton Hill
November 23rd 1780

My Lord

I have the honour to inform your Lordship that I arrived with the whole detatchment eight and twenty miles from town at about ten in the evening. After giving every refreshment to the men that the plantation afforded, I proceeded into the swamp about day light, and, after the dirtiest and most fatigueing march I ever experienced of fifteen miles through bogs, lakes etc, had the mortification to find the enemy flown. They quitted their abode the evening before, robbing every widow and friend's house within the district. On my way down I met with Colonel Tynes, who had just made his escape with some of his officers who were taken at the same time. They have attended me during the day with about twenty others. Since my return more has joined me, and as he has assured me he can collect about a hundred and fifty stanch good men, I have thought proper to remain here untill I shall have the honour of your Lordship's advice how to act. My present situation is a good one, indeed the strongest ground I have seen in this country. The house and out houses are situated upon the top of a high hill, and with the assistance of a few Negroes, which are soon collected in this quarter, I could put it in a posture of defence against any number that may appear. It exactly covers the swamp that these scoundrels have secreted themselves in. The situation of the plantation in the swamp is such that ten men could prevent any number of boats passing the river.

Contigues to this post is a fine grist mill. If your Lordship shou'd think it an object for me to remain here seven or eight days, Colonel Tynes would then have his militia collected and be able to secure this post and in some measure keep the country quiet. His comeing in will be of great service, as he has it in his power to impeach a number of the inhabitants, who I shall apprehend tomorrow and, if agreeable to your Lordship, proceed to justice with them, as your Lordship may be assured the best consequences will insue from it. With the assistance of the militia I hope to get a number of horses. Five has been procured this day, and in a day or two more I hope to remit a pleasing account to your Lordship. Mr Johnston[62] with the few men he has in camp wou'd prove a pleaseing reinforcement and enable me to act with vigour against the rascalls.

The liberty I have taken in dictateing and adviseing to your Lordship will, I hope, be overlooked, as it proceeds from real zeal for the service.

I have the honour to be
Your Lordship's obedient and most humble servant

JN^{O} COFFIN
Captain commanding New York Volunteers

Cornwallis to Rawdon, 25th November 1780 — *82(101): C*

Wynnesborough
November 25th 1780

Rt Hon Lord Rawdon

My dear Lord

I have received yours of the 24th by the detachment of Harrison's. The officers did not look quite so smart as the men, who really make a very soldier like appearance. I had this day a confirmation by two different channels, and both good, of what I told you about Gates, so that I think it cannot be doubted. I enclose to you a note I received from Tarleton[63]. You will be kind enough to exert yourself as much as possible to get intelligence; I have many people employed. If one in a number succeeds, I think myself well off.

If you can comply with the request I made to you in cypher yesterday, you may depend on a speedy return, unless material events should happen, and my keeping a constant look out towards Camden.

Captain Coffin's letter is very sensible and satisfactory. I have seen no particular accounts of McLeroth and conclude you have yet had no communication with him.

In regard to the cloathing coming up I can only say that the regiments are in the utmost want of it. Therefore the safest and speediest method will be best. The 71st are quite naked.

---

62 There were two Johnstons presently serving in the New York Volunteers: Alexander (1764-?), who had been promoted from ensign to lieutenant on 15th August, and William Martin (1757-?), who had entered the regiment as an ensign in 1776 and risen to be a captain on 15th January 1779. Both were Americans, and both would be placed on the Provincial half-pay list at the close of the war. (Treasury 64/23(1), WO 65/164(31) and WO 65/165(2) (National Archives, Kew); Raymond, 'British American Corps')

63 *a note..*: of 24th November, p 343.

I am, my dear Lord,
Most sincerely yours

CORNWALLIS

[*Subscribed*:]

As soon as Haldane can be spared I wish to send him to 96, where by all accounts engineering has been at its lowest pitch.

I understood from Haldane that he had sent the cypher to Colonel Balfour. If not, pray decypher the enclosed[64] before you send it.

Cornwallis to Rawdon, 26th November 1780 — *82(105): C*

Wynnesborough
November 26th 1780
12 o'clock noon

Rt Hon Lord Rawdon etc etc etc

My dear Lord

Nothing new since I wrote last night. I keep two of Harrison's men in case I hear this evening.

In regard to the cloathing, you know the great importance it is of to us. If it was to be lost, the 33rd and 71st Regiments would be rendered totally unfit for service. I cannot guess how many waggons would be wanted for bringing it by land. If a sufficient number could be sent from Camden without distressing the service to McChord's Ferry, it would certainly be a great saving in point of time. If that cannot be, and that[65] it is too bulky to send up all at a time, we must send as much as we can at once and I will send any that I can spare to meet them halfway. You do not mention the first cargo of necessaries, which I hope are by this time at Camden. We shall be glad to receive them as soon as possible.

I am, my dear Lord,
Most sincerely yours

CORNWALLIS

---

[64] *the enclosed*: probably Cornwallis to Balfour, 25th November, p 89.

[65] *that*: the meaning is 'if'. See p 43, note 55.

Rawdon to Cornwallis, 25th November 1780 *4(202): ALS*

Camden
November 25th 1780
One o'clock pm

Earl Cornwallis etc etc etc

My Lord

I have this moment been honored with your letter dated at nine o'clock yesterday evening, in consequence of which the Seventh Regiment shall march in the course of this night.

It will be necessary for me to recall immediately the detachment under Captain Coffin as I should not now be able to relieve him in case he were distressed, neither indeed can I well spare him from this post whilst there is a possibility that the enemy in front could make any attempt against it.

That I may not lose time by having a new return of the troops here made out, I enclose to your Lordship the state which I received from Lt Colonel Turnbull[66]. In addition, there are 270 rank and file fit for duty of the Voluntiers of Ireland, and 150 convalescents are reported to me as fit for the defence of the redoubts. The number will answer very sufficiently in the works, *tho I cannot say much for the quality of some of my forces. It is necessary for me to say that, should the enemy approach in such force as to make me confine myself to the works, the village and stores might be burned without my being able to prevent it. The principal redoubts are so far asunder that resolute troops would pass between them at any time without hesitation and the most timorous might penetrate by night without apprehension. The works likewise, tho defensible, are by no means complete. In short, the post (which was always an infamous one) is not much mended by the entrenchments in their present state, but I will venture to promise that, should the foe attack us, your Lordship shall be satisfied with our behavior*.

I have agitated these points from my ignorance of the force which Gates and Smallwood combined may muster. Possibly they may rather apprehend an attack from us. If they meant any thing against us, by your dates they ought to be very near us at present.

I have the honor to be, my Lord, with great respect and affection
Your most faithful servant

RAWDON

66 *the state..*: not extant.

Cornwallis to Rawdon, 26th November 1780 *82(107): Df*

Wynnesborough
November 26th 1780
9 o'clock pm

Rt Hon Lord Rawdon

My dear Lord

One of my *friends* is just come in who says that he is quite sure that on Thursday Smallwood was at his old quarters at Hewston's and that a woman whom he saw since assured him that he was there on Friday night. Davie's people are certainly gone back from Waxhaw, which gives an appearance of probability to the intelligence contained in Tarleton's note which I sent to you. My *friend* adds that Gates's corps lay somewhere about Mecklenburg, and that the Back Mountain men were to assemble at Lawson's Iron Works to join Sumpter, and that the North Carolina militia say that they will defend their own State but will not march into the south. So much for my gazette.

I never apprehended that Gates intended any serious attack on our army, or any of our principal posts unless he found them much off their guard. I must still consider this as the victorious and superior army, ready to act offensively whenever circumstances and a proper object makes it adviseable. I have a much better army than I had on the 16th, he a much worse, but we must not put too great temptation in his way. The Grand Army and head quarters in an open camp with six hundred men[67] *and nothing within call, not a mounted man, is risking too much*.

Now, my dear Lord, the greatest attention is to be paid to the cloathing. I believe we could send six, and perhaps eight, waggons to McChord's. Now if you could make up enough from Camden for this job, it would make our affairs much easier. You will, however, be better able to judge of the safety of the river than me, and I am sure you must feel as much the importance of the object. The return of the Carolina regiments surprises me. Major Prevost assured me that he mustered above 300 of Hamilton's and 225 of Innes's under arms.

The works may be bad, but you in the enemy's place would not attack without cannon a large corps with redoubts and that could be speedily succoured.

I am, my dear Lord,
Yours most sincerely

CORNWALLIS

67 *six hundred men*: the 23rd, 33rd and 2nd Battalion of the 71st.

Rawdon to Cornwallis, 26th November 1780 *4(211): ALS*

Camden
November 26th 1780

Earl Cornwallis etc etc etc

My Lord

I have the honor to enclose a letter which I have this morning received from Captain Coffin[68]. I sent orders to him yesterday afternoon to return hither. I will write to Tynes to prevent any bad effect which that movement might produce, and will send another detachment to the High Hills as soon as I can ascertain that the enemy do not advance towards us. I was loth to withdraw Coffin even before I received his letter, but I thought no precaution superfluous for the security of this post and no consideration equal to its safety.

The information which I have received this morning from the country rather leads me to think that Smallwood has fallen back beyond Charlotteburg and was in that position joined by Gates on Monday or Tuesday last, but I am grieved to say that notwithstanding the most assiduous pains and liberal payment I cannot get such certain and distinct intelligence from that quarter as I ought to have. I consequently do not suffer my information to influence my precautions.

The necessaries for the 33rd and 71st are arrived and shall be forwarded as soon as possible. Seven puncheons of rum have likewise come up, four of which are on their road to your Lordship.

I have the honor to be, my Lord, with great respect
Your very affectionate and faithful servant

RAWDON

Rawdon to Cornwallis, 26th November 1780 *2(209): ALS*

Camden
November 26th 1780
3 o'clock afternoon

Earl Cornwallis etc

My Lord

Since I had the honor of writing to your Lordship this morning, a rebel serjeant of dragoons arrived with a flag of truce at the picquet. He brought a waggon for the removal

---

68 *a letter..*: not extant.

of Lt Colonel Porterfield, but as Porterfield is unable to travel, I dismissed both the waggon and the serjeant immediately. Among many other letters the enclosed[69] for your Lordship were delivered to me. I took the liberty of opening them, as I thought some information might be drawn from them. I observe those letters, as well as the pass for the waggon, are dated on the 24th instant, yet I suspect that Gates detached them earlier. If that is not the case, he ought to be very near me, and indeed he might have been here by this time by the account which your Lordship received. I have, however, no information of any enemy being in the neighborhood. The serjeant was sifted but was so much upon his guard that nothing could be learned from him. Should the enemy attempt this post, I hope they will find neither want of vigilance nor of firmness in the garrison.

As soon as I can learn any thing further, your Lordship may depend upon hearing from

Your most obedient and affectionate servant

RAWDON

Cornwallis to Rawdon, 27th November 1780 — *82(115): C*

Wynnesborough
November 27th 1780

Rt Hon Lord Rawdon etc etc etc

My dear Lord

A person returned to me this morning who was in the rebel camp on Saturday evening. He says that Gates joined on Thursday and that they were altogether on 6 Mile Run. When he was there he rode all about Smallwood's camp. He supposes them about 1,000. They shewed him where Gates's men lay but he was afraid to venture amongst the Continentals for fear of being too strictly examined. They reported Gates to have 1,300 infantry and 2 pieces of cannon. He believes the people he conversed with, taking him for a firm friend, told him the truth to the best of their knowledge, so that he has no doubt as to the 2 pieces of cannon which they affirmed to be at Gates's quarters but supposes they might not be perfectly accurate as to his numbers. He says he has no doubt of the cavalry under White, Armand and Washington amounting to upwards of 300. He marched some way with the 2 former and counted 150, and says it did not appear to him that he had counted above half.

A man is come in from the back of North Carolina who informs me that the Indians joined by some white people are in arms about the Western Waters, that they do not hurt women and children but carry off all rebels, that Shelvy and Cleveland were gone after them.

---

69 *the enclosed*: Gates to Cornwallis, 24th November, enclosing De Peyster to Cornwallis of the 19th, pp 403-4.

I send you a letter I got this evening from Tarleton[70]. I understand that he has only cavalry and mounted men with him and is gone after the debris of Sumpter, supposed to consist of about 250.

I like Coffin's letter very much and his account of things in that part of the world. I wish much that we may be able to keep up the spirits of our friends there. I sincerely believe Bromfield to deserve the character given of him, but we must buy him out or he will be a 2nd Marion. You may depend on my paying the utmost attention to any movement the enemy may make towards you, and I think now I shall be rather better off for intelligence. Tarleton, whether he has succeeded in his blow or not, is by this time on his way towards us. If the cloathing is not past McChord's, I believe we can by means of waggons of the country send 8 or 10 from hence, but of this you will be the best judge, as you perfectly know whereabouts the cloathing is on the river. I have said so much on that subject that I will not tire you with more.

I forgot to mention that my informant assured me that Davie and his corps were disbanded, their time being out. He himself heard Davie say that now he was a free man. One Taylor[71], he said, was to collect such a corps. On Saturday there was not a man at Waxhaw or any where on this side of 6 Mile Run. I beg you will do what you please, or perhaps what our friends in that country please, about Bradley. Pray assure M[72] of all possible favour from me.

I am, my dear Lord,
Most sincerely yours

CORNWALLIS

[*Subscribed*:]

Any plan of Captain Coffin's for raising men in that country which you think likely to succeed will meet with my approbation.

---

70 *a letter..*: of 25th November, p 345.

71 Colonel John Taylor of the Granville County revolutionary militia had reinforced Davie in late September with 200 infantry and 60 horse. A prominent revolutionary, he had represented his county in the Provincial Congresses which convened in August 1775 and April 1776. (Davie, *Revolutionary War Sketches*, 26; Robinson, *Davie*, 75; Wheeler, *Historical Sketches* ii, 162)

72 *M*: probably Isham Moore.

Rawdon to Cornwallis, 27th November 1780 *4(215): ALS*

Camden
November 27th 1780
11 o'clock forenoon

Earl Cornwallis etc etc etc

My Lord

I have delayed writing to you untill this hour in hopes that I might be able to give you some certain information respecting the enemy. Rugeley has just come in to me. He says that on the night before last he was out with a party in search of Kembill[73] very near Berkley's in Waxhaw and the information he received was that Smallwood had retired beyond Charlotteburg. This agrees with the intelligence which I had before procured. We are, however, very alert and feel every part of the country round us with constant patroles.

My plan of defence would be, after garrisoning the redoubts, to remain with two battalions at least and the field pieces in the village. I should thus be ready to attack any part of the enemy's line that might offer to penetrate. Were all the troops shut up in works, I think they would not communicate sufficiently. This is supposing the enemy so numerous and so cautious as to reduce us to an absolute defence.

Captain Coffin arrived here yesterday evening, having left Tynes satisfied that he could keep matters quiet with his militia till the return of the troops.

The blunder of a conductor has delayed your Lordship's rum, but it proceeds as soon as possible. A portion of the necessaries go up at the same time under escort of some convalescents.

Haldane shall leave this immediately. He has just given directions for a stockade round the body of the village, which will secure our stores. Balfour has your Lordship's cypher.

I shall write again if I learn any thing worth communicating.

In the mean time I have the honor to remain with great respect
Your Lordship's most obedient and faithful humble servant

RAWDON

---

[73] Benjamin Kimball, who may have been a son of Benjamin Kimball Sr (1708-1794) of Camden District, was a leader of an indiscriminate gang of freebooters who were presently plundering and murdering loyalists and who would soon turn their attention to those of the revolutionary persuasion. *The Greene Papers* are mistaken in stating that he was one of Rugeley's militia and captured with him. The extant muster rolls of Rugeley's regiment contain no mention of him, and clearly, if he had been captured with Rugeley on 1st December, he would not have been active later. (*The Cornwallis Papers*; *The Greene Papers*, vi, 606 and note)

[*Subscribed*:]

The 7th Regiment has of course reached your Lordship before this time. I have been honored with your letter of the 25th at night and also with that of yesterday, 12 o'clock.

Rawdon to Cornwallis, 27th November 1780 — *4(213): ALS*

Camden
November 27th 1780
Seven o'clock evening

Earl Cornwallis etc etc etc

My Lord

I have just been honored with your letter dated at nine yesterday evening. I perceive that your Lordship has misunderstood a part of mine of the 25th. *I felt strongly the impropriety of your being left so weak and I could have spared more troops without thinking myself in the least exposed. Were I left here with but one battalion, I would do my best without apprehension, and I seek to do service, not to gain reputation*; but I wished to account for a measure which was unpleasant but in my opinion necessary, *I mean the recalling Coffin. All the troops cannot lie in the redoubts. Those who don't might be surprised as easily as if there were no works. Strong piquets and constant patroles are therefore necessary*. I wanted likewise to explain the difficulty of *securing the stores*, whence arises *my opinion of the post. The redoubts alone would be safe with half my force*.

A serjeant and nine privates of the Legion, who were left with me by Tarleton, and four or five convalescents of the same corps shall join your Lordship tomorrow. To furnish Coffin's detachment I was obliged to borrow the bridles and saddles of all the officers here, but we daily expect an assortment from Charlestown.

The cloathing for the 33rd is arrived at McChord's. As many waggons as can be collected shall be sent for it without delay. England's activity and attention have eased the business of every department here wonderfully, but there was a great deal to do and there is still a great deal to be done. Your Lordship may depend upon our exertions in every particular.

Two persons whom I employ have come in this evening. Their account agrees with your Lordship's intelligence. There was no enemy near Hanging Rock this morning. I should rather doubt the movement of Washington etc as I do not well see any essential purpose in it to counterbalance its inconveniences.

I have the honor to be, my Lord, with great truth and respect
Your very affectionate humble servant

RAWDON

Cornwallis to Rawdon, 28th November 1780 *82(119): C*

Wynnesborough
November 28th 1780

Rt Hon Lord Rawdon etc etc etc

My dear Lord

I received your letters of yesterday dated 11 o'clock forenoon and 7 o'clock evening.

I believe you will find the intelligence I sent you last night pretty correct. I have heard nothing material since nor any news from Tarleton. About 100 of Sumpter's corps under Lacey came over Fishdam Ford on Saturday night and either crossed to the Catawba or dispersed to plunder, I am not sure which. I have sent 5 waggons for the cloathing of the 71st to McChord's this evening and hope to send 3 or 4 more to morrow. *Your ideas of the post at Camden are very just. I mean it as an intrenched camp from whence the country is to be kept and protected. Present necessity obliged me to take what you cannot spare. Situated as I am, they will not probably attack you. My weakness might tempt them to make me move, which would embarrass affairs at present*.

I am plagued for ever about Innes's corps and refer them always to you. You must talk very seriously to Major Fraser from me. I cannot allow men to be kept on the strength of this army who are acknowledged to be unfit for service by age or infirmity or have promise of perpetual furlow, provided only that they appear at a muster. You may say that if that practice continues I shall think myself under the necessity of bringing the commanding officer to a court martial. I have kept this letter open in hopes of Manley's return, but as it is now growing late, I despair of him 'til to morrow.

Yours, my dear Lord, most sincerely

CORNWALLIS

Rawdon to Cornwallis, 28th November 1780 *4(227): ALS*

Camden
November 28th 1780

Earl Cornwallis etc etc etc

My Lord

I have been honored with your letter of yesterday by Whittles. As he returns, I write a line to let your Lordship know that all is quiet here. I heard from Tynes this morning. He had collected a tolerable corps and there was no enemy near him. I shall write again in the course of the day.

In the mean time I remain
Your Lordship's very affectionate and faithful servant

RAWDON

Rawdon to Cornwallis, 28th November 1780 — *4(221): ALS*

Camden
November 28th 1780
Eight at night

Earl Cornwallis etc etc etc

My Lord

The dispatch[74] which I have the honor to forward has just arrived. I opened it as it was marked *On Service.*

I have heard from Moore and Richbourg this evening. All is going on well in their quarter and they think the revolution will be general. The movement proposed for McLeroth will, I think, decide the business.

Ten waggons with rum and necessaries set out for Wynnesborough at day break tomorrow. Having been detached for forage into the country, they were detained by a blunder, otherwise the stores would have been with your Lordship by this time. Ten waggons will start at the same time for McChord's to transport the cloathing of the 33rd to your camp. The rum which is in the same boat must come up by water.

I am very glad that I happen to be here at this time, when a little attention is necessary upon many points of consequence. Your Lordship may be assured that we shall be as active as possible.

I give your Lordship much joy upon Balfour's veteran reinforcement[75], and have the honor to subscribe myself with equal truth and respect

Your Lordship's very faithful and affectionate humble servant

RAWDON

---

74 *The dispatch*: Balfour to Cornwallis, 24th and 25th November, p 91.

75 *Balfour's veteran reinforcement*: the two old Hessian generals, to which Balfour's above dispatch refers.

[*Subscribed*:]

B——[76] and M——[77] never liked one another, so I hope it is not quite so bad.

Cornwallis to Rawdon, 29th November 1780 — *82(125): ADfS*

Wynnesborough
November 29th 1780
12 o'clock noon

Rt Hon Lord Rawdon etc etc etc

My dear Lord

One of my people is come in. He brings nothing but hearsay, but he has certainly been as far as Twelve Mile Creek. He says that every body asserted positively that the rebel army had marched, he believes on Monday morning. The report was current that they were going to Camden. They did not come through the Waxhaws, so that in that case they must come down the Old Salisbury Road or go by Linches Creek. My opinion is that they have marched only to their left. I have, however, already sent out two people towards Hanging Rock, and from thence to go upwards on the road, and shall send as many more as I can get to go. You will of course try all means to procure intelligence, but I have no faith in their attacking Camden.

Yours ever, my dear Lord, most sincerely

CORNWALLIS

Rawdon to Cornwallis, 29th November 1780 — *4(232): ALS*

Camden
November 29th 1780
1 o'clock afternoon

Earl Cornwallis etc etc etc

My Lord

I have just been honored with your letter of last night. Some persons have just been with me who left Salisbury on the 22nd. They assert that the infantry which marched from thence with Gates amounted to no more than six hundred, his cavalry were about three hundred, and

---

76 Balfour.

77 McLeroth.

he had two pieces of cannon. The report in North Carolina is that a second army, stronger than that of Lesslie, has landed in Virginia. It is said likewise that Lesslie had taken Williamsburg and that Gates was ordered back to Virginia.

Mr Haldane is desirous of remaining here till the day after tomorrow, by which time he will have put matters into such a train that his workmen cannot go astray. I had detained the dragoons in order that they might have accompanied him to Wynnesborough, but as he postpones his departure, I now send them.

All is quiet here. It is said that Harrington is moving to join Gates, but I have no certainty of it.

I have the honor to be, my Lord, very faithfully and respectfully
Your most obedient servant

RAWDON

Rawdon to Cornwallis, 29th November 1780 — *4(234): ALS*

Camden
November 29th 1780
9 at night

Earl Cornwallis etc etc etc

My Lord

I have just received your Lordship's letter of this day giving me intelligence which was brought to you respecting a movement of the enemy. About an hour ago two of my spies came in. They had not been in the enemy's camp but sent a woman thither, who returned to them yesterday morning, reporting that she had left Gates and Smallwood at Six Mile Run on Monday night. I am disposed to credit this intelligence. If these spies do not deceive me, there was no enemy upon the Old Salisbury Road or on the Waxhaw Road this morning. It is reported in the country that Gates is to move immediately to a mill upon Wild Cat Creek, which runs into the eastern branch of Lynches Creek. The country around it is full of corn and forage, and his present position is eaten bare. Your Lordship may be assured that we shall not fail in vigilance.

I am under some apprehension that Harrison and his corps will get into a scrape. The day before yesterday Major England ordered Harrison to send a patrole to the first run on the Cheraws Road. Instead of that, Harrison marched with his whole force and has not yet returned. I should not be able to guess where he was, were it not that at least a dozen terrified militia men have been with me to swear that a thousand rebels in blue and red coats and three corner'd hats were scouring the whole country between the branches of Lynches Creek. I should be grieved on many accounts that any misfortune should happen to them, but they thoroughly merit a little chastisement. If they do not get themselves beaten or dispersed, they will probably soon return, and if the enemy has moved in that direction, they must bring me certain information of it.

I have the honor to be, my Lord, with great respect
Your very affectionate humble servant

RAWDON

Cornwallis to Rawdon, 30th November 1780 — *82(138): A(in part) C*

Wynnesborough
November 30th 1780

Rt Hon Lord Rawdon etc etc etc

My dear Lord

I have received your letters of yesterday at one and 9 o'clock pm. Every thing that I have heard to day makes me believe that Gates has certainly not moved. I have ordered the 63rd to Camden. They will march from Shirar's Ferry to morrow or next day. As the Legion have lost many horses by action and fatigue, I have directed that they should give up all their horses to them except twenty which I have ordered them to take with them to Camden to help to mount the New York Volunteers. Colonel Cruger informs me that he has sent twenty to you from Augusta[78]. *The Legion will remain on Broad River between the forks and Shirar's Ferry*.

I have sent 4 more good waggons of the country to bring him cloathing from McChord's.

I am, my dear Lord,
Yours most sincerely

CORNWALLIS

[*Subscribed*:]

I enclose a letter to Balfour[79], which you will be kind enough to direct the express to give him on the road if he meets him.

I hear that Hampton, the brother to the man who keeps the store, is gone off to the rebels with his Negroes. I don't know what steps we can take except employing people to watch the store and observe the contents and the removal of them.

---

78 *Colonel Cruger informs me..*: on 27th November, p 275.

79 *a letter..*: of 30th November, p 95.

Rawdon to Cornwallis, 30th November 1780 — *2(248): ALS*

Camden
November 30th 1780

Earl Cornwallis etc etc etc

My Lord

I have received your Lordship's letter of last night[80]. That which I enclose from McLeroth will shew your Lordship that he does not mean to risque any thing, but I really have a better opinion of the disposition of that country than he expresses.

I have the honor to lay before your Lordship a dispatch from Major Harrison[81]. By the account of the people who came from him there was certainly no enemy yesterday upon Lynches Creek, and if I may trust my spies, there were none below Twelve Mile Creek. I have many people out and I think I must have certain information directly of their movements. I have ordered Harrison back, as I do not think him likely to do much service where he is and he might get into a scrape.

I have the honor to be, my Lord, with great respect
Your very affectionate servant

RAWDON

Cornwallis to Rawdon, 1st December 1780 — *83(1): ADfS*

Wynnesborough
December 1st 1780

Rt Hon Lord Rawdon etc etc etc

My dear Lord

I received this day yours inclosing the reports from McLeroth and Harrison. My apprehensions on account of the former are quite over. Upon the whole I am better pleased that he is on the Santee than on the Pedee. As to Harrison, I shall be perfectly satisfied if he does not lose the good blue coats. My intelligence reports Smallwood at his old camp and a doubt whether Gates was not gone back to Charlottetown. My informant was on Wild Cat Creek yesterday morning. He said that it had been reported that Gates intended to come to one Murphy's on that creek, but that it was not believed, as the enemy had already drawn a great deal of forage from that neighbourhood. The necessaries and rum are arrived. I cannot

---

80 *your Lordship's letter*..: no extant copy.

81 Neither McLeroth's letter nor Harrison's is extant.

get any certain account of the clothing of the 71st. I have sent an officer of that corps to McChord's to assemble the nine waggons which I sent and take care of them and to send forward to find out where the clothing is. As soon as that is ascertained, I have directed him to proceed with the waggons and bring up the clothing by land. I think that McLeroth, considering his strength, is rather too fond of detaching, neither do I apprehend that the compound which he mentions of 64th and Hessians is likely to make good light infantry. This easterly wind must produce something good.

I am, my dear Lord,
Most sincerely yours

CORNWALLIS

Rawdon to Cornwallis, 1st December 1780 — *4(265): ALS*

Camden
December 1st 1780

Earl Cornwallis etc etc etc

My Lord

I have the honor to send to you by Mr Haldane two hundred guineas which were sent for your Lordship by Lt Colonel Balfour. They were brought hither by Major Doyle. He is surprisingly recovered, but I believe must take another trip to Charlestown, for he has not gotten a sixpence for the regiment, and without this fleet from New York brings cash, we shall all be pennyless. He left town on Saturday evening, at which time there was nothing particular. A corporal of the 57th (ordered for garrison duty in Bermuda) came in the transport with the Hessian generals. He asserts positively that he saw his own regiment embarked for Charlestown, as likewise the Regiment of Bunau. The generals know nothing of the matter either way. It is a fortnight this day since the fleet sailed; there were sixteen transports. I have heard nothing of the enemy this morning but hope in the course of the day to transmit some news.

I forward some letters which have just arrived here from Buckhead, and have the honor to remain with great respect

Your Lordship's most obedient and very affectionate servant

RAWDON

[*Subscribed*:]

I took the liberty of opening the dispatches[82], as your Lordship desired, but will not delay Haldane by saying any thing concerning them.

---

82 *the dispatches*: Balfour to Cornwallis, 29th November, p 96, enclosing Clinton to Cornwallis, 5th and 6th November, pp 14 to 23.

Rawdon to Cornwallis, 1st December 1780 — *4(259): ALS*

Camden
December 1st 1780
3 afternoon

Earl Cornwallis etc etc etc

My Lord

I enclose to your Lordship a letter which I have this moment received from Colonel Rugeley. I have examined Makey[83], who is very clear and positive in his intelligence. He understood that the corps encamped at Simpson's (which consisted both of infantry and cavalry) was commanded by Morgan. He says that the enemy marched down the road which leads to Rockey Mount and that they had carriages of some kind with them. A Negro (who says he came in on purpose to give me the information) asserts that a party of the rebel cavalry under the command of Major Marshall[84] lay last night at Murphey's beyond Lynches Creek, 25 miles from hence. He further says that Harrison's people, upon hearing of this party, immediately went off down Lynches Creek. I think it very probable that an attempt is in agitation against Rugeley's post. I have therefore desired the colonel to send out parties all around him, and if he finds any large body of the enemy near him, I have advised him to retire hither directly. Your Lordship may be assured that we will be strictly upon our guard here, and I will lose no time in forwarding any further intelligence that I may receive. A serjeant of rebel dragoons, with a flag of truce and a pass from Smallwood dated the 28th, arrived at the outpost this day. I have detained the serjeant for the present.

I have the honor to be, my Lord, with great respect
Your very obedient and affectionate servant

RAWDON

---

83 Perhaps Samuel McKee (1736-1808), who married Jennett McCullough and may have been related to James McCullough (see below). In October 1772 he had left Belfast in the *Pennsylvania Farmer* and settled on what became a 200-acre plantation on the north side of Broad River, South Carolina. After the war he remained in the Back Country and was buried in the cemetery of Hopewell Church, Chester County, where his headstone bears the name 'Makee'. (Jean Stephenson, *Scotch-Irish Migration to South Carolina, 1772: Rev. William Martin and His Five Shiploads of Settlers* (Clearfield Publishing, 2001), 28, 74; Virginia Draffin Waites, *Strong and Allied Families...* (privately published, Chester Co SC, 1980), 111, 175-7, 215; Pre-revolutionary Plat Folder 1209, 6th January 1773, and Royal Grants, Book 30, 249 (SC Department of Archives and History))

84 Perhaps John Marshel, who had been major in Joseph Kershaw's Camden regiment of the South Carolina revolutionary militia and went on to serve as a colonel in Sumter's Brigade. (Moss, *SC Patriots*, 656)

Enclosure
Rugeley to Rawdon, 1st December 1780 ***4(267): ALS***

Camden
1st December 1780

My Lord

On Wednesday I sent up one Makey to Mr James Simpson's in the Waxaws. He returned this morning and informed me that there was 600 of the rebels encamped at Mr Simpson's house the night before last, that yesterday they kept passing in small parties by there downwards, and that he himself saw some of them encamped at Mr Simpson's house last night before he set off to come down.

This Makey is recommended to me by Captain McAllough[85] as a man I might put confidence in. Have therefore sent him down to your Lordship that if your Lordship thinks proper he may be further examined respecting his intelligence.

I have the honor to be with the greatest respect, my Lord,
Your Lordship's oblig'd humble servant

HEN[Y] RUGELEY

Rawdon to Cornwallis, 1st December 1780 ***4(261): ALS***

Camden
December 1st 1780
Seven at night

Earl Cornwallis

My Lord

A deserter from Washington's dragoons has just come in to me. By his account Washington with an hundred cavalry lay at Murphy's last night and, this morning three miles above Rugeley's, joined Morgan, who had marched with six hundred infantry by the Rockey Mount Road. The plan is to storm Rugeley's post this night. This deserter was sent to try a ford across the creek behind Rugeley's. Having arrived there, he slipped from his guides and, galloping up to Rugeley, gave him notice of the enemy's intentions. A patrole of mine arriving at that time, Rugeley forwarded the deserter to me, assuring me that, as he found the enemy had no cannon, he would defend himself to the utmost. By the description which he

85 A friend of Alexander Chesney, James McCullough (?-1812) was a captain in Henry Rugeley's Camden regiment of the royal militia. Before the revolution he had migrated from County Armagh, Ireland, to what is now Lancaster County, South Carolina. Whether he was now to be discreditably captured with Rugeley is uncertain, but by September 1781 he was receiving pay as a refugee militia officer in Charlestown. When the town was evacuated in December 1782, he returned to Ireland. He later moved to Canada, where he was granted land and died. (Clark, *Loyalists in the Southern Campaign*, i, 111, 136, 138, 147)

gave me of his house I do not believe it could possibly be forced without artillery. I was much tempted to try a stroke against Morgan, but considering the importance of the stake here, I have determined not to risque any thing upon information which may be deceitful. I have therefore only sent a small party of mounted men, instructing them to approach as near as possible to Rugeley's and (if the house is attacked) to throw a few random shots upon the enemy's rear. This may perhaps make Morgan suspect that from the information of the deserter I have marched out with intention to cut him off. I have told the party (in case any of them should be taken) that I was just going to march thro' the woods with a large body of infantry. The deserter is Irish. He says Gates with his Continentals and four pieces of cannon (all they have) are gone back to Charlotte. Smallwood waits the event of this attempt at Six Mile Creek with the militia.

I have the honor to be, my Lord,
Very respectfully and affectionately yours

RAWDON

½ past seven

I had just finished the above when Rugeley's Negroes and the man whom I had sent to advise him to fall back came galloping in to me. The enemy advanced suddenly towards Rugeley's blockhouse, then, halting at some distance, summoned him to surrender. He said he would defend himself to the last and ordered his Negroes and the express to make the best of their way to Camden. I do not think yet that I can with propriety take any other steps than what I have done. If Rugeley's people once begin to fire, they will find themselves safe; and the enemy, knowing the alarm to be spread, will not remain long there. Perhaps I miss an opportunity of making a creditable blow against the enemy, but when I weigh the consequences of any misfortune, I strengthen myself in the resolution of leaving nothing to hazard. I think your Lordship will approve my determination. I will not make excuses for the hurry in which I have written, as it proceeds from desire of satisfying your Lordship upon this affair as soon as possible.

I have the honor to be, my Lord, very faithfully
Your Lordship's most obedient servant

RAWDON

Cornwallis to Rawdon, 2nd December 1780 *83(3): C*

Wynnesborough
December 2nd 1780

Rt Hon Lord Rawdon etc etc etc

My dear Lord

I received your letters of yesterday dated three in the afternoon and seven and ½ past seven in the evening. I own I tremble for Rugely and most heartily wish that he had retired as you desired him. I am very anxious to hear the event, for altho' the intrinsic value of his garrison may not be great, yet their being taken will contribute to damp the spirits of the militia. I approve totally of the part you took. You had much more to lose than to gain, and a great part of your troops are not such as I wish to trust in an affair by night. To have carried a decided superiority against the enemy you must have left Camden very weak.

I enclose to you the copy of your letter of which General Washington complains to Sir Henry Clinton and of which Sir Henry desires to be informed of the authenticity[86]. I shall write to the Commander in Chief in a day or two, not that I know of an opportunity of sending it, but that I wish to have it ready. Poor Money died last night. He is a great loss to me and to his country. The 63rd marched from Shirar's Ferry for Camden this morning.

I am, my dear Lord,
Most faithfully yours

CORNWALLIS

Rawdon to Cornwallis, 2nd December 1780 — *4(271): ALS*

Camden
December 2nd 1780

Earl Cornwallis etc etc etc

My Lord

The party of mounted infantry which I sent out towards Rugeley's has returned. The officer who commanded them reports that he went up to the post and found the last logs of the house burning. I therefore take it for granted that Colonel Rugeley surrendered. His post was the barn which your Lordship may reccollect at the end of the field near the road. It was built of strong logs, loopholes were cut thro' it, a platform erected inside for an upper tier of musquetry, earth thrown up against the outside, and a strong abbatis well pinned down around it. In short, it was a post that ought not to have been touched without cannon. The officer of the New York Voluntiers thinks he discovered the enemy's fires about a mile beyond Rugeley's. I think it most probable that they retired very early this morning. I have spies out and constant patroles. I learn that Marion has taken this opportunity to cross Black River. His force is called three hundred. I must try to move him as soon as I can be assured that my front is clear.

I have the honor to be, my Lord, with great respect and affection
Your Lordship's very faithful servant

RAWDON

---

86 *your letter..*: Rawdon to Rugeley, 1st July, p 18.

[*Subscribed*:]

I have opened this letter again to add that two of my spies are come in. Rugeley surrendered without firing a shot, and the enemy are gone back.

Cornwallis to Rawdon, 3rd December 1780[87] *83(7): C*

Wynnesborough
December 3rd 1780

Rt Hon Lord Rawdon

My dear Lord

Your account of Rugely vexed me altho' it did not surprise me. I think he must be a traitor, or he would have come away when you desired him. I will have an inquiry made into his conduct and would have his Negroes secured, as that will be the only forfeiture we shall probably get from him.

As I mean to write in a day or two to New York, I should be much obliged to your Lordship for a copy of the first letter you sent to Sir Henry[88].

I trust, my dear Lord, that you will have a constant eye to McLeroth, who by his letters requires much looking after. A blow to any British regiment cuts deep. I have not any intelligence that I can depend on from your side of the water. I have people out, but none are returned.

I find that five of the waggons which I sent for the cloathing of the 71st are returning with that of the 33rd, the 71st's cloathing not being arrived at McChord's. I sent 4 others from hence, and McArthur 4 from Shirar's Ferry, and I directed the officer when those waggons arrived at McChord's, if the cloathing was not there, to find out where it was and proceed with the waggons to greet it. I likewise ordered him, if he wanted more waggons, to try to press them in the country and, if he could not, to send an express for assistance to Camden. The 71st is in the greatest want of their necessaries. I should be much obliged to you if you could find out where they are and get them conveyed to the regiment by the most expeditious means, otherwise I am much afraid it will soon be unfit for service.

I am, my dear Lord,
Yours most sincerely

CORNWALLIS

---

87 The first paragraph is published in Ross ed, *Cornwallis Correspondence*, i, 71-2.

88 *the first letter..*: of 29th October (as sent), vol II, p 57.

[*Subscribed*:]

I find that no rice has as yet been sent for the use of the hospital at Camden. You will be so kind as to order Stedman to send some over by the first opportunity. As cattle grew scarce in this neighbourhood, I was obliged some days ago to order up one hundred of those which were sent to the Congarees.

Rawdon to Cornwallis, 3rd December 1780 — *66(25): ALS*

Camden
December 3rd 1780

Earl Cornwallis etc etc etc

My Lord

An emissary upon whom I place much dependence has this morning returned from the neighborhood of Six Mile Run. He is too well known to have ventured into the enemy's camp, but he sent his niece thither, and her report I now transmit to your Lordship.

Some days ago General Sumpter joined that army. He had a wound in his shoulder but it was nothing dangerous. Upon his arrival a council of war was held, in result of which Gates fell back to Charlotte. The daughter of a Colonel Haggins[89] told my informant that her father had imparted to her the design of that movement, which is that Gates is to cross the Catawba at Tuccaseecha Ford.

Sumpter's being alive and the project of crossing the Catawba appear to me very problematic. In other respects this person's intelligence corresponds with what I have before transmitted to your Lordship, both as to the number and the position of the enemy's different corps.

I have been honored with your Lordship's letters of the 1st and of yesterday 9 pm. My account of Rugeley's fate will before this have reached your Lordship. A deserter from Morgan's corps (a Scotchman) asserts that Rugeley surrendered to the light horse alone, Morgan with the infantry being three miles distant. The light horse had not even a carbine to attack the post with. Rugeley knew that I was advertised of the enemy's approach and he had full time to retire in case he did not mean to defend himself. *I am confident he has betrayed his men*. I have thought it likely to happen and have always had my precautions. Morgan etc are returned to Six Mile Run. A feu de joye was fired for the victory.

The intercepted letter is mine. It certainly is not such as I would have wished should be ushered to the public, merely on account of what relates to the Voluntiers of Ireland. It was

89 Lt Colonel William Heaggins of the Mecklenburg revolutionary militia, whose surname has been otherwise spelt as Hagins or Higgins. (Davie, *Revolutionary War Sketches*, 8; Lee, *Memoirs*, 176; Hunter, *Sketches of Western NC*, 102, 105, 112; Wheeler, *Historical Sketches*, ii, 190)

an ostensible letter written to Rugeley after consultation with him upon the point, and I have reason to believe that it was of much service. The expression may be loose, but the intent I need not vindicate to your Lordship, for I will indulge myself in the belief that your Lordship is convinced I have zealously and to the best of my judgement consulted the public good in whatsoever line my station has called on me to act. To the Commander in Chief it will be necessary that I should make a more formal avowal. I shall therefore tomorrow send to your Lordship another letter upon this subject.

I sent Coffin yesterday with forty mounted to support Tynes. Fifty infantry follow this night and a larger detachment is in readiness to march according as information may advise. The death of Money grieves me most sincerely.

I have the honor to be, my Lord, with great respect and affection
Your very faithful servant

RAWDON

[*Subscribed*:]

103 rank and file were taken with Rugeley.

Cornwallis to Rawdon, 4th December 1780 — *83(11): C*

Wynnesborough
December 4th 1780
9 o'clock pm

Rt Hon Lord Rawdon etc etc etc

My dear Lord

I received your letter this morning and agree perfectly with you in opinion about Rugely.

I hear that Washington returned to camp with the prisoners but that a body of the enemy still remained about Wade's Mill. I am not sure whether Morgan is there but have taken all means in my power to know. Nothing under his corps would be worth striking at.

My friend doubts the information about the crossing the Catawba and is positive that Green is either arrived or hourly expected to relieve Gates.

McArthur says that there are some men of the 71st who are reported to be in such a state as to be unfit for service this winter but who by quiet quarters may be rendered usefull by the spring. I have directed an officer to take them to Charlestown and shall desire Balfour to let them garrison Sullivan's Island. The cloathing of the 33rd and rum is arrived. The twelve waggons return to morrow to McChord's in quest of 71st cloathing and any thing else that may offer.

I am informed that a boat is arrived at Friday's Ferry, Congarees, with salt and salt pork, and that 15 waggons are come from Charlestown with goods for Hampton's Store. I have ordered the waggons to be pressed to bring up the greatest part of the salt hither, the remainder of it and the pork to Camden, and the rest of the waggons to be detained for the publick use, as it is likely that we may at this juncture have occasion for them.

Be so kind as to ask McLeroth by the first opportunity whether the 64th Regiment is supplied with necessaries and otherwise prepared for an active winter campaign in case they should be called upon. If that is not the case, I wish him to take the speediest method of getting the men supplied.

One of Ferguson's men is just come in from Sumpter's camp. He positively says that Sumpter was yesterday on this side of the Catawba but that they were in hopes of getting him over the river in a chair in a day or two. He confirms a report I heard this morning that Rutledge is with that corps.

I am, my dear Lord,
Most sincerely yours

CORNWALLIS

Rawdon to Cornwallis, 4th December 1780 — *4(277): ALS*

Camden
December 4th 1780

Earl Cornwallis etc etc etc

My Lord

I have the honor to enclose to your Lordship a letter which I have this day received from Lt Colonel Balfour respecting McLeroth. I likewise send a letter from McLeroth himself.[90] The 64th Regiment is not wanted here at present, nor do I imagine that your Lordship would wish it to join you. I therefore shall leave McLeroth where he is till I have your Lordship's directions. I think you would wish the recruits and convalescents to join you from Neilson's, but as the time of their arrival there is not certain, no time will probably be lost by my waiting to learn your Lordship's desire. I do not think McLeroth in any danger of being attacked, but I believe I must send Coffin with his light company to support him and for the present remain with him. It was after that party of 200 which McLeroth mentions that I sent the detachment from hence. Coffin joined Tynes (who had seventy men) in the night and, marching immediately, reached the rebel camp by day break. The enemy had received notice of the movement and had gone off with great precipitation about half an hour before. Coffin pursued them smartly for several miles but could not come up with them. He then fortified

---

[90] Neither Balfour's letter nor McLeroth's is extant. Balfour's was addressed to Rawdon (see Cornwallis to Balfour, 5th December, p 99).

Tynes's house for him and left him in perfect security. I have been honored with your Lordship's letter of yesterday and shall fulfill all the commands contained in it. The cloathing of the 7th Regiment is arrived at McChord's and shall be transported to Wynnesborough with all dispatch.

I have been informed to day of a body of rebels near Rugeley's. It does not tally with my intelligence from other quarters and I believe at most it can only be a scout of Waxhaw plunderers. My wish to ascertain this point has delayed my writing this morning. I will not detain Lieutenant L'Estrange[91] lest he should not get to Wynnesborough tonight, but I will send an officer with the copy of the first letter to Sir Henry this night.

I have the honor to be with great respect
Your Lordship's affectionate servant

RAWDON

[*Subscribed*:]

I enclose poor André's trial lest your Lordship should not have seen it, and will beg to have it again when you have done with it.

Cornwallis to Rawdon, 5th December 1780 — *83(19): C*

Wynnesborough
December 5th 1780

Rt Hon Lord Rawdon etc etc etc

My dear Lord

I by no means wish McLeroth to join me at present, nor do I conceive that you want him at Camden, so that he will for the present continue to secure the communication and to correspond equally with your Lordship, in which I should hope by degrees you will bring him to be a little more minute and particular. I think Major Irwin and his militia must have been very hard hearted.

I think I may possibly take the 64th with me hereafter, as I do not consider them just the properest corps for the service they are now employed in but think of substituting Watson's light infantry, who cannot easily be employed as such with the army without a perpetual interference with Tarleton in command. I find there are six puncheons of rum and 170 bushels of salt. I have ordered the rum and 100 bushels of the salt to be brought hither, the remainder of the salt and pork to Camden. You will allow for the six puncheons in your supplies.

---

91 Commissioned an ensign in the 54th Regiment on 26th October 1775, Thomas L'Estrange had been promoted to lieutenant in the 7th Regiment (Royal Fusiliers) on 18th August 1778. (*Army Lists*)

The recruits I should wish to join their regiments as soon as they conveniently can, but with good cloaths on their back and a good supply of necessaries. I am a little apprehensive that those at Nelson's Ferry may have been sent too hastily from Charlestown. I had received a copy of the trial and therefore return yours with thanks.

A person who returned to me this morning assured me that there was no enemy in the neighbourhood of Rugely's. It is not, however, first rate intelligence. Sumpter's corps is on Allison's Creek at one Watson's – not numerous. Rutledge was over to visit Sumpter but had repassed the Catawbaw. I forgot I told you this before.

Yours ever most sincerely

CORNWALLIS

Rawdon to Cornwallis, 5th December 1780 — *4(281): ALS*

Camden
December 5th 1780
7 o'clock pm

Earl Cornwallis etc etc etc

My Lord

I have the honor to enclose to your Lordship some reccommendations for commissions in the North Carolina Regiment which Lt Colonel Hamilton gave in to me[92].

The 63rd Regiment is arrived and makes me feel my force very formidable. They delivered to me the twenty horses intended for the New York Voluntiers, but unfortunately not one of the steeds or one of the saddles is fit for any kind of service. It is necessary for me to mention this that your Lordship may not be surprized at our not being forwarder in mounting the New York Voluntiers. England has been indefatigable. He has bought up ninety horses and we have procured none by any other channel.

Small parties of the enemy are committing every barbarity around us. Two brothers of Major Harrison's, who were ill of the small pox, lay at a house about eight miles in our rear. Last night a scouting party of rebels burst into the house, shot both the sick men in their beds, tho' they were incapable of making the least defence, and afterwards murdered the old man of the house in the same manner. This day an officer whom I had sent to patrole in my front reported to me that, having come up to a house which a party of rebels had just quitted, he found it stripped of every thing that could be carried off. Such articles as could not be taken away were destroyed, the woman was left standing in her shift, even her stockings and shoes having been pulled off of her, and her four children were stripped stark naked. These are the enemies who talk of the laws and usages of war.

---

[92] *some reccommendations..*: omitted. They were enclosed with Rawdon's letter of the 6th but are not extant.

McLeod has just arrived from Charlestown. He has no letters, no message, no news. He therefore proposes halting tomorrow to settle every thing here and will proceed to Wynnesborough early on the 7th.

The furlough men of the South Carolina Regiment come in daily, so that I shall be able to settle every thing about that corps, without speaking harshly.

A Captain Gassaway[93] of the Maryland line has returned hither, his leave of absence being expired. He says there were some proposals of exchange between him and Captain De Peyster and requests me to remind your Lordship of it.

I have been honored with your Lordship's letter of last night. Stedman tells me that Hampton has gone off to the enemy, and I have sent him orders to secure the goods till he has your Lordship's further directions.

I have the honor to be, my Lord, with great respect and affection
Your very faithful servant

RAWDON

Cornwallis to Rawdon, 7th December 1780 *83(27): C*

Wynnesborough
December 7th 1780

Rt Hon Lord Rawdon etc etc etc

My dear Lord

I received very late last night yours of the 5th. No recommendations for the North Carolina Regiment were inclosed. The accounts of the cruelty of those rascals is really shocking, and if it is capable of aggravation, their impudent accusation of us makes it the more provoking. Lieutenant Woods[94] of the 7th Regiment having set out this morning to go by the shortest road to Charlestown, I sent by him my letters for New York[95], not that it's now of any vessel going, but I wished to have them ready as the General would not be pleased if any man of war went without his hearing from me.

---

93 John Gassaway (?-1819) was a captain in the 1st Maryland Continental Regiment, where he had served as an officer since December 1776. Captured at the Battle of Camden, he would not be exchanged but be paroled till the close of the war. In later life he resided in Anne Arundel County, Maryland, and was granted a revolutionary pension. (Heitman, *Historical Register*, 243-4)

94 Thomas Wood was adjutant of the 7th Regiment (Royal Fusiliers). (WO 65/164(6) (National Archives, Kew))

95 *my letters for New York*: Cornwallis to Clinton, 3rd and 4th December, pp 24 and 27.

From Tarleton's account of the horses of the 63rd I did not expect they would be of much use to you, but I wonder those from 96 are not arrived, as Colonel Cruger informed they had set out. Bad as the horses were of the 63rd Regiment, some account should if possible be kept of them as they belonged to Tynes's militia.

I have heard nothing from Captain De Peister about his exchange with Captain Gassaway.

I grow very impatient for the arrival of Leslie.

Yours, my dear Lord, very sincerely

CORNWALLIS

PS

I have no material or certain intelligence. The report is that the Continentals are at Charlottetown and that Green is arrived.

Rawdon to Cornwallis, 6th December 1780 — *4(289): ALS*

Camden
December 6th 1780
8 at night

Earl Cornwallis etc etc etc

My Lord

I have many excuses to make to your Lordship for omitting to enclose in my letter of yesterday evening a paper to which I referred. I mean the reccommendations from Lt Colonel Hamilton, which I now transmit[96].

My letter was prevented from going last night by the attempt of a party of rebels to carry off Colonel Cary. Lieutenant McLeod will inform your Lordship that the enemy were disappointed and were very near suffering for their boldness. I hear that Morgan and Washington are near Wade's Mills. Of Smallwood I have no recent intelligence.

I find that Rugeley did not receive the letter which I wrote to him upon getting information of Morgan's march, but I had before particularly reccommended to Rugeley to fall back to me whensoever he should hear that any considerable body was moving towards him. The neighbors seem to suspect collusion between Rugeley and the enemy. McLeroth is at Jacks Creek.

---

[96] *the reccommendations..*: see p 196, note 92.

I have the honor to be, my Lord, with great respect
Your most obedient and very faithful servant

RAWDON

[*Subscribed*:]

I have had the honor to receive your Lordship's letter of yesterday.

Cornwallis to Rawdon, 7th December 1780 — *83(29): C*

Wynnesborough
December 7th 1780

Rt Hon Lord Rawdon etc etc etc

My dear Lord

I received your letters[97] by McLeod. I enclose your letter to Sir Henry Clinton with a line from myself to him. You will please to fasten the seal and send it on to Major Benson to go with the dispatches[98] which I sent to day by Mr Wood. I enclose likewise Washington's letter to Sir Henry[99] and his answer[100], which you will please to return to me. Now, my dear Lord, the reason of my sending the letter to Sir Henry under a flying seal is that I wish and hope that upon duly considering the matter you will leave out the 11th line beginning at *and* and concluding with *measure*. I have got Hamilton's recommendations.

I was informed that Washington and Morgan were at Wade's Mill, but, on examining my informant more closely, he seemed to think that Washington was not there and even doubted as to Morgan, but said there was a party there, but promised me farther information. This was on the 4th. I have heard nothing since. I should have thought it worth some inconvenience and fatigue to the Legion, who are much worn down, to have made a stroke at the *two gentlemen*, but it would not answer to have merely a chance of catching some militia.

As Mr Lancaster, the printer, is rather idle, it might answer to make him publish some copies of Arnold's Address to the People of America and his proclamation relative to his raising his corps etc.

---

97 *your letters*: one of them, dated 5th December, is no longer extant in the Cornwallis Papers but was published in Ross ed, *Cornwallis Correspondence*, i, 501-2. It was addressed to Cornwallis for the benefit of Clinton, not directly to Clinton as Cornwallis loosely states. The subject of the letter was Rawdon's of 1st July to Rugeley (p 18), on which Clinton had sought advice (p 14).

98 *the dispatches*: see p 197, note 95.

99 *Washington's letter to Sir Henry*: of 16th October, p 17.

100 *his answer*: of 23rd October, p 19.

I am, my dear Lord,
Most sincerely yours

CORNWALLIS

Rawdon to Cornwallis, 8th December 1780 *4(291): ALS*

Camden
December 8th 1780

Earl Cornwallis etc etc etc

My Lord

I have had the honor to receive both your Lordship's letters of yesterday. I return two of the enclosures with many thanks. The others I have forwarded to Charlestown.

Colonel Tynes arrived here this morning exceedingly frightened. His militia, upon some report of Harrington's approach, excepting twenty, deserted his new fort. He thought the twenty who remained too small a garrison and therefore deserted them. He says that he is convinced he can do nothing with the militia and on that account begged leave to resign his command. I accepted his resignation. That line of interest has failed us; we must now try another. I have the honor to enclose a plan for a kind of fencible regiment, which Coffin and Moore are of opinion will take effect. I mean that Richbourg, Singleton[101] and all that connection should be the captains, inducing them to regard the business as opposition to a gang of freebooters, and not shewing it to them in the light of a decided step in the great line of policy. Coffin and Moore set out tomorrow to carry the scheme into execution. Your Lordship must consider the project rather as a measure of resource than of choice.

I have had a letter from McLeroth dated yesterday. He knows not of any enemy in force near him.

Mrs Clay[102] of this town says that she had your Lordship's permission to meet her

---

101 Of the Singletons who were not presently in arms, Rawdon is probably referring to Robert (1734-1820) or James, both of whom were brothers of Matthew (see vol II, p 211, note 5). (Information from George Lightfoot Singleton, 30th July 1999)

102 Ann Clay was the wife of Joseph Clay (1741-1804), a native of Yorkshire, who at the age of nineteen had settled in Savannah and gone on to prosper as a merchant and planter. A committed revolutionary, he had served in 1775 on a council of safety and in the Georgia Provincial Congress besides taking part in the raid on the Crown powder magazine at Savannah. In August 1777 he was appointed a deputy paymaster general to the southern Continental forces, a post which he still held, presumably in the vicinity of Charlotte. Ann, for her part, was a refugee from Georgia who had taken up residence in Camden before the battle of 16th August. She at once admitted to her house (already occupied by two ladies and a number of children) some 20 or 30 wounded revolutionary officers, including Thomas Pinckney and Charles Porterfield, 'to whom... this amiable lady behaved like a mother, sharing with us every comfort they had and depriving herself for our accommodation'. She would outlive her husband, who in later life held several important offices, including State Treasurer, Judge of the Inferior Court, and one of

husband at Rugeley's and afterwards to return hither. I think she is ill situated at this post, for she may easily be the means of keeping up illicit correspondence, especially after the opportunity of laying the plan with her husband.

The horses which were brought to me by the 63rd have not been turned adrift but were sent to Congarees by Major England that they might have every chance of recovery. England has discharged several certificates of horses taken for the 63rd Regiment from friends, but it runs to a great amount and he does not know whether he ought to proceed.

Lieutenant Vallancey[103] of my regiment is returned from Charlestown perfectly recovered. He is very skillful as an engineer in case your Lordship should want any body in that line.

I forward a letter[104] with two English newspapers from Lt Colonel Balfour, and have the honor to be with great respect

Your Lordship's very obedient and very affectionate servant

RAWDON

[*Subscribed*:]

I must add this half sheet to thank you, my dear Lord, for your goodness in pointing out to me a passage in my defence which I feel was exceptionable. I have erased it and have forwarded the letter to Charlestown.

The expence of the Santee corps would be high and we should have little or no service from them, but I thought it was adviseable to make such appointments for officers as might make it an object for persons of influence to accept them. If by retaining the leaders of the people we can once establish the tranquillity of the district, the expence may be either partially reduced or totally stricken off, for the corps must naturally be diminished in proportion with the difficulties which give birth to it. Perhaps I may err in my politics, but I see no hope of service from the *militia*, and if they do not act with us, they will be forced to take part against us. Nothing will be finally decided till I have the honor of hearing from

---

the first trustees of the state college which became the University of Georgia. Both are buried in Colonial Park Cemetery, Savannah. (Information from the Georgia Historical Commission; Cashin Jr and Robertson, *Augusta, passim*; Thomas Pinckney to Judge James, 31st July 1822 (Collections of the South Caroliniana Library, Columbia SC))

103 Having been commissioned an ensign in the 16th Regiment, Charles Vallancey had transferred to the Provincial line in 1778, entering the newly forming Volunteers of Ireland as a lieutenant. He survived the war and was a captain in the regiment when it was taken on to the British establishment in August 1782. Of Huguenot descent, he was no doubt a son or close relation of Charles Vallancey, the chief engineer in Ireland, an inference to be drawn not only from his sharing the same name but also from his having engineering skills and serving in a regiment with Irish connections. (*Army Lists*; Raymond, 'British American Corps'; Monica Nevin, 'General Charles Vallancey, 1725-1812', *Journal of the Royal Society of Antiquaries of Ireland*, cxxiii (1993), 19-58)

104 *a letter*: Balfour to Cornwallis, 4th December, p 104.

your Lordship.

R

Enclosure
Plan for a kind of fencible corps *4(294): D*

Plan for a Corps of Voluntiers to serve under Isham Moore Esq

The men shall engage to serve (submitting themselves to military regulation) for the term of six months. The corps is destined for the protection of their own district and the men shall not be obliged upon any occasion, without their own consent, to pass either the Pedee or the Santee Rivers.

Each private shall be allowed six pence sterling per day; each corporal eight pence; each serjeant a shilling. A dollar bounty shall be given to each man upon his engagement, and a pair of stockings, a pair of shoes and a blanket or rug shall be issued to each.

A captain and a lieutenant shall be allowed for every thirty men. The former shall receive a dollar per day, the latter half a dollar. An adjutant and quarter master shall likewise be allowed at three shillings sterling each per day.

The commandant of the corps, with the rank of major, shall receive ten shillings sterling per day.

The pay shall be issued every two months.

Establishment of a Company

Captain	Lieutenant	Serjeants	Corporals	Privates	Daily Pay
1	1	2	2	26	£1. 3*s*. 1*d*[105]

---

105 On this basis a dollar was equivalent to 4*s*. 6*d* sterling.

Cornwallis to Rawdon, 9th December 1780 — *83(34): C*

Wynnesborough
December 9th 1780

Rt Hon Lord Rawdon etc etc etc

My dear Lord

Your letter enclosing Balfour's etc arrived this morning. I have sent him an answer[106], which I hope will meet him on the road. I am sorry to hear so bad an account of Tynes and his militia. We must try Isham Moore, for, although I much doubt his success and have often had some doubts of himself, yet I would try every possible means of raising a force in this country. If any thing could succeed as a beginning, very good consequences might ensue. If I consented to Mrs Clay's meeting her husband at Rugely's and returning to Camden, it must have been when things were very differently circumstanced, so that I now submit that affair entirely to your Lordship's determination.

I understood that the horses of the 63rd were so bad as to be mostly unserviceable. I therefore thought they had better be returned to the owners than be paid for by Government. I have no doubt that many of the claims will be fraudulent, that is, that those who have not *actually* been enemies will, as good friends, claim the horses of those that have. I should be sorry that a heavy charge should be brought against Government for horses of little or no value. As you can judge better of the worth of the horses, and of the claimants, I shall beg of you to settle this business in the most œconomical manner to the *publick* (I do not mean by that word the Department) without doing any act of injustice or oppression to our friends.

I have no good intelligence, but my reports say that the Continentals are falling back. The most horrid accounts come in daily of the cruelties committed about the Waxhaws. I shall send duplicates of my letters to New York.

Yours, my dear Lord, most sincerely

CORNWALLIS

Rawdon to Cornwallis, 9th December 1780 — *4(298): ALS*

Camden
December 9th 1780

Earl Cornwallis etc etc etc

My Lord

I have dispatched Coffin this morning with seventy men to communicate with McLeroth and to settle matters on the High Hills. I have made an arrangement which satisfies all

[106] *an answer*: of 9th December, p 105.

parties, and it only wants your Lordship's approbation. Till I know your sentiment, nothing is decided. I propose that Isham Moore should be colonel of militia for the district, Tynes lt colonel, and that Bromfield should continue major. They will each occasionally command the corps which is to be raised, but pay is to be allowed for one only, and as they are to take field alternately, the person actually on service is to receive the allowance. If all three turn out, they are to divide the ten shillings. I must beg your Lordship to observe that I feel the expence of this plan to be too great for any long continuance, but I think this coalition of parties will reduce matters to such a state as will enable me very soon to abridge the extent of the scheme.

One Anderson, master of a New York privateer who was taken by the rebels, has made his escape hither from Richmond jail. He says that a body of troops passed thro' Salisbury towards Charlotteburg on Tuesday last. They were called 1,300, all militia. Many of them were the prisoners taken under Ferguson and elsewhere, who are now forced to bear arms on the rebel side. He heard of no Continentals in the whole country between Richmond and the Yadkin. I am told that Smallwood is at Charlotteburg, but for some days past my intelligence has failed me much.

I have the honor to be, my Lord, with great affection
Your very faithful and respectful servant

RAWDON

Cornwallis to Rawdon, 11th December 1780 — *83(38): C*

Wynnesborough
December 11th 1780
9 o'clock pm

My dear Lord

I did not write yesterday, having nothing material to say, and I deferred it to the last this evening in hopes of hearing from Charlestown. I agree to any mode that you think most likely to succeed in the District of the High Hills.

My intelligence has of late been as bad as possible. The cruelties that have been exercised by the scouting parties of the rebels have so terrified all my people that I can get nobody to venture far enough out to ascertain any thing.

The 7th Regiment have a number of convalescents at Camden they wish to get up to some house in the neighbourhood of camp — as many of them as are likely to become serviceable soon — that they may equip them properly. I have directed the officer of that regiment to make application to your Lordship about it.

The cloathing of the 71st is arrived and every regiment here has received its winter appointments, so that we want only to hear of [Leslie].

I received England's letter[107] and am very sensible of his great attention and exertions for the good of the service. His account of the New York Volunteers gives me great satisfaction. I am convinced that a good force mounted is absolutely necessary for you.

I am, my dear Lord,
Most sincerely yours

CORNWALLIS

Rawdon to Cornwallis, 10th December 1780 — *4(308): ALS*

Camden
December 10th 1780

Earl Cornwallis etc etc etc

My Lord

I have the honor to forward to your Lordship a letter from General Phillips and another from General Smallwood[108] which were brought to the out post this morning by a flag of truce. They were accompanied by a certificate of Brigadier General Du Portail's exchange for General Gall[109] of the Brunswic troops and there was a passport annexed, of which I transmit a copy. I shall wait your Lordship's orders before I send the passport to Monsieur Du Portail, as it may be necessary to particularize his route.

Two of my emissaries came in today. They report that Smallwood, Morgan and Washington were yesterday at Six Mile Run. The Continentals under Green were at Charlotteburg. The Waxhaws are full of small plundering parties. As soon as I get the swords for Coffin, I shall hope to punish Kembill's gang for the horrid murders which they daily commit.

Carey makes a proposal for raising a kind of district troop of light horse. I have rejected the plan on the footing which was proposed by him, but if he comes down to decent terms, I shall lay it before your Lordship.

I have the honor to be, my Lord, with great respect and affection
Your very faithful servant

RAWDON

---

107 *England's letter*: see p 253.

108 For Smallwood's letter of the 8th, see p 405.

109 Colonel of the Hesse-Hanau Regiment Erb-Prinz, Wilhelm Rudolph von Gall had served as a brigadier general during Burgoyne's offensive. He was among the troops who surrendered at Saratoga on 19th October 1777.

[*Subscribed*:]

The tenor of Du Portail's exchange is such that he cannot serve till he gets to Philadelphia.

Enclosure (1)
Phillips to Cornwallis, 4th November 1780 — *4(23): ALS*

November 4th 1780

His Excellency Lt General the Earl Cornwallis

My Lord

I writ some time since to your Lordship respecting an American prisoner of war, Colonel Ball of Virginia. I repeat the request made in that letter that you would have the goodness, my Lord, to permit Colonel Ball going to Virginia or elsewhere upon his parole. I shall be happy by this instance to return civilities I received from that gentleman during a residence I made at Frederickburgh while with the troops of Convention.

I apprehend this letter will reach your Lordship by the same express which will carry the account of Mr Du Portail's release and permission to pass to Philadelphia.

I have the honour to be, my Lord, with great respect
Your Lordship's most obedient humble servant

W PHILLIPS

Enclosure (2)
Passport, 2nd November 1780 — *4(307): C*

Passport annexed to the Certificate of Brigadier General Du Portail's Exchange

November 2nd 1780

Approved, and His Excellency Lt General the Earl Cornwallis or officer commanding at Charlestown will please to permit Brigadier General Du Portail to pass to Philadelphia by the most convenient rout consistent with the situation of the King's forces in South and North Carolina.

H CLINTON

Cornwallis to Rawdon, 12th December 1780 *83(40): C*

Wynnesborough
December 12th 1780

Rt Hon Lord Rawdon etc etc etc

My dear Lord

I received yours last night enclosing General Phillips's and Smallwood's letters etc. I have sent passports for Du Portail and Colonel Ball as I think it uncertain whether the Commandant will be at Charlestown.[110]

The little intelligence which I have been able to procure agrees pretty much with yours, but I have the utmost difficulty in forcing any body over the Catawba.

I have no opinion of Carey's raising any good cavalry. However loyal he may be, he certainly is not much of a soldier. I should think the best way will be to put the cavalry raised for the 96 District under Dunlap, and that for Camden under Coffin. Cavalry is not only a very expensive arm but requires skill and vigilance in the management. I should expect to hear that Carey and his troop were surprised and his horses and appointments all taken the first week.

The easterly wind to day gives me some hopes, but I am really very uneasy about Leslie.

I am, my dear Lord,
Very sincerely yours

CORNWALLIS

Rawdon to Cornwallis, 12th December 1780 *4(314): ALS*

Camden
December 12th 1780
7 morning

Earl Cornwallis etc etc etc

My Lord

Not having had any thing to communicate to your Lordship yesterday from this post, I waited in hopes that the arrival of some express from Charlestown or Santee would enable me to transmit some news. Nothing, however, came in excepting three letters from McLeroth, and unfortunately they did not furnish matter for a single period.

---

[110] See Cornwallis to Balfour, 12th December, p 107.

As Mr McDonald of the Legion goes to your camp this morning, I will not omit saying by him that all is well at this post.

Ensign Cunningham[111] of the Voluntiers of Ireland has by repeated misconduct made the other subalterns refuse to do duty with him. I endeavored to persuade him to quit the regiment quietly, but as he refuses to do it, I must sollicit your Lordship that he may be brought before a court martial. The subalterns have given in their charge against him: 'for ungentlemanlike and unsoldierlike behavior'.

I have the honor to be, my Lord, with great respect
Your most affectionate humble servant

RAWDON

[*Subscribed*:]

I have the honor to forward some letters from town which have this instant arrived.

Cornwallis to Rawdon, 13th December 1780 — *83(42): C*

Wynnesborough
December 13th 1780

Rt Hon Lord Rawdon etc etc etc

My dear Lord

I received your letter enclosing one from Balfour[112]. I send you the extracts that relate to the arrival of Leslie.

Balfour had not received my letter of the 5th[113], in which I informed him of my intention of taking the 64th with the army and leaving Watson's light infantry under your orders on the communication.

I do not see the use of having those recruits at Nelson's and should think it much better for them and for the service that they should be with their respective regiments a few days before they march. I do not apprehend that you will want McLeroth at Camden. The recruits therefore will not be required to fill the place of the 64th. McLeroth should either order his

---

[111] John Cunningham had been commissioned an ensign in the Volunteers of Ireland in December 1778. He had ceased to be an officer in the regiment when it was taken on to the British establishment in August 1782. (Raymond, 'British American Corps'; *Army Lists*)

[112] *one from Balfour*: of 9th December, p 108.

[113] *my letter of the 5th*: see p 99.

necessaries to Nelson's Ferry or to meet him at Camden when Watson's corps arrives to replace him, as you and he may think most convenient.

I know that I do not make you a great present in the person of Colonel Watson, but as his corps is called light infantry and must of course act as light troops, there would be a constant difficulty of command between him and Tarleton. Now your Lordship can make him obey you, his men must be as good as those of the 64th, and himself as good a partisan and as intelligent a correspondent as McLeroth.[114] I beg, my dear Lord, that, notwithstanding these ideas of mine about the recruits, 64th etc, that you will give any directions and make any alterations in the disposition that you may think proper. 48 hours makes such an alteration in affairs here that it is impossible to give orders at a distance, and I am sure I need not repeat assurances of the confidence I have in you. If therefore you think you can make any use of the recruits, I beg you will do it. I will send an order for a general court martial on Ensign Cunningham, and am, my dear Lord, with very sincere regard

Most faithfully yours

CORNWALLIS

[*Subscribed*:]

The detachment of the 16th serving with the guns are quite naked. McLeod means to get those from Camden and to send to you those of your regiment. If you can procure any cloaths for them for an order to receive theirs at Charlestown, or think of any means of covering those poor people, it will be great charity.

Rawdon to Cornwallis, 13th December 1780 — *4(321): ALS*

Camden
December 13th 1780
10 morning

Earl Cornwallis etc etc etc

My Lord

I have had the honor to receive your Lordship's letter of yesterday, as likewise that dated on the 11th.

I have had a report this morning from Coffin, who has been obliged to fall back to Swift Creek. He tells me that Marion with a considerable force (reported 500) was at Singleton's Mills yesterday. Information was given to Coffin that he was to be attacked in the night, and a large body of the enemy approached very near to him in the evening. Under these

114 The reference to Watson and McLeroth is ironic. The implication is that Rawdon will be no worse off with the former than with the latter.

circumstances Coffin judged it best to retire. I do not conceive that Marion's force can amount to what is above represented. If it does, still I should consider McLeroth (who has 270 rank and file) more than equal to them. However, we must endeavor to remove the enemy from that station immediately. My intelligence of the enemy in front is not sufficiently good for me to venture drawing from this post the number of troops that would be necessary to surround Marion and force him to action. It is likewise difficult for me to prescribe any share in a combined movement to McLeroth because, before the plan could be put in execution, circumstances might intervene to prevent the performance of my part. I have therefore thought it best to augment Coffin's detachment to 130 and have ordered him to make a movement as if he meant to get between Marion and Black River. He is not to risque himself, but if Marion retires hastily or in separate parties, he may make some little stroke. In this, however, we are much embarrassed from want of swords. Isham Moore's house was plundered and much mischief of that nature was done in the settlement. I did not hear of any attempt being made upon the boats, but I much fear something of that nature will have happened. Your Lordship shall hear from me the moment I learn any thing further upon this subject.

I have the honor to be, my Lord, with great respect and affection
Your very faithful servant

RAWDON

Rawdon to Cornwallis, 13th December 1780 — *4(323): ALS*

Camden
December 13th 1780
8 at night

Earl Cornwallis etc etc etc

My Lord

I have the honor to enclose a letter which I have just received from Captain Coffin. It is so hastily written that it is necessary I should explain it from my knowledge of the circumstances. The reinforcement is one sent from this to Coffin, which was close to him when his express came away, so that before this he has marched with an hundred and forty mounted. I understand that McLeroth sent to Coffin for reinforcement. In that case he had either beaten off the enemy or was only skirmishing with them, otherwise his messenger could not have gotten thro'. If he has repulsed Marion, Coffin has orders to cross upon the enemy's route to Black River and retard their march, sending notice to McLeroth that he may pursue. If the enemy still hang about McLeroth, Coffin's approach must move them, and with his assistance McLeroth may press Marion to the utmost. I rather believe that the enemy have been recconnoitring McLeroth in the strong post at Singleton's and that there probably has been firing at his piquets or from his cannon, but I do not think the report bears the semblance of having arisen from any serious attack. Your Lordship shall have immediate information as soon as I learn any thing further.

I have the honor to be, my Lord, with sincere affection and respect
Your very faithful servant

RAWDON

Enclosure
Coffin to Rawdon, 13th December 1780 — *4(319): ALS*

English Plantation
December 13th 1780

My Lord

I have just received an express informing me Major McLeroth was attack'd this day by seven hundred rebels. The attack began at twelve o'clock at Singleton's Mills. He has sent for a reinforcement, which I understand is at hand, and shall proceed with all expedition.

I am, my Lord,
Your Lordship's obedient and most humble servant

J COFFIN
Captain, New York Volunteers

Rawdon to Cornwallis, 14th December 1780 — *4(327): ALS*

Camden
December 14th 1780
9 at night

Earl Cornwallis etc etc etc

My Lord

I have with much impatience waited till this hour in expectation of news from the High Hills. Not even a rumor, however, has yet reached us. I think that circumstance has rather a favorable appearance. Had any thing happened amiss, it is most probable that I should have had earlier notice of it, and the delay of a report from that quarter may admit supposition that Coffin and McLeroth are too much occupied in following the enemy to have leisure for transmitting intelligence.

I am happy that I have some pleasing information to communicate. Kinloch came here about an hour ago, having left Charlestown on Monday last. He says that two ships, both from England in six weeks, arrived just as he was quitting the town. They both ran aground on the bar and sent up a boat for assistance. From the persons in the boat Kinloch learned that Ross arrived safe in England after a passage of thirty three days, and one of these ships has brought out dispatches in answer to those which Ross carried. Kinloch, finding that it would be some time before the dispatches could be brought up to town, proceeded on his journey. The people to whom he spoke were very stupid and could not tell him any news.

Two hundred and fifty recruits and convalescents are on their way from town and will be at Neilson's on Saturday. They shall there receive directions from me according to the news that I may hear from McLeroth. I understand that the recruits of the 33rd are in that party.

I have been honored with your Lordship's letter of yesterday. As to a certain gentleman, he certainly shall neither disgrace nor injure the service with impunity, and as (from former circumstances) I think he will suspect the ground he stands on, the station destined for him appears on every account the most eligible. I have been fortunate in anticipating your Lordship's wish about procuring cloathing for the 16th additional gunners. I sent their serjeant to town some time ago to get it and expect him daily. Should he not succeed, I can manage to supply the whole from hence. I keep an express ready to dispatch with the first news from McLeroth.

I have the honor to be, my Lord, with sincere affection and respect
Your most obedient and faithful servant

RAWDON

Cornwallis to Rawdon, 16th December 1780 — *83(50): C*

Wynnesborough
December 16th 1780
9 o'clock pm

Rt Hon Lord Rawdon etc etc etc

My dear Lord

I own your letter of the 13th made me a little uneasy about McLeroth, but I was satisfied by that of the 14th that nothing material could have happened. The return of Coffin was certainly unlucky, but I should think the hearing of the arrival of a considerable detachment at Nelson's Ferry will alone oblige Marion to decamp. Captain Kerr of my regiment, who commands the recruits, served in Germany and is a carefull and attentive officer, but Captain Ingram[115], who is with him and whose opinion will have weight, has served the whole war with the light infantry and is very intelligent. Our expresses are very slow, taking 20 hours to perform 40 miles. Fixing 2 or 3 horses at Dukes's with a person to take care of them would expedite the business very much and sometimes save a few anxious hours. The wind

[115] James Ingram had recently been serving as a captain lieutenant in the 70th Regiment, having been promoted there from the 33rd on 25th October 1779. He had entered the 33rd as an ensign on 22nd February 1768, rising to lieutenant in the regiment on 10th June 1771. On the recommendation of Cornwallis he was now rejoining the 33rd to fill a captaincy vacated by the death of Richard Cotton. (*Army Lists*; *The Cornwallis Papers*)

has been so long fair that I cannot doubt the arrival of Leslie and expect every instant to hear of it. No news of Kinloch to day. Every thing in our front remains very quiet and I have heard nothing since the 9th from Ninety Six.

I am, my dear Lord,
Your most faithfull and affectionate servant

CORNWALLIS

[*Subscribed*:]

You will be kind enough to allow a flag of truce to Mrs Murchison[116], a poor distressed widow, to go to North Carolina. About twenty prisoners marched from hence to day for Camden, most of them taken by Tarleton. I believe it will be best to send them by the first favorable opportunity to Charlestown.

Rawdon to Cornwallis, 15th December 1780 — *4(337): ALS*

Camden
December 16th 1780[117]
8 at night

Earl Cornwallis etc etc etc

My Lord

I began to be uneasy at not hearing from McLeroth, when to my great surprize I saw him enter the room. The matter has been nearly as I suspected. Marion has been recconnoitring him and there was some loose firing at his out-posts. Captain George Kelly[118] and two privates of the 64th were wounded. The rebels lost ten or a dozen. Coffin joined McLeroth near Singleton's but no pursuit of the enemy was undertaken in consequence of this junction. McLeroth seems to think that there would have been no chance of getting up to them. The

116 Janet Murchison's elderly husband is believed to have died in jail in North Carolina, having been consigned there by the revolutionaries for his loyalism. Janet would receive some relief. After the war, when she may have settled near her son Duncan in Lancaster, Ontario, the Crown awarded her compensation of £193-16*s*-0*d* for her losses in North Carolina together with a small pension, which she continued to receive till her death around 1820. (The Hon Judge John Matheson, 'Murchison, Duncan Uel' (Internet, 30th December 2005); DeMond, *Loyalists in NC*, 255, 257-261)

117 According to an annotation, the letter was written on the 15th.

118 Having entered the 44th Regiment as an ensign on 3rd July 1772, George Kelly was promoted to lieutenant there on 10th February 1776 before transferring as a captain to the 64th with effect from 5th October 1778. By 21st December he would be dead of his wound. (*Army Lists*; *The Cornwallis Papers*)

64th under Captain Dennis Kelly[119] are posted at Waring's on the High Hills. Coffin's detachment has returned hither, which I could have wished otherwise. Marion (whose force is about 600) lies between Neilson's Ferry and the 64th, sixteen miles from the latter. I must drive Marion out of that country but I cannot yet say what steps I shall take to effect it. One good consequence has arisen from this scramble: Moore and the Richbourgs have taken so decided a part, and have in consequence been so plundered by the enemy, that they are now very much in earnest for us, and I see the prospect of much service from that line of connection. I expect swords tomorrow for my cavalry, and then we shall take the field again.

Smallwood and Morgan were at Six Mile Run yesterday, Greene at Charlotteburg.

I have the honor to enclose a letter from Balfour[120], to the contents of which I have attended. I have some English letters for your Lordship but I keep them to go very early tomorrow morning by Captain Kinloch. I send an English paper which Balfour transmitted for your Lordship. I have written this in great haste that I might remove any anxiety about McLeroth as soon as possible.

I have the honor to be very truly
Your Lordship's very obedient and affectionate humble servant

RAWDON

Rawdon to Cornwallis, 16th December 1780 — *4(343): ALS*

Camden
December 17th 1780[121]
One o'clock afternoon

Earl Cornwallis etc etc etc

My Lord

I have the honor to forward a letter from Lt Colonel Balfour[122] which I have this moment received. It was accompanied by one to me giving me notice of General Lesslie's safe arrival, with all his army in perfect health. Some dispatches from the Commander in Chief for your Lordship were sent to me at the same time, but as I perceive that they are only

---

119 Dennis Kelly had spent his entire service in the 64th Regiment. Commissioned an ensign on 28th May 1774, he was promoted to lieutenant on 3rd May 1776 and to captain on 13th April 1778. He would remain with the regiment in South Carolina, taking part in the Battle of Eutaw Springs in September 1781 and commanding the ambush near Combahee Ford in August 1782 in which John Laurens was killed. (*Army Lists*)

120 *a letter..*: of 11th December, p 111.

121 The letter was written on the 16th according to Rawdon's of the 19th. See p 218.

122 *a letter..*: of 13th or 14th December, p 112.

copies of those which your Lordship has already received and that therefore no purpose is to be answered by sending them, I will detain them till I have an opportunity of sending them in perfect security. I shall immediately detach an escort of mounted men to Thompson's[123].

I have received no report this day from the High Hills. I therefore trust that all is quiet. Captain Kelly has fifty of Harrison's, mounted, with him. I must immediately dislodge Marion, but as McLeroth has not quite enterprize enough, I shall let him go to Charlestown (which he wishes) to hurry up the necessaries for his regiment and shall send an officer from hence to command the detachment. Lt Colonel Doyle would answer my purpose admirably, but as he has not yet entirely conquered his ague, I fear that, were he to undertake the service, his falling sick might eventually embarrass it. I believe therefore that I shall employ Major Campbell, upon whose zeal and steadiness I can place full reliance. If I send Campbell, I will detach the light company of my own regiment with him to make his appointment to that command appear the more natural. If Marion was once forced to retire so as to give our new party time to reccollect themselves and to form, I think our interest in that country would take a very different complexion from what it has hitherto borne. In short, I think the scale would be decidedly in our favor, not perhaps from attachment to us, but from weariness of the long disquiet in which a contrary conduct has kept the district.

I have the honor to be, my Lord,
Your most faithful and obedient servant

RAWDON

[*Superscribed in Cornwallis's hand:*]

A person just come in reports that Morgan with the cavalry has crossed the Catawba to collect the debris of Sumpter's corps. I do not believe it.

Cornwallis to Rawdon, 17th December 1780 — *83(53): C*

Wynnesborough
December 17th 1780

Rt Hon Lord Rawdon etc etc etc

My dear Lord

It will be convenient to the regiments here to receive their recruits on account of cloathing as soon as Mr Marion is disposed of. I would not, however, wish this consideration to interfere with any material object you may have in view.

I have for some days heard a report of Morgan's passing, or being expected to pass, the Catawba. I have, however, no certain account of his having passed. My intelligence is,

---

123 *an escort..*: to meet Balfour and accompany him to Winnsborough.

however, miserably bad. Colonel Ballantyne[124] is very ill, who was the most active in that line, and Colonel Phillips is so taken up with a business which is likely to hang Colonel Wynne[125] that he cannot be brought to attend to any thing else. My best intelligence insisted, last time that he went out, that he should be paroled on his return, so that I now am quite in the dark.

Balfour cannot come on from Thompson's in a day with an escort, nor do I think he has occasion for one. I shall tell him so and try to save your horses.

I am, my dear Lord,
Yours most sincerely

CORNWALLIS

[*Subscribed*:]

McLeod sends 2 waggons to bring up 20,000 musket cartridges. Your Lordship may keep part of the escort that went with the prisoners to come back with them.

Rawdon to Cornwallis, 18th December 1780 — *4(355): ALS*

Camden
December 18th 1780

Earl Cornwallis etc etc etc

My Lord

I did not write to your Lordship yesterday, as I had nothing particular to mention and as I was in hourly expectation of news from the High Hills. Major Campbell went thither very early yesterday morning with forty of the light company from my regiment, mounted for the occasion. By my not hearing from thence, I imagine that Marion has retired to a greater distance.

I have better hopes of that country than I ever had before. Henry Richbourg is thoroughly incensed against the enemy and has thrown himself decidedly into our party. By the accounts of McLeroth and Coffin he is as active and as popular an officer as Marion, with more abilities. Isham Moore says that the country is very eager to have Henry Richbourg at their head and he advises the measure strongly, resigning all competition on his own part. I have

---

124 William Ballentine of Orangeburg had very recently been promoted from captain to lt colonel in Daniel Clary's Dutch Fork Regiment of the royal militia. (Clark, *Loyalists in the Southern Campaign*, i, 230-1)

125 John Winn (*c.* 1732-1814) had at one time been colonel of a regiment of revolutionary militia whose catchment area was bounded by the lower Broad and Wateree Rivers. At its centre lay Winnsborough. He was now a prisoner. (Moss, *SC Patriots*, 1005; Lambert, *SC Loyalists*, 287)

written very fully to Richbourg and have taken every other step that I thought likely to conciliate the minds of his party; and I endeavor (I hope with success) to make the people forget the original ground of contest and look upon Marion merely as a destroyer of their property. In justice to McLeroth I should mention that his mild and equitable behavior to the inhabitants of that country has been of great service. His regiment is in high health and very keen. I think your Lordship will find them an useful battalion, and they will be supplied in time with what necessaries are wanted.

I sent orders to Captain Kerr to join your Lordship with the recruits by McCord's Ferry. Circumstances might alter so exceedingly, in the interval between dispatching orders from hence and the time of their receipt at Neilson's Ferry, that I would not at this particular time risque any thing by employing that corps against Marion.

What would your Lordship have done with the two three pounders attached to the 64th, when that regiment comes hither?

Major England will wait upon your Lordship tomorrow to receive your commands respecting his department.

I have the honor to be, my Lord, with great respect
Your most obedient and very affectionate servant

RAWDON

[*Subscribed*:]

I received your Lordship's letter of the 16th 9 pm.

Cornwallis to Rawdon, 19th December 1780 *83(57): C*

Wynnesborough
19th December 1780

Rt Hon Lord Rawdon etc etc etc

My dear Lord

I received your letter this morning, and this evening England arrived. I am glad to hear every thing bears so favourable an aspect in the Low Country. If we can get an enterprizing man to act against Marion and fight him with his own countrymen, it will be a great object. Colonel Goodwin arrived here this afternoon. He says he has been very ill used and confined by the rebels, and that they would not let him see his brother. I have directed him to go to you and mention a person in the camp of Sumpter's corps who may be usefull. He says that Smallwood is gone to the northward, I think probably to appear against Gates. Morgan succeeds him in the command of the North Carolina militia and the camp at Six Mile Run. No cavalry has passed the Catawba and every thing in our front remains in the same situation that it has done for some time. I forgot whether I told you of Clarke etc being in Long Cane settlement with about 400 men. Colonel Allen with 150 soldiers, and Brigadier General Cunningham with 250 militia, marched against them and totally defeated them. Clarke was certainly wounded this time, for Colonel Twiggs, who came in with a flag of truce, said that he had extracted the ball. The cavalry acoutrements will come up by land in waggons from McChord's for the dragoons arrived from the northward. I write in great haste now and will mention the three pounders tomorrow.

Yours, my dear Lord, most sincerely

[CORNWALLIS]

Rawdon to Cornwallis, 19th December 1780 — *4(361): ALS*

Camden
December 19th 1780
8 pm

Earl Cornwallis etc etc etc

My Lord

A person having come in from the enemy's army whose information seems pretty clear, I will transmit his report to your Lordship. Yesterday morning Smallwood was at Six Mile Run; Morgan and Davison were with him. Their joint force was called 1,000. The time of Davison's people was out but he was engaging them anew. Washington was at Wild Cat Creek with the cavalry, rated at 200 or 250. Davie is collecting a new corps at Ramsower's Mills. Greene, with the principal force (called 2,000), is building huts at Charlotteburg and professes to be waiting for reinforcement, which is said to be on its march under Stevens or Muhlenberg. My informant says that he saw ten pieces of cannon in the enemy's camp, but in that point I think he is mistaken. He heard it reported that Sumpter (who is recovered) is to have the command of the corps now under Marion. I think that the *news of Leslie's being on his way to join you must cause* an immediate movement of their army. England will have informed your Lordship that Rutledge is said to be at Cheraw Hill and that the enemy are hutting there. I have not heard from Campbell, but I am told that Marion lay at Luten's the day before yesterday and that his corps was divided into a number of small parties. I have been honored with your Lordship's letter of the 17th and had before perceived my mistake in affixing that date to a letter which I wrote on the 16th. The want of a cathedral in Camden prevents our correcting our lunar calculation by the dominical letter, for at present neither inhabitant nor sojourner could tell you when Sunday comes.[126]

I have the honor to be, my Lord, with sincere affection and respect
Your very obedient servant

RAWDON

---

[126] Rawdon had believed he was writing the misdated letter on a Sunday (the 17th), but was unable to check in the manner described.

Cornwallis to Rawdon, 20th December 1780 *83(59): C*

Wynnesborough
20th December 1780

Rt Hon Lord Rawdon etc etc etc

My dear Lord

Your letter with the information of the positions of the enemy came this morning. A person who came from North Carolina had mentioned Davison's being at Ramsouer's raising militia. I dare say he mistook the name, as your account is the most probable. Goodwin mentioned that Mulenburgh was expected, but that is all militia. I agree with you in disbelieving the ten pieces of cannon. By their hutting every where on the frontiers and building the log fort on Turkey Creek, the enemy certainly do not expect any material forward movement. The arrival of Leslie must, I think, make them suspect it. I have agreed to the exchange of one McJunkins[127], a prisoner sent from hence to Camden, and beg that you will be kind enough to order him to be released.

I am, my dear Lord,
Most sincerely yours

[CORNWALLIS]

[*Subscribed*:]

I enclose a copy of an extraordinary order of Major Frazer's[128] which I think will furnish Washington with better materials for complaint than he has had. I desire you will be so kind as to express my disapprobation of it in the strongest manner to Major Frazer and desire that it may be immediately recalled. I should be glad to see a list of the officers of that corps. It is very extraordinary if Parris is a captain in Colonel Innes's corps, as he assured me in June last that Parris was one of the greatest scoundrels in the whole country[129].

---

[127] Of the McJunkin family it is Daniel (1756-1825) to whom Cornwallis is referring. While serving in the South Carolina revolutionary militia he had taken part in several engagements. His more famous brother Joseph (1755-1846) had been serving as a major under Thomas Brandon, while his father Samuel (*c*. 1725-1808) would be elected to the Jacksonborough revolutionary assembly as a Member for the Upper District between the Broad and Saluda. (Moss, *SC Patriots*, 630-1; McCrady, *SC in the Rev 1780-1783*, 559)

[128] *an extraordinary order..*: no extant copy.

[129] *he assured me..*: see Innes to Cornwallis, 15th June, vol I, p 117.

Cornwallis to Rawdon, 21st December 1780 *83(63): C*

Wynnesborough
21st December 1780

Rt Hon Lord Rawdon

My dear Lord

I inclose to you a letter which I have sent to meet Leslie at Nelson's Ferry[130], where he will arrive on Saturday. I am anxious to hear what Campbell has done with Marion. The boat with the swords had a very narrow escape.

On considering seriously your situation, and being convinced that it is of the greatest importance to make you as strong as possible, I have determined to leave the 64th Regiment as well as Watson's corps under your command, and desire your Lordship to take the command of all the troops from Georgetown to Augusta, both inclusive. You will be kind enough to order Hamilton's corps to be ready to march with Leslie and explain to him my sentiments about baggage, of which I hear he has a great quantity.

I propose taking with me 4 six pounders and 2 three and intended that you should have on the east of Santee two brass six and one three, leaving only one brass three at Ninety Six after the iron guns arrive there, consisting of one six and two three, and removing the two brass three pounders from Augusta to Savannah. I believe that the two three pounders coming with Leslie are on the two wheel carriages, which are much the best. In that case I would have you keep one and send the other up for Tarleton. If you wish to keep more three pounders, you are welcome to them. If not, there will remain to be sent to Charlestown the two guns with the 64th, Tarleton's old gun, and an heavy three pounder from 96. All this arrangement is subject to any proposals of alteration which you may think proper to make.

I am, my dear Lord,
Very sincerely yours

[CORNWALLIS]

[*Subscribed*:]

A captain and about 12 men of Simcoe's are arrived. I understand the captain has orders to compleat a troop to serve to the southward. It seems an odd plan but we may as well avail ourselves of it. I have therefore directed that the captain should proceed to Georgetown and endeavour to compleat his troop in that neighbourhood. You will judge afterwards whether you can send him to any other place where he is more likely to succeed.

---

130 *a letter...*: of 21st December, p 367.

Rawdon to Cornwallis, 21st December 1780 *4(370): ALS*

Camden
December 21st 1780
8 am

Earl Cornwallis etc etc etc

My Lord

Nothing occurred yesterday that was worth transmitting to your Lordship. In the night I received a letter from Major Campbell. He had not fallen in with the enemy, but the movements which he was making, joined to the presence of a corps at Nelson's, must, I think, make Marion retire immediately across Black River. Campbell's letter was dated on the 19th at night. He was then within fourteen miles of Wright's Bluff, so that no longer obstruction of the navigation is to be apprehended. No damage has been done excepting the burning of one empty boat, of which Lt Colonel Balfour will have informed your Lordship. Campbell thinks very favorably of our prospects in that country. I am grieved to report to your Lordship that Captain George Kelly of the 64th is dead of his wound.

I have been honored with your Lordship's letter of the 19th. I have had pretty good information that Washington with the cavalry has quitted Wild Cat Creek and has gone across Great Lynches Creek. I do not comprehend the movement.

I have the honor to be with equal truth and respect
Your Lordship's very faithful and affectionate servant

RAWDON

Rawdon to Cornwallis, 21st December 1780 *4(368): ALS*

Camden
December 21st 1780
7 pm

Earl Cornwallis etc etc etc

My Lord

I have the honor to forward to your Lordship a letter which was received at the outpost this afternoon[131]. It was an officer (a Lieutenant Bruff[132]), attended by a dragoon, who

[131] *a letter..*: Greene to Cornwallis, 17th December, p 406.

brought it. Altho' I thought it had been understood that officers were not to be sent upon such business to our posts, I have given Mr Bruff the reception due to the bearer of a flag of truce. As it was too dark for him to make any observations of consequence about the works, I had him brought in to Colonel Hamilton's house. After he and his horse have had some refreshment, he shall be sent out again. I shall, however, request that no other officer may be sent with a flag of truce to this post untill your Lordship shall have decided whether you admit that form.

I have received your Lordship's letter of the 20th and have spoken to Fraser in the manner you wished. He owned the impropriety and was much distressed at it, but he begged me to assure your Lordship that the order was only meant to be shown to the friends of the delinquents in the hopes that they might advise the latter to avoid the penalty by returning to their duty. The affair of Dougherty and Captain Lindsay was prior to this order, and not in consequence of it, as might be suspected from the memorandum being tacked to the copy. An express will be dispatched tomorrow to revoke the instructions. Fraser says that Paris is not a captain in the regiment but only bears that title for the performance of his present commission. A list of the officers properly belonging to the South Carolina Regiment shall be sent to your Lordship.

By different accounts which I have received, Muhlenberg ought to have reached Charlotteburg yesterday or today. I cannot learn his real force, but as the country calls it 4,000, I suppose it may be near 1,000. The rebels say that 800 more are on their march from Virginia.

I have the honor to be, my Lord, with great respect
Your very affectionate servant

RAWDON

Rawdon to Cornwallis, 22nd December 1780 — *4(374):ALS*

Camden
December 22nd 1780

Earl Cornwallis etc etc etc

My Lord

The officer who came with the flag of truce let drop some information which your Lordship may not have yet received from any other quarter. He said that before he left the

---

[132] Since December 1776 James Bruff had been serving as a lieutenant in the 6th Maryland Continental Regiment now commanded by Lt Colonel Benjamin Ford. Transferring to the 5th Maryland in January 1781, he would be promoted to captain lieutenant the following month and be wounded and taken prisoner at the Battle of Hobkirk's Hill in April. Although he was reported in late May to be still weak and in danger, he recovered and, being exchanged, was promoted to captain with effect from 8th September, the date of the Battle of Eutaw Springs. In later life he would serve for thirteen years in the US Army as a captain in the artillery and engineers. He retired to Baltimore County, Maryland, and was awarded a revolutionary pension. (Heitman, *Historical Register*, 128; *Maryland Historical Magazine*, xviii (December 1923), 309, 310)

camp at Charlotte (on the 18th), Major Lee's cavalry had arrived there. Some militia had likewise joined. The reinforcement[133] of which we have had intelligence is commanded by Major General the Baron de Steuben[134], to whom Muhlenberg is second. It is the new-raised Virginia line – therefore, I suppose, not very numerous. This corps had not joined the army when the officer left it, but was expected in a few days. Virginia was left quite bare of troops. This officer is but just arrived from Maryland with recruits for their line. He says that Washington was understood there to be encamped near Bergen but there had not been any action.

People from the country assure me that all the militia are gone from Six Mile Run. Whether they have retired to Charlotteburg or have moved by their left I cannot yet ascertain. There is some cavalry upon Wild Cat Creek and Kembill is near Wade's Mill.

Late last night I received your Lordship's letter of yesterday. I have many thanks to return to your Lordship for the important trust which you have done me the honor to repose in me, and shall endeavor, by application at least, to prove that your Lordship's confidence is not misplaced.

Hamilton's regiment will be in readiness to march whenever it may be called upon, and I have given a hint about the baggage.

I have the honor to be, my Lord, with great respect
Your most obedient and very affectionate servant

RAWDON

---

133 In early December Steuben had forwarded some 400 troops from Virginia to join Greene, but he did not accompany them. (*The Greene Papers*, vi, 525-6n)

134 Born in Magdeburg, Freiherr Friedrich Wilhelm von Steuben (1730-1794) had served as a junior infantry and staff officer in the Prussian army during the Seven Years' War. He then went on to serve as a court official in a minor German principality, but by 1777 he was unemployed. Encouraged by Beaumarchais, Franklin and Silas Deane, who recognised his military abilities, he began to look to the revolutionary war as a field for displaying them. Coming out to America later that year, he profoundly impressed both Congress and Washington and was soon appointed Inspector General of the Continental Army with the rank of major general. During the next two years he proved to be indispensable in training the troops to form an effective and highly disciplined force. Sent south with Greene, he would remain in Virginia as Greene's second and be responsible for forwarding men and supplies to the southern army. It would be a disagreeable task, beset partly by Arnold's, Phillips' and Cornwallis's invasions and partly by a deterioration in his relations with the Virginia revolutionary government. He would, however, have the satisfaction of being present at the siege of Yorktown. After the war he adopted American citizenship and settled in New York, where he became one of the most popular figures in the social life of the city and state. He died of apoplexy and was interred on his estate in the Mohawk country. (*DAB*; *The Greene Papers*, vi-ix, *passim*)

Cornwallis to Rawdon, 23rd December 1780 *83(71): C*

Wynnesborough
December 23rd 1780

Rt Hon Lord Rawdon etc etc etc

My dear Lord

I have received your letters of 21st, 8 am and 7 pm, and one of 22nd. It will be better to keep to the rule of not admitting an officer with a flag of truce. I am informed that a reinforcement, supposed to be Back Mountain men, of about 500 has joined Lacey on Turkey Creek. I have heard nothing in particular from the east of Catawba. I sent a trusty man about 3 days ago to Wild Cat Creek, who is not yet returned. I should wish to watch the motions of the enemy very attentively for this next week. After that, *there is no danger of their attempting any thing seriously offensive*. I had not received any certain account of the arrival of Major Lee's cavalry. I should wish Leslie's march to be as expeditious as possible.

It is certainly true, my dear Lord, that you are one of the last men whom I would place in an embarrassing situation, but upon the most mature consideration of the affairs of this province I think it so necessary that your force should be respectable that I am convinced it is for the good of His Majesty's Service that the 64th should remain with you.

I am with great truth
Most sincerely yours

CORNWALLIS

Rawdon to Cornwallis, 24th December 1780 *4(386): ALS*

Camden
December 24th 1780
8 pm

Earl Cornwallis etc etc etc

My Lord

I have had the honor to receive your letter of yesterday. In consequence of it I have written to General Lesslie, informing him of your Lordship's having expressed a wish that he should expedite his march as much as he could with convenience. From a sentiment similar to your Lordship's I wrote to Major Campbell three or four days ago, directing that, either upon Marion's retiring or upon Watson's crossing the river, he should send the 64th Regiment to me without delay. I have received a letter from Campbell dated Wright's Bluff on the 21st in which he tells me that Marion had fallen back without having been able to do any other mischief than burning the empty boat. I therefore conclude that the 64th is now on its march towards me. I do not neglect any means of gaining intelligence, yet for two or three days past I have had none upon which I can fully depend. I did not write to your Lordship yesterday, having had nothing to say.

I have the honor to be, my Lord, with great respect
Your very affectionate and faithful servant

RAWDON

Cornwallis to Rawdon, 25th December 1780 — *83(79): C*

Wynnesborough
December 25th 1780
9 o'clock pm

Rt Hon Lord Rawdon etc etc etc

My dear Lord

I received yours of yesterday and am glad to find that Marion has left the coast clear as I think he would only have delayed our business. The recruits, I fear, were stopped by Balfour and will probably join Leslie. If, however, you can manage by a forced march or two (if they come by Camden) to get them to us a day or two before we march, it will be a great convenience. I cannot hear of any material move of the enemy. The accounts differ so much about the Back Mountain men that I am not certain whether any have passed or not. By the best intelligence I can get, the principal posts of the enemy remain much in the same state. They are removing the corn they had collected at Turkey Creek to Watson's or Bullock Creek, and they do not as yet appear to expect a forward move from us.

I am, my dear Lord, with the greatest regard
Most sincerely yours

CORNWALLIS

[*Subscribed*:]

I send duplicates of my New York letters[135] and a letter or two[136] to take their chance of being in time for the *Blonde*, which you will be kind enough to transmit to Charlestown.

---

[135] *my New York letters*: Cornwallis to Clinton, 3rd, 4th and 22nd December, pp 24 to 29.

[136] *a letter or two*: Cornwallis to Germain, 18th December. p 43, together with letters of possibly a private nature.

Rawdon to Cornwallis, 25th December 1780 *4(390): ALS*

Camden
December 25th 1780
7 pm

Earl Cornwallis etc etc etc

My Lord

I have no news to transmit, but I write because it will be satisfactory to your Lordship to learn that all remains quiet here. The enemy had several scouting parties pretty close in my front last night and all my spies were driven in without having been able to gain any intelligence. I therefore pushed an officer's patrole beyond Rugeley's this day and have had parties out a good distance on the other roads, but they did not hear of any thing but plundering militia. England has told me what quantity of rum your Lordship talked of carrying with you. We have thirty puncheons here. There is none at Thompson's, but I hope there is a stock at Neilson's. I have plenty of meal.

I have the honor to be with great respect
Your Lordship's very faithful and very affectionate servant

RAWDON

[*Subscribed*:]

I have this instant received a letter from Neilson's Ferry dated on the 24th at night. The 64th *is at Luten's*. *Leslie came last night to Nelson's but his corps lay at Martin's*. Marion is upon Black River.

Cornwallis to Rawdon, 26th December 1780 *83(81): C*

Wynnesborough
December 26th 1780
9 o'clock pm

Rt Hon Lord Rawdon etc etc etc

My dear Lord

I received yours of yesterday. This is fine weather for the march of Leslie and I hope he will make good use of it. None of the people whom I sent out are yet returned, but a man who was long prisoner with us and was sent out by Despard about 3 weeks ago on promise of returning and bringing intelligence came this morning from within a few miles of Charlottetown. He says that Green marched on Wednesday last towards the Cheraws to join Caswell and that on Thursday and Friday last Morgan and Washington passed the Catawba at Bigger's Ferry to join Sumpter's corps. I do not believe him, but still the report is worth some attention. I enclose a letter to General Green[137]. Your Lordship will read it and fasten the seal.

I am most sincerely yours

CORNWALLIS

Rawdon to Cornwallis, 26th December 1780 — *4(402): ALS*

Camden
December 26th 1780

Earl Cornwallis etc etc etc

My Lord

As there is a person going up to Wynnesborough, I will just mention to your Lordship that I have not learned that the main body of the enemy has made any movement.

Lt Colonel Hamilton reccommends a voluntier Newton for an ensigncy in the Royal North Carolina Regiment.[138]

I have been honored with your Lordship's letters of yesterday.[139] Whilst Balfour was with you, I had some thoughts of giving your Lordship assurances upon the point to which your private letter alludes, as there had been some little coldness between Balfour and me. I dropped the idea, however, from the confidence that your knowledge of my way of thinking would enable your Lordship to answer for me in the manner which you have so kindly done. Depend firmly, my Lord, upon my sense of what is necessary for the public service and upon the affection with which I have the honor to be

Your Lordship's most faithful servant

RAWDON

---

[137] *a letter...*: of 27th December, p 408.

[138] Hamilton's recommendation was not acted upon.

[139] There is no copy of Cornwallis's private letter.

Extract
Cornwallis to Rawdon, 27th December 1780 ***83(85): C***

Wynnesborough
December 27th 1780

Rt Hon Lord Rawdon etc etc etc

My dear Lord

The intelligence which I sent to you last night is certainly true. Green marched the Cheraw Road. You will lose no time in endeavouring to procure the best accounts of his situation and strength. If you address any persons, you may send *to Westfield*[140] *at Cheraws. He will give you accounts you may depend on*.[141]

I am very sincerely yours

CORNWALLIS

Rawdon to Cornwallis, 27th December 1780 ***4(411): ALS***

Camden
December 27th 1780

Earl Cornwallis etc etc etc

My Lord

I have not heard any thing this morning respecting the enemy, nor have I news from any other quarter, but I will not let Mr Coffin go up to Wynnesborough without sending a line by him to your Lordship.

Your Lordship will probably want some engineer to act under the direction of Mr Haldane. Lieutenant Barrette may immediately join his regiment without any inconvenience to me, as Vallancey shall superintend whatever is to be done without expecting any pay.

I take it for granted that General Lesslie either has your Lordship's orders for the steps which he is to pursue or that they will meet him upon his arrival here.

---

140 John Westfield had been one of the early migrants from Virginia to the Pee Dee. He lived on the west side of the river above Cheraw. Evidently a covert loyalist, who would go undiscovered, he appears to have done as little as possible to keep in with the revolutionaries, limiting himself to the supply of corn and acting for a time as a waggoner. Sometime after 1783 he returned to Virginia, where he died. Westfield Creek in Chesterfield County, South Carolina, was named after him. (Gregg, *The Old Cheraws*, 62n, 430; Moss, *SC Patriots*, 980-1)

141 According to an annotation, the rest of the letter was of a private nature.

I have the honor to be, my Lord, very truly
Your faithful and most obedient servant

RAWDON

Cornwallis to Rawdon, 28th December 1780 — *83(89): C*

Wynnesborough
December 28th 1780

Rt Hon Lord Rawdon etc etc etc

My dear Lord

I received yours by Mr Coffin and desire that you will please to order Mr Barrett to join the army. Blair[142], the miller, is arrived and confirms the account I sent you. Upon reflection I do not think it necessary to make any alteration in my plan. I cannot conceive it possible that Green will attempt any thing materially offensive. It is impracticable for him to push any force over the Santee; he must get into a cul de sac to go to George Town, from which he could not easily escape; and although you may not be quite strong enough in point of quantity and quality of troops to manœuvre against him in the field, you need not fear an attack from him, especially as there is no danger of your being called upon to succour Ninety Six until I have passed the Catawba.

By a letter which I have received from Lt Colonel Brown at Augusta[143], he seems to have cut out work enough for the Back Mountain men with his Indian friends. The only difficulty is your subsistence until Green is taken off your hands. I really think you may draw enough from Congarees to preserve you from absolute want 'til the time comes that Green must positively retire. If I heard of his advancing, I could pass the Catawba and march directly to Cheraws. I beg you will be kind enough to send to Leslie to desire him to come in to Wynnesborough and leave O'Hara to bring on the corps, as I wish to explain my march to him. I should wish the Yaghers, Guards and Bose to be passed over the Wateree the day after their arrival at Camden. To save time you may send Hamilton's corps over the day before. I intend they should march by the road that Captain Hovenden did to the Cross Roads. I should be glad that the recruits for the regiments here and the detachment of the 17th Dragoons would join us by forced marches as soon as possible. The hospital waggons and the proportion of rum that is to come from Camden will march with Leslie's corps. I enclose a note which you will forward to Leslie[144].

---

[142] James Blair (*c.* 1738-1789) was a Scotch-Irish Presbyterian who had migrated from County Antrim to the Waxhaw settlement before the revolution. He was the owner of Blair's Mill on the eastern side of the Catawba. (Information in part from John A Blair, 'Blair Genealogy' (http://blairgenealogy.com, 1st November 2002)

[143] *a letter..*: of 17th December, p 295.

[144] *a note..*: of 28th December, p 369.

Macleod sends for ten thousand musquet cartridges and materials for making ten thousand more. I have desired Balfour to forward a supply to you as soon as possible.

Yours, my dear Lord, most sincerely

CORNWALLIS

[*Subscribed:*]

I should wish that Leslie's corps might be supplied if possible with six days' meal, four of which the men must carry. There is much more meal at the Congarees than we can possibly carry with us, from which you may replace what you spare to Leslie. As I intend to take England with me, I must desire you to keep Savage[145]. I enclose a paper relative to the publick departments[146], which you will please to communicate to the heads of each under your command.

Rawdon to Cornwallis, 27th December 1780 — *4(409): ALS*

Camden
December 27th 1780
9 pm

Earl Cornwallis etc etc etc

My Lord

I have had the honor to receive your letter of last night. Just as it reached me, intelligence had been brought to me of Greene's having marched towards Cheraws upon the day which your Lordship's information specified. The person who brought me the account saw the column which marched under Greene. It did not appear to him to be very large and he saw only thirty cavalry, who were attending on the General. Another person whom I had sent out has since come in to me. He was in the enemy's camp at Charlotteburg and saw them march from thence. Greene moved on Wednesday last and Morgan followed him towards the Cheraws the next day. My emissary did not venture to examine too nicely, or to ask too many questions, lest he should be discovered not to belong to them, but he heard Greene's Continentals rated at seven hundred and Morgan's rifle men at an hundred and fifty. He saw the latter parade and thinks the account was pretty just. Having been taken ill, he could not leave Charlotteburg till Monday last, at which time Washington with all the cavalry remained there, and my informant did not observe any preparations for moving among them. Kembill

---

145 Commissioned a lieutenant in the army on 15th October 1759, Henry Savage had entered the 37th Regiment on 8th June 1768 and been promoted to captain there on 15th April 1774. He was now serving on secondment to the Quartermaster General's Department. (*Army Lists*; *The Cornwallis Papers*)

146 *a paper..*: no extant copy.

and Wade[147], finding the harvest scanty among the Tories, have plundered the Liberty Folks in Waxhaw and Meclenburgh County so abominably that Greene was obliged to send out parties of cavalry to bring them prisoners before him. The banditti, however, have evaded the pursuit, and there was a report of their having waylaid a party of the dragoons and killed several of them. I have dispatched persons to Cheraws to find what the enemy is doing. There was nothing between the branches of Lynches Creek this morning.

Major Doyle arrived here today. He left Charlestown on Sunday. A schooner with a clearance from New York to the West Indies had just come in, by which there is an account of the arrival of a pacquet from England at New York. The passengers did not reccollect any news excepting a report that the two battalions of the Royals, the 14th, the 2nd, the 18th and the 59th Regiments were embarking in England to reinforce your Lordship.

Captain Kerr with the recruits will, I fancy, be at Wynnesborough the day after tomorrow, having pursued the route which I gave him by McChord's Ferry. What would your Lordship have me do with the printing press?

I hope to receive better paper tomorrow from town. This is all that Camden affords and I fear it will give your Lordship trouble to read what I have written.

I have the honor to be very respectfully
Your Lordship's most affectionate servant

RAWDON

Rawdon to Cornwallis, 28th December 1780 — *4(415): ALS*

Camden
December 28th 1780
9 pm

Earl Cornwallis etc etc etc

My Lord

I have the honor to forward to your Lordship a letter from Balfour[148] and I likewise enclose one which I have received from General Lesslie[149]. There has been a strange delay about the 64th, which ought to have moved towards me upon Marion's retreat. Major Campbell writes me word that Marion lies on this side of Black River and that he means to

---

[147] Wade, the freebooter, has not been identified.

[148] *a letter..*: of 26th December, p 116.

[149] *one..*: Leslie to Rawdon, 26th December, p 367.

press Watson to push him directly. Should the movement specified in Benson's letter[150] take place, Marion may be in a scrape.

A report is brought to me that a Colonel Gulph, who had just raised a corps of light horse on Pedee, has been surprized by a party of friends to Government, who defeated him and killed thirty-four of his men upon the spot. The account is very circumstantial, but I require strong vouchers for any story at present.[151]

Two deserters from Greene came in today. They left him five days ago on the road to Cheraws. They say that Morgan took the same road but turned back suddenly, it is supposed towards Ramsower's. I have several people out, so that I hope to give your Lordship good information immediately.

By a letter of McKinnon's to England I fear that the waggons which were sent for the appointments of the 17th Dragoons have been detained with those articles to move in the slow procession of General Lesslie's corps.

I have the honor to be, my Lord, with great respect
Your most obedient and very faithful servant

RAWDON

Cornwallis to Rawdon, 30th December 1780[152] — *83(97): C*

Wynnesborough
December 30th 1780

Rt Hon Lord Rawdon etc etc etc

My dear Lord

I cannot express my feelings on the generosity and friendship of your letter[153]. If it had been possible to have raised my esteem for you, it would have done so.

---

150 *Benson's letter*: of 22nd December, p 117.

151 Neither has Gulph been identified nor the report corroborated. His name may have been corrupted from Gough, Goff or the like, and the incident, perhaps much exaggerated in the telling, may have been a minor one involving, for example, Captain Richard Gough of Marion's Brigade. Before joining Marion, he had, in February 1779, been commissioned a captain in a regiment of light dragoons being raised by the South Carolina revolutionary authorities. In July 1782, having ventured, apparently on private business, to a part of the Pee Dee frequented by loyalists, he would have his fate lamented by Governor John Mathews. (McCrady, *SC in the Rev 1775-1780*, 298; Gibbes, *Documentary History*, ii, 200, iii, 232; Moss, *SC Patriots*, 376)

152 Extracts from this letter are published in Ross ed, *Cornwallis Correspondence*, i, 76-7.

153 *your letter*: not extant. Part was no doubt of a private nature.

What you say as to driving Green is perfectly just, but from every thing which I hear of his force I do not think it possible for him to strike any blow that would materially affect my movements, and by advancing on the west of Catawba I should, I think, oblige Morgan and Washington absolutely to quit the country before me. Such corps as Sumpter's, it is true, might get out of my way and return as soon as I passed the Catawba, but I do not think Morgan and Washington could play that game. I understand there are but two fords below Coulson's, which last is very deep and only passable in dry times; but I am frightened at the report of the French at Cape Fear. That would greatly embarrass our operations and engage us in a naval expedition, which I fear we are but ill prepared for.

I enclose a paragraph of a letter which I received from the Admiral by the *Camilla*. That added to Green's movement makes me suspect it to be too true.

A few days must ascertain this fact. I likewise think I must hear from New York relative to the embarkation said to be taking place there. From a private letter which I received from Phillips I think it highly probable that he is going to the Chesapeak. If there is no French landing and Phillips is in the Chesapeak, we may make a great change in the southern colonies in these next four months.

I send you my packet to Balfour[154] under a flying seal, which you will please to forward to him.

I am, my dear Lord,
Yours most affectionately

CORNWALLIS

Rawdon to Cornwallis, 29th December 1780 — *4(419): ALS*

Camden
December 29th 1780
8 pm

Earl Cornwallis etc etc etc

My Lord

Your letter of yesterday has just reached me. Mine of the same date[155] will already have informed your Lordship in some degree how I consider myself circumstanced with regard to the enemy. I have only to say in addition that I have taken care to lay up here a sufficient stock of provisions to support the garrison for many days in case I should at any time be reduced to the necessity of keeping close within the works, and I am continually adding to

---

[154] *my packet..*: enclosed with a letter to Balfour of 29th December, p 118.

[155] *Mine..*: see note 153 above.

that hoard by collecting from the country much more than is necessary for our ordinary consumption. However, in a few days I hope my force will have acquired a more active quality by the equipment of our new cavalry, and should the enemy take any incautious step, I might possibly avail myself of it.

We have had a little *alert* today. About noon two of the militia came galloping in and declared that they had been made prisoners by a picquet of Continental infantry, which they described as being regularly posted in front of Saunders's Creek with sentries advanced. They said that they had broken away from this picquet and had been fired upon by the sentries. In proof of this, one of them showed the mark of a ball thro' his clothes and produced his horse wounded. I had just before seen a man who left Cheraws the day before yesterday and had heard nothing of Greene. I therefore thought it very possible that Greene might have made this double. Further information soon confirmed the story of the militia men, and all the reports concurred in describing the picquet to be dressed in blue trimmed with white and equipped with caps and white manes. Very fortunately, forty swords arrived in that moment, with which I instantly armed the light company of the New York Voluntiers and sent them out to feel the country. They proceeded as far as Rugeley's and returned by Chesnut's, having only learned that this supposed picquet had had horses and had gone off towards Lynches Creek. A patrole which went ten miles up the Cheraws Road saw nothing. I have sent another to try the whole country between the two roads. I am glad that this affair happened as it showed me that every thing was in order immediately without hurry to receive the enemy. Our young troops wore a very good countenance, and sixty militia appeared under arms directly, requesting to be employed. I sent to hasten the 64th Regiment. I received an answer, by which I find they will be here tonight after a march of more than thirty miles, for they were stopped at Singleton's Mills (to secure some meal that was prepared for General Lesslie) till some of the Guards relieved them. I do not think that Greene is in my neighborhood. If he is, I am fully strong enough. Every thing respecting General Lesslie and his corps shall be performed as your Lordship wishes.

I have the honor to be, my Lord, with great respect
Your very affectionate and faithful servant

RAWDON

Cornwallis to Rawdon, 31st December 1780 — *83(101): C*

Wynnesborough
December 31st 1780
9 pm

Rt Hon Lord Rawdon etc etc etc

My dear Lord

I desired Governor Martin to acknowledge the receipt of your letter of the 29th as I had nothing particular to say. Morgan and Washington with their respective corps and some militia are at Grimes's Mill about 3 miles south of Pacolet. They give themselves out for 3 thousand and say they are going to Ninety Six. Colonel Allen and Brigadier General Cunningham firmly believe them and are frightened accordingly. I do not enter much into their terrors. My anxiety is great to know about the Cape Fear business. If you should hear nothing to discredit the report, I should wish you to keep Leslie's corps a day or two at Camden, as I think by that time we must hear with certainty. As Green is gone, there can be no harm in their moving a few days after us. I hope you have turned over the consequences of that event in your thoughts. If they are in possession of that harbour, and Phillips is not gone to the Chesapeak, it would be madness to think of penetrating into North Carolina. At the same time I think with horror of an embarkation and naval cooperation, nor do I conceive our friend Gayton, altho' an excellent man, at all calculated to carry on a business of that sort. I should be glad to hear your thoughts upon it.

I forgot to mention that Pickens has broke his parole and joined Morgan, taking with him 2 majors, a captain and about 100 men. I have heard a confused account of some people rising about Bryar Creek in Georgia to attack some of our boats going up to Augusta, and that they missed the boats but attacked an officer's party and killed or took 12 of them. I trust that the fair winds we have lately had must bring something either from New York or from England.

It will be necessary to send with the Yaghers some proper powder for the rifles. Macleod says there is some at Camden.

Yours, my dear Lord, most sincerely

CORNWALLIS

[*Subscribed*:]

I am in hopes of seeing Leslie to morrow.

Rawdon to Cornwallis, 31st December 1780 — *4(429): ALS*

Camden
December 31st 1780

Earl Cornwallis etc etc etc

My Lord

You have made me very happy by the kind construction which you have put upon my sentiments. You bind me doubly to act up to my professions lest I should forfeit the merit which your partiality has attributed to me.

I can at last give your Lordship certain intelligence about Greene. Yesterday at noon he was encamped beyond the Pedee opposite to Cheraws Hill. On this latter spot he has a post of thirty light dragoons, which I believe to be all the Continental cavalry at present with him.

There are no troops between me and Meclenburg County but about eighty militia under Marshall on Wild Cat Creek, and I have grounds to think that there is nothing at Charlotteburg.

I rather suspect that Morgan will have passed Broad River and will keep very wide of the track which your Lordship would wish to pursue. From particular intelligence which I have received, I am tempted to imagine that the enemy have made a false move. I really believe that Greene, when he left Charlotteburg, had no information of General Lesslie's being on his march to join you – at least he had no idea of the route. Admitting that supposition, his plan possibly might have been to pass down Lynches Creek and, being reinforced by Marion, to cut off my communications east of Santee. Thus situated, he might have two views: if your Lordship followed Morgan, Greene might propose to force Georgetown at least, perhaps to try Camden, in conjunction with a move of Steuben's upon my front, whilst Lacey should break in on Congarees; if you crossed the Wateree, Greene would probably endeavor to get behind the Pedee, but Morgan would in the mean time strike seriously at Ninety Six. The news of Lesslie's march, the uncertainty of its object, and the fear lest a move from Camden should throw him between two fires might have decided Greene's resolution to take in reality that step which was, before, his ostensible purpose and to put himself in safety across Haley's Ferry. This is all surmise, but it would account for a movement for which only one other motive (rather, I think, unlikely) could be supposed. I have seen some persons very lately from Cross Creek (I cannot reccollect the day) and they had heard no rumor of any troops landed at Cape Fear.

Should a body of French be really landed in North Carolina, I do not think that it will much interfere with your Lordship's views. They could not join Greene for some time, during which period your Lordship's operations would be going on and we should be strong enough to prevent his doing much mischief on the Santee. For Georgetown alone, on account of its distance, I cannot answer. By the time the junction could be made, the situation of your army would probably forbid any attempt against this place, and should the combined force endeavor by a rapid march to gain the Santee with intent to cross it, I should think it necessary to move against them whatsoever might be their numbers, delaying them if they opposed me, striking at them if they did not give attention to me, at worst crippling them in some degree should they give me a beating. In short, my Lord, every body under you seems to be in earnest, and that being the case, it must be no trifling disparity of force that sinks the scale against us.

At this instant I have received a letter from General Lesslie. In consequence of what I said to him he has pressed forward so vigorously that I think it probable his army will reach Camden tomorrow. They shall proceed the day after by the route which your Lordship mentions in your letter to Balfour[156]. Having dispatched a subaltern and twenty dragoons yesterday morning for Lesslie's escort, I expect *him* here tonight.

Ten waggons with blades pressed close are ordered to join your Lordship from Congarees. Would you have any empty waggons from hence, or would you have any rum exclusive of what will accompany Lesslie?

---

[156] *your letter..*: of 29th December, p 118.

I did not write yesterday. I mention it lest your Lordship should conceive a letter had miscarried.

I have the honor to be, my Lord, with sincere respect
Your very faithful and affectionate servant

RAWDON

Cornwallis to Rawdon, 1st January 1781 *84(3): C*

Wynnesborough
January 1st 1781

Rt Hon Lord Rawdon etc etc etc

My dear Lord

Mr Oldfield is just arrived and brought me your letter. If I could flatter myself that, supposing the report to be true about the French, their intention was to join Green, I should most exceedingly rejoice at the event; but I apprehend their design to be to establish themselves at Cape Fear as they have done at Rhode Island, to possess the post, and to prevent our making any use of the Cape Fear River to Cross Creek and of course our establishing ourselves with ease and security in North Carolina. For this reason I should wish to ascertain the fact before I embarked too far and thought it advisable to let Leslie's corps remain a few days at Camden. I have ordered up the ten waggons with pressed blades from Congarees, and the remainder of our complement to make up the fifty which are to come from Camden will march with Leslie's corps and carry the hospital stores, rum and salt. The men must carry 4 days' meal upon their backs, in addition to which two days' in the waggons will bring them to the mills, where I hope to have a fresh supply ready for them, and shall direct Mr Knecht to send by the express which is going to the Congarees to secure some for you.

On considering seriously the state of Ninety Six and of the 7th Regiment, which will not march above 230 men, and many of those not near so healthy and robust as the rest of my corps, I have determined, when I march, to send them to 96. I think that reinforcement will ease the despondency which prevails in those parts and overbalance the defection of Mr Pickens.

I would have the printing press sent to Charlestown to come round to Cape Fear. As to money, I must spare you £200 from the £1,500 that Leslie has brought up, and must refer you for further assistance to Balfour, who is on the point of bankruptcy.

I trust to hearing certain accounts of the Cape Fear business in a day or two from Charlestown.

Yours, my dear Lord, most affectionately

CORNWALLIS

Rawdon to Cornwallis, 1st January 1781 — *67(3): ALS*

Camden
January 1st 1781
11 at night

Earl Cornwallis etc etc etc

My Lord

I sit down to answer your Lordship's letter of last night. I cannot fullfill that purpose in part better than by reciting what has just been asserted to me by a person who left Cheraws yesterday evening. My informant says that he not only sent a man thro' Greene's camp but that he himself approached so near as to reckon the artillery in park, which amounted to four pieces. He maintains that General Morgan rode close by him at Cheraws three days ago, and tho' I told him it was impossible, he persists in it, saying that he is too well acquainted with Morgan to have been mistaken. By the best accounts he rated the Continentals at 800 and the militia at little more. He says that the time of the latter is out on the 20th and that they have generally declared they will not be forced to serve any longer. The most material part of the report is what follows. He says that, hearing a report in the country of the French having landed at Cape Fear, he took it for granted that it was the debarkation of General Lesslie's army which had caused the rumor. Therefore he resolved to proceed instantly to Cape Fear and give General Lesslie information how we were situated. He had actually set out when he met one McCrae (a true friend of Government), who left Wilmington on Christmas Eve, and McCrae assured him that at that time no troops of any kind had appeared on the coast.

All this intelligence may be deceitful, and indeed I do not much depend upon the author. Therefore, in obedience to your Lordship's desires, I will reason upon the supposition that the French have actually landed. I think an expedition by sea to Cape Fear not only hazardous at this season, and from the peculiar circumstances of our squadron liable to a thousand disappointments, but even of very doubtful policy should the best success be ensured to the naval operation. I think the French would by no means attempt to join Greene untill they had established and strongly fortified a post for the protection of their vessels and stores. If you employ a small corps against them, it will have very little chance of success. Should you detach a large body, you expend your force upon a point which, when gained, is of no decisive advantage. It might not be expedient to commit yourself deeply in North Carolina, yet an active movement in that province would be the best means of securing this. Perhaps if you got Greene between you and the coast, there might be a hope of driving him to distress in those desarts, that is, if the inhabitants could be prevailed on to follow you with provisions. Should Phillips land in Virginia, you might without risque take such steps as would give a fair trial to the temper of the North Carolinians, and a favorable issue from the experiment would decide the fate of the French.

If it appears necessary that General Lesslie's army should remain for some time on this side of the Wateree, might it not with safety take a position on Lynches Creek, where it would awe the lower district and live upon the country instead of our depôt?

I have sent up one of the light three pounders for Tarleton with the 17th Dragoons. I have kept the other, and would wish also to keep one of McLeroth's three pounders if your Lordship has no objection.

I have the honor to be, my Lord, with great respect
Your most faithful and obedient servant

RAWDON

[*Subscribed*:]

I have just received your Lordship's letter by Mr Oldfield and am happy to find that what I have said above corresponds in some measure with your sentiments.

Cornwallis to Rawdon, 3rd January 1781 — *84(8): C*

Wynnesborough
January 3rd 1781

Rt Hon Lord Rawdon etc etc etc

My dear Lord

On the evening of the 1st I received accounts that Washington had surprised and routed a party of militia near Williams's stockaded house on the 30th and that Brigadier General Cunningham had abandoned the house in the night. It was reported that Morgan was marching with two pieces of cannon to Ninety Six. I immediately ordered Tarleton to cross Broad River with the Legion and 1st Battalion of the 71st and to proceed with the utmost dispatch to the relief of Ninety Six or pursuit of Morgan. Tarleton was last night at Sommers's House about six miles from Brierly's Ferry. I hope and trust that no mischief can happen at 96 before his arrival.

Balfour in his letter of the 29th[157] says not a word of Cape Fear, which, joined to your account and Leslie's saying that the *Delight* with 3 or 4 sail appeared off that harbour with French colors, makes me pretty easy about that business. I shall therefore march as soon as I know the issue of Tarleton's expedition.

7 o'clock pm

I have just heard from Tarleton at Menses Mill about 14 miles from the ferry. He has no intelligence of the enemy. A young man who brought me a letter from Colonel Allen dated on the 31st, but who says he left 96 on Monday morning at 9 o'clock, tells me that all he knew of the enemy was that some people said Washington's light horse were at Williams's Fort and some, who I believe were nearest the truth, that they had burnt the fort and gone

---

[157] *letter of the 29th*: see p 120.

back. I have ordered the 7th Regiment to Bryerly's Ferry, which is on their road to 96, and, if I cannot conveniently send the old Legion 3 pounder to Camden, shall direct them to take it with them to 96. I have no objection to your keeping one or both of McLeroth's guns if you think fit. The two iron 3 pounders which I ordered to 96 were going up without escort; eight or ten men stopped the waggon about 30 miles from thence and knocked the trunnions off and burnt the carriages. I hope now to be able to move in two or 3 days and will let Leslie march a day or two after me that he may not be too hard for your depot. I shall be anxious for Balfour's getting off the expedition to Cape Fear as soon as possible. I think about 200 men will do, and that he will make them out from scraps that can be collected of one sort or other. If he wants any little help from you, I need not say that I recommend it. England will come up with Leslie. I intend that *Sutherland*, the engineer, should go to Cape Fear. We shall not want much engineering with the army and it is necessary to have an intelligent person to fix the proper place to cover the shipping, victuallers, etc. Be so kind as to communicate this to him and desire him in consequence to repair to Charlestown. You will please to order Mr Barrett to 96, and Mr McPherson[158] will join the army with General Leslie unless Sutherland wishes to take him with him, which I will readily agree to.

I am, my dear Lord,
Yours very sincerely

CORNWALLIS

Rawdon to Cornwallis, 5th January 1781 — *67(12): ALS*

Camden
January 5th 1781

Earl Cornwallis etc etc etc

My Lord

I have had the honor to receive your letter of the 3rd by Captain McKinnon. Two Highlanders who left Cross Creek on the 28th of last month arrived here last night. They say that they heard nothing in the country of any troops having landed at Cape Fear, so that I think there can be nothing in the report.

Captain Savage says that it was not intended he should remain in this district and presses earnestly for permission to go to New York. With Rankin[159] or any other of the assistants

[158] McPherson, like Barrett, was probably an officer of the line acting temporarily as an assistant engineer. There is no record of him in the Corps of Engineers. His was a common surname, possessed by four junior officers serving in the south: Charles, lieutenant, 1st Battalion, De Lancey's; Donald, captain, British Legion infantry; Donald, ensign, 2nd Battalion, 71st; and Hugh, lieutenant, New York Volunteers. Of these, he was not the captain (see p 360, note 77). (*Army Lists*; Raymond, 'British American Corps')

[159] William Rankin had been commissioned an ensign in the 45th Regiment on 30th October 1777 and been promoted to lieutenant in the 16th on 20th August 1778. He was now serving on secondment to the Quartermaster General's Department. In the Battle of Hobkirk's Hill he would act as an aide-de-camp to Rawdon, who would warmly praise him for his services during the action. (*Army Lists*; *The Cornwallis Papers*)

I should manage as well as with Savage.

Your Lordship may reccollect an old Frenchman, Dusseron, who lives beyond Rugeley's. Whilst the army lay at Waxhaw and Charlotteburg, every party that came up to us foraged at his house and very few gave him receipts. The estimate which he has made of his losses is exorbitant, but as he has behaved himself irreproachably, I imagine your Lordship would wish that some compensation should be made to him.[160]

I send to your Lordship a state of this corps and hope in the course of the day to receive and forward the dispatches from the *Medea*[161].

I have the honor to be very faithfully
Your Lordship's most obedient and affectionate servant

RAWDON

---

[160] No further information about Dusseron has come to light.

[161] *the dispatches..*: see p 124, note 105.

Enclosure
State of the troops at Camden, 1st January 1781 — *103(14): DS*

STATE of the Regiments under the Command of Colonel Lord Rawdon at Camden, the 1st January 1781							
Ranks	*Regiments*						*Total*
	63rd	*64th*	*V of I*[162]	*NYV*[163]	*SCR*[164]	*NCR*[165]	
Officers present:							
Commissioned							
Colonels	-	-	-	-	-	-	-
Lt Colonels	-	-	1	-	-	1	2
Majors	-	-	1	-	1	-	2
Captains	1	2	1	3	2	5	14
Lieutenants	2	3	6	4	5	6	26
Ensigns	4	3	7	2	3	5	24
Staff							
Chaplain	-	-	-	-	1	-	1

[162] Volunteers of Ireland

[163] New York Volunteers

[164] South Carolina Royalist Regiment

[165] Royal North Carolina Regiment

Adjutant	1	1	-	1	1	1	5
Quarter Master	-	-	-	1	1	1	3
Surgeon	1	1	-	1	-	1	4
Mate	1	-	1	1	1	1	5
Effective Serjeants, Drums and Rank & File:							
Present fit for duty							
Serjeants	11	6	17	13	13	20	80
Drums	13	9	12	5	9	10	58
Rank & File	155	250	328	167	204	255	1,359
Absent or Command and Recruiting							
Within the District							
Serjeants	5	13	4	2	7	1	32
Drums	1	5	1	-	-	-	7
Rank & File	48	147	36	25	60	21	337
Without the District							
Serjeants	2	1	-	4	-	-	7
Drums	1	-	-	2	-	-	3
Rank & File	33	11	4	69	-	11	128
Prisoners with the Rebels							
Serjeants	-	1	-	-	3	-	4
Drums	-	-	-	-	-	-	-
Rank & File	25	11	23	16	16	54	145

Sick							
Serjeants	6	3	7	-	2	2	20
Drums	1	2	3	-	-	-	6
Rank & File	114	66	91	16	69	38	394
Wounded							
Serjeants	-	-	2	1	-	-	3
Drums	-	-	-	-	-	-	-
Rank & File	26	2	19	3	-	1	51
Total effective							
Serjeants	24	24	30	20	25	23	146
Drums	16	16	16	7	9	10	74
Rank & File	401	487	501	296	349	380	2,414
Wanting to compleat:							
Serjeants	-	-	-	10	5	7	22
Drums	-	-	6	3	1	-	10
Rank & File	47	-	59	234	181	180	701
Alterations since last return:							
Enlisted	41	-	6	-	1	14	62
Transferred	-	-	-	-	-	-	-
Dead	4	-	1	-	2	1	8
Discharged	-	-	-	-	-	-	-
Deserted	-	-	-	-	-	-	-

Killed	-	-	-	-	-	-	-
Wounded	-	-	-	-	-	-	-

RAWDON
Colonel

Cornwallis to Rawdon, 6th January 1781 *84(22): C*

Wynnesborough
January 6th 1781

Rt Hon Lord Rawdon

My dear Lord

As Tarleton is not quite ready and our waggons not arrived from the Congarees, I deferred my march til Monday. I shall desire Leslie to move on Tuesday and to proceed by the best route to Bullocks Creek. I doubt whether six days' meal will be quite sufficient for him and could wish that you would lend him two waggons for the 2 first days. I will get the best information I can to morrow about his march. I have been writing all day and can only add that I am much obliged to you for your private letter. I have nothing to do with the settling whether Savage or McKinnon was to take charge of the department. Having appointed England to go with me, it was not agreable to me to change, but as Savage wishes to return to New York, that will make all easy. You will keep Rankin or who you please. I will write again to morrow.

Yours most sincerely

CORNWALLIS

Cornwallis to Rawdon, 7th January 1781 *84(27): C*

Wynnesborough
January 7th 1781

Rt Hon Lord Rawdon etc etc etc

My dear Lord

I am not sure whether you saw the copy of T———'s[166] intelligence. From good authority I am informed that Lee's Legion was on Wednesday sevennight at Guilford Court House, where it waited for orders. Whether it was intended to proceed to Charlottetown or Haley's Ferry on Pedee was uncertain, but it was rather thought the latter.

I shall march to morrow for Bullock Creek. Leslie, I understand, will come into our road at the Cross Roads. I will take care that if he is in want, he shall be supplied with meal there. I shall continue writing to you as long as there is communication. The account I have of roads etc is very satisfactory. I almost give up all hopes of Ross but shall not dispair as long as there is a possibility of his joining.

---

166 de Treville's.

I am, my dear Lord,
Very sincerely yours

CORNWALLIS

[*Subscribed*:]

Leslie may depend on meal at the Cross Roads.

Cornwallis to Rawdon, 8th January 1781 — *84(35): C*

McAllister's Plantation
8th January 1781
6 o'clock pm

Rt Hon Lord Rawdon

My dear Lord

I received your letter[167] by Mr Gore[168]. In regard to your recommendations, as I can have no doubt of Sir Henry's approving of them, I will give them out in orders to act untill the Commander in Chief's pleasure is known. I shall halt here tomorrow, move to the Cross Roads on Wednesday, perhaps halt there on Thursday, and then make two days' march to Bullocks Creek Meeting House. I inclose a letter to Fanning[169]. As you will know where to find Leslie tomorrow night, may I beg that you will tell him the plan of my march that he may know where to find me. Tarleton was last night on King's Creek, Ennoree, waiting for his baggage. He heard that Morgan was throwing up works at Grindal's Shoals on Pacolet. I do not believe it.

Be assured, my dear Lord, of the constant good wishes of
Your very assured friend

CORNWALLIS

---

167 *your letter*: not extant.

168 Probably Ralph Gore, who had been commissioned an ensign in the 33rd Regiment on 16th April 1778. Serving as a captain in the same regiment was William Gore, but if Cornwallis had been referring to him, he would most likely have stated his rank. (*Army Lists*)

169 *a letter to Fanning*: of 8th January, p 467.

Cornwallis to Rawdon, 9th January 1781 — *84(44): C*

McAlister's
January 9th 1781
3 pm

Rt Hon Lord Rawdon etc etc etc

My dear Lord

Nothing new since yesterday. Our accounts still place Morgan on Pacolet. The weather will, I fear, be inconvenient to Leslie.

Mr McDonald, the commissary at Camden, is particularly complained of for treating the inhabitants ill who go to him with receipts, particularly some of our Orangeburg friends. I should be obliged to you if you will give him a lecture upon that subject.

There is now a great quantity of meal barrelled up at Congarees, which you may order to Camden. From every account I have great reason to think that I shall not be distressed either for meal or forage on my march.

I am, my dear Lord,
Very sincerely yours

CORNWALLIS

[*Subscribed*:]

Downes[170] was with me yesterday with some proposals about the uncaptured part of Rugeley's militia. I referred him to your Lordship.

Cornwallis to Rawdon, 10th January 1781 — *84(49): C*

McAlister's
January 10th 1781
8 pm

Rt Hon Lord Rawdon etc etc etc

My dear Lord

As the late rains will have very much impeded the march of Leslie and of Tarleton, I think it prudent to remain here a day or two longer; otherwise, by the corps on my flanks being so

---

170 Major William Downes, a former officer of the Royal Irish Artillery who had settled as a blacksmith near Camden, now held, or would soon hold, a commission in the royal militia. Just before the Battle of Hobkirk's Hill a large party of revolutionaries surrounded his home and demanded that he surrender. He and his overseer defended the house, killing several of the attackers with firearms loaded by his wife and children. She later testified that, when he surrendered, the attackers granted him a Georgia parole, that is to say, they 'fired nine balls into him'. (Lambert, *SC Loyalists*, 201-2)

far behind, I should be in danger of losing my communication. I have not heard from Tarleton this day, nor am I sure whether he has passed the Ennoree. I have not as yet been able to procure any satisfactory intelligence of the enemy nor of Colonel Lee's destination.

I am, my dear Lord,
Very sincerely yours

CORNWALLIS

Rawdon to Cornwallis, 11th January 1781 *67(14): ALS*

Camden
January 11th 1781

Earl Cornwallis etc etc etc

My Lord

I have had the honor to receive your Lordship's letters of the 8th and 9th and am to express my obligations very warmly for your assent to the promotion in the Voluntiers of Ireland. I have forwarded all your Lordship's letters[171] to Balfour and I this day send some dispatches from him[172] to overtake General Lesslie. In the mean time I transcribe in cypher such particulars as I think will be satisfactory to your Lordship to know immediately. All is quiet in our neighborhood, and I have so many persons watching Greene that I think he cannot make any movement without my receiving early notice of it. As to the dispatches, be assured, my Lord, that attention shall be paid to every object (tho' it should not be within the limits of my command) in the manner which I shall conceive will be most consonant to your wishes. I beg my best remembrances to Governor Martin and the rest of your family, and have the honor to be, my Lord, with sincere affection and respect

Your very faithful and obedient servant

RAWDON

Cornwallis to Rawdon, 12th January 1781 *84(57): C*

McAlister's
January 12th 1781

Rt Hon Lord Rawdon

My dear Lord

I received yours of yesterday with the extracts of Balfour's letters. The rains have impeded all operations on both sides. Morgan is at Scull's Shoals on Pacolet, and Tarleton

---

[171] *all your Lordship's letters...* See, principally, ch 30 and 31

[172] *some dispatches..:* see Balfour to Cornwallis, 7th January, p 131.

I believe still on the south of Ennoree, unable to pass either that river or the Tyger. The Broad River is so high that it is with difficulty a canoe can pass. If Leslie had not been likewise detained, I might have tried to stop Morgan's retreat, but the corps which I have with me, altho' very good, will not afford a strong detachment to take care of baggage and provisions. I think it very doubtfull whether Leslie will even reach Rocky Mount tomorrow, and untill he gets there, I cannot trust to any assistance from him, so very precarious is our trade and on so many unforeseen events does it depend.

I am much pleased with the detachment proposed by Balfour for the expedition and with the commanding officer, of whom I have heard much good.

I should be very glad to have the troops of dragoons raised to serve under Captain Coffin in the Camden District, to whom I would give the same sort of rank of major that I gave to Dunlap and Maxwell, which I believe in fact is no rank but gives them some credit with the people of the country. I would even engage the men for one year only, and not during the war, and limit their services to the Roanoke, or only to Cape Fear River if they preferr'd it. In short, I would leave no means unattempted to arm America in our favour, which is the only chance of putting a favourable end to this war.

I shall move tomorrow to the creek where we halted before, seven miles short of the Cross Roads. My next march will depend on what I hear of the enemy and of Leslie.

I am, my dear Lord, with the greatest regard
Most faithfully and affectionately yours

CORNWALLIS

[*Subscribed*:]

I inclose a letter from Colonel Fisher relative to Mr McDonald and an account of meal at Congarees.[173]

Rawdon to Cornwallis, 14th January 1781 — *67(20): ALS*

Camden
January 14th 1781

Earl Cornwallis etc etc etc

Most sincerely, my dear Lord, do I congratulate you on the enclosed intelligence, and your friends[174] shall join you tho' five such armies as Greene's should stand in the way.

---

173 There are no extant copies of the enclosures.

174 *your friends*: Major Ross and Captain Brodrick on their arrival from England.

Colonel Fanning has been here but is gone back to Charlestown. He feels much obliged to your Lordship for your wish to make his situation agreable and sees perfectly the impossibility of his being employed here. His desire at present is to take a trip to England for the sake of his health. I did not think Coffin would have gone from hence, as (tho' I left him at liberty to do it) I rather dissuaded him from it; otherwise I should have written by him. Two of your expresses likewise went off without waiting for letters. I am raising militia corps upon pay, which I think will answer well, and you may depend upon every exertion from my knowledge of your sentiments. I am told that Marion is with Greene beyond Pedee, but intelligence is stopped by the floods. I have told the express that you would reward him in proportion to the expedition he uses. It is now twelve o'clock. Excuse my haste, for I only write whilst the messenger's horse is preparing, and the news of an event so very agreable to your Lordship has given a lively spring to the spirits of

Your very faithful and affectionate servant

RAWDON

[*Subscribed*:]

An escort is gone to meet Ross.

Cornwallis to Rawdon, 21st January 1781 — *84(78): ADfS*

Buffalo Creek
January 21st 1781

Rt Hon Lord Rawdon etc etc etc

My dearest Lord

The late affair has almost broke my heart. Morgan is at Gilbertown. I shall march tomorrow with 1,200 infantry and the cavalry to attack or follow him to the banks of Catawba. General Howard remains at Cherokee Ford with all baggage, knapsacks included, ready to meet us at Ramsoure's. I was never more surrounded with difficulty and distress, but practice in the school of adversity has strengthned me. Write to me and to Howard and communicate with 96. England is with Howard.

I would have the Cape Fear business go on. Communicate this to Balfour.

Your truly affectionate friend

CORNWALLIS

Cornwallis to Rawdon, 25th January 1781 *84(83): ADfS*

Ramsoure's

January 25th 1781

Rt Hon Lord Rawdon etc etc etc

My dear Lord

Morgan's movements have been too rapid for me and he has passed the Catawba at Sherrill's Ford. My situation is most critical. I see infinite *danger in proceeding but certain ruin in retreating. I am therefore determined to go on, unless some misfortune should happen to you, which God forbid.*

Whilst Green remains on Pedee, I would have you act with great caution and even suffer insults east of Santee, taking great care that Watson may not receive a check, which, as I understand Lee[175] has joined Green, is but too probable. But you should use all possible exertion to get a stock of provisions from Congarees; that is the point I am most uneasy about.

As soon as Green quits the lower Pedee, I think you may make a forward *move unless you see objections of which I cannot judge. You must at the same time send 200 men to Ninety Six. I should recommend Fanning's corps, in which case the redoubt at George Town might be occupied by sixty of the worst marchers of the 64th under Gratton and 40 Hessians from Charlestown. If you do not approve of this, alter it as you please, but do not send either Watson or Innes's corps. The former would not be proper to command, the latter would relapse into militia. I find it impossible to take on waggons. I have therefore determined to burn all my waggons except those loaded with rum, salt, spare amunition and hospital stores.* O'Hara's brigade sets the example of rigid discipline and perfect good will on all occasions. Our men are healthy and full of zeal. If an opportunity offers, I trust I shall send you good news. Let me hear from you as often as possible.

---

175 Henry ('Light Horse Harry') Lee of Virginia (1756-1818) had entered the Continental service as a captain of horse in 1777. Promoted to major in command of his own corps of cavalry in April 1778, he had come to lead the augmented Legion which was commonly named after him (see vol I, p 44, note 4). A decisive and resourceful officer, he had brilliantly led the force which surprised the British post at Paulus Hook, New Jersey, in August 1779, an event which gained him one of only eight gold medals awarded by Congress during the war. Now a lt colonel, he had been recently sent south with his Legion to reinforce Greene and would play a consummate, and mostly distinguished, part in the events of 1781 in the Carolinas. His reputation would, however, be sullied by his involvement in the inhuman butchery of a band of unresisting loyalists led by Dr John Pyle, an event commonly known as 'Pyle's massacre', which occurred in late February near the Haw River, North Carolina. Engaging in politics after the war, he was elected to the Virginia legislature and Continental Congress and also served a term as Governor of Virginia. A poor businessman, he was imprisoned for debt in 1808-09, a period when he embarked on writing his memoirs of the revolutionary war in the south. In his final years he suffered from ill health, spent a considerable period in the West Indies, and, while on his way home from there, died at Cumberland Island, Georgia. In 1913 his remains were transferred to the Lee chapel at Washington and Lee University, Lexington. (*DAB*; Boatner, *Encyclopedia*, 607-610; *Appletons'*; 'Joseph Graham's Narrative', *The Murphey Papers*, ii, 273-6)

I am, my dear Lord,
Yours most sincerely

CORNWALLIS

[*Subscribed*:]

I do not write to Balfour but trust to your giving him information.

I hear that Sumpter's people are assembling at Crowder's Creek, meaning to march down the fork. I wish you to pay attention to them and think that I shall soon take Green off your hands.

Fornay's Plantation
6 miles west of Beatty's Ford
January 29th 1781

The Catawba is swelled but will be passable in a day or two. We shall perhaps meet with some opposition, but I hope no great difficulty. Morgan is said to be at Sherrill's, and Davidson at Beatty's Ford. I hear from good authority that Green is marching towards Salisbury. I will lose no time in passing the Yadkin.

§ - §

3 - From Richard England

England to Cornwallis, December 1780 — *4(257): ALS*

Camden
December 1780[176]

Lt General Earl Cornwallis

My Lord

Since my return here I wou'd have often done myself the honor of reporting to your Lordship different matters relative to the department under my care, but, sensible of your having many more important matters to occupy you, omitted troubling you particularly as there was so constant a correspondence between your Lordship and Lord Rawdon, who I acquainted with every circumstance that I considered a trial and who I believe reported them

176 Written on or around the 9th. See Cornwallis to Rawdon, 11th December, p 204.

to your Lordship. I have been very anxious to return to Head Quarters and imagined that the chief purpose of my jaunt here wou'd have been accomplished before now, but have met with an unaccountable delay in getting from Charles Town the saddles and other articles necessary for the New York Volunteers, tho to remove a possibility of delay I sent waggons sufficient for that purpose to town immediately after my arrival here. That corps has now got one hundred and twenty horses that wou'd not disgrace any regiment of cavalry, exclusive of those intended for them by the 63rd Regiment, which I have sent to the Congarees to recover, they not being fit for any immediate service nor a probability of their recovering shortly, their backs being much injured from the saddles and frequent use. And if they are not too far gone, idleness and the forage in that country will recover them. The saddles shall be repaired and made serviceable when the necessary articles for that purpose can be procured. Tho much distressed for want of them, they cannot be brought into use.

I have received from Colonel Browne eighteen horses and daily expect more by Colonel Cruger's letter. Those I have received are appropriated to the department as they were not fit for the New York Volunteers. There are twelve waggons at the Congarees collecting a magazine as directed by your Lordship, and I have one hundred and forty worn down horses there in order to recover, and I have here fit for immediate service near thirty waggons exclusive of those daily employed by the engineer and barrack master here daily. They shall be constantly employed in removing the quantities of rum and salt from McCord's or in executing any of your Lordship's commands, as they are able to go thro any service. I have sent some days since a waggon on purpose to Charles Town for the four hundred pairs of shoes your Lordship ordered *thro* Colonel Tarleton for the infantry of the Legion and expect them in the course of next week. Whenever Captain McKinnon favours me with the articles I wrote for to appoint the New York Volunteers, I shall go to Head Quarters. In the mean time, shou'd be happy to receive any commands your Lordship may honor me with.

I inclose to your Lordship a letter sent me by Captain Roorback[177] and shall forward him any answer you direct.

I have the honor to be, my Lord, with great respect
Your Lordship's very faithful humble and obedient servant

R^D ENGLAND

§ - §

---

[177] The letter is not exant. Barent Roorbach (1748-?) was from New York and on 24th October 1776 had been commissioned a captain in Cruger's 1st Battalion, De Lancey's Brigade. He had previously entered college to study medicine and been in practice. When the battalion was disbanded at the close of the war, he was placed on the Provincial half-pay list and settled at New York. Despite receiving half pay, his circumstances had become needy by 1806 and he joined the Venezuelan revolutionary, Francisco de Miranda, in a failed attempt to cause a revolution at Caracas. (Treasury 64/23(9), WO 65/164(33) and WO 65/165(7) (National Archives, Kew); Sabine, *Biographical Sketches*, 241)

4 - Return of troops remaining in South Carolina under Rawdon

15th January 1781

103(16): D

STATE of the Troops left in South Carolina under the Command of the Rt Hon Colonel Lord Rawdon, 15th January 1781

	British Regiments or Corps				*Total*
	17th[178]	*63rd*	*64th*	*84th*[179]	
Dates of Returns	1 Jn 81	1 Jn 81	1 Nov 80	15 Jn 81	
Officers present:					
Commissioned					
Colonels	-	-	-	-	-
Lt Colonels	-	-	-	-	-
Majors	-	-	1	1	2
Captains	1	1	3	3	8
Lieutenants	-	2	7	2	11

178 A detachment

179 Four companies

Ensigns	2	4	2	-	8
Staff					
Chaplains	-	-	-	-	-
Adjutants	-	1	1	1	3
Quarter Masters	-	-	1	1	2
Surgeons	-	1	1	-	2
Mates	1	1	-	1	3
Effective Serjeants, Drummers, Rank & File:					
Present fit for duty					
Serjeants	9	11	16	4	40
Drummers	2	13	11	2	28
Rank & File	99	155	249	113	616
Absent on Command and Recruiting					
Within the District					
Serjeants	-	5	3	4	12
Drummers	-	1	1	2	4
Rank & File	-	48	46	63	157
Without the District					
Serjeants	-	2	-	-	2
Drummers	-	1	-	-	1
Rank & File	-	33	-	-	33
Prisoners with the Rebels					
Serjeants	-	-	1	-	1

Drummers	-	-	-	-	-
Rank & File	-	25	11	-	36
Sick					
Serjeants	1	6	4	-	11
Drummers	-	1	4	-	5
Rank & File	4	114	80	32	230
Wounded					
Serjeants	-	-	-	-	-
Drummers	-	-	-	-	-
Rank & File	-	26	-	-	26
Total effective					
Serjeants	10	24	24	8	66
Drummers	2	16	16	4	38
Rank & File	103	401	386	208	1,098
Wanting to compleat:					
Serjeants	-	-	-	-	-
Drummers	-	-	-	-	-
Rank & File	-	167	182	-	349
Alterations since last return:					
Inlisted or Recovered	-	-	-	15	15
Transferred	-	-	-	-	-
Dead	-	-	-	-	-
Discharged	-	-	-	-	-

Deserted	-	-	-	-	-
Killed	-	-	-	-	-
Wounded	-	-	-	-	-

	Provincial Regiments or Corps								*Total*
	Lt Infantry[180]	*NYV*[181]	*3rd, Skinner's*	*1st, Delancy's*	*KAR*[182]	*PWAR*[183]	*V of I*[184]	*SC*[185]	
Dates of Returns	1 Jn 81	1 Jn 81	15 Nov 80	15 Dec 80	1 Jn 81	15 Jn 81	1 Jn 81	1 Jn 81	
Officers present:									
Commissioned									
Colonels	-	-	-	-	1	-	-	-	1
Lt Colonels	1	-	1	1	-	-	1	-	4
Majors	1	-	-	-	1	1	1	1	5

180 Watson's corps

181 New York Volunteers

182 King's American Regiment

183 Prince of Wales's American Regiment

184 Volunteers of Ireland

185 South Carolina Royalist Regiment

Captains	6	3	2	2	6	1	1	2	23
Lieutenants	7	4	6	1	8	3	6	5	40
Ensigns	4	2	4	1	6	1	7	3	28
Staff									
Chaplains	-	-	-	-	-	-	-	1	1
Adjutants	1	1	1	1	1	-	-	1	6
Quarter Masters	1	1	-	1	1	1	1	1	7
Surgeons	1	1	1	-	1	1	-	-	5
Mates	-	1	-	-	1	1	1	1	5
Effective Serjeants, Drummers, Rank & File:									
Present fit for duty									
Serjeants	16	13	18	9	17	10	17	13	113
Drummers	6	5	5	4	8	6	12	9	55
Rank & File	200	167	186	59	246	40	328	204	1,430
Absent on Command and Recruiting									
Within the District									
Serjeants	-	2	3	5	-	11	4	7	32
Drummers	-	-	3	1	-	1	1	-	6
Rank & File	-	25	6	68	-	104	36	60	299
Without the District									
Serjeants	-	4	3	1	3	1	-	-	12
Drummers	-	2	-	-	1	-	-	-	3
Rank & File	3	69	28	14	89	17	4	-	224

Prisoners with the Rebels									
Serjeants	-	-	1	3	-	4	-	3	11
Drummers	-	-	1	-	-	1	-	-	2
Rank & File	-	16	46	49	20	16	23	16	186
Sick									
Serjeants	-	-	1	1	7	3	7	2	21
Drummers	-	-	-	-	-	2	3	-	5
Rank & File	6	16	18	9	48	52	91	69	309
Wounded									
Serjeants	-	1	1	-	-	1	2	-	5
Drummers	-	-	-	-	-	-	-	-	-
Rank & File	-	3	1	-	-	9	19	-	32
Total effective									
Serjeants	16	20	27	19	27	30	30	25	194
Drummers	6	7	9	5	9	10	16	9	71
Rank & File	209	296	285	199	403	238	501	349	2,480
Wanting to compleat:									
Serjeants	-	10	3	11	3	-	-	5	32
Drummers	-	3	1	5	1	-	6	1	17
Rank & File	31	234	275	361	157	292	59	181	1,600
Alterations since last return:									
Inlisted or Recovered	-	-	-	-	-	2	-	7	9
Transferred	-	-	-	-	-	-	-	-	-

Dead	-	-	-	-	-	-	-	6	6
Discharged	-	-	-	-	-	-	-	-	-
Deserted	-	-	-	-	-	-	-	6	6
Killed	-	-	-	-	-	-	-	-	-
Wounded	-	-	-	-	-	-	-	-	-

	German Regiments or Corps				*Total*	*Combined Total (British, Provincial and German)*
	Dittfurth	*Angelleli*	*Huyne*	*Artillery*		
Dates of Returns	15 Jn 81	15 Jn 81	15 Jn 81	15 Jn 81		
Officers present:						
Commissioned						
Colonels	1	-	1	-	2	3
Lt Colonels	1	-	1	-	2	6
Majors	1	1	1	-	3	10
Captains	3	4	5	-	12	43
Lieutenants	6	3	4	3	16	67
Ensigns	5	4	4	-	13	49
Staff						
Chaplains	1	-	1	-	2	3
Adjutants	1	1	1	-	3	12
Quarter Masters	1	1	1	-	3	12
Surgeons	1	1	1	-	3	10

Mates	5	5	5	-	15	23
Effective Serjeants, Drummers, Rank & File:						
Present fit for duty						
Serjeants	54	44	55	4	157	310
Drummers	18	12	13	1	44	127
Rank & File	389	258	390	40	1,077	3,123
Absent on Command and Recruiting						
Within the District						
Serjeants	-	-	3	2	5	49
Drummers	-	1	1	-	2	12
Rank & File	-	15	23	4	42	498
Without the District						
Serjeants	2	-	-	-	2	16
Drummers	1	-	-	-	1	5
Rank & File	19	-	-	-	19	276
Prisoners with the Rebels						
Serjeants	-	-	-	-	-	12
Drummers	-	-	-	-	-	2
Rank & File	-	48	-	-	48	270
Sick						
Serjeants	4	14	1	1	20	52
Drummers	3	4	1	-	8	18

Rank & File	46	109	43	6	204	743
Wounded						
Serjeants	-	1	-	-	1	6
Drummers	-	-	-	-	-	-
Rank & File	-	13	3	-	16	74
Total effective						
Serjeants	60	59	59	7	185	445
Drummers	22	17	15	1	55	164
Rank & File	454	443	459	50	1,406	4,984
Wanting to compleat:						
Serjeants	-	1	1	1	3	35
Drummers	-	5	-	-	5	22
Rank & File	71	127	66	15	279	2,228
Alterations since last return:						
Inlisted or Recovered	-	41	1	-	42	66
Transferred	-	-	-	-	-	-
Dead	-	3	2	-	5	11
Discharged	-	-	-	-	-	-
Deserted	-	-	-	-	-	6
Killed	-	-	-	-	-	-
Wounded	-	-	-	-	-	-

Not included in the above:

Detachment of Royal Artillery	*Majors*	*Captains*	*Subalterns*	*Staff*	*Serjeants*	*Drummers*	*Rank & File*
	1	*1*	*1*	*3*	*4*	*3*	*85*

§ - §

CHAPTER 33

Correspondence with Ninety Six and Augusta

---

1 - Between Cornwallis or Haldane and Cruger or Allen

Cruger to Rawdon, 1st November 1780 ***4(7): ALS***

Ninety Six
November 1st
11 o'clock am

The Rt Hon Lord Rawdon etc etc etc
Wynnesborough

My Lord

This morning I received intelligence that the rebels were collect'd a little beyond Ennoree. Three hundred they are called, and intended advancing. We having not more than 100 militia in arms (at Williams's plantation), I proposed Major Wemyss marching immediately to support our post at Williams's, to encourage the militia to turn out, they, as soon as capable, to pursue. Major Wemyss' appearance, I flatter myself, will have all those good consequences. I expect him in every minute from his quarters to proceed on. This step, I am happy to find, corresponds with your Lordship's intentions in respect to the use to be made of the mounted 63rd, as directed by your Lordship's letter of yesterday, which I have this instant the honor of receiving and to which due and full attention shall be paid. Your Lordship's letters of the 26th and 28th of last month I answer'd on the 30th.[1]

---

[1] For the letters referred to, see vol II, pp 201 and 203-6.

Major Clary told me yesterday that he does not apprehend any difficulty in getting men for the two troops, but horses they have not. Quakers, protected men and old men have the horses that would answer. In what manner to possess ourselves of those, I told him, rested with the Commander in Chief. Your Lordship's directions for mounting our dragoons I hope to have soon. The difficulty of raising the infantry (militia) obliges me to repeat my wish that a third troop may be added.

I have the honor to be with the highest respect, my Lord,
Your Lordship's most obedient humble servant

J H CRUGER
Lt Colonel commanding 96

Cornwallis to Cruger, 4th November 1780 — *82(8): C*

Wynnesborough
November 4th 1780

Lt Colonel Cruger commanding at Ninety Six

Sir

I have given directions to Captain Dunlap relative to the raising some cavalry for the protection of 96, which he will explain to you. The militia must be encouraged. I would give three months' back pay to those who have been actually employed during that time and did not quit their regiments without leave, at the following rates: a captain £50, a lieutenant £30, an ensign £20 a year, a private 3 dollars a month, the prisoners to receive their share. It will be difficult to ascertain every man's right exactly, but you will do it in the best manner possible. I am convinced, without some douceur of this sort, that we shall totally lose the service of the militia. I have explained my intentions to Colonel Balfour, so that he will assist in procuring you the money from Charlestown[2].

I am, sir,
Your most obedient etc

CORNWALLIS

---

2 *I have explained..*: on 1st and 4th November, pp 59-61.

Cruger to Cornwallis, 8th November 1780 *4(76): ALS*

Ninety Six
November 8th 1780

Rt Hon Earl Cornwallis etc etc etc

My Lord

I am very happy in being again honor'd with a letter from your Lordship of the 4th instant by Captain Dunlap, who has explain'd to me the plan of raising some cavalry in this neighbourhood. I think your Lordship's order quite necessary for the horse accoutrements at Savannah, as I am very doubtful of Sir James Wright's parting with them on any other conditions. I would then immediately send a troop (3 serjeants, 3 corporals and 40 privates) off for them as the safest and most expeditious way to get them.

I will call for returns from the militia to find out those who have actually been employ'd for three months past that they may be paid agreeable to your Lordship's intentions. Lt Governor Graham was here the last week. From him I received the inclosed abstract, which points out not only the number but the manner how the inhabitants are disposed of on the Ceded Lands. I promised Mr Graham to communicate to your Lordship Sir James Wright's wish and his that Colonel Brown's corps was advanced as far forward as Broad River on the Ceded Lands in the fork nearly opposite Fort Charlotte, and that the duty at Augusta should be constantly done by 100 or 150 militia.

I have the honor to be with the highest respect, my Lord,
Your Lordship's most obedient and very humble servant

J H CRUGER
Lt Colonel commanding 96

Enclosure *4(75): C*

Inhabitants of the Ceded Lands in Georgia, viz:

255 loyal and form'd into a regiment under Colonel Waters

159 left in the settlement for whom hostages are taken and carried to Savannah

21 the above hostages gone to Savannah

42 prisoners sent to Charles Town by Governor Graham

57 persons in the settlement, characters not known

49 notorious and active rebels laying out and to be destroy'd as speedily as possible, persons and property

140 persons with Clark when he went away
723

NB

The wives and children to be immediately sent after the husbands who have left the province. The prisoners sent to Charles Town by Colonel Cruger are not included in the above number.

Cornwallis to Cruger, 11th November 1780[3] *82(24): C*

Wynnsborough
November 11th 1780

Lt Colonel Cruger

Sir

I have just received your letter of the 8th. You will by this time, I hope, have seen Major Prevost and received my letter by Captain Gibbs[4] giving some account of Major Wemys's affair at Fishdam Ford. The serjeant major of the 63rd, who was left with a flag of truce, is returned and assures me that when day broke there was not a rebel to be seen and that it was full two hours before two men came to the house where Major Wemys was left, so that if our people had staid till daylight they would have found themselves in full possession of the enemy's camp and would have brought off the major and the rest of the wounded and the victory must have been indisputable, which in this war is of the utmost importance. As it is, they were surprised, their loss was 3 times more than ours, and they were drove from their camp, where our people never meant to remain. I have sent Major McArthur with the 1st Battalion of the 71st, the 63rd and some cavalry to Shirar's Ferry. He has cannon and his corps is good and respectable in point of numbers. McArthur's battalion is strong and the 63rd are commanded by my aid de camp, Mr Money, an intelligent and spirited officer. I expect Colonel Tarleton in three or four days. I think the corps under Sumpter etc will not in the present circumstances venture to attack 96. If they disperse near the Broad River to plunder, Money with the cavalry and mounted men will cross and fall on their parties. In short, I will pay every attention to the protection of that quarter consistent with the safety of the whole. Major Wemys is paroled and coming hither. I have the satisfaction to hear that his wounds are not so dangerous as they were at first represented, although his situation is very doubtfull.

The cavalry acoutrements are arrived at Charlestown. Although I promised Colonel Tarleton the picking of them, yet I think it of so much consequence to have some shew of cavalry at 96 that I shall give a line to Dunlap to desire Balfour to let him have forty six setts,

---

3 Extracts from this letter are published in Ross ed, *Cornwallis Correspondence*, i, 67-8.

4 *my letter by Captain Gibbs*: no extant copy.

and agree to engage the men and officers on the terms which Dunlap informs me are those only by which they can be procured, viz, that the men are to serve only twelve months, to receive no bounty, and the officers to be paid as infantry. I have directed Major McArthur and Mr Money to send you every intelligence they can procure of the movements of the enemy. The accounts I receive from Colonel Kirkland[5] of the supineness and pusillanimity of our militia takes off all my compassion for their sufferings. If they will allow themselves to be plundered, and their families ruined, by a banditti not a third of their numbers, there is no possibility of our protecting them. I hope and trust, however, that Colonel Kirkland exaggerates their demerits to raise his own merit.

I am, sir,
Your most obedient and faithfull servant

CORNWALLIS

Cruger to Cornwallis, 14th November 1780 — *4(116): ALS*

Ninety Six
November 14th 1780

Rt Hon Earl Cornwallis etc etc etc

My Lord

Yesterday and the day before I was honor'd with your Lordship's letters of the 10th and 11th[6]. Captain Gibbs ought not to have troubled your Lordship about an exchange for Lieutenant Ford[7] on parole, as I had already told him and their connections that a Lieutenant Thomas[8], who Colonel Kirkland had improperly paroled from this place when I was in Georgia, should continue at his house on his parole, provided Ford was suffer'd to continue on his, or I would order Lieutenant Thomas back to jail, and so I would wish the matter to remain. I will make enquiry for such men as your Lordship describes of Colonel Innes's corps, defend them against the arbitrary proceedings of their officers, and encourage their entering into the militia service, where they may be of some use.

---

5 *The accounts..*: Cornwallis has in mind Kirkland's letters of 8th and 10th November, pp 380-3.

6 As to the letter of the 10th, see note 4 above.

7 John Ford Jr was a lieutenant in Zacharias Gibbs' Spartan Regiment of the royal militia. (Clark, *Loyalists in the Southern Campaign*, i, 282)

8 Perhaps Abram or Robert Thomas, both of whom were sons of Colonel John Thomas Sr (see vol I, p 259, note 28). Abram would be wounded, and Robert killed, in the action at Mud Lick on 2nd March 1781. Taken prisoner, Abram would die in Camden jail. ('Jane Thomas' in Elizabeth F Ellet, *The Women of the American Revolution* (New York, 1848); Moss, *SC Patriots*, 924, 926; McCrady, *SC in the Rev 1780-1783*, 114)

I am exceedingly obliged to your Lordship for the account you are pleased to give me of the business at Fish Dam Ford, but distress'd that we were so unfortunate as not to avail ourselves of every circumstance, which might have been great and productive of happy consequences. Major McArthur's situation will awe in some measure the Colonels Clark, Thomas, Brandon, Candler etc with about 400 men (between Tyger and Ennoree) in advancing. Sumter composes the second detachment, and Campbell with the Mountain men the third, of all which your Lordship has undoubtedly better intelligence than mine. Plundering and destroying the country appears to me the grand object of the rebels, in which, from the inhabitants, I can't find that they'll have much opposition in any quarter. Kirkland's account of the fork people I fear is too just. The old man, for his zeal and industry and good disposition towards the royal cause, your Lordship may be assured, has merit.

Captain Dunlap is now here. He means to be in Charles Town by Sunday next to send up from thence the horse accoutrements. Clary tells me he has the men for his troop ready. I mean to have them muster'd this week by Mr Brice[9], who is expected here every day. Major Prevost came to us on Sunday and will leave us for Augusta on Thursday.

Just after my return from the Ceded Lands I intimated to Colonel Balfour a wish for leave of absence to go [to] Charles Town. Poor Ferguson's misfortune soon after and other circumstances have hitherto in Colonel Balfour's opinion, corrisponding with my own, stopt me. By Colonel Cunningham from town I received a message from Colonel Balfour that he desired to see me, General Williamson and Colonel Pickens, who have held themselves in readiness to go with me when ever I should go, which most probably may be about Sunday or Monday next, but I shall not presume to stir till I acquaint your Lordship with it, as well as to know if your Lordship will have any particular commands for me in town.

Captain Dunlap informs me that it is your Lordship's pleasure that Serjeant Major Blew[10],

9 Rigdon Brice was born in Craven County, North Carolina, the grandson of Colonel William Brice, who died there in 1719. Like John Hamilton (see vol I, p 55, note 22), he appears to have been expelled from North Carolina for his loyalism in 1777 and to have made his way to New York. There he was appointed one of two Deputy Muster Masters on the staff of the Inspector General of Provincial Forces and was taken on Archibald Campbell's expedition to Georgia in late 1778. He had since been responsible for mustering British American corps in the Southern Department and was still performing this duty in 1782. He would soon accompany Cornwallis on the winter campaign but would not proceed with him to Virginia. At the close of the war he was placed on the Provincial half-pay list and claimed £1,000 from the royal commission for property confiscated in North Carolina. He was awarded £39-12*s*-0*d*. (Julia French Wood, 'French-Wood Genealogy' (Internet, 29th December 2000); Rigdon Brice to Edward Winslow, 24th August 1781 and 25th January 1782 (The Edward Winslow Papers, University of New Brunswick, Reel 152, 2-34 and 2-42); Clark, *Loyalists in the Southern Campaign*, i, *passim*; Treasury 64/23(21), WO 65/164(6) and WO 65/165(15) (National Archives, Kew); DeMond, *Loyalists in NC*, 251)

10 Perhaps from North Carolina, Daniel Blue was a serjeant major in the Provincial line who had been seconded to Ferguson's corps. By order of Ferguson he had acted for some months as adjutant to the royal militia in the Back Country and, while serving with intrepidity under Dunlap's command, had been wounded. His good conduct had brought him to the notice of Cornwallis, who would specially award him four months' pay as adjutant. Soon he would be promoted acting quartermaster to the corps of irregular horse being raised by Dunlap, a position which would lead to his being placed on the Provincial half-pay list, not as of right, but as being among those very few officers in his situation 'who appeared to have served with zeal and to have suffered from wounds or otherwise'. In 1786 he would settle in Nova Scotia on a 200-acre plantation on the eastern bank of the Musquodoboit River about two and a half miles from its mouth. (*The Cornwallis Papers*; Treasury 64/23(38) (National Archives, Kew); Ann Moser, 'History of Meagher's Grant' (http://www.rootsweb.com/~nsmusquo/, 4th December 2005))

whom Colonel Ferguson had appointed to act as adjutant to the militia, should be paid four months' pay out of the money I have in hand for the militia.

Lt Colonel Allen, who will command here (if your Lordship pleases) in my absence, is well known to Major McArthur and is a gentleman on whom your Lordship may rely with the utmost confidence.

I have the honor to be, my Lord, most respectfully
Your Lordship's most obedient and very humble servant

J H CRUGER
Lt Colonel commanding 96

Cornwallis to Cruger, 16th November 1780 — *82(50): C*

Winsborough
November 16th 1780

Lt Colonel Cruger commanding at Ninety Six

Sir

I last night received your letter of the 14th. You will have heard from Major McArthur that a Negroe came to me on Tuesday positively saying that General Smallwood was on your side of the river with three pieces of cannon. Every intelligence that I have been able to procure contradicts him as to Smallwood, and indeed I can hardly doubt his being on the Salisbury Road. The Negro still obstinately persists about the cannon and says he will be content to be hanged if it proves to be a lie. I can, however, hardly believe him. The lad who brought me your letter talked so much of rebel parties that I am afraid, having no cypher with you, to write very fully. You will find things in two or three days take a very different turn in your district, of which you will have notice, and perhaps you may be able to cooperate. I should by no means approve of your going to Charlestown at present. Altho' I have a great respect for Colonel Allen's character, it is very proper that you should both be on the spot. Kirkland may have merit for his loyalty but I suspect that he is caballing amongst the militia to serve private views. He has been the cause of their plaguing me with several improper petitions[11], and from the character I have always heard of him I cannot consider him a proper person to be placed at the head of the militia of Ninety Six. I must if possible put Cunningham in that station.

I am, sir,
Your most obedient and faithfull servant

CORNWALLIS

---

[11] *several improper petitions*: only one is extant. See p 395.

Cruger to Cornwallis, 16th November 1780 *4(141): ALS*

Ninety Six
November 16th 1780

Lt General Earl Cornwallis etc etc etc

My Lord

This will be deliver'd your Lordship by Colonel Cunningham, to whom I have communicated Colonel Balfour's proposal of appointing him to the command of all the militia in the District of 96 in order by draft to raise one third the militia for constant service and while on duty to be paid: a captain (at the rate of) £50, a lieutenant £30 and an ensign £20 per annum, privates 3 dollars per month. Cunningham will undertake it and is certainly by far the properest hand, but previous to his going to work he wishes to be indulged with an interview with your Lordship in which he may fully explain his own particular situation and relate some circumstances that may remove every kind of impediment hereafter. He has suffer'd so much already in the cause of Government that from what I can learn he cannot engage farther without pay adequate to the expensive nature of his command. Your Lordship's being troubled with this application is to avoid the delay that would consequently attend an application to Colonel Balfour, time now being precious.

The 14th I did myself the honor to write your Lordship, advising of Colonel Balfour's message to me by Cunningham to come to Charles Town, which I have repeated in a letter I received from him yesterday evening. I shall wait your Lordship's commands. Mr Brice (Muster Master) came in here yesterday and went with Major Prevost this morning for Augusta. Some of our neighbours in the Long Cane settlement have join'd the rebels. They were of the protection or parole kind. Cunningham will procure in the fork, as he goes through, the best intelligence of the enemy. I beg to refer your Lordship to him as I know nothing very important.

I have the honor to be most respectfully, my Lord,
Your Lordship's obedient and very humble servant

J H CRUGER
Lt Colonel commanding 96

Cornwallis to Cruger, 23rd November 1780 *82(89): C*

Wynnesborough
November 23rd 1780

Lt Colonel Cruger

Sir

I sent on the 16th an answer to your letter of the 14th, which I hope arrived safe. Cunningham yesterday delivered me yours of the 16th. I have made him a brigadier general of militia with the command of the militia of the District of Ninety Six and he returned full of zeal and perfectly satisfied. I think Kirkland should have some little douceur for the active part he has taken at this critical time[12]. I believe him very loyal, but he certainly is not a very proper man to be at the head of the militia. You will have heard, long before this reaches you, of Colonel Tarleton's success on the 20th against Sumpter at Blackstokes on Tyger River. I had not received the account when Cunningham was with me.

I desired Colonel Tarleton to apply to you if he thought any cooperation from your post would be usefull to him, as well as for any assistance of militia. I think at all events if the militia could seize any of the stragglers from Sumpter it would be of consequence to do it as they have been guilty of the most horrid outrages.

I mentioned in my letter of the 16th that I thought you had better postpone your intention of going to Charlestown 'till affairs were a little more settled. I propose sending Mr Haldane to 96 in a few days, as soon as he can be spared from Camden. I should be desirous of his seeing you there that you might talk over the state of the present works and the propriety of any additional ones.

I think if you had two iron six pounders for the works and a brass 3 pounder for any excursions into the country, it might answer better than keeping the two brass six pounders. I am not sure whether there is one or two pieces of brass ordnance at Augusta, but unless the garrison was much augmented, I should be of opinion that it would be more proper for them to have iron only. Indeed I consider 96 as the security of Augusta. As I apprehend that the fork is by this time pretty well cleared of rebel parties, you had better send the horses to Major England at Camden under escort of the militia as he will want them as soon as possible. Forage being scarce here, they had better not pass by this place, which is out of the way, but proceed directly to Camden.

I am, sir,
Your most obedient humble servant

CORNWALLIS

Cruger to Cornwallis, 23rd November 1780 — *4(181): ALS*

Ninety Six
November 23rd 1780

Rt Hon Earl Cornwallis etc etc etc

My Lord

From the country reports received yesterday and this day I presume the communication between this and Shirer's Ferry is again open and shall therefore trouble your Lordship with

---

12 *some little douceur..*: see Cornwallis to Kirkland, 30th November, p 387.

a letter, tho' nothing of any consequence has occurr'd since I had the honor of writing by Colonel Cunningham the 16th instant. I am exceeding anxious to get some authentick accounts of Colonel Tarlton's success; my expectations have been great; the prospect from the assurance of the rebels was favorable.

Last week Colonel Brown sent here from Augusta twenty horses for the Quarter Master General's Department. I immediately acquainted Major England with it, and that Brown would send in about ten days fifty more. We are increasing daily (tho' moderately) our stock of provision.

Last week Colonel Allen lost a serjeant and private, who, contrary to orders, were strolling through the country and taken off by some sculking fellows.

I hope soon to be honor'd with a letter from your Lordship. The last I received was the 16th.

A few of the inhabitants on Long Cane have been plunder'd. Many more deserved it for their pusilanimous behaviour. About forty to fifty rebels frighten'd the whole regiment. Two or three loyalists are kill'd and many disarm'd. I think I shall never again look to the militia for the least support and I am convinced that it is the King's troops only that can hold this country.

I have the honor to be most respectfully with the greatest deference, my Lord,
Your Lordship's most obedient and very humble servant

J H CRUGER
Lt Colonel commanding 96

Cornwallis to Cruger, 25th November 1780 — *82(99): C*

Wynnesborough
November 25th 1780

Lt Colonel Cruger commanding at 96

Sir

I informed you by a letter of the 23rd of Colonel Tarleton's success. You will no doubt by this time have heard all the particulars. I should wish to have as many of the militia as possible sent to Colonel Tarleton. If any body can put spirit into them, he will.

I am glad to hear from Mr Brice, the Muster Master, that your garrison was so healthy. I will as soon as possible send you an engineer. Mr Haldane is detained at Camden by the illness of Mr Barrett, his assistant. You will be kind enough to give notice to Brigadier General Cunningham about the militia.

I am, sir,
Your most obedient humble servant

CORNWALLIS

Cruger to Cornwallis, 27th November 1780 *4(217): ALS*

Ninety Six
November 27th 1780

Rt Hon Earl Cornwallis etc etc etc

My Lord

I am honor'd with your Lordship's letter of the 23rd. Am exceeding happy to find Cunningham with zeal take to the militia. I think that if any thing can be done with them, it will be through him, tho' in the day of trial I shall ever suspect them hereafter. Old Kirkland's having a temporary command was from absolute necessity. I shall look for the pleasure of Mr Haldane's company this week, after which I presume it will not be contrary to your Lordship's pleasure to suffer me to go to town, *provided always* that no new matter turns up to make it improper, in which case your Lordship may be assured I should never offer to stir. I must take the liberty to intercede with your Lordship for keeping the two *three* pounders we have here. The name only of guns, cannon, is terrible to the ear of a cracker[13]. We are now said to be fortify'd with field pieces. We can't afford to lose any part of our consequence, tho it may be somewhat ideal. At Augusta there are two three pounders brass, and some iron ordnance, I believe not good for much. There again, my Lord, the sound of *artillery* tells through the country.

The twenty horses for Major England are gone to him this day at Camden, as directed by your Lordship, under an escort of militia.

I received a letter last Saturday from Colonel Tarleton signifying your Lordship's wish to have the District of 96 clear'd as soon as possible of the rebels, and that a detachment from this garrison was necessary to move immediately into the Long Cane settlement with some militia to affect this purpose. Colonel Allen with an hundred men march'd accordingly yesterday morning and will be join'd this day or tomorrow by 100 to 150 of King's regiment who have been in arms for sometime past but too cautious ever to go near the enemy, who I imagine are now all off.

Kirkland means to retire towards Savannah. His regiment is amazingly ill off for officers, which, unfortunately for us, is too much the case throughout the militia. I think there is more than a possibility of getting a certain person in the Long Cane settlement[14] to accept of a command, and then I should most humbly be of opinion that every man in the country should

---

[13] *cracker*: see vol 1, p 34.

[14] *a certain person*..: Colonel Andrew Pickens.

be obliged to declare and act for His Majesty or quit. Of the expediency of this measure, as well as the proper season for it, your Lordship is the best and only judge.

I have the honor to be most respectfully, my Lord,
Your Lordship's obedient and very humble servant

J H CRUGER
Lt Colonel commanding 96

Cruger to Cornwallis, 28th November 1780 — *4(225): ALS*

Ninety Six
November 28th 1780

My Lord

My last respects to your Lordship were by Captain Taylor and Mr Stevens[15] of Colonel Ferguson's late corps, who left this yesterday morning for head quarters. I am this instant honor'd with your Lordship's letter of the 25th. I apprehend Mr Brice has given our garrison too much credit for health. He must have form'd his judgment from the number that were brought on the parade, many of whom are convalescents and are still plagued with the fever and ague, of which we have had a great deal, but nothing like, by many degrees, to that horrid country Georgia.

I have just wrote agreeable to your Lordship's directions to Brigadier General Cunningham concerning the militia. By information from a man this morning from Long Cane, I learn that the rebels lately infesting that country have broke into small bodies, I imagine to go off. I have not heard from Colonel Allen since he march'd. I have limitt'd him to a week's excursion unless some unexpected matters should make a longer stay necessary. General Williamson is just come in. He becomes more and more what we would wish. He has declared the same sentiment to me that I took the liberty to mention to your Lordship yesterday. The country once more wholly clear'd of the rebels, I think new measures may be adopted that will prove beneficial. I fear I am going beyond my province, but if your Lordship will be pleased to pardon me, I'll go no farther than to declare myself with the highest deference most respectfully, my Lord,

Your Lordship's most obedient and very humble servant

J H CRUGER
Lt Colonel commanding 96

---

15 *Stevens*: Cruger means Lt William Stevenson, 2nd Battalion, New Jersey Volunteers, who with Taylor had been captured at the Battle of King's Mountain. Ill-treated by their captors, they had fled Bethabara on 5th November and arrived at Ninety Six eighteen days later. (Draper, *King's Mountain*, 355-6 and 513-5)

Cornwallis to Cruger, 30th November 1780 *82(131): C*

Wynnesborough
November 30th 1780

Lt Colonel Cruger

Sir

I have received the favour of your letters of the 27th and 28th and hope that now your district will enjoy some quiet. I should be very glad to hear that the person you allude to would take a command, and I then think that this would be a very proper time to insist on the declaration you propose. Without it there can be no hopes of the settlement remaining long at peace. The garrison of Augusta is certainly weak to be trusted with 2 brass guns. I do not like the idea of losing artillery and consequently am averse to having a greater proportion of it than of troops. I will not, however, immediately determine this business.

I enclose 2 letters which I received from Captain De Peister[16], by which he seems to intimate that the gentlemen who came from Salem broke their paroles. They deny it with so much confidence[17] that I hope it is not so, otherwise they must be sent back. I must desire that you will please to send waggons with a flag of truce to bring in the sick and wounded of Major Ferguson's corps who remain near King's Mountain, and, if you can, that you will send some necessaries and blankets to the prisoners. Mr Haldane is not yet arrived from Camden. As soon as he comes, I shall send him to you, and after you have seen him, I give my consent to your going to Charlestown if nothing new should happen in this part of the world. I must, however, beg that you will stay there as little time as possible. I wrote a few civil lines to Kirkland[18], but he seems so dissatisfied that I think it will be better that he should go away.

I am, sir,
Your most obedient and faithfull servant

CORNWALLIS

---

16 *2 letters..*: only that of 19th November, p 403, is extant.

17 *They deny it...* for Taylor's and Stevenson's representations of 30th November, see p 459.

18 *I wrote..*: on 30th November, p 387.

Cruger to Cornwallis, 3rd December 1780 *4(273): ALS*

96
December 3rd 1780

Rt Hon Earl Cornwallis etc etc etc

My Lord

My last respects were in answer to your Lordship's letter of the 25th of last month, since which nothing material has occurr'd in this quarter. Colonel Allen with his detachment return'd yesterday, not having seen a rebel during his excursion. He left in arms about 100 of our militia (King's regiment), who have promised to patrol on the frontiers of Long Cane and watch the motions of the enemy.

Thursday night last I received from Colonel Balfour 150 blankets, 200 jackets, 200 overalls, 200 hats, 200 pair shoes, 191 French musquets, 2 cask cartridges, 1 of flints, and 83 bushells of salt, which were intended for a twelve month's regiment of militia, but as that plan can not be accomplish'd and Brigadier General Cunningham tells me he intends raising or calling out the militia in classes to serve 2, 4 and 6 weeks at a time, I beg your Lordship's orders respecting the cloathing etc. The arms and ammunition the fork militia will require, if they would make use of them and not give them again to the rebels.

I have the honor to be most respectfully, my Lord,
Your Lordship's most obedient and very humble servant

J H CRUGER
Lt Colonel commanding 96

Cornwallis to Cruger or Allen, 7th December 1780 *83(25): C*

Wynnesborough
December 7th 1780

Lt Colonel Cruger or officer commanding at 96

Sir

I received your letter of the 3rd and am glad to hear that every thing is quiet in Long Cane.

Cunningham writes me an account of his distresses, want of arms, cloathing etc[19]. I looked on your letter to be the key to it, as you mention what you have received from Charlestown. I have lost so many arms by the militia that I am much afraid of trusting them.

---

19 *Cunningham writes..:* on 3rd December, p 392.

Indeed I suspect that those who complain of want of arms either do it to excuse their not turning out or in order to make a property of ours. I must therefore refuse them to any who will not enter into more permanent engagements than the militia.

In regard to the cloathing, blankets etc, you must first consider what will be wanted for the cavalry, and then perhaps it may be proper to assist those who were taken with Ferguson, and if any remain that Cunningham can dispose of without making a jealousy among the militia, I have no objection to his doing it, but it appears to me that great caution should be used in this business, as it is much to be apprehended that if any militia man who was not with Ferguson should get a share of the cloathing, the rest will refuse to turn out unless they get the same. I beg you will shew this letter to Cunningham and state the danger I mention strongly to him and let me know whether he can point out any method of evading it.

Some salt and salt pork arrived at Friday's Ferry, as I was informed for 96. I ordered it, however, to Camden and desired Colonel Balfour to direct that any supply of that sort intended for 96 should be sent up by the Savannah River. You will please to talk to Colonel Balfour about it.

In regard to cannon, I intend to send 2 iron three pounders to 96, and to give you one of brass, which will be as much as you can want for any excursion that the garrison can afford. The iron guns are full as good for the defence of the work.

I cannot be of opinion that it is proper to have any brass gun at Augusta. I desire that Lt Colonel Brown may be directed to procure ammunition if wanted for his iron guns and to state a requisition of what he thinks necessary, and then I would have his brass guns sent down the river to Savannah.

I am, sir,
Your most obedient and most humble servant

CORNWALLIS

[*Subscribed*:]

If Colonel Cruger should be gone to Charlestown, Colonel Allen will be pleased to send a copy of as much of this letter as may concern any arrangements he may make with Colonel Balfour.

Cruger to Cornwallis, 5th December 1780 — *4(287): ALS*

Ninety Six
December 5th 1780

Earl Cornwallis etc etc etc

My Lord

I was the night before last honor'd with your Lordship's letter of the 30th November.

Williamson and Pickens have for some time past been waiting to go to town with me. Indeed, the same cause that made it improper for me to go sooner they conceived ought to detain them. When we get to town, we will with Colonel Balfour, if your Lordship approves, settle the business there both for the *command* and the *declaration*. The former should be first establish'd if he[20] can be prevail'd on to accept, and then would your Lordship mean to have all the inhabitants of this district called on and, to save your Lordship the trouble, the proclamations for the purpose to come from Colonel Balfour?

I hope the officers who made their escape from Salem may be able to maintain their very positive assertions of not having forfieted their words or in any shape violated their honor, for should they be obliged to go back, more than savage cruelty, I fear, will be their fate.

Lieutenant Hatton[21] of the Jersey Volunteers with a flag of truce will go with four waggons tomorrow to bring in the sick and wounded of Major Ferguson's corps who remain near King Mountain, but for the prisoners it appears impossible to send necessaries, they being by the last accounts so far as Moravian Town and to be immediately removed from thence.

I thank your Lordship for your permission to go to town after seeing Mr Haldane, and have the honor of being with the greatest deference most respectfully, my Lord,

Your Lordship's obedient and very humble servant

J H CRUGER
Lt Colonel commanding 96

Cruger to Cornwallis, 9th December 1780 — *4(300): ALS*

Ninety Six
December 9th 1780

Rt Hon Earl Cornwallis etc etc etc

My Lord

As Mr Haldane fully writes by this opportunity every thing relative to this post, I will not trouble your Lordship with a repetition. In a day or two Mr Haldane and myself purpose

---

20 *he*: Pickens.

21 The son of a wealthy South Jersey loyalist, John Hatton Jr (1756-?) had fled in July 1776 to Virginia, where he was commissioned a lieutenant in the Queen's Own Loyal Virginia Regiment raised by Lord Dunmore. With it he accompanied the deposed Governor to New York, and when the regiment was incorporated into the Queen's Rangers, he transferred as a lieutenant to what became the augmented 3rd Battalion, New Jersey Volunteers, under Lt Colonel Isaac Allen. He would serve with the battalion for the rest of the war and be wounded at the siege of Ninety Six between May and June 1781. At the peace he was placed on the Provincial half-pay list but reentered active service several years later as an officer in the 23rd Regiment (Royal Welch Fusiliers). His property in Gloucester County, New Jersey, was confiscated by the revolutionary authorities. (Nan Cole and Todd Braisted, 'A History of the 6th Battalion, New Jersey Volunteers' (*The On-Line Institute for Advanced Loyalist Studies*, 5th December 2005); Sabine, *Biographical Sketches*, ii, 528; Audit Office 12/85(43) (National Archives, Kew))

leaving Ninety Six. By tomorrow I am in hopes of getting together as many militia as will be able to drive Clark, Twiggs etc with between two and three hundred men from the Long Cane settlement. They came into it last Monday night. On Wednesday morning they sent for General Williamson and have since detain'd him. As our friends abandon the country where the rebels go, our intelligence is very bad. Yesterday I had brought to me two of the Long Cane gentry, two more are mortally wounded and one kill'd, all paroled or protection men. They fell in with some of our militia who were coming here.

I was yesterday honor'd with your Lordship's letter of the 7th. Proper attention shall be paid to its contents and, as far as relates to General Cunningham, be communicated to him. I beleive your Lordship might entrust the disposal of some arms for the militia to Cunningham, particularly for those men who were taken with Major Ferguson, most of whom are return'd. I shall write Colonel Brown this day your Lordship's sentiments respecting the brass guns at Augusta etc.

I have the honor to be most respectfully, my Lord,
Your Lordship's most obedient and very humble servant

J H CRUGER
Lt Colonel commanding 96

Haldane to Cornwallis, 9th December 1780 — *4(296): ALS*

Ninety Six
9th December 1780

Lt General Earl Cornwallis etc etc etc

My Lord

I had the honour to receive yesterday your Lordship's letter of the 7th[22]. I arrived at this place early on Wednesday morning and found the works in a much better state than I expected. Tho' they are not so entirely conformable to rule, yet they may answer the present purpose as well as the best executed work. When I have the pleasure of seeing your Lordship, which I hope will be in a few days, I shall be able to explain to you more perfectly their situation and what I have recommended to be done for the present and what in future may be done to render this post more respectable and more convenient to the garrison, which I have marked out on the ground, that, if your Lordship approves of it, [it] may be carried into execution. Lt Colonel Cruger has informed me you propose to order two iron three pounders to be sent to this place. If six pounders could be spared, they would be of more service as they would command much better a hill that is opposite to this post.

Agreeable to your Lordship's directions, I am making a cypher for the correspondence with this garrison. I hope the Governour is well. I must beg the favor of your Lordship to present my best respects to him, and

22 *letter of the 7th*: no extant copy.

I have the honour to be, my Lord,
Your very humble and most obedient servant

HENRY HALDANE

Cornwallis to Cruger or Allen, 11th December 1780 — *83(33): C*

Wynnesborough
December 11th 1780

Lt Colonel Cruger or officer commanding at Ninety Six

Sir

In consequence of the very good character I have heard of Serjeant Major Blue, who acted as adjutant of the militia under Major Ferguson, I desire you will please to allow him four months' pay as adjutant out of the money lodged in your hands for the use of the militia.

I am, sir,
Your most obedient and most humble servant

CORNWALLIS

Cruger to Cornwallis, 15th December 1780 — *4(335): ALS*

Ninety Six
December 15th 1780

Rt Hon Earl Cornwallis etc etc etc

My Lord

Last Tuesday week I heard of a party of rebels under Clark, Few[23], Twigs, Candler etc crossing the Saluda into Long Cane settlement. They reported themselves 4 to 500. One of

[23] Born in Harford County, Maryland, Benjamin Few (1744-1805) was brought by his parents to the Eno River in North Carolina when aged fourteen. In 1764 the family moved to a farm near Hillsborough, from where they became involved in the War of the Regulation. The day after the Battle of Alamance in 1771, Benjamin's brother James was hanged by order of Governor Tryon, an event which may have instilled in Benjamin a hatred of the Crown. Beset by difficulties resulting from their support of outlawed Regulators, the family moved on to Georgia in 1773 and settled near Wrightsborough. Benjamin went on to receive several land grants in the Ceded Lands and became a colonel in the up-country revolutionary militia. Although he is said to have taken part in the ill-fated East Florida expedition in 1778, the unsuccessful siege of Savannah in 1779, and the equally unsuccessful attempt on Augusta in September 1780, he is chiefly remembered for his involvement in partisan warfare and for his failure to support Clark and McCall in the present action near White Hall (which Cruger's letter later describes). After the war he was quite active in the public affairs of Georgia before moving in 1803 to Alabama, where he died. (*DGB*, i, 304-5, 307-8)

their objects was to get the inhabitants to join them, for which purpose they order'd Williamson, Pickens and the principal people of the country who were on parole to attend them, alledging that we had violated the capitulation. They used both soothing and threatening arguments to those gentlemen, who, I have the pleasure to inform your Lordship, behaved like men of honor and persisted in a different opinion. Some idle, worthless chaps join'd them, but not, from what I can learn, one man of character.

Last Monday morning was the soonest I could get together any militia, when Brigadier General Cunningham brought over with him about 160 – Kirkland's and King's regiments furnished about 110 – to which I added 150 rank and file of this garison with one field piece under Colonel Allen and sent them off on Monday night at 11 o'clock in hopes of surprizing the enemy, who we had reason to beleive lay at General Williamson's, but unluckily found no body there, but received intelligence that they were encampt six miles farther on, for which the march was immediately continued, but here again we fell short by about three miles. A halt was then made, the day being far spent. A party of militia was sent out for forage and were driven by the rebels, who, having received not the least intimation of any soldiers being on the ground, run headlong into our camp so sudden and rapidly that the soldiers had but just time to form. They gave one fire and rush'd on with their bayonets. A rout ensued and soon became general. Our militia avail'd themselves of this circumstance and pursued for two miles with spirit. The soldiers follow'd those of the enemy who had not time to get on their horses. The first rebel that arrived in their camp sett the rest agoing, and in an instant they were all off, leaving six waggons and 30 head of cattle, and on Wednesday morning recross'd the Saluda. Their loss, kill'd, is reported from 30 to 50. Prisoners taken: one major badly wounded and 8 privates chiefly wounded. The Colonels Clark and McCall[24] are wounded but escaped. Our loss: 2 militia men kill'd, 6 wounded, and 3 soldiers wounded. Colonel Allen and the soldiers will be in this evening or tomorrow morning. The militia I have desired to continue scouring the country. I will intrude no farther for the present on your Lordship's time than to beg leave to refer your Lordship to Mr Haldane for every thing relating to this post, and have the honor to be most respectfully with great deference, my Lord,

Your Lordship's obedient and very humble servant

J H CRUGER
Lt Colonel commanding 96

---

24 Born in Pennsylvania, James McCall (1741-1781) was the son of Irish immigrants who removed by way of Virginia to Anson County, North Carolina. In 1771 James migrated to a branch of Long Cane Creek in South Carolina and was later to see distinguished service in the revolutionary militia. A lt colonel by mid December 1780, he had taken part in the defeat of Alexander Innes at Musgrove's Mill in August, the assault on Augusta in September, and the actions at Fishdam Ford and Blackstocks in November. Wounded in the present action near White Hall, he would go on to participate in the Battle of Cowpens and the capture of James Dunlap at Beattie's Mill. In April 1781 he contracted small pox and died the following month. (McCrady, *SC in the Rev 1775-1780* and *1780-1783, passim*; Heitman, *HistoricalRegister*, 363; Ron Crawley, 'Military Exploits of James McCall', The Iron Scouts Inc (Internet, 12th November 2005))

Allen to Cornwallis, 19th December 1780 — *4(359): ALS*

Ninety Six
December 19th 1780

The Rt Hon Lt General Earl Cornwallis

My Lord

I have this moment received intelligence, *by an officer* who went with *a flagg to North Carolina* and has just returned, that Colonel Campbell has assembled seventeen hundred men at Remsaur's twenty miles above King's Mountain and has called for a draught from Tryon, Mecklenburg and Berk's Counties for a secret expedition supposed by the informant (a friend of Government in that province) to be for some of our outposts. This gentleman was within seven miles of *Charlotte*, where *General Green* lies with a small force.

Probably Campbell intends to reinforce him. I thought it my duty to give your Lordship the earliest intelligence I could of this body of the enemy. General Cunningham has about two hundred militia collected and expects as many more in a few days, but many of his men who were made prisoners at King's Mountain are without arms and cloathing. I am perswaded that, had he arms and a small supply of cloathing, he would put the militia in a respectable situation in a few weeks. These people have been with me in two excursions and behaved extremely well, and I have a good opinion of their loyalty and spirit. Should Campbell bend his course this way with the force he is reported to have, the whole *fork* will be overrun, and this *post* may be in *danger* if he should bring *cannon*.

The works are extensive but the want of *water* I should most fear.

I did myself the honor to apply to your Lordship by Mr Haldane respecting some men of mine who were made prisoners at Augusta[25], and shall be particularly obliged to your Lordship for an answer upon this subject.

I have the honor to be, my Lord,
Your Lordship's most obedient and most humble servant

ISAAC ALLEN
Lt Colonel commanding 3rd Battalion, New Jersey Volunteers

---

[25] According to a memorandum of 16th December (102(4)), the men comprised 1 major, 1 lieutenant, 3 serjeants, 1 drummer and 11 privates.

Haldane to Allen, 22nd December 1780 *83(65): ACS*

Head Quarters
Wynnesborough
22nd December 1780

Lt Colonel Allen or the officer commanding at Ninety Six

Dear Sir

Lord Cornwallis has directed me to acknowledge the receipt of your letter of the 19th and at the same time to communicate to you his answers to several queries that I received from Lt Colonel Cruger.

That Serjeant Major Bleu is to receive pay as a British adjutant.

That Doctor Ross is to receive pay as a surgeon for the time he has attended the militia.

That the militia are to receive arms, ammunition and a blanket, provided that Brigadier General Cunningham will be responsible that they return them into store at Ninety Six when their time of service is expired or that they deliver them to the men that relieve them.

Lord Cornwallis consents to your sending out an equal number of prisoners for the officers and men of yours who are on parole or to exchange them by cancelling the paroles of an equal number of the enemy who are in that situation.

I have mentioned to his Lordship the necessity of a reinforcement for your post[26] and have reason to think he will consent to it, and he wishes that in the mean time you will be pleased to order the Negroes to cut abattis to be layed at about 30 yards from the ditch and to include the gaol within the abattis.

I am, dear sir,
Your very humble and most obedient servant

HENRY HALDANE
Aid-de-camp

[*Subscribed*:]

(In cypher) A.6

Instead of placing a letter as a key to the cypher, substitute the following marks for the vowels: (A, |), (E, +), (I, ✓), (O, ∧), (U, *).

---

[26] According to the memorandum of the 16th December (102(4)), Allen considered '500 men requisite for the defence of the country and post at Ninety Six'. See also his letter of 29th December to Haldane, p 287.

Lord Cornwallis has also ordered me to inform you that the officers of militia are not to consider their rank as entitling them to command when acting with the officers of the regular troops.

HENRY HALDANE
Aid-de-camp

Allen to Haldane, 25th December 1780 — *4(394): ALS*

Ninety Six
December the 25th 1780

Dear Sir

I received yours of the 22nd and shall order the blacks to cutt the abattis as fast as possible, but am doubtfull whether you mean the abattis should be layed thirty yards from the present ditch or the line you marked out when here. Should be glad to hear from you and have that matter ascertained.

We have no rebel prisoners here for exchange but militia, and most of them have been guilty of crimes of so atrocious a nature that Colonel Cruger order'd them to Charles Town. I supposed that Colonel Tarleton had paroled and left a number sufficient to exchange my men at Lynches Creek and in the attack on Sumpter last August. My idea was to send a flag and inform them that an equall number of those people should be released from their parole. If this was done, I should have no scruple about my people taking up arms.

I have been very much indisposed since you left Ninety Six but am much better. Petitions are continually coming from the people who came with Clark, Few etc begging to be received into favor again. Many of these people have violated their parole. I shall be glad of my Lord's directions whether they should be received or not. It is the opinion of many of the inhabitants that if they are pardoned most of them will return.

I am with respect
Your friend and humble servant

ISAAC ALLEN
Lt Colonel commanding at 96

Haldane to Allen, 29th December 1780 — *83(91): AC*

Head Quarters
Wynnesborough
29th December 1780

Lt Colonel Allen

Dear Sir

I received your letter yesterday evening of the 25th. Lord Cornwallis has directed me to inform you that he has received intelligence of Morgan and Washington having passed Broad River.

His Lordship will pardon those men that joined Clarke and Few, provided they come in and give their parole, which if they violate again and are taken, they may depend on its being punished with the greatest severity.

If you send a flag of truce to the enemy relative to the prisoners, you will be pleased to obtain from them the names of those people who are released from their paroles on their side and transmit them to head quarters. They must not be of the militia paroled by the capitulation of Charlestown.

The abattis may be layed just without the line that I traced out.

I have the honor to be etc etc

[HENRY HALDANE]

[*Subscribed*:]

Lord Cornwallis wishes you could send to Colonel Browne at Augusta a copy of your cypher and to acquaint him that Lord Cornwallis will write to him by the way of Charlestown.

Lord Cornwallis also desires you will be pleased to inform Colonel Browne that he approves of every thing he has done and that he is to keep the brass one pounders at Augusta.

Allen to Haldane, 29th December 1780 — *4(426): ALS*

Ninety Six
December the 29th 1780

Dear Sir

I received yours and have ordered the abbatis cut, but King's work like church work goes on slow. The poor naked blacks can do but little this cold weather. Colonel Pickens, who you saw here, has gone to the rebels. He is said to be a good soldier and may give us some trouble in this quarter. I am told the rebels are making works and collecting magazines near Love's Ford. This, I dare say, you have full information of. Mine is so vague and uncertain both as to their designs and numbers that I hardly think any thing I can say worth communicating. However, I *allow*, as the crakers say, that Green propose to keep à body upon your left to fall on your rear whenever my Lord determines to press forward into North Carolina or perhaps take hold of this province by way of exchange. You know my opinion of the force that wou'd be necessary to repel any thing that may come this way and keep up our militia, a matter in my judgment of some importance if we intend to keep the hold we have of this country. The revolt of the Long Cane settlement will make this matter more difficult. The regiment commanded by *Pickins was always esteemed the best in the rebel service*. Most of them will join him and from their *knowledge of the country* may be very *troublesome*, but I am still of opinion that five *hundred*, such as I mention'd to you, ad'd to our *militia* will be sufficient. Unless this is done, *we shall* soon be *confined* to *Ninety Six*. If we don't take the *field* soon, they will *gain* both numbers and *confidence*. A gentleman has just [come] in who says the rebels have taken two pieces of cannon that were going from Savannah to Augusta and killed seven of the party. General Williamson is at home, much distressed with the perfidious behaviour of his friend Pickins. I hope we shall now have done with protection and paroles. I beleive the rebels will not exchange my people for their militia. Cou'd we not pick a few honest *Hibernians* from the Provost in Charles Town who wou'd *celebrate* next *Saint Patrick's Day* with my *Lord Rawdon*?

I am with respect
Your very humble servant

ISAAC ALLEN
Lt Colonel commanding at 96

Allen to Cornwallis, 29th December 1780 — *4(422): ALS*

Ninety Six
December the 29th 1780

My Lord

I have received certain information that Colonel Pickins, Major Boyce[27], Major Noble[28] and Captain Anderson[29] with about one hundred men have left the Long Cane settlement and joined the enemy. These are all men of *influence* with the *rebels* and will be such an

27 Perhaps David Boyse (*c.* 1740-?), who migrated to America in 1764 from Newry, County Down, Ireland, and settled with his wife and three sons in the Long Cane settlement. (Earnest Boyce, 'The Genealogical Record of One Branch of the Boyce Family in America' (np, 1972))

28 Alexander Noble (1733-1802) was Andrew Pickens' brother-in-law. (Moss, *SC Patriots*, 730)

29 Perhaps Henry Anderson (1731-1781), who served as a captain under Pickens and was murdered by loyalists in October of the following year. (Moss, op cit, 19)

accession of *strength* to those who had left the country before and are now embodied near the iron works as will make them much *too powerfull* for *our militia*, which will render our *supplies* at this *post* very *precarious*.

I have this moment received an express from General Cunningham informing me that General Morgan with fifteen hundred men is now at Grimes's Mills two miles on this side Pacolet on his way to this post. How true this information may be I cannot say, but the General beleives it. *If a speedy check* is not *given to the enemy, I fear* this *country* will be *lost*. The *militia* will not *collect* in *force* without a *regular* force to *support* them. I shall be glad of your Lordship's directions upon this point.

I have the honor to be, my Lord,
Your Lordship's most obedient most humble servant

ISAAC ALLEN
Lt Colonel commanding at 96

Haldane to Allen, 31st December 1780 — *83(99): ACS*

Head Quarters
Wynnesborough
31st December 1780

Lt Colonel Allen or the officer commanding at Ninety Six

Dear Sir

Lord Cornwallis has directed me to inform you that *if Morgan moves towards Ninety Six, he will detach a sufficient force to your relief*.

By the intelligence Lord Cornwallis has received, Morgan has about 150 or 200 Continentals and Washington about 120 horse. The rest of his force must be militia. His Lordship always wishes you will communicate to him from time to time any intelligence you can procure.

His Lordship wishes to know *what guns were taken between Savannah and Augusta and whether yours are arrived at Ninety Six*.

I am, dear sir, etc etc

HENRY HALDANE

[*Subscribed*:]

I perceive by your letter you did not thoroughly comprehend my meaning respecting *the cypher*. This appears to me to be *more unintelligible if taken*.

Allen to Cornwallis, 31st December 1780 — *4(435): ALS*

Ninety Six
December 31st 1780

My Lord

The intelligence I did myself the honor to communicate to your Lordship in my last proves to be too true. Morgain and Washington have advanced and took possession of Williamson's Fort[30], which the militia abandoned at their approach. Washington's light horse yesterday surprized and totally routed the militia about seven miles above the fort. The number of killed and taken I have not been able to ascertain. They certainly behaved very ill. *Bad as they* are, *I fear we cannot live in this country* without them. General Cunningham is here with *sixty men. The whole country over* Saluda *is in possession* of the *enemy*. The *Long Cane revolt* will give great strength and spirit to the *enemy*. Whether they will come to *this post* I cannot say, but I flatter myself *water is* all I shall *want*. I need not point out to your Lordship the *necessity* of a speedy *reinforcement to* this *quarter*. I sent to your Lordship an *intelligent person* this day who will be *able* to *give full information*.

I shall send to Colonel Brown what your Lordship requests the first good opportunity.

I am with great respect
Your Lordship's most obedient and most humble servant

ISAAC ALLEN
Lt Colonel commanding at 96

Haldane to Allen, 4th January 1781 — *84(10): ACS*

Head Quarters
Wynnesborough
4th January 1781

Lt Colonel Allen

Dear Sir

Lord Cornwallis has directed me to acquaint you that *he has ordered the Fuzileers to Ninety Six with a brass field piece. This force will render your post very respectable. Lieutenant Barrette, an assistant engineer, will bring intrenching tools to compleat the works*.

If you will send to Lt Colonel Balfour a return of your men that are on parole, Lord Cornwallis will give directions to Colonel Balfour to send out an equal number of Continentals. When you receive advice that they are sent, your men may consider themselves exchanged.

---

30 *Williamson's Fort*: a slip of the pen. The reference is to Williams's Fort.

I am, dear sir, etc etc

HENRY HALDANE
Aid de camp

[*Subscribed*:]

The two field pieces at present at 96 are to remain. An iron six is ordered up.

Haldane to the officer commanding, 9th January 1781 *84(42): ACS*

Head Quarters
9th January 1781

The officer commanding at Ninety Six

Sir

Lord Cornwallis has directed me to acquaint you that you are to consider yourself under the command of Lord Rawdon and that you will be pleased to report to him on all occasions and at the same time to inform Lt Colonel Balfour of any material circumstance that might occur in that part of the province.

I have the honour to be, sir,
Your most humble and very obedient servant

HENRY HALDANE
ADC

Cornwallis to Cruger or Allen, 16th January 1781 *84(66): C*

Hillhouse's Plantation near Turkey Creek[31]
January 16th 1781

Lt Colonel Cruger or officer commanding at Ninety Six

Sir

The present situation of this part of the province requires in my opinion the utmost attention of the commanding officer at Ninety Six. All auxiliary force from other provinces is expelled by the King's troops. The banditti under the chiefs who style themselves colonels

[31] On leaving William Hillhouse's plantation, Cornwallis had it demolished. Born near the Catawba River, William (1760-1848) had served in the South Carolina revolutionary militia since December 1775 and had lately been involved in the actions at Rocky Mount, Hanging Rock, and Camden Ferry. When his company commander was wounded at Hanging Rock, he was promoted to captain. During 1781 he would take part in several engagements in South Carolina. After the war he moved on, eventually to Starkville, Mississippi, where he was buried in the Odd Fellows' Cemetery. (Moss, *SC Patriots*, 447; Mississippi State Society DAR, 'Located Graves of Revolutionary War Soldiers in Mississippi' (Internet, 19th November 2005))

such as Bratan, Brannan, Wynne, Clarke, Few etc etc have betaken themselves to their hiding places and the power is now totally in our hands. You have a formidable body of good soldiers at Ninety Six. You must now use your utmost exertion to prevent a renewal of the same kind of troubles and calamities which have so long oppressed the deserving inhabitants of your district.

To effect this desirable purpose you should in my opinion hold out the sword and the olive. You should rigidly disarm as many of the enemy, and make as few desperate, as possible, but above all things you must carefully attend to those colonels. Get people at any price to observe their haunts. Offer privately considerable rewards for securing their persons, and on the first report of their attempting to assemble their gang, send a considerable detachment of your regulars with a proportion of militia to remain on the spot and to make the most diligent search after those who may be suspected of being concerned in the insurrection. I most strongly recommend that those detachments should observe method and order in their severity, that the strictest discipline should be observed, and the quiet inhabitants molested as little as possible. Unless you should be called upon for other services by Lord Rawdon, which is not probable, you may afford to have considerable detachments constantly out, and I should advise that they should never be weaker than 150 men, and generally stronger, and that the greatest attention should be paid to the choice of proper officers to command them without any attention to roster. If complaints should arise in consequence of it, you may quote my authority. You will please to consider all my directions as subject to the controul of Lord Rawdon, to whom and to Lt Colonel Balfour you will report every material occurrence.

If Colonel Pickens has left any Negroes, cattle or other property that may be usefull to Mr Cruden or to the supply of the troops, I would have it seized and applied accordingly, and I desire that his houses may be burnt, and his plantations, as far as lies in your power, totally destroyed, and himself, if ever taken, instantly hanged.

I shall be very happy to hear that the plan of raising dragoons under Major Dunlap is likely to succeed and most sincerely wish you success in every undertaking.

I am, sir,
Your most obedient and most humble servant

CORNWALLIS

Cornwallis to Cruger or Allen, 21st January 1781 — *84(77): ACS*

Buffalo Creek
January 21st 1781

Lt Colonel Cruger or officer commanding at 96

Sir

I desire you will be vigilant but not alarmed. Lord Rawdon and myself will keep a watchfull eye on 96. I will contrive to substitute some reinforcement in lieu of the 7th

Regiment. I march tomorrow to attack the enemy.

I am, sir,
Your most obedient humble servant

CORNWALLIS

§ - §

2 - Between Cornwallis and Dunlap

Dunlap to Cornwallis, 8th November 1780 *4(65): ALS*

Ninety Six
8th November 1780

Lt General Earl Cornwallis

My Lord

If I recollect justly, I inform'd your Lordship that the terms on which Colonel Cruger and Major Clary proposed raising the cavalry were that they should serve during the rebellion. In this I misunderstood Colonel Cruger. He now informs me that they are to serve only for twelve months, the men to receive no bounty, and the officers to be paid as infantry; and I find it will be impossible just now to engage them to serve for any longer space. However, Colonel Cruger thinks it absolutely necessary they should be raised at all events. I shall therefore proceed with all possible expedition. Colonel Cruger is of opinion that Govenour Wright will not deliver the horse accoutrements to any other than your Lordship's positive order. If your Lordship should think proper, I would be glad that the order might be for 46 instead of 40, which will include the six non commissioned officers and will cleverly compleat the first troop. The most safe and expeditious method of getting the accoutrements from Savannah will be, after the troop is embodied, to let them fetch them on their own hack horses, which they can very easily perform before cloathing etc can be provided for them.

I have the honor to be with respect
Your Lordship's obedient servant

J DUNLAP

Cornwallis to Dunlap, 11th November 1780 *82(26): C*

Winsborough
November 11th 1780

Major Dunlap

Sir

I received your letter of the 8th. The cavalry accoutrements are arrived at Charlestown in bad order and many of them plundered. However, I am so anxious to shew some cavalry at 96 that I would have you send in the most expeditious manner for 46 setts, which Colonel Balfour will let you have on seeing this letter. I have agreed to the troops being raised on the terms which Colonel Cruger mentioned.

I am, sir,
Your most obedient humble servant

CORNWALLIS

Dunlap to Cornwallis, 30th November 1780 *4(242): ALS*

Charles Town
30th November 1780

Lt General Earl Cornwallis

My Lord

When I last had the honor of waiting on your Lordship, I took the liberty of mentioning the situation of Sergeant Major Blue, who had for some months acted as adjutant to the militia by order of Major Ferguson. Your Lordship then signifyed your desire that he should receive four months' pay as adjutant from Colonel Cruger out of the monies lodged in his hands for the use of the militia. This I mentioned to Colonel Cruger but he declined payment untill he should receive an order from your Lordship to that purpose.

The particular situation of Sergeant Major Blue, the intrepidity of his behaviour under my command at the time he was wounded, and his present necessitys importune me to mention him again to your Lordship. I really believe him to be a young man very worthy of encouragement.

The *Crown* galley not having yet arrived detains me in Charles Town (I can assure your Lordship) much against my own inclination. Colonel Balfour thinks it absolutely necessary I should remain till the accoutrements arrive. Nothing, my Lord, would give me more pleasure than having it in my power to second my Lordship's wishes in shewing a respectable cavalry at Ninety Six.

I have the honor to be
Your Lordship's most obedient servant

J DUNLAP

§ - §

3 - From Brown

Brown to Cornwallis, 17th December 1780 ***4(345): ALS***

Augusta
December 17th 1780

My Lord

I have the honor to inform your Lordship that, in consequence of a talk I sent to the Cherokee nation, the friendly Indians and those who were formerly in the rebel interest have chearfully agreed to attack the plunderers and banditti who have taken forcible possession of their hunting grounds on the Watoga, Holstein, Caentuck, Nolachuckie, Cumberland and Green River. The chiefs of twenty five hundred Cherokees who left this place last month promised to march immediately against the abovementioned places and to continue at war during the winter on condition I would supply them with arms and ammunition and their families with clothing etc during their absence. This I consented to and have already sent off a quantity of ammunition to the nation.

I have employed a proper number of whitemen and traders to head the different war parties under the command of the commissaries, who understand the Indian language and customs and will be capable of preventing the commission of wanton outrages to which their savage ferocity might hurry them.

The kings and chiefs have promised to confine their attacks to men in arms *without the legal boundary lines of the provinces* and to implicitly follow such orders as they may receive from me through the medium of their commissaries.

A party of the Upper Creeks have marched to assist the Cherokees. In my conference with the kings and chiefs of the two nations I adjusted their respective quarrels and prevailed on the dissaffected Creeks and Cherokees to take an active part in favor of Government. I told them in very spirited terms that if they persevered in their former madness and folly, I would not permit a trader to live in, or a single article of merchandize to go into, their towns. This reprimand and menace brought them, I believe, to their senses.

About 500, who were down here at different times offering their service, I have provided with ammunition and arms and have instructed the commissaries to send them off under proper trusty men towards Holstein to harrass the mountaineers and divert their attention from the loyalists in North and South Carolina to their own immediate concerns.

I transmitted to Colonel Balfour an estimate of the expences which will be incurred by employing extra officers on such services and supplying the Indians with arms and ammunition and their families with clothing during the absence of the men at war, which he approved of.

I beg leave to suggest to your Excellency the difficulties I have laboured under from having been obliged to defray all the expences of the Indian Department for this twelvemonth last past on my own credit to the great prejudice of my private fortune by such expenditures.

The last year's accounts are preparing to be laid before your Lordship since the period of settlement by Sir Henry Clinton. In future I hope your Lordship will be so obliging as enable me to settle the Indian accounts every two months, as the purchases of rations, expence of expresses, repair of arms and extra officers and interpreters (as allowed by Sir Henry Clinton) for war parties reduce me to many inconveniences after the loss of provisions taken by the rebels.

One hundred and forty Cherokee and Creek men and women are now with [me?], being left sick with the small pox and fever. They are daily recovering with much nursing.

Inclosed I have the honor to transmit your Lordship extracts of letters from General Campbell from Pensacola and Major De Peyster commanding at Detroit.

In a fortnight I shall send off an express to the Cherokees to be forwarded to Detroit. If your Lordship should have any dispatches for this place or Quebec, they can be conveyed with great facility and safety to the former and from thence to the latter. In four months an Indian express may be sent from this place to Quebec.

The inclosed are copies of letters from the Governor of Virginia and Don Galvez. The covers and directions being destroyed, and supposing them intended for (as they accompanied a letter to) one of my commissaries in the Cherokees, I examined them and found on perusal they were designed for the Governor of Pensacola. As they contain some intelligence of consequence, I took the liberty of transcribing them for your Lordship.

I have in consequence of these letters given directions to the Abenahkies, a tribe of northward Indians who live in the Cherokees, to keep out parties constantly on the River Ohio to obstruct the navigation, as well as that of the Mississippi.

The Cherokees attacked some boats on their passage down the river on their way to Orleans, killed the guard and have sent down some women and children to this place who accompanied them. I commended the Indians for this instance of their humanity and obedience to the orders they received, and rewarded them as they deserved.

Fourteen days ago 200 Indians were detached to Green River to annoy the plunderers and mountaineers. Your Lordship has probably heard by some of the frontier inhabitants of this incursion.

From Colonel Cruger I have the honor of receiving your Lordship's orders to send down to Savannah two brass (one pounders) field pieces. I found them extremely useful in our engagement with the rebels, particularly in dislodging them from the houses they occupied.

Your Lordship will be pleased to pardon my soliciting permission to recruit in South Carolina, as it has been my constant endeavor to procure as many men as my purse and interest would enable me for His Majesty's Service. I have every reason to think, from a general knowledge of the inhabitants, I can engage as considerable number as any person in the province.

I have the honor to be, my Lord, with just respect
Your Lordship's most obedient and most humble servant

THO^{S} BROWN
Lt Colonel commanding King's Rangers

Enclosure (1)
Extract from Campbell to Brown, 15th November 1780 *4(349): C*

Head Quarters
Pensacola
the 15th November 1780

Sir

On the evening of the 12th instant I received your obliging favor of the 21st ultimo and sincerely thank you for your speedy communication of such pleasing and gladdening intelligence; and I cannot omit observing your attention to me and to the good of the King's Service by your diligence and dispatch in immediately forwarding news that must have their effect on all minds in exhilerating or depressing them. It requires not then to be remarked of how much importance this critical arrival of good news may be in determining the savage Indian to the part he shall act, and I trust the present joyous tidings will be of consequence (in this point of view) with the Chactaws in adding weight to the British interest, for with them the Spaniards and us are suspended in the ballance.

I have now to inform you that I have every reason to believe the Spaniards will soon invade Pensacola. I trust then you will take every step to secure to me (on my intimation to your commissaries of such an event) a speedy and effectual reinforcement of Creek Indians. They have already been a principal cause in deterring the Spaniards last spring from attacking this place, and they have it still in their power by frequent attacks and constant alarms, in short by continually harrassing and hanging on the enemy's rear in case of siege, greatly to impede the operations, if not totally defeat and disconcert the designs, of any force they can send against us. Your prudence and discernment have already suggested the precaution of instructing the Indian chiefs to this effect.

I have the honor to be with regard, sir,
Your most obedient and most humble servant

JOHN CAMPBELL
Major General

Enclosure (2)
Extract from De Peyster to the Commissary of Indian Affairs in the Upper Cherokees, 5th April 1780 *4(352): C*

Detroit
April 5th 1780

I am glad to hear that the Indians in your way are zealous for the King's Service, and have the pleasure to inform you they are no less so here. The Canada Indians exert themselves on all occasions and the five nations have much annoyed the enemy. The Mechilimakinac Indians and from thence to the Sioux country are staunch for the King and propose attacking the Illinois soon. I am convinced they will act with humanity, which principle I have greatly instilled in their minds. The Shawnees, Hurons, Wiandots, part of the Delawares, Mingoes etc have just struck a capital stroke, headed by interpreters from this post. They defeated a Colonel Rogers[32] on his way with a convoy for[33] New Orleans to Pitsburg. Rogers landed his men consisting of fifty five rebel soldiers and made the first attack, but was soon routed by the Indians and lost his life together with 45 of his men. John Campbell[34], colonel of

---

[32] David Rogers (?-1779) was an Irishman who had migrated in his youth to America and settled at Oldtown, Maryland, where he became a merchant. In 1775 he went on to found a settlement at Wheeling on the Ohio and in 1776 and 1777 was elected to the Virginia revolutionary assembly. In March 1777 he was appointed County Lieutenant of Ohio County but soon resigned. Two years later he was charged with undertaking a mission to New Orleans, the nature of which is apparent from the following enclosures. On the way back to Fort Pitt his party had reached a sandbar on the Ohio River near what is now Dayton when it was attacked in October by native Americans and Rogers was killed. (Information from the Glenn Black Laboratory of Archæology, Indiana; Mann Butler, *History of the Commonwealth of Kentucky* (Lousiville, 1834), 102 et seq; Jim Reis, *Pieces of the Past*, vol i (Kentucky Post, 1988))

[33] *for*: a slip of the pen. The sense suggests 'from'.

[34] Born in Ireland, John Campbell (1735-1799) had come to America as a young man and established himself as a trader on the western frontier. He also acted as an agent in supplying British outposts in the Ohio River valley. Having been involved in laying out Fort Pitt in 1764, he was living there thirteen years later when he opted to support the revolutionary party. Becoming a Justice of the Peace and a colonel in the revolutionary militia, he had joined David Rogers on the mission to New Orleans and was captured on the way back (see above). He was to remain a prisoner with native Americans for more than three years. At the close of the war he opened a tobacco warehouse and began operating the first public ferries on the Ohio River at Louisville. In 1792 he attended the state convention and was afterwards elected to the Kentucky Senate, becoming its Speaker in 1798. Campbell County, Kentucky, is named after him. (Jim Reis, op cit, vol i: Robert M Rennick, *Kentucky Place Names* (University of Kentucky Press, 1984))

militia, and one lieutenant taken prisoners with some Canadians, and some of our men retaken. This affair will be severely felt by the garrison of Fort Pitt, as the convoy was their sole dependence for the ensuing winter. I must not forget to tell you that the great Huron chief, Sasterassee, is returned from Niagara and brings belts with him from the five nations to be sent to the Southern Indians, requesting them not to make peace with the Virginians 'till required to do so by the great King of Great Britain. The Cherokees are charged with this message to their nation and to the Creeks, Chickesaws and Chuctaws.

The prisoners taken from the southern nations are not willing to return, finding themselves happy in their present situation.

A^{T} DE PEYSTER[35]
Major to the King's Regiment

Enclosure (3)
Henry to Galvez, 14th January 1779 — *4(350): C*

Williamsburgh
Virginia
January 14th 1779

Sir

I have taken the liberty to trouble your Excellency with several letters lately which went by sea, and considering how liable our vessels were to be taken by the British cruisers and that the intercourse with New Orleans was precarious in that route, I informed your Excellency that I should send a messenger to wait on you by way of the Mississippi. Colonel David Rogers will have the honor to wait on you with this and to receive such commands as your Excellency may please to have on that river, which, by opening an easy and safe communication with the Gulf of Mexico, invites to that intercourse and correspondence, between the subjects of His Catholic Majesty and the good people of this Commonwealth, which, I flatter myself, may be managed to the advantage of both. An infant state engaged in a formidable war, procuring with difficulty many articles necessary for maintaining it with vigor, must feel considerable distresses. These Virginia feels, and thanks be to heaven they are not greater than her courage to encounter them. Her own internal resources aided by perseverance have removed some of them, while others have been alleviated by the friendly interposition of the Spanish and French nations, and signal successes have in many instances

---

35 Born in New York City, Arent Schuyler De Peyster (1736-1832) was the uncle of Abraham and Frederick De Peyster, who appear elsewhere in these Papers. Having entered the 8th Regiment in 1755, he had served in various parts of North America under his uncle, Colonel Peter Schuyler, and was now a major commanding at Detroit. The native Americans of the North-West were at first hostile to the Crown, but by his tact and conciliatory measures he had entirely weaned them from the revolutionaries. After eventually taking command of his regiment and rising to the rank of colonel, he would retire to Dumfries, where he resided till his death. During the French Revolution he enlisted and drilled the 1st Regiment of Dumfries. One of its original members was Robbie Burns, who dedicated to him his poem 'Life' and at one time carried on with him a poetical controversy in the columns of the Dumfries *Journal*. (*Appletons'*)

crowned the American arms. Sensible of the value of that friendship which your nation hath tendered to Virginia and of the favors received from you, I am anxious to make the best returns in my power. I beg your Excellency to consider whether the uniting West Florida to American confederacy will not greatly distress the English West India settlements and hinder their progress of rivalship to Spain. I am told they get supplies of lumber and some provisions and other things from the Mississippi. These the Americans can easily stop if it would be acceptable to your nation.

I have thought it necessary for securing the intercourse with New Orleans to build a fort somewhere near the mouth of Ohio, but that shall depend upon what your Excellency shall please to write me upon the subject.

The inland navigation of the Ohio and Mississippi, though at present subject to many inconveniences, has this great advantage, that the British cruisers cannot infest it. Our trade by sea is very much distressed by them, which occasions the want of woollens (particularly blankets), linen and military stores. In order to supply these Colonel Rogers will receive such goods as your Excellency may please to send by him and which in your letter to Congress were said to be lodged at New Orleans for that purpose.

The operations of war with England have been carried on to a great extent insomuch that the expences of it become heavy. This induces me to ask your Excellency whether it would be possible for you to furnish this State with a sum of money on loan, suppose one hundred and fifty thousand pistoles or what other sum, whether this sum would be most conveniently advanced at New Orleans, the Havannah, Cadiz or what other place. Your Excellency will naturally enquire what I have to give in exchange for these advances. I answer the gratitude of this free and independant country, the trade in any or all of its valuable productions, and the friendship of its warlike inhabitants. At present I know not on which of these things you set the greatest value, but they are tendered to you and you will have a right to chuse that which will be most acceptable.

I beg leave to refer you to Colonel Rogers for any matters you may wish to know concerning this Commonwealth and the progress of the war. He is a gentleman in whom your Excellency may place confidence. He will be able to give satisfaction in many things which cannot fall within the compass of a letter. I must entreat your Excellency's peculiar favor and protection to this gentleman, and that in his progress homewards he may meet with every assistance his situation and circumstances may require.

Six hundred thousand people of all ages are subjects of this Commonwealth, a very small proportion of our country, which is as yet uncultivated. We have more lands than can be settled for many ages to come, our manufactures are yet in their infancy, but agriculture hath flourished to great value and extent and enables us to spare commodities of great variety. For an enumeration of them I must refer you to my former letters. I wish that such proposals may be related by your Excellency, in return for the goods and money I ask on loan, as may best suit your occasions and that I may have the earliest information on the subject.

With sentiments of perfect esteem, I have the honor to be, sir,
Your Excellency's most obedient and very humble servant

PATRICK HENRY[36]

Enclosure (4)
Galvez to Henry, undated *4(353): C*

A Monsieur Patrice Henry

Monsieur

Le Colonel Monsieur David Rogers a son arrivée en cette ville me remis votre lettre du 14 janvier de cette année, a laquelle je repondrai article par article, mais avant vous me permetrez d'aplaudir le choix que vous avez fait en la personne du dit colonel pour une commission si interessante. Ses merites lui rend digne d'une estimation generale. Je lui ait offere mes services en tout ce qui pourroit lui etre agréable et ne les a employé en rien qui ait pu me laisser la satisfaction de lui avoir ete util.

Vous me dites par le premier article de votre lettre que, vu les grandes difficultes de pouvour etablir par mer une communication entre ses[37] etats et cette province, vous vous flattez qu'elle pourroit se faire par le fleuve Mississipi a l'avantage des sujects de mon Souverain et de ceux de ses contrées. Je vous avoue que je ne ressentiroit pas de satisfaction plus grande si la chose se verifioit, mais il y a un inconvenance qui empeche cette communication, qui est, que les Anglois etablir et fortifier dans les postes de Manchak et Natchez ne permetroient pas surement (tant qu'ils y seroient) la descente d'aucun Ameriquain par le fleuve. Le Colonel Rogers vous communiquera l'embarras et le danger qu'il a couru pour arriver a cette place.

Ce que vous me dites par le 2e article m'est d'une singuliere satisfaction, et je suis persuadé que par la valeur, persevérance et autre secours, ses provinces reussironts a jouir de ce qu'elle desirent.

Je vous rend mil graces des offres d'amitié que vous avez la bonté de me faire, et je ne doute pas que vous soïez bien persuadé que les miens en retour sont des plus sinceres.

Par l'article 4e vous me dites d'examiner si, en unissant la West Florida a la confederation de ses etats, les etablissements anglois ne se trouveront pas reduits a l'extremité, si on coupoient les progres de la rivalité de ceux cy avec l'Espagne, et que la quantitée de bois,

---

36 One of the most influential political leaders in the revolutionary movement, Patrick Henry (1736-1799) had become the revolutionary Governor of Virginia in June 1776 and remained in office until the summer of 1779. He would continue to play a prominent part in public affairs till his death. (*DAB*)

37 *ses*: a mistranslation of the Spanish 'sus'. Here and elsewhere in the letter the third person possessive or the demonstrative adjective is used to translate 'your'.

provisions, et autres effects dont vous etes informé qu'ils tirent du Mississipi pourroient etre facillement interrompée par les Ameriquains si l'Espagne la prouve. Il ni a pas le moindre doute qu'en separant la West Florida de la domination britanique qu'on oteroient aux Anglois toute communication dans les ports du Golfe du Mexique (d'ou ils peuvent tenter quelque expeditions) ainsï que tous les avantages qu'ils tirent du Mississipi. Ce qui je crois ne deplairoit a l'Espagne; au contraire, il est naturel qu'elle le desire.

Vous me dites par le cinquieme article que pour assurer une correspondence avec la Nouvelle Orleans vous juge qu'il seroit apropos de construire un fort dans quelque endroit d' l'embouchure de l'Ohio, et que cette objet dependra de la reponse que je ferai. Je considere cet etablissement tres util pour faciliter la navigation du Mississipi, et quoique aujourdui elle ne peut se faire si ont ne remedier pas aux inconvenance expliqué au premier article de cette lettre, ce fort serviroit toujours a contenir les sauvages amis des Anglois, sans les secours desquelles ils n'oseroient pas inquieter si facilement ceux qui voyagent d'un endroit a un autre.

Vous m'exposé que pour remedier a la necessite de laines, toilles et munitions que cette province soufre, cause par la quantité de corsaires anglois dont la mer est infestée qui en empeche l'introduction, vous m'envoyé le Colonel Rogers pour recevoir les effets que j'ai destiné pour ses etats, surquoi je doit vous informer qu'il est certain que j'en avoit une certaine quantitée de ramasser, mais, comme j'en donnai ci devant avis au Congré, et que celui cy m'ecrivit de les livrer au Sieur Oliver Pollock, son agent en cette ville, il y a long temps qu'il les a recu et envoyé par les occasions le plus sur qui se sont presentée, tant par mer comme par le fleuve.

Il n'y a pas de doute que la longue guerre que ses etats soutienent doit les avoir constituer dans des depenses enormes. Je suis tres mortifié de ne pouvoir pas moi meme condescendre a la demande que vous faite de vous avancer cent cinquante mil pistoles, ceci etant un object qui depend entierement de mon Souverain. Je lui envoyerez votre lettre a fin que sa volonté royale ait a determiner ce qu'elle jugera a propos, et selon ce qui me sera ordonné je vous en avisirai promptement. Si la quantitée n'etoit pas aussi considerable, et que je n'eusse pas donné au dit Sieur Oliver Pollock l'argent dont je pouvoit disposer qui etoit de surplus de celui assigné annuellement pour les depenses de cette colonie, de l'instant pour vous complaire et servir cet etat je vous en auroit pu donner une partie, ce qui m'est impossible d'executer maintenant, n'aiant pas de fond.

Vous me dites que, comme il est a croire que je veuille m'informer de ce que vous aurez a donner en recompense de ses avances, vous m'offrez la reconnoissance, le commerce d'une ou touts les riches productions du païs, et l'amitié de ses inhabitants. La generosité du Roy, mon maitre, est connu de tout le monde, et son principal interêt sera la gloire d'avoir faciliter ses secours a une nation dans le besoin.

J'ai eu plusieurs conferences avec le Colonel Rogers sur l'etat de la guerre actuelle, ainsi que sur divers autres pointes il participera a son retour.

Je vois avec joie la nombreuse population de cet etat, et son accroissement dans l'agriculture, et je ne doute pas de celui de manufactures soit peu.

Comme les effets que j'avoit ici ont eté envoyé au Congré, et que le prêt que vous me demande depend de la Cour, si Sa Majesté a pour agréable de vous l'accorder, elle designera les productions de ce paїs qui lui conviendront pour son remboursement. J'ai repondu par triplicate a votre lettre du 20 8bre de l'annee derniere, et comme il est a presumer qu'une au moins vous sera parvenue, je crois pouvoir me dispenser de repeter ici ce que je vous disoit alors.

Je vous souhaite le plus grand success dans votre gouvernement, et je serait flatté que vous m'occupiez en tout ce qui pourroit tendre a votre avantage et dont mes facultes me permettroit.

J'ai l'honneur d'etre etc

BERNARD DE GALVEZ

PS

Le papier ci-joint est la traduction en francois de cette lettre.

TRANSLATION

Patrick Henry Esq

Sir

On his arrival in town Colonel David Rogers delivered to me your letter of 14th January this year, to which I shall reply point by point, but first permit me to compliment you on your choice of the colonel for so interesting a mission. His abilities entitle him to general esteem. I have offered him my services in whatever may be agreeable to him and have employed them in whatever was able to give me the satisfaction of being of use to him.

As to the first point in your letter, you say that, considering the great difficulties of establishing a communication by sea between your States and this province, you flatter yourself that it might be effected by way of the Mississippi River to the advantage of the subjects of my Sovereign and those of your country. I confess that I would feel no greater satisfaction if this were to be so, but there is a difficulty which impedes the communication, namely that the British, who are stationed and fortified in the posts of Manchac and Natchez, would surely not permit (whilst they were there) any American to descend the river. Colonel Rogers will convey to you the difficulty and danger he faced in reaching this place.

As to the second point, what you say gives me uncommon satisfaction, and I am persuaded that by valour, perseverance and the assistance of others your provinces will succeed in enjoying what they desire.

May I tender a thousand thanks for the offers of friendship which you kindly make, and I doubt not that you are convinced mine in return are most sincere.

As regards the fourth point, you beg me to consider whether uniting West Florida with the American confederacy will not greatly distress the English settlements and halt the progress of their rivalry with Spain; and you say that the supplies of lumber, provisions and other things you are told they get from the Mississippi could easily be stopped by the Americans if it were acceptable to Spain. I have not the slightest doubt that severing West Florida from British control would deprive the British of all communication with ports in the Gulf of Mexico (from which they are able to attempt expeditions) and of all the advantages they derive from the Mississippi. I do not believe Spain would be displeased with this. On the contrary, we would naturally welcome it.

As respects your fifth point, you say that you think it appropriate to build a fort somewhere at the mouth of the Ohio for securing the intercourse with New Orleans, and that this shall depend on my reply. I believe the post would be very useful for facilitating the navigation of the Mississippi, and although the navigation cannot at present be effected until the difficulty set out in my second paragraph is resolved, the post would nevertheless check the savage friends of the British, without whose help they would not venture to harass so easily those who are repairing from one place to another.

You advise me that the want of woollens, linen and military stores affecting your province, caused by the many British cruisers infesting the sea and preventing their importation, has led you to dispatch Colonel Rogers to me to receive the goods I intended for your States. On this point I have to inform you that I certainly had a quantity assembled, but, as I previously advised Congress of them, and as they wrote me to hand them over to Mr Oliver Pollock, their agent here, he long ago received them and dispatched them by the safest opportunities that offered, both by sea and by the river.

There is no doubt that the long war being waged by your States must have involved them in enormous expenses. I am very mortified that I myself am unable to consent to the request you make for an advance of one hundred and fifty thousand pistoles, this being a matter entirely for my Sovereign. I shall send Him your letter that His royal pleasure may determine what is thought appropriate, and I shall advise you promptly of His commands. If the sum were not so large and I had not given Mr Oliver Pollock the money at my disposal which was left over from that assigned annually for the expenses of this colony, then, to gratify your wishes and serve your State, I would have at once been able to give you a share, but I find it impossible to do so now, not having any funds.

You say that, as I may probably wish to enquire what you have to give in exchange for these advances, you offer gratitude, the trade in any or all of the country's valuable productions, and the friendship of its inhabitants. The generosity of my master, the King, is known to everyone, and His principal interest will be the glory of having facilitated His assistance to a nation in need.

I have had several discussions with Colonel Rogers on the present state of the war as well as on various other points he will impart on his return.

I note with pleasure the numerous population of your State and its growth in agriculture, and I do not doubt its growth in manufactures may be small.

As the goods I had here have been dispatched to Congress, and as the loan you request depends on the Court, if His Majesty is agreeable to grant it, He will designate the productions of your country suitable for repayment. I have replied in triplicate to your letter of 20th October last, and as I assume that at least one will have reached you, I think I may dispense with repeating here what I said there.

I wish you the greatest success in your government, and I shall be flattered if you will involve me in everything that may tend to your advantage and is within my power.

I have the honour to be etc

BERNARDO DE GALVEZ[38]

PS

This is a French translation of the letter.

§ - §

[38] Born in Málaga, Don Bernado de Gálvez (1746-1786) had pursued a military career before becoming Governor of Louisiana in February 1777 and providing, for some two years, covert aid to the American revolutionaries. When war finally broke out between Spain and Britain in June 1779, he was soon afforded the opportunity of again displaying his military talents and received the full support of Charles III due in part to his influential family connections. His uncle, Don José de Gálvez, was President of the Council of the Indies (akin to a colonial secretary), while his father, Matias, was soon to be appointed Captain General of Guatemala. Although the date of Bernado's present letter is not given, he evidently wrote it sometime before September 1779, when he reduced the British posts of Manchac, Natchez, and Baton Rouge. In March 1780 he captured Mobile, and in May 1781 he would reduce Pensacola. A year later New Providence in the Bahamas fell to him. As a result of his campaigns Spain obtained both West and East Florida in the peace settlement of 1783. He was rewarded by appointment as Captain General of Cuba while retaining the governorship of Louisiana and the Floridas. Shortly after, he succeeded his father, who had died in office, as Viceroy of Mexico. On his death his heart was placed in an urn in the Cathedral of Mexico while the rest of his remains were interred next to his father's crypt in the Franciscan Church of San Fernando, Mexico City. (*DAB*; *Appletons'*; Robert H Thonhoff, 'Who was Bernado de Gálvez?' (HispanicAmericanHeroesSeries.com/who.php, 22nd November 2005))

CHAPTER 34

Correspondence with British officers in the field

---

1 - Between Cornwallis and Wemyss, Stark or Money

Money to Wemyss, 1st November 1780 ***82(3): ACS***

Head Quarters
Wynnesborough
November 1st 1780

Major Wemyss
63rd Regiment

Dear Sir

In addition to the directions sent yesterday by Lord Rawdon for the movement of the 63rd[1], I am directed by Lord Cornwallis to acquaint you that it is his opinion you should cross Broad River to protect the mills and at the same time be in communication with this army. His Lordship this morning received yours of the 29th October[2].

I am, dear sir, etc

J M

---

1 *the directions..*: see Rawdon to Wemyss, 31st October, vol II, p 225.

2 *yours..*: see vol II, p 224.

Stark to Cornwallis, 9th November 1780 — *4(80): ALS*

Davis's House
9th November 1780

The Rt Hon Lord Cornwallis etc etc etc

My Lord

I have the honour to acquaint your Lordship that at six o'clock last night Major Wemyss march't from Dansby's plantation with the 63rd Regiment consisting of 135 rank and file, and 30 dragoons, with an intention to surprize General Sumpter, who was encamp't at More's Mill near Fish Dam Ford with a corps of militia, the strength of which by the different accounts was supposed from 400 to 900 men.

On arriving near that place, intelligence was brought in that the enemy had moved the preceding night. Altho' this deprived Major Wemyss of one essential advantage, which was a perfect knowledge of the ground, open and proper for cavalry to act in, his zeal for the publick service would not allow him to overlook any opportunity that offered for attacking them. He therefore continued his march to Fish Dam Ford, which he reached about one o'clock this morning and immediately attack't the enemy, who were posted on very strong ground with picquets advanced on the hills around, by which they were alarmed a little before our approach.

Their line, formed on the low ground, immediately gave way and were pursued into the ford, but, being galled by a very severe fire from every height and swamp from which it was found impracticable to dislodge them, and Major Wemyss having received two wounds, in his knee and arm, which rendered him incapable of giving any farther directions, after remaining an hour in that situation and perceiving the enemy had taken a position by which they must have pick't off the whole with their rifles as soon as daylight appeared, I determined, with the concurrence of all the other officers, to return, which was effected without the smallest molestation. From the want of any kind of conveyance I was under the disagreable necessity of leaving the wounded in a house near the field. I left the surgeon with a flag of truce to take care of Major Wemyss and, as he was in want of every kind of necessary, afterwards sent Lieutenant Campbell with a flag to deliver his baggage, who is not yet returned. Our loss is two serjeants and 20 rank and file killed and wounded. That of the Legion, expeting Lieutenant Hovenden, who is wounded, I cannot even guess at. The loss of the enemy I imagine does not exceed forty from their keeping so much out of reach.

As the plantation of Colonel Wynne was formerly pointed out by Major Wemyss as an eligible situation, I shall move there this evening, where I shall remain untill I receive your Lordship's directions.

I am with the greatest respect
Your Lordship's most obedient servant

H B STARK[3]
Lieutenant commanding 63rd Regiment

Cornwallis to Money, 11th November 1780 — *4(92): ADfS*

Winsborough
November 11th 1780

Dear Money

If the horses and mares mentioned in the inclosed notes[4] are or have been in your corps, you must either return them or give the bearer receipts to be paid a fair price. You will be particularly carefull not to be surprized before Major McArthur joins you, and don't let desire of revenging the last affair hurry you too far. Try every means to procure intelligence, and above all things don't forget that you are infantry and that good infantry may make bad cavalry. What I have said proceeds from my anxiety for you and not from want of confidence.

Yours very sincerely

CORNWALLIS

Cornwallis to Money, 11th November 1780 — *4(100): ADfS*

Winsborough
November 11th 1780

Dear Money

Your serjeant major's account of Wemys gives me great satisfaction, but he has added to my regret about the unfortunate business by assuring me that at day break there was not an enemy to be seen. If you hear positively of the enemy's march to 96, you will try to inform the commanding officer. I wrote to you just now by some country people.

Yours sincerely

CORNWALLIS

---

3 As indicated elsewhere in this volume, Henry Bethune Stark's part in the affair at Fish Dam Ford would displease Cornwallis. He had been commissioned an ensign in the 63rd Regiment on 29th September 1775 and been promoted to lieutenant on 7th October 1777. For the last five months he had been acting as the regiment's quartermaster. At the Battle of Hobkirk's Hill in April 1781 he would act as an aide-de-camp to Rawdon, who would warmly praise him for his services during the action. (*Army Lists*; *The Cornwallis Papers*)

4 *the inclosed notes*: no extant copies.

[*Subscribed*:]

Pray return my thanks to the 63rd for their good and gallant behaviour.

Cornwallis to Money, 13th November 1780 — *4(112): ADfS*

Winsborough
November 13th 1780

Dear Money

I received this evening your letter begun on the 11th and finished this morning[5]. Captain O'Neal is just arrived and I find the terror as great as possible. Tarleton alone can settle matters. He was at Camden last night and I hope his corps will pass tomorrow. It is probable the 63rd Dragoons[6] may be of his party. I have sent for him to come here, but his corps must keep at a distance or they will eat us up. Despard is arrived, Lord Rawdon and England gone to Camden. The Volunteers of Ireland marched to day.

Yours sincerely

CORNWALLIS

[*Subscribed*:]

Put McArthur in mind to send constantly to me. The Governor and all here send best compliments.

§ - §

5 *your letter...*: not extant

6 *63rd Dragoons*: a droll reference to the 63rd Foot. They were to join Tarleton as mounted infantry.

2 - Between Cornwallis and McArthur

McArthur to Cornwallis, 13th November 1780 — *4(114): ALS*

Camp at Byerly's Ferry (formerly Shirar's)
November 13th 1780, 10 am

The Rt Hon Lt General Earl Cornwallis
Head Quarters

My Lord

I have the honor to inform your Lordship that I arrived here yesterday morning and found Lieutenant Money had secured the boats. They consist of two flatts, capable of carrying 30 men each, and two canoes. Lieutenant Money had passed the night at Sommers's Mill three miles lower down the river. I have left an officer's guard to protect the mill, and the two corps are encamped close to this ferry. By the information of two emissarys sent over yesterday, who returned in the night, I learn that Sumpter was at Hawkins's Mill on Tyger River, that his numbers were not much short of one thousand (though I take this to be too high a computation), and they gave out they inten[d]ed for Ninety Six. When I was at the mill yesterday, there was a considerable quantity of meal ground and two waggons ready to receive it, but [they] could not proceed for want of casks or baggs to contain it. I sent them some casks from hence and hope they went off in the night. The cattle that were to be sent with us by Colonel Philips's people have not yet appeared. However, we have had no want. The ferryman here has a little rum, which I have secured for the detachment, but as he is a true friend, it costs very dear. The distance from this ferry to the nearest ford on Ennoree (Kelly's) is nine miles and from thence to Hawkins's Mill on Tyger River eight miles.

I have the honor to be, my Lord,
Your Lordship's most obedient humble servant

ARCH[D] McARTHUR

Cornwallis to McArthur, 13th November 1780 — *82(36): C*

Winsborough
November 13th 1780
7 o'clock pm

Major McArthur

Dear Sir

I have received the favor of yours dated this morning. By your account the mill seems to serve no better than the commissaries. Tarleton is returned to Camden and I hope we shall soon put a stop to Mr Sumpter's bragging and to the terror of our friends. I am glad you have got cattle and rum. I shall not grudge the price of the latter, especially in this weather. I have had a letter from General Leslie, who will be ready to come to any place where he can be useful to us. Balfour says that the carriages and horses are in so bad order that he is afraid he cannot answer half the demands made by the regiments. However, he says he will send up all the most material and useful articles as soon as possible. Captain O'Neal, who is just arrived, confirms the account of the general terror. Let me hear constantly from you and I will in return send you all intelligence that I receive.

I am faithfully yours

CORNWALLIS

Cornwallis to McArthur, 14th November 1780 — *82(41): C*

Winsborough
November 14th 1780

Major McArthur
71st Regiment

Dear Sir

A Negro is come in who says he left Smallwood with three pieces of cannon near Lawson's Iron Works on Saturday last and that he was certainly going for 96. I wish you to send out every body you can to ascertain this fact as soon as possible, and to keep a look out on the fords above you, especially Lisle's Ford. I hope Tarleton will be up to morrow.

I am faithfully yours

CORNWALLIS

Cornwallis to McArthur, 14th November 1780 — *82(43): C*

Winsborough
November 14th 1780

Major McArthur

Dear Sir

I beg you will endeavour to communicate to Colonel Cruger by some trusty messenger the intelligence which I sent you this morning, if you have not already done it. The Negroe is so very circumstantial, and describes so particularly the march of Smallwood's corps and his cannon, that altho' all other intelligence, which indeed is not good, puts him on the other side of the Catawba, I am very apt to give credit to the Negroe. Should his account prove true, it will certainly occasion our moving your way, so that I should wish you to detain the waggons that are now at the mill untill you hear farther from me. I need not press your taking every possible step to get intelligence and watching the fords above you.

I am most faithfully yours

CORNWALLIS

[*Subscribed*:]

Desire Cruger to have an eye to the roads towards Augusta.

McArthur to Cornwallis, 15th November 1780 — *4(137): ALS*

Camp at Bryerly's
November 15th 1780, 7 am

The Rt Hon Lt General Earl Cornwallis
Head Quarters

My Lord

I was honored with your Lordship's letter last night and shall use every possible endeavour to ascertain the point you mention. I am happy to find your Lordship has heard from General Leslie.

Advice was brought me yesterday morning between one and two o'clock that a party of the rebels had crossed at Fish Dam and were plundering Mobily's setlement, that they were about one hundred in number and were got within 12 or 13 miles of us. I immediately detached Lieutenant Money with the 63rd in quest of them, who returned last night at 7 o'clock after having marched above four and forty miles, but could not come up with them as they staid but a few hours at one place; and on his return it appeared they had crossed at Lisle's Ford on Monday night, so well do the militia there do their duty, though Major Alcorne[7] tells me Colonel Philips gave orders to Captain Hill[8] to keep a guard of his

7 The inference to be drawn is that 'Alcorne' was major in John Phillips' Jackson's Creek Regiment of the royal militia, but no other reference to this effect has come to light. He may have been Robert Alcorn (*c.* 1728-1797), whose father migrated from Ireland in 1721 and settled in Virginia. About 1755 Robert moved on from Montgomery County, first to the Pee Dee and Mecklenburg County, North Carolina, and then in 1772 to the South Carolina Back County, where he was granted 300 acres along Little River near its confluence with the Broad, together with 50 acres at the mouth of Sandy River. Both land holdings lay within the catchment area of Phillips' regiment. During the war in South Carolina Robert acted for a time as a commissary to the revolutionary forces, while some sons served in the revolutionary militia. In 1788 he removed to Kentucky, where he died in Madison County. (Elsie, Lloyd and Malvern Alcorn, 'Supplement to "Robert Alcorn and His Descendants"' (Internet, 18th December 2005); *The Cornwallis Papers*)

8 Apart from being a captain in Phillips' regiment of the royal militia, Hill has not been identified.

company constantly at that ford. I have sent orders to Hill and informed him he is to be answerable this is done. The night Money arrived here he sent off three waggons for the wounded of the 63rd, but the drivers got *scared* before they got to them, left their waggons and came home yesterday with their horses. I should think the best way of bringing them will be by waggons with a flagg from head quarters, as it would be difficult to procure waggons or drivers here. A man from Commissary Bloxham came here last night and says three waggons with flour from beyond the river will be here this day. I shall forward them immediately.

I have the honor to be, my Lord,
Your Lordship's most obedient humble servant

ARCH^{D} McARTHUR

[*Subscribed*:]

I wrote to Colonel Cruger on Monday.

[*Endorsed*:]

The three waggons with flour are come.

McArthur to Cornwallis, 15th November 1780 — *4(128): ALS*

Camp at Byerley's
November 15th 1780, 10 am

The Rt Hon Lt General Earl Cornwallis etc etc etc
Head Quarters

My Lord

I did myself the honor to write to your Lordship at 7 this morning. I am now honored with your letter directing me to communicate to Colonel Cruger the intelligence you mention and a trusty messenger will instantly set off with it. I this moment receiv'd the enclosed from Colonel Kirkland, but without your Lordship's orders I don't think myself at liberty to detach so far and I shall write him accordingly.

I have a man of approved fidelity ready to go off towards Lawson's Fork, where the iron works are. I have ordered off a guard of the militia from this place to Lyel's Ford as those of Hill's company have been so negligent. I detain the three waggons with the flour and have sent directions to the mill to stop any that may be there.

I have the honor to be, my Lord,
Your Lordship's most obedient humble servant

ARCH^{D} McARTHUR

Enclosure
Kirkland to McArthur, 14th November 1780 — *4(130): LS*

Fort at Williams
November 14th 1780

Major McArtur commanding at Shires Ferry

Sir

I am sorry to acquaint you that Colonel Cunningham, a man that might be of the greatest service of any man in this fork, is doing every thing in his power to make a division amongst the people to keep them from imbodying in defence of this post. I have not now more than 100 men, nor don't expect more than 20 to our relief, and from all probility I may expect to be attack'd this night as Clark with his hole body consisting of 25 colonels[9] and about 500 men join'd Sumpter at Hendricks Mill on Enary about 20 miles from this fort. If I should avacuate it, the whole strength of the militia of the Destrict of Ninety Six will amediately be in possession of the rebells and Colonel Cruger's supplys of provision will be amediately cut of. I cauld upon him last night for support. I this moment received his answer that he cannot spare one man but desired that I would amediately write to you for support. The only thing that can be done, if it was agreeable to his Lordship, would be to put Sumpter to the rout. It would give fresh spirits to the militia and they would raise in a great body and pursue them. On Thursday last Clark was in camp on Fare Forrest at Flichhal's Mill when the news came to them of Sumpter's defeat. The amediately decamp[ed] and retreated 20 miles that night. Pray give me a positive answer wheathe I shall be supported if I am attacked.

Your most obedient and very humble servant

MOSES KIRKLAND
Lt Colonel Militia

Cornwallis to McArthur, 16th November 1780 — *82(51): C*

Winsborough
November 16th 1780

Major McArthur
71st Regiment

Dear Sir

I yesterday received your letters dated at 7 and 10 am. I have received so many positive accounts that Smallwood is on the other side of Catawba that I cannot doubt it. However,

---

[9] *25 colonels*: a nonsense. Perhaps a mistake by Kirkland's transcriber.

the Negroe persists and says that he will be content to be hanged if there are not three pieces of cannon with the enemy on the other side of Broad River. I cannot, however, believe him. Tarleton will be with you to morrow. He will cross with the Legion and 63rd Regiment and will open the communication with the country so as to ascertain the fact. If they have cannon, they must be in force and have most of their Continentals, in which case I shall come to you. If not, Tarleton with some cooperation from 96 will be equal to the business. I am unwilling to quit this position as the communication from Camden to McChord's, and indeed the whole fork, would be greatly exposed. The necessaries for the 71st, 33rd and Volunteers of Ireland were embarked at Nelson's Ferry on the 11th. I hope they will come safe, but I had much rather have heard of their coming by land. As we have sent off the sick to Camden, I am not strong in waggons. I therefore desired Major Despard to propose to you to send the drivers and horses back with a flag of truce to the waggons they have left. I likewise ordered the surgeon of the 63rd to go early this morning to dress them. As my moving is very uncertain, I would have the waggons sent to me from the mill, a proportion of the flour and every thing to go on as usual. I fear you will not get much good service out of Phillips's militia.

I am with great regard
Your most obedient and faithfull servant

CORNWALLIS

McArthur to Cornwallis, 17th November 1780 — *4(147): ALS*

Camp at Byerley's Ferry
November 17th 1780

The Rt Hon Lt General Earl Cornwallis etc etc etc

My Lord

I was honoured with your Lordship's letter of yesterday and in consequence five waggons with flour and three with meal set off last night. I have kept one waggon load of flour here. I am sorry to inform you that one of the people that set off to ascertain the point you mentioned is just returned, not finding it practicable to cross the Ennoree. He met a man he could depend on who informed him that the militia is collecting fast to Sumpter but that in his camp they had heard nothing of the approach of Smallwood. I hope that a man who is gone up this side of the river and was to cross high up may be more successfull. The inclosed proclamation[10] was brought me this moment by a discharged soldier of Delancey's who lives four miles beyond the ferry. It was brought to the house he lives at this morning

[10] *The inclosed proclamation*: not extant.

at two o'clock by four men, who ordered him to deliver it to one Turly[11] in that neighbourhood, but he chose to bring it here. I was yesterday at Lile's Ford, where I found a proper guard of Captain Hill's company, who assured me he never received any order from Colonel Philips to keep a guard there. I have ordered another guard to be placed three miles higher up at a ford called Marbury's, and when I proposed to keep a guard at the Fish Dam Ford, Hill and his people said nothing less than one hundred men would be sufficient there, as they were more afraid of the people in their rear than of Sumpter's men, but they promise to patrole there frequently and keep a confidential person always on the spott.

I have the honor to be, my Lord,
Your Lordship's most obedient humble servant

ARCH[D] McARTHUR

McArthur to Cornwallis, 18th November 1780 *4(153): ALS*

Camp at Bryerley's Ferry
November 18th 1780, 6 pm

The Rt Hon Lt General Earl Cornwallis
Head Quarters

My Lord

I have the honor to inform your Lordship that, a party of the rebells having come within two miles of the ferry this morning, I was just going to pass over with 150 men when Colonel Tarleton arrived at nine o'clock, and I countermanded my party. The rebells had the audacity, in half an hour after, to come close to the river and fire at our men who were washing in the flatts. Luckily the most of them had retired before the firing began, so there was only one soldier of the 63rd wounded sligtly and a waggon horse hurt. They blackguarded us a great deal, but no return was made them except one shott by a militia man without orders. At two o'clock the infantry of Tarleton's corps passed at this ferry and only one shott was fired at them, which hurt nobody, for care was taken to fire several cannon shott across, which dispersed the enemy, and I have this moment received advice from Colonel Tarleton that his mounted people have passed at the Mill Ford three miles lower down without opposition and the 63rd were ready to follow. The rebells appeared at the other side of the river opposite the mill earlier than here, and Captain Hill informs me they shewed themselves at Liles's Ford about the same time they came opposite to us. Tarleton has left his baggage herc and taken the cannon I had with me, it being in better condition than his own, which he has left with me. He proposed going between four and [five?] miles only this evening. It gives me concern that the emissary who was to cross pretty high up the river returned this evening, not

---

11 Perhaps Peter Turley, who came to South Carolina before the revolution from Fairfax County, Virginia. He appears to have settled in the Back Country, where his wife Elizabeth (née Hiatt) died in 1837 at the age of ninety-two. He has left no record of service in the royal or revolutionary forces. (Katie Bond, 'Family of John Hiatt/Heydt' (Internet, 17th November 2005))

daring to pass at Fishdam or Love's Fords, finding them both too well guarded, so that I have no hopes of being able to ascertain the desired point.

I have the honor to be, my Lord,
Your Lordship's most obedient humble servant

ARCH^D McARTHUR

Cornwallis to McArthur, 19th November 1780 — *82(65): C*

Wynnesborough
November 19th 1780
11 o'clock am

Major McArthur
Brierly's Ferry

Dear Sir

I received your letter this morning. The country people had reported that they had heard firing, but I was not uneasy. I send a dragoon who went with a flag of truce to Sumpter. He was at Sumpter's camp on the 16th and saw his corps and Clarke's on the march. I have every reason to believe that there is not the least foundation for the report of Smallwood or the cannon. I beg you will not allow the dragoon or the men of the 63rd to proceed to join Tarleton unless you think they can do it safely.

I am
Your most obedient and faithfull servant

CORNWALLIS

McArthur to Cornwallis, 21st November 1780 — *4(177): ALS*

Camp at Bryerley's Ferry
November 21st 1780

The Rt Hon Earl Cornwallis etc etc etc

My Lord

I have been honoured with your letters of yesterday and the day before[12]. The only certain accounts I have of Colonel Tarleton are that he passed the Ennoree the day before yesterday and encamped at night near the river and marched next morning. Some small

---

[12] *your letters..*: of that of the 20th there is no extant copy.

partys of the rebells are still prowling on the other side of this river, and on Sunday night they rendered the two mills opposite to ours useless, though I am told the expence of repairing them will not be considerable. The supply of rum was very welcome.

I have the honor to inclose Mr Burns', surgeon's mate, 71st, letter to me. If your Lordship cannot receive his resignation[13], I request you will be pleased to countersign and forward the inclosed memorial[14].

The express that carried my letter to Colonel Cruger, I learn from Colonel Cunningham, was taken by the rebells.

I have the honor to be, my Lord,
Your Lordship's most obedient humble servant

ARCH^{D} McARTHUR

Cornwallis to McArthur, 22nd November 1780 — *82(85): C*

Wynnesborough
November 22nd 1780

Major McArthur
71st Regiment

Dear Sir

I would have you move on to morrow morning very early to Calley's[15] Ford on Ennoree with your battalion and the baggage of Colonel Tarleton's corps and send an express to Colonel Tarleton to let him know that you will forward his baggage from thence with an escort of a captain and 50 men, but if he wishes your battalion to follow, you will do it with the utmost expedition. In the meantime let the baggage and escort go on. I send Stewart as I understand there are several wounded. If Tarleton does not want your battalion, I would have you return to Bryerly's Ferry and acquaint me with it.

I am most faithfuly yours

CORNWALLIS

---

13 David Burns' resignation was not accepted. He was still serving with the 71st in 1783. (WO 65/164(15) (National Archives, Kew))

14 *the inclosed memorial*: neither it nor Burns' letter is extant.

15 *Calley's*: a misspelling of 'Kelly's'.

McArthur to Cornwallis, 22nd November 1780 — *4(179): ALS*

Camp at Bryerley's Ferry
November 22nd 1780
12 at noon

The Rt Hon Lt General Earl Cornwallis
Head Quarters

My Lord

Captain Risingar is this moment arrived from Colonel Tarleton and, his letter to your Lordship[16] being open, I took the liberty to read it and find that Tarleton had wrote to me to pass and bring his baggage with me, which I shall do without loss of time. The horses of the Legion and 63rd waggons are out a-foraging, so that I can go but a litle way this evening. I shall leave an officer and twenty men to protect the mill and leave the care of this ferry to the militia. Risingar informs me Tarleton's express to me set off yesterday morning before day, so there is no doubt of his being taken.

I have the honor to be, my Lord,
Your Lordship's most obedient humble servant

ARCH^D McARTHUR

McArthur to Cornwallis, 24th November 1780 — *4(191): ALS*

Camp at Kelly's Ford on Ennoree
November 24th 1780, 6 am

The Rt Hon Lt General Earl Cornwallis
Head Quarters

To be forwarded by Captain Risingar

My Lord

I was honoured with your Lordship's letter by Dr Stewart after I had passed Bryerley's Ferry the night before last. I wrote to Colonel Tarleton, before I received your Lordship's, that I had passed the ferry on my way to join him, and yesterday morning I wrote him that I would forward his baggage with an escort of a captain and 50 of the 71st agreable to your Lordship's commands, and yesterday at noon his baggage with the escort passed this ford, but at seven o'clock last night I received a letter from him desiring I would join him with all possible expedition *as he has something else to do near the mountains before he returns.* He tells me Colonels Clark and Chandler were killed and Sumpter mortally wounded, that the

---

16 *his letter..*: of 21st November, p 340.

enemy's loss amounted to 120 killed and wounded, and some people who passed here this day affirm Sumpter is died of his wounds. I would have marched immediately on receipt of Tarleton's letter but this ford is too deep and stony to pass in the night. We are just preparing to pass the ford and hope to make a good day's march of it.

I have the honor to be, my Lord,
Your Lordship's most obedient humble servant

ARCH^{D} McARTHUR

McArthur to Cornwallis, 25th November 1780 — *4(204): ALS*

Camp at Skelton's
November 25th 1780, 5 pm

Earl Cornwallis etc etc etc

My Lord

Major Manly overtook me this day at one o'clock. In consequence I encamped at the first proper place, not a mile farther on, and sent an officer forward to Tarleton, who was moving. He desired I would remain here till I heard from him again, which shall be complied with. I am within seven miles of his camp. Mr McBean is just arrived and has delivered your Lordship's verbal message, which shall be observed without delay so soon as I have permission. The distance from Ennoree to this place is not thirty miles, I mean from Kelly's Ford.

I have the honor to be, my Lord,
Your Lordship's most obedient humble servant

ARCH^{D} McARTHUR

Cornwallis to McArthur, 30th November 1780 — *82(136): C*

Wynnesborough
November 30th 1780

Major McArthur
71st Regiment

Dear Sir

You will please to remain until further orders with the 1st Battalion of the 71st at Brierly's Ferry. Lt Colonel Tarleton will go lower down on Broad River for the convenience of forage with the Legion. The 63rd Regiment will march either to morrow or Saturday, as you shall think most convenient, with the wounded men to Camden. As I do not intend to continue any of the British regiments mounted, they will give up their horses for the use of the Legion to any officer who shall be appointed by Lt Colonel Tarleton to receive them, except twenty, which they will take with them to Camden and deliver to Lord Rawdon for the use of the New York Volunteers. You will please to signify to the officers and soldiers of the 63rd my acknowledgments for the spirit with which they have supported the very fatiguing service on which they have been employed for these last three months.

As I find poor Money is much worse than I supposed, and that[17] nothing is so likely to be of use to him as rest, I should wish him to remain with you under the care of Stewart until he can be moved with perfect safety to Camden. I shall be glad to hear frequently from Stewart how he goes on.

I expect some necessaries for your battalion this day or to morrow, which shall be immediately forwarded to you, and I will use every endeavour to get up your cloathing, which I believe is by this time at McChord's Ferry. If you can press any waggons in your neighbourhood for the purpose of bringing your cloathing from McChord's, you may promise them 13*s.* a day and a discharge as soon as that service is performed.

If you can collect any wheat flour, I beg you will do it as it may be very usefull for a move. I shall be glad to hear from you frequently and am with great regard

Your most obedient and faithfull servant

CORNWALLIS

McArthur to Cornwallis, 2nd December 1780 — *4(269): ALS*

Camp at Byerley's Ferry
December 2nd 1780

The Rt Hon Lt General Earl Cornwallis
Winnesborough

My Lord

I was honored with your Lordship's of the 30th ultimo. The 63rd marched at eight this morning with the wounded. They delivered their horses yesterday agreable to your Lordship's order, reserving the number prescribed for the New York Volunteers. As it is at all times a disagreable office to be the harbinger of bad news, I am extremely sorry to be under the necessity of informing your Lordship that poor Money died last night about eleven o'clock. I shall see him decently interred this day. Dr Stewart carries with him a memorandum

---

[17] *that*: the meaning is 'as'. See p 43, note 55.

book[18] and some other papers found in his letter case which I thought you would chuse to peruse.

I have got four waggons in readiness to set off tomorrow morning for McChord's Ferry to bring the cloathing of the 71st. I send a serjeant with them. They go down the west side of the river and I have ordered them to cross at Camden and leave cloathing there for the sick and convalescents of the regiment. Our surgeon's mate at Camden informs me there are a considerable number of men of the 71st there that are capable of doing garrison duty but very unfit for a winter campaign. If your Lordship approves of it, I would wish to send them to Charles Town under care of one officer for both battallions – or, could it be done, rather to Sullivan's Island, where they would be more out of harm's way – and probably in the spring they may be fit for active service. I shall use every endeavour to procure some flour, though I cannot flatter myself with being able to collect any considerable quantity as so much has already been got from this neighbourhood. Our rum is just done.

I have the honor to be, my Lord,
Your Lordship's most obedient humble servant

ARCH^D McARTHUR

Cornwallis to McArthur, 3rd December 1780 — *83(5): C*

Wynnesborough
December 3rd 1780

Major McArthur
71st Regiment

Dear Sir

I have ordered your necessaries with some rum to be forwarded to you. The cloathing of the 71st was not arrived at McChord's. I have sent the best directions I could to the officer to expedite that business. Camden is vastly out of the way for the waggons and must make a difference of at least fifty miles, and the road is much worse. I have no objection to your plan for the convalescents who will not be equal to the winter campaign, and will desire Balfour to send them to Fort Moultrie.

Tarleton will be some time below you upon Broad River. He will shift his ground from time to time on account of forage. I should wish you always to know where he is in case of any thing extraordinary.

I am, dear sir,
Your most obedient and faithfull servant

CORNWALLIS

---

18 *a memorandum book*: Money's Journal, vol II, pp 356-366.

McArthur to Cornwallis, 16th December 1780 *4(339): ALS*

Camp at Byerley's Ferry
December 16th 1780

Rt Hon Lt General Earl Cornwallis
Winnesborough

My Lord

I have the honor to inform your Lordship that a Mr Lane[19], who was taken some time ago, going express from me to Colonel Cruger, returned to his habitation two days ago, being paroled and limited within five miles of his house. He has sent me notice that the rebels under Colonel Lacey were busy making a stockade redoute on a high hill on the upper side of Turkey Creek, that they had collected about five hundred bushells of corn at that place and expected by the 17th instant a reinforcement of between 4 and 500 men from beyond the mountains, that Sumpter was sent to Charlotte and still continues very ill.

A young man named Caldwell[20] from near Ennoree informs me that at dusk the evening before last a party of between forty and fifty rebells commanded by a Colonel Hayes[21] attacked twenty five of our militia under Major Buffington[22] at Widow Duggan's three or four miles south of Ennoree on Indian Creek, who as usual had no centry out. Buffington is mortally wounded, three more much wounded, and seven or eight carried off. Hayes had with him in all about 250 and is supposed to have repassed Ennoree yesterday.

I have the honor to be, my Lord,
Your Lordship's most obedient humble servant

ARCH[D] McARTHUR

---

19 Lane possessed such a common surname in South Carolina that he cannot be positively identified. He may, for example, have been Thomas Lane, who would enlist as a private in the South Carolina Royalist Regiment on 12th March 1781. (Clark, *Loyalists in the Southern Campaign*, i, 13, 14)

20 Perhaps Matthew Caldwell (1763-?), a young man whose parents had settled in the vicinity of the Enoree. (Audrey McDowell ed, 'Union County, SC, Genealogy' (Internet, 28th November 1998))

21 Having settled to the south of the Enoree, Joseph Hayes had served first as a captain and then as a lt colonel under James Williams. On the latter's death at the Battle of King's Mountain he had succeeded to the command of Williams' men and would soon take part in the Battle of Cowpens. On 19th November 1781 he would be granted a 'Georgia parole' by Bloody Bill Cunningham, when, having surrendered at Hayes' Station on condition of being treated as a prisoner of war, he would be summarily strung up and, when the pole broke, hacked to death. (Draper, *King's Mountain*, 467-8)

22 Although badly wounded, Moses Buffington (1751-1782) survived. He belonged to a family of Back Country loyalists and in autumn 1779 had taken part in the defence of Savannah as an ensign in the South Carolina Royalist Regiment. By now he had resigned his commission and for the last twelve days had been serving as major in Daniel Clary's Dutch Fork Regiment of the royal militia. During the siege of Ninety Six in May and June 1781 he would be promoted to colonel. By early July he would have fled to Charlestown, where he was paid as a refugee militia colonel until his death in August or November of the following year. (Moses Buffington to his father Peter, 8th December 1779 (The Moses Buffington Papers, Georgia Historical Society); Clark, *Loyalists in the Southern Campaign*, i, 233, 491 et seq, 550)

Cornwallis to McArthur, 17th December 1780 — *83(52): C*

Wynnesborough
December 17th 1780

Major McArthur
71st Regiment

Dear Sir

I received your letter of yesterday and had before heard that the rebels were making a log fort on Turkey Creek. The remissness and constant misfortunes of our militia are very provoking. You will please to take every opportunity in your power to procure intelligence. I have the pleasure to inform you that General Leslie is arrived at Charlestown and I believe the fleet has not suffered in its passage. Your 2nd Battalion is gaining strength every day.

I am, sir,
Your most faithfull servant

CORNWALLIS

McArthur to Cornwallis, 20th December 1780 — *4(364): ALS*

Camp at Byerley's Ferry
December 20th 1780

Rt Hon Lt General Earl Cornwallis
Winnesborough

My Lord

The only thing I have learned respecting the enemy, since I last did myself the honor to write you, is that a person arrived here yesterday who left Turkey Creek two days ago and says the rebels had pressed all the waggons in that neighbourhood and gave out they were to be sent to Salisbury for salt.

I have the honor to send your Lordship a litle sketch of the ground where the rebels have made the redoute on Turkey Creek. Lieutenant McDonald[23] has made it from the information of Mr Lane, who was at the place when prisoner. He does not know the size of it but is positive there was no place for cannon. I likewise inclose a plan of the action at Black Stocks drawn by Lieutenant McDonald, which is pretty near the mark.

I have the honor to be, my Lord,
Your Lordship's most obedient humble servant

ARCH^{D} McARTHUR

---

23 Angus or Robert McDonald, both of whom were lieutenants in the 1st Battalion, 71st (Highland) Regiment. (*Army Lists*)

Plan of the Rebel Stockade near Turkey Creek and of surrounding area

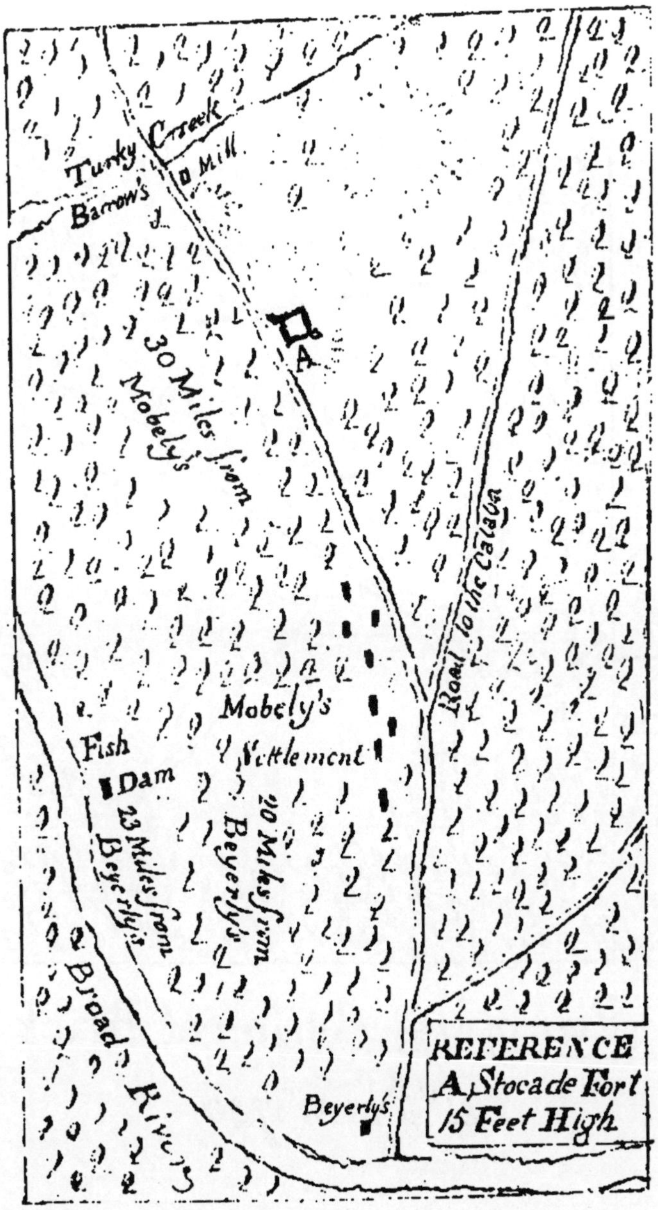

Plan of the Action at Blackstocks, 21st November 1780

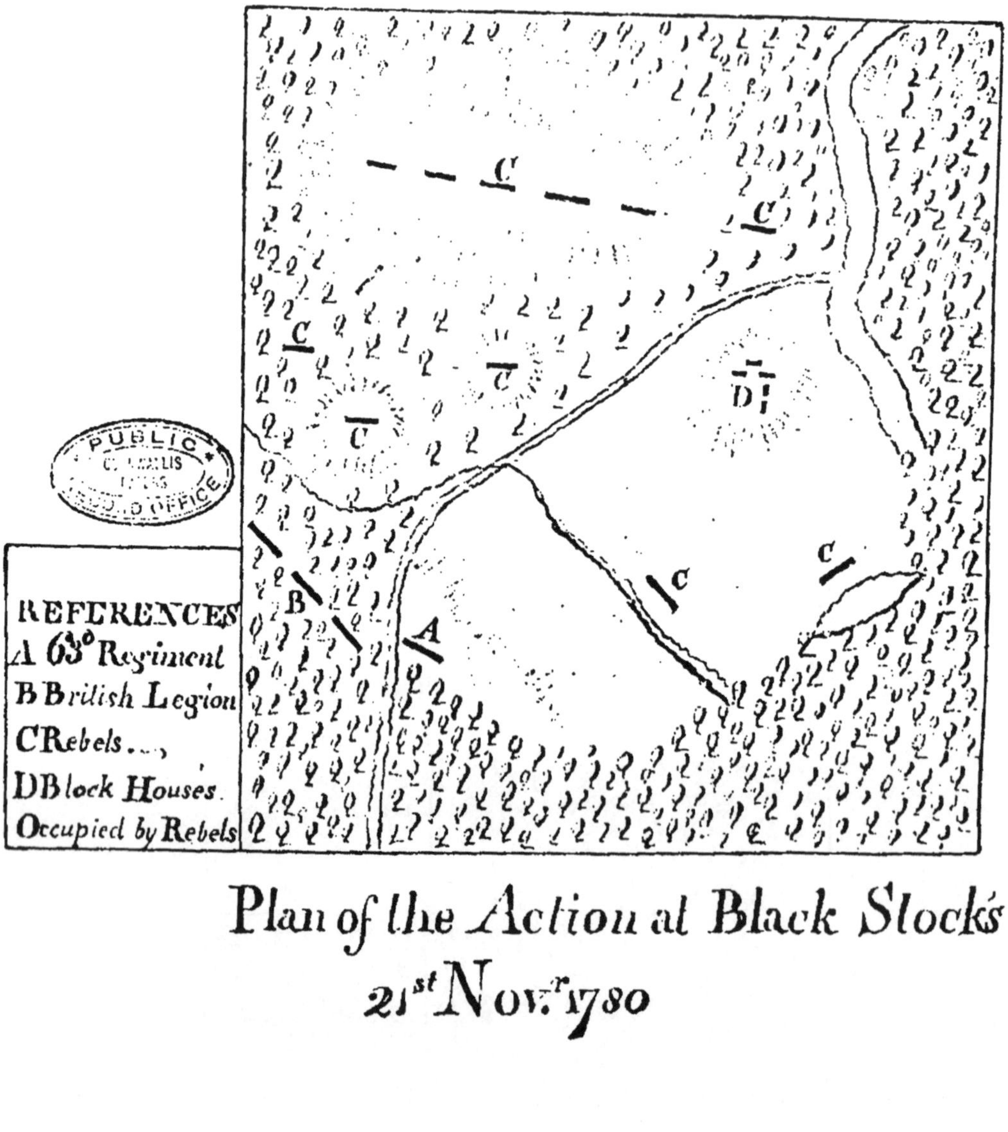

Plan of the Action at Black Stock's
21st Novr 1780

Haldane to McArthur, 22nd December 1780 — *83(67): ACS*

Head Quarters
Wynnesborough
22nd December 1780

Major McArthur commanding the post at Bryerley's Ferry

Dear Sir

Lord Cornwallis having received intelligence that Colonel Campbell is near King's Mountain with a considerable body from the back of the mountains, his Lordship therefore desires you will be pleased to march tomorrow morning and take post at Owens' plantation and to do every thing in your power to procure intelligence, and that if you are informed by creditable authority that there is any considerable force within 50 miles of you, you will be pleased to march and join his Lordship, but without hurry or any appearance of retiring, which might discourage the country.

Lord Cornwallis has received your letter inclosing the sketches of Black Stoakes and Turkey Creek.

I have the honour to be, dear sir,
Your very humble and most obedient servant

HENRY HALDANE
Aid-de-camp

McArthur to Cornwallis, 22nd December 1780 — *4(378): ALS*

Camp at Byerley's Ferry
December 22nd 1780

Rt Hon Lt General Earl Cornwallis
Winnesborough

My Lord

I hope your Lordship will excuse the liberty I have taken in sending Lieutenant Fraser[24] to Charlestown this day. Had I waited for your Lordship's permission, he could not have overtaken Lieutenant Grant[25] in Charlestown and consequently the return for forage money could not have been made till Lieutenant Grant returned.

---

24 Three Frasers with the rank of lieutenant were serving in the 71st (Highland) Regiment. All were in the 1st Battalion (now with McArthur), two of whom were named Alexander and one Edward. (*Army Lists*)

25 Of the Grants with the rank of lieutenant in the 71st, three were still serving with the regiment: John in the 1st Battalion; and John and Robert in the 2nd. It is probably the first to whom McArthur refers. He had entered the 1st Battalion as an ensign on 27th November 1775, rising to lieutenant on 14th October 1778. (*Army Lists*)

I have learned nothing about the enemy worth troubling you with since my last. I don't find they cross the Ennoree so frequently since the check at Long Canes.

I have the honor to be, my Lord,
Your Lordship's most obedient humble servant

ARCH^{D} McARTHUR

Haldane to McArthur, 23rd December 1780 — *83(69): ACS*

Head Quarters
Wynnesborough
23rd December 1780

Major McArthur commanding the post at Owens' Plantation

Dear Sir

Lord Cornwallis has directed me to acquaint you that he has received intelligence that 500 men have joined Lacey, but as they are only mounted militia, his Lordship thinks that this reinforcement to the enemy need not occasion your moving.

I am, dear sir,
Your very humble and most obedient servant

HENRY HALDANE
Aid-de-camp

McArthur to Haldane, 24th December 1780 — *4(384A): ALS*

Camp at Owens's Plantation
December 24th 1780

Lieutenant Henry Haldane
Aid de camp to Lord Cornwallis
Head Quarters

Dear Sir

I received your letter of yesterday at six in the evening. Please inform my Lord Cornwallis that I sent out several people for intelligence the moment I received the order to come here. I have ordered the militia to keep a guard at the ferry and I keep a guard of our own men at the mill, to which I am as near as when at Byerley's. Half a dozen of rebells came within three miles of the ferry the day before yesterday. They fired at one man, who is much wounded in the body, took his gun and rode off. Green[26] was the leader.

---

[26] Green has not been identified. His surname was common in South Carolina.

I am, dear sir,
Your most obedient servant

ARCH^D McARTHUR

McArthur to Haldane, 25th December 1780 — *4(388): ALS*

Camp at Owens's Plantation
December 25th 1780

Lieutenant Haldane
Aid de camp to Lord Cornwallis
Head Quarters

Dear Sir

As my Lord Cornwallis may probably have heard that there was some firing yesterday morning near Lisles's Ford, please inform him that I got notice of it yesterday between three and four in the afternoon from a man who came in great haste *and fear* and told me 30 or forty shotts were fired near the ford. I immediately sent two trusty men to know the cause. They came back early this morning and brought me a letter from Captain Hill of the militia acquainting me it was a party of Captain Gillam's[27] company of militia who began so early to celebrate Christmass by firing their pieces, and I have learned from the men sent that the militia had got plenty of rum, which made them *feel bold*.[28]

I am, dear Haldane,
Yours etc

ARCH^D McARTHUR

---

27 Apart from being a captain in the royal militia, Gillam has not been positively identified. He may have been William Gillam, who, when the Judicial District of Ninety Six was established in February 1779, was named in the petit jury list for the Spartan division, an area comprising the present-day counties of Cherokee, Spartanburg, and Union.

28 The discharging of guns on Christmas Eve was a custom in the Dutch Fork at this time and for many years after. Writing in the early 1890s, John Abney Chapman remarked, 'Sixty years ago the young men of the Dutch Fork retained many of the wild, frolicksome habits which their forefathers brought with them from the Fatherland. Perhaps the wildest of these customs was to ramble throughout the night of Christmas Eve in companies of a dozen persons from house to house, firing heavily charged guns, and having thus aroused the family, they would enter the domicile with stamping scramble to the blazing fire, greedily eat the *praetzilies*and *schneckilies*,imbibe, with many a rugged joke and ringing peal of laughter, heavy draughts of a compound liquor made of rum and sugar, butter and alspice stewed together, and then,

"With monie an eldritch screetch an' hollo",

rush out into the night to visit the next neighbor.' (John Belton O'Neall and John A Chapman, *The Annals of Newberry* (Newberry SC, 1892), 556, 660)

McArthur to Cornwallis, 26th December 1780 — *4(396): ALS*

Camp at Owens's Plantation
December 26th 1780

Rt Hon Lt General Earl Cornwallis
Winnesborough

My Lord

I have the honor to inform your Lordship that a person who is come from Turky Creek, which he left on Thursday, says the rebels are building a redoute at Bullock Creek; that a considerable reinforcement was coming from beyond the mountains, but that expresses came after them acquainting that the Indians had rose and destroyed eleven familys, upon which the reinforcement went back; that 300 North Carolina militia were daily expected but he had not heard of any that lately arrived. I beg leave to inform your Lordship that George Harvey, who was serjeant major to the 2nd Battalion 71st and deserted at Bonnamtown[29] and was an officer of cavalry with the rebels, was lately taken on board a privateer and carried into York. Captain Duncanson[30] brought him to Charlestown and he is now in the Provost there. If your Lordship thinks him a proper subject for a general court martial, there are several officers of the 71st now at Charlestown that can prove the fact.

We had a man killed yesterday by the fall of a tree during the high wind at the quarter guard.

I have the honor to be, my Lord,
Your Lordship's most obedient humble servant

ARCH^D McARTHUR

McArthur to Cornwallis, 1st January 1781 — *67(1): ALS*

Camp at Owens's
January 1st 1781

Earl Cornwallis etc etc etc
Winnesborough

My Lord

Since I did myself the honor of writing to your Lordship this morning[31], I have seen a

---

29 Bonhamtown, New Jersey.

30 Robertson Duncanson had been commissioned a lieutenant in the 2nd Battalion of the 71st on 1st December 1775 and was promoted to a captaincy in the 1st Battalion on 12th November 1778. He would be captured with the battalion at the Battle of Cowpens in January 1781. (*Army Lists*)

31 The letter is not extant.

Lieutenant Pierson[32] of the militia from beyond Broad River, who informs me that one Campbell, a neighbour of his whose veracity he can depend on and who was taken in the skirmish of Saturday and made his escape from the rebels, told him General Cunningham and his people quitted the fort on Saturday night and marched for 96 and that the rebels took possession of it yesterday morning at eight o'clock – that only four or five were killed, and between 20 and 30 taken, on our side.

I have the honor to be, my Lord,
Your Lordship's most obedient humble servant

ARCH[D] McARTHUR

Haldane to McArthur, 2nd January 1781 — *84(5): AC*

January 2nd
¼ past 8 am

Dear Sir

I arrived here at about 5 this morning with Lord Cornwallis's orders to Lt Colonel Tarleton to pass the Broad River if his intelligence from the Dutch Forks should render it necessary, and at the same time his Lordship directed me to transmitt to you his orders that, if Lt Colonel Tarleton judged it necessary to pass the river, that you would likewise pass with 1st Battalion 71st Regiment at Bryerley's Ferry. Lt Colonel Tarleton proposes moving immediately and will join your battalion at the ferry. Lord Cornwallis desired you would leave your heavy baggage at the encampment of the Legion.

[HENRY HALDANE]

§ - §

32 No record has come to light of a Pierson, or person of like name, serving with the rank of lieutenant in the royal militia. McArthur is probably referring to Captain Joseph Person or Ensign Thomas Pearson, both of whom were members of Patrick Cuningham's Little River (Saluda) Regiment. Williams' stockaded fort, now abandoned by Patrick's brother Robert, lay within the regiment's catchment area. (Clark, *Loyalists in the Southern Campaign*, i, 265)

3 - Between Cornwallis and Tarleton etc

Tarleton to Cornwallis, 1st November 1780 *4(52): ALS*

Camden Ferry
November [1st]
7 o'clock pm

My Lord

My baggage being in Camden, I have no paper excepting Colonel Turnbull's cover[33]. I shall pass to morrow and move according to your Lordship's *meaning*. I have sent to *Rugely's* Mills. To morrow I shall converse with Colonel Turnbull, a letter from whom I inclose[34]. I shall desire him to garrison the redoubt on this and the intended one on the other side with troops and not militia. Your Lordship's intention relative to his post, forage, cattle, flour etc and my movement I shall make known to him.

I have the honor to be
Your Lordship's most devoted servant

BAN TARLETON

Cornwallis to Tarleton, 2nd November 1780 *82(5): C*

Wynnesborough
November 2nd
3 o'clock

Lt Colonel Tarleton

Dear Tarleton

I can make nothing of Turnbull's letter to you, as he only seems to describe parties of ten or twelve rebels, which of course it is not intended to employ the Legion to hunt. Our supplies here seem very precarious, and of course our stay. We have as yet received nothing from the Broad River mills. You will of course not be long absent, and let me hear from you constantly. I cannot hear of any considerable body of the enemy. A man just come in from the middle of the Waxhaw settlement could hear of nothing but plundering parties.

Yours faithfully

CORNWALLIS

---

33 *Colonel Turnbull's cover*: of a letter from him to Tarleton.

34 *a letter..*: not extant. According to Cornwallis's reply of the 2nd, it was addressed to Tarleton.

Tarleton to Cornwallis, 3rd November 1780 *4(16): ALS*

November 3rd 1780

My Lord

I have the honor of your Lordship's letter. Every precaution you charged me with I have given to Colonel Turnbull and have advis'd him to let 2 companies sleep and constantly remain in each redoubt. Haldane is arrived and will enforce the argument.

I have had Major Cooke with me. I sent for him to place proper people on the Wacsaw roads to give immediate information of any move of the enemy. Smallwood *all* confirm to be at the 12 Mile Run. Davie has been nearer. Numbers pretty much the same as told to your Lordship at Winsborough. I will watch them, my Lord, with an eager eye. I have made use of every necessary prevention of their abrupt approach to Turnbull. I will not go far from him, and I think a move up Linches Creek of the Legion troops, if convenient for forage, and the severe season will force all the militia home. I shall see Major Harrison or some intelligent part of his people tomorrow morning. I can move, if any object presents itself, at a moment's warning. Colonel Turnbull I shall give a sketch of my plan to morrow morning that he may provide foragers, waggons etc etc and I mean to move that evening or next day eastward of his flank.

Colonel Turnbull has informed me now of people assembling at Singleton's on Wateree. I can't believe it but have sent to learn facts, which I shall receive tomorrow morning at 6 o'clock.

In short, my Lord, I will advertize your Lordship most frequently and will exert both my abilities and enterprize on this cruise.

I have the honor to be
Your Lordship's most devoted servant

BAN TARLETON

Tarleton to Turnbull, 5th November 1780[35] *4(63): ALS*

Cross Roads near Singleton's Mills
9 am, November 5th

My dear Sir

No enemy at Singleton's. The people of the country appear every where dark and mysterious. A Negro has just told me of a party at Jacks Creek. I shall proceed to General Richardson's, and if I get no satisfactory intelligence before I arrive there, I shall take post and destroy the country between there and Kingstree down to Nelson's etc etc.

---

[35] Enclosed with Turnbull to Cornwallis, 8th November, p 137.

It has been a general revolt below the Santee Hills, but Mr Marian, hearing the light horse were come to Camden, pass'd over the Black River.

Nothing will serve these people but fire and sword. All are out except such as have the small pox. *Now* they are swamp'd[36], to return again upon our communications when I return to the army. They have had a look out and intelligence ever since I left Camden.

The only treatment I can propose or think of, if I am spared long enough here, is, according to the ancient scripture, saving only the salt which we *cannot* spare.

Pray send any letter which may have come for me from head quarters by the bearer. Forage and beef might be obtained in our rear.

Yours with the greatest esteem

BAN TARLETON

Cornwallis to Tarleton, 8th November 1780[37] — *82(12): C*

Wynnesborough
November 8th 1780

Lt Colonel Tarleton

Dear Tarleton

I received this day your letter of the 5th to Turnbull. I am not sanguine as to your operations in that country. The enemy, I believe, is in no great force, and Marrion is cautious and vigilant. If a blow could be struck at any body of the rebels it might be attended with good consequences, but I do not see any advantage we can derive from a partial destruction of the country. If there is no considerable force of the enemy in that quarter, it will be right to send back the light company of the New York Volunteers immediately to Camden as they may be usefull in collecting provisions, forage etc. I mean to mount the whole of the New York Volunteers to assist in keeping that country quiet. As to your movement, I am not sufficiently acquainted with the country or the state of provisions or forage to direct you. If you could move up between Lynches Creek and Pedee high enough to make the enemy on Twelve Mile Creek jealous for their left, it might be attended with some advantage. If not, you must use your discretion and live as well as you can, keeping within reach of Camden and within a few days' call of us in case we should want you, always endeavouring to strike some blow if an opening should offer, and taking up all that have been violent against us to change for our friends, who have been every where seized and most cruelly treated. If you should hear of Smallwood's passing the river, of course you will come to us. Wemyss with

36 *swamp'd*: hiding out in the swamps.

37 An extract from this letter is published in Ross ed, *Cornwallis Correspondence*, i, 65.

the 63rd and 40 dragoons with young Hovenden is gone to night to attack Sumter. Captain Hovenden is very ill and I fear will never be fit for any service. Notwithstanding our scarcity, his troop has hitherto been well foraged, and we have contrived to rub on, sometimes with meal and sometimes without. Lord Rawdon is going to command at Camden and takes his corps with him and I shall let poor Turnbull go. You say nothing to me about your rank of lt colonel, which, if it is true that you have it, I take very ill, as you must be convinced that it is an event in which I feel myself much interested.

I am with very sincere regard etc

CORNWALLIS

Cornwallis to Tarleton, 9th November 1780[38] — *82(15): C*

Wynnesborough
November 9th 1780

Lt Colonel Tarleton

Dear Tarleton

Major Wemyss attacked Sumpter at Fish Dam at one o'clock this morning contrary to his plan, which was to wait till daylight. The consequence is that Wemyss is wounded and left, and about 20 men. Lieutenant Hovenden is wounded, but I believe the Legion have not lost much. I must beg of you to return immediately, leaving some horses for mounting men at Camden. I am under the utmost anxiety for Ninety Six and trust you will lose no time in returning to me.

I am yours sincerely

CORNWALLIS

Cornwallis to Tarleton, 10th November 1780[39] — *82(20): A(in part) Df*

Wynnesborough
November 10th 1780

Lt Colonel Tarleton

Dear Tarleton

You will have received my letter of yesterday, since which we have intelligence that Sumpter has passed the Broad River and joined Clarke, Brannon etc. They talk of expecting

[38] Published in Ross ed, op cit, i, 65.

[39] A short extract comprising the first three sentences is published in Bass, *The Green Dragoon*, 117.

some of the mountaineers. As they have excellent horses, we can't hurt them, and unless they receive some check they will be very troublesome. Notwithstanding my anxiety to have you in this part of the province, still my cares are of so extensive a nature that, if by stepping aside for a day or two you can strike any material blow, I wou'd have you do it. A man whom I sent to the Waxhaws reported that Washington and Morgan were gone to Black River. It was only hear say report and I don't believe it. I wish it was true for your sake. If, however, no material objection occurs, I wish to see you here as soon as you conveniently can come. The country about Broad River is pretty full of forage and you had better eat it than the rebels. The security of the navigation of the Santee is so very essential to our existence that I am sure you will leave some cavalry at Camden for a time if you think, which I fear is the case, that the navigation cannot be secure without it. The supplies of necessaries which are coming to the army, and which are so material at this time, depend totally upon it. Hovenden's troop lost only one man wounded in Wemys's affair, but young Hovenden has a painfull wound in the knee and his brother continues exceedingly ill. The 63rd are well mounted for infantry and may occasionally ride in your train. They behaved vastly well and only wanted a commander. Out of 5 shots which were fired from the picquet, one broke Wemys's arm and another his knee. The command then devolved to a young lieutenant who knew nothing of the place or the ground or force of the enemy, and all was confusion. After what I have said, I am sure I may depend on your acting for the best on the general plan of the welfare of the army. My best wishes will always attend you.

I am yours very sincerely

CORNWALLIS

[*Subscribed*:]

Memorandum

With duplicates of the letters of the 8th and 10th Lord Cornwallis wrote a third letter dated November 11th to Lt Colonel Tarleton, reciting the particulars he had since heard of Major Wemys's affair and containing only this paragraph that was material: 'We can do no good without you. I trust to your coming immediately unless you see something still more materially pressing.'

Tarleton to Cornwallis, 11th November 1780[40] *4(96): ALS*

Singleton's Mills
November 11th 1780

My Lord

I have the honor to inform you that I am so far returned from my expedition after Colonels

---

40 An inaccurate transcript appears in Bass, op cit, 112-3.

Marion, Horry[41] etc. The insurrection wou'd have been general and dangerous to Camden and the communication of the army had [it] not been nipp'd before it arrived at maturity. The enemy had just issued proclamations saying your Lordship was dead, that the whole cavalry with 600 infantry and your humble servant were cut to pieces, and that Camden was press'd by a northern army.

No intelligence to be depended upon cou'd I possibly obtain of the enemy's situation or number. Every inhabitant between Santee Hills, Nelson's Ferry and Kingstree Bridge, besides many from St Stephen's Parish, had either join'd thro' affection, hid themselves thro' dislike to, or were prisoners to Marion and his adherents.

As I was disappointed in my attack at Singleton's Mills, the place where 4,000 were said to be collected, I kept my numbers concealed, advanced on the roads, fell back again, shew'd tokens of fear, by leaving camps abruptly and provisions cook'd, in order to draw the enemy, of whom I cou'd gain no news, either to attack or approach me. I so far deceived Marion that he wou'd certainly have attacked on the 7th instant in the evening, had he not been prevented by some treacherous women (Mrs Richardson[42] etc), with from 400 to 500 men. A prisoner who escaped from him in the night came into my camp just before day on the 8th and informed me that he wou'd have attacked me had he not obtained intelligence of my numbers at Richardson's, but on that account he had alter'd his route in confusion. The corps under my command were ordered under arms immediately and made a rapid march of 26 miles thro' swamps, woods and fastnesses towards Black River without a halt. The enemy, by being all mounted, obtaining so much time previous to the pursuing, and owing to the difficulties of the country, cou'd not be brought to action. I had the mortification not to fight them but I had the pleasure in a great measure to disperse them. A few prisoners were taken from the swamps by Harrison's corps. I returned on my steps and laid the houses and plantations of violent rebels waste about Richardson's and Jacks Creek. The country seems now convinced of the error of insurrection. People join me from the swamps. The torch is stopp'd and I have issued the enclosed proclamation. Thus, my Lord, I have used my best ability to settle the affairs of this part of the province, but if there had been one individual of the country attached to our cause and exempt from fear, the total destruction of Mr Marion had been accomplish'd.

---

41 Of the Horry brothers serving under Marion, Tarleton is probably referring to Peter Horry (1747-1815), a South Carolina plantation owner and a Continental officer since 1776. He was presently serving in Marion's Brigade as a colonel commanding mounted troops. In later life he would hold a number of political offices in South Carolina and collaborate with Mason Locke Weems on a life of Marion, a work from which he soon tried to disassociate himself in the light of Weems' heavily editing his recollections and fictionalising the work in part. Peter's brother Hugh also served as an officer under Marion, but it is less likely that Tarleton is referring to him. (*The Greene Papers*, ix, 7; Boatner, *Encyclopedia*, 679; Rankin, *Marion, passim*)

42 Mary Richardson (née Cantey) was the widow of Richard Richardson (1704-1780), a brigadier general in the South Carolina revolutionary militia, who had died of natural causes in September. She had married him in 1738. Besides herself, her son Richard Jr (1741-1818), a captain in the revolutionary forces who had been granted parole, was the mode of conveying intelligence of Tarleton's presence to Marion. Perhaps in retaliation, Tarleton torched the family's dwelling house, outbuildings, grain and fodder and drove off or burnt the stock. According to one account, he disinterred General Richardson's remains on the pretext that 'he might examine the features of a man of his decided character, but it was in fact from a mean suspicion that the family plate was buried there'. (Rogers Jr, *Georgetown County*, 63n; Moss, *SC Patriots*, 812; James, *Marion*, 61-3; Johnson, *Traditions*, 162; Rankin, *Marion*, 112-5)

I am to acknowledge the honor of your Lordship's letters of the 4th, 5th and 8th dates[43]. In your last you chide me for not informing you of my advancement. A letter from Liverpool by a private ship from a very near relation dated 10th August says that 'the King has honor'd you with the rank of lt colonel in the army and your brevet is on board the South Carolina packet'.

Your praises, my Lord, have exalted me. I hope my future services will merit your past commendation. Those actions ought to be the best which are founded on gratitude.

BAN TARLETON

Enclosure **4(95): ACS**

PROCLAMATION[44]

Singleton's Mills
November 11th 1780

Be it known to all people concerned in the late revolt between Nelson's Ferry, Kingstree Bridge and Santee Hills that a general and free pardon is held out to all the said delinquents in case they will return home between the date hereof and twenty fifth of this month. Upon their arrival at home they must separately acquaint the officers of the loyal militia of their intention to live peaceably at their plantations and in case of any future insurrection or incursion to give notice thereof, which determination (of the late deluded people) the said officers of loyal militia must transmit to the officer commanding His Majesty's troops at Camden.

It is not the wish of Britons to be cruel or to destroy, but it is now obvious to all Carolina that treachery, perfidy and perjury will be punished with instant fire and sword.

BAN TARLETON
Lt Colonel commanding British Legion

43 *your Lordship's letters..*: of those of the 4th and 5th there are no extant copies.

44 An inaccurate transcript appears in Bass, op cit, 111-2.

Cornwallis to Tarleton, 13th November 1780[45] *82(39): C*

Winsborough
November 13th 1780
Seven o'clock pm

Lt Colonel Tarleton

Dear Tarleton

Sumpter is at Hawkins's Mill on Tyger River with what he calls a thousand men, bragging much of his victory. Our friends are all in the utmost terror and running down to the Congarees as fast as possible. I shall be glad to see you, but your corps must keep at a distance, as they would consume our whole substance in half an hour. I rather think the Legion had better march up the Wateree, as you will then threaten Davy, Smallwood and Sumpter, and perhaps most the two former, and I believe you can subsist. I may probably see you the day that your corps passes the ferry. Lord Rawdon and England will explain to you all my wishes, my expectations, and present difficulties, amongst which the establishing a post on Black River is not the least. I fancy that you will have found that Morgan and Washington are quite out of your reach.

I am, dear Tarleton,
Very sincerely yours

CORNWALLIS

[*Subscribed*:]

Captain O'Neal is just arrived from 96 and describes the terror of our friends beyond all belief. He brings a letter from Kirkland[46], who commands the militia, and looks on all as lost. My correspondence from that quarter is quite pleasant and agreable[47]. Lose no time in passing the ferry for fear of a fresh in the river.

Cornwallis to Tarleton, 14th November 1780 *82(45A): C*

Winsborough
November 14th 1780

Lt Colonel Tarleton

Dear Tarleton

A Negro is just come in who was taken with Ferguson. He is clear in his story, and sticks

45 A transcript, which omits the subscription and is otherwise materially inaccurate, appears in Bass, op cit, 117.

46 *a letter..*: of 12th November, p 384.

47 *is quite pleasant and agreable*: an ironic description.

to it, that he left Smallwood on Saturday last near Lawson's Iron Works on the other side of Broad River, that he had 3 pieces of cannon with him and was certainly going to 96. This intelligence alarms me much for the safety of that place. I therefore wish you would, if on the road to me yourself, order on the Legion by the shortest route to Shirar's Ferry. If you are not set out, I wish you to come to me immediately and leave those orders for the corps.

Yours sincerely

CORNWALLIS

PS

Send this letter on to Lord Rawdon.

Tarleton to Cornwallis, 21st November 1780[48] *4(173): ALS*

Camp at Blackstokes, Tyger River
November 22nd, Tuesday[49]
7 o'clock am

My Lord

I have no baggage, consequently no cypher. I trust this short letter to accident. I yesterday cut Sumpter's rear guard to pieces on Ennoree. I pursued his trail with great rapidity and had an action on this ground last night with the cavalry and 63rd only.

Sumpter is defeated, his corps dispersed, and himself dangerously wounded. The ground was difficult. Thick night came on and for want of more infantry I could not immediately pursue the blow. Three young men who were of Ferguson's corps have promis'd to fix Sumpter immediately. I have promis'd them for the deed 50 guineas each in case he falls into my hands.

But, my Lord, I have lost men – 50 killed and wounded and officers which are losses to the public service. Poor Money is wounded but not dangerously, Gibson and Coke kill'd, Mr Munroe[50], Legion, wounded, and every officer's horse, my own included, kill'd or wounded.

The rebels were commanded by Sumpter, Clarke, Lacy, and Brannon's men were present - 1,000 in all – and were attack'd by 190 cavalry and 90 infantry on most unapproachable

---

48 A materially inaccurate transcript appears in Bass, op cit, 121. It is followed by Cornwallis's reply of the 22nd, of which there is no copy in *The Cornwallis Papers*.

49 Tuesday was the 21st, the day after the action. Tarleton had a habit of misdating letters.

50 Duncan Munro had been commissioned a lieutenant in the cavalry of the British Legion on 25th June 1780. By January he would have recovered from his wounds. (WO 65/164(38) (National Archives, Kew); *The Cornwallis Papers*)

ground. I have wrote to McArthur to pass and bring my baggage. I shall take every immediate step totally to suppress insurrection.

I have the honor to be
Your most devoted servant

BAN TARLETON

NB

The enemy attack'd the 63rd and forced me to action before the cannon, Legion and light infantry cou'd be brought up.

BT

Tarleton to Cornwallis, 22nd November 1780[51] *4(189): ALS*

Near the Head of Tiger
Wednesday, November 24th 1780[52]
10 o'clock am

Earl Cornwallis etc etc etc
Winsboro

My Lord

I believe my last action had many good consequences. The rebels have disbanded. Sumpter is mortally wound'd, one colonel of theirs kill'd, and about 120 kill'd, wounded and prisoners of the rebel army. Night and want of infantry prevented a pursuit. Many prisoners came in yesterday who had escaped them during the engagement and several of the [rebels] have sent in for terms. One adjutant and 12 men submitted themselves yesterday.

There is a report of Colonel Selvey, but it is, I am persuaded, a rebel one. All the people about here say that their whole force was at Blackstokes, 10 colonels, 1,000 men etc etc.

It was difficult for me to manœuvre for want of intelligence and I had to pass the Ennoree three times before I cou'd strike at Sumpter. You will see, my Lord, by my letter of yesterday that I cou'd only bring up 80 of 63rd and 190 cavalry. I did not mean to attack Sumpter, only to harrass and lay close to him till I cou'd bring up the rest of the corps, as he would have pass'd the Tiger if I had not acted so. The 63rd were attacked by the enemy, which brought on the affair. I will write more fully when I get more paper. I order'd Major McArthur to Blackstokes on hearing of victory with our waggons to take off the wounded.

B TARLETON

---

51 A grossly inaccurate transcript appears in Bass, op cit, 122-3

52 Wednesday was the 22nd, which Cornwallis in his reply confirms was the date of the letter.

[*Superscribed*:]

Sumpter's wound is thro both shoulders. People this instant have reported him dead.

[*Subscribed*:]

Several of Ferguson's have made their escape, and one of 63rd taken at Fishdam. Money is as well as can be expected.

Cornwallis to Tarleton, 23rd November 1780[53] *82(93): C*

Wynnesborough
November 23rd 1780

Lt Colonel Tarleton

Dear Tarleton

I have this instant received your letter dated the 24th but which should have been dated the 22nd. The express said he left you last night. I have no doubt but your victory will be attended with as good consequences to our affairs as it is with honor and credit to yourself. I shall be very glad to hear that Sumpter is in a condition to give us no farther trouble. He certainly has been our greatest plague in this country.

You will have got my letter in regard to McArthur's battalion[54]. If you have reason to think you shall have any occasion for it with you, I beg you will order it up. If not, of course I had rather have it within reach of me. I repeat what I said yesterday for fear of accidents: that the baggage is ordered up with a captain and fifty men of the 71st, and McArthur with the remainder of the battalion is to remain at Calley's[55] Ford on Ennoree to come up to you if you want him – if not, to return to Shirar's Ferry. I have sent Stewart to assist in the care of your wounded. I am very happy to hear so good an account of Money. Assure him of my best wishes if he is still with you.

I do not hear of any alteration in the enemy's position on the other side of Catawba. I have people to watch the Lands Ford – at least who tell me that they watch it and are paid accordingly. All here join in best compliments and congratulations.

I am, dear Tarleton, with the most sincere regard
Ever faithfully yours

CORNWALLIS

---

53 Part of the first paragraph is published in Bass, op cit, 123.

54 *my letter..*: no extant copy.

55 *Calley's*: Kelly's.

Tarleton to Cornwallis, 24th November 1780 — *4(206): ALS*

On Tiger
November 26th[56]
6 o'clock am

My Lord

I have the honor of your Lordship's letter of the 22nd[57]. I believe you have not received my other letters, which relate many good circumstances besides Sumpter being mortally wounded and Clarke and Chandler dead.

My Lord, in the course of this night I have learned that Washington and Davie, Caswel and Grimes[58] are to reinforce the debris of Sumpter's at the iron works. I shall take the liberty to order up Major McArthur's and be with them[59] as soon as my wounded are sufficiently covered. One other affair will settle these parts. I have ordered out the militia under General Conningham and every thing seems in spirits in this part of the province.

BAN TARLETON
Lt Colonel

[*Superscribed*:]

Money is as well as can be expected. His [wounds] dress'd yesterday. Stewart [attends?]. Baggage will be here today.

[*Subscribed*:]

My great reason for desiring Major McArthur to come to Blackstocks is to cover the wounded officers and men. The militia have been so frighten'd and dispers'd since poor Ferguson's affair that it is difficult [*illeg*].

---

56 According to an annotation, the letter is misdated. It was written on the 24th.

57 *your Lordship's letter..*: see p 340, note 48.

58 William or Joseph Grimes was a field officer in the Mecklenburg revolutionary militia. In September Ferguson had dispersed a body of men which Grimes was raising near Gilbertown and had taken many prisoners. (William Lee Anderson III, 'Notes about Scotch-Irish and German Settlers in Virginia and the Carolinas' (Internet, 13th October 2005); E Alfred Jones ed, 'The Journal of Alexander Chesney, a South Carolina Loyalist in the Revolution and After', *Ohio State University Bulletin*, xxvi (October, 1921), 4)

59 *them*: the enemy at the iron works.

Cornwallis to Tarleton, 25th November 1780 *82(103): C*

Wynnesborough
November 25th 1780

Lt Colonel Tarleton

Dear Tarleton

The account of Gates was confirmed to me by two different channels, both good. I trust to your discretion and that you will not forget us here.

I hope *soon to hear of McArthur's being on his way towards us.*

Yours most sincerely

CORNWALLIS

[*Subscribed*:]

I hope your baggage has brought you some blacker ink. My best wishes to Money.

Cornwallis to Tarleton, 26th November 1780 *82(109): ADfS*

Wynnesborough
November 26th 1780
9 o'clock pm

Lt Colonel Tarleton

Dear Tarleton

Davie's corps certainly fell back from Waxhaw some days ago. Smallwood was at his old camp on Friday evening and Gates said to be in the neighbourhood of Charlottetown. All this may correspond very well with the intelligence you sent me. I likewise heard, but not from authority, that the Back Mountain men were ordered to assemble at Lawson's Iron Works to support Sumpter before his defeat was known.

I think the enemy meant Ninety Six. If they detach in force towards you, I will assist in any possible means you can propose to strike at them.

I am yours etc

CORNWALLIS

Tarleton to Cornwallis, 25th November 1780 — *4(246): ALS*

On Tiger
November 25th 80, 4 pm

My Lord

I have just received your letter of 23rd. The troops are now in line of march to attack the enemy to morrow.

Money is as well as can be expected. My reason for ordering McArthur to move was to cover the wounded and baggage. I hope to morrow to compleat the destruction of our enemies in this district. Sumpter is now reported dead. Colonels Thomas[60], Clarke and Chandler are dead. Brigadier General Cunningham and the militia have not yet join'd. I wrote to Colonel Cruger to send Colonel Allen and part of his battalion with Kirkland etc to end the disturbances in Long Cain settlement.

Cunningham I will employ in settling the district as soon as I have beat the enemy, after which I will return towards your Lordship.

I have the honor to be
Your Lordship's most devoted servant

BAN TARLETON

Cornwallis to Tarleton, 27th November 1780 — *82(117): C*

November 27th
6 o'clock pm

Lt Colonel Tarleton

Dear Tarleton

I have just received your letter of the 25th and most anxiously hope to hear good news from you very soon. I am informed from pretty good authority that Gates joined Smallwood

---

60 John Thomas Jr (1751-1819) was, like his father (see vol I, p 259, note 28), a settler in the Fair Forest area of the South Carolina Back Country. Rather than enter into a parole or risk imprisonment, he had gone off with some sixty disaffected men of his father's regiment and, adopting the rank of colonel, had led them in a rout of loyalists in the first action at Cedar Creek on 13th July. Joining up later with Sumter, he had served under him in the very recent action at Blackstocks, to which Tarleton's letter refers. With Sumter incapacitated from a wound received in that affair, Thomas would soon go on to take part under Morgan in the Battle of Cowpens before rejoining Sumter on the latter's return to the field. About 1800 he moved from South Carolina to Illinois and settled at Turkey Hill in St Clair County. A very active Methodist, he became a founder of Shiloh Church there. When Illinois was admitted to the union in 1818, he was very probably the John Thomas who became the first Treasurer of the state, dying in office one year later. In the Royal Collection of Firearms at Windsor there is a Pennsylvanian rifle belonging to him which was captured in the action at Blackstocks. The silver escutcheon plate is engraved with the initials 'JT', while the small but prominent cheek rest is inlaid with a thirteen-pointed silver star bearing the words 'STATES UNITED WE ARE ONE'. (T W Lipscomb to the editor, 23rd August 1977; Draper, *King's Mountain,* 73-5; *The Greene Papers*, vii, 153; Hanger, *An Address to the Army*, 85; Howard L Blackmore, *Royal Sporting Guns at Windsor* (HMSO, 1968), 38-9, plate 34)

on the 28th[61] and that the whole were encamped on 6 Mile Run on the evening of the 25th. Gates has 2 pieces of cannon, which we must take. Washington, White and Armand, I am assured, exceed 300 cavalry, a breakfast for the Legion! Nothing new here, nor have I more to say than I have already expressed by Manley and Mr McBean.

Yours ever most sincerely

CORNWALLIS

Reisinger to Cornwallis, undated — *4(256): ALS*

To Lord Cornwallis

This is to inform your Lordship that the last express that was directed to Lieutenant Cor^{nl} Tatleton was taken the 28th of this instant about six mils from Henereeses Mell and if your Lordship sends any other express it must be a man that is well acquented with the woods or els he cannot git along onless he is taken and likewise I do acquent you that I am very unwell myself.

FEIGHT RISINGER
Capt

Tarleton to Cornwallis, 28th November 1780[62] — *4(223): ALS*

28th November
6 o'clock am

My Lord

All affairs in this district are settled. McArthur is a day and *a half march on his return. I march this day and leave Conningham with proper orders*.

I have the honor to be
Your Lordship's most devoted servant

BAN TARLETON

---

61 *the 28th*: a miscopying of the 23rd, a Thursday. See Cornwallis to Rawdon, 27th November, p 176.

62 Published in Bass, op cit, 124.

Cornwallis to Tarleton, 4th December 1780 — *83(13): C*

Wynnesborough
December 4th 1780

Lt Colonel Tarleton

Dear Tarleton

Rugely will not be made a brigadier. He surrendered, without firing a shot, himself and 103 rank and file to the cavalry only. A deserter of Morgan's assures us that the infantry never came within 3 miles of the house. They say that Gates is going to pass the Catawba at Tuckasiege Ford. Smallwood remains at 6 Mile Run. The object of this move must be that, in case you pursue any parties that they may send forward to make incursions into Ninety Six District, they may retire upon him. In case I advance, he will then retire, and Smallwood by moving by Linches Creek towards Harrington, Marion etc will endeavor to alarm Camden and the communication to Nelson's Ferry, McLeroth and George Town. These are my suppositions on a supposed move. I wish you to try all you can about intelligence. You know I am as generous about that business as in the article of *table money*. If you can for a time live well above McArthur, it will certainly answer very good purposes and prevent the enemy trying the same game upon Cunningham as they have upon Rugely — not that I suspect he would behave like him.

If you should find it convenient to stay a few miles above Brierly's Ferry, I have no objection to your taking McArthur along with you if you see any reason for desiring it. Correspond with Cunningham.

A deserter, one of Burgoyne's Brunswickers, is come in. He speaks very little English. He says he belongs to Major Lee. I shall send him to you. His horse, sword etc may be of use to you. The enemy fired a feu de joye for their victory over Rugely.

Yours most sincerely

CORNWALLIS

Tarleton to Cornwallis, 4th December 1780 — *4(283): ALS*

Woodford's Plantation
December 5th[63]

My Lord

I have given Haldane an escort for Ninety Six.

---

63 According to an annotation, the letter is misdated. It was written on the 4th.

The forage about here is pretty good but I am afraid we shall not find any rum in this neighbourhood. A reinforcement of that kind wou'd highly oblige the light troops.

I am anxious to hear General Rugely's fate, and the news of arrivals at Charles Town wou'd be highly satisfactory. I am going to send 2 waggons to Charles Town for our wants and 2 to Camden.

I have the honor to be
Your Lordship's most devoted servant

BAN TARLETON

[*Subscribed*:]

I have heard from General Cunningham. Every thing well in his quarter.

Cornwallis to Tarleton, 5th December 1780 — *83(21): C*

Wynnesborough
December 5th 1780

Lt Colonel Tarleton

Dear Tarleton

You will find I had anticipated your wishes about Rugely and rum. I will always try to give you your share of the latter when it can be got to you. I saw a letter from Balfour to Lord Rawdon of the 1st[64]. No news of Leslie. Nine sail were coming over the bar, supposed to be the remainder of the New York fleet.

They say that Green is certainly coming to relieve Gates. I hear nothing of the move to Tuckasiege Ford. Sumpter was at the house of one Watson's on Allison's Creek two days ago. Rutlidge had been to visit him but had repassed the river, and it was intend[ed] to try to get Sumpter himself over the Catawbaw if he could bear the motion of the chair, which, however, they much doubted. I heard that as much of his corps as could be assembled was at Barrows Mill on Turkey Creek.

I send you the Brunswicker fully accoutred. I will let you know when anything new comes from Charlestown.

Yours most sincerely

CORNWALLIS

---

64 *a letter..*: see p 194, note 90.

Tarleton to Cornwallis, 5th December 1780 *4(285): ALS*

Woodward's
December 5th 1780

My Lord

I am sorry your letter contained no better news. I think Rugely's affair very immaterial. The arrivals at Charles Town will be very pleasing.

The position your Lordships wishes, I will take to morrow or next day, and intelligence I will procure.

At present we are exceedingly busy. No iron for shoes to be obtained here. I am obliged to send for it from Camden.

I have order'd Cunningham to write to me daily. He is collecting the militia fast. The Brunswicker your Lordship mentions I have not yet seen. Some rum to day or to morrow wou'd be received with a heartfelt welcome.

I have the honor to be
Your Lordship's most devoted servant

BAN TARLETON

Cornwallis to Tarleton, 6th December 1780 *83(24): C*

Wynnesborough
December 6th 1780

Lt Colonel Tarleton

Dear Tarleton

The Brunswicker would not go to you, and as he had been a grenadier, and not an hussar, I did not think it of much consequence. We purchased his horse, saddle, sword etc for sixteen guineas and an half, which I believe you will not think dear.

I am told that Branan, Lacey etc are busy in building block-houses on Turkey Creek. If they place much confidence in them, it may produce some good.

I am etc

[CORNWALLIS]

Tarleton to Cornwallis, 14th December 1780[65] *4(325): ALS*

Woodward's
December 14th 1780, 7 am

My Lord

I am still upon my old ground. Yesterday patroles were sent into the neighbourhood in order to review the stock of forage etc.

The officer who was detached to the country above Byerly's Ferry reported that there was not above six loads of forage for seven miles above that place.

It is full as convenient to the corps to remain here as move, except to the Congarees - that, I fear, is too far.

I have this morning detached Lieutenant Willett[66], with 160 guineas in his pocket to buy horses, down between the conflux of the rivers. I hope he will be succesful and accomplish his business without any references or disputes.

After having deliver'd all the supposed friends to Government that the real ones cou'd point out, I am still entangled with prisoners which Blackstokes threw into my hands. I have therefore sent them on to your Lordship's camp in order that they may [be] transmitted on or receive such doom as your Lordship shall judge right.

I have the honor to be
Your Lordship's most devoted servant

BAN TARLETON

[*Subscribed*:]

Captain McDonald of the Legion has particular business with Major Small if your Lordship will allow him to go to Charles Town.

---

65 A transcript, which omits the subscription and is otherwise inaccurate, appears in Bass, op cit, 124-5.

66 Walter Willet (1747-1812) was born in Flushing, Long Island, from where his family moved to Bucks County, Pennsylvania. In 1778 he obtained a commission in the Bucks County Light Dragoons, and after their absorption into the British Legion he entered the corps as a lieutenant of horse on 24th December 1779. He would soon take part in the winter and Virginia campaigns and be among the troops who capitulated at Yorktown. In 1783 he settled at Granville, Nova Scotia, having had his small farm in Southampton Township, Pennsylvania, confiscated by the revolutionary authorities. His remains were interred in Upper Granville Cemetery. (Donald J Gara, 'Biographical Sketches on Cavalry Officers of the British Legion 1778-1782' (*The On-Line Institutefor Advanced Loyalist Studies*, 24th June 2005); WO 65/164(38) (National Archives, Kew))

Cornwallis to Tarleton, 15th December 1780 — *83(48): C*

Wynnesborough
December 15th 1780

Lt Colonel Tarleton

Dear Tarleton

I should be sorry that the want of forage should oblige you to fall farther back than where you are now, as I am convinced the District of 96 would immediately relapse into the situation in which it was when you crossed Broad River. Besides that, I should not like to leave McArthur at Brierly's Ferry unless you was within a few miles of him. I am a little afraid that your foragers will clash with ours, which must go towards Broad River. You know of how much consequence it is to me to keep this position until every thing is ready. Every day's forage that you can any how get is a great object. You will be best able to find out whether you can possibly effect this by any movements except retrograde ones. At the same time I see at present no reasons but those of forage for wishing you to move. If it should happen that any of your foraging parties should go to any of the sequestered estates on which a deputy of Mr Cruden's may be placed, you will direct your officer to make application to that deputy for the forage and give him the receipt.

I have no material intelligence, and, I am sorry to say, none that I can depend on, from the enemy or our part. If you can meet with any persons more enterprising than those I can find, I beg you will employ them. No news from 96 or General Cunningham since you left us. I saw yesterday your convalescents. Some of them I thought hardly fit to join, and there were rather more black attendants, both male and female, than I think you will like to see.

As soon as I hear any thing material of Leslie or McLeroth you shall hear from me.

I am with great regard
Most faithfully yours

CORNWALLIS

Tarleton to Cornwallis, 17th December 1780 — *4(357): ALS*

Daniels Plantation
December 18th 1780[67]

My Lord

I moved from Woodward's this morning to this place. Forage was my only motive. I have not alter'd my distance from Winsboro above 4 miles and about an equal number from

67 According to an annotation, the letter is misdated. It was written on the 17th.

Byerly's. The roads, owing to the bad weather and the poverty of my waggon horses, render'd the movement indispensably necessary. In the place I am now I cannot obtain, by carrying it 6 or 7 miles, above three days' forage, but, however, I shall use every means not to retire much farther. I have sent two people out into your Lordship's front. Forage and intelligence must be obtained.

I will send a man to Major McArthur (he knows of my move) to ascertain the ground. I wish to hear of McLeroth. I hope he has come off handsomely.

News from Charles Town will be exceedingly pleasant, as the troops are now near ready to second your Lordship's wishes.

I have the honor to be
Your Lordship's most devoted servant

BAN TARLETON

Cornwallis to Tarleton, 18th December 1780[68] *83(55): C*

Wynnesborough
December 18th 1780

Lt Colonel Tarleton

Dear Tarleton

Lord Rawdon has received intelligence, which, however, he does not credit, that Morgan's corps and the cavalry had passed the Catawba. I have sent out every body that I could engage to go, but the friends hereabouts are so timid and so stupid that I can get no intelligence. I have heard nothing from 96, but a man who came here from near Broad River says that General Cunningham has beat Clarke and wounded him mortally. I shall be glad to hear a confirmation of this.

I apprehend we must first dislodge Lacey etc from Turkey Creek and then march up the west side of Catawba to some of the fords above Tuccaseege. I wish you would take pains to inform yourself as thoroughly as possible of the state of the roads, provisions, forage, mills etc. I hear a good account of our recruits in general and hope to march from hence 3,500 fighting men, leaving those I mentioned to you upon the frontiers.

Lord Rawdon has very readily agreed to undertake Watson, so that we shall be relieved from that plague.

I trust you will make every possible shift rather than go much farther back, as I should in that case be uneasy about McArthur; and as soon as you have been able to get information about the country, I should be glad to see you to talk over our march.

---

[68] An inaccurate transcript appears in Bass, op cit, 139-140.

I am, dear Tarleton,
Very sincerely yours

CORNWALLIS

Haldane to Tarleton, 23rd December 1780 — *83(73): ACS*

Head Quarters
Wynnesborough
23rd December 1780

Lt Colonel Tarleton

Dear Tarleton

I neglected to mention to you yesterday that Lord Cornwallis desired you would procure every intelligence respecting the state of <u>the roads on the east</u> and <u>west sides</u> of <u>Broad</u> River.

Lord Cornwallis has been informed that Mulenburgh and Lee's cavalry have joined Green.

Believe me ever, dear Tarleton,
Yours most sincerely

H HALDANE

Tarleton to Haldane, 24th December 1780 — *4(383): ALS*

December 24th 1780

My dear Haldane

I have sent H—— out to enquire about the other side. I have just got intelligence from 2 of my people of the state of the roads etc on this side thro Maply settlement up the Broad River to Sandy River and the Cross Roads. The roads are good. Forage likewise is to be obtained. The road as far as Sandy River runs paralell to the Great Road at the distance of 17 miles (the best road for the light troops), then lessens and tends to the Cross Roads.

I feel pleasure from the news of Mulenburg's and Lee's arrival. The more difficulty, the more glory.

I cannot go to see, but I have sent Lieutenant Forbes to Major McArthur to day.

Believe me most faithfully yours

BAN TARLETON

[*Subscribed*:]

Forage grows very scarce near me.

Enclosure **4(384): D**

Sketch of Roads surrounding and to east of Broad River

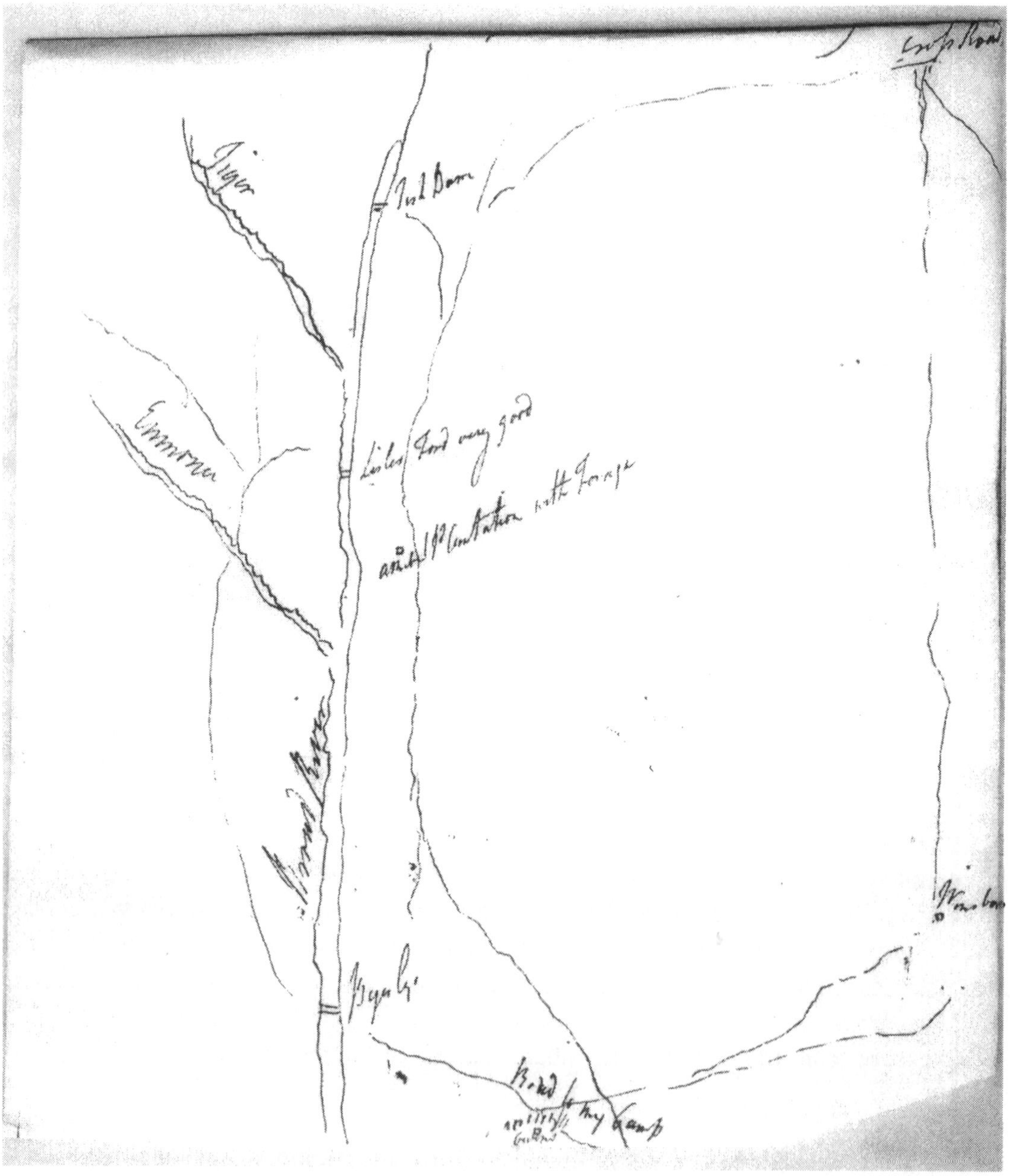

Haldane to Tarleton, 24th December 1780 — *83(75): ACS*

Head Quarters
Wynnesborough
24th December 1780

Lt Colonel Tarleton etc etc etc

Dear Tarleton

Lord Cornwallis thanks you for your information respecting the roads. He wishes you not to move at present if you can obtain forage sufficient to maintain you for a short time longer.

Believe me ever, my dear Tarleton,
Yours most sincerely

HENRY HALDANE
Aid-de-camp

Tarleton to Cornwallis, 26th December 1780 — *4(404): ALS*

Daniels Plantation
December 26th 80

My Lord

I am sorry your Lordship has cause to complain of the plundering of the Legion. The oppress'd have kept me in ignorance, or steps should have been taken immediately to suppress it.

We forage at a very great distance. I have this day sent all my waggons for long forage to Saluda.

The two inclosed letters I have just received. They confirm the assembly at Ramsour's Mill. Morgan, I apprehend, is gone to head them. H—— is not yet come in. I will inform your Lordship as soon as I hear of him.

General Leslie is, I suppose, by this time arrived at Camden. The enemy's movement may alter your Lordship's plan.

I have the honor to be
Your Lordship's most devoted servant

BAN TARLETON

Enclosure (1)
Cunningham to Tarleton, 24th December 1780 *4(406): ALS*

Williams's
24th December 1780

Colonel Tarleton at camp

Sir

From the best authority am convinced the rebels are embodying at Ramsour's Mill, in all probability intend moving their opperation towards this quarter. I shall exert ev[ery] faculty to disconcert their diabolical plans, a[m no]w moving towards them with my militia, am sorry to say I lack the necessary accoutriments, wish and shall endeavour a daily corrispondence with you.

I am, sir,
Your most obedient humble servant

ROB^{T} CUNNINGHAM
Brigadier General of Militia

Enclosure (2)
McArthur to Tarleton, 26th December 1780 *4(407): ALS*

Owens's Plantation
December 26th 1780

Lt Colonel Tarleton etc etc

Dear Sir

Mr Greer[69] would inform you of the firing heard at Liles's Ford and of my having sent to know the cause of it, which proved to be nothing more than a parcel of our militia who had got too much rum and began to celebrate Christmass so early by firing their pieces. We lost a man yesterday, killed outright by the fall of a tree at our quarter guard in the great squall.

I am, dear sir,
Your most obedient servant

ARCH^{D} McARTHUR

---

69 There is no record of a Greer in the *Army Lists* or in the Roll of officers of the British American corps. He may have been a Back Country loyalist, perhaps George Greer, who was to serve as a private in the royal militia, or James Greer, who was a private, perhaps on furlough, in the South Carolina Royalist Regiment. (Clark, *Loyalists in the Southern Campaign*, i, 24-5, 32-3, 112)

Haldane to Tarleton, 27th December 1780 — *83(86): ACS*

Head Quarters
Wynnesborough
27th December 1780

Lt Colonel Tarleton commanding the British Legion

Dear Tarleton

Lord Cornwallis has desired me to inform you that he has received a confirmation of the intelligence he transmitted to you yesterday.[70]

Believe me ever, dear Tarleton, etc

H HALDANE

[*Subscribed*:]

If it would not be inconvenient to you, his Lordship would wish to see you tomorrow.

Cunningham to Tarleton, 30th December 1780 — *66(43): ALS*

Williams's
30th December 1780

Colonel Tarleton at camp

Sir

From undoubted authority General Morgan is now on Pacolett with 500 of the Virginia riflemen, all on foot. Am convinc'd he is join'd by Few, Brandon, and Pickens, who leads forth all the protectioners from Long Cane. The destination of this crew I cannot yet learn. By the best intelligence, believe Ninety Six to be their object.

I am, sir,
Your most obedient humble servant

ROB[T] CUNNINGHAM
Brigadier General of Militia

---

70 Extracts from Cornwallis's two letters of the 26th appear in Bass, op cit, 141. They state, *inter alia*, that Morgan and Washington had crossed the Catawba at Bigger's Ferry and were now beyond Broad River.

Tarleton to Cornwallis, 3rd January 1781[71] *67(11): ALS*

Somers's Plantation
January 3rd
½ past 6 am

Lt General Earl Cornwallis
Winsboro

My Lord

I am well here. I move directly towards Monses Mill, a proper course, as I have *no intelligence*.

I have the honor to be
Your Lordship's most devoted servant

BAN TARLETON

[*Subscribed*:]

If the 7th or 71st *battalion was at Bylerly's, it wou'd be well*.

Cornwallis to Tarleton, 3rd January 1781 *84(39): ADf*

Wynnesborough
3rd January 1781

Lt Colonel Tarleton

[Dear Tarleton]

I received yours of this morning.

I suspect that the enemy are retired. If so, I would lose no time. Which side of Broad River do you think it best for you to march? The 7th Regiment are ordered to Byerly's.

Yours etc

[CORNWALLIS]

[*Subscribed*:]

Be quite sure that 96 is safe. 7th Regiment will take your old gun to Ninety Six.

---

71 Published, with Cornwallis's following reply, in Bass, op cit, 144.

Allen to Tarleton, 4th January 1781 — *100(14): ALS*

December the 4th 1780[72]

Colonel Tarleton

My dear Sir

I rejoice to hear of you. Am very sorry you have not the cypher. Not knowing your force and your intention, I am at a loss to know what to say. I shall communicate my sentiments to the bearer, who may be depended upon. He returns immediately. Your time is too precious, I suppose, to make a visit to Ninety Six. If it should be otherwise, I should be very happy to have a few hours' conference with you respecting this country. Some good I think may be drawn from the late defeat and fright of our militia.

I am with great truth and respect
Your very humble servant

ISAAC ALLEN
Lt Colonel commanding at 96

[*Subscribed*:]

The enemy have retired and are now at Henderson's, as I am told, about 1,000.

Cornwallis to Tarleton, 5th January 1781[73] — *84(15): ADfS*

Wynnesborough
January 5th 1781

Lt Colonel Tarleton

Dear Tarleton

I received your letter dated yesterday, 7 o'clock am[74]. *I have ordered the baggage of your corps to Byerley's Ferry under the care of the 7th Regiment. I propose marching on Sunday next. You will contrive to correspond with me, keeping on my left flank, either on the*

---

72 The letter was written on 4th January 1781. Allen did not assume command at Ninety Six until 17th or 18th December 1780 when Cruger temporarily departed for Charlestown. The defeat of the militia to which the letter refers took place near Williams's stockaded house on 30th December 1780.

73 An inaccurate transcript appears in Bass, op cit, 145.

74 *your letter..*: the original is not extant, but an extract from Tarleton's copy appears in his *Campaigns*, 245. Encamped 20 miles from Brierley's Ferry, he wished principally to coordinate his push against Morgan with the commencement of Cornwallis's march, which he recommended should head for King's Mountain.

east or west of Broad River as you will judge best according to the intelligence you may receive. McArthur will of course march with you.

Yours etc

CORNWALLIS

[*Subscribed*:]

Your baggage is order'd to Byerley's Ferry under the care of the 7th Regiment. I propose marching on Sunday.

[*Annotated*:]

The postscript of this was repeated by a letter written on the same evening[75].

Tarleton to Munro, 5th January 1781 — *100(13): ALS*

Brooks's Plantation
January 5th

My dear Munro

Bring up the men's baggage and the officers'. You must get waggons for that purpose either from head quarters or press them. Newlands[76] may have some Congaree waggons, which must be kept and paid. You will receive directions from head quarters relative to the escort etc. Captain McPherson[77] bears this. He will order the convalescent men and women to Charles [Town] as per list. The 17th I hope will come with you etc. A guide comes with McPherson.

I know you will be as expeditious as possible.

Yours with regard

BAN TARLETON

---

75 *a letter*..: written at 8 pm, it appears in Tarleton, *Campaigns*, 246. It acknowledges receipt of a letter from Tarleton dated 2 pm, 5th January (not extant) and adds that Tarleton has done exactly what Cornwallis wished and has understood his intentions perfectly.

76 Newlands was quartermaster to the British Legion. (*The Cornwallis Papers*)

77 Born in Scotland, Donald McPherson (1743-?) had been commissioned a lieutenant in the 4th Battalion, New Jersey Volunteers, on 15th January 1777. He later transferred as a lieutenant to Patrick Stewart's company of the British Legion infantry and was promoted to captain of his own company on 24th October 1780. Now, in early January, he was departing on the recruiting service and so would avoid capture at the Battle of Cowpens, though he may have been taken prisoner in the capitulation of Yorktown. At the close of the war he was placed on the Provincial half-pay list and may have settled at Shelburne, Nova Scotia. (Treasury 64/23(2), WO 165/164(39) and WO 65/165(3) (National Archives, Kew); Raymond, 'British American Corps'; Tarleton, op cit, 246; Sabine, *Biographical Sketches*, ii, 555-6)

[*Subscribed*:]

McPherson's escort will return with you.

[*Superscribed*:]

Take care of my wine etc etc.

Cornwallis to Tarleton, 6th January 1781[78] — *84(23): ADf*

Wynnesborough
January 6th 1781

Dear Tarleton

I received yours of yesterday[79]. You will see that some part of your wishes are already anticipated. I am told that you have already three of the Quarter Master General's waggons at Byerley's. I send another empty and two loaded with rum and salt. You will easily conceive that we have not many to spare. By my letter of yesterday you will see my intention. *I shall march on Monday and direct my course for Bullock Creek. Leslie will march on Tuesday by the river road for the same place*. I approve of your proposal relative to the 7th Regiment and shall send orders to the commanding officer accordingly.

Yours etc

[CORNWALLIS]

Cornwallis to Newmarsh, 6th January 1781 — *84(21): C*

Wynnesborough
January 6th 1781

Captain Newmarsh[80] or officer commanding the Royal Fuzileers

Sir

I have sent two waggons loaded with rum and salt and one empty for the use of Lt Colonel Tarleton's corps. He requested four empty, but as I am informed that there are three

---

78 An inaccurate transcript appears in Bass, op cit, 147.

79 *yours..*: not extant.

80 Timothy Newmarsh was a long-serving officer who had entered the 7th Regiment (Royal Fusiliers) on 30th December 1755 and been promoted to captain on 18th July 1766. Now in charge of the regiment in the absence of Alured Clarke, who was commanding in Georgia and East Florida, he would soon be wounded and taken prisoner, along with the rest of the regiment, at the Battle of Cowpens. News of his promotion to major in the 4th Battalion, 60th (or Royal American) Regiment, effective from 10th August 1780, had apparently not yet reached South Carolina. (*Army Lists*)

of the Quarter Master General's with Mr Munroe, he will keep them for the purpose of carrying up the baggage of the Legion. You will please to follow such directions as you may receive from Lt Colonel Tarleton in regard to the march of the Fuzileers.

I am, sir,
Your most obedient and most humble servant

CORNWALLIS

Cornwallis to Tarleton, 7th January 1781[81] — *84(29): C*

Wynnesborough
January 7th 1781, 8 pm

Lt Colonel Tarleton

Dear Tarleton

I have received yours of yesterday, 10 am[82]. Your Quarter Master Newland has distressed us exceedingly. He went to Congarees, where he pressed all the Quarter Master General's waggons to which I trusted for getting off this ground. In vain the commissaries represented that they were the waggons of the army employed by my order in the publick service. He swore he did not care, that he had Colonel Tarleton's orders to press waggons, and he would have them and appealed to the *ratio ultima* of the broad sword. You must be sensible that unless he is severely dealt with, the conducting this army through the country will be impracticable. What he has done with the waggons, or where they are, God knows! By the great assiduity of Phillips and his militia, and the fortunate arrival of some country waggons, I am enabled to move to morrow, not without leaving a quantity of meal behind. So much for scolding, but you must be very grave with your people upon this business.

Lee's Legion was at Guilford Court House on Wednesday sevennight. Whether they were to join Morgan or to go to Haly's Ferry on Pedee was uncertain. I rather think the latter. Your little friend[83] —— was very near being hanged. I believe he can venture out no more. I do not exactly know where I shall halt to morrow or what stages I shall make, but will lose no time *in getting to Bullock's Creek, from whence we must take a fresh departure*.

I have just heard that the Quarter Master General's waggons are gone from Congarees with a fresh load of forage to Daniels Plantation. You see the consequence of my being superseded by Quarter Master Newland.

---

81 An inaccurate extract from this letter appears in Bass, op cit, 147.

82 *yours..*: not extant.

83 *Your little friend..*: de Treville. See Cornwallis to Rawdon, 7th January, p 246.

I shall write to you every day and shall be glad to hear from you as often.

I am yours very sincerely

CORNWALLIS

Cornwallis to Tarleton, 8th January 1781[84] *84(37): C*

McAlister's Plantation
8th January 1781, 7 pm

Lt Colonel Tarleton

Dear Tarleton

I have just received yours, 7th January, 3 o'clock pm[85]. *I shall remain here tomorrow, march on Wednesday to the Cross Roads, halt Thursday, and reach Bullock Creek Meeting House on Saturday.*

Yours etc

[CORNWALLIS]

Cornwallis to Tarleton, 9th and 10th January 1781[86] *84(47): A(in part) C*

McAlister's
January 9th 1781, 3 pm

Lt Colonel Tarleton

Dear Tarleton

Nothing new since yesterday. Some of Washington's cavalry who had been escorting prisoners to Charlotte Town returned over Broad River. I have taken every means in my power to find out Morgan's movements and whether he repasses Broad River.

---

84 The original of this letter is published in Tarleton, op cit, 247. It contains the following concluding paragraph: 'I have no news.'

85 *yours*..: not extant.

86 Omitting the postscript and otherwise containing a minor inaccuracy, a transcript is published in Bass, op cit, 148.

I received yours, January 8th, 10 am[87].

Yours very sincerely

CORNWALLIS

PS, January 10th 1781

As the rain will delay you and Leslie, I shall not march so fast as I intended. There is a report that Lee was to join Morgan between Broad River and Catawba this day.

Cornwallis to Tarleton, 11th January 1781 — *84(50): ADfS*

McAlister's
January 11th 1781, 3 pm

Lt Colonel Tarleton

Dear Tarleton

I received last night yours of the 9th, 4 pm[88]. I fear the waters have been much more swelled since you wrote it. At present I think I shall move on Saturday to Cross Roads. I can hear nothing of Morgan. They say there are several ferrys high up Broad River where he may pass, particularly Talbot's Ferry. Leslie is much retarded by the waters.

Yours etc

CORNWALLIS

Cornwallis to Tarleton, 14th January 1781[89] — *84(63): ADfS*

Bull Run
Sunday, January 14th 1781, 10 pm

Lt Colonel Tarleton

Dear Tarleton

I received yesterday morning your letter dated Duggins's, Indian Creek, January *11th*, 5 am[90]. By the report, however, of the man who brought it I conceive it ought to have been

---

87 *yours..*: not extant.

88 *yours..*: not extant.

89 An inaccurate transcript appears in Bass, op cit, 149. Of the inaccuracies, the major one is the mistranscription of 'Sandy River' as 'Tardy River'.

90 *your letter..*: not extant.

dated January *12th* as he assured me that he left you on Friday morning.

I shall march tomorrow to the head of Sandy River, and the next day to Hillhouse near Bullock Creek Meeting House. Leslie is at last out of the swamps and reached this day the neighbourhood of Rocky Mount. I have not heard of Morgan's moving but conclude he will now cross Broad River as I hear it has fallen very much.

Yours sincerely

CORNWALLIS

Cornwallis to Tarleton, 16th January 1781[91] — *84(76): ACS*

Hillhouse's Plantation between Turkey and Bullock Creeks
January 16th 1781

Lt Colonel Tarleton

Dear Tarleton

I have not heard from you since the 11th. I fear Morgan has too much the start of you. I have ordered meal to be ground and propose marching in three or four days to Beatty's Ford. Leslie will join me tomorrow or Thursday. Ross and Brodrick are on their road to camp and expected tomorrow.

Yours etc

CORNWALLIS

Tarleton to Cornwallis, 16th January 1781[92] — *67(28): ALS*

Pacolet
January 16th, 8 am

Lt General Earl Cornwallis etc etc etc etc
Head Quarters

My Lord

I have been most cruelly retarded by the waters. *Morgan is in force and gone for Cherokee Ford*.

---

91 The body of this letter, omitting the final sentence, appears in Bass, op cit, 150.

92 Published in Bass, op cit, 151.

I am now on my march. I wish he cou'd be stopp'd.

I have the honor to be
Your most devoted servant

BAN TARLETON

Stewart to Cornwallis, 23rd January 1781 — *67(32): ALS*

Cow Penn
January 23rd 1781

My Lord

Give me leave to inform your Lordship of the situation of the wounded. When I arrived here, I found a surgeon and a commissary of the American army left by General Morgan to provide for them in the best manner possible, but the country is so poor and wretched, and the surgeon is so ill furnished with medicines and other necessaries, that they have suffered much. I have forwarded the flag to General Morgan and at the same time wrote to him, requesting to have the wounded removed within our lines. The reason that urged me to it was the great scarcity, nay almost the absolute want, of provisions, even of meal, in this part of the country. The answer is not returned yet, but if he grants it, it will be necessary to send waggons from the army to carry such as are not able to walk, as there is not one in all this settlement. In my letter to General Morgan I presumed so far as to say that I would grant a receipt for such as were carried off and that they would be accounted for by your Lordship's commissary of prisoners. Should your Lordship not approve of this, please to send me instructions.

I have the honour to be with the greatest respect, my Lord,
Your Lordship's most obedient and most humble servant

J STEWART

§ - §

4 - Between Cornwallis and Leslie or Howard after their arrival in South Carolina

Cornwallis to Leslie, 21st December 1780 — *83(61): C*

Wynnesborough
21st December 1780

Hon Major General Leslie

My dear General

I should have written to you sooner, had I not waited for Balfour's arrival. He came last night and has informed me of your march. I had my doubts of your being able to pass the swamp at Nelson's and the road between it and Jacks Creek. Balfour thinks, from what he heard of the state of it, that you will certainly be able to do it and that any repairs that the causeway or road may want will not delay you above a day or two. I intend that the corps under Lt Colonel Watson should serve with that part of the army which is under Lord Rawdon. You will, however, bring them with you as far as Camden unless Lord Rawdon should request of you to dispose of them otherwise.

I will let you know on your arrival at Camden what I think will be the best and most convenient march for you to join me.

If you should meet with insurmountable difficulties in passing at Nelson's, I should then wish you to proceed to Fryday's Ferry at Congarees, leaving the corps under Lt Colonel Watson at Nelson's Ferry untill he receives directions from Lord Rawdon.

I am, my dear General, with great truth
Most faithfully yours

[CORNWALLIS]

Leslie to Rawdon, 26th December 1780[93] — *4(398): ALS*

Nelson's
26th December 1780

My Lord

I had the honor to receive yours of the 22nd on the road two days ago.

---

[93] Enclosed with Rawdon to Cornwallis, 28th December, p 231.

The troops all arrived here this morning. Colonel Watson's corps are now all crossed the river. The 64th and your Lordship's light company move to night to Jacks Creek.

I have ordered the light company of the Guards *on* to Singleton's Mills with a comissary to provide indian meal for the troops, the biscuit falling short of the quantity supposed to be here.

The 64th etc have orders to lose no time in getting to Camden. Major McLeroth and a serjeant per company are gone to Charles Town to provide for the regiment and to bring up their miserable recruits.

The swamp is in some degree repaired, but I fear we shall find it difficult to get the baggage and waggons well over it. The repairing it was only begun two days ago, otherwise I could have brought the troops faster on.

Your Lordship must not suppose us on our march from Sumpter's before Friday morning, and we will take six days to get to Camden without there's an absolute necessity to leave the baggage to follow, for our horses are good for nothing and our waggons not very light.

That you may know where to find us I send your Lordship the route:

Friday	at Jacks Creek
Saturday	at Major James's
Sunday	at Shanks Creek
Monday	at Mrs James's
Tuesday	at Refton Creek
Wednesday	at Town Creek, but if possible to Camden.

I have the honor to wish you many returns of the season and to assure you that
I am, my Lord,
Your most faithfull humble servant

A LESLIE

PS

I have just received your Lordship's of the 24th and if possible make my march in a shorter time, but if it's necessary, please inform me.

Cornwallis to Leslie, 28th December 1780 — *83(88): C*

Wynnesborough
December 28th 1780

Hon Major General Leslie

Dear Sir

If you are quite stout and are not afraid of a long ride, I should be very glad to see you here to explain my intended march to you, and in that case you will direct Brigadier General O'Hara to proceed with the troops to Camden. If you apprehend any inconvenience from the fatigue of the ride, I will send Haldane to meet you at Camden.

I should be glad that the recruits for the regiments here and the detachment of the 17th Dragoons were sent up with all possible expedition, and I wish to know whether the carriages of the 3 pounders with you have two or four wheels.

I am, dear sir, with great regard
Your most obedient and faithfull servant

CORNWALLIS

Cornwallis to Leslie, 6th January 1781 — *84(20): C*

Wynnesborough
January 6th 1781

Hon Major General Leslie

Dear Sir

I have deferred my march 'til Monday. I would, however, wish you to move on Tuesday unless you should have some particular reason for staying another day. You will direct your course to Bullock Creek. I desired Lord Rawdon to lend you waggons for two days's meal above the quantity I mentioned. As you have several creeks to pass, a day's rain might delay you. I am so tired with writing that I can only assure you that I am

Very sincerely yours

CORNWALLIS

Cornwallis to Leslie, 8th January 1781 *84(33): C*

McAlister's Plantation
January 8th 1781

Hon Major General Leslie

I shall remain here to morrow and march on Wednesday to Cross Roads, where I believe I shall halt on Thursday and march on Friday and Saturday to the meeting house on Bullock's Creek. I will take care that there shall be some meal ready for you at Cross Roads, or even nearer if you should want it, or any other assistance in the article of provisions that you may desire.

I have written to Fanning.

Yours very sincerely

CORNWALLIS

Cornwallis to Leslie, 10th January 1781 *84(48): C*

January 10th 1781

These rains will, I think, impede your march. I shall therefore stay here[94] longer than I intended. There will be meal for you at the Cross Roads or nearer and any assistance of provisions you may want. Send to me here, and if I am gone forward, the messenger may follow me.

CORNWALLIS

Cornwallis to Leslie, 12th January 1781 *84(53): C*

McAlister's
12th January 1781

Major General Leslie etc etc etc

Dear Sir

I have just received yours of last night[95]. I hope you will have reached Wateree Creek this day and that you will be able to proceed to Rocky Mount tomorrow, to which place I

---

94 *here*: McAlister's plantation.

95 *yours..*: not extant.

have sent 4000 weight of meal and some salt. I shall be glad to hear from you every day. I intend moving about five miles forward tomorrow. Morgan is still on Pacolet at Scull's Shoals. The Broad River exceedingly high, I have not heard from Tarleton since Tuesday. I believe he is as much embarrassed with the waters as you are.

I am etc

CORNWALLIS

Leslie to Cornwallis, 13th and 14th January 1781 — *67(16): ALS*

Upper Ford of Wateree Creek
Saturday evening, 7 o'clock

Earl Cornwallis etc etc etc

My Lord

With exertion we are only *here*. The difficulty of heading creeks, making bridges, and repairing and cutting out new roads has impeded our progress much.

I expect to get 11 miles tomorrow to one Smith's, where there is plenty of forage, and I am told there are hogs there for us, found by your comissary.

I have several letters for your Lordship signed N Balfour, but affraid to send them by a single guide, and I have no dragoons. I fancy, reckoning the 4000 lb of indian meall, we can do to the 17th inclusive.

10,000 bal cartriges have overtaken us. They came by land from Charles Town. I am sorry to say the salt had not arrived at Camden and now I dispair of its coming up. We brought from Camden *19* puntions of rum and *33* bushels (all they had) of salt. Your Lordship shall hear from me dayly, and

Believe me to be
Most faithfully yours

A LESLIE

[*Subscribed*:]

6 o'clock, Sunday morning

The guide your Lordship sent can't be found, otherwise this ought to have gone last night.

Cornwallis to Leslie, 14th January 1781 *84(59): C*

Bull Run
14th January 1781, 3 pm

Dear Sir

I received your letter from the upper ford of Wateree Creek dated this morning, six o'clock. I do not exactly know where Smith's plantation is, nor can I find any person that can give me information of it. I conclude, however, it must be at or very near Rocky Mount, as the hogs were ordered from Wynnesborough thither. If I am right, you are twenty five miles from the Cross Roads, the last ten of which are but indifferent, but they say you may avoid the bad part by going four miles about, turning off to your left at the road that crosses to go to Walker's Mill. I shall march by Steward's Cross Roads, about four or five miles from the Old Cross Roads, and am told that you will have a better road, from where you turn to your left, to go directly thither, leaving the Old Cross Roads on your right hand. I think there can be no doubt of your reaching Stewart's Cross Roads by the 17th at latest. I shall perhaps move on to Bullock Creek Meeting House, leaving 4000 weight of meal for you at Stewart's Cross Roads. As I can only leave a guard of militia, which may be easily scared, I could wish you to send on the light company of the Guards with all convenient expedition to take charge of the meal. I shall wait at Bullock Creek Meeting House for your joining me.

I am with great regard, dear sir,
Yours very sincerely

CORNWALLIS

[*Subscribed*:]

I have sent several parties to drive cattle to you, but if you apprehend any want, let me know it.

I mean by Stewart's Cross Roads those nearest to Broad River and to the waters of Sandy River. I am informed that the other were known by the name of Stewart's Cross Roads as a man of that name settled at both, but they are now distinguished by the Old Cross Roads.

Cornwallis to Leslie, 14th January 1781 *84(61): C*

Bull Run
Sunday, 14th January 1781, 10 pm

Hon Major General Leslie etc etc etc

Dear Sir

I inclose to you a duplicate of the letter I sent this afternoon for fear of accidents. The bearer thinks he knows where you are and that he is acquainted with the country. I am not, however, sure that he is right in either of those points. I believe you have the best guides with you. I have only to add that I submit to the judgement you will form from the report of your guides what road is best for you to take to get to Stewart's New Cross Roads, recommending it to you not to halt near my present camp on account of forage. I propose marching tomorrow to the waters of Sandy River about three miles beyond Stewart's.

I forgot to mention that Lord Rawdon sent me extracts in cypher of the most material parts of Balfour's letters[96], so that I am in no haste to get them.

I am, dear sir, with great regard etc

CORNWALLIS

Cornwallis to Leslie, 15th January 1781 — *84(64): C*

Harding's Plantation, Sandy River
15th January 1781, 6 pm

Hon Major General Leslie

Dear Sir

I have just received yours dated this day at 12 o'clock[97]. As this place is but two miles from Stewart's Cross Roads, I brought on the meal with me and shall send to the light company of the Guards to come on in the morning. You may probably reach this place tomorrow, in the neighbourhood of which you will find forage. I shall go tomorrow to Hillhouse's plantation, 11 miles from hence. I shall probably wait there for you. You will find the roads very bad. Ross and Broderick are arrived and will be at Camden this night.

Yours very sincerely

CORNWALLIS

[*Subscribed*:]

You will find forage down Sandy River. We have taken very little here.

---

96 See Rawdon to Cornwallis, 11th January, p 249.

97 *yours*..: not extant.

Leslie to Cornwallis, 16th January 1781 *67(26): ALS*

Laird Bevens
Tuesday morning

Earl Cornwallis etc etc etc

My Lord

I had your Lordship's last night and give you joy on the arrival of your two friends. I shall certainly get to Harding's plantation to day. The guide's horse was tired last night, so could not proceed.

My fingers are so cold I must finish.

Yours, my dear Lord,

A LESLIE

Cornwallis to Leslie, 16th January 1781 *84(74): C*

Hillhouse Plantation
January 16th, 3 pm

Hon Major General Leslie etc

Dear Sir

I have just received your two letters of last night and this morning[98]. I think you will find it difficult to come on to this place tomorrow from the account you give of your horses. You will do as you please, it is not material, and you may probably be determined by the facility of getting forage where you are. There is no good halting place between us. If you should not come on tomorrow, I should be obliged to you if you will send on the grenadier company of the Guards, as I may want to station them and the light company at some of the neighbouring mills.

Morgan was on Sunday night six miles from Grindal's Shoals on Pacolet, on the road leading to Broad River.

Etc

CORNWALLIS

---

98 *your two letters..*: that of the preceding night is not extant.

Cornwallis to Howard, 22nd January 1781 — *84(79): C*

Steis's Plantation
January 22nd

Brigadier General Howard

Dear Sir

Upon receiving certain information that Morgan marched yesterday on the road to Ramsoure's, I changed my route and mean to march as fast as possible to Ramsoure's. I should wish you to begin your march to morrow for the same place, where I think you may arrive in three days. I hope to get there the day after to morrow. Please to acknowledge the receipt of this as soon as possible.

I am, sir,
Your most obedient humble servant

CORNWALLIS

Howard to Cornwallis, undated[99] — *67(30): ALS*

Little Creek near Cross Roads

Earl of Cornwallis

My Lord

At seven this morning I had the honor of receiving the duplicate sent me by your Lordship, the first letter not having yet reach'd me. I shall immediately march as you have directed and in every other respect punctually comply with your orders.

I have the honor to be
Your Lordship's most obedient and most humble servant

J HOWARD
Brigadier General

PS

Several of the waggons yesterday broke down on account of the extreme badness of the road, and our march consequently much obstructed.

---

[99] According to an annotation, the letter was written on 23rd January.

Howard to Cornwallis, 24th January 1781 *67(33): ALS*

Justice Arspy's Plantation
January 24th 1781

Rt Hon Earl Cornwallis etc etc etc

My Lord

As I am informed the distance to Ramsouses from hence is near 15 miles, I shall endeavour if possible to comply with your Lordship's orders. We are come late this evening to our ground and several of the waggons are in want of repair, but hope every thing will be in readiness to move as early as possible in the morning.

I have the honor to be
Your Lordship's most obedient and most humble servant

J HOWARD
Brigadier General

§ - §

CHAPTER 35

Correspondence between Cornwallis and the Royal Militia

1 - With or concerning Kirkland

Kirkland to Cornwallis, 31st October 1780 ***3(346): ALS***

Camp at Williams Plantation
October the 31st 1780

To the Honrabel Earl Cornwallis

May it pleas your Lordship –

To give me leave to acquaint your Excelency that onless sum amediate assistance is sent in order to astablish a post in the upper end of the fork between Braud and Saludy River, you loose the hole support of the malitia and it is to be feared the greatest part will revolt. Some semeth ripe forit and others will be under a nesesaty to submit to superior force as many of the prinsabel men are removing with their effects. Head I not come hear with my regment and taken the command of the malitia, the hole fork wolde have bean in posesion of the rebels in a verry few days time, but I hope by to morro night I shall have threehundred men imbodied, and if you will send orders to Maj^{r} Wims or any other detachment to suport me, I wold march amediately to Waffords Iron Works on Losons Fork and take post their, as it semeth the most convenint place to cover this cuntry, and their arect a strong stockade fort and collect all the provition and other nessary stores, and then I shall be abel with the malitia to defend the upper part of this cuntry, and if a post their is properly mand, a very few men will do at 96. I hope Col^{n} Cruger mentioned my intention to you in his letter. Your Lordships removeing so low down in the cuntry hath very much dispirated His Majestys subjects and imboldens the rebels, who hath got in their posesion all the cuntry on the north side of the Enoree, and I can allso in form your Lordship that Clarke and Brandon joind their detachments yesterday near Mosgroves Mill consisting of a hundred and sixty men each.

I am with great respect
Your Lordships most obedient and fathfull servent

MOSES KIRKLAND
Leu^{t} Col^{o} Militia

PS

For farder perticulers I refer you to the barer, Capt Gibbs.

Cornwallis to Kirkland, 2nd November 1780 — *82(4): C*

November 2nd 1780

Lt Colonel Kirkland

Sir

I received yours of the 31st by Captain Gibbs and am much obliged to you for the active part you have taken at this time. The want of provisions obliged me to come so low down the country. I am determined to give every encouragement in my power to the militia and have explained myself on that head to Captain Gibbs. In the mean time I should advise you to be very cautious, as it would be attended with the worst of consequences if the corps with you met with any check.

I am, sir, etc

CORNWALLIS

Kirkland to Wemyss, undated[1] — *4(439): C*

Major Weyms commanding 63rd Regiment

Sir

I am credibly inform'd some of your men have taken horses from Mr William Griffin, a very aged gentlman and has been many years a cripple and has ever been a faithful and loyal subject to His Majesty. His sons have been very active in His Majesty's Service and one of

---

1 Written in early November 1780 when Wemyss was in the vicinity of Kirkland's post at Williams's stockaded house.

them under Colonel Ferguson receiv'd a wound which renders him forever incapable of getting his living. As I am convinced you would not wish to distress such people, I hope you will order your men to deliver up the horses to the owners.

I am, sir,
Your most obedient humble servant

MOSES KIRKLAND
Lt Colonel Militia

Kirkland to Cornwallis, 6th November 1780 *4(72): LS*

Fort at Williams's
6th November 1780

The Hon Earl Cornwallis etc etc etc

Per Captain O'Neall

Sir

I had the honour of yours by Captain Gibbs dated the 2nd instant and beg leave to present you my humble thanks for your encouragement to the militia.

Colonel Balfour has honoured me so far as to offer me the command of a regment to be raised out of the militia for nine or twelve months for the defence of this province. He has omitted sending me a commission or warrant, for which reason I am at a loss how to proceed till I receive instructions from your Lordship. I must beg leave to give them some little encouragement according to the time they engage for. I have embodied between two and three hundred men, and the men seem now a little spiretted and bigen to come in. I have erected a stockade fort and am collecting provisions. If your Lordship is pleas'd to give me the command of all the militia in this district and allow me to draft, which Colonel Balfour recommends, I should soon be at the head of a very beautiful regiment. I beg the favour of you to give Lieutenant John Hattan of Colonel Allen's core leave to quit that core and join me as commander of a company. I beg leave to recommend to your Lordship Mr Benj° Smith[2] to be appointed assistant commissary and hope the Commissary General will send him instructions by Captain O'Neall.

I would also beg leave to recommend Captain Henry O'Neall of undoubed honesty as paymaster to the regiment and militia, and that he might be the keeper of a publick store, which would be of the greatest benefit to those militia when he is enabled to furnish them with those necessaries they most need out of their pay.

---

[2] Smith has not been identified.

Further particulars I refer to Captain Henry O'Neall, and conclude

Your Lordship's most faithfull and obedient humble servant

MOSES KIRKLAND
Lt Colonel Militia

Cornwallis to Kirkland, 8th November 1780 — *82(11): C*

Wynnesborough
November 8th 1780

Lt Colonel Moses Kirkland

Sir

I received by the hands of Mr O'Neal your letter of the sixth. As I left the regulation of the affairs of the militia to Colonel Balfour on my leaving the province, it is necessary that I should know what steps he has taken. After I have heard from him, I shall endeavour to settle matters on the most satisfactory footing for the militia. I beg leave to assure you, sir, that I have the best opinion of your loyalty and zeal for His Majesty's Service. I shall keep a considerable force in this quarter untill the frontiers of South Carolina are put into a respectable state of defence. For that reason alone I returned from North Carolina. I beg you will do every thing in your power to animate and encourage the militia. With proper exertions on their part we cannot fail of success.

I am, sir,
Your most obedient humble servant

CORNWALLIS

Kirkland to Cornwallis, 8th November 1780 — *4(67): LS*

Fort at Williams's Plantation
November 8th 1780

The Hon Earl Cornwallis

Per Captain Gibbs

My Lord

I thought it my duty to inclose you the copys of two letters directed to two of the worst rebells that were in the fork, and I know that a rebell Colonel Hampton had a conference with them about three weeks ago. Lightner is taken and Summers is flead. The letters was taken out of a young women's pocket who was suspected to be a spy. Your Lordship may depend the rebell scheam is for Sumpter to lay on the south side of Broad River, if possible to prevent your Lordship sending any reinforcements this way, while won of their main bodys from North Carolina to join with those already in the fork is to dislodge me and then take 96. Then the greatest part of the inhabitants of this province will be under their command, and then they would be round your Lordship on all sides. The spirit of the militia of this fork is sunk so low that no incouragement that can be giving will raise it without first giving the rebells a suden check. They are eavin afraid of staying with me in the fort for fear of being be sieged. I have only 115 of my own rigement that I can put confidence in to gard the fort, where their is 2,000 men living convenient. But [with] Colonel Faugerson's defeat, and Colonel Cunningham, his brother and other leading men refusing to take any command over their rigements and companys, but were making of with their effects before I came here, which quite dispirited the militia, I shall ever be glad to receive your Lordship's commands.

I am, sir, with great respect
Your Lordship's most obedient and very faithful servant

MOSES KIRKLAND

Enclosure (1)
Liles to Lightner, 3rd November 1780 — *4(69): C*

November 3rd 1780

To Captain Michael Lightner

Dear Sir

I make bold with you to request of you to collect all the men that is frend to their country to immediately embody and repair to join General Sumpter at Shirer's Ferry, which I hope will be by Sunday next without fail. They that will not must abide by the consequence. It is not that I would wish you to come to any dammage but purely through good will to you and the rest of the good people of the regiment, neither would I recommend it for any one to stay at home, thinking they will meet with any indulgence hereafter, which they will not, but the behaviour of men will let us know what their principles is. For farther satisfaction you may apply to [*torn*].

I am, sir, with due regard
Your very humble servant

JAMES LILES[3]

---

3 Of James Liles little is known. He was an officer in Sumter's Brigade and had taken part in the action at Hanging Rock. (Moss, *SC Patriots*, 569)

Enclosure (2)
Sumter to Summers, 3rd November 1780 *4(71): C*

Camp at Stallions's
3rd November 1780

Major Adams Summers

I hope you will cheerfully embrace this oppertunity, to which heaven has favour'd you with, to attempt the release of your oppress'd country. Your character is such as to leave no room for me to doubt either your zeal or vigilence. I therefore request you will be pleas'd to give the most speedy notice to the people in your regiment, and otherways if convenient, that they are call'd on once more to declare themselves either as friends or enemies to the State. [Towards] those who are reasonable and just enough to offer themselves as friends and demonstrates their sincerity by their good conduct you will proceed with mildness, not with threatnings. Let them cooly deliberate what choice to make. They may depend on being treated accordingly.

Have the men gathered by Monday at or near Shirer's. I shall be glad that you will direct some propper person to have collected a quantity of flour for the use of the army.

If you know any thing of the movements of the enemy from Ninety Six or else where, please to let me know the perticulars by express.

I am, sir,
Your most humble servant

THO^S SUMPTER

Kirkland to Cornwallis, 10th November 1780 *4(82): LS*

Fort at Williams Place
November 10th 1780

The Hon Earl Cornwallis
Commander in Chief of His Majesty's army in the Southern Department

My Lord

From the best intilligence I can git from every part of this destrict I have reason to beleive that the whole rebell party, boath purrole[4] and protection men, do mean a general revolt and to take up arms against us. The friends of Goverment seems sensible of it, [so] that they think it needless making any resistance, and the greater part incline to be hiding in swamps,

---

4 *purrole*: parole.

and many others appear to be making their peace with them, so much that it is out of my power to gother any body of men out of any regements exsept a part of my own. [From] four companys of my own regement joining Long Cain settlement I can not git one man. Major King [can] not raise one man. Major Clary has not yet joined me with any.

I beg leave to sign my self
Your Excellency's most obedient and very dutifill servent

MOSES KIRKLAND
Lt Colonel Militia

Cornwallis to Kirkland, 11th November 1780 *82(28):C*

Winsborough
November 11th 1780

Lt Colonel Kirkland

Sir

Major Wemys surprized General Sumpter in his camp at Fishdam Ford and killed and wounded a great number of his men. The remainder fled from the field, and for two hours after day break not a rebel was to be seen near their camp. However, unfortunately, Major Wemys was most dangerously wounded by the first fire, and the command devolving on a very young officer, he came away before day and left the major and about 13 men who were badly wounded in a house near the place of action, so that he lost all the credit of a most compleat victory. Sumpter, I am informed, has joined Clarke etc. I have sent a strong detachment of horse and foot with cannon to Shirar's Ferry, and I do not think that the present force of the rebels, which when united cannot exceed 700 men (all militia), will venture to attack 96. If our militia are so timid and supine to suffer themselves to be plundered by a force so much inferior to what they could raise, it is certainly their fault. I shall keep a watchfull eye on the movements of the enemy and recommend it to you to be vigilant and not be taken in your fort.

I am, sir,
Your most obedient humble servant

CORNWALLIS

Fort at Williams
November 12th 1780

Lord Cornwallis
Commander in Chief of the Southern Department

My Lord

Yesterday morning before day, the block house on the Indian line commanded by Captain Pain[5] the rebell Colonel Clark whent to take with four hundred men, but Pain, having notice, sot them on fire and retreated of[6] with his party; and Clark amediately made for Musgrove's Mill, where a hundred more join'd him, where he [was] in camp last night and sent four men as spys to know the strength of this fort; and we have taken one [of] them of the name of W^m^ McHarry[7], who has confest their whole scheam and strength; and they are to attack this post, if possible to git it on fire as it is made of old rails, and I have but one hundred men to defend it. If I am taken or are ablidge[d] to avaculate it, the whole Destrict of 96 will amediately be in possession of the enemy and Colonel Crugar's provision intirely cut off, and all expatitions[8] of the militia of this destrict will then be lost. Several of their partys was with in six miles of me last night.

I am with respect to your Lordship
Your most obedient and very humble servent

MOSES KIRKLAND
Lt Colonel Militia

---

5 William Payne was a captain in Patrick Cuningham's Little River (Saluda) Regiment of the royal militia. Whether he was the William Payne who had been a leading Regulator in Orange County, North Carolina, is uncertain, but by 1775 he had settled at Cane Brake in Ninety Six District, South Carolina. In the same year he was serving as an officer in Thomas Fletchall's Upper Saluda Regiment of the royal militia, which, to a man, refused to sign the Continental Association subversive of the Crown. Maintaining his loyalty, he was captured during the Snow Campaign later in the year and was among the prisoners sent to Charlestown, being considered one of the leading and most active members of the loyalist party in the Back Country. Now, in 1780, part of his company had been captured in the Battle of King's Mountain, but he did not take part. Instead, he had been assigned to the command of the blockhouse on the old Indian line, which he had now abandoned. When the Back Country was given up in the summer of 1781, he would flee to Charlestown and by May 1783 was residing in East Florida. From there he presented a claim to the royal commission for the loss of 300 acres, a house, etc in South Carolina. (Clark, *Loyalists in the Southern Campaign*, i, 253, 256, 300, 525-6; Wheeler, *Historical Sketches*, ii, 14; Lossing, *Pictorial Field-Book*, ii, 367; Coldham, *Loyalist Claims*, 141, 293, 382; McCrady, *SC in the Rev 1775-1780*, 38; Gibbes, *Documentary History*, i, 249-253)

6 *of*: off.

7 No information about McHarry has been found apart from that now provided by Kirkland.

8 *expatitions*: expeditions?

PS

Musgrove's Mill is but 20 miles of. There is two rebells, Colonel Cambell and Colonel Christy[9], [who] was four days ago at Gilbert Town with a large army coming this way.

Cornwallis to Kirkland, 13th November 1780[10] — *82(34): C*

Winsborough
November 13th 1780

Lt Colonel Kirkland

Sir

I have just received your letter of yesterday's date by Captain O'Neal. I have taken every possible measure for the security of 96, and if our friends will have confidence in me, I have no doubt but they will soon see their enemies driven with loss and disgrace out of their province; but if those who say they are our friends will not stir, I cannot defend every man's house from being plundered, and I must say that when I see a whole settlement running away from 20 or 30 robbers, I think that they deserve to be robbed.

I am, sir,
Your most obedient humble servant

CORNWALLIS

Kirkland to Cornwallis, 25th November 1780 — *4(207): LS*

Ninety Six
25th November 1780

Erl Corn Walles, Lt General etc etc

Sir

I am happy to find your Lordship has had influence enough over Colonel Cunningham to get him to take the command of the militia of this district. It is but a few weeks ago since Colonel Cruger and all the friends he had could not prevail on him to take the command of the militia in the fork when there was not more than 50 rebels imbodied within the fork. He

---

9 *Christy*: Major Gilbert Christian (*c.* 1734-1793), who lived in the Holston country and had taken part in the Battle of King's Mountain. (Draper, *King's Mountain*, 417, and Williams, *Tennessee during the Revolutionary War*, *passim*)

10 Published without the first sentence in Ross ed, *Cornwallis Correspondence*, i, 69.

then was advising his brothers and other friends to move off with their effects to the lower parts of Carolina or Georgia and was about doing so himself. Major Gibbs and the officers of his regiment and Plommer's, finding they were not to be supported by Cunningham's regiment, did fly off with their familys and effects and almost all the friends of Government in their regiment. This alarms me. I knew, if Cunningham's regiment broke, that the rebels wou'd increase so as to overrun the whole district. I waited on Colonel Cruger and acquainted him of the danger, who did me the honour, as he cou'd not get Cunningham to do any thing, to take post in the fork, which I did with part of my regiment. Colonel Cunningham, finding me between him and his enemy, quit moving away and went to Charles Town[11]. His brother, Patrick Cunningham, and almost every other captain in his regiment did so much disapprove of his conduct that they petition'd your Lordship[12] to have the command of all the militia of the district given to me, and as my commission was senior to his and my rank superior, I expected your Lordship wou'd have done me that honour, which wou'd [have] oblidged me to remain in this district and, as my matters is much unsettled about Savannah and Charles Town, wou'd have been much to my disadvantage. I therefore beg the favour of you to let me resign the command of the regiment of militia you have been pleased to honor me with. I further beg your Lordship wou'd be pleased to consider those poor militia men in my regiment who I have had almost constantly on duty since I have been in this district and have them paid, particularly those who had the misfortune to be made prisoners with Colonel Ferguson. Many have got home almost naked. If your Honor wou'd be pleased to order Major Frazier of 71st, acting Deputy Quarter Master General, to settle with me and repay me the money I advanced for his horses and waggons I bought for him by his own request, the receipts of which I have, it wou'd enable me to put my son to school in Charles Town this winter, for which favour you will ever oblidge

Your Lordship's most obedient and most humble servant

MOSES KIRKLAND
Lt Colonel Militia

PS

On the day Colonel Tarleton march'd up the fork, Colonel Cunningham apply'd to me for all the men that was mounted at the fort to pursue after the enemy, which I gave him the command off to the number of 70, which guarded him to Shirey's Ferry, where he left them at their own disposal; and on his return as a general officer, he call'd at the fort, dismissed me with orders for me to discharge every man under my command, which has prevented me from joining Colonel Tarlton with that force I intended.

---

[11] After 'Charles Town' the following is deleted: 'to get his commission'.

[12] For the address, see p 395.

Cornwallis to Kirkland, 30th November 1780 *82(134): C*

Wynnesborough
November 30th 1780

Lt Colonel Moses Kirkland

Sir

From the best information I could procure it appeared to me to be for the good of His Majesty's Service to place Brigadier General Cunningham at the head of the militia of the 96 District. I therefore thought myself bound in duty to my King and country to give him that command. If you find yourself in any shape aggrieved by it, I can assure you that I am sorry for it, but in my station I cannot put the desires of any individual in competition with the publick good.

I beg you will accept of my thanks for the spirited and active part which you took on the late invasion of the district. I shall be always ready to bear testimony of your merit on that occasion.

I enclose a request to Major Fraser that he will settle your accounts and pay you the balance, and a note to Colonel Balfour to desire that he will present you with fifty guineas in consideration of the expences incurred by you in your late command.

I shall still hope that you will give every support and assistance to the cause in which we are engaged, and am, sir,

Your most obedient and most humble servant

CORNWALLIS

Enclosure (1)
Cornwallis to Fraser, 30th November 1780 *82(133): C*

Camp at Wynnesborough
November 30th 1780

Major Fraser
Deputy Quarter Master General

Sir

I desire that you will please to settle the accounts you have with Lt Colonel Kirkland and pay him what balance may be due to him.

I am, sir,
Your most obedient humble servant

CORNWALLIS

Enclosure (2)
Cornwallis to Balfour, 30th November 1780 *82(130): C*

Camp at Wynnesborough
November 30th 1780

To Lt Colonel Balfour
Commandant of Charlestown

Sir

You will please to pay to Lt Colonel Moses Kirkland or his order the sum of fifty guineas on account of the expences incurred by him in his late command of the militia.

I am, sir,
Your most obedient servant

CORNWALLIS

Fraser to Cornwallis, 12th January 1781 *5(37): ALS*

Savannah
12th January 1781

My Lord

I had this day the honor of your Lordship's orders by Colonel Kirkland relative to his acompts with the Quartermaster General's Department, and I am sorry that it is not in my power at present to pay him the entire ballance of it, having not so much of the publick money in my possession. The only sum that I was directed to draw at Charlestown was for the purchase of horses since the 1st of January 1780. That I have almost paid all away. I assured Colonel Kirkland how soon the acompts of this district of the department would be settled in the office and money granted to answear the demands upon it, that his acompt, as far as depended upon me, would be fully and speedily paid. I offered likewise to give him an order upon the office at New York for the ballance due him, remiting at the same time a copy of his acompt for the information and aprobation of the officer preciding there, but he will not accept of that. I have paid him at sundry times £133-11-10 to acc^{t}. The amount of his claim is £342-7-6, as your Lordship will see by the enclosed copy, which I received this morning and which contains an addition of £126 more than a former copy of his acompt which I received some time ago, but I objected to none of his charges, though perhaps some of them may not be sustained in the office.

It hurts me that your Lordship should be troubled with representations of this kind, and the more so as it is not in my power to prevent it. However, I hope to return in a few days to Charlestown and proceed to York to have my acompts in the department finally settled. Then I hope to be able to satisfy every demand.

I have the honor to be, my Lord,
Your most obedient humble servant

SIMON FRASER

Enclosure
Kirkland's claim ***5(39): C***

Major Fraser of the 71st Regiment, acting Quarter Master General, in $^{a}/_{c}$ curr[d] with Moses Kirkland

D[r]

1779		£	s	d
	To hire one waggon, my own property, from 16th January to 31st March both days inclusive, 75 days @ 1/9 per day	6	11	3
	Hire of 3 horses, my own property, from 16th January to 31st March, 75 days at 1/9 per day	19	13	9
	Hire of one horse, my own property, from 16th January to 31st March at 1/9 per day (75 days)	6	11	3
	Hire of one waggon, bought of Israel Ruser, from 16th January to 31st March, 75 days at 1/9*d* per day	6	11	3
	Hire of one horse, my own property, from 16th January to 31st March, 75 days @ 1/9*d* per day	6	11	3
	Hire of one waggon, bought of Dorothy Trail, from 16th January to 31st March, 75 days @ 1/9*d* per day	6	11	3
	Hire of 4 horses, my own property, from the 17th January to the 31st March, 64 days at 1/9*d* per day for each horse	22	8	0
	Hire of 4 horses, my own property, bought of Ja[s] McGerth, from 30th January to 31st March, 61 days at 1/9*d* per day each horse	21	7	0
	Hire of one waggon, bought of W[m] Tanner, from 16th February to 31st March, 44 days at 1/9*d* per day	3	17	0
	Hire of two horses, bought of ditto, from 16th February to 31st March, 44 days at 1/9*d* per day each horse	7	14	0
	Paid W[m] Tanner for waggon driving from 16th February to 31st March, 44 days at 1/9*d* per day	3	17	0
	Paid James Tanner for waggon driving from the 1st to 31st March, 31 days at 1/9*d*	2	14	3

Date	Particulars			£	s	d
	Hire of one horse, bought of Joseph Strable, from 19th January to 31st March, 72 days at 1/9			6	6	0
	Hire of one waggon, bought of Jo Ramsheart, from 16th January to 31st March, 75 days at 1/9*d* per day			6	11	3
	Hire of 1 waggon, bought of Christopher Sepra, from 19th January to 31st March, 72 days at 1/9*d* per day			6	6	0
	Hire of two horses, bought of ditto, from and to the dates above, 72 days @ 1/9*d* each			12	12	0
	Hire of 1 waggon, bought of James Cruise, from the 24th January to 31st March, 72 days at 1/9 per day			6	6	0
	Hire of two horses, bought of ditto, from and to the above dates, 72 days at 1/9*d* per day for each horse			12	12	0
	Paid John Friday the 25th April in part of account for making and mending gears			1	1	9
April 1st	Sold you all the waggons and horses I had in the service, viz:					
	Sold	1 waggon purchased of J° Ihly	7-0-0			
	"	3 horses purchased of ditto	14-0-0	21	0	0
	"	1 waggon, my property, bought of Israel Ruser		5	18	9
	"	2 horses, my ditto, delivered into the service, 16th January		10	16	9
	"	1 waggon bought of Dorothy Trail		5	18	9
	"	4 horses delivered to the waggon master at Sweetwater Creek on the 27th January last		21	15	0
	"	4 horses purchased of James McGerth		8	14	0
	"	1 waggon purchased of Wm Tanner	9-0-0			
	"	2 horses purchased of ditto	13-13-9	22	13	9
	"	1 horse purchased of Joseph Strable		6	14	0
	"	1 waggon purchased of J° Ramsheart		5	18	9
	"	1 waggon purchased of Christopher Sepra	5-0-0			
	"	2 horses purchased of ditto	6-2-0	11	2	0
	"	1 waggon bought of Samuel Crouse	6-0-0			
	"	2 horses bought of ditto	8-2-0	14	2	0
May 30th	"	1 horse bought of Matthew Black		5	0	0
June 9th	"	1 horse bought of Thomas Hooper		2	3	6
	"	1 waggon and gears bought of Joel Wallee (for 4 horses)		15	0	0
	Hire of my Negro Harry from 16th January to 28th April for driving a waggon, 103 days at 1/-			5	3	0

		£	s	d
	Hire of my Negro James from the 16th January to 30th September, 258 days at 1/- per day	12	18	0
	Hire of Negro Henable for driving a cart from 29th April to 25th May, 27 days at 1/- per day	1	7	0
		342	7	6
	To ballance due me as per contra brought foreward	208	15	8
	My own pay as Assistant Quarter Master General under your direction from 1st January 1779 to 1st August following, 212 days at [*blank*] per day			

C[r]

		£	s	d
1779	By cash received of you in Savannah, December 18th	42	9	4
1780	Ditto received 40 guineas @ 21/9 each, February 15th	43	10	0
1780	Ditto received at Cambden 30 guineas @ 21/9*d* each, August 28th	32	12	6
1781	Ditto received at Savannah, January 6th	15	0	0
	Ballance due me	208	15	8
		342	7	6

§ - §

2 - With Robert Cunningham

Cornwallis to Cunningham, 22nd November 1780 *101(5): Df*

By Charles, Earl Cornwallis, Lt General of His Majesty's Forces etc etc etc

To [Robert] Cunningham Esq

Greeting

By virtue of the powers and authorities in me vested, I, reposing especial trust and confidence in your courage, loyalty and good conduct, do hereby nominate, constitute and appoint you the said [Robert] Cunningham Esq to be Brigadier General of the Militia of the District of 96. You are therefore to take under your charge and command the militia of the said district and to form and array them in such manner and numbers as you shall see expedient for His Majesty's Service and the protection of this province. And you are hereby required to observe and obey all such orders as you shall from time to time receive from me, the commanding officer of His Majesty's forces within this province for the time being, or any other your superior officer according to the rules and discipline of war.

In pursuance of the trust hereby reposed in you —

Given under my hand and seal this 22nd of November 1780
and in the twenty first year of His Majesty's reign

[CORNWALLIS]

Cunningham to Cornwallis, 3rd December 1780[13] *4(275): ALS*

Saludy
3rd December 1780

The Rt Hon Earl Cornwallis, Lt General etc etc etc
Head Quarters, Wynnsburgh

My Lord

I am collecting the militia in order to dispose of them as your Lordship will direct, but they are very ill provided with guns and amonition and Colonel Cruger is not able to supply us. There appears one third of the men without guns. The rebels have collected above the ironworks between four and five hundred men and expects to be speedily reignforced with more from Burk County and the other side of the mountains. There is a considerable number of our men has returned from their captivity with Campbell and would gladly join us but is intirely naket for want of cloathing and blankets.

I am, my Lord, with real regard
Your Lordship's most obedient servant

ROB[T] CUNNINGHAM
Brigadier General of Militia

Cunningham to Cornwallis, 20th December 1780 *4(363): ALS*

Williams's Place
96 District
20th December 1780

Earl Cornwallis

My Lord

I am sorry to trouble your Lordship twice on one occasion but necessity compels me in my present critical situation.

---

13 Cornwallis to Cruger, 7th December, p 278, served as a reply.

Campbell from good authority has cross'd the mountains and is near Ramsour's Mill with (it is said) fifteen hundred men. If so many, many that are now a head of us will undoubtedly join him, and the scarcity of arms and amunition incapaciates me to give him that reception I would wish. The militia consider themselves neglected in equipment. While they remain so, they cannot be depended on.

I am with the greatest respect
Your Lordship's most obedient humble servant

ROB^{T} CUNNINGHAM
Brigadier General of Militia

Haldane to Cunningham, 25th December 1780 — *83(77): ACS*

Head Quarters
Wynnesborough
25th December 1780

Brigadier General Cunningham commanding the militia

Sir

I transmitted to Lt Colonel Allen on the 22nd Lord Cornwallis's directions respecting the militia, which were as follows: 'that the militia are to receive arms, ammunition and a blanket, provided that Brigadier General Cunningham will be responsible that they return them into store at Ninety Six or that they deliver them to the men that relieve them.'

I am, sir,
Your very humble and most obedient servant

HENRY HALDANE
Aid-de-camp

§ - §

3 - With others

Gray to Cornwallis, 5th November 1780 *4(98): ALS*

Post at Colonel Thompson's
5th November 1780

My Lord

I am credibly informed that Captain Oates[14] of my regiment was hanged lately on Peedee by the rebels. Your Lordship's generous interposition in favour of Colonel Cassils and myself, when prisoners in their hands, I shall ever remember with gratitude, and being convinced that your Lordship wishes to extend your influence and protection to all His Majesty's subjects indiscriminately who adhere to their duty, I beg leave to address you on this subject.

This province, having revolted and been conquered by His Majesty's arms, has again become a British province, and the inhabitants British subjects. In the preamble to an Act of the rebel Assembly of this province passed in 1777, it was observed that protection and allegiance were reciprocal duties, that, the British Government being overturned and the people owing the protection of their lives and properties to the Constitution then established, their allegiance was transferred from the former to the latter, and therefore they were required to take an oath of fidelity to the Government at that time in force. If this position is well founded or warranted by the law of nations, the most inveterate rebel will hardly deny its operating in full force in favour of the British Government when once re-established. Indeed they have established a precedent on a similar occasion which sets the matter in the clearest point of view, the State of South Carolina having uniformly treated the Georgians who fell into their hands after the reduction of that country as prisoners of war and exchanged them as such. Their deviating from this conduct lately I have reason to believe proceeds from General Harrington, who treated Colonel Cassils, myself and the other gentlemen at that time in confinement with us as State prisoners and even confessed to us that General Gates would have treated us as prisoners of war had it not been for the reasons he himself had suggested to him. But from whatever quarter this conduct may proceed, so repugnant to the practice of civilized nations and hostile to the rights of humanity, I flatter myself your Lordship may be able to put a stop to it, if avowed by the rebel Governments, as the number of prisoners in your hands leaves them exposed to retaliation. If they continue this outrage it will be productive of the worst effects. The loyal part of the people who have hitherto withstood the general delusion of their countrymen will lose all confidence if they find themselves doomed to the halter when captives whilst the rebels in the same condition are treated by the humanity of the British nation as prisoners of war and foreign enemies.

---

[14] Of Edward Oates little is known besides what is revealed in these Papers. His estate would be confiscated by the revolutionary authorities in South Carolina, but part given to his widow, Elizabeth. (Draper, *King's Mountain*, 340n, 607; Sabine, *Biographical Sketches*, ii, 121)

Captain Oates's fate is the more to be regretted as he possessed great influence over the militia on the frontiers where he resided. The use he made of it, when General Gates entered South Carolina, was so remarkable that a detachment of the rebels from King's Tree was sent against him, whom he attacked and dispersed. When Major Wemyss was at the Long Bluff, he brought in a party of the militia from Little Peedee, was made a prisoner upon his return and ignominiously put to death. Several others have met with the same fate, while others have been subjected to rigorous corporal punishments.

I am with the greatest respect, my Lord,
Your Lordship's most obedient most humble servant

ROBERT GRAY
Colonel of Cheraw militia

Address of the militia of Ninety Six, undated[15] *4(74): DS*

To his Exelencey Hon Earl Cornwallis
Commander in Chief of His Majesty's forces in the Southern Departments

The humble remonstrance of the militia of Ninety Six Destrict humbley sheweth that in the unhappy strugle be[t]ween Great Britain and her American colonies many of His Majesty's subjects have been killed and maimed in His Majesty's service and many taken prisoners, in consequence of which there familys is reduced to the most reched condition, and as the legislature of this province under the Old Constitution hath made provision for such destressed persons, we hope you will take the case of such as is above mentioned into your consideration and grant such aditional relief as their unhapy condition may require.

We crave leave to represant to your Exelencey that the militia of this cuntrey have ben very much destressed by the rebels during their administration, by which they ware much impoverished, and since the reduction of Charles Town they manfully suppressed rebelion in the uper parts of this province, hopeing that suckcess of His Majesty's arms would soon restore us to peace and good order, but as the war is likely to continue, we find that it is out of our power to suppoart our selves and familys any longer unless some provision is made for officers and soldiers. We also hope that the disobidient, both officers and soldiers, may be subject to the same penaltys as was inflicted by the Old Constitution under they King. We also hope that you'l appoint officers as was under the Old Constitution, viz, a colonel, lt colonel and major, and cause that the militia be divided into three divisions who may serve alternately and two months at a time.

We would also beg leave to solicit your Excellencey to use your indeavours for an immediate exchange of our brethern and fellow subjects who unfortunately have or may hereafter fall into the hands of the rebels in time of action.

---

15 The address was delivered by Henry O'Neaill with Kirkland's letter of 6th November, p 379.

And further we beg leave to recomend to your consideration the erection of a garison near the iron works, as we conceive it would shelter the suffering loyalists from the shocking ravages of those rascall banditti whose greatest mercies are bloody cruelties.

We also crave leave to represent to your Excellencey that it's necessary for the publick safety that the militia of this destrict should be commanded by some person that may superintend the whole militia of the said destrict. The person that we crave leave to represent to your Excellencey is Colonel Mosses Kirkland.

P CUNINGHAM	JACOB ADAM, Captain	H RODGERS, Captain Militia
HENRY O'NEAILL	JOHN NABOURS, Captain	WILLIAM MELTON, Captain Lieutenant
DAVID REES, Captain	COLBERT ANDERSON, Captain	JN^O BROWN, Captain
JAMES GIBBS, Captain	HECTOR DICKIE, Lieutenant	CH^R NEELLY, Captain
BARTON HARRIS, Captain	WILLIAM GRIFFIN, Captain	THOMAS GOODE, Captain Lieutenant
	RICH^D JONES, Captain Lieutenant	

Cornwallis to petitioners, 8th November 1780 — *82(10): C*

Wynnesborough
November 8th 1780

To the officers of the militia
who signed the address presented to me by Captain Henry O'Neal

Gentlemen

I received an address, signed by several officers of the militia of the District of Ninety Six, by the hands of Captain Henry O'Neal. Most of the proposals contained in it appear to me perfectly reasonable and proper. I shall not fail to pay the most serious attention to them and hope in a few days to send satisfactory answers to each of them. I see the necessity that the officers and soldiers when on duty should receive some fixed pay and can have no objection to the militia being regulated according to the Old Constitution of the province.

I am, gentlemen,
Your most obedient and most humble servant

CORNWALLIS

Coleman to Cornwallis, 21st November 1780 *4(170): ALS*

November 21st 1780

Earl Cornwallis

I desier to inform your Lordship that on this day I parted with Coronel Tarelton on Tyger River, where he the day before fought Sumter's Brigade of rebels, ho he disperst. Coronel Tarlton retreated aboubt a [mile?], which gave the rebels an opertunety of returning and carry'd of their did and wound[ed], 'tho I saw som ded and som wounded. The General Sumter is sayd to be mortaly wounded. I also would wish to inform you that on the forth instant the rebels tuck me prisener and treated me in the most unhumanist maner they could whilst[16] the 20th, on which the Ganaral giv me a sort of parol, which I send to you[17] to let your Lordship see the form thereof, which I exsepted of with the forfit of all that Ey had. I have no more to rite but that I would gladly com before you but I am wounded and very unwell. God save the King.

All from your most humbel

CHRIS COLEMAN[18]

Mills to Cornwallis, 28th November 1780 *4(229): ALS*

Charles Town
28th November 1780

My Lord

Agreable to your Lordship's orders I proceeded on the expedition commanded by Major Weymss down Black and up Peedee Rivers to the Cheraws, where the Major halted for ten or twelve days to assist in collecting and forming my regiment so as to enable me to keep the peace and check the rebells in that part of the country. This we found impossible to be effected from the general spirit of rebellion that prevailed in that quarter from its vicinity to

---

16 *whilst*: until.

17 *parol..*: not extant.

18 Christopher Coleman had migrated in 1768 from Lunenburg or Mecklenburg County, Virginia, to the Back Country of South Carolina, where he settled on Mill Creek, a branch of the Pacolet River, and established 'Christy's Tavern'. He was presumably still living there in February 1779, when the Judicial District of Ninety Six was created and he was named in the grand jury list for the Spartan division. Sometime later he left the Back Country to enter the South Carolina Royalist Regiment as major and by April 1780 was receiving half pay in Savannah. At that time he was sent into the Back Country to drum up support for the Crown, and like other officers in the regiment, he resigned his commission, being succeeded on 10th August by Thomas Fraser. He may have died in Charlestown in December 1781. His sister Frances was married to Zacharias Gibbs. (Trisha Carden, 'Descendants of Thomas Draper 1690-1735' (Internet, 20th December 2005); Clark, *Loyalists in the Southern Campaign*, i, 47, 545; WO 65/164(40) (National Archives, Kew))

North Carolina, where Mr Harrington had a number of rebell militia collected. In this situation the Major recommended to me to move my family and the few effects the rebels left me to the southward. And having captured a number of Negroes from those concerned in the second rebellion on his march, he ordered them to the southward for greater security and, seeing the losses I had sustained by the burning of two saw mills, a grist mill, all my buildings, and by the rebels who carryed off from me fifty seven Negroes, thought proper to give me a hundred of those taken to indemnify me. A copy of his certificate I beg leave to inclose to your Lordship. On my return from Peedee with the troops I came to Camden and obtained a licence to stay at Laurens' plantation on Santee with my distressed family. There I was taken ill and remained about four weeks very sick, when I was routed by a party of Marion's and came to Charlestown and there reported those hundred Negroes, with 160 others that I had also under my care for your Lordship's disposal, to Mr Cruden, whom I observed your Lordship had appointed Commissioner for taking into his custody rebel property. He then informed me he had no interference with the estates of persons concerned in the second rebellion, but since the Commandant has thought proper to order all those Negroes to be detained, I apprehend, untill your Lordship's pleasure shall be known respecting them.

I have therefore taken the liberty of giving your Lordship this trouble, requesting your Lordship will be pleased to confirm Major Weymss' grant of the Negroes to me for the many very heavy losses I have sustained for my attachment to His Majesty's Government, or for such other directions as your Lordship shall think proper to give on this occasion.

I am with the greatest respect, my Lord,
Your Lordship's most obedient humble servant

W^M^ H^Y^ MILLS

Enclosure
Certificate to appropriate slaves, 26th September 1780 — *4(231): C*

Cheraws
September 26th 1780

This is to certify that I have given to Colonel Mills of the Cheraw militia one hundred Negroes (rebel property) to indemnify him for the losses he has sustained by his attachment to His Majesty's Government.

J WEMYSS
Major commanding 63rd Regiment

Haldane to Fisher, 27th December 1780 *83(83): ACS*

Head Quarters
Wynnesborough
27th December 1780

Colonel Fisher commanding the militia in the Orangeburg District

Sir

Lord Cornwallis desires you will be pleased to order cattle to be collected in your district and drove to Fryday's Ferry in the Congarees.

I am, sir,
Your very humble and obedient servant

HENRY HALDANE
Aid-de-camp

§ - §

CHAPTER 36

Correspondence with the enemy, intercepted papers, and intelligence

---

1 - Correspondence with the enemy

Clark to Cornwallis, 4th November 1780 *4(20): ALS*

4th November 1780

To the Hon Earl Cornwallis,
Commander in Chief of the British forces in South Carolina

By Major Hampton)
Lieutenant Awbrey[1])

By various complaints from the inhabitants of North and South Carolina daily sitting forth, I am induced to write by Major Hampton[2], who is the bearer, as plundering have daily been practised by the soldiars of the Brittish and American troops and individuals been robed and much destresed who have not been active in this present war.

And as armies marches through the country and soldiars from the different corps much destressed the good inhabitants thereof, it is well known that plundering or destresing of

---

[1] How one of the Hamptons and one of the Aubreys, both South Carolinians, came to be carrying a letter from Elijah Clark, a Georgian, is uncertain, but the real purpose of both would have been to spy out the post at Winnsborough. (For the Hamptons, see p 75, note 27; for the Aubreys, see Moss, *SC Patriots*, 31-2)

[2] After 'Major Hampton' the words 'and Lieutenant Awbrey' are superscribed.

individuals of private property will in no measure support a war and will in the greatest measure lay the officers under censure. I shall indeavour to put a stop to such pernicious practices and have issued the most strenious orders imaginable to prevent the same.

I make no doubt the Brittish officers commanding the different corps will take such measures to prevent the like practices as they in there wisdom shall think fit. An answer to this flag we hope to receive by the bearer, Major Hampton, and Lieutenant Awbrey, whom we expect will have permission to pass and repass without fire armes.

From, sir,
Your humble servant

E CLARK
Colonel Commandant

Cornwallis to Smallwood, 10th November 1780[3] *91(9): ADfS*

Camp
November 10th 1780

Brigadier General Smallwood

Sir

Your letter of the 24th of last month[4] by some mistake was not forwarded to me for several days. I understand that some prisoners who were on their march from Camden to Charlestown made their escape, but have not yet had an opportunity of informing myself whether those mentioned in your letter were of the number. If they are still in our possession, I will agree to exchange them for persons in similar situation and circumstances. I must now observe that the cruelty exercised on the prisoners taken under Major Ferguson is shocking to humanity, and the hanging poor old Colonel Mills, who was always a fair and open enemy to your cause, was an act of the most savage barbarity. It has also been reported to me that Captain Oates of Colonel Gray's militia, who was taken near the Pedee, was lately put to death without any crime being laid to his charge. From the character which I have heard of you, sir, I cannot suppose that you can approve of these most cruel murders, but I hope you will see the necessity of interposing your authority to stop this bloody scene, which must oblige me in justice to the suffering loyalists to retaliate on the unfortunate persons now in my power.

I am not conscious that any persons have hitherto been executed by us unless for bearing arms after having given a military parole to remain quietly at home or for enrolling themselves voluntarily in our militia, receiving arms and amunition from the King's Store and

---

3 An extract from this letter is published in Ross ed, *Cornwallis Correspondence*, i, 67.

4 *Your letter..*: not extant.

taking the first opportunity of joining our enemies. The only persons who were hanged at Camden after the actions of the 16th and 18th, except some deserters from our army, were two or three of the latter description who were pick'd out from about thirty convicted for the like offence on account of some particularly aggravating circumstances which attended their case.

I would willingly exchange any of the North or South Carolina militia who may be prisoners with us for those who were taken on King's Mountain.

I am, sir,
Your most obedient and most humble servant

CORNWALLIS

Cornwallis to Sumter, 15th November 1780 *91(11): ADfS*

November 15th 1780

General Sumpter

Sir

I sent on the 12th instant two dragoons to Lands Ford on Catawba River with a flag of truce and an answer to a letter which I received from General Smallwood. On their return they reported to me that a detachment of your corps surrounded White's Mill, where they had stopped to get some refreshment for themselves and their horses, and by force took away their horses, saddles, pistols and blankets. As I am convinced that this outrage must meet with your highest disapprobation, it is needless for me to make any comments upon it, and I can have no doubt but you will give immediate orders for the restitution of the horses and effects and the punishment of the offenders.

I am, sir,
Your most obedient and most humble servant

CORNWALLIS

Gates to Cornwallis, 24th November 1780 *4(200): LS*

Camp
24th November 1780

The Rt Hon Earl Cornwallis

My Lord

Captain Dorsey[5] of the artillery, who was so badly wounded in the action near Camden, had your Lordship's permission to come from thence upon parole for four months. His knee is now so contracted that he can make no manner of use of his left leg, and it is very doubtful if he will ever be able to walk upon it. He requests I would solicit your Lordship to extend his parole until his wound is so recovered as that he can be able with convenience to obey your Lordship's summons, or until he is regularly exchanged.

I am your Lordship's most obedient humble servant

HORATIO GATES

PS

The letter for your Lordship from Captain D' Peyster from King's Mountain came to my hands only this morning.

Enclosure
De Peyster to Cornwallis, 19th November 1780 *4(163): ALS*

Salem, Surry County
November 19th 1780

Lord Cornwallis

My Lord

I have long wished for an opertunity to acquaint your Lordship with the particulars of the action near King's Hill but imagine those gentlemen that left me have done it. I make no doubt they have before this endeavoured to make an apology to your Lordship for their

---

5 In the Battle of Camden Captain Richard Dorsey (?-1799) had commanded the 1st Maryland Continental Artillery Company, which formed part of the 1st Continental Artillery Regiment. He would be permitted by Cornwallis to remain on parole and would repair to Maryland to convalesce. Unfortunately, he would be so disabled as to be unable to follow any occupation after the war, in consequence of which the General Assembly of Maryland at its November session in 1791 authorised the Governor and his successors to make him regular payments of half the pay which he received in the Continental service. (Heitman, *Historical Register*, 201; W T R Saffell, *Records of the Revolutionary War containing the Military and Financial Correspondence of Distinguished Officers* (Kessinger Publishing, 2005), 231; *Laws of Maryland*, cciv, 630)

conduct in leaving this after they had given their word to remain in the quarters they were directed to by Colonel Campbel[6]. The only one they can offer is the ill treatment recieved from some of the militia, which was truly such as no gentlemen ever experienced before. The particulars, I suppose, they have acquainted your Lordship, tho some of the militia endeavoured to make things as agreable as circumstances would admit of. The melancholy situation the officers and soldiers are in they have surely related to your Lordship. This, together with being detachments from different corps and the fatigues they have already undergone, some of whom have been upwards of fourteen months in the field and most ardently wish for an opertunity again, makes us hope your Lordship will be pleased to think of us. As I have every reason to believe your Lordship is acquainted with our present circumstances, shall defer mentioning particulars. Since I wrote your Lordship the 11th of October[7], upwards of twenty soldiers have made their escape.

I wrote to General Gates the 3rd instant, acquainting him with our situation, and requested paroles to Charles Town or wherever the British army were that we might be able to provide ourselves with necessaries. This day was handed me his answer, with orders to march with Captain Wood[8] to Hills Borough, where I should recieve every reasonable indulgence, at the same time acquainting me I might write to your Lordship, the great necessity of which will, I hope, sufficiently apologize for this.

I have the honour to be, my Lord,
Your Lordship's most obedient humble servant

A DE PEYSTER
Captain, King's American Regiment

Cornwallis to Gates, 1st December 1780[9] — *91(13): ADfS*

December 1st 1780

Major General Gates

Sir

In consequence of your application for Captain Dorsey I consent to his remaining at home on parole untill he is recalled by the Commanding Officer of His Majesty's forces in the Southern District or the Commandant of Charlestown.

---

6 *an apology..*: see p 459 for the representations of Stevenson and Taylor.

7 *Since I wrote..*: see vol II, p 166.

8 Perhaps Samuel Wood, who was a captain in the Salisbury District of the North Carolina revolutionary militia and had taken part in the Battle of King's Mountain. (Heitman, *Historical Register*, 603; Hay ed, *Soldiers from NC*, 406)

9 An extract comprising the final paragraph is published in Ross ed, *Cornwallis Correspondence*, i, 71.

I sent a letter dated the 10th of last month to General Smallwood in answer to one which I received from him. Whilst two dragoons who carried the flag were refreshing themselves at White's Mill on Fishing Creek, the house was surrounded by some of General Sumpter's men, who took away their horses, saddles and pistols. I wrote to General Sumpter to complain of this violation of the flag and to desire the restitution of the horses etc, but received no answer.

I think it proper to represent to you that the officers and men taken at King's Mountain were treated with an inhumanity scarcely credible.[10] I feel myself under the disagreeable necessity of making severe retaliation for those unhappy men who were so cruelly and unjustly put to death at Gilbert Town.

I am, sir,
Your most obedient humble servant

CORNWALLIS

Smallwood to Cornwallis, 8th December 1780 — *91(19): LS*

Camp
December 8th 1780

Earl Cornwallis

Sir

Upon the receipt of your letter dated the 10th ultimo it was immediately transmitted per express to General Gates, who at that time had reached Salisbury, from an impression that the subject matter therein would be more properly addressed to him as the Commander in Chief of the American forces in the Southern Department, at the same time requesting his answer, which he promised to forward; but having just understood he declined this, I think proper to acquaint your Lordship that I shall take the earliest opportunity of laying your letter before General Green, who has succeeded to the command in this department, viewing myself not authorized to accede to your propositions respecting an exchange of the prisoners taken on King's Mountain for those of the North and South Carolina militia in your possession.

The prisoners I solicited a partial exchange for had made their escape as you suggested.

I was a stranger to the abuses you complain of exercised on the prisoners taken under Major Ferguson. These were committed by persons in the capacity of volunteers not immediately subject to my command but amenable to the States, nor have I heard upon what principle they acted. Therefore, was I authorized, I could not with propriety reply before this matter was properly investigated, but this will come before, and be more properly accounted

10 The following passage is deleted: 'The officers particularly mention the brutal insults of Colonel Cleveland. Should this behaviour be suffered to continue, you must easily foresee the consequences.'

for by, the Commander in Chief of this department. I ever have, and hope I ever shall, make it my particular duty to discountenance acts of inhumanity, which can have no other tendency on either side of the question but inflaming the parties and sullying the reputation of an officer.

I am, sir,
Your most obedient and very humble servant

W SMALLWOOD

Greene to Cornwallis, 17th December 1780[11] *91(21): ALS*

December 17th 1780

The Rt Hon the Earl Cornwallis

My Lord

Your Lordship's letter of the 1st instant addressed to Major General Gates I had the honor to receive, he having left this department before it came to hand.

I have written General Sumter respecting the violation of the flag mentioned in your letter and am persuaded he will take such measures as will be satisfactory to your Lordship, as well for restoring the honors of the flag in the present instance as for preserving it inviolate in future.

I am too much a stranger to the transactions at Gilbert Town to reply fully on that subject. They must have been committed before my arrival in this department and by persons under the character of volunteers who were independant of the army. However, if there was any thing done in that affair contrary to the principles of humanity and the law of nations and for which they had not the conduct of your army as a precedent, I shall be ever ready to testify my disapprobation of it. The first example was furnished on your part, as appears by the list of unhappy sufferers which I have the honor to enclose, and it might have been expected that the friends of the unfortunate would follow it. Punishing capitally for a breach of military parole is a severity that the principles of modern war will not authorize, unless the inhabitants are to be treated as a conquered people and subject to all the rigor of military government.

The feelings of mankind will forever decide when the rights of humanity are invaded. I leave them to judge of the nature and tendency of your Lordship's orders to Lt Colonel Balfour after the action near Camden[12], of Lord Rawdon's proclamation[13], and of Lt

---

[11] Published without the enclosure in *The Greene Papers*, vi, 591.

[12] See p 18, note 9.

[13] See p 18.

Colonel Tarlton's conduct in laying waste the country and in distressing the inhabitants[14], who were taught to expect protection and security if they observed but a neutrality.

Sending the inhabitants of Charles Town to St Augustine contrary to the articles of capitulation is a violation which I have also to represent and which I hope your Lordship will think yourself bound to redress.

It is my wish to soften the rigors of war as much as possible, and it shall be my study to lessen the sufferings of the unfortunate on either side. For this purpose I should be happy to promote an exchange of prisoners on just and equal principles and, where exchanges cannot immediately take place, to grant paroles to the officers in captivity.

I am, my Lord,
Your Lordship's most obedient humble servant

NATH GREENE

Enclosure — *91(21): D*

A List of Persons executed by the Enemy

William Stroud and M Dowel	Executed near Rocky Mount without a trial by order of Lt Colonel Turnbull
Rich[d] Tucker Sam[l] Andrews and John Miles	Hanged in Camden by order of Lord Cornwallis
Mr Johnston	Hanged since the action of Blackstocks by Lt Colonel Tarlton
Adam Cusack	Hanged at Pedee by one Colonel Mills
About thirty persons	Hanged at Augusta by Colonel Brown

[14] *Tarlton's conduct..*: during his incursion east of the Wateree in early November.

Cornwallis to Greene, 27th December 1780[15] *91(27): ADfS*

Wynnesborough
December 27th 1780

Major General Green

Sir

I received your letter of the 17th of this month. I shall not enter into a detail of facts, which can avail but little unless proof could be brought of their authenticity. If truth could be heard, the feelings of mankind would decide that in the southern provinces the rights of humanity have been invaded by the enemies of Great Britain. Whether they were volunteers in cruelty is not for me to determine, nor should I have thought it necessary to have said any thing further on the subject had you not alluded to an order of mine to Lt Colonel Balfour, which I suppose to be the same which General Washington transmitted to Sir Henry Clinton. The order was directed to Lt Colonel Cruger and not to Lt Colonel Balfour, who was at that time Commandant of Charlestown. That error, however, is immaterial, but the order itself is essentially altered, which you will see by the authentic copy which I inclose to you. If you have inserted the forged copy in any of your publications, I trust to your candour to publish that which I now send.

I can with truth assure you, sir, that no man abhors acts of cruelty more than myself or would more reluctantly adopt measures of severity. The proving to the suffering loyalists that I am in earnest to protect them, and to retaliate on their inhuman oppressors, is a duty which I owe to my country.

You have been greatly misinformed if you have ever been told that any inhabitant of this country has been punished by us for observing a neutrality, but you will find instances enough of the most inhuman persecution, and even tortures, inflicted on those who refuse to take arms on your side.

I have only to add that I shall observe the same rule of conduct which you do in the treatment of the officers and soldiers of the army, the militia, and the inhabitants of the country.

I am, sir,
Your most obedient and most humble servant

CORNWALLIS

---

15 Published in *The Greene Papers*, vii, 5. There are no differences.

de Cambray to Cornwallis, 6th January 1781 *71(17): ALS*

Haddrel's point
6 janvier 1781

My lord Earl Cornwallis

My lord

J'ai eu l'honneur de vous écrire il y a environ six semaines. N'ayant point reçu de reponse, j'ai tout lieu de croire que ma lettre a été égarée. Ainsi je ne crains point de vous importuner par une nouvelle lettre, d'autant plus que ma situation est si pressante qu'elle ne me permettra de repos que lorsque j'aurai obtenu de vos bontés ce que j'en attends.

La situation de ma santé, my lord, l'épuisement de mes finances et l'ignorance ou je suis de mes affaires, n'ayant pas pu recevoir une seule lettre de mes amis depuis que je suis prisonnier, sont les motifs que je mets en avant pour que vous me soyés favorable.

Ma parole d'ailleurs est pour la ville de Charlestown, mais je ne puis en jouir. Je suis retenu par vos ordres à Haddril's point.

Je vous aurai la plus grande obligation si vous m'accordés de changer ma parole contre un'autre qui s'étende jusqu'à Philadelphie, ou bien si vous m'accordés une permission limitée d'y faire un voyage pour me procurer ce qu'il me faut pour supporter une plus longue captivité.

Vous mettrés, my lord, le comble à vos bontés si vous me permettés en mème tems de m'en aller par mer dans quelqu'un des flags qui sont arrivés dernierement, cette voye étant la seule qui puisse convenir à l'état épuisé de mes finances.

Je suis avec un profond respect, my lord,
Votre très humble et tres obéissant serviteur

LE CHEVALIER DE CAMBRAY
Lt Colonel of Engeneers

TRANSLATION

Haddrell's Point
6th January 1781

Earl Cornwallis

My Lord

I had the honor of writing to you some six weeks ago.[16] Having received no reply, I have every reason to suppose my letter miscarried. Therefore I have no fear of troubling you with a further letter, all the more so as my situation is so pressing that it will allow me no rest until I receive by your kindness what I expect.

The state of my health, my Lord, the drain on my finances and my ignorance of my affairs, having been unable to receive a single letter from my friends since becoming a prisoner, are the reasons I advance for your treating me favourably.

My parole, by the bye, extends to Charlestown, but I cannot enjoy it. I am confined by your orders to Haddrell's Point.

I shall be under the greatest obligation to you if you will permit me to exchange my parole for another extending to Philadelphia, or if you will otherwise grant me restricted permission to travel there to procure what I need to sustain a longer period of captivity.

You will consummate your kindness to me, my Lord, if you will permit me at the same time to go by sea in one of the flag vessels which have arrived recently, this being the only way which may answer the exhausted state of my finances.

I am with profound respect, my Lord,
Your very humble and very obedient servant

LE CHEVALIER DE CAMBRAY
Lt Colonel of Engineers

§ - §

16 The letter is not extant.

2 - Intercepted papers

Davidson to Locke, 30th October 1780 — *3(320): LS*

Camp, New Providence
October 30th 1780

General Matthew Lock[17]
Rowan County

Sir

As a considerable quantity of property was taken from the Tories during last summer, you will much oblige me by informing me what was done at last session of Assembly respecting such property, as I have never had any thing but verbal accounts of what was done concerning that matter. This application is made in consequence of a quantity of the above property being taken under colour of military, which I would now wish to be delivered to that of the civil.

Sir, your most obedient servant

W[M] L DAVIDSON

PS

Saturday morning the enemy were at Lee's plantation, continuing their retreat. Their destination, whether to Camden, Charlestown or 96, not known. They appeared to be in distress from want of provision and their force daily weakening.

---

[17] Born in the north of Ireland, Matthew Locke (1730-1801) migrated to Rowan County, North Carolina, where he engaged in conveyance by waggon. A staunch revolutionary like his fellow Scotch-Irish immigrants, he became a member of his county's committee of safety in 1774 and served in the Provincial Congress in 1775-6. Since 1777 he had been a member of the lower house of the North Carolina revolutionary legislature and would continue to sit in one house or the other until 1792. He then served in Congress from 1793 to 1799. Presently a brigadier general in the revolutionary militia, he had not played a material part in the war militarily nor would he do so. A planter and extensive landowner by the time of his death, he was interred at Thyatira Cemetery near Salisbury. (Joel D Treese and Dorthy J Countryman, *Biographical Directory of the United States Congress 1774-1996* (Cq Pr, 1996); Wheeler, *Reminiscences*, 399, 400)

Smallwood to Davie, 3rd November 1780 *4(18): ALS*

Camp
November 3rd 1780

Colonel Davie
Waxhaw

Dear Sir

Previous to the receipt of your favor of the first instant I had ordered down sixty men properly officered from General Davidson's command, and in compliance with your request detached yesterday another company from General Jones's brigade[18], and circumstances now induce me to believe that even this number will not be adequate fully to the execution of your instructions as the men imployed thereon must go in large parties and may require strong covering parties.

I have this morning received intelligence that the Tories of the districts in which your duty is comprized are now busily imployed in conveying away their property to Camden and that a large body of four hundred now lie at the Hanging Rock for the purpose of covering the parties removing the same. The intelligence comes pretty direct, though not to be certainly depended on, but as it is probable, and such a measure would be politic in them, I have thought proper to order down the light infantry with a party of rifle men, and the Continental cavalry, to destroy or disperse them as well as cover you whilst in the execution of your orders. If the Tories are really embodied and advanced for this purpose, this step is essentially necessary; and if otherways, it will give greater security to your parties and have a good effect in other respects, whilst the troops will be more benefited by such a tour than lying inactive in camp. General Morgan with this command will set off about the middle of the day. Pray, if you possibly can, engage one or two trusty persons properly adapted to the trust of going in to Camden to obtain a true account of their strength, situation, works and resources, and in like manner engage a trusty person or two well adapted to obtaining similar intelligence of the army under Lord Cornwallis and his views. To accomplish these views proper stages had better be established that information might be conveyed to you otherways than immediately by the person who obtains it, which might subject him to suspicion. Perhaps if a Tory or two could be gained over in whom dependance could be put upon

---

18 Born in what is now Halifax County, North Carolina, Allen Jones (1739-1807) was the son of an Attorney General of the province and is said to have been educated at Eton. Before the revolution he attained local prominence as Clerk of the Superior Court for Halifax District and as a Member for Northampton County in the Commons House of Assembly from 1773 to 1775. In 1771 he assisted Governor Tryon in the suppression of the Regulators. His contribution to the revolutionary cause was almost entirely at the political level. From 1774 to 1776 he represented Northampton County in the Provincial Congress, sat on many important committees, and was involved in framing North Carolina's revolutionary constitution. From 1777 to 1779 he sat in its Senate, and in 1779 and 1780 was a delegate to the Continental Congress. Soon, in 1781, he would be appointed to North Carolina's Council Extraordinary charged with the conduct of the war. Although in 1776 he was commissioned Brigadier General of Halifax District's revolutionary militia, a post which he would hold till the end of the war, he had made, and would continue to make, no material contribution to the revolutionary cause militarily. In later years he would remain prominently involved in political affairs and by 1790, as a large property owner, he would possess 177 slaves, the fourth largest slaveholding in North Carolina. He died at his seat, Mount Gallant, in Northampton County. (*DAB*)

promising a pardon and their being reinstated in their priviledges and possessions, they might become the most proper *instruments*, but this I shall leave intirely to your judgment, and am with sincere regard

Your obedient humble servant

W SMALLWOOD

Thorpe to Locke, 6th November 1780 — *4(51): ADS*

Specific Supplies for the Southern Army
Quota of North Carolina

To furnish against the first of January next:

3000 Barrels of beef
7000 Ditto of pork
2000 Ditto of flour
4000 Gallons rum or other spirits equivalent

To furnish on or before the first of March:

1000 Barrels of flour
2000 Gallons rum

Against the first of May:

2000 Barrels of flour
4000 Gallons rum
991 Bushels salt

Against the 15th July:

1000 Barrels of flour
11000 Gallons rum

10000 C:weight of beef to be delivered to the order of the Commissary General

---

NB

An accurate account ought to be kept of all the beeves, hogs, sheep etc taken either from Whig or Tory or at least the number of rations supplied by our State – which will all stand part of our quota and be charged to the Continent.

W^M THORPE[19] 6th November 1780

[*Endorsed*:]

Mathew Locke Esquire

Smallwood to Davie, 14th November 1780 *4(124): ALS*

Camp
November 14th 1780

Colonel Davie
Waxhaw Settlement

Favor'd by Major Moore

Dear Sir

Major Moore[20] with a detachment of near two hundred men I have ordered to join you this evening. Their detention has been owing to the bad weather. This reinforcement, I hope, will secure you 'till one more powerfull arrives, which you may expect as soon as the *weather* appears *settled*. At present I am apprehensive of more rain and the waters swelling much. I hear General Gates with the Continental troops was at Fyfer's on Sunday evening. This reinforcement will enable us to detach largely and accomplish all the objects in view, provided it meets with his approbation. This, as he is so near, it will be necessary for me to obtain before any enterprize is undertaken.

You have not as yet mentioned the quantity of forage and provision which you have procured. It will be necessary for me to know this in order to govern myself with respect to the number of troops and supplies to be ordered from this quarter. In your present situation

---

19 William Thorpe was a resident of Guilford County, apparently now connected with the North Carolina Commissariat General.

20 A major in Colonel William Moore's Granville County Regiment of the North Carolina revolutionary militia, Elijah Moore had marched with his men in mid September to augment the revolutionary forces in and around Charlotte. While on their march by way of Hillsborough and Salisbury a party had been detached to the Shallow Ford on the Yadkin but had arrived too late to take part in the defeat of the loyalists there. Now all at Charlotte, they would see service in the vicinity until mid December when their three-month tour of duty would expire. (Revolutionary pension application R 3767 made by Sowell Frazer of Stokes County, North Carolina, on 5th September 1832; Revolutionary pension application W 1763 made by Paul Haralson of Randolph County, Illinois, on 4th December 1832)

and circumstances I imagine you cannot extend your views towards the completion of your orders. Your strength will not admit of foraging so remote. It therefore may be necessary to secure what may lie more contiguous to your encampment 'till a larger force arrives. I have also ordered an officer and twelve horse, who came from Guilford, to join you. I recieved your letter inclosing Lord Cornwallis['s][21] with a flag. You will please give the earliest intimation of any intelligence respecting the enemy you may recieve at Wynsborough and Camden[22]. From those at the former place you have little to apprehend, and I have no doubt of your being sufficiently upon your guard against any attempts from the latter.

I remain with great regard
Your very obedient humble servant

W SMALLWOOD

NB

Please forward the inclosed letter[23] to the gentlemen who are at or near Lands Ford.

§ - §

3 - Intelligence

Unaddressed, unsigned and undated *4(70): D*

S Liu^t John Hutton of Allon corps to have leave to joyn Kirkland corps.[24] The rebles is svorn in North Carolina to meet on the Cotoba River 13th November 1780. The sceme is to atack 96, plunder Augsta.

[*Endorsed*:]

Last Satarday and Sunder 3 or 4 hundred rebels lay at Capt Gibbs's on Fair Forrest under the command of Clark, Thomas, Brandon, Candler, Hampton, Few, Col^os.

---

21 *Lord Cornwallis['s]*: of 10th November, p 401.

22 *any intelligence..*: Smallwood means any intelligence respecting the enemy at Winnsborough and Camden that Davie may receive.

23 *the inclosed letter*: not extant

24 See Kirkland to Cornwallis, 6th November, p 379.

George to Cornwallis, 11th December 1780 *66(33): ALS*

Fork of Broad and Tyger Rivers
December 11th 1780

To General Earl Cornwallace
Commander in Chief of the Southern Posts

May it please your Excellency

With the utmost humility I have undertaken to write a few lines to inform your Excellency of some of the menovers of the rebels. I had put my self to the trouble of fixing of three waggons and teams to set of[25] to Charles Town, had got some of my load in, and was about to finish loading the said waggons on Thursday last, when there came up a number of arm'd rebels, seized all the horses they cou'd find that was fit for service, drive of two of the waggons and plunder'd me of many other things, took me a prisoner, and carryed me over Broad River at Love's Ford and from there up to the mouth of Bullocks Creek, in order to send the waggons over Broad River to where the rebel Colonel Brandon lay with, as they told me, about two hundred or two hundred and fifty men, who lay at one John Cunningham's in the fork between Brod and Packolate Rivers. The corn, as I understood by the company, was to be carried to Barrows Mill on the head of Turky Creek, where the rebels are about to build store houses and a fort. They have waggon'd of[26] a bundance of the subjects' corn about Love's Ford and for some distance above and below Love's Ford on Broad River. The rebels, if they are let alone a little longer, will distress all the subjects in this part of the country. We have no commanding officer in the rebel Colonel Brandon reigement since the defeat of our worthy friend, Colonel Ferguson. Major Plummer was wounded and taken prisoner at that defeat. We are in a most melancholy situation, there being so many rebels gone of out of the fork of Tyger and Enoree Rivers and of Indian Creek below the Enoree River, and they are often a-comeing in to their familyes, and when they go of, they distress us very much. While they had me a prisoner among them, they were inform'd that their wives was to be sent of out of this province. I heard many of them swearing, if their wives was sent of, they wou'd come in and carry of the subjects' wives and children. They say that General Morgan with his rifle men have got to Barrows Mill and join'd Colonel Lacy with about five hundred men. The truth of it I no not. General Green is come to Charlotte to take General Gateses place. I cou'd not find out the number of men he has brought with him. I was told that about twelve hundred of his men had got to Charlott last Friday and the hole was expected in last Saturday. I heard some of the rebel officers teling some of the others that Colonel Campbell over the mountains and all the mountain men was to join them at Barrows Mill about the seventeenth day of this instant. I fear they will ruin me totally soon if there is not a stop put to their coming in among us, and I am afraid to offer to move away, for if I was to offer to move of and the rebels was to *hear of it, they wou'd follow me* and take of every thing I possess. Brandon and Lacy might be very easily drive of. Brandon's men is always scouting about. The bearer is very uneasy awaiting for me. I hope your Excellency will excuse hast.

---

25 *of*: 'off', as elsewhere in the letter.

26 *waggon'd of*: taken off by waggon.

I am your Earlship most obedient humble servant

DAVID GEORGE[27]

George to Cornwallis, 30th December 1780 *66(44): ALS*

North side of Tyger River
December 30th 1780

To General Earl Cornwallace
Commander in Chief of His Majesty's forces in the Southern Districts

Noble Earl

My wife's sister last night came to my house out of strong rebel settlement up at Prince's Fort[28]. By her I have heard the design and intention of the rebels as far as their captains has any knowlege. As she came, she informs me that she got into some of their camps on the south side of Packolate River at one Grimeses Mill about ten or twelve miles below the iron works on Loson's Fork. She understood from Captain Francis Prince's and Henry Prince's wives that they were a-waiting for Colonel Morgan and Colonel Washington, who was on their march in order to join them; Morgan with five or six hundred light horse had cross'd Broad River at Smith's Ford a few days a goe; and Washington with their arteliry and footmen was to cross Broad River at the same ford yesterday; that they intended to march against Ninty Six and Augusta. They say they will have three thousand men to go against them places, but I have alwayes observed that they alwayes make the most of there men......

If it was consistant with your Excellency's wisdom and policy to have about five or six hundred militia men and some of the British troops stationed near Lyles Ford on Broad River and to keep out spyes in order to find out the movements of the rebels, it is possible it might answer a very good end.

---

27 Having migrated from Hanover County, Virginia, David George had settled in 1774 on a 2,200-acre plantation abutting the south side of Brown's Creek, a western tributary of the Broad River between the Tyger and Pacolet Rivers. Nearby was a plantation owned by Zacharias Gibbs. Towards the close of 1775 David took part in the uprising of Back Country loyalists, was captured during the Snow Campaign, and was imprisoned at Charlestown for several months. Perhaps soon to be driven from his property, he may have been the David George who in late February 1781 was recorded as having enlisted as a private in the South Carolina Royalist Regiment. (Phil Norfleet, 'Biographical Sketches of David George, John Mayfield, and Charles Sims', South Carolina Loyalists and Rebels (Internet, 4th January 2006); Clark, *Loyalists in the Southern Campaign*, i, 2, 3, 5, 16)

28 Prince's Fort lay seven miles north-west of the later town of Spartanburg upon a commanding height near the head of a branch of North Tyger River. In the early settlement of the Back Country, some twenty years before, it had served as a place of neighbourhood resort in time of danger from native Americans. Named after William Prince, a Virginian who had settled nearby, it was circular, built of heavy timbers from twelve to fifteen feet high, and surrounded by a ditch, the dirt from which was thrown against the wall. In front it was secured by an abatis. Briefly during the summer of 1780 it was occupied by James Dunlap and a body of royal militia but it had to be abandoned in mid July. As asserted later in David George's letter, all members of the Prince family were committed revolutionaries. Francis had already been supplying gunpowder to the enemy and he would possibly soon join Henry and William in serving in the revolutionary militia. (Draper, *King's Mountain*, 80, 501; Landrum, *History of Upper SC*, 31; Moss, *SC Patriots*, 788-9)

I have been inform'd that one William Love[29] has come from the rebels and has or wants to join your Excellencyes camps. I fear he is a traitor, for on the elevinth day of November last he was at my house with a number of rebels who plunder'd me of three good horse creatures, about fifteen gallons of rum and about six gallons of French brandy, some sugar and many other things. The said Love was very active in takeing of the sugar and rum, which did not appear to be good behaviour in a subject.

The woman informs me that one William Prince brought up a waggon load of salt, rum etc a few dayes before Christmas. I am at a loss to no how he cou'd procure a pass to go to town when every one of the Princes has been strong rebels from the first commencement of the rebellion. They must have forg'd a pass from a subject, and I am of the opinion that he surely got his load from Wade Hamton at the Congarees.

I humbly implore your Excellency to give orders to have a number of passes printed and put into the hands of the field officers and justices of the peace and not suffer any man, woman, boy or girl to ride any distance, unless they can procure a pass, under the penalty of being sent to jale, which wou'd prevent the rebels from giting so much intiligence from the rebels that is at home, which I fear are as much predejudice to the subjects as those that are gone of. Excuse hast.

I am your Earlship's most obedient humble servant

DAVID GEORGE

George to Cornwallis, 30th December 1780 — *66(46): ALS*

December 30th day 1780

To General Earl Cornwallace
Commander in Chief of His Majestyes forces in the Southern Districts

Noble Earl

Since I wrote to your Excellency this morning I have got a more certain account of the rebels, and finding the bearer of my other letter was not set of with it, I have sat down to acquaint you with what I have heard a few moments agoe. Morgan and Washinghton had join'd the party that lay at Grimes' Mill yesterday and they all moved to Colonel Henderson plantations about a mile this side of the mill, and I am well inform'd that they intend to march as fast as they can to Ninty Six. I don't believe they have as many men as it is reported to my wife's sister. They have call'd in Brandon's, Lyle's, Hayses, Shelvey's, Clerk's and co reigements and they were all together in camps yesterday at the place above mentioned.

---

[29] Love was a common surname in South Carolina. Of those listed in Moss, *SC Patriots*, five with the first name William saw service in the revolutionary forces, of whom the one living in the New Acquisition may be the person referred to here. No William Love was admitted into the royal militia.

I am your Earlship's very humble servant

DAVID GEORGE

Filinghauzen, 2nd January 1781 — *102(6): ADS*

Situation of the American Army Headquarters, Charlote

General Green's command:

8 brass field pieces

1,200 regular troops of Mariland, Delawar and new levee

300 Virginia militia

200 ditto North Carolina

200 ditto in Cross Kreek, waiting for orders

120 cavalery with Green

Baron de Stuben commands in Virginia some militia. Some are to be mounted.

General Lincoln is reported to be on his march for the southern. No troops with him.

On the 29th Marion and his party wher at the 3 Bridgess. He consists of 3 or 400, mostly mounted.

General Green's army is in a very bad condition for cloading, blankets, and he wants wagons and horsess.

Major Lee with is Legion is sartainly on his march for Charlote.

Morgan has drafted from the army a detachment of 200 men for marksmen.

There's at New Burn greadill[30] of provitions, cloding and tobaco in one stanby stor[31] purchased for the army, also at Wilmington. No troops in anny of thoze placess.

---

[30] *greadill*: great deal.

[31] *stanby stor*: standby store.

Marion has order to keep himself in the rear of the British army if the[32] pass Charlote. He is to be joined by another party. Ruteledg is apointed major general.

FILINGHAUZEN[33] January 2nd 1781

§ - §

---

[32] *the*: they.

[33] *Filinghauzen*: the *nom de guerre* of an emissary sent out by Clinton. See Clinton to Cornwallis, 20th May, vol I, p 48.

CHAPTER 37

Letters to or from Savannah, Pensacola, St Augustine, New Providence and Bermuda

---

1 - To or from Savannah or Pensacola

Wright to Cornwallis, 20th November 1780[1] *4(166): ALS*

Savanah in Georgia
the 20th of November 1780

The Earl of Cornwallis, Commander in Chief etc etc etc

My Lord

I most heartily congratulate your Lordship on the recovery of your health and resuming the command of the army.

I presume it needless for me to give your Lordship an account of the situation of affairs in this province as you will have had it from Colonel Clarke, Colonel Cruger and Colonel Brown, and from which, and the change of circumstances both here and in Carolina since I had the honor to write your Lordship[2], I hope your Lordship will be of opinion that a troop of 50 horse is really necessary for the protection of this province and that establishing a small post at Augusta is not and cannot be a sufficient check on the rebels. In a former letter[3] I

---

[1] For Cornwallis's response, see the postscript to his letter to Balfour, 9th January 1781, p 130.

[2] See Wright to Cornwallis, 28th and 31st July, vol I, pp 351 and 353.

[3] *In a former letter*: that of 28th July (see above).

gave your Lordship my reasons why this province is at present unable to bear the expence of it, and if your Lordship will be pleased to agree to pay the expence and to order 50 of the saddles and accoutrements here which were lately sent from England and partly meant for this province, we can raise the men and get the horses here, so that in that respect it cannot interfere with any views your Lordship may have in raising horse men in Carolina. We are all clearly of opinion that a troop of horse is absolutely necessary, and I trust your Lordship will be so too, and must request to be favoured with an answer.

Our inlets have for some days past been infested with 2 rebel row galleys, which carry some swivels and from 40 to 50 men each and row with 22 oars each. They have already taken 2 vessels off Tybee light house and landed at a Mr Tho[s] Young's[4] and taken him and 39 Negro's and all his household furniture etc and we have not a vessel or boat of any kind to send after them, and they may rob and plunder every settlement on the sea islands or inlets and it's not in our power to prevent them. I applied to Admiral Arbuthnot when he was at Charles Town for a galley, but nothing was to be spared for *this* province.

My Lord, mere perplexity and necessity urge me to acquaint your Lordship that we have at Augusta about 40 rebel prisoners represented to me as notorious villains and which we really don't know what to do with. Mr Graham says these are people who must not on any account be let at liberty. They are at present prisoners to Colonel Brown, but if sent here, we have no prison or prison ship, wherefore, if your Lordship would be pleased to order them to be kept at any of the military posts, it would be of signal service to this province, as it is not possible for the civil power to confine them. We must either try or discharge them, and Mr Graham says, if let at liberty, they will certainly do much mischief, being incorrigible.

I have the honor to be with perfect esteem, my Lord,
Your Lordship's most obliged and obedient servant

JA WRIGHT

Clarke to Cornwallis, 29th November 1780 — *4(236): ALS*

Savannah
November 29th 1780

Earl Cornwallis etc etc etc

My Lord

Not having any thing particular to communicate and knowing how fully your Lordship's time must have been occupied by affairs of moment, I have not trespassed on it by writing

---

4 A firm loyalist, Thomas Young was an Englishman who had settled about 1767 in what was to become Bryan and Chatham Counties, Georgia. By now he was a prominent planter. His loyalism would lead to his banishment, and to the confiscation of his property, by act of the Georgia revolutionary assembly in May 1782. (John F Wise, 'Pioneers of Bryan County, Georgia' (Internet, 4th March 2006); The Georgia Banishment and Confiscation Act 1782)

for some time past, but now have the honor to acknowledge the receipt of yours of September the sixth[5] sent me by Doctor Hayes (whose illness prevented my receiving it for a long time after it was written), in consequence of which I have broke up the hospital at this place and ordered the gentlemen belonging to it to Charles Town except one mate, who I thought it absolutely requisite to keep here for the attendance of the soldiers of the artillery – such men as belong to absent corps — and the servants of the different departments, who would otherwise have been without any medical assistance whatever, which I hope will meet with your Lordship's approbation.

The garrison of St Augustine was formerly supplied with provisions by a particular contract through Mr Shirley[6], who is Commissary of Stores and Provisions for East Florida. He resides in England and a Mr Will[m] Brown is his deputy, who informs me he sent a contingent account (which it seems was formerly allowed) to your Lordship but it was returned to him with directions from Captain Ross to present it to me. This he has done and some of the articles appear reasonable, but there is a charge of a *store cooper* amounting to upwards of sixty pounds a year, which I don't think necessary as the business is transacted wholly by Mr Wier's deputys. Therefore don't chuse to pay it unless it meets with your Lordship's concurrence. Mr Brown is strongly recommended as a very deserving man who has suffered much during the rebellion.

Lt Governor Graham informs me that £150 is due to him as Inspector of Refugees for this province and requests I will ask your Lordship if Sir Henry Clinton has signified his approbation of its being paid. He says he had the honor of mentioning it to you when at Charles Town.

I can with great sincerity assure your Lordship that I heard of your being ill with infinite concern and was as truly rejoiced when I learnt that you was sufficiently recovered to again enable your undertaking the fatigues to which your situation exposes you.

The works that are erecting for the protection of this town go on very fast. At the request of the Governor, Council etc I consented to its being a parapet with redoubts instead of a stockade. They furnish four hundred Negroes with carpenters etc for the completion of it and are to defray every expence above what I before had the honor to mention to you[7], which being the case, added to its being much stronger and pleasing the people very much, I hope the alteration may not be thought improper by your Lordship.

We have just received the pleasing intelligence of my friend Tarleton's success against Mr Sumpter. His active and enterprizing spirit does him the greatest credit and makes him a proper person to act under your Lordship's directions.

---

5 *yours..*: see vol II, p 303.

6 The *Army List for 1780* confirms that Henry Shirdley was Commissary General of Stores and Provisions for East Florida at an annual salary of £273-15*s*-0*d*.

7 See Clarke to Cornwallis, 5th October, vol II, p 305.

I have the honor to be with the highest respect, my Lord,
Your Lordship's most obedient and most faithful humble servant

ALURED CLARKE

Cornwallis to Clarke, 4th January 1781 — *84(12): C*

Wynnesborough
January 4th 1781

Lt Colonel Clarke commanding in Georgia and East Florida

Dear Sir

I am much ashamed of not answering sooner your letter of the 29th of November but I have had much business, and as there was nothing very pressing in the points which you submitted to me, I trust you will forgive me.

In regard to Mr Wm Brown's charge of sixty pounds a year as *stores cooper*, if Mr Brown has other good appointments and is in tolerable circumstances I would discontinue an expence which you think useless. If he is on the contrary much reduced by his sufferings and rather a distressed man, I do not think that salary an object of reformation.

In a letter which I wrote to Sir Henry Clinton in June last[8] I requested his directions relative to Lt Governor Graham, but the Commander in Chief took no notice of that paragraph in his answer to my letter. As his answer was written in an hurry, perhaps he overlooked it. I will remind him of it when I write again to New York.[9]

I refer you for news to Balfour and your correspondents in Charlestown. The Royal Fuzileers are gone to Ninety Six. They are much improved in health and their recruits are good. Every thing at present wears a promising aspect in this quarter. This is, however, a war of such uncertainty that I have left off being too sanguine.

I am with great regard, dear sir,
Your most obedient and faithfull servant

CORNWALLIS

---

[8] *a letter..*: of 30th June 1780, vol I, p 160.

[9] See Cornwallis to Clinton, 6th January, p 33.

Clarke to Balfour, 29th December 1780 *62(12): ALS*

Savannah
December 29th 1780

Many thanks, my dear Balfour, for your two last letters, one by Mr Stuart, the other arrived last night by the *Arbuthnot* galley. I suppose you are by this time returned to Charles Town, where I hope you will find every thing in the same good order that I am sure you left it, after having arranged matters with Lord Cornwallis to both your satisfactions and the publick advantage. The bearer, Captain Breley[10] of the 60th, was formerly in the 54th Regiment. He is a very good natured man and has been long in the service, which he now seems inclined to quit. I have therefore given him permission to go to New York in order to present memorials to that effect and am to request you will assist him in procuring an early passage.

I was rejoiced to hear the cavalry appointments were at last safely arrived, for I really began to think they were in the hands of the philistines. The galleys etc that are stationed between this and Charles Town will certainly secure every thing betwixt us, but I am sorry to say our communication with East Florida will be very uncertain without the assistance of the *sloop* or *frigate* you mention. Therefore hope it may be sent soon.

I cannot conclude without thanking you for all sorts of intelligence you are so good as to communicate to me, and begging that you will not suppose I hear what is going on from any body else, when you have a spare half hour to bestow on me.

I hope they have sent cash from York as I shall not be able to send you any more, for what with Major Frazer, contingencies from Augustine, pay for the Hessians, and demands from the different departments I am well nigh a bankrupt.

Adieu, my dear Balfour, and believe me
Very truly yours

ALURED CLARKE

[*Subscribed*:]

Enclosed you have a letter relative to victualling the militia when on duty[11], to which I must beg an answer as soon as convenient.

---

10 Commissioned an ensign in the 54th Regiment on 17th August 1761, Alexander Breley was promoted to lieutenant there on 5th October 1770. On 2nd February 1780 he became a captain lieutenant in the 3rd Battalion, 60th (Royal American) Regiment, which formed part of the garrison of St Augustine. His resignation would be accepted. (*Army Lists*)

11 *a letter*..: not extant.

A rebel privateer is cast away near St Augustine and the crew made prisoners. The captain is one Harrison, who I am informed was on *parole* with you and that he *broke* it. Major Glasier has very properly on that account confined him in the fort. Most of the sailors are old country men and seem inclined to serve with our fleet. Therefore think our men of war should send for them. The captain being (by all accounts) a notorious fellow, I think something should be done with him and wish you would send for him by the first opportunity. Was it intended that the prisoners at Augustine should have rum delivered from the King's Stores, or is it a mistake, as I understand they receive it by directions from you? If so, well and good, but otherwise it should be rectified, never having been customary.

Once more adieu
Yours

ALURED CLARKE

Clarke to Balfour, 2nd January 1781 — *62(14): ALS*

Savannah
January 2nd 1781

Lt Colonel Balfour

My dear Balfour

I last night received a letter of intelligence (of which the enclosed is an abstract) from Mr McIntosh[12], Deputy to the Super Intendant of Indian Affairs, residing in the Creek nation. And this morning a Doctor William Burnet arrived, who brought me a letter from General Campbell of the 10th of November[13] from whence I conclude Pensacola is attacked long before this time. I also send by this express General Campbell's dispatches for Lord Cornwallis etc which came by this gentleman, who gives me a very sensible, intelligent account of matters in West Florida, and who, from the opportunities he has had of conversing with many Spaniards of note, both civil and military, is clearly of opinion that the reduction of Pensacola is to be followed by the immediate attack of St Augustine. Under these circumstances I must request that you will advert to the situation of the prisoners at that place, which, with the addition of those taken from the wrecked vessel, amount to 130. Having said so much, it rests with yourself to act as you please respecting them and I will do all in my

---

12 William McIntosh was a member of a prominent family in Savannah and had been sent into the Creek nation to secure their loyalty to the Crown. He would return to Savannah when the fate of the war was sealed. He was the father of Chief William McIntosh Jr (1775-1825), a future leader of the Creeks, whose mother Senoya was a member of the Wind Clan. (Alastair McIntyre, 'Scots around the World: Chief William McKintosh' (Internet, 24th December 2005))

13 *a letter..*: a repetition (4(86)), as far as the word 'passage', of Campbell's letter of 14th November 1780 to Cornwallis, p 428. It concludes by recommending the bearer, Dr Burnet, to Clarke's countenance and protection as a long-standing loyal and worthy resident of West Florida.

power to coincide with your wishes.[14]

I yesterday received intelligence from Colonel Lechmere that McKay[15] with upwards of 100 horse-men was at Port Royal Ferry; and this morning, by a man of Colonel Brown's corps, who was in one of them, I am informed that three boats going from hence for Augusta were attacked by this same party and taken on Christs-Mass Day. Two of them had provisions and rum for the back posts, the loss of which will be very distressing to them. In short, the navigation of the River Savannah is so infested with these partys that I don't know what to do, and unless the militia of South Carolina can give some attention to the banks of it from Ebenezer towards Briar Creek, the communication will be totally stopped as I cannot send sufficient escorts with the boats, having only 211 men fit for duty.

I am anxious to get to St Augustine in order that my best efforts may not be wanting towards the defence of that place and yet am under difficulties in leaving this province to be commanded by *one* who seems totally unacquainted with the laws by which it is governed. Mr de Porbeck[16], who I seldom see, this morning sent me a message by his adjutant to say he had received a commission appointing him a colonel, the drift of which you will plainly see. However, having a letter of service which will justify my acting as heretofore for the publick good, I shall not take any further notice of the message untill Lord Cornwallis shall signify his pleasure concerning it. Colonel de Porbeck was a younger lt colonel than myself and many others. I therefore make no doubt but justice will point out some mode by which the Commander in Chief may prevent *our being superceeded* by those (who have been our juniors) in the service of the Landgraffe of Hesse.[17]

It is probable that you have sufficient authority to open Campbell's letter to Lord Cornwallis. If so and it contains *any* thing that you think would be useful to me, pray let me know it; and that you may be the better judge of the matter I send you a copy of the letter I have received from him. Pray order Mr Townshend to send a sufficiency of rum to East

---

14 Annotated in another hand: 'To keep prisoners at St Augustine unless a serious attack, in which case to send them here by the inland navigation.'

15 James McKay was captain of a revolutionary band of Georgia irregulars who haunted the swamps along the Savannah River, attacking traffic on the neighbouring highway and supply boats bound for Augusta. He and his men had a reputation for severity and for the pursuit of plunder as much as for their support of the revolutionary cause. When Lieutenant Camp and ten of the King's Ranger's surrendered to him in January 1781, Camp and several of the prisoners were tortured before being granted a 'Georgia parole', that is to say, murdered in cold blood. Not surprisingly, McKay was by late May 1782 in fear of his life, warning John Martin, the revolutionary Governor, that three different parties of loyalists had left Savannah with the intention of killing him. (Cashin Jr, *Augusta*, 44, 53, 72; Cashin, *The King's Ranger*, 125-7, 144; *The Cornwallis Papers*)

16 Friedrich von Porbeck had served for most of the war as Lt Colonel of the Garrison Regiment von Wissenbach and had come south with it to Georgia in late 1778 as part of Archibald Campbell's expedition. Ten months later his involvement in breaking the siege of Savannah led to his being mentioned in Prevost's dispatches. Now promoted to colonel, he would not supersede Clarke but would remain in town with his regiment as part of the garrison. (Edward J Lowell, *The Hessians and the other German Auxiliairesin the Revolutionary War* (New York, 1884), ch xxi; *The Cornwallis Papers*)

17 Annotated in another hand: 'Hessian colonel not to supersede letter of service. Lord Cornwallis will agree to his going to St Augustine whenever he sees occasion, but I hope no danger to Pensacola.'

Florida immediately and such other articles as may be necessary. The former cannot be supplied from hence, not having more than will serve this province for one month. Adieu, my dear Balfour. Let me hear from you directly. I send this by an express boat as thinking the water passage safest.

Ever yours

ALURED CLARKE

Enclosure (1)
Extract from McIntosh to Clarke, 12th December 1780 *4(312): C*

Lower Creek Nation
December 12th 1780

Sir

I take the liberty by express to transcribe a paragraph of a letter which I receiv'd four days ago from General Campbell dated Pensacola, November 22nd 1780, advising me that he has receiv'd certain intelligence that a large armament consisting of five frigates, a King's xebeck, with fifty one victuallers, and transports, with troops and military stores, sail'd from the Havannah the 16th of last month for the invasion and attack of Pensacola. They met with a storm the fifth day from their departure, which dispersed them, in consequence whereof two of them have actually been taken and brought into this harbour and their papers have given us the above information.

WILL^{M} McINTOSH

Enclosure (2)
Campbell to Cornwallis, 14th November 1780 *4(122): LS*

Head Quarters
Pensacola
14th November 1780

The Rt Hon Lt General Earl Cornwallis

My Lord

Since my last (by our quarterly express, Joseph Dawes) no material circumstance that we are apprised of has occurred in this part of the world, only that the cargo of a polacre bound from the Havannah to Mobile, captured by one of our cruisers the 30th ultimo, together with what can be learned from the prisoners taken on board her, plainly indicate the approaching attack of this place. The prize is chiefly laden with provisions, but has also a staff of commissaries and their suit sufficient to act for an army, an ordnance storekeeper with his retinue and attendants, together with timber and plank requisite for a train of battering or field artillery, and informs that an artillery vessel must have arrived lately at Mobile, at which place the Spaniards have had for these two months past a large train of artillery embarked in readiness to join the armament from the Havana destined for the attack of Pensacola. And when the polacre sailed from that place, Don Bernard de Galvez, Governor of Louisiana and nephew to Don Joseph de Galvez[18], President of the Council of the Indies and a principal if not prime minister of Spain, was there present in person to superintend the embarkation of the reinforcements he was to receive for the expedition, and they suppose that he is now at sea on his passage. As these circumstances would only be a repetition of repeated intelligence already conveyed to his Excellency Sir Henry Clinton, I have not troubled him therewith by this occasional conveyance, but should your Lordship think the intelligence that may be inferred from the above particulars of sufficient importance to be communicated to the Commander in Chief, I request that favor of your Lordship by the first opportunity.

I have the honor to be with deference and respect, my Lord,
Your Lordship's most obedient and humble servant

JOHN CAMPBELL
Major General

Clarke to Cornwallis, 2nd January 1781 — *5(25): ALS*

Savannah
January 2nd 1781

Lt General Earl Cornwallis etc etc etc

My Lord

I have just received a letter from General Campbell[19] by Doctor Burnet, who left Pensacola on the eighteenth of last month. The accounts from thence (as your Lordship will probably find by a letter[20] which I have the honor to forward by express) strongly indicate an immediate attack of that place, and the accounts given me by the gentleman above mentioned, who seems a very sensible, intelligent man and is strongly recommended to me by General Campbell, puts it beyond a doubt that it must have taken place before this time and that the reduction of West Florida will be followed by an immediate attack of St Augustine. Mr Burnet has resided some time amongst the Spaniards and says their chiefe object (declared on every occasion) is the uniting the two Floridas to the Spanish settlements

---

18 As Campbell says, Don José de Gálvez (1729-1786) was President of the Council of the Indies (akin to a colonial secretary), an office which he had held since 1775. Uncle of Don Bernado de Gálvez (see p 305, note 38), he was influential in obtaining Charles III's support for his nephew's campaigns. (*Appletons'*)

19 *a letter..*: see p 426, note 13.

20 *a letter*: see enclosure (2), p 428.

and that no stone will be left unturned to accomplish it. These circumstances make me particularly anxious to get to St Augustine and I would set off for it immediately but from the difficulties that I am under in leaving the command of the troops etc of this province to *one*[21] who seems totally unacquainted with the laws by which it is governed. Your Lordship, I fancy, has had some knowledge of the character of the gentleman alluded to, or should think it necessary to apologise for having said so much where no charge is meant against the person in question but merely a hint which I think it necessary to give for the benefit of the service. I have written to Balfour[22], who I am sure will do all in his power towards preventing any wants at St Augustine, and desired him to advert to the situation of the Carolina prisoners and those taken from the wreck of a rebel vessel, in all amounting to 130. I make no doubt but General Campbell will send another express on the appearance of Don Galvez's armament, on the arrival of which I shall at all events set off for East Florida if I have not done so before, and if my taking fifty to one hundred men with me should prove necessary, I hope your Lordship will let them be replaced by a few from Carolina, as Savannah would otherwise be extremely ill off, having at present only *211* men fit for duty. I have this morning received a message from Colonel de Porbeck by his adjutant to inform me that he has received a commission from his Prince appointing him a colonel, the drift of which will be obvious to your Lordship. I sent him a message of congratulation and shall take no further notice of it untill I know your pleasure. And that your Lordship may be the better able to judge of the matter, I have taken the liberty to enclose a part of the letter of service I had from Sir Henry Clinton on his ordering me to assume this command. Colonel de Porbeck was younger than myself, consequently than Webster, and some others of the lt colonels serving in America, which makes this promotion of the Landgraffe's rather a hardship. I am therefore persuaded your Lordship's kindness and good wishes towards many of us who have had the honor to serve under your command will render us every assistance in your power if any mode could be adopted (unattended with bad consequences to the service at large) by which it might be prevented that we should be commanded by such as have so recently been our juniors. The above idea having occured, I took the liberty of mentioning it and hope your Lordship will excuse my having done so when I assure you that nothing can be more foreign than any improper motives having induced me to it.

I cannot conclude without congratulating you on the arrival of General Lesslie and the reinforcement with him, which I hope may soon give your Lordship an opportunity of adding to those laurells you have already gained. The intelligence of my friend Ross's being appointed a major gave me great pleasure, and I am persuaded his merit will do justice to your patronage on every occasion.

I have the honor to be with the greatest respect, my Lord,
Your Lordship's most obedient and most faithful humble servant

ALURED CLARKE

---

[21] *one*: Colonel von Porbeck.

[22] See p 426.

Enclosure
Extract from Clinton to Clarke, 20th May 1780 *4(84): C*

Head Quarters
Charles Town Neck
May 20th 1780

To Lt Colonel Alured Clarke
of His Majesty's 7th (or Royal Fusilier) Regiment of Foot

Sir

Major General Prevost having obtain'd my leave to go to Europe on his private affairs, and judging it necessary for the King's Service that a British officer should command the troops in Georgia, I have thought proper to appoint you to that service.

You will therefore be pleas'd to proceed forthwith to Savannah and there take upon you the command of His Majesty's troops, both British and foreign, in the province of Georgia as soon as Major General Prevost shall please to assign it, and they are hereby required and directed to obey you as their commandant.

[H CLINTON]

Clarke to Balfour, 5th January 1781 *62(18): ALS*

Savannah
January 5th 1781

Lt Colonel Balfour

My dear Balfour

Enclosed you have a letter from General Campbell to General Dalling[23], and being informed it is of some importance, I must request you will forward it by the first opportunity.

This goes by Mr McDonald[24] belonging to the Ordnance Department, by whom I have sent a message to Major Traile respecting the artillery detachment at this place, which is but five in number, and those, all but one, have been unfit for duty for many months past. As I am to have so few, they surely should be good men. I therefore beg you will use your interest towards procuring me a proper non commissioned officer and six or seven *good men* in lieu of those already here, who, as I have before said, are totally useless.

---

23 *a letter..*: no copy.

24 Alexander McDonnell was a clerk of stores in the civil branch of the Ordnance. (WO 65/164(6) (National Archives, Kew))

For God's sake do something towards ridding the country of that scoundrell McKay and his party, without which our communication with the back posts is totally cut off. And I shall be afraid to send any thing from hence 'till the passage is a little cleared.

Pray let me hear from you, and give me *hints* of what is going forward if you don't venture to speak out. Pray beg of Benson to send me some good paper for your own sake, for this is so bad that it is difficult to read it.

Adieu
Ever truly yours

ALURED CLARKE

[*Annotated in another hand*:]

Campbell's letter sent to Lord Cornwallis but little hopes of an answer soon, as his Lordship is advanced beyond communication with this.

Respecting artillery, Major Trail has wrote and done the utmost in his power.

Hope the posts at Pocotalligo and Augusta will free you from plunderers and keep open the communication of the river.

Stationary.

Wright to Balfour, 5th January 1781 — *62(20): ALS*

Savanah
the 5th of January 1781

Lt Colonel Balfour etc etc etc

Sir

Your letter of the 8th of December I had the honor to receive on the 28th, and the disposition [which] you are pleased to acquaint me has been made for the protection of South Carolina by stationing the galleys and building batteries etc at proper places is certainly very judicious and well calculated for the defence of the inlets, rivers and inhabitants of *that province*, but I must beg leave to observe that the station of the galley sent here would be of very little or *no use to this province*, viz, from Tybee to Callibogue, and in consequence of Captain Barkley's letter to me I have *recommended* a quite different station and cruize to Mr Scallion[25], which he seems very ready to observe.

---

25 Scallion has not been identified.

I gave directions, and made all the inquiry I could, about the Negros etc [who] you mentioned you were apprehensive were brought into this province with a view to sell or ship off, but could not discover that any were. Anxious to promote your wishes to the utmost of my power, I issued the inclosed proclamation[26].

I have the honor to be with much esteem, sir,
Your most obedient servant

JA WRIGHT

[*Annotated in another hand*:]

The advantage of a post[27] from Georgia meeting ours at Pocotaligo every Wednesday.

§ - §

2 - From St Augustine

Tonyn to Cornwallis, 24th November 1780 — ***66(3): LS***

St Augustine
24th November 1780

The Rt Hon Earl of Cornwallis

My Lord

I have been in great anxiety on a report circulating here that your Lordship was dangerously ill and am greatly relieved by letters I have this day received from Colonel Balfour without any mention of such disagreeable misfortune and therefore hope that you are in a perfect state of good health.

As the inclosures will acquaint your Lordship of the particulars relative to the rebel prisoners, it is unnecessary to trouble you further on that head, and I have only to desire your Lordship's attention to that part of my letter to Colonel Balfour mentioning the behaviour of

26 *the inclosed proclamation*: no extant copy.

27 *a post*: a mail delivery.

Doctor Turnbull[28] towards the rebels here and that I could have wished that some of His Majesty's well affected subjects had been rewarded with the appointment of Commissary of Provisions instead of Mr Turnbull[29], who with his father have been in constant opposition to Government.

I sincerely congratulate your Lordship on the arrival of the King's forces in Virginia, which I hope will prove of such additional strength to the army under your command as will be sufficient for carrying your plans of operations into completion.

May every hour be propitious to your Lordship.

I have the honour to be with great respect and esteem, my Lord,
Your Lordship's most obedient and most humble servant

PAT TONYN

Enclosure (1)
Tonyn to Balfour, 24th November 1780 *66(5): CS*

St Augustine
24th November 1780

Sir

By the *Sandwich* frigate I have this day the honour of receiving your letter of the 14th instant[30].

It is with great propriety the Earl of Cornwallis thought of the expediency of sending the heads of the rebels to this garrison. These incendiaries can do little mischief here, and that

---

[28] Born and educated in Scotland, Dr Andrew Turnbull (*c.* 1718-1792) settled in Smyrna, Asia Minor, where he practised medicine for many years. In 1766 he became interested in promoting the cultivation of sub-tropical products in East Florida, was granted 20,000 acres there, and two years later brought over an indentured collection of some 1,400 Minorcans, Greeks and Italians to establish the colony of New Smyrna at Mosquito (now Ponce de Leon) Inlet. By some accounts he treated the indentured immigrants abominably, a sizeable number of whom soon revolted and tried unsuccessfully to flee in a schooner to Havana, whereas hundreds of others died of malaria, scurvy and gangrene while undertaking improvements of the land. Appointed to HM Council for East Florida, he was sympathetic to the approaching revolution in the other North American provinces and became a leader of a faction opposed to administration. Eventually his differences with Lt Governor John Moultrie led to his resigning his seat on the Council in the early 1770s. Denounced later as disloyal by Governor Tryon, he was away in England, protesting his innocence, when Tryon broke up the New Smyrna colony in 1776, drafting many of the immigants into the militia and galleys and welcoming the rest to St Augustine. On his return to the province Turnbull was soon sued for debt and was detained for two years for want of the bond that Tonyn imposed. Released by surrendering all but a fraction of New Smyrna, he would eventually sail for Charlestown, where he practised medicine till his death. (Carita Doggett Corse, *Dr Andrew Turnbull and the New Smyrna Colony of Florida* (Great Outdoors Publishing Co, 1967), *passim*; *DAB*; Johnson, *Traditions*, 327)

[29] Nichol Turnbull was the eldest son of Dr Andrew Turnbull (see above). After the war he became a planter and slaveowner in Georgia. (Daniel Schafer to the editor, 17th May 2006)

[30] *your letter..*: no extant copy.

their opinions and principles may as much as possible be confined to themselves they are kept by me at a great distance, and to have a friendly intercourse with them is considered as disrespectful to His Majesty and displeasing to me. Doctor Turnbull and a Mr Martin are the only gentlemen that have shewn them countenance. The former under colour of his profession, although two rebel physicians are prisoners and no sickness amongst them, passes daily some hours, and, frequently appearing on the parade with them, I am convinced his behaviour proceeds not only from principle but from other reasons. The other is a man of different sentiments but of particular cast and passions, actuated by a former acquaintance and gratitude for former favours.

I was in hopes the offices under His Majesty in this province would have been confined to such as were known to be well attached to the British Constitution. The appointment of Mr Turnbull, the doctor's son, to be acting commissary for the King's troops cannot be considered in this light, as the father has invariably reviled every measure of Government for the suppression of the rebellion and was a principal of a faction here in opposition to this, and the son no less active as far as his power and abilities, and his behaviour since in office continues agreeable to his former conduct, in some instances very improper.

The sanction of religion sometimes is made to answer very bad purposes, and the rebel prisoners were begining to hold meetings under such specious pretences. I therefore thought it best and expedient to stop such proceedings in the first outset, and I have the honour of inclosing a copy of my letter to the commissary upon that subject, and relying upon the generals and admirals for the security and protection of this province from the depredations of the enemy, the internal peace cannot be much disturbed by the machinations of these prisoners without[31] their being soon checked.

The arrival of the forces in Virginia will have considerable effect in support of Lord Cornwallis's operations, and by the removal of the most turbulent and disaffected from Carolina the situation of affairs in that country must become more quiet and easy, and it will give me great pleasure that by their residence in this the King's Service will be forwarded, and it will add to his Lordship's peace of mind and your satisfaction.

I am very sorry for the unfortunate disaster that happened to Colonel Ferguson's corps, and that it has had such unfavorable consequences of apostacy.

The plan you purpose to adopt for the supply of this garrison will be very effectual if once a sufficient quantity of provisions is established in store, and that portion constantly kept up will remove many anxieties.

It is of little moment to repeat my assurances and wishes of assistance to you in whatever you think of publick utility, and that I shall have great pleasure in conducing to your personal welfare, having the honour to be with great regard and esteem, sir, etc

PAT TONYN

---

[31] *without*: a slip of the pen. The sense suggests 'with'.

Enclosure (2)
Tonyn to Brown, 18th November 1780 ***66(7): CS***

St Augustine
18th November 1780

William Brown Esquire
Commissary for Prisoners of War

Sir

Having been informed that the rebel prisoners, forgetful of their paroles, have very improperly held private meetings for the purpose of performing divine service agreeable to their rebellious principles, and as such proceedings are thought highly injurious to His Majesty's Government and of seditious tendency and an infringement of their pledge of honour, I desire you will acquaint them that such meetings will not be allowed and that seats shall be provided for their reception in the parish church, where it is expected they will observe the utmost decency.

You are also to mention to those gentlemen that I consider messages delivered by you of sufficient weight and authenticity and that it is in compliance of your request that I descend to this manner of satisfaction, which Lt Colonel Glazier also desires may be understood to be expressive of his sentiments.

I am, sir, etc

PAT TONYN

§ - §

3 - To or from New Providence

Necessaries wanting for defence, 5th July 1780 ***63(91): DS***

New Providence
July 5th 1780

An estimate of necessarys wanting for the defence of the Island of New Providence, viz:

250 soldiers (not invalieds)

30 matrosses and 1 officer

~~A doctor, mate and medicines~~

1,000 musketts, cartouch boxes etc

6 or 8 reams cartridge paper

300 spades

100 hoes, 100 pick and 100 falling[32] axes

	(6 twenty-four pounders	)
Iron	(	) with carriages, shott etc
	(12 eighteen pounders	)

	(4 brass six pounders	)
Field pieces	(	) with ditto
	(4 grass hoppers	)

JOHN MAXWELL[33]

[*Subscribed*:]

Six months' provisions is in the fort, and no allowance for *prisoners* or any extra *service*.

Maxwell to Cornwallis, 31st August 1780 — *63(90): LS*

New Providence
August 31st 1780

The Rt Hon Charles Earl Cornwallis,
Lt General of His Majesty's forces etc etc

My Lord

I repeatedly gave information to Sir Henry Clinton of the miserable state of the garrison under the command of Captain Grant[34] but received no answer. I since applied to General

[32] *falling*: a misspelling of 'felling'.

[33] Having previously served in the military line, John Robert Maxwell had entered upon the office of Governor of the Bahamas earlier in the year. He would cease to be Governor on 8th May 1782, when the defenceless islands were captured by Don Bernado de Gàlvez. He would remain a prisoner of the Spanish until 19th April 1783, but then resumed the office of Governor after the restoration of the islands to Britain. He was replaced in 1784.

[34] John Grant was a captain in the Royal Garrison Battalion, which had been formed on the Provincial establishment in October 1778 out of invalids unfit for campaigning. He had previously been a lieutenant on half pay. In December 1778 he arrived at New Providence with two companies to form the garrison there. (*Royal American*

Paterson (hearing your Lordship was upon an expedition) for sundry stores and the garrison to be relieved, it being waisted away to 68 from 260 on landing in December 1778.

I have the mortification now to find Captain Grant has had so much weight with your Lordship as to have the stores that where shiped unloaded as unnecessary without my receiving an answer to my letter. I must therefore request your Lordship will send an officer to report to you the true state of this miserable garrison, forts etc.

That Captain Grant is displeased with the inhabitants of this Government I can readily believe from the treatment he has received, such as being twice posted for a coward and once boxed of the fish wharf for wrangling. He disobey'd my orders in not sending a small party to guard some stores, which I have represented to Sir Henry Clinton, not that I mean to prosecute him but hope he may never have a command where I am. His conduct and the state of the island I have represented to the Minister. Whatever may be the consequence of my not being supported, I cannot be answerable for.

Colonel and Lt Colonel Kershaws are arrived by your Lordship's permission. I dare say they will behave themselves, but I beg your Lordship will send no more as my garrison is exceeding weak and no ship of warr of any kind in the harbour to protect me.

I have the honor to be, my Lord,
Your Lordship's most obedient servant

JOHN MAXWELL

Cornwallis to Maxwell, 21st November 1780 — *82(77): ADfS*

Wynnesborough, South Carolina
November 21st 1780

His Excellency Governor Maxwell
Providence

Sir

I received a few days since your letter of the 31st of August and beg leave to assure you that you could not have mortified me more than by supposing that Captain Grant had any influence with me. I only saw that gentleman once at Charlestown for an instant and had not the least conversation on business with him. My reason for not sending the stores shipped by order of Brigadier General Paterson were: 1st, that they must have gone in an unarmed vessel without convoy; 2ndly, as you represented your garrison to be so weak as to be incapable of making any defence, I thought the stores could be of no real use to you and might possibly tempt an enemy to make you a visit.

Gazette (New York), 6th October 1778; A Sketch of an Establishment for a Garrison Battalion, The Mackenzie Papers, William L Clements Library; The Clinton Papers, 121(3); Nan Cole and Todd Braisted, 'Royal Garrison Battalion' (*The On-Line Institute for Advanced Loyalist Studies*, 11th February 2006))

In regard to your requisition of thirty artillery men and two hundred and fifty infantry, not invalids, I can only say that I am in great want of reinforcement myself and that there is not the smallest probability of my being able to spare you a man from this province.

I am, sir,
Your most obedient and most humble servant

CORNWALLIS

Maxwell to Cornwallis, 27th December 1780 — *4(413): LS*

N° 2

New Providence
December 27th 1780

Rt Hon Earl Cornwallis

My Lord

I had the honor of your Lordship's letter dated the 21st November, and had I not had so much presumptive proof as to lessen me in the eyes of the people I am to govern, I shou'd not have thought it incumbent on me to justify myself as to the propriety of my requisition.

The inclosed extract of a letter from a master of a vessell belonging here will, I flatter myself, justify my supposing Captain Grant had some information, having gone the day before to the vessell that was loading and threathned the master with what did happen the day after, for it appears the stores where ship'd and reshiped and the captain paid a demurrage.

I hope your Lordship will believe me when I assure you there is not a general officer in America I have, and always had, so high an opinion of as yourself, and when I had the honor of writing to your Lordship I was then, as I now am, without a garrison, artillery, or provissions.

The Minister in his dispatch of June last gave me a particular account of the Havanna being considerably reinforced and desires me to apply to Sir Henry Clinton or any other general officer for such assistance as the place may require. In answer Sir Henry tells me I am to depend on the loyal inhabitants and that stores will be shiped. Your Lordship tells me, as there is no garrison, stores are needless. In part I agree, but at same time am of opinion the stores and provissions necessary for *sixty invalids* cou'd not be an object of any temptation to our neighbouring enemys, especially as they have received during the summer such plentifull supplys, and I have it only to regret that an old soldier must if attack'd capitulate without firing a shot.

I have the honor to be, my Lord,
Your Lordship's most obedient servant

JOHN MAXWELL

Enclosure
Extract from Lightbourn to Maxwell, 20th July 1780 *4(417): C*

Charles Town
July 20th 1780

A few days after my arrival a commissary of artillery inform'd me that in consequence of your Excellency's requisition to General Patterson a supply of stores were to be shiped in my vessell. I soon after received on board a great part of them and had them stowed away. The next day Captain John Grant, who had just arrived from Providence, came on board and, finding I had stores for the garrison, exclaimed much against the inhabitants of the place and threathned to be of as much disservice to the island and inhabitants as he cou'd. A day or two after, I was order'd to stop taking in till further orders. Upon my asking the reason, was told some person had been speaking to Lord Cornwallis against the people and place, and intimated no body more likely than Captain Grant, as he had conversed with him as well as Major Trail. I waited on Major Trail, who gave me positive orders to reland what I had taken on board, being orders from Lord Cornwallis, which I complied with and received for my detention of time £11 4/- sterling.

PAUL LIGHTBOURN
Captain

§ - §

4 - From Bermuda

Bruere to Cornwallis, 27th November 1780 ***4(219): LS***

St George's, Bermuda
Government House
27th November 1780

The Rt Hon Lord Cornwallis etc etc etc

My Lord

The situation these isles are in oblidges me to intrude on your Lordship in the midst of your most glorious successes, which I very heartily congratulate your Lordship on.

The turn the people here have always had to navigation has left a grateful soil much neglected, so much that one winter in this rebellion many died for want, since which some evil minded people here have made a handle of then necessitys to carry on under pretence of seeking provisions a salt and other trade with the rebel colonies, not confining it merely to those that grew corn but extending it to tobacco etc to the southward and lumber to the northward, sometimes directly here, often by St Eustatia, and by other complicated manœvres, more especially during the ilness of my father and the interval between his decease and my arrival.

At this moment I have information from eye witnesses that from ten to fourteen sail were within these four months at Boston with salt, which was of infinite service to the French fleet and army, who paid these bad people in hard dollars.

At the same time I had the honor to be appointed Lt Governor, His Majesty was pleased to appoint a new Collector, a Judge of the Admiralty and an Attorney General. The two former are now here, the other much wanted. We have seized four vessels and mean to seize every rebell trader we can lay our hands on, thereby to knock up practices so injurious to the British Empire. If your Lordship will be pleased to allow the Bermudians to import indian corn, rough rice, tar and lumber, they will not have the shadow of an excuse, and our severitys will at once force them out of rebell trade, possibly into privateering against them.

Two gentlemen very well connected here, and cousins to Mrs Montresor[35], were made prisoners at Charles Town, the one a regular physician (brother to my brother in law), Doctor Thomas Tudor Tucker[36], the other a very young man, Mr Cornelius Hinson[37]. I flatter my self that indulgence to them would convince many of past error and therefore request your Lordship to allow them to come here on their parole.

---

[35] Frances Montresor (1744-1826) was the only child of Thomas Tucker of Bermuda, a lieutenant in the British Army, whose head was shot off by a cannonball in 1745. When aged almost twenty, she married in New York John Montresor, an officer in the Corps of Engineers who went on to become Chief Engineer in America until he resigned his commission in 1778. She was presently residing with him in England, where she would presumably remain until her death at Rose-hill near Sittingbourne, Kent. In the 1770s surviving portraits of both her and her husband were painted by the American artist, John Singleton Copley. (*ODNB*; 'Journals of Captain John Montresor (July-October, 1764)', *Collections of the New-York Historical Society for the Year 1881*, 5)

[36] Born in Port Royal, Bermuda, Thomas Tudor Tucker (1745-1828) was the son of Colonel Henry Tucker, a prominent Bermuda merchant and a leading political figure opposed to administration. After studying medicine at the University of Edinburgh, he moved to South Carolina, where he began to practise as a doctor. A member of the South Carolina revolutionary legislature in 1776, he became subject to the capitulation of Charlestown four years later and was now acting as a physician and surgeon to the Continental hospital there, although he held no formal appointment in the Continental medical service. When the cartel for the exchange of prisoners came into effect in June 1781, he accompanied his patients to Williamsburg, Virginia, where he assumed direction of what was the main Continental hospital in the Southern Department. In the following September his position was regularised. After the war he served several terms in the South Carolina legislature, and several in Congress, before being appointed United States Treasurer in 1801, an office which he held till his death. He is interred in the Congressional Cemetery. (Joel D Treese and Dorthy J Countryman, *Biographical Directory of the United States Congress 1774-1996* (Cq Pr, 1996); Mary C Gillett, *The Army Medical Department 1775-1818* (Lightning Source Inc, 2002))

[37] Cornelius Hinson (*c.* 1750-*post*-1808) of Pembroke Parish, Bermuda, was a member of an extended family which, besides being related to the extended family of Tuckers, was prominent in the political and social life of Bermuda. His father, also named Cornelius, had been a Member of the General Assembly there. Cornelius, the son, would soon return from South Carolina to Bermuda, where he would reside till his death. ('Descendants of Cornelius Hinson' and 'A Survey of the Inhabitants of Bermuda: Pembroke Parish - Part Two' (www.rootsweb.com, 20th November 2005))

A safer opportunity will offer in a few days, when I hope to be able to send your Lordship a turtle. If all Bermudians taken trading with the rebells by our men of war or privateers were confined on board a prison ship, the others would be intimidated from any further commerce, although the gain is all most irrisistable to such men as most of them are.

I have the honor to be with the utmost respect
Your Lordship's most devoted humble servant

GEORGE BRUERE[38]
Lt Governor

§ - §

[38] George Bruere (1744-1786) had until recently pursued a military career. During the Seven Years' War he had served in the 14th Foot, and during the revolutionary war he had taken part in the Battle of Bunker Hill as a lieutenant in the 18th (Royal Irish) Regiment. He was wounded in the affair and his elder brother John, who was also serving in the regiment, was killed. In 1776 he was promoted to captain in the 3rd Battalion, 60th (Royal American) Regiment, and saw service in East Florida. Three years later he was wounded in the action at Beaufort, South Carolina, and returned to England to convalesce. There he quit the military line and was appointed Lt Governor of Bermuda, but on arriving at Port Royal in October 1780, he found that his father, George James Bruere, who held the office of Governor, had died the previous month. Beset by difficulties arising from widespread sympathy for the American revolutionaries, he would head the Island's administration until January 1782, when William Browne, a native of Salem, Massachusetts, who was in high office prior to the revolution, succeeded him as Governor. Returning shortly after to England, he eventually moved on to Scotland, where he died at Alderston, a district of Haddington in East Lothian. His eldest sister Frances was married in 1770 to Henry Tucker Jr, a brother of Thomas Tudor Tucker (see above). (G K Armstrong, 'The Hallowes Genealogy' (Internet, 20th November 2005); *Army Lists*; Phillip Hamilton, *The Making and Unmaking of a RevolutionaryFamily: The Tuckers of Virginia, 1752-1830* (University Press of Virginia, 2003), 17)

CHAPTER 38

Miscellaneous letters etc

---

1 - To or from Cruden etc

Balfour to Cruden, 20th November 1780 ***7(28): C***

BY Nisbet Balfour Esq,
Lt Colonel of His Majesty's Twenty Third Regiment of Foot
and Commandant of Charlestown etc etc etc

TO JOHN CRUDEN Esq

YOU are hereby authorized, empowered and directed to seize and to take into your custody and management the estates of those, both real and personal, who have joined the enemy and thereby abandoned their property in this province AND you are also directed, on receiving the return of property on the estates of those of the description above mentioned, to give unto me a list of their names that warrants may be given to you pursuant to the directions and under the limitations and restrictions of the proclamation of Lord Cornwallis bearing date the sixteenth day of September last, excepting always, as is therein excepted, their property in Charlestown, secured to them by the capitulation.

AND for so doing this shall be your sufficient warrant.

GIVEN under my hand at Charlestown
20th November 1780

N BALFOUR
Commandant

Cruden to Haldane, 30th November 1780 *4(250): ALS*

Charles Toun
30th November 1780

Sir

When this toun was taken, my friend and relation, Colonel Abercromby[1], expressed to me his desire in behalf of himself and the army that I should be joined in the commission as Commissarry of Captors with Majors Moncrief and Hay. For many reasons I declined the offer, but in a letter to Colonel Abercromby I stated my ideas on the subject and pointed out the mode I thought most likely to secure to the army a handsome sum of money. I offer'd to take upon me the direction of the business under the name of Agent for the Army, which they wished me to be, but the Commander in Chief, altering the commission of the Commissarry of Captures to that of Agents for the Army, prevented my service from being accepted of.

The moment I received warrants for the seizure of the property of those on Congaree and Wataree Rivers that came within the meaning and intention of Lord Cornwallis' proclamation, I dispatched a person of trust, Mr Alex[r] Speirs[2], with most particular orders to employ hands in securing the crops on the ground and to take evry possible step in removeing the effects to Camden. Afterwards, on finding that the army were near him, I order'd that he should endeavour by every means in his power to send provisions to the army. Mr Speirs has lately wrote me that Mr Stedman was sent by his Lordship for the same purpose, and I find he has removed grain from some of the estates now under sequestration to Camden and has drau'en on Mr Frazer[3] for the expences attending the removal of it, which he refuses to pay[4]. The

---

1 Robert Abercromby (1740-1827) was born into one of those Scottish landed families that were to play an important role in British military and imperial history over the next two centuries. Baptised at the family's Scottish estate near Tullibody, Clackmannanshire, he would enlist as a volunteer at the outbreak of the Seven Years' War and see distinguished service before retiring as a captain on half pay at the close. When the revolutionary war began, he had returned to active service and was Lt Colonel of the 37th Regiment. He went on to serve dependably throughout the war and by late 1780 had seen action at Long Island, Brandywine and Germantown besides being involved in the Charlestown campaign. Soon to be with Phillips in Virginia, he would remain there and command on the left during the siege of Yorktown. Promoted to colonel in 1782, he became an aide-de-camp to the King before going out to India in 1788 with the 75th Regiment to serve again under Cornwallis. When Cornwallis returned home in 1793, Abercromby – by then a major general – succeeded to the office of Commander-in-Chief, having been knighted for his part in the Third Anglo-Mysore War. With his eyesight failing he left India in 1797. By his death at Airthrey near Stirling he had become the British Army's most senior general. (*ODNB*; Boatner, *Encyclopedia*, 2; *Appletons'*; *The Cornwallis Papers*)

2 Like John Cruden, by whom he was now employed, Alexander Speirs was a loyalist from North Carolina. As agent in Cross Creek of Messrs Burgwin & Co, a mercantile firm at Wilmington, he had delivered arms, ammunition, blankets, rugs, provisions, etc to the Scots Highlanders of Cumberland County at the time of their uprising in early 1776 in support of the Crown. Whether as a result of his involvement or as a result of his later declining to take the test oath, he had had to leave North Carolina. (Coldham, *Loyalist Claims*, i, 66)

3 *Mr Frazer*: James Fraser, one of three persons in Charlestown jointly in charge of the Department of Captures.

4 *which he refuses to pay*: presumably because sequestered estates were involved, which were the responsibility of Cruden.

Commandant referr'd to me Colonel Gray of Pedee[5] with an order of his on Frazer, which, considering the nature of the service performed and the merits of Mr Gray, I paid the money for. In order to prevent confusion it will be necessarry that I receive an order from Mr Stedman for the amount of grain deliver'd to the commissarry at Camden that I may be enabled to comply with the directions given me with respect to the property under sequestration.

In the prosecution of the Capture Department it is highly necessarry for the credit of Government that some person should be here to answer the drafts of those employed in the direction of it, and as it may be done by me very easily and without a new commission for that purpose – only an order from his Lordship to keep the accounts seperate from those that are to be laid before the Commandant and Board of Police — I shall most cheerfully, if agreable to his Lordship, take that upon me; and as a mode of reimbursement and the establishment of a fund for the advantage of the army I most humbly beg leave to suggest the following plan of conducting the business.

For all species of provisions[6] that may be furnished the Commissarry[7], receipts should be taken and the same prices allowed as if purchaseing from individuals; for all the horses, grain and forage that may be captured, receipts should be taken from the Quarter Master General in the same manner; which receipts to be transmitted to me from time to time that I may settle with the heads of the respective departments and thereby secure funds necessarry for the prosecution of the business[8] and begin a stock for the advantage of those who merit every attention and emolument that can in justice be given them (I mean the army).

For commoditys of value that may be seized on the march of the army, returns to be made that I may give information of their value and of the best mode of disposeing of them to advantage, which, from the knowledge I have of the trade of the country, may be of service to those concerned. Requesting your forgiveness for this very long epistle, I have the honor to be, sir,

Your most obedient and most humble servant

J CRUDEN

---

5 Gray was now located at Colonel Thomson's near the confluence of the Congaree and Wateree. See p 394.

6 *provisions*: captured provisions.

7 *the Commissarry*: the Commissary General's Department.

8 *the business*: of the Department of Captures.

Balfour to Cruden, 8th December 1780 *7(29): C*

Charlestown
8th December 1780

Lt Colonel John Cruden
Charlestown

Sir

In consequence of your uniformly expressing to me that you would not be able to pay the necessary attention to the duty of a field officer of militia, far less that of commanding a battalion, which I am sensible of from the extent and variety of business on your hands as well as the deficiencies in the companys of the second battalion, I am induced to change the mode of raising the militia of this town.

And I have now to desire that you do forthwith call together the gentlemen volunteers and express to them the high sense I entertain of their zeal and readiness, which I shall not fail to make known to Earl Cornwallis.

And in consideration of their voluntary services I am desirous to give every encouragement and indulgence in my power to them; and, being determined that all persons shall take their part of the duty, and while the inhabitants are embodied by districts, the gentlemen of your battalion shall be drafted into two companies never to exceed one hundred men each and to be commanded by Major Buchannan, the companies by Captains Eccles and Morris, and called the Volunteer Battalion.

And as a further indulgence I leave to the gentlemen themselves the making of such regulations as may be thought by them most effectual in order to preserve discipline and good government in the battalion.

I am, sir,
Your most obedient humble servant

N BALFOUR

Cornwallis to Speirs etc, 12th December 1780 *83(41): C*

Wynnesborough
December 12th 1780

Mr Spiers or Mr Cruden's deputy at the Congarees

Sir

John Lancaster[9] having rendered very essential services to the army, in consequence of which his house was burnt and his wife and family treated with the greatest cruelty, I desire

[9] John Lancaster has not been identified beyond what is revealed about him in this volume.

you will give him temporary use of the plantation of one Taylor[10] at the Congarees or some other plantation that may suit him as well, leaving thereon for the use of the said John Lancaster and his family some corn and cattle and such articles as may be necessary for their present support.

I am
Your most obedient servant

CORNWALLIS

Haldane to Speirs, 9th January 1781 — *84(45): ACS*

McAlister's Plantation
9th January 1781

Mr Speers

Sir

Lord Cornwallis desires you will put the family of Mr Thomas Lancaster[11] in possession of the upper quarter of the plantation of Thomas Taylor (the proprietor being in rebellion). If that part of the plantation is occupied by any loyalist that has previous permission to this, you will be pleased to appoint a proper place to receive the family of Mr Lancaster with 2 or 3 Negroes and 2 cows for their present use. His Lordship also desires you will inform the inhabitants in that neighbourhood that if they attempt to molest the family, person or property granted to the refugees by his Lordship's order, they will be severely punished.

I am, sir, etc

H HALDANE
ADC

§ - §

10 Thomas Taylor (1743-1833) was serving as a colonel in Sumter's Brigade and had recently taken part in the actions at Fishdam Ford and Blackstocks. Born in Amelia County, Virginia, he had been brought to South Carolina in 1754. (Moss, *SC Patriots*, 920; McCrady, *SC in the Rev 1775-1780* and *1780-1783, passim*)

11 Apart from his being a loyalist, little is known of Thomas Lancaster beyond what is revealed in this volume. If he survived the war, he may have been the Thomas Lancaster who went on to settle in what became Maury County, Tennessee.

2 - To or from Commissaries etc

Knecht to Cornwallis, 24th November 1780 — *4(198): ALS*

Cedar Creek
the 24th November 1780

Rt Hon Earl Cornwallis

My Lord

The late successes of Colonel Tarleton (whereon I have the pleasure to congratulate your Lordship) I hope will check that rebel audacity which the pusilanimity of the inhabitants gave birth to. I find the rebells have obtained both money and salt, and perhaps merchandize, by overrunning the Dutch Fork! A few of them have been on Monday last within six miles of Kennerly's Mill. I was under some apprehension about the mill and fruitlessly endeavour'd to get some militia stationed there (all the plantations near the mill being rebel property), and some of the inhabitants (not owners, for they are chiefly absconded) behav'd daringly insolent to Mr Dubber, who has ever since been upon the fret.

Waggons were so scarce in these parts that the corn which was promised us could not be brought to the mill. We were therefore under the necessity of supplying the mill with corn in canoes, and those rebel plantations laying most convenient, we partly had our corn from one William Strother's plantation.

Some days ago, on taking a survey of the crops and produce of those rebel plantations, it pained me to see the waste and embezlement every where. Hogs, cattle and horses were drove and allow'd to fend in the corn fields. I imediatly sent eight Negros and three white labourers into Mr James Kennerly's field to gather the remaining standing corn and I now hear that there will not be above 200 bushels gathered there, which should have rendered about 3,000 bushels. I have been repeatedly inform'd that cattle and hogs are killed upon this plantation and clandestinely carried off, but have no proofs as yet to lay hold on the culprits. It is my opinion, my Lord, that every thing that is fit for the use of the army (yet in due proportion) ought imediatly be taken off from those plantations, but as the greater part of it is rebel property, your Lordship will be pleased to direct by whom it shall be done, should it be approved of. I have myself seen between 30 and forty head of cattle big and small in James Kennerly's fields. These I sent for on this side the river. Shall put them in a good pasture till your Lordship's pleasure is known what to be done with them. If your Lordship approves, I purpose in this neighbourhood to collect and keep by way of reserve a number of cattle, having a much better pasture in view for it than there is about Wynsborough.

My Lord, I have been witness of a distressing scene! The family of Mr John Kennerly's seems to have been a family of mutual affection and harmony. An elderly woman aged 60 or more (who, I soon found, had lived in elegance in Virginia, but through misfortune thought herself happy in passing her life in this family, being somewhat related to it) opened yesterday her bursting soul to me and beg'd me to intercede with your Lordship if they could not be allow'd to remain on the plantation, at least to enlarge the time of evacuation, for the 20 days' notice expire in 9 days hence and this old lady nor three children of said Kennerlys know not where to go. My Lord, I should be happy to be bearer of any grace you may be pleased to bestow on this unhappy family, though I more and more suspect the head of it of disaffection to our gracious Sovereign.

I have the honour to be
My Lord's most obedient and most humble servant

A KNECHT

Cornwallis to Knecht, 27th November 1780 — *82(113): C*

Wynnesborough
November 27th 1780

A Knecht Esq

Sir

I received your letter of the 24th and am sorry that your friends of the fork shewed so much timidity. I hope that Colonel Tarleton's success and our 96 militia appearing again in the field will put an end to the pannick. Mr Wier will tell you that we want cattle. I trust you will send some immediately. It will certainly be right to collect proper proportions of corn and every thing that can be usefull to the army. The people employed by Mr Cruden will be the properest to execute this business. I desire therefore you will apply to them in my name to do it.

I feel much for the distress of Mr Kennerly's family, but if I immediately interfered with Mr Cruden's regulations I should put the whole province in confusion. The greatest attention was paid to the care and maintenance of women and children by my regulations — very different from those of the enemy.

I am, sir,
Your most obedient humble servant

CORNWALLIS

Cornwallis to Stedman, 15th December 1780 *83(46): C*

Wynnesborough
December 15th 1780

Charles Stedman Esq
Commissary of Captures
Congarees

Sir

I desire that you will give a receipt to Mr Cruden or his deputy for all kinds of provisions which you may take for the use of the army in the province of South Carolina, and you will likewise pay the most exact attention to leaving the proportion to the wives and children of the absentees whose estates are under sequestration according to my proclamation of the 16th of September. I should, however, wish you to apply in all cases of the sequestered estates to Mr Cruden's deputy, whom you are required to assist on every occasion and by no means to counteract.

I am, sir,
Your most obedient humble servant

CORNWALLIS

Haldane to Ancrum, 29th December 1780 *83(93): ACS*

Head Quarters
Wynnesborough
29th December 1780

Mr Ancram

Sir

Lord Cornwallis has directed me to acquaint you that whatever cattle you furnish for the use of His Majesty's troops shall be paid for at a fair price, his Lordship having been informed that you have been rather averse to allowing your cattle to be drove in, which he imagines must have proceeded from your thinking that you would not be paid the full value for them. His Lordship also begs the favor you will communicate the contents of this to the gentlemen in your neighbourhood.

I am, sir,
Your most humble and obedient servant

HENRY HALDANE

Haldane to Commissary General, 23rd January 1781 — *84(81): ADfS*

Head Quarters
Steis's Plantation
23rd January 1781

Commissary General

Sir

Lord Cornwallis desires you will pay at sight to Mr Charles Steis[12] or his order the sum of twenty three pounds eleven shillings and sixpence for the under mentioned articles received for the use of His Majesty's army:

100 bushels of oats at 1/6 per bushel	£7-10-0
40 bushels of corn at 1/6 per bushel	£3–0-0
6 head of cattle at £1 17*s* 4*d* per head	£11–4-0
3 head of sheep at £0 12*s* 6*d* per head	£1-17-6
Sterling	£23-11-6

HENRY HALDANE
Aid-de-camp

§ - §

3 - To or from others[13]

Innes to Cornwallis, 31st October 1780 — *3(344): ALS*

Charles Town
31st October 1780

My Lord

I did myself the honor of writing to your Lordship[14] inclosed in the Commandant's packet conveyed by Lt Colonel Doyle. Since that time a severe fever would have prevented

12 Charles Steis's plantation lay half way between Buffalo Creek and Little Broad River at a location forty miles directly west of Charlotte. For him to be paid so directly for the supply of grain and stock it is unlikely that he was of the revolutionary persuasion. (Tarleton, *Campaigns*, map; *The Greene Papers*, vii, 212, map)

13 Exceptionally, the rest of the incoming papers in this chapter are arranged in date order and not necessarily in order of receipt.

14 See Innes to Cornwallis, 10th October, vol II, p 199.

my taking the benifit of the late opportunity to New York had the state of Provincial matters in this part of the Continent admitted of it, which was not the case. I have now sent Captain Prevost, the Deputy Inspector, to visit *if possible* all the Provincial corps in this province and Lt Colonel Brown's at Augusta, and I am to entreat your Lordship will have the goodness to appoint a Deputy Muster Master if Mr Brice cannot be spared to attend Captain Prevost, as without the certificate of the Muster Master the Provincial troops cannot with propriety receive the amount of their abstracts from the Pay Master. Captain Prevost will have the honor of receiving your Lordship's commands, of presenting the state of the Provincial Stores in this place, and reporting the forwardness in which every article order'd by your Lordship is in. Nothing is wanting but a safe mode of conveyance. I shall immediately on Captain Prevost's return to this place take the earliest opportunity of proceeding to New York.

Permit me to join most sincerely in the general congratulations on your Lordship's recovery and in offering my ardent prayers that a life so valuable may long be preserved as a blessing to your country and friends.

I have the honor to be with the greatest respect, my Lord,
Your Lordship's most devoted and obedient servant

ALEX INNES
Lt Colonel

NB

Mr Jones[15] is recommended to your Lordship for a vacancy in the New York Volunteers. So many alterations have happen'd in that corps that Mr Jones comes in a lieutenant without any injustice to the ensigns.

Return of clothing in Provincial Stores, 29th October 1780 *103(5): DS*

RETURN OF CLOATHING received, issued and remaining in His Majesty's Provincial Stores at Charlestown between the 15th and 29th of October 1780

	In Store Oct 14th	*Received since*	*Issued since*	*In Store Oct 29th*
Drummers' suits	8			8
Privates' coats, scarlet	264		247	17
White cloth for waistcoats	90		7	83
Breeches, made	101		9	92

15 Perhaps Lawrence Jones. If so, he did not succeed to the vacant lieutenancy but was commissioned an ensign in the New York Volunteers in February 1781. At the close of the war he was placed on the Provincial half-pay list. (Raymond, 'British American Corps'; Treasury 64/23(1) (National Archives, Kew))

Shoes	928		3	925
Stockings	2,128		382	1,746
Hats	1,033		35	998
Shirts	1,331		13	1,318
Rollers	400		9	391
Epaulets	508			508
Yards of legging cloth	1,687		958	729
Yards of blue cloth[16]	1,140		604	536
Yards of brown cloth	1,435		38	1,397
Yards oznaburgs, dowlas etc etc etc	750		340	410
Haversacks	263			263
Stand of arms	140		171	-
Felling axes	175			175
Hatchets	18			18
Canteens	363			363
Blankets	970	508	239	1,239
Privates' tents	66			66
Camp colours	6			6
Mittens	2,000			2,000
Shoe soles	3,400			3,400
Split shirts	549			549
Linen overalls	703			703
Woolen overalls	-	390	3	387
Blue jackets	400	213	6	607
Light infantry accoutrements	905			905
Battalion accoutrements	543			543
Drum slings	304			304
Drum cases	26			26
Markees	35			35

[16] This and the following entry are annotated: 'Harley and Drummond'.

Serjeants' sashes	82			82
Russia drab jackets	274		1	273
Serjeants' plaid, yards	600			600
Yards of privates' plaid	11,820			11,820
Cavalry Cloathing				
Blue coats (unmade)	350			
Horsemen's cloaks	80			
Saddles	2			
Snaffle bridles	2			
Pairs of boots	56			
Helmets	61			
Forage cords	52			
Carbine belts	30			
Water decks[17]	17			
Yards white plush	130			
Pairs of pistols	40			
Cruppers	23			
Girths	36			
Powder bags	20			

AUG PREVOST
Deputy Inspector General, Provincial Forces

Summary of account, Innes's Department — *103(6): D*

Amount of expenditures and contingent account of the Inspector General's Department from the 1st of January 1779 to the 31st of October 1780 inclusive	£7,125-6-8
By a warrant granted by the Rt Hon Charles Earl Cornwallis on David Thomas Esq, Paymaster General, dated the 28th of July for	£2,000

17 *Water decks*: painted canvas to cover the saddles, bridles and girths of cavalry horses.

Balance due the Inspector General's Department £5,125-6-8

Hayes to Cornwallis, 15th November 1780[18] *4(134): ALS*

Charlestown
November 15th 1780

Rt Hon Earl Cornwallis etc etc etc

Permit me, my Lord, to express my feelings on the dreadfull accounts we have had of your Lordship's health and the joy so universally diffused in every breast at the glorious tidings of your recovery. Tho' worn down by sickness and many relapses, I was upon the point of paying a visit to your Lordship had not the favourable news of your recovery reached us. Thank heaven health is restored and your Lordship once more at the head of an army as distinguished for their attachment to your Lordship as their bravery in the field. May they never experience such anxious moments again.

I have the honor to enclose the last return of the hospitals here, by which your Lordship will see that health once more begins to smile on us. Of the number, 76 are wounded, and several venereal patients. We have received no stores from New York, nor have the surgeon and mates required been sent. Our mates here have been all ill, and some so far reduced as to render a visit to Europe necessary. To supply their places I had been obliged to employ some who I have ordered to join the army with two hundred weight of best powdered bark. Your Lordship, from the necessity of the service, will, I hope, approve of my having employed them. As Mr Huddleston, apothecary, has been, from the reduced state of his health, obliged to leave Camden and Mr Hill will probably have joined the army with his assistants, I humbly submit it to your Lordship's consideration whether it would not be proper, while an hospital is at Camden and so many sick, to send Mr Forster[19] to that post, whose health is so established as to enable him to do the duties of his profession. I shall myself take charge of the surgical patients and shall ever consider it my greatest happiness to render myself in any capacity usefull to the sick or wounded soldier. Our hospitals here are in high order and I hope your Lordship will always find that every attention is paid the sick.

I have the honor to be with the greatest respect, my Lord,
Your Lordship's most obliged and very humble servant

JOHN McNAMARA HAYES

---

18 For Cornwallis's reply, see p 461.

19 In October 1775 Thompson Forster (?-1830) had been appointed a surgeon on the staff of the General Hospital in North America, the department responsible for hospitals other than small regimental ones. He would retire on half pay at the close of the war but return to the active list between 1803 and 1805. Besides serving as senior surgeon to Guy's Hospital, London, he again entered the army medical service as a deputy inspector of hospitals in 1821. He died at Southwell, Nottinghamshire. (Johnston, *Commissioned Officers in the Medical Service*, 47)

Enclosure
Return of HM Hospital at Charlestown ***4(136): DS***

RETURN of Sick and Wounded in His Majesty's Hospital at Charlestown between the 5th and 11th November 1780, both days inclusive						
Regiment or Troop	*Remained last Return*	*Since entered*	*Total*	*Discharged*	*Died*	*Remains*
7th Regiment of Foot	21	2	23	1		22
16th ditto	4		4	1		3
17th ditto	1		1			1
23rd ditto	5	2	7			7
33rd ditto	23	1	24	4		20
63rd ditto	22	1	23	3		20
64th ditto		1	1		1	-
1st Battalion, 71st	9	1	10			10
2nd Battalion, 71st	4		4	1		3
North Carolina Volunteers	6		6		1	5
British Legion	10		10	1		9
Volunteers of Ireland	21	2	23	2	1	20
Prince of Wales' American Regiment	29		29	7	2	20
Guides and pioneers	2		2			2
New York Volunteers	5		5	1		4
Garrison battalion	1	1	2			2
Sailors	9	4	13			13
North Carolina militia	3		3			3

Inhabitants	2		2			2
Servants of the hospital	1		1			1
Women admitted as patients	3	2	5			5
	181	17	198	21	5	172

JOHN McNAMARA HAYES
Physician to the General Hospital

Mathis to Haldane, 21st November 1780 *71(9): ALS*

Tuesday, 21st November 1780

Major Henry Haldane
Camden

Sir

Tho the present subject of this letter may seem troublesome or out of the line of your appointment, yet your great humanity and interest with Lord Cornwallis may induce you to commiserate a truly distressed family.

In the account of sundries taken out of Joseph Kershaw's house[20] I have omitted the flour and corn meal mentioned in that I shewed you, because His Majesty's commissaries had a great deal more provisions from Mr Kershaw's mills and plantations, for which Lord Cornwallis was so good as to order that we[21] should draw provisions from the commissaries. I can not possibly tell the balance[22], therefore have not mentioned any.

Mrs Kershaw[23] would esteem it a very great favour if you wou'd mention to Lord

---

20 *the account..*: not extant.

21 *we*: Mrs Kershaw and Mathis, who were allowed to draw provisions for their immediate needs in return for those appropriated for military use.

22 *the balance*: between the provisions appropriated and those returned.

23 Sarah ('Sally') Kershaw was the daughter of Daniel and Sophia Mathis, Irish Quakers who had settled in the Waterees before the founding of Pine Tree Hill (later renamed Camden). She married Joseph Kershaw (see vol I, p 137, note 33) about 1763. Her house in Camden had been occupied by Cornwallis and would now remain occupied by Rawdon. She and her children were presently residing on a family plantation a few miles to the south, and as evinced by this letter, they were having a hard time of it. When Camden was evacuated in May 1781, the torch was put to public buildings, but although the flames went on to engulf many private ones too, her house was

Cornwallis that she is exceedingly distressed for want of the two first articles (sugar and salt) mentioned in the account and hopes his Lordship will be kind enough to grant her the same in return. If it should not seem pleasing to his Lordship, what ever his Lordship is willing to grant will be very thankfully receiv'd by Mrs Kershaw.

I would likewise acknowledge myself under a very particular *obligation* to your *kindness* if you wou'd represent to my Lord that our crop being entirely destroy'd by the horses belonging to the Royal Artillery, cavalry etc which were turn'd out into the fields before the grain was ripe, and the commissaries not allowing us any part of the toll of grain ground at the mill or wages for the Negroe miller who attends constantly, has so reduced us that we are not able to keep our Negroes at home for want of bread for them. The toll would be quite sufficient to subsist all our Negroes and selves, tho I do not suppose it customary for the commissaries of the army to pay toll for grinding their grain, yet I hope, when my Lord is acquainted with the distress'd situation of Mrs Kershaw and her small children, he will grant an order that Mrs Kershaw may get three or four bushels of corn meal weekly from the mill, which will enable her to keep her Negroes together and get the plantation in order for making provisions for themselves and us that we may not always be an incumberance to my Lord, who has always been so remarkably good to us.

We have no resource but in his Lordship's bounty and your goodness to lay the above circumstances before his Lordship. If I have requested any thing that should prove troublesome or disagreeable, I would wish you to act as your better judgment should dictate.

I am, sir, with the most profound respect
Your most obedient humble servant

SAM^L MATHIS[24]

PS

I wou'd beg leave to remark that Mrs Kershaw is under a very disagreeable situation for want of a little *specie* to answer present demands and would be much obliged for what you should judge convenient to yourself untill you had an opportunity to lay the accounts before my Lord.

SM

---

spared. (The Reverend Charles Woodmason, *The Carolina Backcountry on the Eve of the Revolution*, edited by Richard J Hooker (University Of North Carolina Press, 1953), 144-5 and notes; Johnson, *Traditions*, 463-9)

24 Samuel Mathis would no doubt have been a brother or nephew of Sarah Kershaw (see above).

Representations of Stevenson and Taylor, 30th November 1780 4(254): DS

At camp
Wynsborough
30th November 1780

This to certify that after being taken prisoner by the rebels at King's Mountain the 7th October, we were all close confined with the rest of the prisoners till the morning of the eighth instant[25], then marched under guard till night without any provision, and marched us to Biggenstaff[26] plantation, where we were march'd up to the foot of the gallows, where they made us stand till they executed nine of our prisoners, among which were Colonel Mills, Captain Wilson and Captain Chithood[27]. The next day we were marched off, the day being very bad, our men getting no provision, and marched 30 miles, the road being very bad after the rain. Many of our prisoners were so wearied out that many of them were obliged to give out on the road. They then roll'd them down in the mud and many of them they left there trod to death and many of them cut to pieces. They still kept marching us till they got us to the Morraven[28] Town, where they promised to parole us, but instead of that Lieutenant Stevenson was close confined with several of the officers' servants for stealing a pair of spurs, which Captain Campbell[29] had lost and charged them with having them and threatned taking their lives if they did not get his spurs. There were a house appointed for the officers to be put into. He then order'd Lieutenant Stevenson to the house appointed for them, with a sentinel at the door, where he continued till Captain Depistur[30] came from Salem Town. Then Colonel Campbell and Captain Depustur got other quarters for us, which they allowed us to go to without giving us paroles or limits, and, we being confident that we never had given our words of honour to them, we then did not think ourselves under the least obligation to them, and finding what manner they use our officers — to knock down our surgeon for dressing our wounded men and cut his hand with his sword and throwing a large knife at another of them as he was coming in at the door, which went under his arm and stuck into

---

25 *instant*: ultimo.

26 *Biggenstaff*: Bickerstaff.

27 James Chitwood (1724-1780) was a Virginian of Cumberland County who was still resident there in 1768. Sometime later he migrated with his family to what is now Rutherford County, North Carolina, where he had recently been serving as a captain in the loyalist militia. The manner of his execution and the circumstances leading to it are related in vol II, p 135, notes 150 and 152. His remains were carried half a mile from the site to Benjamin Bickerstaff's plantation, where they were buried on a hill used as a graveyard. (Draper, *King's Mountain*, 340n, 345)

28 *Morraven*: Moravian.

29 That Captain Campbell was a bully or worse is borne out by the entry for 24th October in Allaire's Diary: 'This night Dr Johnson and I were disturbed by a Captain Campbell, who came into our room and ordered us up in a most peremptory manner. He wanted our bed. I was obliged to go to Colonel [William] Campbell and wake him to get the ruffian turned out of the room; otherwise he would have murdered us, having his sword drawn and strutting about with it in a truly cowardly manner.' (Draper, op cit, 512)

30 *Depistur*: De Peyster.

the floor – we then thought ourselves not safe among them, and they seem'd determined to murder some of us, and to prevent a thing of that kind happening we thought we might as soon trust in making our escapes, upon which we concluded to leave them, and likewise Lieutenant Allare[31] assured us that he never had promised nor given his word to them nor laid himself under any obligation of confinement to them.

JOHN TAYLOR
Captain, 1st Battalion, New Jersey Volunteers

WILLIAM STEVENSON
Lieutenant, 2nd Battalion, New Jersey Volunteers

Cornwallis to Turnbull, 3rd December 1780 — *83(9): C*

Wynnesborough
December 3rd 1780

Lt Colonel Turnbull

Dear Sir

I received your letters of the 23rd and 26th[32]. I can with truth assure you that I never have in any manner interfered with the promotions of the army, either British or Provincial, except in the case of augmentations or new levies made in this district. In every other instance I have declined even transmitting the memorials but desired the commanding officers of regiments to apply directly to Sir Henry Clinton.

If any thing could tempt me to break through this rule it would be my desire of obliging Colonel Turnbull and of assisting him in the execution of any plan I might think consistent with the good of His Majesty's Service. I beg you will accept of my sincere good wishes for the recovery of your health, a prosperous voyage and a happy meeting with your family.

I am with great regard
Your most obedient and faithfull servant

CORNWALLIS

---

31 Of Huguenot descent, Anthony Allaire (1755-1838) was born at New Rochelle in Westchester County, New York. Having been commissioned a lieutenant in the Loyal American Regiment on 20th April 1777, he was three years later seconded to Ferguson's corps and taken prisoner in the debacle at King's Mountain. He had now escaped and made his way with Stevenson and Taylor to Ninety Six. At the close of the war he was placed on the Provincial half-pay list and settled in New Brunswick, where he later served for some years in the New Brunswick Regiment. He died on his farm near Fredericton. The diary which he has left is a valuable account of events in 1780, particularly those involving Ferguson's corps. (Draper, *King's Mountain*, 480,484-519; Treasury 64/23(3), WO 65/164(37) and WO 65/165(3) (National Archives, Kew))

32 *your letters...*: not extant.

Cornwallis to Hayes, 5th December 1780 — *83(17): C*

Wynnesborough
December 5th 1780

Dr Hayes etc

Dear Sir

Many thanks for your very kind expressions on the occasion of my illness[33]. As it happened, I am very glad you was prevented from coming. I am now perfectly stout. I am happy to find that Charlestown is again healthy and am well convinced that the management of the hospital cannot be in abler or better hands. My opinion is that, when the care and assistance of a sick soldier is in question, no reasonable expence should be spared, and as I can place the utmost confidence in you, I shall always approve of your procuring mates and such other assistance as you may think necessary for the good of the patients, and beg it may always be considered as done by my orders.

I approve of your plan of sending Mr Foster to Camden. There will probably be a considerable hospital there during the whole winter, as all the troops employed on the frontier of the province must send their sick thither.

I am, dear sir,
Your most obedient and faithful servant

CORNWALLIS

Simcoe to Money, 15th December 1780 — *66(39): ALS*

New York
December 15th 1780

Dear Money

Observing in the rebell papers that a letter was intercepted from General Leslie to Lord Cornwallis, the substance of which they have related to us, I enclose to you a cypher that, if you have no safer mode of conveying any matter that may be requisite, you may make use of. I do this as probably such a matter may not have been thought of. I shall acquaint General Arnold with it.

I beg that you will present my best respects to my Lord Cornwallis and remember me to all friends. Mackenzie desires to join me in good wishes to you.

I am with great truth
Your obedient servant

J GRAVES SIMCOE

---

33 *your very kind expressions..*: see Hayes to Cornwallis, 15th November, p 455.

NB

Mackenzie has the same cypher.

Enclosure
Cipher **66(40): D**

a	b	c	d	e	f	g	h	i	j	k	l	m	n	o	p	q	r	s	t	u
1	s	3	n	m	u	e	f	2	w	x	p	d	z	5	k	&	6	a	4	g

v	w	x	y	z
1	b	h	7	q

In this cypher the same pointing is to be used as in common writing.

The letters of the word *victory* are expressed in figures according to succession, v being 1, i 2, and so on, and the same letters v,i,c,t,o,r,y, are added or interspersed in words to increase the intricacy.

In decyphering, they are to be struck out, as they bear no signification. For example:

T	i	u	6	i	m	n	m	6	t	2	3	x	y
		F	r		e	d	e	r		i	c	k	

O	d	1	c	3	i	x	m	z	t	q	o	2	r	m
	M	a		c		k	e	n		z		i		e

Small to Cornwallis, 22nd December 1780 **4(372): ALS**

Charles Town, South Carolina
December 22nd 1780

Rt Hon Earl Cornwallis etc etc etc

My Lord

I could not regret (but rejoice at) the opportunity that has led me to the honor of serving under your Lordship's immediate command, had I been so fortunate as to have had it in my power to bring with me a battalion which has been unluckilly and uncommonly dispers'd ever since its existence.

I feell a deep concern at the information it behoves me to lay before your Lordship, that the detachment, 2nd Battalion, 84th, I am now serving with is very inadequately compos'd, one company only properly form'd, the remainder recruits. Of this circumstance I requested Colonel Balfour to inform your Lordship by presenting a state of the battalion[34] which I took leave to forward for your perusal.

I have beg'd also of General Lesly (with his accustom'd goodness to me) to represent some other matters respecting the 2nd Battalion, 84th, by laying before your Lordship some injunctions I receiv'd from the Commander in Chief.

I hope to be pardon'd for taking this liberty, which a wish to benefit the publick service can only be offer'd as an apology for presuming to do.

I have the honor to be with the utmost respect and the highest esteem, my Lord,
Your Lordship's much oblig'd and most obedient humble servant

JOHN SMALL

Simpson to Cornwallis, 2nd January 1781 — *67(9): ALS*

Charles Town
January 2nd 1781

The Earl Cornwallis

My Lord

By Major Craig, who arrived here yesterday in the *Medea*, I received a letter from Sir Henry Clinton in which he expresses an uneasiness, and I think some displeasure, at my haveing delay'd to join him at New York and he desires me to come there as soon as possible. I therefore think myself oblidged to embark the first oportunity. If your Lordship hath any commands which I can execute there, either now or at any future time, I shall be honoured by being entrusted with them.

As before the arrival of the *Medea* the *Blonde* was to have sailed as yesterday, Colonel Balfour was so busily employed in getting ready his dispatches that he had not time to inform me of your Lordship's pleasure upon the matters I took the liberty to submit to your consideration in the letters I wrote to you by him[35], excepting what you remarked upon the

---

34 *a state..*: not extant.

35 *the letters..*: not extant.

table of depreciation. I have now the honour to send to your Lordship copies of the work[36] and you will readily perceive there never was the least intention to establish it as an authority or adopt it as a positive rule, neither of which I am convinced can de done but by the interposition of the legislature. The whole therefore, either done or intended, was to ascertain some particular facts, which it would have been dangerous to delay because the proofs, upon which they are founded, every day diminish and become more dificult. As it is a first essay, notwithstanding the care with which it has been compiled, it may probably have errors and defects, which ought to prevent it from being established as a standard or criterion, but if it is tollerably exact, it may occasion future differences to be settled amicably and agreeable to justice.

It gave me great pleasure to learn from Colonel Balfour that your Lordship's health and spirits were so much recruited. With the compliments of the season I most sincerely wish for a continuance of them, and I hope and trust that the year 1781 will crown your Lordship's exertions with such success as will render the most essential services to your country and record your name with honour to the latest posterity.

I am with great truth and regard
Your Lordship's most faithfull and obedient humble servant

J SIMPSON

Gayton to Cornwallis, 2nd January 1781[37] *67(7): ALS*

Romulus off Charles Town
2nd January 1781

My Lord

The arrival of the *Medea* from New York having brought me orders from Vice Admiral Arbuthnot[38] to proceed with His Majesty's ship under my command to Chesapeak Bay with such part of the squadron that may be ready here, exclusive of certain ships that are ordered to remain for the protection of this port, I am to acquaint your Lordship therewith and that I mean to proceed the moment the ships are in readiness and receiving your Lordship's commands.

---

36 *the work*: James Simpson, *An Accurate Table, ascertaining the progressive Depreciation of the Paper-Currency, in the Province of South-Carolina, during the late Usurpation: with a Comprehensive Digest of the Proofs and Evidences, laid before the Commissioners appointed for that Purpose, to which are subjoined a few brief Observations, tending to elucidate so intricate a Subject* (Charlestown,1781). A copy is contained in PRO 30/11/108.

37 For Cornwallis's reply, see p 466.

38 *orders..*: see p 52.

The orders that Captain Barkley has this day received from the Admiral[39] puts me to the stand on the propriety of sending the *Blond* to England, as the *Hyena* and *Sandwich*, two of the ships named in those orders for the protection of this province, are now absent and the *Galatea* in her present state unfit to cruize, and should the *Blonde* leave it also, the trade of this port will be entirely unprotected. Thus situated, I judge it for His Majesty's Service that she should be detained from persuing her present orders, at the same time referring to your Lordship whether your dispatches are of such consequence to require an immediate conveyance.

There will be a convoy made up for England by February and I should wish to learn from your Lordship if that time will be early enough.

I have the honor to be with the greatest esteem, my Lord,
Your Lordship's very obedient humble servant

GEO GAYTON

Wemyss to Cornwallis, 4th January 1781 — *5(29): ALS*

Charles Town
January 4th 1781

My Lord

Permit me to thank your Lordship for the leave you have been so good as to grant me of going to New York.

Altho I cannot with propriety call myself the commanding officer of the 63rd Regiment (being still a prisoner), yet I hope you will think that I am entitled to recommend the officers to fill up the vacant commissions. In a belief that you are of this opinion, I beg to know whether the memorials should be sent to you in order to their being transmitted to the Commander in Chief or whether I should give them in myself on my arrival at York. Should your Lordship entrust me with your dispatches, it would confer an honor upon me.

Although my wounds are perfectly healed, I am still very lame both in my leg and arm and I find my health very much impaired.

I beg leave to assure you that the honor of serving under your Lordship will be an additional inducement for me to return to my duty the instant I am able.

I am with much respect
Your Lordship's most obedient and most humble servant

J WEMYSS

---

39 *The orders..*: see p 49.

Moncrief to Cornwallis, 6th January 1781 *71(15): ALS*

Charles Town
6th January 1781

The Rt Hon Earl Cornwallis etc etc etc

My Lord

Give me leave to return my most grateful thanks for the attention your Lordship as been pleased to honor me with in your very interesting letter in my behalf to my Lord Amherst[40]. I shall always consider myself under the greatest obligations for this as well as many other marks of your Lordship's friendship, and my only wish is to convince your Lordship that I shall always be happy in having the honor to serve in any capacity where your Lordship commands.

By His Majesty's Ship *Medea* I had the honor to receive a letter from my Lord Townshend[41] and one from his Excellency the Commander in Chief aquainting me of my being promoted to the rank of lt colonel. I entertain the highest sense of gratitude for the honor my country has been pleased to confer upon me, and sincerely wishes to have merit deserving this distinguished mark of His Majesty's favour.

I have the honor to be with the greatest respect, my Lord,
Your Lordship's most obedient and most humble servant

JAMES MONCRIEF

Cornwallis to Gayton, 6th January 1781 *84(19): C*

Wynnesborough
January 6th 1781

Captain Gayton

Dear Sir

I this day received your letter of the 2nd and am entirely of opinion that in consequence of the Admiral's directions the *Blonde* should remain. My letters will keep very well 'till the sailing of the convoy. I most sincerely wish you a prosperous voyage, and am with great regard

---

40 *letter..*: no extant copy.

41 Educated at Eton and Cambridge, George Townshend (1724-1807), 4th Viscount Townshend, had served as a brigadier general under Wolfe at Quebec. From 1767 to 1772 he was Lord Lieutenant of Ireland before taking up his present post of Master General of the Ordnance. (*ODNB*)

Your most obedient and faithfull servant

CORNWALLIS

Cornwallis to Fanning, 8th January 1781 — *84(31): C*

McAlister's Plantation
8th January 1781

Colonel Fanning

Sir

I was informed by Lt Colonel Balfour and afterwards by General Leslie that you intended coming to the army.[42] As I have began my march and the communication may not be long safe, perhaps you may not be able to execute your intentions. I see that your situation in this country is an unpleasant one and am concerned at finding that I have no possibility of making it more agreeable. The army in the Southern District is so circumstanced, and the stations of the officers so arranged, that I have no opportunity of giving you a command suitable to the rank you hold in the Provincial line. If it would be agreeable to you to remain at Charlestown or return to New York, I should have no objection or to adopt[ing] any other plan that you may propose which I may think consistent with the good of His Majesty's Service.[43]

I am, sir, etc

[CORNWALLIS]

Mallom to Cornwallis, 14th January 1781 — *67(18): ALS*

Charles Town
14th January 1781

My Lord

I take the liberty of forwarding to your Lordship the inclosed[44], which came directed to my late poor friend Money. I am infinitely obliged to you, my Lord, for your goodness in permitting me to go to Europe, and particularly so for the honor you have done me by intrusting me with the charge of your Lordship's dispatches home.

---

42 For Balfour's comments, see his letters of 15th and 16th December 1780, pp 113-5.

43 For Fanning's reaction, see Rawdon to Cornwallis, 14th January, p 250.

44 *the inclosed*: Simcoe to Money, 15th December 1780, p 461.

I have the honor to be, my Lord, with the greatest respect
Your Lordship's most obedient humble servant

J MALLOM

Turnbull to Cornwallis, 15th January 1781 — *67(22): ALS*

Charlestown
January 15th 1781

Earl Cornwallis

My Lord

It is with the greatest reluctance that I at this [time] trouble your Lordship but necessity oblidges me.

The case is this. At the breaking up of Emmerick's corps in 1779, the Commander in Chief was pleased to order a Captain Althause[45] with his company to join the New York Volunteers, and in December that year before our embarkation he drew a bill of £175 New York currency on our pay master for necessaries he had then purchased for his company. Captain Althause's ship was dismasted and drove to England. He came back by the way of New York and is now in Virginia, having drawn his full pay for himself and company at both these places up to the 24th of December last. It has been signify'd to us from New York that such monies as had been drawn for him by us here should be immediately refunded. Besides, we are a good deal in advance to his wife.

What I have to request of your Lordship is that you wou'd be pleased to order him as soon as convenient to come to Charlestown to settle his acounts with the pay master.

My journey to the northward has been retarded much longer than I expected. However, I hope in a few weeks, perhaps in less, to find a proper ship going that road. Wishing your Lordship a continuation of health and a successfull campaign,

I have the honor to be with the greatest respect
Your Lordship's most faithfull humble servant

GEO TURNBULL

---

45 Born in Germany, Johann ('John') Althause (1734-?) had been commissioned a captain on 25th May 1778 in Andreas Emmerich's Chasseurs, a British American corps. When the corps was disbanded on 31st August 1779 due to incipient unrest, Althause and a rifle company of 57 men were reconstituted and drafted into the New York Volunteers, but on their passage to the south as part of Clinton's expedition their transport was dismasted and driven to England. They had arrived back at New York in early autumn and were now forming part of Arnold's expedition to Virginia. They would remain there and be among the troops who capitulated at Yorktown. At the close of the war Althause was placed on the Provincial half-pay list. (Treasury 64/23(1), WO 65/164(31) and WO 65/165(2) (National Archives, Kew); Raymond, 'British American Corps'; The Clinton Papers, 67(1); Nan Cole and Todd Braisted, 'A History of Emmerick's Corps' (*The On-Line Institute for Advanced Loyalist Studies*, 8th December 2005))

Innes to Cornwallis, 16th January 1781 — *67(24): ALS*

Charles Town
16th January 1781

My Lord

I have the honor to transmit a return of the Provincial cloathing embarked with the detachment under the command of Major Craig and a copy of the instructions I have given to the person who has the stores in charge.[46] The great demands made lately upon us from all quarters has prevented me from sending so large a quantity of jackets and some other articles as I could have wished, but where any deficiency in the proportions may appear, it proceeds from our poverty, as there is not now an article left in store that I thought could be useful. By the general return of all our stores which I had the honor to convey to your Lordship by Colonel Balfour[47] you will see an additional supply of blankets, stockings, shirts, shoes etc may be sent if necessary and some proper regimental cloathing for corps that may be formed. Captain Prevost is gone to Savannah to put the two broken corps there in some order and I have the happiness to acquaint your Lordship that all the Provincials now in this province are very decently appointed and compleatly cloathed.

I have the honor to be with great respect, my Lord,
Your Lordship's most devoted servant

ALEX INNES
Inspector General, Provincial Forces

§ - §

---

46 Neither the return nor the copy of the instructions is extant.

47 *the general return..*: not extant.

Index[1]

[1] The letter 'n' after the number of a page indicates the presence there of biographical or identifying information, whether in a footnote or, in the case of an introductory chapter, in the body of the text. Such information appearing in another volume is indicated in brackets immediately after a person's name.

§ - §

15730502R00289

Printed in Great Britain
by Amazon